THE ORIGIN AND GROWTH

OF THE

ENGLISH CONSTITUTION

𝔄𝔫 𝔥𝔦𝔰𝔱𝔬𝔯𝔦𝔠𝔞𝔩 𝔗𝔯𝔢𝔞𝔱𝔦𝔰𝔢

IN WHICH IS DRAWN OUT, BY THE LIGHT OF THE MOST RECENT
RESEARCHES, THE GRADUAL DEVELOPMENT OF THE ENGLISH
CONSTITUTIONAL SYSTEM, AND THE GROWTH OUT OF
THAT SYSTEM OF THE FEDERAL REPUBLIC
OF THE UNITED STATES

By HANNIS TAYLOR, LL. D.

LATE MINISTER PLENIPOTENTIARY OF THE UNITED STATES TO SPAIN

IN TWO PARTS

PART I.

THE MAKING OF THE CONSTITUTION

"Tum Lælius, nunc fit illud Catonis certius, nec temporis unius, nec hominis esse constitutionem Reipublicæ." — CICERO.

"The new building has been raised upon the old groundwork; the institutions of one age have always been modelled and formed from those of the preceding, and their lineal descent has never been interrupted or disturbed." — PALGRAVE.

"And thus it comes to pass that Magna Carta, the Acts of the Long Parliament, the Declaration of Right, the Declaration of Independence, and the Constitution of 1787 constitute the record of an evolution." — BRANTLY.

"The Government of the United States is not the result of special creation, but of evolution." — FISKE.

BOSTON AND NEW YORK
HOUGHTON MIFFLIN COMPANY
LONDON: SAMPSON LOW, MARSTON & COMPANY (LIMITED)
𝔗𝔥𝔢 ℜ𝔦𝔳𝔢𝔯𝔰𝔦𝔡𝔢 ℜ𝔯𝔢𝔰𝔰, 𝔠𝔞𝔪𝔟𝔯𝔦𝔡𝔤𝔢

To the

MEMORY OF HIS MOTHER,

The Author

DEDICATES THIS BOOK.

PREFACE.

THE task essayed in this work involves an attempt to draw out, within the limits of two octavo volumes, the entire historic development of the English constitutional system, and the growth out of that system of the federal republic of the United States. In the Introduction an effort has been made to emphasize the fact that the constitutional histories of England and of the United States constitute a continuous and natural evolution which can only be fully mastered when viewed as one unbroken story. That story the author has attempted to unfold in the light of the latest researches, — English, German, French, and American, — and in such a manner as to impart to it something of a human interest. The double effort has been made to satisfy the critical student of the "Science of Politics" as to fulness and accuracy of detail, and at the same time to interest every American citizen who desires to read within reasonable limits the entire history of the wonderful constitution under which he lives.

The growth of English and American constitutions, considered as a single progressive development, is a subject of paramount importance and of almost universal interest. By the sixteenth century nearly every effort that had been made to establish representative government upon the continent of Europe had come to an end. In England only, among the Teutonic nations, did the representative system survive; in England only has the representative principle — which has been called "a Teutonic invention" — been able to maintain a continuous existence. In that way the English nation has been able to hand down the representative principle from the barbarian epoch to modern times; in that way England has become the "mother of parliaments," — the teacher of the science of representative government to all the world. Since the beginning of the French Revolution nearly all the states of continental Europe have organized national assemblies after the model of the English parliament in a spirit of conscious imitation. But the typical English national assembly, embodying what is generally known as the bicameral system, was not copied into the continental European constitutions until it had first been reproduced in a modified form and popularized by the founders of the federal republic of the United States. In the several colonial commonwealths founded by English settlers upon American soil, the typical English national assembly reappeared in an embryonic form as the predestined product of a natural process of reproduction; and the framers of the federal constitution of 1787, abandoning the original idea of a federal assembly consisting of a single chamber, adopted the English system of two chambers in the form in which that system had reappeared in the several states. Thus rendered popular by its successful reproduction in the American constitutions, state and federal, the " British political mode was followed by France, by Spain and Portugal, and by Holland and Belgium, combined in the kingdom of the Netherlands ; and after a long interval by Germany, Italy, and Austria." [1] To the student of the "Science of Politics" the typical English national assembly, therefore, appears not simply as the local legislature of the United Kingdom, nor even as the imperial parliament of the British Empire, but higher still, — as the accepted model of popular government throughout the world.

Until recently the attainment of a full and comprehensive knowledge of this all-important subject was beset with serious difficulties, which can be explained only through a brief exposition of the peculiar manner in which the history of the English people has been written. The English language had grown old, and English literature had passed what has been called its Augustan age, before any serious effort was ever made to open up the vast domain of English history. With the richest accumulation of historical records in all Europe — "whether we consider them in relation to antiquity, to continuity, to variety, to extent, or to amplitude of facts and details" [2] — mouldering beneath their feet, English scholars, until very recent times, were content to shed light upon every theme save that involved in the history of their own country. Not until near the close of the last century was any deliberate effort ever made to write the history of the English people.

[1] Sir Henry Maine, *Popular Government,* p. 13.
[2] The words of Sir Francis Palgrave, under whose auspices as deputy keeper the public records were, in 1858, finally brought together under the roof of the present Record Repository.

And when the investigation was at last begun, it was prosecuted according to the method which has prevailed in the exploration of the Nile, whose course has been mapped out by explorers who have slowly ascended from its mouths to its source. Beginning with modern times, the English historians have gradually worked backward until at last the sources have been reached. This assertion can easily be maintained by a few familiar illustrations. Hume began his "History of England" with the accession of the house of Stuart, — the volumes which treat of the preceding period were pinned on as an after-thought. How innocent Hume was of any real knowledge of the early and mediæval history of England he puts beyond all question when he tells us in his autobiography that, prior to the accession of the house of Stuart, "it is ridiculous to consider the English constitution . . . as a regular plan of liberty." Hallam began his "Constitutional History" with the accession of the house of Tudor, — three meagre chapters in the Middle Ages sufficed to contain all he desired to say of the preceding period. The magnificent ruin known as Macaulay's "History of England" really begins with the accession of the house of Stuart, — a single chapter sufficed to contain all that the most brilliant and the most inquisitive of Englishmen cared to say of the ten eventful centuries which precede that event. Some deep and serious reason must certainly have impelled three minds at once so acute and comprehensive to pass so lightly over the early and mediæval history of their country in order to begin their narrations in comparatively modern times. That reason is not hard to find. The truth is, until recently, the real history of early and mediæval England has remained a sealed book. Only within the last fifty years have the charters, chronicles, and memorials in which was entombed the early history of the English people been made accessible; and only within the last twenty years have they been subjected to the final analysis which has at last extracted from them their full and true significance. These facts become more comprehensible when we remember that only within the period last named has the study of history, as a distinct and substantive branch of knowledge, been raised to an independent position at the two great English universities. Not until 1870 was the study of modern history put upon an independent footing at Oxford; and not until 1875 was a separate tripos for universal history instituted at Cambridge. But when the emancipation of history was thus finally brought about, the work was done with genuine English thoroughness. Under the influence of Professors Stubbs and Freeman at Oxford, and Professor Seeley at Cambridge, the scientific study of history has at last been carried to as high a point in England as it has ever reached upon the Continent.[1]

Sharon Turner tells us, in the preface to his "History of the Anglo-Saxons," published between 1799 and 1805, that when his first volume appeared, "the subject of the Anglo-Saxon antiquities had been nearly forgotten by the British public. . . . The Anglo-Saxon MSS. lay still unexamined, and neither their contents nor the important facts which the ancient writers and records of other nations had preserved of the transactions and fortunes of our ancestors had been ever made a part of our general history." The honest effort made by Turner to arouse his countrymen to a sense of interest in the beginnings of their national life was followed in 1800 by an inquiry in parliament into the state of the public records, which resulted in an able report upon the condition of the archives, and in the appointment of a commission "to methodize, regulate, and digest the records." The conduct of the work of preservation and publication proving unsatisfactory in the hands of the Record Commission, its direction was finally intrusted to the Master of the Rolls, who in January, 1857, "submitted to the Treasury a proposal for the publication of materials for the history of this country from the invasion of the Romans to the reign of Henry VIII." Invaluable as are the official publications, which have been prefaced and edited by the most competent critics and scholars that the Master of the Rolls could draw to his aid, they can never overshadow or supersede the works of one who was the real path-breaker into the jungle of early English history. To Kemble belongs the imperishable honor of being the first to bring to light the most valuable of the early records, and to apply to their interpretation the rich results of German research into the childhood of the whole Teutonic race. No matter whether the Germans drove the English into historical scholarship or not, the fact remains that Kemble, who studied under the brothers Grimm at Göttingen, was the first to reject every suggestion of Roman influence, and to clearly perceive the all-impor-

[1] See "The Study of History in England and Scotland," by Paul Frédéricq, professor at the University of Ghent, *Johns Hopkins Studies*, fifth series, x. pp. 17, 32.

tant fact, now generally admitted, that the national life of the English people, both natural and political, began with the coming of the Teutonic invaders who, during the fifth and sixth centuries, transferred from the Continent into Britain their entire scheme of barbaric life. In 1839 Kemble began the publication of his "Codex Diplomaticus Ævi Saxonici," whereby "upwards of fourteen hundred documents, containing the grants of kings and bishops, the settlements of private persons, the conventions of landlords and tenants, the technical forms of judicial proceedings, have been placed in our hands." In 1840 Thorpe published his "Ancient Laws and Institutes of England;" and in 1848 Kemble published his "Saxons in England," in which was embodied the first effort ever made to state in a systematic form the results of the new sources of knowledge which he had done so much to bring to light. A co-worker with Kemble was Sir Francis Palgrave, who in 1832 published "The Rise and Progress of the English Commonwealth," and in 1851–64 the "History of Normandy and England." Kemble may have been guilty of exaggeration; he may at times have been misty in his conclusions. Sir Francis was no doubt often fanciful; at times he was certainly garrulous. And yet the fact remains that these pioneer scholars were the path-breakers who opened the way for the coming of the two English historians who have raised the science of history to as high a pitch, perhaps, as it has ever reached in ancient or modern times. Not until Mr. Freeman had completed his "History of the Norman Conquest," not until Bishop Stubbs had completed the "Constitutional History," the "Select Charters," and "the wonderful prefaces," did the grand inquest into the early and mediæval history of England, which Kemble and Palgrave had inaugurated, reach a definite and final result. Not until the head waters of the mighty river had thus been reached, not until the direction of the stream during its earlier course had been clearly mapped out by competent hands, did it become possible either for the general student of the history of the English people, or for the special student of the English constitution, to begin with the sources, and trace them without interruption to their ultimate conclusion. Until the analysis had ended, it was impossible for the synthesis to begin.

The advent of the new learning touching the early and mediæval history of England — which has rendered obsolete and worthless nearly all of the older disquisitions made before the fresh sources of knowledge had become available — has rendered necessary a reconsideration of nearly every branch of English history from a new point of view.   Not until the early periods, which contain the starting-points of everything, had been fully mastered, was it possible to firmly establish the premises upon which every far-reaching argument touching the social or political life of the English nation must necessarily proceed.   One of the first to perceive the necessity for a recasting of English history as a whole, from the new point of view, was the late John Richard Green, the gentle scholar, whose master hand was the first to trace the entire course of the history of the English people from its long-hidden sources in the "village-moots of Friesland or Sleswick," across the Northern Ocean into Britain, and across the Atlantic into North America.   Several years before the publication of the "History of the English People," the author of this work undertook the humbler and narrower task of drawing out, in the light of the new learning, the entire historic development of the English constitution, — a task which, up to that time, no one had ever attempted.   Since then has appeared the now famous "History of the English Constitution," by Dr. Rudolph Gneist, Professor of Law at the University of Berlin ; and also a work entitled "English Constitutional History," by the late Thomas Pitt Taswell-Langmead, sometime Professor of Constitutional Law and History at University College, London.   It is to the author rather a source of pleasure than of regret that the publication of these meritorious works should have preceded his own.   All attempts so far made to write a complete history of the English constitution are merely tentative, — the historian who is to cast the entire theme in its final form is yet to come.   His coming will finally be made possible through a series of imperfect efforts to execute his task by a succession of historical students, each one of whom will make some advance toward the common goal by utilizing all that is strongest, and by discarding all that is weakest, in the works of his predecessors.

The history of the growth of the English constitution, extending as it does through the annals of fourteen centuries, is by far too vast a theme for any one mind to assail in the way of original research. The best of the modern historical schools recognize the fact that the study of the history even of a single country can only proceed in a truly scientific manner through a system of coöperation based upon a division of labor. Each epoch must first be made the subject of thorough investigation by specialists who work upon the sources (what the Germans call *Quellenstudien*), and extract from them, through a kind of laboratory process, their full and true significance. Not until the original documents and other sources have been taken from the mine and purged of their dross by these special workers do the facts which they contain become available to those who desire to build upon them broad and comprehensive generalizations. In the collection of the materials which have entered into the structure of this work the author has striven to select out of the mass with which the subject is encumbered only such as have passed through the crucible of the latest and most enlightened criticism. In the attempt which has been made to work the materials thus collected into such a combination as will reveal a natural and unbroken sequence of constitutional growth, the method of the historical school has been followed,—a school which dogmatizes but little, which has little or nothing to do with *à priori* theories, and which teaches, with Sir James Macintosh, that "constitutions are not made, they grow." Only by the aid of this method, which recognizes the law of growth as the law of constitutional life, is it possible to trace the mighty stream of Teutonic democracy from its sources in the village-moots and state assembles of Friesland and Sleswick across the Northern Ocean into Britain, and across the Atlantic into North America. Only by the aid of this method is it possible to demonstrate the fact that the federal republic of the United States is the lineal descendant of those ancient German tribal federations of which we catch our first glimpses in the pages of Cæsar and Tacitus. When, in the light of this method, we contemplate this vast and unbroken development, which has affected so profoundly the destiny of mankind, we

> "Doubt not through the ages one increasing purpose runs,
> And the thoughts of men are widen'd with the process of the suns."

Although the historical method, which teaches the unity of all history, necessarily ignores such arbitrary divisions as sever the history of ancient from that of modern times, it nevertheless recognizes the fact that in the history of peoples, and of their institutions, there are epochs of growth so marked that they may be made the subject of separate and distinct treatment. The history of the growth of the

English constitution may be broken into two broad and well-defined periods. The first, which extends from the Teutonic conquest to the end of the Middle Ages, may be termed the formative period, — the period of "the making of the constitution." Although it may be true in a vague and general sense that the struggle of the constitution for existence came to an end in the reign of Edward I., it can hardly be maintained that its structure was complete in any full and perfect sense until its vital organ, the parliament, had developed all of its powers and privileges, — a result which was not reached earlier than the reigns of the Lancastrian kings. To this formative period — which has been made the subject of Bishop Stubbs's "Constitutional History," in three volumes — the author has devoted his first part or volume. To the second period, entitled "the after-growth of the constitution," — one part of which has been treated by Hallam, in three volumes, and another, by Sir Thomas Erskine May, in three volumes, — the author has devoted his second part or volume. Each part of this work may, therefore, be regarded as a complete treatise upon a distinct period of constitutional growth usually considered separately. And yet each part is so constructed that, when the two are taken together, they embrace a consecutive and harmonious treatment of the entire theme viewed as one unbroken development.

During the years which have passed by since the preparation of this work began, the author has received so much of sympathy, encouragement, and helpful criticism from historical scholars, not only in his own but in foreign lands, that he might be justly deemed ungracious should he now fail to make fitting acknowledgments to those from whom he has received special consideration. Some years ago it was his good fortune, during Mr. Freeman's last visit to the United States, to form a cordial acquaintance with the Nestor historian, who has made perhaps the largest and most invaluable contributions to the historical science of modern times. While that lamented and illustrious scholar for a long time consciously contributed very much to this undertaking in the form of encouragement, suggestion, and criticism, he unconsciously revealed to the author the fact that he was a master of that somewhat rare art of bestowing kindness without condescension. To his brother-scholar, the Rt. Rev. William Stubbs, Bishop of Oxford, the obligations of the author, although of a less personal, are not of a less serious character. To the master of the constitutional history of the Middle Ages, who sits alone at the head of his serene science, all students of the English constitution must go for the key, before they can hope to enter into its inner mysteries. While the pages of the "Constitutional History" and the "Select Charters" may not be inviting to the careless inquirer, to the earnest student they are mines of fact and of thought which may be worked without limit and without exhaustion. To Dr. Rudolph Gneist, Professor of Law at the University of Berlin, and to M. Boutmy, member of the Institute, and Director of the School of Political Sciences of Paris, the author desires to make special acknowledgments. Amongst those of his own countrymen who have generously aided him with judicious criticism and friendly encouragement, it is no less a pleasure than an honor to name Mr. John Fiske, of Cambridge; Hon. J. Randolph Tucker, of Virginia; Dr. H. B. Adams, Professor of History and Politics at the Johns Hopkins University; the late Mr. Alexander Johnston, Professor of Jurisprudence and Political Economy at Princeton; Mr. S. M. Macvane, University Professor of History at Harvard; Dr. James C. Welling, President of Columbia College, Washington, D. C.; the late Judge John A. Campbell, of Baltimore, and his peerless daughter, Mrs. Henrietta Campbell Lay; Mr. Richard M. Venable, Professor of Law at the University of Maryland; Mr. Wm. Preston Johnston, President of the Tulane University of Louisiana; Mr. Alfred Goldthwaite, of New Orleans, La.; the Hon. John T. Morgan, United States Senator from Alabama; and the Hon. N. H. R. Dawson, National Commissioner of Education. In his own home the author desires to express his thanks to his friends, the Hon. John Little Smith, the Hon. Fredrick G. Bromberg, and Peter J. Hamilton, Esq., three scholars of whom any city might be proud. And, last and most of all, may he not indicate, even in this public way, to his good wife, — whose loving hands have, during a period of many years, lessened the pain incident to feeble eyesight by transcribing these pages, often again and again, — a sense of gratitude which he "can ne'er express, yet cannot all conceal."

Mobile, Alabama, *September 12,* 1889.

ANALYTICAL TABLE OF CONTENTS.

INTRODUCTION.

ENGLISH ORIGIN OF THE FEDERAL REPUBLIC OF THE UNITED STATES.

BOOK I.

THE OLD–ENGLISH COMMONWEALTH.

CHAPTER I.

THE TEUTONIC ORIGIN OF ENGLISH INSTITUTIONS.

CHAPTER II.

THE FOUNDERS IN THE FATHERLAND.

CHAPTER III.

THE TEUTONIC CONQUEST AND SETTLEMENT OF BRITAIN.

CHAPTER IV

THE GROWTH OF NATIONAL UNITY.

CHAPTER V.

CONSTITUTION OF THE CONSOLIDATED KINGDOM.

BOOK II.

THE NORMAN CONQUEST.

CHAPTER I.

THE NORMAN DUCHY AND ITS DUKES.

CHAPTER II.

THE NORMAN KINGS OF ENGLAND.

CHAPTER III.

HENRY OF ANJOU — THE PERIOD OF FUSION.

CHAPTER IV.

THE WINNING OF THE CHARTERS.

BOOK III.

THE GROWTH AND DECLINE OF PARLIAMENT.

CHAPTER I.

HISTORY OF PARLIAMENT FROM EDWARD I. TO HENRY IV.

CHAPTER II.

HISTORY OF PARLIAMENT FROM HENRY IV. TO HENRY VII.

INTRODUCTION.

ENGLISH ORIGIN OF THE FEDERAL REPUBLIC OF THE UNITED STATES.

1. As the Constitution of the United States embodies a federal union of political sovereignties whose separate existence is older than that of the Union itself,[1] the simplest principle of analysis indicates the fact, that, in order fully to grasp the nature of the composite whole, it is first necessary to comprehend the nature of the units out of whose aggregation it arose. Any exhaustive investigation into the structure of our federal system must necessarily begin with the historical origin of the states that compose it.[2] The leading and practical purpose of this treatise will be to unfold in one unbroken story the gradual process of historical development through which the typical English state in America — the political unit in our federal system — came into existence.

2. A great French orator has said that "words are things," and to this the philologist may add, that, like all other human things, they are subject to the endless variations which are brought about by the changes of time, place, and circumstance. To the student of the "Science of Politics"[3] this truth is of paramount importance, for the reason that the cardinal terms in which he has to deal often represent in one age a train of ideas which completely vanish in another. Of this fact the word "state" may be used as a striking illustration. As employed in modern times the word "state" presents to the mind a political conception which a states-

[1] "They existed before it. They could exist without it." — Bryce, *The American Commonwealth*, vol. i. p. 14.

[2] "To examine the Union before we have studied the states, would be to adopt a method filled with obstacles. . . . The great political principles which now govern American society undoubtedly took their origin and their growth in the state." — De Tocqueville, *Democracy in America* (Bowen's ed.), vol. i. pp. 73, 74.

[3] The word Politics is here used in the sense which it bears in the name of the famous work of Aristotle. In this sense it is used by Bagehot in his *Physics and Politics*, by Pollock in his *History of the Science of Politics*, and by Freeman in his *Comparative Politics*.

man of the ancient world could hardly have grasped, for the reason that the political organization which we call the state had, in the ancient world, no existence. In order clearly to contrast the ancient conception of the state with that which exists in modern times, it will be necessary to utilize the results of recent research into the early history of political institutions. By the marvellous discoveries which have been made within the present century by the masters of the science of language, a great flood of light has been shed upon the earliest forms of social organization which existed in those nations with whose history we are at all concerned.

Compara-
tive philol-
ogy.
Through the labors of the comparative philologists, not only has the original unity of the Aryan race been clearly established, but its prehistoric language has also been so far reconstructed as to distinctly indicate the stage of civilization attained by it before the departure from the common Aryan home. In the words of Peschel, "When the ancient vocabulary of the primordial Aryan age is restored by collecting the roots common to all the members, we at the same time obtain an outline of the social condition of these nations in the most ancient period." [1] This great revelation, which in the history of the intellect has been called "the discovery of a new world," [2] has been brought about by the application of the comparative method to the study of language, whereby the roots common to a large group of kindred tongues have been traced back to a common source. But the comparative method has not been confined to the study of language only ; it has found a new and a broad field for its operation in its application to the comparative study of political institutions, of forms of government. Alongside of the science of comparative philology a new science has lately

Compara-
tive politics.
sprung into existence which has been styled comparative politics. To the votary of this new science "a political constitution is a specimen to be studied, classified, and labelled, as a building or an animal is studied, classified, and labelled by those to whom buildings or animals are objects of study. We have to note the likenesses, striking and unexpected as those likenesses often are, between the political constitutions

[1] Cf. *Enc. Brit.*, 9th ed. vol. viii. p. 622.   the work of Fredrick Schlegel, in
[2] See Max Müller's comments upon   *Science of Language*, p. 165.

of remote times and places; and we have, as far as we can, to classify our specimens according to the probable causes of those likenesses."[1] The most valuable single result so far attained by the application of the comparative method to the study of political institutions is embodied in the discovery that the unit of organization in all of the Aryan nations, from Ireland to Hindoostan, was the naturally organized association of kindred — the family swelled into the clan — which in a settled state assumed the form of a village-community.[2] "The two things, in short, the clan and the village-community, are the same thing, influenced only by those circumstances, geographical or otherwise, which allow one clan or company to adopt a more settled life, while another is driven to linger in, or even to fall back upon a ruder state of things. The γένος of Athens, the *gens* of Rome, the *mark* or *gemeinde* of the Teutonic nations, the village community of the East and, as I have said, the Irish clan, are all essentially the same thing."[3] When we have firmly taken hold of this fact; when we clearly understand that the original unit of organization was the same in all the Aryan nations, whether situated on the shores of the Mediterranean or the Baltic, we have possessed ourselves of the atom or unit, which, in different forms and different combinations, everywhere enters into the structure of the state.

Following the usual historical order, we naturally turn to the Hellenic world, in which the science of politics was born, in order to ascertain the elements of political organization which there existed when authentic history begins. The dominant political idea which we there encounter is embodied in the independent city which stands towards all other cities as a sovereign commonwealth whose internal affairs are regulated by its own domestic constitution. When the internal organization of such a city is examined, the fact is revealed that the city-commonwealth is a composite whole, which has arisen out of the aggregation of village communities. The first stage in the aggregation is represented by the gathering of a group of village communities or clans (γένεα) into a

Unit of organization the village-community.

The Greek city-commonwealth.

[1] Freeman, *Comparative Politics*, p. 23. In this brilliant work the name of the new science finds its origin.
[2] Cf. Sir Henry Maine, *Village-Communities in the East and West*, passim.

The village-community is not, however, an exclusively Aryan possession. — Maine, *Early Hist. of Inst.*, p. 77.
[3] *Comparative Politics*, p. 102.

brotherhood (φρατρία) ; the second by the gathering of brother-
hoods into a tribe; the last by the gathering of tribes into a
city. "Several families formed the phratry, several phratries
the tribe, several tribes the city. Family, phratry, tribe,
city, were, moreover, societies exactly similar to each other,
which were formed one after the other by a series of federa-

Only con-
ception of
the state
that existed
in the Hel-
lenic world.

tions." [1] The aggregate thus made up, the independent city,
embodied the only practical conception of the state which existed in the Hellenic world.[2] To the Greek mind the state,
the city-commonwealth, was an organized society of men
dwelling in a walled city with a surrounding territory not too
large to allow its free inhabitants to habitually assemble
within its walls to discharge the duties of citizens.[3] In this
system of cities, internally organized after one general model,

✓Aristotle,
the founder
of political
science.

were contained the political conditions with which Aristotle,
the acknowledged founder of political science,[4] was brought
into contact ; and, in obedience to his practical temper, he
begins his political speculations with a description of the
forms of government actually existing around him. It is
probable, that in order to collect sufficient data to support
the statements and conclusions contained in his Politics, he
made, as a preparatory study thereto, the collection called
the Constitutions, which is said to have contained a description of the organization, manners, and customs of one hundred and fifty-eight states or cities.[5] However that may have
been, he informs us in the general introduction, which forms
the first book of his Politics, that the state differs from the
household only as to the number of its members, a fact which
will appear from an examination of its elements. Out of the
very necessities of social existence arise the relations of husband and wife, parent and child, master and servant, and thus
the household is formed. Out of a union of households

---

[1] De Coulanges, *The Ancient City*
(Small's trans.), p. 168. See, also,
Comparative Politics, p. 104.

[2] "During the most brilliant times
of the Greek Commonwealths, the
City, and nothing higher or lower, was
the one acknowledged political unit."
Comparative Politics, p. 83.

[3] Aristotle thought that a state
should not be so large as to deny to
its citizens the opportunity to become

familiar with each other. 'Αναγκαίον
γνωρίζειν ἀλλήλους, ποῖοί τινές εἰσι, τοὺς
πολίτας. *Pol.*, bk. vii. ch. iv. 13.

[4] See Pollock, *Hist. Science of Politics*, p. 1.

[5] The main body of materials thus
collected has been lost, but the fragments which remain have been collected and annotated by Neumann, and
are contained in Bekker's Oxford edition of Aristotle.

arises the village or tribe. Out of the union of villages or tribes arises a community of a higher order, the state, which is the natural and necessary completion of the process of aggregation in which the family is the unit or starting point. Neither the family nor the tribe is in itself sufficient for all the wants of social existence; it is only in a union of tribes — the state — that man finds the one form of life that will fully develop all of his capabilities. The conclusion thus attained is embodied in Aristotle's famous maxim that "man is born to be a citizen." The cityless[1] man ($\check{a}\pi o \lambda \iota s$) — the natural man of Hobbes and Rousseau — must be more or less than man, — either superhuman or a monster. Aristotle's political reflections were confined in the main to the constitutions of Greek states, and the typical Greek state was the independent city. It is true that sometimes a Greek city would be reduced to a relation of bondage to another city, and it would sometimes confederate upon equal or unequal terms with other cities; but there was never any such thing as admitting either subjects or allies to a common franchise, there was never anything like a merger of the independent city into a larger aggregation, which, in any proper political sense, could be called a nation.[2]

"Man is born to be a citizen."

When we pass from the Greek to the Italian peninsula, we there find the idea of the independent city to be the leading political idea, and we also find the Italian city to be the resultant of the process of aggregation heretofore described in which the village community or clan is the unit or starting point. In Italy the village-community appears as the *gens*. Out of the union of *gentes* arose the tribe, out of the union of tribes arose the state or city-commonwealth.[3] But the idea of the state as an independent city was never carried out with the same completeness in Italy as in Greece, for the reason that the Italian cities, which were generally smaller than those of Greece, manifested a greater willingness to join together in confederations. In this way the history of ancient Italy is far more a history of confederations than of

The Italian city-commonwealth.

---

[1] "He is the unit out of whom, if there be only enough of them, theorists of the Social Contract school undertake to build up the State. This is an enterprise at which Aristotle would have stared and gasped." — Pollock, *Hist. Science of Politics*, p. 9.

[2] *Comparative Politics*, pp. 84, 91, 92.

[3] See De Coulanges, *The Ancient City*, pp. 131–146, 154–177.

single cities.[1]   And yet it was upon the soil of Italy that a group of village communities grew into a single independent city[2] that centralized within its walls the political power of

the world.   The way in which Rome accomplished this marvellous result was by departing from the exclusive policy of the Greek cities, and by extending the right of Roman citizenship alike to her conquered enemies and to her faithful allies.   The franchise of the Roman city was first extended to Italy, then to Gaul and Spain, and finally to the whole Roman world.[3]   In the end a right so widely bestowed became of course utterly worthless; but the theory upon which the right was conferred was never for a moment lost sight of. The freeman who received the franchise of the Roman city could only enjoy it within her own walls; it was only within the local limits of the ruling city that the supreme powers of the state could be exercised.[4]   And so whether we take for illustration the exclusive Greek city, or the great Latin city extending its franchise to all the world, the ancient conception of the state as the city-commonwealth stands forth clearly and distinctly defined.

3. Out of the settlements made by the Teutonic nations upon the wreck of the Roman Empire has gradually arisen the modern conception of the state as a nation occupying a definite area of territory with fixed geographical boundaries, — the state as known to modern international law.   In the Germania of Tacitus we have the contemporaneous observations of one of the greatest and most accurate of historians upon the social and political organization of the Teutonic race while yet in its childhood.   By the aid of this invaluable sketch it is possible to establish by direct and positive evidence the existence of those primitive elements of organization, common to the whole Aryan world, whose existence in the Greek and Italian peninsulas can only be inferred from

[1] "The Italian confederations had from the beginning a closer union and a nearer approach to national unity than the later and more brilliant confederations of Greece." *Comparative Politics*, p. 96.

[2] Maine, *Early Hist. of Inst.*, p. 84.

[3] Guizot, *Hist. Rep. Govt.*, pp. 181,182. As to the edict of Antoninus Caracalla,

extending the privilege of Roman citizenship to all the free inhabitants of the empire, see Maine, *Ancient Law*, p. 139; Gibbon, *Decline and Fall*, vol. i. pp. 185, 193, 194.

[4] "Within the walls of Rome alone could be consummated all the acts of a Roman citizen." — Guizot, *Hist. Rep. Govt.*, p. 184.

traces and survivals. In the words of Sir Henry Maine, —
"As societies do not advance concurrently, but at different
rates of progress, there have been epochs at which men
trained to habits of methodical observation have really been
in a position to watch and describe the infancy of mankind.
Tacitus made the most of such an opportunity."[1] According
to his account the race now called Teutonic, although of the
same physical type, and speaking the same language, and
although possessed of a common mythology, and a common
system of social, political, and military institutions, did not
possess in its own tongue a common name by which to describe the race as a whole, nor any form of central political
organization.[2] This homogeneous race was broken up into
an endless number of political communities or tribes which
stood to each other in a state of complete political isolation,
except when united in temporary confederacies. The typical
Teutonic tribe — the *civitas* of Cæsar and Tacitus — represented an aggregation of hundreds, while the hundred represented an aggregation of village-communities.[3] The spot
inhabited by the village community is called in German muniments the mark, — an area of land marked out and defined
by settled boundaries. The absolute ownership of the territory embraced within the mark was vested in the community
itself, or in the state of which the mark was a part, while the
right to its common enjoyment was vested in its qualified
members. Territorially the mark was divided into three
parts, — the village lands, the arable lands, and the common
or waste lands. In the centre of the mark was situated the
village in which the markmen dwelt in their homesteads, surrounded by inclosures and out-houses. The possession of
such a homestead was evidence of the fact that its possessor
was a fully qualified member of the mark, and as such entitled to a full share in the enjoyment of every right that belonged to any other member of the community. The arable
mark was usually divided into three great fields, whose cultivation was regulated by a system of minute and complicated
rules, while the use of the woods, pastures, and meadows was
enjoyed in obedience to a scheme of strict proportion. The

Marginal notes: Teutonic tribe, — *civitas* of Cæsar and Tacitus.

The mark.

---

[1] *Ancient Law*, p. 116.
[2] Tac. *Germania*, cc. 1-4.
[3] See below, bk. i. ch. ii. c. 5.

internal affairs of the mark were regulated by a village council or mark-moot in which every markman had his place.   In
the assembly of the mark was transacted all business which
arose out of the system of common cultivation, and out of
Parallel be-
tween the
Teutonic,
Greek, and
Latin tribe. the enjoyment of common rights.[1]   The parallel between the
Teutonic, the Greek, and the Latin tribe seems to be complete.   The γένος, the *gens*, the *mark* represent the same
thing — the village-community; while the φρατρία, the *curia*,
the *hundred* seem to represent the same thing — a group or
union of village-communities.[2]   Out of the aggregation of such
intermediate groups or hundreds arose the tribe itself.   But
here the parallel ceases.   In the Mediterranean peninsulas the
resultant of a union of tribes was the city-commonwealth, —
in Teutonic lands the resultant of a union of tribes was not a
city at all but a nation.[3]   In ancient Greece and Italy the city
became the heart, the centre of social and political life ; while
in countries inhabited by the Teutonic race the idea of the
city never became dominant.   The Teutonic city, if it was to
be found at all, was simply the dwelling-place of part of the
nation who were in no wise privileged above those who dwelt
beyond its bounds.   At the time Tacitus wrote the typical
Teutonic tribe (*civitas*) was a distinct commonwealth, the largest and highest political aggregate.   Not until nearly a hun-
Teutonic
tribes gath-
ered into
nations. dred years later were these scattered tribes gathered into
larger wholes — into nations.[4]   When this stage was reached,
when tribes were fused into the higher political unit — the
nation — the primitive Teutonic conception of the state or
commonwealth widened into its full and final development.
But another stage of growth had yet to be passed before the
new unit, which thus arose out of an aggregation of tribes,
reached the full modern conception of the state as a nation
possessing a definite portion of the earth's surface with fixed
geographical boundaries.   The fact must be borne in mind
that the primary bond which united the people who composed
a Teutonic nation was a personal one, — the national king

---

[1] For the authorities as to the primitive Teutonic mark, see below, bk. i.
ch. ii. c. 7.

[2] *Comparative Politics*, pp. 102–105, 117.

[3] "The Teutons passed from the tribal stage into the national stage without ever going through the city stage

at all." Ibid., p. 101. "In Greece and
Italy the union of tribes formed only
the city; among all the branches of
the Teutonic stock the union of tribes
formed the nation." Ibid., p. 120.

[4] Zeuss, *Die Deutschen und die Nachbarstämme*, pp. 303, 304.

was first among the people, the embodiment of the national being, but not the king of a particular area or region of territory. The idea of sovereignty was not associated in the Teutonic mind with dominion over a particular portion or subdivision of the earth's surface. The Merovingian line of chieftains were not kings of France, they were kings of the Franks; Alaric was king of the Goths wherever the Goths happened to be, whether upon the banks of the Tiber, the Tagus, or the Danube.[1] The leading idea which seems to have prevailed among the conquering nations who settled down upon the wreck of Rome was that they were simply encamped upon the land whose possession they had won. The conception of sovereignty which the Teutons brought with them from the forest and the steppe was distinctly tribal or national and not territorial. The general nature of the transition whereby the primitive notion of tribal sovereignty was gradually superseded by that of territorial sovereignty has been described as a movement from personal to territorial organization;[2] from a state of things in which personal freedom and political right were the dominant ideas to a state of things in which those ideas have become bound up with and subservient to the possession of land.[3] The most striking single result of the transition, — which, for the want of a better term, has been called "the process of feudalization,"[4] — is that the elective chief of the nation, the primitive embodiment of the tribal sovereignty, is gradually transformed into the hereditary lord of a given area of land. The new conception of sovereignty, which thus grew out of "the process of feudalization," did not become established, however, until after the breaking up of the empire of Charles the Great, out of whose fragments have arisen most of the states of modern Europe. The completion of the transition is marked by the accession of the Capetian dynasty in France. When the hundred years' struggle between the Dukes of Paris and the descendants of Charles the Great ended in the triumph of Hugh Capet, he not only assumed the dynastic title of

Tribal sovereignty.

Territorial sovereignty the outcome of "the process of feudalization."

---

[1] Maine, *Ancient Law*, p. 100; Freeman, *Norm. Conq.*, vol. i. p. 53.

[2] Palgrave, *Eng. Commonw.*, pt. i. p. 62.

[3] Stubbs, *Const. Hist.*, vol. i. p. 166.

[4] Maine, *Village - Communities*, lecture v. "The Process of Feudalization" is its title.

King of the French, but he also styled himself King of France.[1] Hugh Capet and his descendants were kings in the new territorial sense; they were kings who stood in the same relation to the land over which they ruled as the baron to his estate, the tenant to his freehold. The form thus assumed by the monarchy in France was reproduced in each subsequent dominion established or consolidated; and thus has arisen the state-system of modern Europe in which the idea of territorial sovereignty is the basis of all international relations.[2] The modern conception of the state is, therefore, an outgrowth of "the process of feudalization" through which the Teutonic nations passed after their settlement within the limits of the Roman Empire.

Growth of the English kingdom.

4. Amongst all the states that have arisen out of the settlements made by the Teutonic nations on Roman soil, there is not one whose political life has remained more pure, or whose political development has been more persistent or more unbroken than that of the English kingdom. This condition of things has arisen in the main out of the special circumstances under which the Teutonic settlements in Britain were made. In the first place the very physical difficulties that had to be met and overcome impressed upon the Teutonic invasion of Britain a character and form at once local and peculiar. The invaders were compelled to cross the sea in ships, and their sea craft and war craft could only transport bodies of men more or less numerous, and not great armies of invasion by which the whole land could be suddenly overrun. All the evidence goes to show that the Teutonic invaders came into Britain in disconnected bands, more or less numerous, each under its own leader, who singled out some

---

[1] "The important change occurred when the feudal prince of a limited territory surrounding Paris began, from the accident of his uniting an unusual number of suzerainties in his own person, to call himself King of France, at the same time that he usurped from the earlier house their dynastic title of Kings of the French."—Maine, *Ancient Law,* p. 104.

Mr. Freeman was at first inclined to challenge this statement. He has since written me as follows: "I should not say that what Maine says about *Rex*

Francorum and *Rex Franciæ* was other than right in a general way. Those things came in gradually. *Roi de France* comes in pretty early, as early as Wace. I doubt whether *Rex Franciæ* is ever used, till Hen. IV's *Rex Franciæ et Navarræ*, as a formal Latin title." See also *Norman Conquest,* vol. i. Appendix, note M, p. 395.

[2] Upon this whole subject of "territorial sovereignty," and its relations to modern international law, see Maine, *Ancient Law,* pp. 99–108.

special district of country for conquest and settlement. Such a leader, with the limited force at his command, necessarily circumscribed his efforts to a narrow area, from which by dint of hard fighting he was obliged to drive the Celtic masters of the soil. In this way, bit by bit, the land was won. Moving from the south, the east, and the northeast, the invaders drove the Britons slowly to the west. The struggle from its very nature was a bitter one. Invasion no longer signified, as upon the Continent, forcible intrusion, — it became, within the districts which the conquerors made their own between the middle of the fifth century and the end of the sixth, practically equivalent to extermination. "The plain fact is that, in utter contrast to the phenomena of Teutonic conquest on the mainland, the Britons were, as a race, exterminated within those parts of Britain which the English occupied while they were still heathens. . . . How far in any particular district the vanquished were slain, how far they were simply driven out, we never can tell. It is enough that they were exterminated, got rid of in one way or another, within what now became the English border." [1] "Though the literal extirpation of a nation is an impossibility, there is every reason to believe that the Celtic inhabitants of those parts of Britain which had become English at the end of the sixth century had been as nearly extirpated as a nation can be. The women would, doubtless, be often spared; but, as far as the male sex is concerned, we may feel sure that death, emigration, or personal slavery were the only alternatives which the vanquished found at the hands of our fathers." [2] Under such favorable conditions as these the whole fabric of Teutonic life was replanted in a practically free and unincumbered soil. In a state of pure barbaric

"The Teutonic theory."

[1] Freeman, *The English People in its Three Homes*, p. 133.

[2] *Norman Conquest*, vol. i. p. 18, 3d ed. As Mr. Freeman is now generally regarded as the champion of "the Teutonic theory," I have preferred to state it in his own language. His latest utterance upon the subject is contained in his *Four Oxford Lectures*, 1887, in which he quotes both of the passages given in the text. See his lecture on *Teutonic Conquest in Gaul and Britain*, pp. 61–112. See also

Green, *Making of England*, p. 132. For the contrary view see, as to the survival of Roman civilization, Coote's *Romans of Britain* (1878); as to the permanence of the Celtic race, Pike's *Origin of the English;* as to Celtic influence upon language, Kennedy, *Ethnological and Linguistic Essays* (1861); as to "The Welsh Element in English Law," *Law Magazine and Review*, No. cclviii. Nov., 1885; Taswell-Langmead, *Eng. Const. Hist.*, pp. 2, 3, and notes.

heathenism the invaders passed, without intermediate probation, from their seats in the far north to their island home,
bearing with them in their blood and bone the primeval
polity of the fatherland. The details of the process by which
the old Teutonic polity was transferred to Britain are not
recorded, but from the state of things which is found to exist
when authentic history begins the conclusion is irresistible

that the Teutonic settlements in Britain were a substantial
reproduction of the older state of things described in the
Germania. The chain of evidence upon which this conclusion rests, "no criticism is strong enough or sharp enough to
sever."[1] The village community which appears in Germany
as the mark, reappears as the tun or township in Britain,
where it becomes the "unit of the constitutional machinery."[2]

The township, like the mark, is at once a cultivating and a
political community, and in its qualified members resides the
power to order their own village and agricultural life. This
power is vested in the village assembly or tun-moot in which
the townsmen regulate the internal affairs of the township by
the making of by-laws, a term which is said to mean laws
enacted by a "by," as the township was called in the northern
shires. The tun-moot elected its own officers, and also provided for the representation of its interests in the courts of
the hundred and the shire, where the gerefa and four discreet

men appeared for the township. In this arrangement appears
the earliest form of the representative principle. "In these
four discreet men sent to speak for their township in the old
county assembly, we have the germ of institutions that have
ripened into the House of Commons and into the legislatures
of modern kingdoms and republics. In the system of representation thus inaugurated lay the future possibility of such
gigantic political aggregates as the United States of America."[3]
Out of a union of townships arose the hundred, out of a union
of hundreds arose the primitive *rice* or kingdom, — the

civitas of Cæsar and Tacitus.[4] But before the historic period
begins these primitive states in which the settlers originally
grouped themselves have ceased to exist as independent com-

[1] Stubbs, *Const. Hist.*, vol. i. p. 71.
[2] Ibid., vol. i. p. 82.

[3] John Fiske, *American Political Ideas*, p. 71.
[4] Stubbs, *Const. Hist.*, vol. i. p. 119.

munities, — they have become bound up in seven or eight larger aggregates generally known as the heptarchic kingdoms. These larger aggregates were finally fused into a single consolidated kingdom, which is the ultimate outcome of the process of aggregation in which the local, self-governing communities descend in status without the loss of their autonomy. The consolidated kingdom represents an aggregation of shires; the shire an aggregation of hundreds; the hundred an aggregation of townships. Upon the substructure thus made up of local, self-governing communities the English political system has ever depended for its permanency, its elasticity, its enduring power. In every one of these communities the idea of local self-government was intensely developed, and in their very structure were imbedded, from the beginning, the germs of the representative system. And from the tendency — conscious or unconscious — upon the part of Englishmen to reproduce these self-governing communities in other lands has resulted the ascendancy and power of the English nation as a colonizing nation. The entire fabric of the new society — out of whose political elements arose in Britain the constitution of the consolidated kingdom — was purely Teutonic. Its language was made up of a set of dialects of the Low German; the only religion which it possessed was the religion of Woden; its only conception of government and law was a purely Teutonic conception. The witness of language, of religion, and of law all point to the one irresistible conclusion that, within the limits which they made their own, the conquerors of Britain "created a Germany outside of Germany."[1] The old Teutonic constitution was thus replanted in its purity in the free and unincumbered soil of an island world, where it has been able to work out its historic development in a state of comparative isolation. So deeply were its foundations laid in its island home that it has been able to survive, and to preserve its identity, through all the vicissitudes of time and of change through which it has passed. In the political history of the world the Teutonic constitution, which thus matured on British soil, occupies the foremost place for two

The heptarchic kingdoms.

The consolidated kingdom.

New society purely Teutonic.

[1] Taine, *Hist. of Eng. Literature*, vol. i. p. 50. Upon the subject of the Teutonic conquest and settlement of Britain, see ch. iii. bk. i.

reasons. In the first place, it has had the most continuous and unbroken development; in the second place, out of that unbroken development has been evolved the most important political principle with which the world has so far become acquainted — the principle of representative government.

Representative principle a Teutonic invention.

Of this principle, which has been justly called a Teutonic invention, the ancient world knew practically nothing.[1] The political systems of all the Teutonic nations, as they appear to us when written history begins, contained germs of the representative principle, — germs which were imbedded in the organization of their local, self-governing communities. And in every one of the modern European states that have arisen out of the settlements made by the Teutonic nations on Roman soil a serious attempt has been at some time made in the direction of representative government. But the remarkable fact is that in every Continental state in which such an attempt was made, it ended at last in failure and disappoint-

Representative government dies out everywhere but in England.

ment. By the sixteenth century every effort in the direction of representative government upon the Continent of Europe had come to an end.[2] In England only among the Teutonic nations did the representative system survive; in England only has the representative principle been able to maintain a continuous existence. In this way the English nation has been able to hand down the representative principle from the barbarian epoch to modern times; in this way England has become the "mother of parliaments" — the teacher of the science of representative government to all the world. Since the date of the French Revolution nearly all the states of continental Europe have organized national assemblies after the model of the English Parliament in a spirit of conscious imitation.[3]

---

[1] "It is the great political invention of Teutonic Europe, the one form of political life to which neither Thucydides, Aristotle, nor Polybios ever saw more than the faintest approach."— Freeman, *Hist. Fed. Govt.*, vol. i. p. 67.

[2] "In the fourth period, on the Continent, all efforts towards a representative system have failed or almost entirely disappeared; pure monarchy prevails. England alone decidedly obtains a constitutional government. This epoch lasts from the sixteenth century to the French Revolution."— Guizot, *Hist. Rep. Govt.*, p. 258. See also p. 15.

[3] "The British political model was followed by France, by Spain and Portugal, and by Holland and Belgium, combined in the Kingdom of the Netherlands; and, after a long interval, by Germany, Italy, and Austria."— Maine, *Popular Govt.*, p. 13.

5. In our own land the case is far otherwise. The representative systems which sprang up as a part of the constitutional machinery of the several provincial states founded by English settlers upon American soil were in no proper sense the result of imitation. Like the states themselves of which they were a part, they were the predestined product of a natural process of reproduction.[1] The constitutional history of these provincial states does not begin with the landing of the English in America in the seventeenth century, but with the landing of the English in Britain in the fifth.[2] The English emigrants who founded upon the eastern coast of what is now the United States a group of colonial commonwealths brought with them in their blood and bone, and in a matured form, that peculiar system of political organization which had been slowly developing in the mother country for centuries. They brought with them ready made the language, the law, the institutions of the old land to be modified and adapted to the changed conditions of the new. The settlements made by the English colonists in America in the seventeenth century were in all material particulars substantial reproductions of the English settlements made in Britain in the fifth. In both instances the settlers crossed the sea in ships in small companies, and in both lands they grouped themselves together in distinct and practically independent self-governing communities.[3]

The tide of Aryan migration, from which has been peopled both the Old World and the New, has traversed no land in its whole westward course more capable of supplying all of the varied wants of a great and growing nationality than that in which the English settlers in America made their homes. The vast expanse of territory now embraced within the limits of the United States offered to the European emigrant not only nearly every variety of soil and climate to which he had

Growth of the English colonies in America.

Physiography of North America, and its effects upon immigration.

---

[1] "The local assemblies in which the colonists were represented 'were not formally instituted, but grew up by themselves, because it was in the nature of Englishmen to assemble.'" — Maine, *Pop. Govt.*, p. 223. Hutchinson says, "This year (1619) a House of Burgesses *broke out* in Virginia." See Seeley, *The Expansion of Eng.*, p. 67.

[2] Freeman, *The English People in its Three Homes*, p. 360.

[3] "Wherever the Anglo-Saxon race has gone, wherever they have carried their language and laws, these communities, each with a local administration of its own selection, have gone with them." — Mr. Justice Brown, in *The People v. Draper*, 15 N. Y. pp. 532, 562.

been accustomed in the Old World, but it also offered him easy access to its heart through a system of mighty waterways navigable through nearly their entire course. The fact that most of the navigable rivers of America flow eastward made the new land easily accessible from the Atlantic to those who had once passed the difficulties and perils of its navigation westward. In addition to such inducements as these America also offered to the European emigrant a new and cheap source of bread with which to sustain the beginnings of life in the wilderness.[1] Early in the sixteenth century a spirited competition began between England, France, and Spain for the possession of that part of North America which is bounded on the north by the great lakes and the St. Lawrence, on the south by the Gulf of Mexico, on the west by the Mississippi, and on the east by the Atlantic. The results of the first period of struggle for the possession of the heart of the New World may be summed up in the assertion that while Spain succeeded in securing a footing upon its southern, and France upon its northern border, every attempt at settlement made by Englishmen in America during the sixteenth century ended before its close in failure and disappointment. The only circumstance from which England could draw any consolation whatever was embodied in the fact that while her rivals had secured a precarious hold upon Canada and Florida, their mutual hostilities and contentions[2] had prevented either from entering into possession of the vast and priceless central district in which the English settlements of the seventeenth century were destined to be established. During that period it was that the permanent English settlements in America were made which were finally incorporated in the thirteen colonies that grew into the Federal Republic of the United States.

Struggle for possession between England, France, and Spain.

In order to regulate the competition for the possession of the New World, and to avoid conflicting settlements, and consequent war with each other, the European nations agreed " to establish a principle which all should acknowledge as the law by which the right of acquisition, which they all asserted,

European nations agree that discovery gives title.

---

[1] As to the "Effects of the physiography of North America on men of European origin," see *Narrative and Critical Hist. of Am.*, vol. iv. pp. x.–xxx.

[2] See Doyle, *English Colonies in Am., Virginia, etc.*, p. 100.

should be regulated as between themselves. This principle was that discovery gave title to the government by whose subjects, or by whose authority, it was made, against all other European governments, which title might be consummated by possession." [1] The principle thus established assumed that the Indian tribes found upon the soil were mere temporary occupants. According to the theory of the English constitution the title to all newly-discovered lands accrued to the king in his public and regal character, and the exclusive right to grant them resided in him as a part of the royal prerogative: "upon these principles rest the various charters and grants of territory made on this continent." [2] The claim of the English crown to the territory upon which the English settlements in America were made was based upon the voyages of the Cabots made along the American coast during the years 1497–98.[3] The first patent issued to the Cabots — the oldest surviving document connecting the old land with the new [4] — gave to the patentees the right to sail under the royal ensign, and to set up the royal banner in any newly discovered land as lieutenants and vassals of the king. The inchoate right thus acquired by discovery at the close of the fifteenth century did not ripen into a perfect title until early in the seventeenth, when the permanent English settlements in America were made. The great title-deed under which the English settlers in America took actual and permanent possession of the greater part of the Atlantic seaboard is represented by a charter granted by James I. on the 10th April, 1606, to certain patentees, wherein he created two distinct corporations; and then, in the same document, granted to the one known as the London Company the section of North American seacoast lying between 34° and 38° N. lat.; and to the other known as the Plymouth Company the section lying between 41° and 45° — each grant having an indefinite western extension. The intervening expanse, lying between 38° and 41°, was placed as a march or border

English crown bases its claim upon voyages of the Cabots.

The great title-deed — James I.'s charter of April 10, 1606.

---

[1] Marshall, C. J., in *Johnson* v. *McIntosh*, 8 Wheat. p. 573.
[2] Taney, C. J., in *Martin et al.* v. *The Lessee of Waddell*, 16 Peters, p. 409.
[3] See *Nar. and Crit. Hist. Am.*, vol. iii. pp. 1–58.

[4] This document, which is dated 5 March, 1495 (1496 new style), is printed in the Hakluyt Society's edition of the *Divers Voyages*, and in Rymer's *Fœdera*.

land between the domains of the two companies, and its common use was made subject to the limitation that neither should plant a colony within a hundred miles of one previously made by the other.[1] Although the two corporations thus intrusted with the mighty work of English colonization in the New World — a work which in the hands of private adventurers had been so singularly unfortunate — were short lived, the fact remains that during the brief period of their existence they not only established representative government upon American soil, but they also brought about the founding of two typical settlements which have moulded the whole after course of American history.   Under the auspices of the London or Southern Company was founded in 1607 the Virginian settlement at Jamestown — the first permanent settlement made by Englishmen upon the soil of the New World. Twelve years later (1619) the management of the London Company passed into the hands of liberal-minded men at home who gave to the infant colony the right to convene the first American representative assembly.[2]   Five years later (1624) the charter of this company, which had thus made its impress upon all time, was brutally revoked through a legal judgment, which was " one of the earliest of those efforts in which the Stuart reigns were so fruitful, efforts to wrest the process of law to the arbitrary purposes of the crown."[3]   Out of the vast territory originally granted to the London Company were carved the domains finally distributed between the five southern colonies of Virginia, Maryland, North Carolina, South Carolina, and Georgia.[4]   Under a license obtained from the Plymouth or North Virginia Company a Puritan settlement was established in 1620 at Plymouth, in the southeastern part of what is now the State of Massachusetts, by a

The London Company and its work.

The Plymouth Company and its work.

---

[1] This charter may be found in *Charters and Constitutions*, compiled under the order of the U. S. Senate, by Ben : Perley Poore, part ii. p. 1888. It is also contained in Stith, and in Hazard's *Hist. Collections.*

[2] The manuscript proceedings of this assembly, contained in the State Paper Office, London, were published in 1874 as a State Senate Document, Colonial Records of Virginia, with notes by T. H. Wynne. They were first published in 1857 in the *Collections of the N. Y. Hist. Society.*

[3] Doyle, *English Colonies in America, Virginia, etc.*, p. 182.

[4] I will here refer once for all to the admirable article upon the United States — " Part I. History and Constitution " — in *Enc. Brit.*, 9th ed., by Prof. Alexander Johnston, of Princeton, to whom I am indebted for several valuable suggestions.

band of separatists from the English Church, who had for a time dwelt in Holland, prior to their final departure from the mother country to their New England home. North of the Plymouth settlement was established at a little later day another, by men of the same general creed, but of a broader culture, which, in March, 1629, was incorporated by royal charter under the name of the Governor and Company of Massachusetts Bay in New England — a charter which was obtained in order to put at rest any difficulty as to the title of the colony originally derived from a grant made to it by the Council of New England.[1] After establishing the colony of Massachusetts Bay, into which the Plymouth settlement was finally incorporated,[2] the North Virginia Company in June, 1635, surrendered its charter to the crown, and out of the territory which had been granted it were carved the domains finally distributed between the four northern colonies of Massachusetts, Connecticut, Rhode Island, and New Hampshire. Out of the march or border land, fixed between the territories of the London and Plymouth Companies by the original grant of 1606, were carved the domains of New York, New Jersey, and Pennsylvania, from the last of which was clipped the State of Delaware. In this wise the heart of North America, which passed to the English crown by right of discovery, was granted, as any royal manor might have been granted,[3] first, to the two trading companies created by the charter of 1606, and, after their dissolution, to the thirteen colonies which united in the making of the Declaration of Independence.[4]

The soil upon which the English colonies in America were planted was granted to them as *terra regis* by the English crown; it was not granted to them as folkland by the English parliament.[5] The charters under which the colonial govern-

The soil granted to the colonies by the crown and not by the parliament.

---

[1] For the history of these settlements, see *Nar. and Crit. Hist.*, vol. iii. pp. 219–384.

[2] October, 1691.

[3] The language of the charter is, "To be holden of us, our heirs and successors, as our Manor of East-Greenwich, in free and common socage, and not in capite."

[4] "Within the period of ten years, under the last of the Tudors and the first of the Stuarts, two trading char-

ters were issued to two companies of English adventurers. One of these charters is the root of English title to the East, and the other to the West. One of these companies has grown into the Empire of India; the other into the United States of North America." — *The Am. Commonw.*, Bryce, vol. i. p. 416.

[5] See *Essays in A. S. Law*, pp. 91–93, 98–100.

ments were organized were likewise royal grants; they were not concessions from the English legislature. In contemplation of English law the whole group of colonial governments in America created or confirmed by royal charters were mere corporations created by the king, and subject like all others of their kind to his visitorial power, and to the power of his courts to dissolve them in a proper case presented for that

Colonies mere corporations with charters irrevocable as to the crown. purpose.[1] Until some cause of forfeiture arose, the grant, as between the crown and the patentees, was irrevocable, — it being the settled doctrine of English law that after a grant of corporate powers made by the crown had been once accepted, the crown could not resume the grant without the consent of those in whom its privileges had been vested.[2] The irrevocable rights thus acquired by the colonists as against the crown were revocable, however, at the hands of the parliament. Under the theory of the English constitution, then as now, "Its power is legally speaking illimitable. It may create, and abolish, and change, at its pleasure, with or without the assent of the people or corporation to be thereby affected."[3] A practical illustration of the exercise of this parliamentary power may be found in the famous Municipal Corporations Reform Act of 5 and 6 Will. IV., by which the whole English municipal system was reorganized and reëstablished. Subject to this illimitable power of the Imperial parliament the English crown organized upon the soil of the New World a group of colonial governments, whose differences of internal organization, and whose greater or less dependence upon the crown, distinguished them broadly from each other.[4] Those colonies to which the crown gave most sparingly the right to regulate their own affairs are generally known as

The royal colonies — Virginia. royal colonies, — a typical representative of which may be found in the Colony of Virginia, whose early constitutional growth happily illustrates the general process of evolution through which the most dependent of the English settlements in America was rapidly transformed from a servile corporation

---

[1] The charter of Massachusetts was cancelled in 1684 by the crown judges in a proceeding begun by *scire facias* (Palfrey's *New Eng.*, vol. iii. pp. 391–393); that of Virginia, by a legal judgment rendered in 1624.

[2] Cf. Dillon, *Municipal Corporations,* vol. i. p. 109, 2d ed., and cases cited.

[3] Ibid., p. 110.

[4] See Fiske's classification of the colonial governments, *The Critical Period, etc.,* p. 65.

into a self-governing state organized upon the model of the English kingdom. The government of the London Company, whose charter granted by James I. in 1606 contained the germs of the Virginian constitution, was vested in a resident council of thirteen appointed by the crown who were authorized to choose their own president, and to govern "according to such laws, ordinances, and instructions, as shall be in that behalf given" by the king. This resident council was subject to the control of a superior council in England, which was also subject to the ultimate ordaining power of the king in council.[1] In the spring of 1609 this complex system of royal government was relaxed in favor of local control through a reorganization of the company whereby the non-resident council was abolished and the government of the colony vested in a single resident council nominated by the king in the first instance, but vacancies in which were afterwards to be filled by a vote of the whole company. Under this council,—which was authorized to choose a governor, and "to make, ordain, and establish all manner of orders, laws, directions, instructions, forms and ceremonies of government, and magistracy fit and necessary for and concerning the government of the said colony,"[2]—the Virginian settlement became almost an independent and self-governing community. In 1612 still further concessions were obtained in favor of the company; and in 1619, under its instructions, the governor summoned an assembly of burgesses from the several hundreds, counties, and plantations embraced within its limits, which met on the 30th of July.[3] The history of the Virginian settlement down to this point clearly illustrates how rapidly even a royal colony slipped from the actual grasp of the crown, and how in its internal organization it involuntarily reproduced the outlines of the ancient constitution. As the basis of its local organization we find the hundred and the shire; in the colo-

(marginal notes:) Ordaining power of the king in council.

First American representative assembly, 1619.

---

[1] As to the distinction between the ordaining power of the king in council and the law-making power of the king in parliament, see below, book iii. ch. i. § 10.

[2] Language of the second charter, see *Charters and Constitutions*, part ii. p. 1899.

[3] On that day "the first representa- tive legislative assembly ever held in America was convened in the chancel of the church at James City or James-town, and was composed of twenty-two burgesses from the eleven several towns, plantations, and hundreds, styled boroughs." — *Nar. and Crit. Hist.*, vol. iii. p. 143.

nial governor we have a reflected image of the kingship; in the royal council — the house of lords; in the house of burgesses — the house of commons.[1] The foundation of the whole fabric was English law; in the original charter it was provided "that all and every the persons, being our subjects which shall go and inhabit within the said colony and plantation, and every their children and posterity, which shall happen to be born within any of the limits thereof, shall have and enjoy all liberties, franchises, and immunities of free denizens and natural subjects within any of our other dominions, to all intents and purposes as if they had been abiding and born within this our realm of England, or in any other of our dominions."[2] In spite of the wanton proceedings by which its charter was annulled by a judgment of the king's bench in June, 1624, and its affairs transferred to the privy council, the Virgi.an settlement survived as a royal colony, and its govern.ent as finally organized was vested in a representative .embly chosen by the people, in a royal council nominate .oy the crown, and in a royal governor armed with a veto .ower upon legislation. Such was the general structure of a royal colony,[3] a type which, originally represented by Virginia alone, came to be the prevailing type before the .everance from the mother country.

English law the basis of the whole fabric.

The cha ter . .ies ..sa- chusetts. In the same sense in which Virginia stands as the typical representative of the royal colonies, Massachusetts stands as the typical representative of the opposite class, — consisting of Massachusetts, Rhode Island, and Connecticut, — generally known as the charter colonies, despite the fact that their foundations were laid without the aid or sanction of charters at all.. As Tocqueville has expressed it, "in general, charters were not given to the colonies of New England till their existence had become an established fact. Plymouth, Providence, New Haven, Connecticut, and Rhode Island were formed without the help, and almost without the knowledge of the mother country."[4] It may therefore be said that their

---

[1] The process of reproduction is well stated by Doyle, *English Colonies in Am.*, *Virginia, etc.*, pp. 215-220. "The colonists proudly looked on the Constitution of their various States as copies of that of the mother country." Green, *Hist. Eng. People*, vol. iv. p. 169.

[2] See *Charters and Constitutions*, part ii. p. 1891.

[3] See *Chalmer's Introduction*, vol. i. pp. 13-16.

[4] *Democracy in America*, vol. i. p. 45 Connecticut has been graphically described as " a State which was born,

free constitutions were older than their charters. The royal charter of 1629 which organized a group of New England settlements into a corporation under the title of the Governor and Company of Massachusetts Bay, and then authorized them to regulate their own affairs as a practically independent and self-governing community, was in fact nothing more than a recognition of a preëxisting state of things.[1] The government of the Massachusetts colony was vested by the charter in the governor, deputy governor, and eighteen assistants, all of whom were to be annually elected by the freemen. The only dependence under which the colony labored at the outset grew out of the fact that it was subject to the control of a corporation in England composed of those by whom its organization had been brought about. With the extinction of this company through the transfer of its charter to America that tie was severed, and Massachusetts became, as far as a colony could become, an independent commonwealth, and continued to be such down to the annulment of its charter in 1684 by a *scire facias.* By the new charter granted it in 1691 its original independence was much curtailed by a provision which gave to the crown the right to appoint a royal governor with an absolute veto upon legislation. Both Rhode Island and Connecticut preserved their free charters unaltered down to the Revolution ; and even then — so completely adequate were they to all their wants — they did not change them. The charter granted to Connecticut by Charles II. in 1662 was continued as her organic law until 1818 ; while the charter granted in 1663 to Rhode Island was continued as her organic law down to 1842.[2]

Between the royal and charter governments stood a middle class known as proprietary, which approached nearer to the latter than the former in respect to their freedom from royal

Internal organization.

Charter annulled in 1684 by a scire facias.

not made, which grew by natural accretion of townships, which formed its own government, made its own laws, engaged in its own alliances, fought its own wars, and built up its own body, without the will of King, Kaiser, or Congress, and which, even at the last, only made use of the royal authority to complete the symmetry of the boundaries it had fairly won for itself." See

"The Genesis of a New England State," Johnston, *Johns Hopkins Studies,* 1st series, XI. p. 6.

[1] " But, if it be not a paradox to say so, the constitution of Massachusetts was older than the existence of the colony." — Doyle, *English Colonies in Am., Puritan, etc.,* vol. i. p. 104.

[2] See *Charters and Constitutions,* part i. p. 252; part ii. p. 1603.

The propri-
etary sys-
tem —
Maryland : control. The proprietary system, which grew out of the idea
that the work of colonization could be better accomplished
by private individuals than by corporate enterprise, rested
upon a series of grants made by the crown to one or more
proprietors of vast tracts of land coupled with an almost unlimited power of government and legislation. The first proprietary government that bore fruit was that of Maryland,
whose constitutional history begins with the grant made in
1632 to the first [1] Lord Baltimore of the tract of land lying to
the north of that actually settled by the Virginia Company.
By this grant the proprietor and his successors were not only
invested with the title to the land, but they were also authorized to make laws with the assent and advice of the majority
of the freemen or their representatives, free from all real dependence upon royal authority.[2] The details of political
organization were in a great measure confided to the discretion of the proprietor, whose original conception of a constitution consisted of a governor, council, and primary assembly,
— a veritable Old-English gemote — in which every freeman
her primary
assembly
supplanted
by a repre-
sentative
system. had the right to represent himself and to vote. Gradually as
the primary plan grew inconvenient it was supplanted by a
representative system, and in 1647 the governing body was
divided into two chambers, the lower consisting of an elective
house of burgesses, the upper of the councillors and of those
specially summoned by the proprietor.[3] In the grant to the
proprietors of Carolina we find the same absoluteness of
sovereignty over the land, and the same freedom from royal
control, with more careful provision however in favor of the
freeholders who were endowed with a charter right[4] to participate in legislation. Here it was that the proprietors attempted to create a political fabric through the aid of Locke
— a philosopher of the Social Contract school — whose
Fundamental Constitutions quickly illustrated how vain it

---

[1] Before the patent passed the seals
George Calvert died, and the charter
was granted to his son Cecilius, second
Lord Baltimore.

[2] "The Province was made a county
palatine; and the Proprietary was invested with all the royal rights, privileges, and prerogatives which had ever
been enjoyed by any Bishop of Durham

within his county palatine." — *Nar.
and Crit. Hist.* vol. iii. p. 520.

[3] As to the history of the early assemblies, see Ibid., pp. 528–531, 536.
See also Doyle, *Virginia, etc.*, pp. 286–
291.

[4] See *Charters and Constitutions,*
part ii. p. 1392.

was to attempt to govern Englishmen by a paper constitu- Carolina
and Locke's
tion [1] whose complicated and artificial details offended the Fundamen-
national instinct by departing from the primitive tradition. tal Constitutions.
When the proprietary system is viewed as a whole the great
landlords to whom the original grants of land and political
authority were made must be looked upon as the mediums or
conduits through which the crown conveyed to the colonists
the boon of local self-government.   The colonies of Maryland,
New York, New Jersey, New Hampshire, Pennsylvania (including Delaware), Carolina, and Georgia were at the outset
proprietary.   But as the proprietors one by one surrendered
their charters to the crown they were all transformed into
royal colonies, except Maryland, Pennsylvania, and Delaware,
which remained proprietary down to the Revolution,[2] — subject to the charter right of their governors to veto legislation.

The fact that the soil upon which the English colonies in American
America were planted came to them through royal grants,[3] colonial
the fact that every form of political organization established rights.
thereon rested upon royal charters, were the foundation
stones upon which the colonists gradually built up, in the
light of their actual experience, their theory of the political
relations which bound them to the mother country.   Their
rights as Englishmen endowed with "all liberties, franchises,
and immunities of free denizens and natural subjects" flowed
from their charters which, as between themselves and the
crown, were irrevocable though not non-forfeitable contracts.
The earliest form of direct legislative control to which any
of the colonies were subjected in the form of ordinances or
instructions for their government emanated, not from the
law-making power of the king in parliament, but from the
ordaining power of the king in council.   And at a later day

---

[1] For the first draft of the Constitutions, see *Carroll*, vol. ii. p. 361 ; for the
later modifications, see the *Shaftesbury
Papers*, under the years in which they
were issued.

[2] "There were thus at last three
proprietary, seven royal [Va., N. Y.,
N. J., N. H., N. C., S. C., and Ga.],
one semi-royal [Mass.], and two charter
colonies" [Conn. and R. I.]. — See
Enc. Brit., 9th ed., vol. xxiii. p. 730.

[3] "The title to the English colonies
was not in the people of England nor
in the state, but in the crown, and descended with it.   The crown alone
could sell or give away these lands.
The crown could make laws for the
inhabitants, and repeal them ; could
appoint their rulers, and remove them.
Parliament could do neither." — *Nar.
and Crit. Hist.*, vol. vi. p. 3.

when the colonial assemblies began the work of legislation on
their own account, the validity of their enactments depended,
not upon the approval of the English parliament, but upon
that of the royal governor who stood as the ever-present representative of his royal master. With the founding of the
colonies, and with the organization of their political systems,
the crown had everything to do; the parliament practically
nothing. Apart from the control which it had exerted from
the beginning over their external affairs in matters of trade
and navigation, the colonies, prior to the latter part of the
eighteenth century, had not been drawn within the widening

The crown
regarded as
the only tie
which
bound the
colonies to
England.

circle of its imperial authority. The whole tendency of their
early experience was to lead the colonies to believe that the
crown was the only tie which bound them to the mother
country, that to each one of them the king stood in the direc
relation of chief executive, that to him alone duties were due
and that the only proper mediums of communication betwee
the crown and the colonies were the colonial parliaments
In their local legislatures the colonists had learned how to
tax themselves, and how to regulate their home affairs through
laws of their own making.[1] Losing sight of the fact that
England had grown into an empire since the work of colonization began, the colonists clave to the earlier conception
which regarded the home parliament simply as the legislative

English
theory of
colonial
rights.

organ of the United Kingdom. As such they held that it
had no right to invade the jurisdictions of their colonial
assemblies in order to legislate directly upon their internal
concerns.   While remoteness and self-interest were alike
intensifying in the colonial mind this reasonable yet narrow
conception, the growth of English dominion was leading
English statesmen at home to elaborate a theory which, in
the gorgeous language of Burke, clothed the English parliament with an "imperial character, in which, as from the
throne of heaven, she superintends all the several inferior
legislatures, and guides and controls them all without annihilating any."[2]   In the hands of a practical tax-loving
statesman like Grenville this imperial theory was not con-

[1] This is well put by Fiske in *The*
Critical Period of Am. History, p. 63.

[2] Speech on American taxation
April 19, 1774.

fined to mere supervision ; in such hands it was held to mean that the Imperial parliament could at any moment override the acts of the colonial assemblies, without consulting their wishes at all, and tax and legislate for the people of Massachusetts and Virginia just as it could for the people of Kent and Middlesex. Out of the conflict which finally arose between the English and the colonial theories as to the practical omnipotence of the Imperial parliament over self-governing communities beyond the four seas, grew the War of the Revolution, and the severance of the colonies from the mother country.[1]

Out of the conflict grew the War of the Revolution.

Having briefly outlined the external relations of the colonies both to the crown and to the parliament, let us return to the question of their internal organization. In the sketch heretofore drawn of the growth of the English kingdom the conclusion was reached that in its matured form it represented an aggregation of shires, — each shire representing an aggregation of hundreds, each hundred, an aggregation of townships. In the examination which will be hereafter made of the making of England the fact will be drawn out that the "unit of the constitutional machinery" was the township — the English form of the village-community — the primary form in which Englishmen group themselves together for self-government. Out of a union of townships grew what was finally known in England as the hundred ; out of a union of hundreds grew the modern shire; out of a union of modern shires grew the English kingdom. The most important fact which this process of state-building reveals is that the Teutonic conquerors of Britain accomplished the work of conquest in small companies, and that, in obedience to the race instinct, they grouped themselves together in townships out of whose coalescence finally arose the larger aggregates. The power to subdue and settle a new country, and then to build up a state by this process of aggregation, constitutes the strength of the English nation as a colonizing nation. By this process,

Internal organization of the colonies.

English kingdom the product of aggregation.

---

[1] The two conflicting theories are clearly stated by Green, *Hist. of the English People*, vol. iv. pp. 226–230. Although this conflict of theory as to the jurisdiction of the Imperial parliament was no doubt the visible and technical cause of separation, was not the real cause that stated by Turgot, who said that "colonies are like fruits, which cling to the tree only till they ripen ? As soon as America can take care of itself it will do what Carthage did."—*Œuvres de M. Turgot*, Paris, 1808–1811, vol. ii. pp. 19, 66.

Federal republic of the United States product of the same general process.

capable under favorable geographical conditions of unlimited expansion, has been built up the federal republic of the United States. "In America . . . it may be said that the township was organized before the county, the county before the State the State before the Union."[1] In order to ascertain how the English colonies in America were constructed, we must look behind their charters at the lives of the men who made the settlements out of which they grew. "Under the shell there was an animal, and behind the document there was a man. . . . The shell and the document are lifeless wrecks, valuable only as a clue to the entire and living existence. We must reach back to this existence, endeavor to recreate it."[2] In the effort to recreate the process through which the English colonies in America were made, we must keep steadily in view the process through which their prototype in Britain was made. The elements of organization in both were the same, and the general principle upon which such elements coalesced was substantially the same. It may be stated as a general rule that the English colony in America, like the English state in Britain, represented an aggregation of counties, and that each county represented an aggregation of townships. The hundred — the intermediate division between the township and the county, — appeared in the structure of some of the colonies, but being unnecessary to the local wants of the new land it passed out of view.[3] In some instances the colony was formed by the coalescence of the local communities before a charter was granted; in others the charter was granted first and the colony then subdivided into districts as the local communities were organized. The fruit of both processes was the same — a dependent state — subdivided into counties and townships as the organs of its local administration. The most striking fact which stands

County and township the organs of local administration.

---

[1] Tocqueville, *Democracy in Am.*, vol. i. p. 49. "Upon the township was formed the county, composed of several towns similarly organized; the state composed of several counties, and, finally, the United States, composed of several states; each organization a body politic, with definite governing powers in a subordinate series." — Address of Mr. Lewis H. Morgan before Am. Ass. for the Adv. of Science, Boston, Aug. 26, 1880.

[2] Taine, *Hist. of Eng. Literature*, vol. i. p. 1.
[3] The hundred existed in Virginia and in Maryland, and may be elsewhere. As to its history in Virginia, see "Local Inst. of Va.," Ingle, *J. H. Studies*, 3d series, II.–III. p. 41. "A Tything-man in each Manor, a Constable in each Hundred." — Bacon, *Laws of Maryland*, 1638.

out in the history of these local communities in the new land is that wherever the one became the active agent of local administration, the other, while it did not cease to exist, became dormant.   In America the county and the township did not reappear as co-working agents dividing the duties of local administration in anything like equal proportions.   In the northern colonies where population became dense, and where the active spirit of the English yeoman and trader reproduced a system of political life as closely organized as it was vigorous, the township became the active organ of local administration for the simple reason that its compact organization was better adapted than that of the shire to the local wants of New England.   In the southern colonies where population was more sparse, and where the southern planter reproduced the more tranquil life of the English gentleman who had little or nothing to do with the life of towns, the county became the active organ of local administration for the reason that it satisfied all of the political wants of a rural population.[1]   To that extent the local organizations of the northern and southern colonies were different from each other.   "Townships and town arrangements exist in every state ; but in no other part of the Union is a township to be met with precisely similar to those of New England.   The farther we go toward the South, the less active does the business of the township or parish become . . . As we leave New England we find that the importance of the town is gradually transferred to the county, which becomes the centre of administration, and the intermediate power between the government and the citizen."[2]   While the township or parish was thus overshadowed in the southern colonies by county organization, the New England county maintained nothing more than a shadowy existence as a local district for certain judicial purposes.[3]   In the middle colonies the two opposing

---

[1] In revising the MS. Mr. Freeman here wrote : "I found in Virginia people spoke of the *county* just as they do here.   In New England the county seemed lost.   There the *town* was the thing, when the *city* had not swallowed it up."   In his "Introduction to Am. Inst. Hist.," *J. H. Studies*, 1st series, I. p. 17, Mr. Freeman, in comparing Virginia with New England, has said that

"the two lands represent two different sides of England.   Virginia more nearly reproduced the England of the time of the settlement.   New England more nearly reproduced the England of an earlier time."

[2] Tocqueville, *Democracy in Am.*, vol. i. pp. 99, 100.

[3] See Washburn, *Judicial Hist. of Mass.*, p. 31, note 1.

Composite system in the middle colonies. systems fought for the mastery, and the result was a composite system which approached nearer than either to the original model by dividing between the town and the county in something like equal proportions the duties of local government.[1]

The township in New England. The remarkable fact is that the township reappears upon the soil of New England rather in the form in which it appeared in Britain when the foundations of the English kingdom were laid than in the form in which it there existed when the migration to America began. The township as it originally appeared in Britain was at once a cultivating and political community in whose qualified members resided the power to elect their own officers and to order their own village and agricultural life. This power was vested in a single village assembly or tun-moot in which the townsmen met to regulate their internal affairs by the making of by-laws, — laws enacted by a "by" — as the township was called in the northern shires. But during the ten centuries which intervened between the Teutonic conquest and settlement of Britain and the making of the English settlements in America the primitive township passed through a marked

Township as the manor, — transformation. In the process of English feudalization the township was transformed into the manor of the lord, and the once free townsmen became the lord's tenants, while the greater part of the ancient jurisdiction of the tun-moot passed to the manorial courts. And more than this, the township in the home land became involved in ecclesiastical as well as

as the parish. in feudal relations. As a division in the territorial organization of the church the township became the parish, and as such its boundaries were used to define the jurisdiction of a single priest, — "in small parishes the idea and even name of township is frequently, at the present day, sunk in that of the parish ; and all business that is not manorial is dispatched in vestry meetings, which are however primarily meetings of the township for church purposes." [2] In this way the tun-

---

[1] "The middle colonies gravitated towards the form of government that obtained in New England or Virginia, as proximity to the one or the other dictated, while the local organization of the Carolinas was of a mixed character such as would naturally have been produced by the manner of their settlement." — "Town and County Government," Channing, *J. H. Studies,* 2d series, X. p. 8.

[2] Stubbs, *Const. Hist.,* vol. i. p. 85.

moot had ceased to exist as a single assembly, and its jurisdiction had been split up and absorbed by the parish vestry
and manorial courts long before the emigration to America
began. It is therefore a remarkable fact, but one perfectly
susceptible of explanation, that when the settlers of New
England reproduced the township in the new world, they
should have reproduced it in its original integrity, unfettered
by the feudal and ecclesiastical restraints by which it had
been hampered for centuries. As a brilliant American scholar
has expressed it, the colonists "were severed now from church
and from aristocracy. So they had but to discard the ecclesiastical and lordly terminology, with such limitations as they
involved, and reintegrate the separate jurisdictions into one, —
and forthwith the old assembly of the township, founded in
immemorial tradition, but revivified by new thoughts and
purposes gained through ages of political training, emerged
into fresh life and entered upon a more glorious career."[1] In
this way the village community common to the whole Aryan
world, which appeared in Britain as the "tun" or township,
where it became involved in both feudal and ecclesiastical
relations, finally reappeared in its primitive simplicity upon
the soil of New England, and there became the active unit of
well organized system of local self-government. The government of the New England town, like that of the Old-English
township, is vested in the town meeting[2] (tun-moot) as a
single assembly in which every adult male residing within
the township is expected to be present and to vote. When
an examination is made of the manner in which a New England town was formed by men bound together by community
of thought and purpose, or by previous neighborhood ; of the
manner in which the townsmen vested the town administration in a body of selectmen ; of the manner in which the early
proprietors held the lands which they parcelled out among
themselves, reserving, to the exclusion of after-comers, certain
portions for common pasture and certain portions for common
tillage ; of the manner in which the town regulated the herd-

Mr. Fiske's statement.

The town meeting.

---

[1] John Fiske, *Am. Political Ideas*, p. 49.

[2] "A New England town-meeting is essentially the same thing as the Ho-
meric ἀγορή, the Athenian ἐκκλησία, the Roman *comitia*, the Swiss *Landes-
gemeinde*, the English folk-moot." —
Freeman's " Int. to Am. Inst. Hist.," *J.
H. Studies*, 1st series, I. p. 16.

ing of cattle and the laying out of highways ; of the manner in which it admitted and excluded members, — the student of the history of the village community is not only reminded of the township as it first appears in Britain in historic times, but of the primitive Teutonic mark as it originally existed in the first home land of the race on the shores of the Northern Ocean.[1]

Manors in Maryland. The fact that the township, stripped of its feudal aspect as the manor, and of its ecclesiastical aspect as the parish, reappeared in its primitive Teutonic form upon the soil of New England, must not lead to the inference that it did not elsewhere appear in each of its discarded characters. In the colony of Maryland, whose constitutional history begins under the aristocratic influence of Lord Baltimore, who had authority to model his colony after the Palatinate of Durham,[2] the township reappeared as the manor with its feudal relations intact, — lord of the manor and his tenants, free and servile, manor-house, church, court baron, court leet and all. The **Proprietor founds the system.** evidence as to the origin and structure of old Maryland manors is of a very clear and satisfactory character. The proprietor under his charter right[3] issued, in 1636, instructions to the governor that every two thousand acres granted to any adventurer should " be erected and created into a manor. . . . And we do hereby further authorize you that you cause to be granted to every of the said Adventurers within every of their said manors respectively . . . a Court Baron and Court Leet, to be from time to time held."[4] By general instructions of this character often repeated, and by special grants made under them to particular individuals, the foundations were laid of a manorial system which "became general, so that English manors, English halls, English lords of the manor were scattered all over"[5] the colony of Mary-

---

[1] For the history of the New England town, see "The Germanic Origin of N. E. Towns," H. B. Adams, *J. H. Studies*, 1st series, II. ; "Town and County Government," E. Channing, 2d series, X.; Fiske, *Am. Political Ideas*, pp. 17–56 ; "Town Meeting," by Fiske, in *Harper's Magazine*, January, 1885 ; Scott's *Development of Constitutional Liberty*, p. 174; Doyle, *Eng. Colonies in Am.*, *Puritan, etc.*, vol. ii. pp. 7–26.

[2] "Although Palatine rights were granted to the Lord Proprietor, yet practically, from the very outset, the government of Maryland was a government by the people."—"Introduction to Am. Inst. Hist.," *J. H. Studies*, 1st series, I. p. 16, in note by Dr. Adams. A special study of the Palatinate of Durham has been made by Mr. Basil Sollers.

[3] See *Charter of Maryland*, art. 19.

[4] Instructions from Lord Baltimore to Governor Calvert, quoted in "Old Maryland Manors," by Mr. John Johnson, *J. H. Studies*, 1st series, VII.

[5] Ibid., p. 7.

land. Coke tells us that, "A court baron is the chief prop and pillar of a manor, which no sooner faileth, but the manor falleth to the ground."[1] In Maryland the court baron was not wanting. From Bozman[2] we learn that "one or two rare instances occurred of the holding both courts baron and courts leet in two distinct manors. 'A court baron was held at the manor of St. Gabriel on the 7th of March, 1656, by the steward of the lady of the manor when one Martin Kirke took of the lady of the manor in full court, by delivery of the said steward, by the rod, according to the custom of the said manor, one messuage, having done fealty to the lady, was thereby admitted tenant.' (MS. Extracts from the records.) This seems to have been conformable to the ancient practice of courts baron in England, on the admission of any tenant of a manor." But what is more important still, in the manuscript records of a court leet and a court baron of St. Clement's manor in St. Mary's County — the property of the Maryland Historical Society[3] — is contained incontestable evidence of the fact that a court leet was held in that manor at intervals between 1659 and 1672.[4] "In 1776 there were still unsold seventy thousand acres of proprietary manors lying in nine counties. In the Maryland Reports is to be found a notable lawsuit over Anne Arundel Manor. The proprietor, Lord Frederick Calvert, sought by means of a common recovery to break the entail upon the manor, and thus prevent its passing into the hands of a natural son of the former proprietor."[5]

The evidence is equally clear as to the existence in New York of the manorial system. The agent which Holland employed in the colonization of New Netherland was the West India Company, whose general government was vested,

A court baron at St. Gabriel's manor;

a court leet at St. Clement's.

Manors in New York.

---

[1] Coke's *Copyholder*, p. xxxi.

[2] *History of Maryland*, vol. ii. p. 581. In an editorial note, p. 25, of "Old Maryland Manors," Dr. Adams says, "Here, then, is instanced by Bozman himself a concrete case of a manorial court, the records of which Mr. Bozman appears to have seen."

[3] These records, presented to the society by Col. B. U. Campbell, are printed as an appendix to *Old Maryland Manors*, pp. 31–38.

[4] "The Court Leet, the existence of which in Maryland has long been de-

nied, was a popular institution, a kind of Town Meeting on the Lord's Manor. Such a manorial survival is, like the old Town Pasture at Annapolis, a connecting link between Province Maryland and Early England." — See note by Dr. Adams to "Int. to Am. Inst. Hist.," *J. H. Studies*, 1st series, I. p. 13.

[5] *Old Maryland Manors*, p. 8. For the case referred to, see 2 Harris and McHenry, p. 279. As to the effect of manorial customs upon the rights of tenants, see *Dorsey* v. *Eagle*, 7 Gill and Johnson, p. 321 (1835).

by the charter granted in 1621, in a board composed of nineteen delegates. In June, 1629, the States-General ratified the document called "Freedoms and Exemptions" previously granted by the governing body of the West India Company "to all such as shall plant any colonies in New Netherland." Under the immunity thus granted and confirmed, each proprietor or "patroon" who planted a colony of fifty souls, upwards of fifteen years old, was not only entitled to a large expanse of territory "as a perpetual inheritance," but he was also authorized to erect it into a seignorial fief or manor within which he was entitled to many of the feudal rights incident to lordship. The colonist, whom the "patroon" was required to furnish with a well equipped farm, was bound in return to pay to the lord a fixed rent, in addition to a portion of the product of the farm and a part of the increase of the stock. The tenant could not sell his produce elsewhere until the lord had first refused to buy it; he was required to have his grain ground at the lord's mill; from the lord he had to obtain a license to fish and hunt within the domain.[1] As lord of the manor the "patroon" was the heir of all who died intestate,[2] and as such he was empowered "to administer civil and criminal justice in person or by deputy within his colonie, to appoint local officers and magistrates; to erect courts and to take cognizance of all crimes committed within his limits."[3] "Theoretically, the patroon was always present in his court baron. Practically, the government of the colony was administered by a court composed of two commissaries and two schepens, assisted by the colonial secretary and the schout."[4] The manorial system thus established by the Dutch in New Netherland was perpetuated under English forms, after the territory was conquered by the English and transformed into the colony of New York. In the patent creating Livingston Manor, granted by Governor Dongan in 1686, authority was given for establishing "in the said Lordship and Mannor one Court Leet and one Court Baron . . . to be kept by the said Robert Livingston his Heirs and assignes for ever or theire or any of theire Stewards

The "patroon" as lord of the manor.

Manorial courts.

Livingston manor.

---

[1] See "Dutch Village Communities on the Hudson River," Elting, *J. H. Studies*, 4th series, I. pp. 12–16.
[2] Broadhead's *Hist. of N. Y.*, p. 305.
[3] O'Callaghan, *Hist. of New Netherland*, vol. i. p. 320.
[4] Broadhead's *Hist. of N. Y.*, p. 305.

Deputed and appointed,"[1] etc. Under the English and Dutch manorial systems thus established in Maryland and New Netherland the proprietors or "patroons" were nothing more nor less than feudal lords who were endowed with the right to exercise within their own manors all of the feudal incidents of tenure and jurisdiction. Thus did the dying feudalism attempt to strike its roots into the free soil of the New World as a permanent institution. The effort was of course short-lived. In spite of the oppressive seignorial rights granted to the lord, the fact remained that the manor was a self-governing community. In the court baron the free tenants acted both as judges and jurors; in the court leet criminal justice could only be enforced against a tenant through the judgment of his peers. In the leet the manorial officers were elected by the tenants, who there enacted by-laws for their own government.[2] The growth of local political life in Maryland and New York, although hampered and retarded for a time by the feudal obstructions by which it was surrounded, soon waxed strong enough to break through them all, and to cast aside as obsolete and worthless the shell in which it had passed the period of its incubation.

The manor a self-governing community.

Having noted the reappearance in New England of the English village community in its primitive form as the township, and in Maryland and New York in its feudal form as the manor, let us turn next to Virginia, where it reappears in its ecclesiastical form as the parish. As the township was the form of local organization specially demanded by the social and economic wants of the settlers of New England, it there reappeared as the primary unit of local self-government. "Upon the township was formed the county, composed of several towns similarly organized; the state composed of several counties,"[3] etc. Thus in New England, as a general rule, we find the state to be an aftergrowth which arises out of a process of aggregation in which the township is the unit or starting-point. In Virginia, which will be accepted throughout as a typical representative of the colonial group to which she belonged, the work of state-building, guided by

The parish in Virginia.

---

[1] *Docs. Relating to Col. Hist. of N. Y.,* vol. ii. pp. 375, 376.

[2] See *Old Maryland Manors,* pp. 14–16.

[3] Mr. L. H. Morgan's Address heretofore cited.

the peculiar social and agricultural wants of the first settlers,

Virginia first divided into counties in 1634.
proceeded upon entirely different principles. In Virginia the colony was first created as an entirety and then subdivided into self-governing districts as rapidly as they were demanded by the growth of population. As early as 1618 the governor and council were ordered to divide the colony into counties ;[1] not until 1634, however, was such a division actually made. In that year the colony was divided into eight shires which were to be governed as English shires were governed, with lieutenants and sheriffs, and "sergeants and bailiffs where need requires." The eight shires[2] "were James City, the country around Jamestown, Henrico, around the settlement of Sir Thomas Dale, Charles City, Elizabeth City, Warwick River, Warrosquayack, Charles River, and on the eastern shore, Accomac. That these counties, as a rule, took their names from and embraced the settlements is a curious phase in English institutions — for it was nothing more or less

Virginia towns grow into counties which are divided into parishes.
than the towns growing into the counties. This was very different from the origin of counties in England and in New England. . . . In 1680 there were twenty counties, a word introduced into the laws in 1639, and the number increased as it became necessary. . . . When the county had finally become crystallized, it was divided into parishes, precincts for the constables, and walks for the surveyors of highways, the last two divisions being subject to such rules and altera- tions as the county court thought fit to make."[3] When the Virginia parish thus appears in its normal shape it is as a subdivision of the county — a subordinate unit subject to the direction and control of the county court. The parish which, like its prototype, thus stood in a subordinate relation to the county, was endowed with all of the ecclesiastical, and nearly all of the civil authority possessed by the English original. "The parish was, as a rule, a division of the county for religious purposes ; but the governing body of the parish, the vestry, had considerable authority in civil affairs."[4] "The township of New England was the parish of England, shorn of its ecclesiastical powers ; the parish of Virginia was the

---

[1] See Rev. P. Slaughter's *History of Bristol Parish*, 2d ed., p. 4 ; *Town and County Govt.*, Channing, p. 43.

[2] Hening, vol. i. pp. 223, 224.

[3] *Local Institutions of Virginia*, Ingle, pp. 81–83.

[4] *Town and County Govt.*, p. 48.

English parish stripped of some of its civil functions. In Resemblance between the English and Virginia parish; Virginia the parish as it existed in England was instituted, although, on account of the peculiar circumstances of the young colony it . . . never possessed civil powers entirely equal to those of the same institution in the mother country." [1] Such local powers as the parish did possess were exercised by the vestry,[2] a body generally composed of twelve members, who were originally elected by the parishioners themselves under the supervision of the sheriff. But as the vestrymen were elected for an indefinite term, and as it was provided by statute in 1661–62 that, in the event of the death or removal of any one of them, his place could be filled by the vestry itself,[3] the governing body of the Virginia parish ceased to be representative, and like its English parent hardened into a close corporation.[4] The executive officers of the parish were two both hardened into close corporations. church wardens whom the vestry elected each year out of their own number. Every fourth year the vestry under the order of the county court divided the parish into precincts, in each of which two persons were appointed to "procession" the lands, that is, to mark anew their boundaries. Twice at least in each year the vestry met to discharge its intermingl. ecclesiastical and civil duties, chief among which was the laying of the annual levy to defray parish expenses. After the parish debts were computed the sum ascertained was divided by the number of tithable persons in the parish, and the sum thus apportioned to each family was paid by its head to the parish collector. It was also the duty of the vestry to hire ministers and to present them to the governor for induction, to provide glebes, parsonages, and salaries, to take charge of the poor, to bind out foundlings or bastards, to present to the court those who offended against good morals, and the like.[5] In the early days, prior to the rise of towns,

---

[1] *Local Institutions of Va.*, p. 52.

[2] In 1643 a statute was passed requiring a vestry to be held in every parish. See Hening, *Stat.*, vol. i. p. 240.

[3] See *Laws in Force in 1769*, p. 2; Hening, vol. ii. p. 44.

[4] For the history of this process in England, see Sir T. Erskine May, *Const. Hist.*, vol. ii. p. 461 ; for its history in Virginia, see *Town and County Govt.*, p. 57. A partial remedy for this

abuse of parochial government in England was supplied in 1831 by Sir J. Hobhouse's Vestry Act, 1 & 2 Will. IV. c. 60.

[5] As to the duties of the vestry, see Slaughter's *Bristol Parish*, xiv.–xix; *Meade*, vol. i. pp. 364, 394, 395 : Peyton's *Hist. of Augusta County*, p. 97 ; *Vestry Book of Henrico Parish*, 1730–1773, edited by R. A. Brock ; *Town and County Govt.*, pp. 42–53.

"The vestries . . . represented all the local and municipal government there was in Virginia,"[1] that is, all local government which was not supplied by the larger and more potential governing body — the county.

The southern county: County administration in Virginia, which was closely modelled after that of England both in its civil and military aspects, was vested in the lieutenant, who under the honorary title of colonel was at the head of the militia, in the sheriff, the executive head of the county, and in the county court, which like its English prototype was charged not only with judicial but administrative functions. As finally organized, the county court consisted of eight or more justices or magistrates appointed by the governor, — four of whom, one being of the " quorum," constituted a court for the dispatch

Its judicial functions; of business. At the time of the Revolution the jurisdiction of the county court extended to all equity causes, and to all cases at common law which did not involve loss of life, limb, or outlawry, and to all matters involving the administration of estates and the care of orphans. In the exercise of its judicial functions it could employ both grand and petit jurors

administrative. according to the course of the common law.[2] Chief among the administrative functions of the county court were its duty to lay the county rate to defray county expenses, to make in connection with the representatives from the parishes by-laws for the county, to build and keep in repair the court-house, public bridges, and causeways, to keep the public roads in order and the water-ways free from obstructions, to license taverns, recommend inspectors of tobacco, to appoint surveyors of highways, and annually to present to the governor the names of three of its members from among whom a sheriff might be appointed for the ensuing year.[3] The meeting of a tribunal which touched the life of the people at so many different points naturally excited general interest.

Court-day. " Court-day was a holiday for all the country side, especially in the fall and spring. From all directions came in the people on horseback, in wagons, and afoot. On the court-house

[1] *Hist. of Augusta County,* p. 97.
[2] As to the early jurisdiction of the county court, see Hening, vol. i. p. 163. As to its later jurisdiction, see *Local Institutions of Va.,* p. 91.

[3] As to its administrative functions, see *Local Institutions of Va.,* pp. 92–97; *Town and County Government,* pp. 45–48.

green assembled, in indiscriminate confusion, people of all classes — the hunter from the backwoods, the owner of a few acres, the grand proprietor, and the grinning, heedless negro. Old debts were settled and new ones made ; there were auctions, transfers of property, and if election times were near, stump-speaking. Virginia had no town meeting as New England, but it had its familiar court-day." [1] Such was the nature and influence of the southern county which in Virginia, and in the other agricultural states of the south and the southwest, dominated local administration as did the township in New England. The essential difference in local organization between the northern and southern colonies was therefore only that which exists between the compact organization of an English town and the laxer organization of an English county. In both, the colonists grouped themselves together for local government upon the old plan, and yet under different circumstances ; and both became not only training-schools for the new political life that was soon to come, but levelling-schools, in which were wiped out all inequalities arising out of prior distinctions of class or nobility of blood. When the appointed time came the indomitable spirit of the new American democracy, which the colonial towns and counties had nourished, went down to the battle of the Revolution ; and, when the battle was won, it embodied itself in the constitution of the federal republic of the United States.

Difference in local organization between north and south.

Neither the New England town nor the southern county is in contemplation of American law a municipal corporation. Both belong to that class of public corporations known as *quasi*,[2] — a term used to denote the fact that the corporate body to which it is applied has not been completely organized as a full corporation. The status of a New England town whose government is administered by the townsmen themselves in town meeting, and through executive officers chosen by themselves, may be compared to that of an English borough that had won exemption from the jurisdictions of the sheriff and the lord, with the right to establish an independent magistracy with a reeve or bailiff as its head, but

Incorporation of New England towns.

---

[1] *Local Institutions of Va.*, p. 90.　*Sears*, 22 Pick., pp. 122, 130 ; *Hooper* v.
[2] See Dillon, *Municipal Corp.*, vol. i.　*Emery*, 14 Maine (2 Shep.), p. 375.
pp. 91–107 ; *Overseers of Poor, etc.* v.

which had not yet completed its municipal character by the election of a "mayor," whose appearance marked in the home land the final transition from the primitive system of township government to the new system in which the borough community appears as a *communitas* or corporation. A like transition takes place in New England whenever a town grows too large for its affairs to be conveniently administered by the whole body of freemen assembled in town

Municipal history of Boston. meeting. A typical illustration of this process may be found in the case of Boston, whose affairs continued to be administered under the primitive system down to 1822, at which time its qualified voters numbered seven thousand. The inconveniences growing out of this state of things finally induced the townsmen to obtain a charter [1] vesting the government of the city in a mayor and elective council, according to the system adopted in London in the reign of Edward I. Impelled by the same reasons, other New England towns, following the lead of Boston, have given up the primitive communal system, which is purely democratic, for a municipal system purely representative.[2] Not until a town community is duly incorporated, and the management of its affairs vested in a mayor and representative council, does it satisfy the American conception of a complete municipal corporation.

Incorporation of southern towns. With the history of the English shire the history of the English town is closely interlaced. The Old-English town or borough was, in fact, nothing more than a subdivision of the shire, " in which men lived closer together than elsewhere; it was simply several townships packed tightly together; a hundred smaller in extent and thicker in population than other hundreds." [3] The burgemot or hustings of the Old-English town was nothing but the hundred court in a slightly different form; its origin was the same, and its procedure substantially the same. The struggle of such a town for municipal existence may be roughly divided into

---

[1] See Josiah Quincy's *Municipal Hist. of Boston,* pp. 28, 41 ; Dillon, vol. i. p. 101, and note.

[2] Although when the population of a town exceeds 10,000 or 12,000 it is usual for it to be incorporated as a city, " the town system is the general one ; the city, or representative sytem,

is the exceptional one," etc. — Dillon, vol. i. p. 101. See, also, *Am. Political Ideas,* p. 33.

[3] Freeman, *Norm. Conq.,* vol. v. p. 312. As to the identity of town and hundred in Virginia in the early days, see *Local Institutions of Virginia,* pp. 43–45.

four stages : first, for emancipation from the jurisdiction of the sheriff ; second, from that of the lord upon whose land the town had grown up ; third, for the right to elect its own magistracy with a reeve or bailiff as its head ; fourth, to elect in the place of the bailiff a "mayor," whose appearance completed the transition from the old system of township government to the new system in which the borough community appears as a *communitas* or corporation, which by the common law had the full right to regulate its own affairs without the aid of any statute.[1] Through a similar though less complicated process the southern town or city usually acquires distinct municipal existence and virtual emancipation from the control of the southern county. The first step is taken whenever a settlement or village in any part of the county has become sufficiently populous to require a more strictly organized form of local administration than that supplied by the general county government. When that point is reached it is usual for the legislature to supply through general[2] laws an inchoate form of incorporation to the new civic community sufficient for its needs during the intermediate period through which it must pass before it is prepared for complete municipal existence. Not until that stage of development is reached is it usual for the legislature, by the grant of a special charter, to raise it to the full dignity of a municipal corporation.

The English self-governing communities which have multiplied so rapidly upon American soil have, in one serious particular, silently passed through a marked transformation which seems so far to have escaped the attention of historians of American law. A great common law judge, in expounding the immemorial and inherent right of every English local community to tax itself for local purposes, has said that : "From time immemorial the counties, parishes, towns, and territorial subdivisions of the country have been allowed in England, and, indeed, required to lay rates on themselves for local purposes. . . . From the foundation of our government, colonial and republican, the necessary sums

American corporations possess no inherent power of taxation.

---

[1] See below, bk. iii. ch. i. § 3.
[2] A good illustration of the process may be found in the legislation of Alabama. See Code of 1886, §§ 1486–1520.

for local purposes have been raised by the people or authorities at home. Court-houses, prisons, bridges, poor-houses,
and the like, are thus built and kept up, and the expenses of
maintaining the poor, and of prosecutions and jurors, are thus
defrayed, and of late (in North Carolina) a portion of the
common school fund, and a provision for the indigent insane
are thus raised, while the highways are altogether constructed
and repaired by local labor, distributed under the orders of
the county magistrates. When, therefore, the constitution
vests the legislative power in the general assembly, it must
be understood to mean that power as it had been exercised
by our forefathers, before and after their migration to this
continent." [1] It seems therefore to be clear that in the home
land every English corporation possessed the immemorial
and inherent power to impose taxes for local purposes without the aid or sanction of parliamentary authority ; and such
seems to have been the law in that American state in which
the English customary law has had its purest and most scientific development. And yet the fact remains that it is now
the settled doctrine of American law that no local corporation, municipal or *quasi*, has any inherent power to levy taxes
for any purpose ; "a municipal corporation has no inherent
taxing power ; the power it can rightfully exercise is that
which the state may deem it expedient to delegate." [2] What
general cause has been at work to bring about a change so
momentous ; and yet a change whose very presence seems to
have escaped observation ? After having sought in vain for
a satisfactory solution of the problem at the hands of several
of our most eminent authorities, the author has contented
himself with the following explanation. From the beginning
of our colonial history down to to-day Americans have been
trained in the belief that legislative power — including the
taxing power — could only be exercised subject to the limitations imposed first by the crown and then by the people upon
the particular assembly by which such power was sought
to be exercised. In the explanation hereafter to be made of
the growth of constitutional limitations the fact will appear
that the colonial assemblies could only legislate subject to

---

[1] Ruffin, J., in *Caldwell* v. *Justices,*
etc., 4 Jones (N. C.) Eq., p. 323.

[2] *Mobile & S. H. R. R. Co.* v. *Ken-
nerly,* 74 Ala., p. 574.

the limitations imposed by the crown in the charters by which such assemblies were created or recognized. When the tie which bound the colonies to the mother country was severed the sovereignty of the crown passed to the people of each state, who revested the legislative power in the state assembly subject to the limitations of the state constitution by which the royal charter was supplanted. When, upon the making of the federal constitution of the United States, this idea of a limited legislative authority, which had existed from the very beginning, was lifted into a higher sphere, it there crystallized into the principle that the federal assembly could legislate only in the execution of powers expressly delegated. In this way the doctrine gained fresh force that in America, as a general rule, no assembly — national or local — possesses any inherent power of taxation at all, — that the authority must come by express delegation from the people. This theory of delegation is the substructure of all the state constitutions which rest upon the principle that the whole legislative power of the state is delegated by the people to the state assembly, which must exercise such power subjected to the limitations of the state and federal constitutions. The American doctrine now is that the state assembly is the reservoir in which the people deposit the entire taxing power of the state, *general and local.* From this premise the conclusion is inevitable that local communities in America possess no inherent power of taxation, for the reason that the people of each local community by becoming parties to the state constitution thereby surrender the right of local taxation to the state assembly. Thus it comes to pass that every local corporation is, in contemplation of American law, a mere agent of the state, endowed with the right to exercise only such taxing power as the state may see fit to delegate.

The representative branch of the English parliament is the outcome of the ancient local systems of election and representation immemorially imbedded in the organization of the shires and towns. When the crown found it convenient for financial reasons to summon to the great council representatives from the local communities, the undertaking was made easy by the fact that the shires and towns to which the writs were addressed had been so long familiar with the practice of

Growth of colonial assemblies,

election and representation in their local courts that they
found no difficulty in applying it to the selection of representatives to speak for them in the councils of the king.   Three
centuries before the English settlements in America were
made the representative system had thus been lifted in the
home land from a lower to a higher sphere.[1]   When the
English settlers in America organized themselves for local
which arise
out of the
organiza-
tions of the
counties
and towns.
purposes in shires and towns upon the old plan, they laid
the foundations for that after-growth of representative assemblies which came into being as rapidly as the political wants
of the several colonies required them.   Such assemblies
"were not formally instituted, but grew up by themselves,
because it was in the nature of Englishmen to assemble." [2]
Each colonial assembly has its own local and personal history,
and yet in their broader outlines there is no great divergence
between them.   Each and every one was composed in whole
or in part of representatives chosen in the local communities;
They as-
sume a bi-
cameral
shape.
and, excepting the assemblies of Pennsylvania, Delaware, and
Georgia, which consisted of a single chamber, they all assumed a bicameral shape.   In Connecticut, Rhode Island, and
Massachusetts the assembly was composed of two houses, the
upper being elected by the people at large, the lower by the
towns.   When the time came for severance from the mother
country the first two did not find it necessary to make any
change in the structure of their assemblies at all.   In New
Hampshire, New York, New Jersey, North Carolina, South
Carolina, Georgia, Virginia, and Maryland, the colonial legislatures consisted of two houses, — the upper being the council
appointed by the crown through the royal governor, the lower
being a representative body elected by the people.   When
the Revolution came these lower houses, under the name of
"provincial congresses," assumed the powers of the state
until, under the recommendation of the Continental Congress,[3] the several colonies could establish independent gov-

---

[1] Upon this whole subject, see below,
bk. iii. ch. i. §§ 3, 4.

[2] Seeley, *The Expansion of England*,
p. 67.

[3] Under this recommendation Delaware, Maryland, New Hampshire,
North Carolina, New Jersey, Pennsylvania, South Carolina, and Virginia

adopted constitutions during the year
1776; Georgia and New York in 1777;
Massachusetts in 1780.   The charter
granted to Connecticut in 1662 was
continued as her organic law until 1818;
while the charter granted to Rhode
Island in 1663 was continued as her
organic law down to 1842.

ernments under formal written constitutions, in every one of which, with the exceptions of Pennsylvania and Georgia,[1] the English bicameral system was reproduced.

When the tie of political dependence which bound the colonies to the mother country was severed, the English provinces in America rose to the full stature of sovereign states. *The colonies transformed into sovereign states,* "When the Revolution took place the people of each state became themselves sovereign." [2] And as soon as they "took into their own hands the powers of sovereignty, the prerogatives and regalities which before belonged either to the crown or the parliament, became immediately and rightfully vested in the state." [3] On the 10th of May, 1776, the Continental Congress recommended to the several conventions and assemblies of the colonies the establishment of independent governments "for maintenance of internal peace and the defence of their lives, liberties, and properties." [4] Before the end of the year in which this recommendation was made, by far the greater part of the colonies had adopted written contitutions in which were restated in a dogmatic form all of the seminal principles of the English constitutional system. Thus ended that marvellous process of growth through which *which are substantial reproductions of the English kingdom.* the English colonies in America were rapidly developed into a group of independent commonwealths in which each individual member was, in its organic structure, a substantial reproduction of the English kingdom. With the adoption of the written constitutions of 1776, the typical English state in America reached its full growth. When the offspring is compared with the parent, when the English state in America is compared with the English state in Britain,[5] the resemblance is too close for the relationship to escape the most careless observer. In both, the political substructure is the same — the ancient Teutonic system of local, self-governing communities composed of the township, the hundred, and the shire. In each, municipal organization rests upon substantially the same foundation. So far as central organization is concerned,

---

[1] In 1789 Georgia adopted the bicameral plan; in 1790, Pennsylvania.

[2] Taney, C. J., in *Martin et. al.* v. *The Lessee of Waddell*, 16 Peters, p. 410.

[3] Ibid., p. 416.

[4] See *Charters and Constitutions*, vol. i. p. 3.

[5] I can here say with Professor Seeley, " By England I mean solely the state or political community which has its seat in England." — *The Expansion of Eng.*, p. 7.

every American state is a mere reproduction of the central organization of the English kingdom with such modifications as have necessarily resulted from the abolition of nobility, feudality, and kingship. In the new as in the old the central powers of the state are divided into the three departments — legislative, executive, and judicial — which, in the same qualified sense, are separate and distinct from each other.[1]

Legislative
department.

So far as the legislative department is concerned, the English bicameral system everywhere reappeared. Our houses of representatives are nothing but the house of commons over again, while our state senates represent the house of lords with the elective principle substituted in lieu of hereditary right.[2] The resemblance extends, however, far beyond the mere form of the assembly. It has ever been an elementary principle of American constitutional law that every state legislature is endowed by its very nature with the omnipotence of the English parliament, save so far as that omnipotence is re-

Constitutional limitations an American invention.

strained by the express terms of constitutional limitations[3] an American invention which rests upon the doctrine of the sovereignty of the people as distinguished from the sovereignty of parliament.[4] Such limitations naturally arose out of the process of historic development through which American legislatures came into existence. From the very beginning the powers of the colonial assemblies were more or less limited through the terms of the charters by which such assemblies were either created or recognized. And even in colonial times, "Questions sometimes arose . . . whether the statutes made by these assemblies were in excess of the powers conferred by the charter; and if the statutes were found to be in excess, they were held invalid by the courts,

---

[1] The English maxim as to the division of powers was followed in the structure of the state constitutions only in the limited and qualified sense in which it was understood in England. See *Federalist*, No. xlvi. Dawson's ed., pp. 334–342. In the light of Madison's exposition I cannot see how Mr. Fiske can suppose that there was a "misconception" upon this subject in the minds of the framers either of the state or federal constitutions. The "literary theory" of the English constitution misled neither Madison nor Hamilton.

See *The Critical Period, etc.*, pp. 289–292.

[2] The ordinary judicial powers of the house of lords were everywhere cut off, except in New York, where the senate was made a supreme court of appeal.

[3] See Cooley's *Const. Lim.*, p. 107 (5th ed.), and cases cited; *Mangan* v. *State*, 76 Ala., p. 60; *Davis* v. *State*, 68 Ala., p. 58.

[4] See *Democracy in America*, vol. i. pp. 123–130; Cooley's *Const. Lim.*, ch. vii.

that is to say, in the first instance, by the colonial courts, or, if the matter was carried to England, by the Privy Council."[1] The statement may be made, as a general rule, that the colonial charter embodied "a frame of government established by a superior authority, creating a subordinate law-making body, which can do everything except violate the terms and transcend the powers of the instrument to which it owes its existence. So long as the colony remained under the British crown, the superior authority, which could amend or remake the frame of government, was the British crown or parliament. When the connection with Britain was severed, that authority passed over, not to the state legislature, which remained limited, as it always had been, but to the people of the now independent commonwealth, whose will speaks through what is now the state constitution, just as the will of the crown or parliament had spoken through the charters of 1628 and 1691."[2]

The elective chief magistrate of an American state simply represents another phase of the general process of reproduction. "The governor of the independent state succeeded the governor of the dependent colony, and he, whether elected or nominated, was essentially a reflected image of kingship. The governor of the state retained the position of the governor of the colony, with such changes as a republican system necessarily required."[3] So far as judicial organization is concerned, there has been but a slight departure from the ancient original. Such differences as do exist are rather differences of detail than of organic structure. In both systems the unit of local judicial administration is the county, where all causes, except equity and probate causes, are tried in the first instance according to the course of English customary law, subject to review in a central

The executive power.

The judicial.

[1] Bryce, *The Am. Commonwealth,* vol. i. p. 243.

[2] Ibid., p. 415. The case of *Trevett* v. *Weeden,* decided in Rhode Island in 1786, seems to be the first case in which a legislative act was declared void by reason of repugnance to the principles of a state constitution. The second case is that of *Bayard* v. *Singleton,* Martin (N. C.), p. 48, decided in 1787. See Cooley (*Const. Lim.*, p..36, note 1), who says, in reference to the Rhode Island case, that it "is worthy of note that the first case in which a legislative enactment was declared unconstitutional and void, on the ground of incompatibility with the constitution of the state, was decided under one of these royal charters."

[3] Freeman, *Hist. Fed. Govt.*, vol. i. p 314, note 1.

appellate court modelled after the great courts at Westminster. It is not the ancient county court, however, that is the local centre of judicial administration. In America as in England the ancient county court is overshadowed by the assize or circuit court held periodically in every county by the itinerant or circuit judge sent to preside in the local tribunals by state authority. In every assize or circuit court held where English law prevails, the jury of presentment and the trial jury enter as component parts into the structure of a tribunal, which, in its modern form, is the special possession of the English race. Each colony started out by adopting the whole body of English statutory and customary law[1] so far as its principles could be adapted to their changed social and political conditions. By a perusal of the colonial codes it is possible to trace the beginnings of the great work of adaptation, which has not yet eliminated all of the obsolete elements of the ancient system. Even in the land law of the United States, which rests upon the broad principle that all lands are held allodially, definite traces of feudal law still survive. Although feudal tenures were abolished by the statute of 12 Car. II. c. 24, the leading principles of the system still survive as the basis of the English and American law of real property. As one of our own jurists has expressed it, — "Though our property is allodial, yet feudal tenures may be said to exist among us in their consequences and the qualities which they originally imparted to estates."[2] When all of these elements of likeness are considered, who can fail to perceive that the typical English state in America is, in a constitutional sense, simply the English kingdom transferred to a new theatre, where it has entered upon a wider destiny with its political horizon unclouded by the waning shadows of nobility, feudality, and kingship.

6. Having traced in some detail the growth of the English colonies in America down to that point in their history at which they appear as thirteen sovereign commonwealths, — each one of which is a substantial reproduction of the English kingdom, — the attempt will next be made to outline the

The assize or circuit court the special possession of the English race.

Feudal principles still linger in American land law.

Federalism as a system of government.

---

[1] "British and colonial statutes made prior to the Revolution continued also in force unless expressly repealed." — *The Critical Period, etc.*, p. 69.

[2] Gibson, C. J., in 9 Serg. and R. (Penn.), p. 333. See, also, 3 Serg. and R., p. 449.

process through which these commonwealths were dra[w]
together first in lax and imperfect confederacies, and fina[lly]
in the most perfect federal union which has ever existed [in]
ancient or modern times. In order the more clearly to com[-]
prehend the process through which federalism has finall[y]
taken on in America its most perfect form, it will be helpful
to glance for a moment at its history as a system of government prior to the making of its last and most successful
experiment. A federal union may be defined to be the
joining together of sovereign states under any form of confederation more permanent than a mere alliance, wherein
each state surrenders a part of its sovereignty for the common good of all, without the surrender of its individual right
to regulate such internal affairs as concern it only. It is the
very opposite of that kind of union which is brought about by
the incorporation or fusion of two or more states or cities
into a single body with equal rights common to all. The
ideal or perfect federal government may be defined to be one **A perfect federal gov ernment.**
which is but a single state in all matters which concern the
federal body as a whole, and yet a group of states perfectly
independent in all matters which concern each member of
the group as a local self-governing community. To the ideal
federal government, the federal commonwealths which have
actually existed in history can only be regarded as more or
less close approximations. Out of the entire group of such
commonwealths four have been specially commended for
study to students of the history of federal government for the
reason that their constitutions illustrate the closest approaches
which have so far been made to the perfect federal ideal.
These four are the Achaian League (B. C. 281–146) ; the **The closest approaches to such an ideal.**
Confederation of the Swiss Cantons (from 1291) ; the Seven
United Provinces of the Netherlands (1579–1795) ; and the
United States of North America (from 1781). "Of these
four, three come sufficiently near to the full realization of the
federal idea to be entitled to rank among perfect federal
governments. The Achaian League, and the United States
since the adoption of the present constitution, are indeed the
most perfect developments of the federal principle which the
world has ever seen." [1] In considering the internal structures

[1] Freeman, *Hist. of Federal Government*, vol. i. pp. 5, 6.

of these more perfect federal systems a sharp distinction must
be drawn between those in which the central power deals only
with the government of states as states, and those in which
the central power acts directly upon all citizens.   According
to the manner in which the central power exercises its special
functions federal governments are usually divided into two
classes.   Those in which the central power is only authorized
to issue requisitions to the state government for each to carry
out are known as " confederated states ;" while those which
are sovereign within their own spheres, and which can enforce
such sovereignty directly upon every citizen, are known as
" composite states." [1]   The scholars who have in our own
time passed beyond the Greece of Thucydides into the Greece
of Polybios,[2] who have passed beyond the period in which the
independent city-commonwealth was the dominant political
idea into the later and less brilliant period of Hellenic freedom occupied by the history of Greek federalism, have at last
put before us in a tangible form the history of at least one
ancient federal league whose internal structure entitles it to
be ranked among " composite states."   Careful analysis of the
constitution of the Achaian League seems to have clearly
established the fact that its government was really national;
that there was an Achaian nation, with a national chief, a
national assembly, and national tribunals; that every Achaian
citizen owed a direct allegiance to the central authority as a
citizen of the league itself, and not merely of one of the cities
that composed it.[3]   The supreme power was vested in a single
primary assembly which met at stated intervals, and in a gen-
eral ($\Sigma\tau\rho\alpha\tau\eta\gamma\grave{o}\varsigma$), elected for a stated term like the American
president, who was assisted by ten magistrates who formed

(margin left:)
Federal
govern-
ments di-
vided into
two classes.

Greek fed-
eralism, —
the Achaian
League,

---

[1] As to the distinction between the
two classes, see J. S. Mill, *Rep. Govt.*,
p. 301; Prof. Barnard, *Lectures on
American War*, Oxford, 1861, pp. 68–
72; Tocqueville, *Democracy in America*, vol. i. pp. 250, 265 *et seq.;* Freeman, *Hist. of Fed. Govt.*, vol. i. pp. 11,
12, and notes. Tocqueville (vol. i. p.
201) says that the constitution of the
United States is neither exactly national
nor exactly federal : it is a novel thing
without a name — " *un gouvernement national incomplet.*"   See upon the whole
subject, *Federalist*, Nos. xxxviii., xxxix.

[2] See Mommsen, *Römische Geschichte*,

vol. ii. p. 427, as to the character of
Polybios as a historian.   Mr. Freeman,
after referring to Grote's depreciation
of " the Greece of Polybios " (vol. xii.
pp. 527–530), laments the fact that his
great work " lies almost untouched in
our universities." — *Fed. Govt.*, pp. 219–
227, note 1.   In Germany the federal
period of Grecian history has excited
more interest.

[3] " The Achaian League was, in German technical language, a *Bundesstaat*,
and not a mere *Staatenbund.*" — Freeman, *Hist. of Federal Govt.*, vol. i. p.
259, citing Helwing, p. 237.

around him a permanent cabinet or council.[1] Although the central assembly did undoubtedly levy federal taxes (αἱ κοιναὶ εἰσφοραί[2]), the probabilities are that such taxes were collected not by federal tax collectors, but through the requisition system under which each city was permitted to raise its quota through its own local machinery. The Achaian League can therefore only hold its place among "composite states" by virtue of the fact that its national government acted directly upon the citizen, and not by reason of the fact that it had passed beyond the requisition stage to that in which a federal government collects its taxes through the direct agency of its own officers.[3] And yet, whatever general resemblance may be traced between the Achaian League (the product of a union of city-commonwealths) and the United States (the product of a union of modern states), the fact remains that the history of the one had no direct or conscious influence upon the making of the other. That the makers of the constitution of the United States had no real knowledge of the history of the ancient league is made certain by that writer in the "Federalist" who tells us that "could the interior structure and regular operation of the Achaian League be ascertained, it is probable that more light might be thrown by it on the science of federal government, than by any of the like experiments with which we are acquainted."[4] The only federal governments with whose internal organizations the builders of our federal republic were really familiar, and whose histories had any practical effect upon their work, were those which had grown up between the Low-Dutch communities at the mouth of the Rhine, and between the High-Dutch communities in the mountains of Switzerland, and upon the plains of Germany.[5] Down to the making of the second constitution of the United States, the Confederation

(marginal notes:) whose national government acted directly upon the citizen.

Makers of our federal constitution had no real knowledge of this ancient league,—

only acquainted with the structures of the Teutonic leagues,—

---

[1] Freeman, *Hist. of Federal Govt.*, vol. i. pp. 263, 282, 285.

[2] Pol. iv. 60.

[3] Mr. Freeman holds that even if the federal taxes were collected through requisitions, that fact should not degrade the "Achaian League from the rank of a composite state to that of a mere confederacy."—*Federal Government*, vol. i. p. 14. See, also, p. 309, and note 2.

[4] No. xviii. That the American Union was not a conscious imitation of the Achaian League is clearly brought out in *Federal Government*, vol. i. p. 319. Such knowledge as the framers did possess of Greek federalism seems to have been chiefly drawn from the work of the Abbé Mably, *Observations sur l'Histoire de Grèce*. See *Federalist*, No. xviii. p. 117.

[5] See *Federalist*, Nos. xix., xx.

of Swiss Cantons, the United Provinces of the Netherlands, and the German Confederation really represented the total advance which the modern world had made in the structure of federal governments. Such advance was embodied in the idea of a federal system made up of a union of states, cities, or districts, — representatives from which composed a single federal assembly whose supreme power could be brought to bear not upon individual citizens, but only upon cities or states as such. The fundamental principle upon which all such fabrics rested was the requisition system, under which the federal head was simply endowed with the power to make requisitions for men and money upon the states or cities composing the league for federal purposes ; while the states alone, in their corporate capacity, possessed the power to execute and enforce them. The first advance made by the English colonies in America in the path of federal union ended with the making of the first constitution of the United States, embodied in what is known as the Articles of Confederation. Up to that point nothing new had been achieved ; the fruit of the first effort was simply a confederation upon the old plan with the federal power vested in a single assembly which could only deal through the requisition system with the states as states.

all of which rested upon the requisition system.

The group of English provincial states, as they appear in America towards the close of the eighteenth century, were a substantial reproduction of that older group of English commonwealths, generally known as the heptarchic kingdoms, as they appear in Britain in the eighth.   Their historical origin was the same, and their systems of political organization substantially the same.   And yet in spite of these likenesses the younger group, in their earlier efforts at union, were unable to look to the political experience of the elder either for light or guidance, for the reason that the widely different geographical conditions by which they were respectively surrounded had prescribed for each a widely different destiny.   Confined within the narrow and impassable limits of an island world, it became "the manifest destiny" of the English states in Britain, advancing in the path of political aggregation, to coalesce in the formation of a single consolidated kingdom.   Situated upon the shores of an almost

Effects of geography on federation.

boundless continent, it became "the manifest destiny" of the English states in America, advancing in the path of political confederation, to unite in the flexible bonds of a federal system capable of unlimited expansion.[1] "The circumstances of the tenth century led the English kingdoms in Britain naturally and necessarily to coalesce in the shape of a consolidated kingdom. The circumstances of the eighteenth century led the English commonwealths in America as naturally and necessarily to coalesce in the shape of a federal commonwealth." [2]

A remarkable fact in the history of the colonies was their rapid growth in population. During the century and a half that intervened between the founding of the first settlements and the close of the French and Indian War the population of the thirteen had swelled to full a million and a half [3] — nearly one fourth of that of the mother country. This rapid increase in population forced upon the early settlements the necessity of continually widening their boundaries. In this way disputes arose not only among the colonists themselves, but with settlers of other nationalities grouped about them whose boundaries were defined in grants from their own sovereigns. The difficulties and dangers growing out of this condition of things brought about the formation of the first American confederacy. No sooner had the four New England colonies of Massachusetts, Connecticut, New Haven, and Plymouth completed their existence than their disputes between themselves, and their hostilities with the Dutch in New Netherland, growing out of encroachments on their territory, with the French in Canada, arising out of conflicting grants, and with the Indians, impelled them, "encompassed by people of several nations and strange languages," to enter "into a consociation for mutual help and strength." The federal constitution of this short-lived league, formed upon the requisition plan, was embodied in formal articles of confederation,[4] eleven in number, which were agreed upon at Boston, in May, 1643. It was provided that the affairs

Effects of the growth of population upon federation.

New England confederation, 1643.

---

[1] See *American Political Ideas*, Fiske, chapter iii., entitled "Manifest Destiny."

[2] Freeman, *The English People in its Three Homes*, p. 186.

[3] "1,200,000 whites and a quarter of a million of negroes." — Green, *Hist. of the Eng. People*, vol. iv. p. 167.

[4] The articles were first printed in 1656 in London, in Governor Eaton's code entitled *New Haven's Settling in New England.*

of the confederacy should be managed by a board of federal commissioners, and that the members of the league should be known henceforth as the United Colonies of New England.[1]   A hundred years and more then passed by before the whole colonial group was for the first time aroused to the necessity for union by the presence of a common danger which also grew out of the question of territorial expansion.   The French, who early in the seventeenth century had possessed themselves of Canada and the St. Lawrence, possessed themselves early in the eighteenth of the Mississippi, founding in 1718 the city of New Orleans.   Between the mouths of the two mighty rivers were placed at points of the greatest strategic value a line of forts which were designed to protect from English intrusion that vast domain called New France, which stretched on the west of the Alleghanies from New Orleans to Quebec.   By such means as these the French hoped to retain for themselves the valleys of the Mississippi and Ohio, and to confine the English colonies within that comparatively narrow strip of country lying between the Appalachian range and the Atlantic Ocean. But when the time for expansion came, when the necessities of the swelling English population impelled them to pass the tops of the Alleghanies in order to possess themselves of the great valleys beyond, upon which France had first laid hold, the fact was revealed that the young giant of the Atlantic had only been bound with the thongs of Lilliput.[2]   When the English colonial system came in collision with the French colonial system, when the new self-governing soldiery which had been reared in the southern counties and in the New England townships went out together under the lead of the mother country to do battle with a colonial power which had never been trained in self-reliance, it "was like a Titan overthrowing a cripple."[3]   France's dream of empire in the west was broken, she was forced to give up her priceless posses-

(marginal note:) New France.

(marginal note:) The struggle for expansion.

---

[1] As to the history and structure of the New England confederation, see "Acts of the Federal Commissioners," which form the ninth and tenth volumes of the *Plymouth Records;* Doyle, *English Colonies in America, Puritan, etc.,* vol. i. pp. 220–265; *Nar. and Crit. History,* vol. iii. pp. 315, 334, 338, 354, 373; *Memorial Hist. of Boston,* vol. i. p. 299.

[2] See *Nar. and Crit. Hist.,* vol. v. ch. viii., entitled "The Struggle for the great valleys of North America."

[3] Fiske, *Am. Political Ideas,* p. 56 See the criticism of this statement in *Nar. and Crit. Hist.,* vol. v. p. 533, note 1.

sions and to retire from North America. The results of the French and Indian War were momentous in their effects upon the cause of union. By the overthrow of the one enemy that they feared, the only real cause for the dependence of the colonies upon the mother country was removed at a blow; by their joint endeavors was won that vast domain beyond the Alleghanies which was destined to become a national possession; in the thick of the fight the new nationality heretofore unconscious of its real character finally awoke to a sense of its oneness. The struggle for expansion thus became the training-school in which the colonists were for the first time made to realize their capacity for concert of action upon which they had mainly to rely in the greater fight that was soon to come. Within two years after the making of the Peace of Paris, by which the French and Indian War was formally terminated, the colonies were called upon to act in concert in resisting the Stamp Act which in February, 1765, had passed the Imperial parliament.[1] When Massachusetts spoke the word for the first American congress, the nine of the thirteen colonies that met in New York in response to the summons took the first step on the way to union. Nine years later, when Massachusetts at the suggestion of Virginia again gave the word, the First Continental Congress assembled in Philadelphia in September, 1774, in which all the colonies were represented except Georgia. In this the first American assembly which was really national, and in which Washington sat in his colonel's uniform, the new-born spirit of union was embodied in a resolution which made the cause of the people of Massachusetts the cause of all by the declaration that if force shall be used "all America ought to support them in their opposition." In the Second Continental Congress which met in the same place in May of the following year all of the colonies appeared, and, in the summer of 1776, all took part in the two great acts[2] which gave

Effects of French and Indian War upon the cause of union.

Stamp Act Congress. Oct. 7, 1765.

First Continental Congress. Sept., 1774.

Second Continental Congress. May, 1775.

[1] It "passed through both houses with less opposition than a turnpike bill." — Green, *Hist. of the Eng. People*, vol. iv. p. 230. The Peace of Paris was the fruit of a treaty signed in Paris in February, 1763. For its history, see Parkman, *Montcalm and Wolfe*, vol. ii. p. 383, etc.

[2] On the 7th of June Richard Henry Lee moved a resolution, which was adopted by congress on the 11th, "That these United Colonies are, and of right ought to be, free and independent states. . . . And that a plan of confederation be prepared and transmitted to the respective colonies for their consideration and approbation."

life and character to the new nationality. By one concurrent act, performed through their representatives in congress assembled, the colonies severed their political relations with the English crown, and thus became independent states, save so far as that independence was limited by the federal relations into which they had entered prior to the making of the Declaration of Independence.[1] What those federal relations were depends upon the nature and extent of the powers of the Second Continental Congress which was the cohesive force which held the states together, and managed their federal affairs from the time of its meeting down to the 1st of March, 1781,[2] when the articles of confederation took effect as a constitution binding on all the states. Down to that time the congress was the national government — such a government as it was — *de jure* and *de facto ;* and the general scope of its powers cannot be more clearly expressed than in the language of Justice Chase, who said that "The powers of congress originated from necessity, and arose out of and were only limited by events, or, in other words, they were revolutionary in their very nature. Their extent depended on the exigencies and necessities of public affairs."[3]

Declaration of Independence. July 4, 1776.

Congress the national government down to March 1, 1781.

Articles of Confederation.

The move upon the part of congress to devise some form of confederation under which the colonies could permanently unite preceded by three weeks the promulgation of the Declaration of Independence.[4] But the task proved a difficult one. Not until after a year and a half had been consumed

[1] "The transformation of the colonies into 'states' was, therefore, not the result of the independent action of the individual colonies. It was accomplished through the 'representatives of the United States;' that is, through the revolutionary congress, in the name of the whole people." — Von Holst, *Const. Hist. of the U. S.,* vol. i. p. 5. To the same effect, see Fiske, *The Critical Period,* p. 91. This seems to be the more reasonable view, but the Supreme Court of the United States, in *Ware* v. *Hylton,* 3 Dallas, p. 224, expressed through Justice Chase a contrary opinion, as follows : " I consider this as a declaration, not that the United Colonies *jointly,* in a *collective* capacity, were independent states, etc., but that *each* of them was a sovereign and independent state."

[2] On that day Maryland signed the articles and completed the constitution.

[3] See *Ware* v. *Hylton,* 3 Dallas, p. 232. Von Holst incorrectly attributes this statement to Jay, C. J.

[4] The committee appointed under the resolution of the 11th of June, 1776, to draft "articles of confederation and perpetual union," completed its work by the 12th of July, but the result was not finally adopted by Congress until November, 1777. " John Dickinson is supposed to have been the principal author of the articles of confederation ; but as the work of the committee was done in secret, and has never been reported, the point cannot be determined." — *The Critical Period, etc.,* p. 93.

in study and debate did the draft of the first constitution of the United States reach completion. Not until November, 1777, were the articles of confederation submitted by congress to the states for adoption, — whereupon they were promptly signed by all except Delaware, New Jersey, and Maryland. Their refusal to enter into the confederacy grew out of the controversy as to the ultimate ownership of the great western territory of which France had been dispossessed. After the Revolution had extinguished the rights of the English crown in this vast domain, Virginia, New York, Connecticut, and Massachusetts undertook to claim it for themselves under conflicting and irreconcilable titles. The three resisting states, whose western boundaries were irrevocably fixed, could never hope to share in this great heritage unless its ownership should be vested in the corporate person of the new nationality. To prevent such a contingency the claiming states had procured an amendment of the articles to the effect that no state should be deprived of territory for the benefit of the United States.[1] Delaware and New Jersey soon withdrew from the controversy, leaving the fight for national dominion over this priceless possession to Maryland alone. In her "Instructions" to her delegates read in congress, May 21, 1779, her position was clearly and distinctly defined. She claimed "that a country unsettled at the commencement of this war, claimed by the British crown, and ceded to it by the treaty of Paris, if wrested from that common enemy by the blood and treasure of the thirteen states, should be considered as common property, subject to be parcelled out by congress into free, convenient, and independent governments, in such manner and at such times as the wisdom of that assembly shall hereafter direct."[2] Fortunately for the future of the country, from this high ground she never withdrew. In January, 1781, Virginia agreed conditionally to yield her claims;[3] on March 1, 1781, New York executed a transfer of her rights to the United States; and on that day Maryland completed the new constitution by giving it her adhesion.[4] Exactly three years thereafter Virginia

The western territory.

Maryland's influence upon the land cessions to the United States.

---

[1] See *Journals of Congress*, vol. ii. p. 304.
[2] See Ibid., vol. iii. p. 281.
[3] *Journal of Va. House of Delegates*, p. 79.
[4] *Journals of Congress*, vol. iii. pp.

conveyed without conditions, and in due time Massachusetts
and Connecticut did substantially the same thing. In this
way the new nationality became the sovereign possessor of
"the whole northwestern territory — the area of the great
states of Michigan, Wisconsin, Illinois, Indiana, and Ohio
(excepting the Connecticut reserve)," [1] which, under the articles of confederation, it had no express right either to hold
or govern.[2] Not until Maryland had been assured that this
great prize should belong to the new confederacy, not until
its right to possess this vast domain as folkland had been
clearly admitted, did she agree to become a member of the
league whose constitution soon proved itself to be more weak,
more worthless, more impotent than that of any of the older
Teutonic leagues after which it had been patterned. In their
first effort American statesmen exhibited no fertility of re-

Character
of the first
federal con-
stitution.

source in the making of federal constitutions. The new
fabric simply embodied the old story of a confederation with
the federal power vested in a single assembly, without an executive head, and without a judiciary. Congress could make
treaties with foreign nations, but it could not force the states
to observe them ; it alone could decide controversies between
the states, and yet it could not enforce the final decree; it
could declare war, but it could raise neither men nor money
save through the old and ineffectual system of requisitions

Interstate
citizenship.

upon the states as states. If there was one feature that
raised the new constitution above its fellows it was the new
system of interstate citizenship which it embodied.[3] But
such a negative virtue as that was not sufficient to save it
from the general condemnation which fell upon it as its deficiencies were day by day revealed in the storm and stress of
protracted war. Federalism, which as a system of government already stood low enough in the estimation of mankind,

581, 582, 591. What has been here said
as to the influence of Maryland in this
great transaction has been chiefly drawn
from the brilliant monograph of Dr.
H. B. Adams, entitled "Maryland's
Influence upon Land Cessions to the
United States," *J. H. Studies,* 3d
series, I.

[1] *The Critical Period,* p. 194.

[2] As to "the exercise of national
sovereignty in the sense of eminent

domain, a power totally foreign to the
articles of confederation," under the
ordinances of 1784 and 1787, see Dr.
Adams's paper cited above, p. 44 ; Fiske,
The Critical Period, pp. 192–207.

[3] See sec. one, art. four, of articles.
"The articles of confederation first
brought in the rule that any one might
at will transfer his membership from one
state to another." — Bancroft, *Hist. of
the Const.,* vol. i. p. 118.

was put in no better plight by the first American experiment. The full significance of that fact naturally fell with the greatest weight upon the heart of the mighty chief whose personality was called upon to supply the unity and cohesion which could not be derived from the new constitution. As Luzerne wrote of him to Vergennes at a little later day, " More is hoped from the consideration of a single citizen than from the authority of the sovereign body." [1] From the very outset Washington saw that no good could come of the new compact unless more adequate powers were vested in the federal assembly. In the month before the articles were finally accepted by Maryland he wrote : " I never expect to see a happy termination of the war, nor great national concerns well conducted in peace, till there is something more than a recommendatory power in congress." [2] So completely had this conviction taken hold of his mind by the close of the war, that he made its expression the most solemn feature in the circular letter which in June, 1783, he addressed through the governors of the states to the whole people as his " legacy " to his country. " The newspapers of the day, as they carried the letter of Washington into every home, caught up the theme, and demanded a revision of the constitution, ' not by congress, but by a continental convention, authorized for the purpose.' " [3] Ere the echo of Washington's great appeal had died away the states, under the lead of Virginia [4] whose conduct he inspired, gathered in the famous federal convention of 1787 in which was framed the present constitution of the United States.

Washington,—

his circular letter of June 8, 1783.

7. The work of the federal convention which met in Philadelphia on May 14, 1787, is generally and justly regarded as the most perfect and the most important piece of political work ever performed by a deliberative assembly in ancient or modern times. In the words of Mr. Gladstone, " As the British constitution is the most subtile organism which has proceeded from progressive history, so the American constitution is the most wonderful work ever struck off at a given

The Federal Convention, May 14, 1787.

---

[1] August, 1783. Printed in Appendix to Bancroft, vol. i. p. 326.
[2] Washington to Sullivan, February 4, 1781. Sparks, vol. vii. p. 402.
[3] Bancroft, vol. i. p. 113.
[4] For the details of the process through which the convention was brought about, and as to the parts taken by Washington and Madison, see *The Critical Period*, etc., pp. 212–229. As to Virginia's initiative, see Bancroft, vol. i. ch. viii.

time by the brain and purpose of man."[1] The men themselves
who accomplished the mighty task seem to have been overcome at its close by the grandeur of their achievement.
When the masses of the people had the opportunity to examine its provisions, and to feel the practical benefits which
it wrought in their political condition, they too became im-
bued with a spirit of intense admiration; they put it upon a
pedestal and made it a popular idol; as a German historian

**Canoniza-
tion of the
constitu-
tion.**

has expressed it, the new constitution soon passed through a
process of canonization.[2] The one evil effect of this ardent
and uncritical spirit was to mislead for a time the minds of
men as to the real character of a work whose true value as
an enduring institution rises higher and higher in the light
of its actual history. The uncritical enthusiasts who looked
upon the framers of the new constitution as demigods and
not as men, and who held up their work as a spontaneous
creation produced under the effects an intellectual inspi-
ration, unwittingly put upon it the gravest reproach to which
it could possibly have been subjected. It is just because it
was no such thing that it has been able to survive all the
vicissitudes through which it has passed, and to stand forth
to-day stronger and better for having passed through the
severest ordeal in which any political fabric was ever tested.

**The consti-
tution not a
"creation."**

To the student of institutions the constitution of the United
States is not a "creation" at all, neither is it a paper constitution in the sense in which that term is usually understood.
If it had been, it would have withered long ago and disappeared along with the many other paper constitutions formu-
lated about the same time by the excited dreamers of the
French Revolution who refused to believe with Sir James
Mackintosh that "constitutions are not made, they grow."
In the light of the calm critical spirit which now prevails, and
with the abundant historical knowledge at the command of
all, there is no reason why any one should be misled as to
the real origin and character of our federal constitution.

[1] This statement is quoted only as
evidence of the esteem in which the
work of the convention is held by the
greatest of statesmen. I believe with
Professor Johnston that, "If the brilliant success of the American constitution proves anything, it does not prove
that a viable constitution can ever be
'struck off at a given time by the brain
and purpose of man.' " See *The New
Princeton Review*, September, 1887, p.
186.

[2] Von Holst, vol. i. pp. 64–70.

From the biographies of the framers themselves it is easy to ascertain what their race-traits were; from the histories of the colonies from which they came it is equally easy to ascertain what had been the character of their prior political training and experience; from the history of the events which had recently preceded their meeting we can derive without any great effort the overshadowing causes which brought them together. As to the secret proceedings of the convention itself, industry has exhausted its resources in gathering together every scrap of existing evidence which can possibly throw light upon the subject.[1] The incomplete Journal of the convention has been edited and published under the sanction of congress; the contemporaneous private correspondence of the members has been gathered together from every quarter; the archives of our own state department have been carefully searched; the archives of the foreign governments that had representatives in the country at the time have been made to yield up their treasures,[2] — until everything calculated to throw light upon what was done in the "secret conclave" has at last been made accessible to every inquirer. In the Federalist papers we have a contemporaneous exposition little less remarkable for intellectual vigor than the constitution itself. Out of such a mass of material it would be easy to spin a volume. The difficult task is to so lift up out of the mass the great central facts and thoughts as to make them present vividly to the mind a clear and simple picture of what actually occurred. Through every great transaction there runs a logical order of thought, as well as a historical sequence of facts. And yet it often happens that a mere narration of the facts in the order in which they occurred will utterly fail to

Proceedings of the convention.

[1] The most important single source of information as to the proceedings of the federal convention is Elliot's *Debates*, in which is contained not only the debates which took place in the state conventions on the adoption of the constitution, but also the Journal of the Federal Convention, Yates' Minutes of the Proceedings, Madison's Journal of the Federal Convention, together with the official letters of many of the leading members in explanation of their conduct, and other documents of the highest historic value. These debates were published "under the sanc-

tion of congress," in 1830-45, and reprinted in Philadelphia in 1888.

[2] In the appendices to Bancroft's *Hist. of the Constitution*, 1883, can be found a rare collection of letters and papers touching the making of the constitution, and the causes which led to the meeting of the convention, very few of which had ever before been published. See Mr. Bancroft's criticism upon the manner in which the incomplete Journal of the convention has been interpolated by its editors. Preface, pp. xiv., xv.

reveal to the mind the full scope of the intellectual process
moving behind them.   This is eminently true of the proceedings of the federal convention.   From the mere record it is
impossible to grasp the full significance of all that transpired.
In attempting to read the mind of the convention, the fact
must be recognized that "under the shell there is an animal,
and behind the document there is a man." [1]   In the light of
this truth the effort will be made to explain within a narrow
compass, first, the sources whence came the great thoughts
that dominated the convention; second, what those great
thoughts were; third, the forms which they finally assumed.

Race-traits of the framers.

An assembly could hardly have been convened in the
United Kingdom more English as to race and political training than that made up of the fifty-five delegates who composed the federal convention.   The Virginia delegation was
simply a brilliant group of English country gentlemen who
had been reared on the right side of the Atlantic.   Alexander
Hamilton and Robert Morris were born English subjects;
the father of Franklin was an English emigrant from Northamptonshire; Charles Cotesworth Pinckney had been educated at Oxford and the Middle Temple; Rutledge had
studied law at the Temple; and James Wilson, the most
far-sighted man perhaps in the whole convention, was born

Political training.

near St. Andrews in Scotland.   As to political training, they
had all been reared under the English system of local self-
government which had grown up alongside of the English
customary law in the several states which they represented.
These states they had helped to transform from English
provinces into independent commonwealths whose constitutions were substantial reproductions of that of the English
kingdom.   In fine, the only practical conception of the state
which they possessed was that embodied in the constitution
of the old land modified as it had been in the new by the
abolition of nobility, feudality, and kingship.   So far as

Blackstone and Montesquieu.

scientific knowledge was concerned, the oracles usually consulted at that day were Blackstone and Montesquieu.   The
"Spirit of Laws" was studied by Washington as a part of his
preparation for the work of the convention; [2] and Madison

---

[1] Taine, *Hist. of Eng. Literature,*
vol. i. p. 1.

[2] Washington drew the outlines of
three new constitutions, each one of

tells us in the "Federalist," that "The British constitution was to Montesquieu what Homer had been to the didactic writers on epic poetry. As the latter have considered the work of the immortal bard as the perfect model from which the principles and rules of the epic art were to be drawn, and by which all similar works were to be judged; so this great political critic appears to have viewed the constitution of England as the standard, or, to use his own expression, as the mirror of political liberty."[1]

The first effort which American statesmen had made to construct a federal constitution had resulted in something which was a radical departure from the whole course of their political experience. They had sought a model for the new structure entirely outside of the political history of the mother country. The result was a fabric whose internal organization violated every political maxim with which they were familiar. It had no executive head; it had no judiciary; it vested and confused the legislative, executive, and judicial powers in one assembly instead of two; it had no power to enforce its mandates. No scheme of government ever elaborated with so much care ever proved a more complete and hopeless failure than that embodied in the articles of confederation. During the war, when executive force and financial promptness were most essential, it had failed to supply either. At the end of the war it found itself burdened with a great debt for which it had no ability to provide — a fact which brought great discredit upon the new nationality. In the hope of restoring the public credit an earnest effort was made in 1782 to give to congress the power to command a permanent revenue through the imposition and collection of a duty on imports.[2] Two years after the refusal of the states to grant that power to congress, Robert Morris, the able financier, who had so long stood up against every difficulty, gave up his hopeless task; and, after informing Marbois,[3] the

Causes which compelled the making of the second constitution.

Financial difficulties of the confederation,

which aimed at the making of a stronger and more perfect union. See *North Am. Review*, xxv. p. 263; Bancroft, vol. i. p. 278.

[1] No. xlvi. p. 334, Dawson's ed.

[2] Such a power could only be bestowed through an amendment of the articles which required unanimous consent. At the close of 1782 all the states had assented except Rhode Island, whose refusal was followed by the withdrawal of Virginia. Subsequently all the states agreed to grant the power except New York, who defeated the last attempt by annexing to her assent, given in May, 1786, the proviso that she should appoint her own collectors.

[3] *Dipl. Cor.*, vol. xii. p. 494.

representative of France in America, that he could not even provide for the interest on the Dutch loan which France had guaranteed, on the first of November, 1784, finally retired from the office of superintendent of the finances of the United States.[1] In the midst of the weariness, inaction, and confusion which existed at this time Marbois wrote to Rayneval: "The people, scarcely escaped from war, are already losing that public spirit which up to this time made good the want of energy in the government. There is neither congress, nor president, nor minister in any department. All matters, and especially those of finance, fall into a worse

Root of the evil the requisition system.

confusion than before."[2] The rock upon which the confederation had gone to wreck was the requisition system, under which the federal treasury was practically dependent upon the states for voluntary contributions. Out of ten million dollars, called for by congress for the four years ending in 1786, only one fourth was actually collected. Under the pressure of such circumstances congress lost both prestige and authority; and by the time of the meeting of the federal convention the government of the confederation had practically disappeared. The country was beginning to be threatened with anarchy,[3] with dangers from within and dangers

Four great motives for union.

from without. The pressure of these dangers brought into the foreground four great motives for union. The English order in council of the 2d of July, 1783, as to the carrying trade between America and the British West Indies made it imperatively necessary that the states should vest in a central government the power to regulate and protect their foreign commerce; while other motives of self-interest made it equally necessary that such central power should be armed with the authority to govern the national domain, to provide a revenue for the satisfaction of the public creditors, and to protect domestic trade by prohibiting the states from impairing the obligation of contracts.[4] As Madison expressed it in

---

[1] See Bancroft, *Hist. of the Const.,* vol. i. p. 165. Morris tendered his resignation to congress in January, 1783, but did not actually give up his post until November, 1784. See Ibid., p. 80.

[2] November 20, 1784. Printed in Appendix to Bancroft, vol. i. p. 396.

[3] This is well brought out by Fiske in *The Critical Period, etc.,* ch. iv., "Drifting toward Anarchy."

[4] For a full statement of the four great motives, see Bancroft, vol. i. p. 146.

a letter written to Lee in November, 1784: "The union of the states is essential to their safety against foreign dangers and internal contention; the perpetuity and efficiency of the present system cannot be confided in; the question, therefore, is, in what mode and at what moment the experiment for supplying the defects ought to be made."[1] The utter worthlessness of the confederation and the pressing necessity for a new federal government were admitted on every hand. The difficulty was to find out how to construct something that would be adequate to the necessities of the new nationality. Experience had shown that a league based upon the requisition system was a mere rope of sand, and yet every other federal commonwealth that had ever existed down to that time had rested upon that impotent expedient. At this point necessity became the mother of invention, — after a painful travail America gave birth to a novel and irresistible political idea, — what the Germans would call a path-breaking idea (*bahnbrechende Idee*). In February, 1783, Pelatiah Webster published at Philadelphia a tract entitled "A Dissertation on the Political Union and Constitution of the thirteen United States of North America," in which he not only advocated permanent courts of law and equity, and a stricter organization of the executive power, but also a national assembly of two chambers instead of one, with power not only to enact laws, *but to enforce them on individuals as well as on states.*[2] A year later this tract, which had been reprinted at Hartford, was followed by another of the same tenor by Noah Webster, of that place, in which he proposed "a new system of government which should act, *not on the states, but directly on individuals, and vest in congress full power to carry its laws into effect.*"[3] This brand-new idea which the Websters seem to have been the first to express, — the idea of giving to the federal government the power to execute its laws not on states in their corporate capacity, but directly on individuals, — embodied the most important and far-reaching political principle to which our career as a nation has given birth. Of this new principle, after its incorporation into the present

The new political idea — the *bahnbrechende Idee:*

Pelatiah Webster;

Noah Webster;

[1] *Madison Papers*, vol. ii. pp. 707, 708.
[2] See P. Webster's *Political Essays*, p. 228.
[3] *Madison Papers*, vol. ii. p. 708. See Noah Webster's *Sketches of American Policy*, pp. 32-38.

Tocqueville.

constitution, Tocqueville said: "This constitution, which may at first be confounded with federal constitutions which have preceded it, rests in truth upon a wholly novel theory which may be considered a great discovery in modern political science. In all the confederations which preceded the American Constitution of 1789, the allied states, for a common object, agreed to obey the injunctions of a federal government; but they reserved to themselves the right of ordaining and enforcing the execution of the laws of the Union. The American states, which combined in 1789, agreed that the federal government should not only dictate, but should execute its own enactments. In both cases the right is the same, but the exercise of the right is different; and this differ-

The new idea becomes the basis of the new constitution.

ence produced the most momentous consequences."[1] The "novel theory," the new self-sustaining principle which became the basis of the more perfect union, and superseded therein the impotent system of requisitions, having been propounded by two political thinkers from three to four years before the meeting of the convention, must have been made the subject of careful consideration beforehand by those who were to give to it its first practical application. That it was the dominant idea in the convention itself is proven by the result, — the framers made it the foundation of their immortal work. That it was so regarded at the time is proven by evi-

Davie.

dence both clear and abundant. Mr. Davie, of North Carolina, in advocating the new constitution in the convention in which his own state finally ratified it, said: "Another radical vice in the old system, which was necessary to be corrected, and which will be understood without a long deduction of reasoning, was, that it legislated on states, instead of individuals. . . . *Every member* saw that the existing system would be ineffectual, unless its laws operated on individuals, as military coercion was neither eligible or practical."[2] In

Hamilton.

the New York convention Hamilton said: "We contend that

---

[1] *Democracy in America*, vol. i. pp. 198, 199, Bowen's ed. A greater than Tocqueville has very recently restated the matter as follows: "Its central or national government is not a mere league, for it does not wholly depend on the component communities which we call the States. It is itself a common-wealth as well as a union of common-wealths, because it claims directly the obedience of every citizen and acts immediately upon him through its courts and executive officers." — Bryce, *The American Commonwealth*, vol. i. p. 13.

[2] Elliot's *Debates*, vol. iv. pp. 21–23.

the radical vice in the old confederation is, that the laws of the Union apply only to the states in their corporate capacity . . . the states have almost uniformly weighed the requisition by their own local interests ; and have only executed them so far as answered their particular convenience or advantage." [1]   In the light of their own painful experience the framers of the new constitution ventured upon the experiment of constructing a federal government that would operate not on the states in their corporate capacity but directly upon individuals — an experiment which drew after it consequences which tended directly to systematize and strengthen the whole fabric into which it entered as a component part.

As soon as it was settled that the new idea was to be made the premise upon which the work of the convention was to proceed, as soon as it was settled that the new government was to be endowed with the power to execute its own laws and decrees directly upon individuals, it became apparent that it must be strictly organized and equipped with machinery adequate to that end.   The builders of the more perfect union were thus forced to give to it a completely organized constitution, "with the usual branches, legislative, executive, and judicial ; with the direct power of taxation, and the other usual powers of a government ; with its army, its navy, its civil service, and all the usual apparatus of a government, all bearing directly upon every citizen of the Union without any reference to the governments of the several states." [2]   When this point was reached, when it became manifest that the new federal commonwealth had to be organized as a "composite state," it was more than natural that the English constitutional system, in the form in which it had reappeared in the several states, should have been adopted as the standard for imitation. [3]   At this point the creative work of the framers ended, and the work of reproduction began.   The first great step in the work of reproduction was taken when the proposition was made to divide the

The new idea forces the construction of a " composite state."

---

[1] Elliot's *Debates*, vol. ii. p. 231.

[2] These are the attributes which Mr. Freeman says a "composite state" should possess. — *Federal Govt.*, vol. i. p. 11.

[3] What the federal constitution owes to the state constitutions has been expressed with great force by Professor Johnston, in an article in the *New Princeton Review* for September, 1887, — an article from which Mr. Bryce has made a copious extract in his first volume.   See p. 666.

The division of the
federal
head into
the three
department-
ments :
Jefferson.

sum of federal power — which under the articles of confederation had been vested in a single assembly — into the three
departments, legislative, executive, and judicial.   The necessity for such a division seems to have been first stated by
Jefferson, who in a letter to Madison written from Paris, December 16, 1786, used this language : "To make us one
nation, as to foreign concerns, and keep us distinct in domestic ones, gives the outline of the proper division of powers
between the general and particular governments.   But to
enable the federal head to exercise the powers given to best
advantage, *it should be organized as the particular ones are,
into legislative, executive, and judiciary*." [1]   Jefferson thus
made it clear that he had found the model for his division of
the federal head into three departments in the constitutions
of the states, each one of which had adopted the political
maxim that the three departments of power shall forever
remain separate and distinct in the same qualified sense in
which that maxim was understood in the English system.
Speaking of the constitution of the mother country, Madison

Division
made ac-
cording to
the maxim
as under-
stood in
England.

said : "On the slightest view of the British constitution we
must perceive that the legislative, executive, and judiciary departments are by no means totally separate and distinct from
each other." [2]   Speaking of the constitutions of the states he
said : "If we look into the constitutions of the several states,
we find, that, notwithstanding the emphatical, and, in some
instances, the unqualified terms in which the axiom has been
laid down, there is not a single instance in which the several
departments of power have been kept absolutely separate
and distinct." [3]   After the federal head had been split into
the three departments, legislative, executive, and judicial, in
the qualified sense in which such division was understood in
the state constitutions, each department was organized in
accordance with English ideas, in so far as they could be

---

[1] See *Jefferson's Correspondence*, by
T. J. Randolph, vol. ii. pp. 64, 65.

[2] *Federalist*, No. xlvi. p. 335.

[3] Ibid., p. 337.   I here repeat what
was said in note 1, p. 46.   The maxim
as to the division of powers was accepted in the qualified sense in which
it was understood by Montesquieu,
who accepted it in the form in which
it existed in the English system.   As

to Montesquieu's views of the English
constitution, see *Spirit of Laws*, bk.
xi. ch. 6.   Speaking of these views, so
far as they relate to the division of
powers, Madison says, "he did not
mean that these departments ought to
have no *partial agency* in, or no *control*
over the acts of each other."   Page 336.
See, also, Paul Janet's *Histoire de la
Science Politique*.

applied to a "composite state" at once federal and republican.

The organization of the executive department of the new government was attended with great difficulty. In the teeth of the prevailing prejudice against monarchy, it was no easy task to devise an acceptable scheme through which the federal chief magistrate could be clothed with the constitutional attributes of an English king. And yet that result was substantially accomplished.[1] Although the president was simply a magistrate to be obeyed within the range of his powers, and personally liable to impeachment if he overstepped them, still he was endowed with as much if not more real power than was possessed even then by the dreaded original. The elective principle, it is true, was substituted for hereditary right, a definite term of office was prescribed, and all the pomp and pageantry of power was sternly cut off, and yet the real resemblance which remained between the two national chiefs was too close to escape the enemies of the constitution, who bitterly assailed it on that ground.[2] And here let the fact be emphasized, that the kingship, whose constitutional attributes the framers reproduced, was not the shadowy kingship of to-day which reigns but does not govern, — "the figure they had before them was not a generalized English king nor an abstract constitutional monarch; it was no anticipation of Queen Victoria, but George III. himself, whom they took for their model. Fifty years earlier, or a hundred years later, the English king would have struck them in quite a different light."[3]

The executive department:

the president and George III.

---

[1] "The president is, beyond doubt, the English king modified by the necessities of a state of things in which hereditary succession was out of the question, and in which even a life term of office would have awakened the greatest jealousy." — Freeman, *The English People in its Three Homes*, p. 375.

[2] See Hamilton's brilliant reply to this attack, in the *Federalist*, Nos. lxvii., lxviii., lxix.

[3] Maine, *Popular Govt.*, p. 212. Mr. Fiske, when he says that, "curiously enough, what they copied in creating the office of president was not the real English executive or prime minister, but the fictitious English executive, the

sovereign" (*The Critical Period, etc.*, p. 289), loses sight of the fact that at the time the copy was made the *real* English executive was the *king* and not the prime minister. Maine's statement covers the whole matter. If any one fancies that George III., even during the ministry of Pitt, was a "fictitious executive," let him read May's first chapter, entitled "Influence of the Crown during the Reign of George III." *Const. Hist.*, vol. i. pp. 15-104. Since the above was written I find that Mr. Bryce says: "In 1787, when the constitutional convention met at Philadelphia, the cabinet system of government was in England still immature. It was

In the organization of the legislative department, the framers of the constitution departed from the old idea of a federal
assembly consisting of a single chamber, in order to adopt
the English system of two chambers, in the form in which
that system had reappeared in the several states.   The
adaptation of this dual system to the complicated interests
of a federal republic gave rise to difficulties which at one
time seemed to be insurmountable.   The convention which
framed the constitution was divided into two parties generally known as nationals and federals.   At the head of the
nationals stood the delegates from Virginia, who came to the
convention with a well-considered scheme known as "the
Virginia plan," which contemplated the abolition of the confederation and the substitution in its stead of a consolidated
national government.   This plan, constructed in the main by
Madison, at the instance of Washington, was laid before the
convention by Edmund Randolph,[1] the governor of Virginia,
in a weighty speech which emphasized the necessity of making the new government operate directly upon individuals
through the medium of laws enacted by a national assembly
in which the American people instead of the American
states should be represented, — an assembly whose members
should be apportioned according to population, and elected
by the people and their representatives.   Such assembly was
to be divided into two houses, — the members of the lower
house to be elected directly by popular vote, while the members of the upper house or senate were to be chosen by the
lower out of persons nominated by the state legislatures.
This plan which contemplated the creation of a national executive, and a national judiciary, and the vesting of the legislative power in a national assembly which could be dominated and controlled by a combination of a few of the greater
states, and which was to be endowed not only with original
powers of legislation in all cases in which the powers of the
states were insufficient, but also with a negative on state laws

so immature that its true nature had
not been perceived." — *The American
Commonwealth*, vol. i. p. 273.
[1] Elliot's *Debates*, vol. i. pp. 180–182.
Randolph's resolutions were offered
on May 29th.

[2] In the course of his speech Randolph said that " the confederation was
made in the infancy of the science of
constitutions, when the inefficiency of
requisitions was unknown." — Elliot,
pp. 126–128.

naturally met with a storm of opposition from the smaller states who were to be denied corporate representation in both chambers. When the momentous issues thus presented were so divided that they could be considered in detail a resolution, which originated with Virginia, was adopted without debate which settled the fact as a starting-point, that however the respective branches of the national legislature should be constituted, it should consist of two houses instead of one.[1] As to the composition of the houses themselves, the question which first arose was whether or no the lower house should be organized on a popular basis after the model of the English house of commons. After a debate in which such men as Gerry, Sherman, Martin, and the Pinckneys expressed grave distrust of the wisdom of the people, the convention was induced by Madison,[2] Hamilton, Wilson, and others to decide that the members of the lower house should be chosen directly by popular election. When this difficulty was removed the convention was free to grapple with the vital question before it, — the question whether or no the states as such were to be represented in the new assembly. If "the Virginia plan," which was supported by Pennsylvania, Massachusetts, and North Carolina, was to prevail, the lesser states, which under the articles of confederation were entitled to an equal vote, would be placed at the mercy of their more powerful associates. At this stage of the proceedings, as a counter-blast to the Virginia scheme, the smaller states under the lead of William Patterson brought before the convention "the New Jersey plan,"[3] which proposed nothing more than a reformation of the articles of confederation. This plan contemplated the continuance of the old federal assembly consisting of a single chamber in which each state had an equal vote; an executive in the form of a council; and a federal judiciary with a limited and inadequate jurisdiction. When angry and protracted debate between the two opposing parties, who had now reduced their conflicting

Adoption of the bicameral system.

"The New Jersey Plan."

---

[1] This resolution was opposed only by Pennsylvania. — Elliot, vol. i. p. 187; Gilpin, p. 753.

[2] Madison adjusted the basis of representation as between the north and the south through his famous three fifths compromise which he had invented at an earlier day for the purpose of adjusting between the sections the basis of taxation.

[3] Elliott's *Debates*, vol. i. pp. 208–210. Patterson's propositions were offered June 15th.

views to definite propositions, had brought the convention to "the verge of dissolution," Roger Sherman and Oliver Ellsworth suggested the famous "Connecticut compromise" which proposed that the national principle contended for by the greater states should prevail in the organization of the lower house, and that the federal principle claimed by the smaller states should prevail in the organization of the upper house or senate. The new proposal, which at first met with but little favor, was referred to a committee with Elbridge Gerry as chairman, and on the 5th of July[1] the committee reported in favor of the compromise. After eleven days of debate the report was adopted on the 16th of July by a majority of only one vote.[2] The supreme conflict between the two opposing parties in the convention thus happily ended in an arrangement in which the theories of both were allowed to prevail. It was finally agreed that the legislative department of the new government should be divided into two chambers, one of which should be organized upon a federal, the other upon a national basis. As a recognition of the federal principle each state was to be allowed an equal representation in the senate ; as a recognition of the national principle the representation of each state in the house of representatives was to be determined by the extent of its population.[3] In the organization of the senate the elective principle of course took the place of hereditary right. Thus modified by republican and federal ideas the English bicameral system, in the form which it had assumed in the several states, passed into the constitution of the United States.

The most consummate and, with a single exception, the most original work accomplished by the framers of the constitution was in the organization of the federal judiciary.[4]

Marginal notes:

"The Connecticut Compromise."

The senate organized upon a federal, the house upon a national basis.

The judiciary department.

---

[1] Elliot's *Debates*, vol. i. p. 226.

[2] Connecticut, Delaware, Maryland, New Jersey, and North Carolina voted in the affirmative; Georgia, Pennsylvania, Virginia, and South Carolina in the negative. Massachusetts' vote was divided, and New York was absent. — Elliot, vol. i. p. 238.

[3] "The principle of the independence of the states triumphed in the formation of the senate, and that of the sovereignty of the nation in the

composition of the house of representatives." — De Tocqueville, *Democracy in Am.*, vol. i. p. 148. As to the respective constitutions of the two chambers, see *Federalist*, Nos. lii. to lxvii.

[4] "The work was chiefly done in committee by Ellsworth, Wilson, Randolph, and Rutledge, and the result did not differ essentially from the scheme laid down in the Virginia plan." — *The Critical Period, etc.*, p. 300.

Section one of article three of the constitution provides that, "The judicial power of the United States shall be vested in one supreme court, and in such inferior courts as the congress may, from time to time, ordain and establish." The inferior courts contemplated in this section were established by the provisions of the Judiciary Act of 1789.[1] The organization of the federal judicial system rests, therefore, in part upon the express provisions of the constitution, and in part upon congressional legislation. The most potent and unique element in the system is its head. The supreme court of the United States has no prototype in history.[2] Judicial tribunals have existed as component parts of other federal systems, but the supreme court of the United States is the only court in history that has ever possessed the power to finally determine the validity of a national law. Such a jurisdiction necessarily arises out of the American system of constitutional limitations upon the legislative power, — a system under which all judges, both state and federal, possess the power in their respective spheres to pass upon the validity of every law that can emanate from a state or federal legislature.[3] In the English system such a jurisdiction could not exist for the reason that the English constitution imposes no limitation upon its legislative assembly; there is no "higher law" by which the English courts can test the validity of an act of parliament.[4] The great federal court, thus endowed with the very highest judicial functions, has from its birth been the watchful guardian of the national constitution, and its beneficent influence has been steadily displayed not only in checking the encroachments of the federal legislature,[5] but in rendering more harmonious the relations of the states with

Supreme Court of the United States has no prototype in history.

The guardian of the constitution.

---

[1] "That great act was penned by Oliver Ellsworth, a member of the convention which framed the constitution, and one of the early chief justices of this court. It may be said to reflect the views of the founders of the republic as to the proper relations between the federal and state courts." — Mr. Justice Field, in *Ex parte Virginia*, 100 U. S. p. 325.

[2] "The supreme court of the United States . . . is not only a most interesting but a virtually unique creation of the founders of the constitution." — Maine, *Popular Govt.*, p. 217.

[3] See above, p. 46, note 3. See, also, Bryce's chapter on "The Courts and the Constitution," *Am. Commonwealth*, vol. i. pp. 237–254.

[4] Austin holds that an act of parliament, which violates fundamental principles, though legal and binding, may still be unconstitutional. See *Province of Jurisprudence*, lect. vi.

[5] In this connection I refer with pleasure to an able essay, entitled "The Supreme Court in Politics," read by my distinguished friend, the Hon. H. A. Herbert, before the Alabama State Bar Association in August, 1883.

Inferior
courts a
mere repro-
duction of
the English
itinerant
system.

each other. The jurisprudence which regulates the procedure and moulds the decrees of this high court is English jurisprudence, and in this way it has become a new fountain not only of federal but of English law. The system of inferior federal courts is a substantial reproduction of the English system of itinerant judicature. The national judge goes down into the districts and the circuits to try cases over which the federal jurisdiction extends, with or without juries, according to their character. In law causes, both civil and criminal, the federal courts proceed according to the course of the English customary law, while in equity and admiralty causes they cling with equal tenacity to the general body of English jurisprudence.

National
citizenship.

8. From a purely scientific point of view the constitution of the United States never reached its logical completion until after the adoption of the fourteenth amendment. As heretofore pointed out, the new principle which became the basis of the more perfect union, and which imparted to it its distinctive character, was that the sum of federal power vested in the new constitution should operate not upon states in their corporate capacity, but directly upon individuals. If that principle had been carried, at the time of its adoption, to its logical conclusion, it would then have been settled that the individuals upon whom the new government was to act should be primarily its own citizens.[1] Even in such a federal system as the Achaian League, "Every Achaian citizen stood in a direct relation to the federal authority, and was in full strictness a citizen of the league itself, and not merely of one of the cities which composed it."[2] And yet at the time of the adoption of the present constitution the sense of nationality had not sufficiently developed to permit the statement of the ultimate and inevitable conclusion, that every citizen of the Union is primarily a citizen of the United States, and not merely of one of the states which compose them. The one particular in which the first confederation rose above the older Teutonic leagues after which it had been patterned was embodied in the new principle of interstate citizenship

---

[1] No greater logical anomaly can be imagined than a federal government acting directly upon individuals, and yet a government without citizens.

[2] Freeman, *Federal Government*, vol. i. p. 259.

which it originated.[1]   Section one of article four of the articles of confederation provided that, "The better to secure
and perpetuate mutual friendship and intercourse among the
people of the different states in this Union, the free inhabitants of each of these states, paupers, vagabonds, and fugitives
from justice excepted, shall be entitled to all privileges and
immunities of free citizens in the several states."   The substance of that provision was reproduced in section two of article four of the present constitution which provides that,
"The citizens of each state shall be entitled to all privileges
and immunities of citizens in the several states."   Beyond
that point the framers of the more perfect union were not
prepared to go.   They did not attempt to do more than establish an interstate citizenship to which they imparted the
qualities of uniformity and equality by denying to every state
the right to discriminate in favor of its own citizens as
against those of any other state.   There was no attempt
whatever, either in the constitution itself or in any act of
congress passed after its adoption, to establish or define
citizenship of the United States as such, as a distinct and
independent thing from state citizenship.   "That the constitution itself has defined citizenship of the United States by
declaring what persons, born within the several states, shall
or shall not be citizens of the United States will not be pretended.   It contains no such declaration."[2]   In the absence
of any positive assertion by federal authority of any such
thing as a primary citizenship of the United States as such,
there was really no substantial basis upon which to maintain
its existence.   If any such thing as a federal or national citizenship existed at all, it was nothing more than a secondary
and dependent relation.   The better view is that prior to the
adoption of the fourteenth amendment a man was a citizen
of the United States only by virtue of his citizenship in one
of the states composing the Union.   In the famous case of
Dred Scott it was held that no state had the power to raise a
man of African descent to the rank of a citizen so as to make
him a citizen of a state or of the United States.[3]   While there

---

[1] "The principle of inter-citizenship infused itself neither into the constitution of the old German empire, nor of Switzerland, nor of Holland." — Bancroft, *Hist. of Const.*, vol. i. p. 118.

[2] Mr. Justice Curtis in *Dred Scott* v. *Sandford*, 19 Howard, p. 575.

[3] See the opinion of the court in this case, p. 406.

can be no doubt that the leading motive which led to the adoption of the fourteenth amendment was to reverse the results of the Dred Scott case, and to secure the right of citizenship to the African race, — the fact remains that the first section of the amendment, without making any direct reference to the question of race at all, contains the first positive definition ever given of citizenship of the United States as a primary and substantive thing, independent of state citizenship.[1] The first section of the amendment provides that, "All persons born or naturalized in the United States, and subject to the jurisdiction thereof, are citizens of the United States and of the state wherein they reside. No state shall make or enforce any law which shall abridge the privileges or immunities of citizens of the United States ; nor shall any state deprive any person of life, liberty, or property, without due process of law ; nor deny to any person within its jurisdiction the equal protection of the laws." When, in what are commonly known as the "Slaughter-House Cases," this new provision of the constitution came for the first time before the supreme court of the United States for construction, a far-reaching discussion arose which touched the very foundations of the Union itself.[2] After great deliberation the court announced through Mr. Justice Miller a weighty judgment which, while it fully upheld the supremacy of the federal authority within its proper sphere, pointedly recognized the fact that neither the civil war, nor the three amendments in which its political results were embodied, had materially altered the constitutional relations of the state and federal governments to each other. While it was admitted that the amendments had imposed additional limitations upon them, it was held to be clear that there was no intention "to fetter and degrade the state governments by subjecting them to the control of congress, in the exercise of powers heretofore universally conceded to them of the most ordinary and fundamental character."[3] In this judgment the fact was rec-

First section of the Fourteenth Amendment first defines national citizenship.

"Slaughter-House Cases."

---

[1] "No such definition was previously found in the constitution, nor had any attempt been made to define it by act of congress." — *The Slaughter-House Cases*, 16 Wallace, p. 72.

[2] The profound argument of the Hon. John A. Campbell for the plaintiffs in error attracted scarcely less attention than the judgment of the court itself.

[3] *The Slaughter-House Cases*, 16 Wallace, p. 78.

ognized, that the order of citizenship had been reversed ; that under the fourteenth amendment the primary citizenship in this country is to the United States ; and the secondary, to the state of the citizen's residence.[1] It was further held that the two citizenships were separate and distinct from each other. In the words of the court, "It is quite clear, then, that there is a citizenship of the United States and a citizenship of the state, which are distinct from each other, and which depend upon different characteristics or circumstances in the individual."[2] Only the privileges and immunities which belong to a citizen of the United States as such are placed by the fourteenth amendment under the protection of the federal constitution ; "those belonging to the citizen of the state as such, . . . must rest for their security and protection where they have heretofore rested ; for they are not embraced by this paragraph of the amendment."[3] Thus through the conservative and sagacious judgment of the great federal court, over whose high threshold the waves of passion have seldom broken, the logical symmetry of the constitution was completed by the recognition of a primary and independent federal citizenship whose privileges and immunities were wisely limited to those only "which owe their existence to the federal government, its national character, its constitution, or its laws."[4] While the legitimate results of the civil war were thus firmly upheld, the constitution was at the same time carefully guarded against the centralizing tendencies to which it had imparted a fresh and menacing force.

Under the Fourteenth Amendment primary citizenship due to the United States, — a principle

which completes the logical symmetry of the constitution.

9. The attempt has now been made to put in a clear and positive light three propositions of the highest historic value. First, that the English colonies in America, which were finally transformed into independent commonwealths through their severance from the mother country, were in a legal and constitutional sense involuntary and unconscious reproductions of the English kingdom, — inevitable products of a natural process of political evolution. The process of growth through which the typical English state in America passes before it takes on its final form is broken into three stages. It first

Summary.

---

[1] See dissenting opinion of Mr. Justice Bradley, *The Slaughter-House Cases* p. 112.

[2] Same case. Opinion of the court, p. 74.

[3] Ibid., p. 75.

[4] Ibid., p. 79.

appears as a mere corporation created by royal authority with only such powers of local self-government as the crown sees fit to delegate. Out of the corporate body thus created emerges the colonial government with an executive head, a judiciary, and a legislative assembly which can do everything but violate the limitations imposed by the charter from which the dependent community derives its political existence. When the tie of dependence which binds the colony to the mother country is severed, the free community finally rises to the full stature of a sovereign state, wherein the people and not the crown are the source of all political authority. The royal charter is then either supplanted by or continued as the state constitution, wherein the people delegate to the three departments the right to exercise the sum of political power vested in them, subject to such restrictions only as are imposed by express constitutional limitations. Second, that when the sovereign commonwealths thus created were driven by the pressure of a common danger to unite in a confederacy, their first experiment resulted in the formation of a league, based upon the requisition system, which represented no advance whatever in the science of federal government; that this first departure from the entire course of their prior political experience soon ended in weariness, failure, and disappointment. Third, that when in the presence of the anarchy which the failure of the articles of confederation threatened, the English states in America were driven to make a fresh effort to construct a more efficient federal system, the exigencies of the occasion brought forth the most important and far-reaching political principle to which our career as a nation has so far given birth. That principle, which was that the federal head should operate directly on individuals and not on states, drew after it the most momentous consequences by forcing the construction of a "composite state," divided, as the individual states were divided, into three departments, legislative, executive, and judiciary. At this point the creative work of the framers ended and the work of reproduction began. In the organization of the three departments the framers of the present federal constitution reproduced, as far as it was possible, the English constitutional system in the form in which it had reappeared in the constitutions of the several states. The analysis which has been made therefore results at last in the conclusion that the typical English state in America was the fruit of a process of involuntary and unconscious growth, — that the federal republic of the United States was the fruit of a process of voluntary and conscious reproduction. The second federal constitution was made, as far as it could be made, after the English model; but it might have been made as the earlier and laxer union was made on an entirely different model. Such a contrary course might have been pursued, and yet it was more than natural that men of a highly conservative temper, who were intimately familiar with the English constitutional system in the form in which it had reappeared in the several states, should have applied it, so far as it could be applied, to the organization of the federal republic. "Although the framers of our constitution were without any grasp of the modern conception of the historical continuity of the race, they revered the ancient constitutional traditions of England. And thus it came to pass that Magna Carta, the Acts of the Long Parliament, the Declaration of Right, the Declaration of Independence, and the Constitution of 1787, constitute the record of an evolution." [1] If that be true, then the Constitution of the United States was not a spontaneous creation; it was the final product in a new soil of a sturdy plant transplanted from an island world where, in comparative isolation, it had been slowly maturing for centuries. In the open sunlight of the new land the later growth has been both strong and rapid; in the vast domain of the New World the old plant has found room for unlimited expansion. The history of this later development cannot be severed from that of the earlier and more tedious process of growth which made it possible. The life of the plant is an indivisible whole, and unless it is studied as a whole its real history can never be fully mastered. That conviction has imparted to the weary task essayed in this work a definite and practical purpose. In attempting to unfold the history of the constitutional growth of the English kingdom in one unbroken story the author has followed the only plan upon which, in his humble view, can ever be written an exhaustive commentary upon the constitution of his country.

"The government of the United States is not the result of special creation, but of evolution."

[1] W. T. Brantly's essay on the "Formation of the Federal Constitution," in *Southern Law Review*, August, 1880, vol. vi. p. 352.

BOOK I.

THE OLD-ENGLISH COMMONWEALTH.

———◆———

CHAPTER I.

THE TEUTONIC ORIGIN OF ENGLISH INSTITUTIONS.

I. DURING the fifth century, four of the Western provinces of the Roman Empire — Britain, Gaul, Italy, and Spain — were in turn overrun by successive hordes of Teutonic invaders who came to settle down permanently on the conquered soil.[1] Out of the fusion of the Teutonic settlements made in Britain between the middle of the fifth century and the end of the sixth has grown the English nation;[2] out of the rude systems of social and political life which the settlers brought with them in their blood and bone from the fatherland has grown the English Constitution. With the founding of the Teutonic settlements in Britain the history of English institutions really begins. In order fully to grasp the early history of these settlements, in order clearly to point out the several vital particulars in which they differed from all other Teutonic settlements made upon Roman soil, it will be necessary to resort to a contrast for the sake of illustration. Within the continental provinces of Italy, Gaul, and Spain, Rome had made a profound impression upon the whole fabric of social and political life. The language, the laws, the institutions, of the people were thoroughly Roman. Roman roads led to Roman cities, in which were contained

General character of Teutonic conquest on the Continent.

---

[1] For a list of the monarchies established by the Teutonic invaders during the interval which elapsed between the beginning of the fifth century and the end of the sixth, see Guizot's *Hist. Rep. Government*, p. 27.

[2] Freeman, *Origin of the English Nation*, part ii.

all the objects of Roman art, — cities which were governed by Roman municipal institutions.[1]   By the end of the fourth century the fabric of this society was not only Roman, — it was fast becoming Christian.   The ancient paganism had already broken down before the aggressive force of the Christian Church.   In the provincial cities were fixed the sees of Christian bishops, who formed a part of an ecclesiastical system based upon the dominant faith.[2]   The three great streams of Teutonic invasion, which spread in successive waves over these Latinized and Christianized provinces of the empire, were unequal both in force and effect.   In Gaul the Teuton made his deepest impression, in Italy the least, while in Spain his influence occupies a middle place between the two.   But the general character of his influence was everywhere the same ; it only varied in degree.   Wherever we find the Teutonic invaders conquering and entering into possession of a continental province, we have an example of a new nation intruding itself into the midst of an older nation and settling down by its side upon the conquered soil.[3]   The invaders came as conquerors, it is true ; but they came rather as imitators than as mere destroyers.   They had long been in contact with Roman civilization ; they had tested the power of the Roman arms ; they had felt the charm of the Roman name ; and they had nearly all become converts to the Christian religion before the invasions began.[4]   And, besides, the invaders were nowhere opposed by any fierce or prolonged native resistance.   The consequence was that conquest nowhere assumed the form of extermination.[5]   The land was generally divided between the conquerors and the conquered

Italy, Gaul, and Spain Latinized and Christianized by the end of the fourth century.

Teutonic invaders settle down in the midst of the continental nations.

Conquest nowhere assumed the form of extermination.

[1] As to the history of the Roman municipal system, see Guizot, *Hist. Representative Gov.*, lect. xxii. part i. ; Savigny's *Hist. of the Roman Law*, vol. i. pp. 16–98 ; De Coulanges, *The Ancient City*, pp. 470–519.

[2] "At the end of the fourth century and the beginning of the fifth, Christianity was no longer a simple belief ; it was an institution, — it had formed itself into a corporate body.   It had its government, a body of priests ; a settled ecclesiastical polity for the regulation of their different functions ; revenues ; independent means of influence."— Guizot, *Hist. of Civilization*, vol. i. p. 48.

[3] A full treatment of this subject will be found in Freeman, *Norm. Conq.*, vol. i. ch. ii. ; Stubbs' *Const. Hist.*, vol. i. ch. i. ; *Origin of the English Nation*, part ii.

[4] The invaders first became acquainted with Christianity in its Arian form ; in Italy, Africa, Spain, and Gaul, they were for a long time involved in that heresy.   In the end, however, they everywhere embraced the orthodox faith.   Gibbon, *Decline and Fall*, vol. iii. pp. 547, 573.

[5] The Teutonic conquerors styled themselves *guests* of the conquered. Ibid., vol. iii. p. 315.

according to certain fixed proportions.[1] The Roman native was permitted to enjoy his own laws, while the conqueror retained for himself his own barbaric code.[2] In this way Teutonic life and law settled down by the side of Roman life and law, and a struggle for the mastery was the natural consequence. By an analysis of the result must be determined the extent to which the different elements prevailed.

So far as language is concerned the conquerors everywhere adopted the tongue of the conquered. Out of the old Latin speech the Romance languages — French, Spanish, Italian, and the rest — were born.[3] The Romance languages are nothing but Latin, with a deep infusion of Teutonic words.[4] So far as religion is concerned the conquerors everywhere adopted the creeds of the conquered. Only in the domain of polity and military organization can the Teutonic element claim in the new combination a position of dominant importance. The leading principles which are worked out in the constitutional histories of France and Spain are Teutonic, — an assertion which may be applied in a modified form to the states of Northern and Southern Italy.[5] After making due allowance, however, for Teutonic influence upon polity and military organization, the predominant fact must be recognized in the general result that the framework of the older society survived ; it remained in the end Roman and Christian ; it did not become heathen and Teutonic. In the history of the continental provinces there is no lack of historical continuity. We do not find upon the Continent, as we shall hereafter find in Britain, a century and a half of heathenism, darkness, and legend intervening between the overthrow of the Roman province and the beginning of the new Teutonic society.[6] In Italy, Spain, and Gaul the older civilization, while taking to itself many elements of Teutonic life, not only

Conquerors adopt the language and creeds of the conquered.

The older society remained Roman and Christian : it did not become heathen and Teutonic.

---

[1] Hallam, *Middle Ages*, vol. i. p. 149.
[2] "The Frank was judged by the Salic or Ripuary code; the Gaul followed that of Theodosius." — Ibid., vol. i. p. 154.
[3] Max Müller, *Science of Language*, pp. 170, 195.
[4] Freeman, *Norm. Conq.*, vol. i. p. 11.
[5] Stubbs, *Const. Hist.*, vol. i. p. 2. "The republican history of the North

and the feudal system of the South, the municipalities of Lombardy, and the parliaments of Naples, are much more German than Roman." — Ibid., vol. i. p. 7.
[6] "Concerning all the other provinces of the Western Empire we have continuous information. It is only in Britain that one age of fable completely separates two ages of truth." — Macaulay, *Hist. of Eng.*, vol. i. p. 6.

continued to be Roman and Christian, but preserved throughout its identity and continuity.

General
character
of Teutonic
conquest in
Britain.

2. In Britain the continental aspects of Teutonic conquest
completely disappear; such conquest there assumed a character and form at once local and peculiar.   This changed
condition of things resulted, in the main, from two causes.
In the first place, apart from its insular character, the very
remoteness of Britain from the seat of empire necessarily
weakened the tie which bound it to the life of Rome.[1]   It
is, therefore, easy to understand why Roman civilization in
Britain took such shallow root.   In no other province did the
language, the laws, the institutions of Rome rest upon such
superficial foundations.[2]   And yet all the externals of Roman
life were there.   The *municipia* and *coloniæ* sprang up within
the area which the legions had reduced to subjection,[3] and a
net-work of Roman roads by which the country was inter-
sected connected them with each other.   The cities were, no
doubt, thoroughly Romanized, but it is extremely doubtful
whether Roman civilization ever made any serious impression
upon the mass of the Celtic provincials.   The language of
Rome was doubtless spoken in the cities and towns, and by
the wealthy classes outside of the towns, but it is hardly
possible that it could ever have been spoken by the main

Roman civ-
ilization in
Britain
nothing but
an exotic.

body of the people.[4]   Roman civilization in Britain was
nothing but an exotic, with no real, self-sustaining hold upon
the native Celtic race.   Consequently, when the power and
support of Rome were withdrawn, it collapsed from lack of
power to maintain an independent existence.   The Teutonic
invaders of what had been Roman Britain never came in
contact with the full force of Roman civilization; they only
encountered a set of superficial influences already in a state
of disorganization and decay.   In the second place, the invaders came directly into Britain from their seats in the far

---

[1] Green, *Making of Eng.*, p. 6.

[2] "No otherwise can we even plausibly account for the instantaneous collapse of the imperial authority : it fell,
with one vast and sudden ruin, the moment the artificial supports, upon which
it relied, were removed." — Kemble,
Saxons in Eng., vol. ii. p. 284.

[3] Ibid., vol. ii. p. 265.

[4] Green, *Making of Eng.*, p. 12.
"Latin was undoubtedly the speech of
the cities, the speech of government, literature, and polite life.   Welsh was
under a cloud, just as English was, ages
after, in the days of Norman rule." —
Freeman, *Origin of the Eng. Nation*,
p. 102.

North, where they had lived completely removed from the power and influence of Rome. Excepting perhaps a single expedition, the legions had never been seen upon their shores; with Roman standards and with Roman missionaries they were equally unfamiliar. They possessed no conceptions either of government or of law except such as were indigenous to the race; they knew no religion except the religion of Odin. In this state of pure barbaric heathenism the invaders entered, without intermediate probation, upon the conquest of Britain. Such conquest necessarily differed from every continental conquest in the manner in which it was undertaken, and it also differed as to the native resistance which it encountered. The invaders were compelled to cross the sea in ships, and their sea craft and war craft could only transport bodies of men, more or less formidable, and not great armies of invasion by which the whole land could be suddenly overrun. All the evidence goes to show that the Teutonic invaders came into Britain in disconnected bands, each under its own leader, who singled out some special district of country for conquest and settlement.[1] Such a leader, with the limited force at his command, necessarily circumscribed his efforts to a narrow area, from which, by dint of hard fighting, he was obliged to drive the Celtic masters of the soil. In this way, bit by bit, the land was won. Moving from the south, the east, and the northeast, the invaders drove the Britons slowly to the west. The struggle, from its very nature, was a bitter one; invasion no longer signified forcible intrusion; it became the equivalent of extermination. Everything goes to show that the first stage of Teutonic conquest in Britain signified the utter annihilation of the native race within the limits which the conquerors defined with their swords.[2] Before the invader settled down the Celt was either expelled or exterminated, and with him disappeared whatever he had acquired of the civilization, language, religion, or law of Rome.[3] In the general wreck, even the Roman

The invaders cross the sea in small companies.

Invasion became the equivalent of extermination, within certain limits.

---

[1] "The story of the conquest confirms the English tradition that the invaders of Britain landed in small parties, and that they were only gradually reinforced by after-comers. Nor was there any joint action among the assailants to compensate for the smallness of their numbers." — Green, *Making of Eng-*land, p. 128; Freeman, *Origin of Eng. Nation*, p. 107.

[2] This restatement of the "Teutonic theory" must be taken with the qualifications put upon it in the Introduction. See above, p. 11.

[3] "The proofs of such a displacement lie less in isolated passages from chron-

municipalities perished.[1]   The Teuton came into Britain as a
mere destroyer ; and of the Romanized natives of the land he
learned absolutely nothing.

Result of
the con-
trast.
3. Under these favorable circumstances the whole fabric of
Teutonic life was replanted, in its primitive purity, on a free
and unincumbered soil. ' " While the Germans of Gaul, Italy,
and Spain became Romans, the Saxons retained their language, their genius, and manners, and created in Britain a
Germany outside of Germany." [2] By this statement the difference between Teutonic conquest and settlement in Britain
and Teutonic conquest and settlement upon the Continent is
clearly defined.   In the one case the invaders were absorbed
in the mass of the conquered ; Teutonic life simply became
an element in the older Roman society.   In the other the
invaders absolutely annihilated, within the limits which they
made their own while they were still heathens, every vestige
of the existing civilization, and established in its stead their
whole scheme of barbaric life.   The Teutonic polity thus
established in Britain in its purity has been able to survive,
and to preserve not only its identity but its primitive instinct
in all the vicissitudes of change and of growth through which
it has passed.

" A Ger-
many out-
side of
Germany."

English na-
tion Teu-
tonic as to
race.
4. The invaders, who thus established a new nationality in
Britain, were of the purest Teutonic type, and all spoke dialects of the Low-German.   From the earliest period in their
insular history, these settlers knew themselves as " the English kin ;" [3] and out of their union has arisen the English
nation, which, through all the vicissitudes of internal growth
and external influence, has preserved both its national character and its identity.   In the course of its history it has
received many infusions, it is true, — for the most part, however, from other branches of the Teutonic stock.   No nation
can claim absolute purity of blood; foreign elements are
present in the veins of every people.   But the national
character is never lost so long as the paternal element is
strong enough to absorb all other elements and to impress

icle or history than in the broad features of the conquest itself." — Green,
Making of Eng., p. 132.
    [1] Kemble, *Saxons in Eng.*, vol. ii.
p. 295; Stubbs, *Const. Hist.*, vol. i. p. 61.

[2] Taine, *Hist. of Eng. Literature,*
vol. i. p. 50.
    [3] Freeman, *Norm. Conq.*, vol. i. p. 15;
citing the entries in Chronicle under the
years 443, 449, and 473.

upon the nation, as a whole, its own image and instincts. The very fewness of Celtic words in the English language shows how small the admixture must have been from that source.[1] When the Danes came to commingle their blood with that of their advancing English brethren, it was simply the blending together of men of the same Low-Dutch stock, the one heathen, the other Christian. With the coming of the Normans, the English nation entered upon its first real struggle for national existence. And yet the Norman himself was originally a Teuton ; " he was a Dane who had gone into Gaul to get covered with a French varnish, and who came into England to be washed clean again."[2] But the Norman struggled hard to maintain the peculiar type which he had assumed in France, and he left nothing undone to make it the predominant element in the national character. But he failed ; the conquerors were absorbed into the mass of the conquered ; the Normans became Englishmen.[3]

All after-comers of the Low-Dutch stock.

The Normans became Englishmen.

5. Out of the fusion of the Teutonic settlements in Britain the English nation was born ; out of the fusion of the dialects spoken in those settlements the English language was born. English is not the dialect of Kent, Wessex, or Mercia ; it is the result of the union of all the Low-Dutch dialects spoken in Britain in one composite whole,[4] which has preserved, through a long period of change and of growth, its organic structure and its identity. The greatest period of trial through which the English language has ever passed began with the Norman Conquest. For a long time after that event the lordly foreign tongue reigned in the castle and the hall, while the humbled native speech reigned in the cottage and the hamlet. But, in the end, the lordly speech passed away, and the English tongue survived with a deep infusion

English language the result of the fusion of all the Low-Dutch dialects into one whole.

---

[1] The Celtic words in our language only number about thirty ; and by far the larger part of these refer to some object or occupation peculiar to females. Cf. Fowler's *English Grammar*, ed. 1881, pp. 76–78 ; Creasy, *Eng. Con.*, p. 29.

[2] Freeman, *Origin of the Eng. Nation*, p. 53.

[3] "The Norman found in the land substantially the same English nation which still exists, occupying substantially the same territory which it occu-pies at present. He found it already exhibiting in its laws, its language, its national character, the most essential of the features which it still retains. Into the English nation which he thus found already formed his own dynasty and his own followers were gradually absorbed. The conquered did not become Nor-mans, but the conquerors did become Englishmen."—Freeman, *Norm. Conq.*, vol. i. p. 6.

[4] Max Müller, *Science of Language*, p. 67.

of Romance words.   The following epitome of the origin and history of our English tongue is from the graphic pen of one

of its greatest living masters: "If we speak of the language of England, we ought, no doubt, to know something of the political history of the British Isles, in order to understand the present state of that language.   Its history begins with the early Britons, who spoke a Celtic dialect ; it carries us on to the Saxon conquest, to the Danish invasions, to the Norman Conquest; and we see how each of these political events contributed to the formation of the character of the language. The language of England may be said to have been in succession Celtic, Saxon, Norman, and English.   But, if we speak of the history of the English language, we enter on totally different ground.   The English language was never Celtic, the Celtic never grew into Saxon, nor the Saxon into Norman, nor the Norman into English.   The history of the Celtic language runs on to the present day.   It matters not whether it be spoken by all the inhabitants of the British Isles, or only by a small minority in Wales, Ireland, and Scotland.   A language, as long as it is spoken by anybody, lives and has its substantive existence.   The last old woman that spoke Cornish, and to whose memory it is now intended to raise a monument, represented by herself alone the ancient language of Cornwall.   A Celt may become an Englishman, Celtic and English blood may be mixed ; and who can tell at the present day the exact proportion of Celtic and Saxon

blood in the population of England ?   But languages are never mixed.   It is indifferent by what name the language spoken in the British Islands be called, whether English or British or Saxon ; to the student of language English is Teutonic, and nothing but Teutonic. . . . In the English dictionary the student of the science of language can detect, by his own tests, Celtic, Norman, Greek, and Latin ingredients, but not a single drop of foreign blood has entered into the organic system of the English language.   The grammar, the blood and soul of the language, is as pure and unmixed in English as spoken in the British Isles, as it was when spoken on the shores of the German Ocean by the Angles, Saxons, and Jutes of the continent."[1]

[1] Max Müller, *Science of Language*, p. 79.

6. The " English kin " transferred to Britain, as a whole, Institu-
tions. that rough yet vigorous system of political and military organization which everywhere prevailed among the Teutonic tribes of the fatherland. Wherever a district of country was won from the native race, the conquerors encamped upon the soil ; and then, after having divided the land upon the basis of that peculiar system which rested at once upon military and tribal divisions, they organized themselves into political communities.[1] The unit in the system, as we shall see more fully hereafter, consisted of a narrow tribal division, originally united by the family tie, whose members possessed the power to regulate their own local and domestic concerns. A group of such units, or village communities, when bound together, constituted the next largest political division ; in this combination appears the earliest form of the representative principle.[2] By the union of these larger divisions were formed the numberless petty states into which the settlers were originally subdivided. The Teutonic political system as a whole rested upon the collective weight of individual freemen acting together in an expanding series of popular assemblies whose jurisdictions, beginning with the smallest local affairs, so widened as to embrace the gravest national concerns. The foundations of this primitive system, composed of these local, self-governing communities, were so deeply laid in Britain, that the system itself has been able to survive all the mutations through which the English nation has passed. When the Norman came he seized the central powers of the state, but the local Teutonic system remained unshaken by the assault. Upon this local system as a substructure the Norman built up his administrative system as a superstructure ; and out of the fusion between the two has grown the modern constitution. Just as the Romance words which the Norman brought with him were woven into the woof and warp of the English tongue, so the Norman's ideas of law and of administration were woven into the primitive constitution.

General
character of
the Teu-
tonic polit-
ical system.

The sub-
structure of
the English
constitu-
tion.

---

[1] " It was this military organization of the tribe that gave from the first its form to the civil organization. In each of the little kingdoms which rose on the wreck of Britain, the host would camp on the land it had won, and the divisions of the host supplied here, as in its older home, a rough groundwork of local distribution." — Green, *Making of Eng.*, p. 169.

[2] Green, *Hist. of the Eng. People,* vol. i. p. 14.

In the same sense in which the English language is Teutonic the English constitution is Teutonic.[1] That strong local system, as originally established in Britain by the Teutonic invaders, has never ceased to exist. It has passed through a long process of change and of growth, it has taken on many new forms, it has borne great fruit, it has controlled the destinies of a nation, " which, while reforming in all directions, has destroyed nothing ; which has preserved both its trees and its constitution, which has lopped off the dead branches without levelling the trunk ; which alone, in our days, among all nations, is in the enjoyment not only of the present, but of the past." [2]

The problem to be worked out. 7. The problem, then, which the student of English political institutions is called upon to work out involves an examination of the entire process of historic development through which the primitive Teutonic constitution has passed under the combined action of internal growth and external influence. The starting-point in the solution of the problem necessarily consists of a close insight into the nature of the primitive system as originally established in Britain, — without that all attempts to work out the subsequent development will fail. But we cannot obtain that insight by relying entirely upon the insular history of the English nation ; we must look beyond to the homes of the "English kin" in the fatherland ; we must begin with the brief history of the childhood of the whole Teutonic race as contained in those terse sketches of the ancient freedom which have been drawn by the Roman historians.

[1] "The German element is the paternal element in our system, natural and political." — Stubbs, *Const. Hist.*, vol. i. p. 11.

[2] Taine, *Hist. of Eng. Literature*, vol. ii. p. 517.

CHAPTER II.

THE FOUNDERS IN THE FATHERLAND.

1. THE earliest account of the Teutonic tribes in general, and of the Suevi in particular, is contained in the military memoirs of Cæsar, who has condensed into a few passages of his Commentaries such information as he had been able to derive from his own observations, and from the reports of the Gallic provincials.[1] But, as Cæsar's sketch is vague and general, and as it varies in at least one serious particular from the more extended account given, a century and a half later, by Tacitus, it cannot be safely followed wherever it departs from the later narrative. It is almost impossible to believe that the whole Teutonic people could have been in the purely nomad state described by Cæsar, when we find them, only a century and a half later, dwelling in villages as permanent cultivators of the soil. The moving, restless tribes which hovered upon the Roman frontier, and with which Cæsar was naturally most familiar, may have been, and likely were, in the unsettled state described by him.[2] But the soundest critics refuse to accept his statement as true in this respect, even in his day, of the whole Teutonic race.[3] One of the most striking features in Cæsar's sketch is the contrast which he draws between the abstemious, poverty-loving, and warlike Germans, and their more cultivated, yet less warlike, neighbors, the Gauls. It is somewhat such a contrast as Tacitus drew at a later day, between the barbaric virtues of the Germans and the voluptuous degeneracy of his own countrymen.[4]

---

[1] Cæsar, *De Bello Gallico*, vi. 21, 22, 23, 24. As to the Suevi, iv. 1, 3.

[2] Stubbs, *Select Charters, etc.*, p. 52.

[3] "But so deeply does the possession of land enter into the principle of all the Teutonic institutions, that I cannot bring myself to believe in the accuracy of Cæsar's statement." — Kemble, *Saxons in England*, vol. i. p. 39. Zeuss maintains that Cæsar's account

was true of some earlier period. — *Die Deutschen und die Nachbarstämme, von Kaspar Zeuss* (München, 1837), p. 52 *et seq.*

[4] The contrasts contained in the *Germania* are so frequent and so pointed that it was at one time regarded as a satire on Roman manners. "With regard to their moral hue, Tacitus has painted the Germans, as Mon-

Cæsar's
sketch.

2. Cæsar, after indulging in some inaccurate assertions concerning Teutonic mythology,[1] begins by saying that the Germans pass their lives in hunting and in the pursuit of arms ; from childhood they are inured to labor and to a hardy habit of life.[2]   And then, after speaking of their chastity and

Chastity of
the Ger-
mans.

its supposed effects upon physical development, he remarks that they do not apply themselves to agriculture, — milk, cheese, and flesh being their chief articles of food.[3]   No one has a fixed quantity of land, or boundaries that he can call

Annual al-
lotments of
land.

his own, but the magistrates and chiefs annually set apart to the several communities, united by the family tie or by common religious rites, for occupation during a single year, a portion of land whose amount and location is fixed according to circumstances.   The next year they compel the group to remove to some other place.[4]   Many reasons are then given for this peculiar habit of unrest, all of which go to show that such a system was perpetuated in order to preserve the martial spirit of the people from the enervating influences which flow from fixed habitations, and from the enjoyment of personal comfort ; and also from the discontent resulting from the unequal distribution of money and estates.[5]

Aversion to
neighbors.

The greatest prestige which the several states or tribes can possess consists in the extent of the uninhabited lands surrounding their territory, which they themselves have laid waste.   They take it as a tribute to their courage that their old neighbors have abandoned their homes through fear of them, and that no one else will take their place.   And this state of things adds to their safety, for the danger of sudden invasion is thereby taken away.[6]   Whenever a state engages in war, defensive or offensive, magistrates, with the power of life and death, are chosen for that particular emergency.   In

---

taigne and Rousseau the savages, in a fit of ill humor against his country ; his book is a satire on Roman manners." — Guizot, *Hist. of Civilization*, vol. i. p. 418.   This fancy has now passed away. — Waitz, *Deutsche Verfassungs-Geschichte*, i. 21 ; Stubbs, *Const. Hist.*, vol. i. p. 17.

[1] Kemble, *Saxons in England*, vol. i. p. 40.

[2] Cæsar, *De Bello Gallico*, vi. 21.

[3] Ibid., vi. 22.

[4] " Neque quisquam agri modum certum aut fines habet proprios ; sed magistratus ac principes in annos singulos gentibus cognationibusque hominum, qui una coierunt, quantum et quo loco visum est agri attribuunt atque anno post alio transire cogunt." — *De Bello Gallico*, vi. 22.   See Laveleye, *Primitive Property*, pp. 102–105.

[5] Cæsar, *De Bello Gallico*, vi. 22.

[6] Ibid., vi. 22.

time of peace there is no common magistracy, but the chiefs of the several districts administer justice and discourage litigation.   Plundering expeditions beyond the borders of one's own state are not considered dishonorable, but, on the contrary, they are commended as good schools in which to exercise the young men, and to diminish idleness.   When a chief offers himself in the public assembly as the leader of such an enterprise, and calls upon all who so desire to follow him, those who approve the cause and the man promise their aid amid the applause of the multitude.   If those who enter into such an engagement fail to perform it, they are regarded as deserters and traitors, and no faith is afterwards reposed in them.

No common magistracy in times of peace.

Fidelity to the war-leader.

To violate the rights of hospitality is considered a sacrilege; strangers who come among them, from whatever cause, are considered sacred, and are protected from injury; the homes of all are open to them, and every one is ready to share his meal with them.[1]   There had been a time when the Gauls surpassed the Germans in valor; they had even sent colonies across the Rhine and pressed war upon the Germans without provocation.   But the Gauls were conquered in so many battles, and gradually became so accustomed to defeat, that they ceased even to compare themselves in prowess with the Germans.[2]   Such is the brief initial outline which the great Roman statesman has drawn of that mighty race of which the English is a part.   For an enlargement of that outline we must look to the Germania of Tacitus, and to the subsequent researches by which its meaning has been illustrated.

Hospitality.

The Gauls.

3. During the century and a half which intervenes between the account of Cæsar and that of Tacitus, knowledge of the German tribes must have greatly increased at Rome. Just before the beginning of the Christian era a determined effort was made under the leadership of Drusus, the step-son of Augustus, to make Germany a Roman province.   The effort of Drusus, which his sudden death interrupted, was continued, in turn, by Tiberius, Varus, and Germanicus, until the results which followed a battle, near Minden, A. D. 16, put an end to all attempts upon the part of the Romans to conquer

Germania of Tacitus.

The attempt to make Germany a Roman province.

[1] Cæsar, *De Bello Gallico*, vi. 23.   [2] Ibid., vi. 24.

Germany.[1] And, apart from the knowledge which must have been obtained during these frequent attempts at conquest, the contact upon the frontier was continuous. The precious accumulation of facts contained in the Germania is, however, the surest indication of just how far a knowledge of the Germans had advanced at Rome up to the time when the narrative of Tacitus was written. Leaving out of view special notices of particular tribes, this invaluable summary contains a brief abstract of the manners, customs, and institutions common to the German race as a whole. As Montesquieu has expressed it, it is the work of a man who has condensed everything because he knew everything.[2] A narrative so broad and comprehensive in its character must necessarily be lacking in fulness of detail. But such evidence as the Germania does contain is of the rarest historic value, for it consists of the contemporary observations of a cultivated historian made upon the customs and institutions of a mighty race while yet in its childhood.[3] If we will but picture to ourselves the historian Bancroft, in his library at Washington, making an abstract of the customs and institutions of the Indian tribes upon our frontier, we shall possess a reasonably correct idea of the relation which existed between Tacitus and the barbarians beyond the Rhine.

Germania an abstract of manners, customs, and institutions ;

its rare historic value.

Distinctive race-traits.

4. According to the Germania the race which is now called Teutonic was pure and indigenous, unmixed by intermarriage with any foreign stock, of the same physical type, speaking the same language, possessing a common mythology, and a common system of social, political, and military institutions, — and yet, possessing no collective name in its own language by which to describe the race as a whole, nor any form of central political organization.[4] The word German[5] is prob-

---

[1] Sime, *Hist. of Germany*, pp. 12–14.

[2] *Spirit of Laws*, bk. xxx. ch. 2.

[3] "As societies do not advance concurrently, but at different rates of progress, there have been epochs at which men trained to habits of methodical observation have really been in a position to watch and describe the infancy of mankind. Tacitus made the most of such an opportunity." — Sir Henry Maine, *Ancient Law*, p. 116.

[4] Tac., *Germania*, cc. 2, 4.

[5] Tacitus indicates that the name German was first applied by the Gauls to the Tungri, and finally to the whole race. *Germania*, c. 2. See Waitz, *D. V. G.*, i. 24. According to Grimm (*Geschichte der Deutschen Sprache*, p. 787) the word signifies "good shouters"; according to some other authorities, "East-men" or neighbors. When, in after times, the German tribes had realized their unity of tongue and descent, they spoke of their language simply as the "Lingua Theotisca," the

ably of Celtic origin, and is supposed to have been first applied by the Gauls to a particular Teutonic tribe, and finally to the whole race. The great national virtue was chastity and respect for the marriage tie. To be content with one wife and true to her was a part of the German instinct.[1] The great national vices were drunkenness and gambling. To be drunk for days was a disgrace to no man, while the ruined gamester would, at last, put even his liberty at stake, and allow himself to be sold into slavery.[2] The Germans had no cities, but dwelt in villages, or in homesteads near villages.[3] Their chief property consisted of flocks and herds, in which they felt the greatest pride.[4] Their peculiar system of agriculture will be examined hereafter.

The word German probably of Celtic origin.

Absence of cities.

5. This homogeneous race, although possessed of a common system of social and political institutions, was nevertheless broken up into an endless number of states or political communities, which stood in relation to each other in a state of complete political isolation, except when united in temporary confederacies. In their general descriptions of the German people, both Cæsar and Tacitus had constantly in their minds the existence of these disconnected states into which the race, as a whole, was subdivided.[5] In order, therefore, to grasp the full import of these descriptions, this fact must be kept constantly in view. Both writers attempted to convey a distinct idea of the form which Teutonic society assumed among a given number of the German people politically united in what each termed the *civitas ;* with the further explanation, that what was true of the race in one state, was true of the race in all the states ; excepting, perhaps, the few particulars in which the monarchical states differed from the non-monarchical. The attempt will therefore be made to render the picture of Tacitus less abstract, by applying what he says of the German race, as a whole, and of the states in general, to one particular portion of the race, bound together in such a distinct political organization as he called the

The state and its subdivisions.

The civitas of Cæsar and Tacitus.

---

language of the people (*theod*) ; whence the name "Deutsch."—Max Müller, *Lectures on the Science of Language*, ii. 230 ; Stubbs, *Const. Hist.*, vol. i. pp. 17, 38, and notes.
[1] Tac., *Germ.*, c. 18.

[2] Tac., *Germ.*, cc. 22, 23.
[3] Ibid., c. 16.
[4] Ibid., c. 5.
[5] Cæsar, *De Bello Gallico*, vi. 23 ; Tac., *Germ.*, cc. 8, 10, 12, 13, 14, 15, 19, 25, 30, 41.

civitas. A great many terms have been used by the English writers as equivalents of the *civitas* of Cæsar and Tacitus. Political community, tribe, state are, however, the terms usually employed to express the idea. But no word in our language will express the exact idea unless it be attended by special qualifications indicating the precise sense in which it is used. The primary bond which united the people in what will be called for convenience the state was a personal one ; the king of the state was the first among the people, the head of the race ; and not the king of a particular area or region of territory. And yet, in the time of Tacitus, the states, into which the German race was broken up, were permanently occupying districts of country which were defined by definite boundaries. And so the conception of the state, although resting upon the idea of personal connection, must also have been associated with the idea of territorial possession. As the distinction has been well expressed : "The idea of the state was not merely a personal but a geographical idea, if not in theory at least in fact."[1] Let us, therefore, present to our minds such a state, composed of a number of the German people, great or small, occupying a definite area of country, surrounded, perchance, by an uninhabited expanse, which the people of that particular state have themselves laid waste.[2] This is the condition in which the primitive Teutonic state appears when written history begins. The largest division of such a state has been designated by many terms. In Latin the word usually employed is *pagus ;* in German, *gau* or *gá ;* in Old-English, *scir* or shire.[3] But all these terms finally gave way on the Continent to the word *hundred,* which will be employed whenever it is necessary to describe the largest division of the continental Teutonic state. These divisions or districts which will be called hundreds were, in their turn, subdivided into village-communities — the *vici*[4] of Tacitus — whose origin and structure will be specially considered hereafter.

Having now defined the nature of the state and its sub-

The state as a personal organization

occupying a definite area of territory.

The largest division of the state — the pagus, gau, or hundred.

The vici of Tacitus.

---

[1] *Essays in Anglo-Saxon Law,* p. 3 (Boston, 1876).

[2] " Civitatibus maxima laus est, quam latissime circum se vastatis finibus soli-tudines habere." — Cæsar, *De Bello Gallico,* vi. 23.

[3] Kemble, *Saxons in England,* vol. i. p. 72 ; *Essays in A. S. Law,* p. 5.

[4] Tac., *Germ.,* cc. 12, 16.

divisions, an examination will next be made of the account which Tacitus gives of the different ranks into which the people were divided; and of the general structure of their social, military, and political institutions.

6. The whole fabric of Teutonic society rested upon two fundamental conceptions: the possession of land, and distinctions of rank. These two ideas are so interlaced that they can hardly be severed from each other. As the man who was not free could, at first, hold no land within the limits of the village-community; so the man who held no land in the community was not entitled to the full measure of freedom, however high may have been his rank or station.[1] According to Tacitus, Teutonic society was divided into four ranks or classes: the nobles, *nobiles;* simple freemen, *ingenui,* freedmen, *liberti;* and slaves, *servi.*[2]

Distinctions of rank: nobles, freemen, freedmen, and slaves.

The simple land-owning freeman, though not of the highest order in the state in respect to privileges, may be justly regarded as the base upon which rested the whole structure of social and political life.[3] Such a freeman was certainly endowed with every political right which the state could bestow.[4] As a fully qualified member of the local community he was entitled to his due portion of land in the annual allotment, and to the enjoyment of all common rights incident thereto.[5] As such land-owner he had also the right to be present and to participate in all public assemblies, great or small, where his own interests, and those of the community of which he was a part, were discussed and determined. He was endowed with the right to bear arms, and to wear them on all occasions, public and private,[6] and with them to defend his life and his honor. He possessed the right of private war, either alone or with the aid of his kindred. In the long hair which floated over his shoulders he wore the

The simple freeman

shares in the annual allotment;

his right to bear arms;

---

[1] Kemble, *Saxons in England*, vol. i. p. 35.

[2] Tac., *Germ.*, cc. 7, 24, 25.

[3] "The base of Roman society here as everywhere throughout the Roman world was the slave, the peasant who had been crushed by tyranny, political and social, into serfdom. The base of the new English society was the freeman whom we have seen tilling, judging, or fighting for himself by the Northern Sea."—Green, *Hist. English People*, vol. i. p. 32.

[4] "The *ingenuus* or simple freeman is in every point, except descent, the equal of the noble."—Stubbs, *Const. History*, vol. i. p. 22.

[5] G. L. von Maurer, *Dorfverfassung*, i. pp. 61–65; *Markenverfassung*, pp. 59–62; *Einleitung*, pp. 93, 97.

[6] Tac., *Germ.*, cc. 11, 13.

his wergild. badge of his freedom.   By his wergild his social position was measured.[1]   In peace he had his place in the public assemblies : in war he was a member of the host, a defender of the

The noble. state.

The noble was simply a freeman with certain special privileges which accrued to him by virtue of his blood.   His political status was in nowise superior to that of a simple freeman, but his personal status was certainly attended with great dignity and advantage.[2]   In the monarchical states the kings were chosen on account of their nobility of blood.[3]   In honor of illustrious birth the son of a famous father was often called to the dignity of prince or chief ; and even the *comitatus* was based in its arrangements upon different degrees of rank and station.[4]   Upon the life of the noble, a higher price was set than upon that of an ordinary freeman.

Emancipation of youths. The youth upon attaining his majority, whether the son of a noble or of a simple freeman, did not pass into the full possession of freedom until he had been first emancipated by the state.   Until he reached the proper age he was considered simply as a member of the household.   When the proper time arrived he was introduced in the state assembly, and there invested, either by a magistrate or by some near relative, with shield and spear.[5]   Thus endowed with the right to bear arms, he ceased to be a mere member of the family, — he became a member of the state.   It is not likely, however, that such a youth, even after his emancipation, entered into the full enjoyment of all political rights until he had become the possessor of rights in land.[6]

Freedmen. The freedmen were not of much higher consideration than actual slaves.   They obtained no rank in their master's family ; and, if we except that part of Germany in which monarchy was established, they never participated in public affairs.[7]   It is not to be presumed that this class enjoyed the possession of political rights.

The unfree : Among the Germans the unfree, the *servi*, were divided

---

[1] Kemble, *Saxons in England*, vol. i. pp. 133, 134.
[2] Ibid., vol. i. p. 135.
[3] Tac., *Germ.*, c. 7.
[4] Ibid., c. 13.   In debate a noble was entitled to precedence.   Ibid., c. 11.
[5] Ibid., c. 13.   For a full account of

this ceremony, see Sohm, *R.- und G. V.*, Beilage I.
[6] Waitz, *D. V. G.*, i. pp. 323, 324; Sohm, *Fränkische Reichs- und Gerichtsverfassung*, pp. 545–558; Stubbs, *Const. Hist.*, vol. i. p. 22.
[7] Tac., *Germ.*, c. 25.

into two classes which represented two distinct grades of servitude.[1] The higher class were mere agrarian dependents *agrarian dependents.* who were obliged to furnish their masters a certain quantity of grain, cattle, or clothing. Such dependents, however, were allowed their own separate homes, and their management. They obeyed their masters, but it was an unusual thing for them to be whipped or punished in any way. It sometimes happened that the master, in his rage, killed his dependent, and then it seems that the crime passed unpunished, and without compensation to any one.[2] This class, no doubt, resulted in the main from conquest, especially in those cases in which the conquerors occupied the land of the conquered, and reduced the original possessors of the soil to a condition of dependence, in which they might still maintain themselves while they toiled for their lords.[3]

The condition of the lowest class of the unfree repre- *Slaves.* sented the full measure of abject servitude. This class seems to have been composed of those who had fallen victims to the national vice of gambling.[4] When the German had lost his all at play, he would put even his person and his liberty at stake. If he lost, he yielded himself up to a slavery in which he could be chained and exposed for sale. To the victims of play may be added such prisoners of war as were reduced to a state of predial or menial servitude ; and to these may possibly be added slaves by reason of crime.[5]

7. The results of recent investigation into the early history *Ownership* of institutions, and into the primitive forms of ancient law, *of land :* have been fruitful indeed. By the light of the knowledge *the village-* thus attained it is now possible to define the primary forms *community.* of political union and of land-ownership[6] prevalent among

---

[1] Tac., *Germ.*, cc. 24, 25 ; G. L. von Maurer, *Hofverfassung*, i. p. 5 *sq*.

[2] Tac., *Germ.*, c. 25.

[3] Kemble, *Saxons in England*, vol. i. ch. viii. ; Stubbs, *Const. Hist.*, vol. i. p. 23.

[4] Tac., *Germ.*, c. 24.

[5] Kemble, *Saxons in England*, vol. i. pp. 194, 200.

[6] " We at length know something concerning the beginnings of the great institution of Property in Land. The collective ownership of the soil by groups of men either in fact united by blood-relationship, or believing or assuming that they are so united, is now entitled to take rank as an ascertained primitive phenomenon, once universally characterizing those communities of mankind between whose civilization and our own there is any distinct connection or analogy." — Maine, *Early History of Institutions*, p. 1. See, also, Laveleye, *Primitive Property*, pp. 102–110.

those races with whose legal history we are at all concerned. It seems to be clear that the earliest tie which bound men together in communities was the tie of kinship,—the earliest form of social and political organization, that of the family,[1] whose members were either actually united by blood relation-

The patriarchal theory.

ship, or assumed to be so. The first form of authority which existed in such a community was vested in its patriarchal head or chief.[2] The first idea, therefore, of sovereignty which existed in the family, or in the clan into which the family widened, was a personal or tribal sovereignty as distinguished from a territorial one.[3] It is assumed that this tribal constitution of society first prevailed among nomad communities; and it is probable that its original principles entered upon a gradual process of change so soon as the tribal community finally settled down upon a definite area of land. From that time the land begins to be the basis of society instead of the kinship.[4] The theory seems to be well settled that this

Collective land ownership

archaic form of organization and of collective land-ownership by groups of men, united by the family tie, was common to all the races which compose the Aryan family.[5] The traces of such a system have been established from Ireland to Hindoostan.[6] Such a type of organization could only continue to exist in its primitive form among a people whose

yields to individual ownership.

social condition was stationary. With the first advance in the path of civilization the principle of collective land-ownership naturally gave way to the principle of individual ownership. And such has been the transition through which the village-community in most countries has passed. The first step was taken when each man became the individual possessor of his homestead; the next, when the arable land ceased to be held in common subject to allotment; the last, when the pasture lands were finally divided. In this way the

[1] Maine, *Early History of Institutions.* See lecture iii., "Kinship as the Basis of Society."

[2] As to the Patriarchal Theory, see Maine, *Ancient Law,* p. 118 *sq.*

[3] Ibid., p. 99.

[4] Maine, *Early Hist. of Institutions,* p. 72.

[5] But this form of organization is not exclusively an Aryan possession. Ibid., p. 77. Society in primitive

times, "In fact, and in the view of the men who composed it, was *an aggregation of families.* The contrast may be most forcibly expressed by saying that the *unit* of an ancient society was the Family, of a modern society the Individual."—Maine, *Ancient Law,* p. 121.

[6] See Maine, *Village-Communities in the East and West,* pp. 13, 80.

waste lands alone remained the common property of the Waste
lands the
last to be
divided. community.[1] From the evidence which has been recently brought to light in the different countries in which this system has been examined, it is now possible to study its history in every stage of development and decay. In those countries in which the progress of civilization has been most marked, its traces are the faintest; in those of which the contrary is true, its form is most distinct. In Russia[2] and *The Rus-sian mir.* in India the structure of this system can still be viewed in its integrity. Wherever the village-community has existed among the races of the Aryan family it is possible to trace *The village council.* the existence of the village council, the organ, which, in its archaic form, corresponds to what is now called the legislature. To this embryo can be traced the origin of the most famous senates of the world.[3] The history of the village council is closely interlaced with the early history of institutions in Germany and in England.

Tacitus tells us that the Germans did not dwell in cities. *Teutonic villages: the mark system.* Some dwelt in villages, *vici*, but not after the Roman fashion, with a series of connected buildings, for every homestead stood detached, with a vacant space of ground about it. Others dwelt apart from the villages in isolated homesteads, wherever a grove, meadow, or spring happened to attract them.[4] In another and famous passage, which has given rise *German method of agriculture.* to a vast amount of learned discussion, is described the German method of agriculture : "The fields are alternately occupied by the whole body of cultivators according to their number, and these they afterwards divide among themselves according to their individual dignity."[5] The extent of the waste lands

---

[1] Maine, *Early Hist. of Institutions,* p. 81 ; Stubbs, *Const. History,* vol. i. p. 52.

[2] In a recent work, entitled *Russia,* by Mr. D. Mackenzie Wallace, is contained a very interesting chapter (viii.) in which is described the present condition of the Russian "mir" or village-community.

[3] "From this embryo have sprung all the most famous legislatures of the world, the Athenian Ekklesia, the Roman Comitia, Senate, and Prince, and our own Parliament, the type and parent of all the 'collegiate sovereignties' (as Austin would call them) of

the modern world, or, in other words, of all governments in which sovereign power is exercised by the people or shared between the people and the king."— Maine, *Early Hist. of Institutions,* p. 388.

[4] Tac., *Germ.,* c. 16 ; Waitz, *D. V. G.,* i. p. 108.

[5] There are two readings of this very difficult passage, c. 26 : "Agri pro numero cultorum ab universis in vices [*al.* vicis] occupantur, quos mox inter se secundum dignationem [*al.* dignitatem] partiuntur." As to the proper interpretation of this passage, see Waitz, *D. V. G.,* i. pp. 132–137 ; G. L.

rendered this method of partition easy: "They change the arable land, from year to year, and there is land to spare."[1] Thus the Germans dwelt together, either collectively in villages, or upon separate farms in the vicinity of villages.

The vicus identical with the mark.

The *vicus* of Tacitus represents the Teutonic form of the village-community,[2] and constitutes an important link in the chain of its history. If we could accept as of undoubted authority Cæsar's statement in reference to the community of kindred, occupying, subject to allotment, a given area of land for one year which it abandoned the next,[3] we would have a perfect picture of the Teutonic village-community, while its members were still in a purely nomad state. However this may be, it is quite certain, that at the time Tacitus wrote the annual migrations have ceased; the village-communities have settled down upon definite areas of land, the arable part of which is cultivated according to the scheme of annual allotment which Tacitus has described. But it is impossible to work out the history of the Teutonic cultivating community by relying exclusively upon the brief outline contained in the Germania, — its full history must be interpreted by the light of later facts, and by the aid of generalizations based upon the record of usages, and upon the general analogies of Scandinavian law.[4]

The mark in the time of Tacitus.

Structure of the mark.

The portion of territory occupied by the community of kindred cultivators was termed in the German muniments the mark, — something, as the term denotes, marked out and defined, and having settled boundaries.[5] The absolute owner-

---

von Maurer, *Einleitung*, pp. 5, 6; Stubbs, *Const. History*, vol. i. p. 19; *Select Charters*, p. 59.

[1] "Arva per annos mutant, et superest ager," c. 26. "It implies no more than this, that within the mark which was the property of all, what was this year one man's corn-land, might the next be another man's fallow." — Kemble, *Saxons in England*, vol. i. p. 40.

[2] Maine, *Village - Communities*, p. 10.

[3] Cæsar, *De Bello Gallico*, vi. 22.

[4] Stubbs, *Const. History*, vol. i. pp. 35, 48.

[5] See Kemble's chapter upon "The Mark," *Saxons in England*, vol. i. p. 35. But since Kemble's day this whole subject has been worked out in great detail by G. L. von Maurer, in a series of works of the highest authority. — *Einleitung zur Geschichte der Mark-, Hof-, Dorf-, und Stadt-Verfassung und der öffentlichen Gewalt*: München. *Geschichte der Dorfverfassung in Deutschland*: Erlangen. *Geschichte der Frohnhöfe, der Bauernhöfe und der Hofverfassung in Deutschland*: Erlangen. *Geschichte der Markenverfassung in Deutschland*: Erlangen. *Geschichte der Städteverfassung in Deutschland*: Erlangen. See, also, Nasse, *Agricultural Community, etc.*, Ouvry; Maine, *Village-Communities*, lects. i., iii.; Hearn, *The Aryan Household;* Seebohm, *The English Village Community;* Laveleye, *Primitive Property.*

ship of the territory embraced within the mark was vested
either in the community itself or in the state within which
the mark was embraced, while the right to its common enjoyment and possession was vested in its qualified members.
The mark might be located either in the forest or in the
plain, according to the nature of the country in which the
kindred chanced to fix their settlement ; and its border land,
according to circumstances, consisted either of wood or
waste.[1] The mark was divided into three parts, — the village, the arable lands, and the common or waste lands.[2] In
the centre of the mark was situated the village in which *The village.*
the mark-men dwelt in their homesteads, surrounded by
their inclosures and outbuildings.[3] Within the precinct
of the family dwelling-place the head of the family was supreme. No one had the right to enter there except himself
and those under his paternal authority. It could not be in- *Sacredness*
vaded even by officers of the law.[4] The possession of such a *of the homestead.*
homestead was evidence of the fact that its possessor was a
fully qualified member of the mark, and as such entitled to a
full share in the enjoyment of the arable, the pasture, the
meadow, and waste lands belonging to the community.[5] The
arable land embraced within the mark was usually divided *The arable lands.*
into three great fields ; and it was so arranged that, in the
rotation of crops, each field could lie fallow once in three
years.[6] In the fields under cultivation in any given year,
every householder had allotted to him his equal share, which
he cultivated separately by his own labor, together with that
of his sons and slaves. But he was required to cultivate
according to fixed rules ; he was obliged to sow the same
crop with the rest of the community and to allow his portion
of the uncultivated field to lie fallow with the rest.[7] The rules
regulating this system of cultivation were both minute and
complicated. The woods, pastures, and meadows which were *The common or waste lands*
embraced within the mark were undivided, and employed in

[1] Konrad Maurer, *Kritische Ueber-schau,* i. 65–72.

[2] Maine, *Village-Communities,* p. 78. The author of *Village-Communities* has condensed into a few pages of that work a summary of Von Maurer's con-clusions as to the structure of the mark, pp. 77–82.

[3] G. L. v. Maurer, *Einleitung,* p. 21.

[4] *Village-Communities,* p. 78.

[5] *Dorfverfassung,* vol. i. pp. 61–65.

[6] See Laveleye, *Primitive Proper-ty,* p. 110, as to the time of the intro-duction of this triennial rotation of crops.

[7] *Village-Communities,* pp. 79, 80.

common, and, originally, without restriction.[1] When this
primitive condition of things ceased, however, the use of the
common lands was regulated by strict proportion, and an
elected or hereditary officer watched to see that the common
domain was equitably enjoyed.[2]

The mark-moot.

Such was the mark in its agricultural aspect, and such were
the relations which the mark-men bore to each other as common cultivators of the soil. We must next consider the political aspect of the mark, and the character of the assembly
in which its internal affairs were considered and determined.
Every free mark-man had his place in the village council or
mark-moot, which, if the assumption of Kemble be followed,
must have had jurisdiction, in the early stages of social development, over all causes which could in any way affect the
interests of the individuals composing it.[3] But in historic
times the marks appear as members of larger communities,
and in the assemblies of such communities was vested the
judicial power. In the mark-moot was transacted all the business which arose out of the system of common cultivation, and
out of the enjoyment of common rights. The annual allotment of the arable lands, the rotation of crops, the choice of
the meadow, the admission of a new member into the mark,
were all questions which were determined in the mark-moot.[4]

Theory of aggrega-tion :

Within the limits of the mark are found dwelling together,
in the peculiar corporate relations which have just been described, all grades of Teutonic life, — nobles, freemen, freedmen, and slaves, — constituting a naturally organized, self-
governing community. A group of families or households
settled upon a given portion of land, and bound together in
the organization of the mark, probably represented the orig-

---

[1] G. L. v. Maurer, *Markenverfas-sung*, p. 142.

[2] *Village-Communities*, p. 79. "Village cow-herds, swine-herds, and goose-
herds are still employed in many parts
of Germany." See " The Germanic
Origin of New England Towns,"
Adams, *J. H. Studies*, 1st series, II.
p. 15.

[3] Kemble, *Saxons in England*, p. 55.
Bishop Stubbs says that, " It is unnecessary to suppose that there was
a period when the village marks administered justice among themselves.

. . . But the initiatory stage of legal
proceedings may well have been gone
through, complaints heard, and presentments drawn up, in the village
council." — *Const. History*, vol. i. p. 51.

[4] G. L. von Maurer, *Einleitung*, pp.
141–150. " It is with a reverence such
as is stirred by the sight of the head-
waters of some mighty river that one
looks back to these village-moots of
Friesland or Sleswick. It was here
that England learned to be a ' mother
of Parliaments.' " — Green, *History of
the English People*, vol. i. p. 13.

inal basis upon which rested all Teutonic society.[1] And if that theory be accepted which begins with the marks as the units of organization, it becomes easy to work out the process through which the larger divisions arose out of their aggregation. In the attempt heretofore made to describe the structure of the Teutonic state, as it first appears in the written history of the race, it was necessary to begin with the state as an existing political organization occuping definite geographical limits, without reference to the questions involved in the origin of its subdivisions, and in the process through which it was evolved out of their gradual coalescence. The unwritten history of this process rests upon the theory of aggregation ; and as that theory depends, in a great measure, for authority, so far as English history is concerned, upon the great names of Kemble and Freeman, it may be well to state it in their own language. In the words of Kemble : " Next in the order of constitution, if not of time, is the union of two, three, or more marks in a federal bond for purposes of a religious, judicial, or even political character. The technical name for such a union is in Germany a gau or bant ; in England the ancient name gá has been almost universally superseded by that of scir or shire. . . . The gá is the second and final form of unsevered possession ; for every larger aggregate is but the result of a gradual reduction of such districts, under a higher political or administrative unity, different only in degree and not in kind from what prevailed individually in each. "[2] In the words of Freeman : " We must remember that the kingdom, like all our ancient divisions, from the shire, perhaps from the hundred upwards, was formed by the aggregation of smaller divisions. The unit is the mark, roughly represented by the modern parish or manor. The shire must not be looked on as a division of the kingdom nor the hundred or the mark as a division of the shire. The hundred is in truth formed by an aggregation of marks, the shire by an aggregation of hundreds, and the kingdom by the aggregation of shires. The aggregation of marks into shires is indeed mainly to be inferred from local nomencla-

as stated by Kemble ;

as stated by Freeman.

[1] Kemble, *Saxons in England*, vol. i. p. 53. See, also, Seebohm, *English Village Community*, preface, x.

[2] Kemble, *Saxons in England*, vol. i. p. 72.

ture and from the analogy of other Teutonic countries, but the aggregation of shires into kingdoms is matter of recorded history." [1] If we accept, therefore, the primitive Teutonic community, represented by the mark, as the unit, and then apply to its union with other units of the same class the theory of aggregation, the making of the Teutonic state becomes at once obvious and easy.

The hundred, and the hundred court: 8. The mark has now been considered as an isolated, self-governing community, and also as the smallest subdivision of the Teutonic state.   In the ascending order it is necessary to examine the structure of the next largest division — the hundred.   By the union of two or more marks was formed the *pagus, gau,* or shire, known in later times as the hundred, — a word which, in some form, enters into all of the Germanic constitutions.   When the written history of the primitive Teutonic state begins, the formative period has ended ; the state is an existing organization, occupying definite geographical limits, while the original units out of whose aggregation it arose have descended to the status of mere divisions and subdivisions.   Connected in this way with the occupation of definite areas of land, these divisions and subdivisions represent forms of organization not only personal but territorial.[2]   their names have varied in different countries. The name of the territorial district represented by the hundred has varied in different countries, and the name of its court, composed of all the freemen residing within the district, has varied nearly as much as that of the district itself.   That fact must not be allowed, however, to mislead us as to the true character of either; for the hundred, and the hundred court, in respect to both judicial and administrative functions, were of all Teutonic institutions the most enduring and the most important.[3]   The faithful investigations of

---

[1] Freeman, *Norm. Conq.*, vol. i. p. 66.

[2] " At the time when German law and society were first brought within the view of history, the German popular assembly consisted, and to all appearance had always consisted, of the free inhabitants of a fixed geographical district." — *Essays in A. S. Law*, p. 3.

[3] " The hundred, and the principle that the hundred community is a judicial body, outlived the storms of the folk wanderings, the political creations of Clovis, the reforms of Charlemagne, the dissolution of the Frankish empire, the dissolution of the county system, the dissolution of public authority by feudalism, the complete beginning of a wholly new development in the isolated territories.   The hundred constitution gave way at last only to a more powerful enemy, — the awakening legal science of the sixteenth century." — Sohm, *Altd. R.- u. G. Verf.*, i. p. 541. See *Essays in A. S. Law*, p. 20.

the German scholars into their own legal antiquities have Their importance as institutions. finally established the fundamental principle, that the whole Teutonic race, from the earliest period of its history, vested both the administration of law and political administration in the hands of popular assemblies. The smallest of these assemblies is represented by the mark-moot; the circle then widens as we ascend to the assembly or court of the hundred until, in the state assembly, appears the highest development of popular power. The hundred court, like all other The hundred court a popular assembly. Teutonic courts, was a popular assembly, composed of all the freemen resident within the district. In this court was administered regularly and frequently the customary law. It met perhaps once a month, and, in addition to its judicial duties, it discharged many administrative functions.[1] Tacitus tells us that each hundred, *pagus*, sent a hundred warriors to the army, called hundreders; and that this name, at first numerical only, became in time a title of honor.[2] In President of the hundred court chosen in state assembly. the state assembly a chief was chosen to act as magistrate in each hundred. He presided in the hundred court, and with him were associated a hundred companions or assistants, chosen from the body of the people, who attended to give their advice and to strengthen the hands of justice.[3]

9. As by the union of two or more marks the hundred was The state assembly: formed, so by the union of two or more hundreds the state was formed. The supreme powers of the state were vested in a state assembly, in which every freeman had his place. The character of this assembly and the methods of its procedure are described in the Germania with some detail. In the assembly of the hundred the people met in council, mainly for the purpose of judicial administration; in the state assembly they met together mainly for the purpose of political action.[4] In the deliberation of the assembled peo- its functions chiefly political; ple every man had an equal voice; and it was the custom for all to appear fully armed. The state assembly met at fixed and stated intervals, unless sooner called together by

---

[1] *Essays in Anglo-Saxon Law*, p. 5.
[2] Tac., *Germ.*, c. 6.
[3] Ibid., c. 12. The duty of attendance upon the courts and the obligation of military service resulted from the possession of personal freedom,

and were of universal application. — Sohm, *Die fränkische Reichs- und Gerichtsverfassung*, vol. i. p. 333; Roth, *Geschichte des Beneficialwesens*, p. 42.
[4] Sohm, *Fr. R. G. V.*, pp. 1–8.

some sudden emergency. When the people had assembled in sufficient numbers the business began after silence had first been proclaimed by the priests, who possessed the co-ercive power to enforce it. The business presented to the consideration of the assembly was all prepared beforehand by a permanent council. This council was composed of the magistrates, *principes*, who decided all minor questions, re-serving only the graver ones for the consideration of the whole people. When the proper time arrived, the debate was opened by the king, or a chief, and then the rest were heard in turn, according to age, nobility of descent, renown in war, or fame for eloquence. No one could dictate to the assembly, — all could persuade, no one could command. When a proposition was put forward to which the people were opposed they expressed their dissent in loud murmurs; when it pleased them, they expressed their approval by the clash of arms.[1] Here the magistrates, *principes*, were chosen to administer justice in the marks and hundreds, —*pagos vicosque*.[2]

its business prepared beforehand by a permanent council, which settled all minor questions.

Criminal law:

10. In the state assembly, as a high court of justice, ac-cusations were exhibited and capital offences prosecuted.[3] Those guilty of treason and desertion were hanged, those guilty of cowardice and unnatural vices were suffocated in the mud. In the infliction of these penalties the spirit of the law was, that crimes against the state should be made notorious, while the infamous forms of vice should be buried out of sight. All other offences could be atoned for by fines, a part of which were paid to the king or state, and a part to the person injured, or to his family.[4] The Germans felt bound to take up both the enmities and friendships of their parents and relatives. But in their enmities they were not implacable. Injuries were adjusted by a settled measure of compensation. Even homicide was atoned for by a fixed number of cattle; and, in this way, the whole family received satisfaction, — a useful institution to the state, as it served to curb that spirit of revenge, which naturally results from too much liberty.[5] And the value of this method of settling

All offences, except trea-son and effeminacy, could be atoned for by fines.

---

[1] Tac., *Germ.*, c. 11.
[2] Ibid., c. 12.
[3] Sohm, *Fr. R. G. V.*, p. 5.

[4] Tac., *Germ.*, c. 12.
[5] Ibid., c. 21.

difficulties is increased when we reflect upon the fact that convivial meetings were frequent in which drunken brawls generally ended in a scene of blood.[1]

11. Tacitus makes it very clear that each state had its own **Kingship:** constitution and that these constitutions were substantially the same in every particular except one, — in some of the states kingship prevailed, in others it did not.[2] In the monarchical states the kings were chosen from among those of noble blood, while the generals, *duces,* were chosen from among those who possessed the greatest military fame. The power of the king was neither arbitrary nor unlimited, while the general commanded more by exhibitions of valor than by positive authority.[3] Although in war the sole command was not vested in the king, and although in peace his powers were very limited, yet he was certainly surrounded at all times with attributes of great dignity and privilege. He represented in his person the national unity, he was the noblest of the people, the head of the state.[4] As a perquisite he received a portion of the fines imposed in the courts of justice.[5] But the most important consideration arising out of this primitive kingship is the principle of election involved in it. **principle of election.** The king was simply one of the people made eligible by noble blood to an office which the people only by election could bestow. Noble blood simply made the candidate eligible ; while the title to the office rested alone upon election. The operation of this complex principle pervades the whole history of English kingship.

In the non-monarchical states the conception of national **Sovereignty** unity was embodied solely in the idea of the *civitas,* working **in states** through the state assembly, and through the magistrates **non-monarchical.** chosen by it for local administration. In such a state, in time of peace, all ordinary matters were determined by the permanent council composed of the magistrates ; in the event of war the great council was convened and generals chosen by it for its management. Under this form of government, that portion of the fines accrued to the state which in the monarchical states passed to the king.[6]

---

[1] Tac., *Germ.,* c. 22.
[2] Ibid., cc. 7, 12, 25.
[3] Ibid., c. 7.

[4] Kemble, *Saxons in England,* vol. i. p. 137.
[5] Tac., *Germ.,* c. 12.
[6] Ibid., c. 12.

Military or-
ganization :

12. So closely did the scheme of military organization, common to all of the Teutonic tribes, resemble the system of political organization upon which the state was constructed,

its likeness
to political
organiza-
tion.

that a comparison has been happily made between the state in its territorial aspect and the army in permanent encampment.[1] In the social and political order the narrowest form of local organization was represented by the kindred grouped together in village-communities. In one of the elements of which the army was composed, the same principle of cohesion appeared. The mass of the people fought together in "families and affinities ; "[2] in these groups of kindred appeared upon the battle-field the village-communities. The larger divisions of the state were also distinctly represented. Each *pagus* or hundred contributed its quota of a hundred warriors to the host. These warriors, chosen from the flower of the youth, constituted the infantry, which was looked upon as the basis of the national strength.[3]

The *comi-
tatus:*

The third element of the army consisted of bands of professional warriors, united to a leader of their choice in a close and peculiar personal relation which Tacitus has described with terse and graphic force. The leader of such a band was the *princeps*, his war-like followers, the *comites ;* and it was no disgrace to any man to be seen among the followers of a

its divisions
of rank ;

chief. The clanship or *comitatus* thus formed had its divisions of rank, which were fixed by the *princeps*. There was great emulation among the *comites* of every *princeps* as to who should hold the highest place in his esteem ; and among the *principes* as to who should have the most numerous and bravest following. To be always surrounded by a band of chosen young men — in peace an ornament — in war a bulwark — was the greatest dignity and power that a chief could

Relative
duties of
princeps
and *comites.*

possess. Upon the battle-field it was a disgrace for the *princeps* to be surpassed by his *comites*, and it was a disgrace for the *comites* not to equal their leader in valor. To survive a battle in which their chief had fallen was eternal infamy. To defend and protect the *princeps*, to make even their own renown subservient to his, was the highest and holiest duty of the *comites*. The chieftains fought for victory, the *comites*

---

[1] Stubbs, *Const. Hist.*, vol. i. p. 31.   [2] Tac., *Germ.*, c. 7.   [3] Ibid., c. 6.

for their chief. The *comitatus* could only be kept together by violence and war, for the *comites* were entirely dependent upon the bounty of their chief. At one time they demanded from him that war-horse, at another, this bloody and victorious lance. The table of the chief, though rude, had always to be bountiful, for it was the only pay of his followers. War and plunder supply the means of liberality.[1] In the bonds of this strange military association, the chief and his followers were united by the closest ties of mutual interest and honor. Both in peace and war the *comites* were required to serve the *princeps* even to the death, and in return the *princeps* shared his spoils with them and gave them bread.

In the structure of the *comitatus* was imbedded the germ of a great after-growth. The relation of lord and vassal, the first outcome of the *comitatus*, was purely a personal one. But in the process of time, when the lord makes a grant of land to his vassal in consideration of past services and upon the further consideration that the vassal will hold such land upon the tenure of military service, a new relation becomes involved with the old one. When the two relations become inseparably welded together the result is feudalism.[2] But we are now only concerned with the *comitatus* as an element in the host, — its growth and influence belong to later times. *Origin of feudalism.*

The host was therefore composed of three distinct elements: the main body of the people fighting in groups united by the tie of kinships; the chosen infantry contributed by the hundreds; and the bands of mounted warriors, each under the leadership of its own trusted chief. When the whole people were in arms we have "popular assembly, parliament, law court, and army in one."[3] The close relationship thus existing between the systems of political and military organization is, in one respect, worthy of special attention. It is easy to understand how an army of invasion, composed either of the whole people of a state, or of a single subdivision, embodied in its very organization the primitive political system, which it would naturally reproduce wherever a settlement was made in the conquered territory. If the expedition happened to be *The host composed of three elements.*

[1] Tac., *Germ.*, cc. 13, 14. See Kemble's chapter (vii.) on "The Noble by Service," *Saxons in England*, vol. i. p. 162.

[2] Freeman, *Norm. Conq.*, vol. i. pp. 58–63.

[3] *Essays in A. S. Law*, p.

Divisions of the host give form to civil organization.

composed of a single group of kindred, upon a settlement being made in a new land, its members would naturally draw together upon the old plan in a village-community.[1] If the expedition happened to be composed of many groups, united under a common leadership, a cluster of village-communities would as naturally result. After the units of organization had thus been reproduced and brought into contact, through the ordinary law of federation, first the hundreds and last the state would reappear. When the attempt shall be made hereafter to reason out, upon scanty evidence, the probable form in which the earliest Teutonic settlements in Britain were made, the foregoing theory will constitute a serious factor in the argument.

Teutonic heathenism; its influence upon national character.

13. No conception of the primitive Teutonic constitution can be at all rounded and complete that does not embrace some insight into the national character which pervaded everything, impressed itself upon everything.[2] With the very warp and woof of that national character the forces of Teutonic heathenism were subtly interlaced. In all the vicissitudes of life, the fierce barbarians of the north felt impressed with a sense of reverence and of awe in the contemplation of the great forces of nature about them, — these they regarded as personal divinities.[3] There can be no doubt about the fact that the true interpretation of every mythology depends, to a great extent, upon a correct observation of the physical phenomena out of which it arose.[4] The light, sensuous aspects of nature about the shores of the Mediterranean Sea reappeared in the mythology of the versatile Greek, idealized but yet unaltered. And so the stern aspects of nature about the shores of the Northern Ocean reappeared in the mythology

---

[1] "And as they fought side by side on the field, so they dwelled side by side on the soil. Harling abode by Harling, and Billing by Billing; and each 'wick' or 'ham' or 'stead' or 'tun' took its name from the kinsmen who dwelled together in it." — Green, *Hist. of the English People*, vol. i. p. 10.

[2] See Kemble's chapter (xii.) on "Heathendom," *Saxons in England*, vol. i. p. 327.

[3] "The primary characteristic of this old Northland mythology I find to be impersonation of the visible workings of nature. . . . What we now lecture of as science, they wondered at, and fell down in awe before, as religion. The dark, hostile powers of nature they figured to themselves as Jötuns (giants), huge, shaggy beings, of a demoniac character. Frost, Fire, Sea-Tempest, these are Jötuns. The friendly powers, again, as Summer-heat, the Sun, are gods. The empire of this universe is divided between these two; they dwell apart in perennial internecine feud." — Carlyle's *Heroes and Hero-Worship*, p. 16.

[4] Buckle, *History of Civilization in England*, vol. i. pp. 118–124.

of the Greek's Aryan brother, and impressed upon his serious character a deep sense of reverence, fidelity, and faith. From Tacitus we learn that the Teutonic race possessed a common mythology,[1] but we can derive from the Germania no adequate conception of its character. Geographically this mythology once extended over all Scandinavia, including Iceland, over England, and over considerable portions of France and Germany.[2] When the Teutonic nations separated, the form of the original faith, which each horde of emigrants took with them, became modified, of course, by the local circumstances of the particular country in which it was finally replanted. The Niebelungen-Lied was its offspring in Germany, the song of Beowulf its offspring in England.[3] As Christianity advanced, Teutonic heathenism retreated before it, step by step, to the north, until the circle of its influence was at last narrowed down to the limits of Ultima Thule. Here it expired after recording its purest traditions in the literature of Iceland. In the Eddas is preserved the genuine record of the ancient faith. In the forms of the Norse gods who move through the mighty epic, all the great forces of nature were vividly personified. Each god impersonated some physical or moral force, and according as it was friendly or unfriendly to man, it was adored as a divinity or dreaded as a demon. The roaring of the storm was to the Northman the coming of the angry Thor, whose chariot wheels shook the universe which the light of his eyes illumined. To his mind the whole life of the world consisted of a great struggle between the gods of good and light on the one side, and of evil and darkness on the other. Out of this struggle creation began; through the results of the struggle everything in the end was to be destroyed. Everywhere the struggle was majestic, the powers terrible, the results profound, — everything was huge, vast, terrific. Still, behind the sombre veil of grandeur and of gloom there was the hope of a resurrection, and of a life beyond the grave. The noble and heroic were borne after death to Valhalla, the base and cowardly

Geographical extent of Teutonic mythology.

The song of Beowulf reveals the moral temper of the English.

Each Norse god impersonated a physical or moral force.

The hope of a life beyond the grave.

---

[1] *Germ.*, cc. 2, 7, 10.
[2] Anderson, *Norse Mythology*, p. 34.
[3] "But the thin veil of Christianity which he has flung over it fades away as we follow the hero-legend of our fathers; and the secret of their moral temper, of their conception of life, breathes through every line." — Green, *Hist. of the Eng. People*, vol. i. pp. 17, 18.

were dragged down to Naströnd. It has been said by a Danish poet[1] that the Asa Faith unfolds in five acts the most glorious drama of victory ever composed by mortal bard. In the religion of the Northman there was nothing frivolous or sensuous, — everything was earnest, sincere, heroic. The greatest of the Norse gods was Odin, the progenitor of kings, the lord of battle and of victory. In this stern and high-thoughted system of mythology we see reflected as in a mirror the moral, social, and intellectual characteristics of

The primitive religion as a source of principles and morals.

that mighty race of which the English people is a part. In its traditions we possess a record of their earliest thoughts and feelings, and in these we discover the sources of their proud self-consciousness, their love of liberty and strife, their heroism, and their power. "In the old Gothic religion were embodied principles . . . and morals that in due course of time and under favorable circumstances evolved the Republic of Iceland, the Magna Carta of England, and the Decla-

A century and a half of English heathenism.

ration of Independence."[2] The Teutonic invaders transplanted into Britain the primitive religion, and the history of the English race begins with a century and a half of unbroken heathenism. The possession of Woden's blood was, among the first settlers, an indispensable prerequisite to kingship. Every royal house in every Old-English kingdom traced its descent from Woden,[3] — his name is a part of the national epos. But in the names of the days of the week is perpetuated the most enduring memorial of the ancient faith.

14. Thus far only such matters have been considered as relate to the history of the Teutonic race as a whole. Let us now gather together the few existing fragments which

Engles, Saxons, and Jutes.

relate to the individual histories of the three tribes — Engles, Saxons, and Jutes — by whom the whole fabric of Teutonic life was transplanted from the Continent into Britain. The Saxons are not mentioned by Tacitus, but of the three tribes

Saxons: our earliest knowledge of them derived from Ptolemy.

their history is most complete. For our earliest knowledge of this tribe we are indebted to Ptolemy, from a passage in whose geography it appears that, about the middle of the second century, there was a people called Saxons dwelling at

---

[1] Grundtvig.
[2] Anderson's *Norse Mythology*, p. 129.

[3] Kemble, *Saxons in England*, vol. i. p. 335.

the north side of the Elbe on the neck of the Danish peninsula, and on three small islands at the mouth of that river.[1]
From this account it is plain that the Saxons had not then
attained to any great importance. About a century and a
half later we have the account of Eutropius, who describes *Account of*
Eutropius.
the Saxons as actively engaged in piratical warfare on the
coast of Gaul, A. D. 287.[2] Sixty years afterwards we hear of
Magnentius attempting to strengthen his precarious hold
upon power by an alliance with the Franks and Saxons,
whom, in return, he protected and encouraged.[3] It seems to
be probable that, by the fourth century, in the names of
Frank and Saxon had been merged the names of many other
tribes occupying the same seats, and better known in earlier
times than either. The tendency seems to have been for the
tribes on the Lower Rhine to become Franks, while those
between the Rhine and the Oder were becoming Saxons.
But the mere common name as yet implied no common
organization, certainly nothing beyond an occasional union
for temporary emergencies.[4] Only a portion of the Saxons *Only a por-*
tion of the
passed over into Britain, the bulk remaining in their old *Saxons pass*
into Brit-
homes to play an important part in the history of northern *ain.*
Europe, upon which the great Saxon Confederation has made
an abiding impression.[5]

The Angles or Engles are the only one of the three tribes *Engles:*
only one of
mentioned by Tacitus, but only as one of a number of North *the three*
tribes men-
German tribes, whose positions he does not define.[6] Accord- *tioned by*
ing to Ptolemy, the Engles and Saxons were situated in the *Tacitus.*
second century between the Elbe, the Eyder, and the War-
now.[7] At the time of the migrations the Engles, or at least
a portion of them, were residing in the district of Angeln or

[1] Cf. Ptolemæus, *Georg.* lib. ii. c. 2.
A little after Ptolemy's account, Mar-
cianus of Heraclea assigns to the Saxons the same position on the neck of
the peninsula. See Turner's *Hist. of*
the Anglo-Saxons, vol. i. p. 76.

[2] Eutropius, ix. 21 (*Monum. Hist.*
Brit., p. lxxii.).

[3] Turner, *Hist. of the Anglo-Saxons,*
vol. i. p. 106.

[4] Stubbs, *Const. Hist.,* vol. i. pp. 38,
39. "In their homeland between the
Elbe and the Ems, as well as in a wide
tract across the Ems to the Rhine, a

number of German tribes had drawn
together into the people of the Saxons,
and it was to this people that the
pirates of the Channel belonged." —
Green, *Making of England,* p. 15.

[5] "Of all productions of the German
mind within the domain of law, the
Sachsenspiegel was the purest and the
greatest." — *Essays in Anglo-Saxon*
Law, p. 6.

[6] Tac., *Germ.,* c. 40.

[7] "In the modern duchies of Hol-
stein, Lauenburg, and Mecklenburg." —
Stubbs, *Select Charters,* p. 5.

Engleland in Sleswick, while the main body lay probably in what is now Lower Hanover and Oldenburg.[1] It would seem from the deserted state of the district of Angeln, as it appeared hundreds of years afterwards, that the whole tribe of the Engles passed over in a body into Britain, leaving but a slight trace upon continental history.[2] And this idea is strengthened by the very wide extent of their British conquests. To the new nationality, born of the union of the three tribes by whom Britain was won, the Engles gave their name, — the conquered land became Engla-land or England.

Whole tribe probably passed into Britain.

North of that portion of the Engle situated in Sleswick, were the seats of the Jutes, whose name is still preserved in the district of Jutland. Under the name of Danes the Jutes reappear in later history. The three tribes were of the purest Teutonic type, and all spoke dialects of the Low-German.

Jutes reappear as Danes in later history.

[1] Green, *Hist. of the English People*, vol. i. p. 7.

[2] Bæda, *Hist. Eccl.*, i. 15.

NOTE. — The fact should be borne in mind that the criticisms of the German village community theory — more than once stated in the text — by Fustel de Coulanges, Enama - Sternegg, Ross, and others have had their influence upon the views of the English writers. In 1883 appeared Mr. Seebohm's work on the English village community, in which he finds the manor to be the direct outcome of the Roman villa. His theory is that the rank and file of the people were from the first slaves, in a condition of servile dependence upon an overlord, and that, therefore, their condition was one of progressive amelioration instead of progressive degeneration. The insufficiency of the evidence upon which Seebohm's assumption rests was first set forth in a critical manner by Professor Allen, of the University of Wisconsin, in a paper upon the Village Community and Serfdom in England. Then Mr. T. E. Scrutton, in reviewing the Influence of Roman Law upon the Law of England, finds that the proof of a Roman parentage for the English manor is so incomplete as to leave the burden of proof still upon Mr. Seebohm. In the mean time a reviewer (Professor Kovalensky) of Mr. Paul Vinogradoff's untranslated Russian work, entitled *Inquiries into the Social History of Mediæval England*, states it to be Mr. Vinogradoff's opinion, in which the reviewer concurs, that Mr. Seebohm's theory has failed. Last comes Mr. John Earle, who, in his Introduction to the land charters and other Saxonic documents, concludes that the English manor is of composite origin; that the Roman villa supplied the dominical element, while the free churls settled beside it, and received from the hand of the superior officer who occupied it the lands which they cultivated after the agricultural customs derived from the continent.

CHAPTER III.

THE TEUTONIC CONQUEST AND SETTLEMENT OF BRITAIN.

1. ABOUT the middle of the fifth century the first perma- Roman Britain. nent Teutonic settlements in Britain were made, — with that event the history of English institutions really begins. With that part of the history of Britain which precedes the making of these settlements we have no direct concern, save so far as that history is necessary to a full comprehension of their character.[1] In order the more clearly to explain the nature of these settlements, a brief review has already been made of the precedent history of the settlers themselves. Let us now glance for a moment at the precedent history of the land that they won.

The great tide of Aryan migration never ceased to flow The Roman conquest. westward until its Celtic wave, spreading over the British Isles, reached at last the western shores of Ireland. This whole island-world is found in the possession of Celtic peoples when its history begins.[2] The two incursions which Cæsar; Cæsar made into Britain resulted in nothing more than the bringing of this dim and distant realm within the domain of Roman history.[3] During the distractions of the civil war which ensued, Britain for a long time passed out of view. Not until a century after Cæsar's invasion, when the republic had become the empire, was the subjugation of Britain undertaken in earnest by the emperor Claudius by the hand of his general Aulus Plautius.[4] Nearly forty years then elapsed be-

---

[1] "The English conquest of Britain cannot be thoroughly understood without some knowledge of the earlier history of the Celt and the Roman." — Freeman, *Norm. Conq.*, vol. i. p. 2.

[2] It is more than probable, however, that the Celts were not the original inhabitants of the British Isles. As to the existence of a pre-Aryan people, see W. W. Kinsley's *Views on Vexed Questions*, p. 151.

[3] Froude's *Cæsar*, p. 237. See, also,

Gneist, *Eng. Parliament*, p. 2 (Shee's trans.).

[4] Tac., *Agric.*, c. 13; *Annals*, bk. xii., cc. xxxi.-xxxix. Dr. Guest says as to the origin of London: "When in the autumn of 43 Aulus Plautius drew the lines of circumvallation round his camp, I believe he founded the present metropolis of Britain." — "Aulus Plautius," *Archæol. Journal*, vol. xxiii. p. 180.

Aulus
Plautius
and Ag-
ricola.
fore the work begun by Plautius was completed by Agricola,
by whom Britain was really reduced to a state of subjection.
Before his recall by his jealous master the whole island had
been overrun, and by far the greater part of it had passed
under the rule of Rome.   Although Tacitus states in his life

Britain be-
comes a
province.
of Agricola that the southern part of Britain was reduced to
the form of a province under the auspices of Plautius and
Ostorius Scapula,[1] yet it is not to be supposed that its organization was fully accomplished until the peaceful age of the
Antonines, when all the provinces became the objects of special care upon the part of the central administration.[2]   An
attempt has heretofore been made to sketch the general aspects of Roman civilization in Britain for the purpose of
pointing out the marked character of its influence upon the

Superficial
character of
Roman civi-
lization.
life of the cities, and the superficial character of its influence
upon the greater mass of the rural population.   And the fact
was then observed how the whole adventitious fabric collapsed and disappeared as soon as the foreign support, by
which it had been nourished and sustained, was taken away.
The very remoteness of Britain from the seat of empire, its
insular position, the harshness of its climate to men of the

A mere
military de-
partment.
south,[3] its border warfare, — all conspired to make it a mere
military department.   It was simply a place to be plundered
and enslaved.   "'Levies, Corn, Tribute, Mortgages, Slaves,'
— under these heads was Britain entered in the vast ledger
of the empire."[4]   And under these heads only could her contributions be recorded, for to the intellectual resources of the
Roman world she contributed absolutely nothing.[5]

The de-
fences of
Britain.
And yet, oppressive as may have been Roman rule in
Britain, its masters were careful to guard it against its foes.
In the north the walls of Hadrian, Antonine, and Severus
were constructed to bridle the constant incursions of the Picts.

Barrriers
against the
Picts.
Despite these barriers, however, these marauders, about the
middle of the fourth century, penetrated into the very heart
of the province, and almost tore it from the empire ere the
general Theodosius could drive them back to their fastnesses

---

[1] Tac., *Agric.*, c. 14.
[2] Gibbon's *Decline and Fall*, vol. i.
p. 42; Green's *Making of England*,
p. 2.
[3] See Ibid., p. 7.

[4] Kemble, *Saxons in England*, vol.
ii. p. 278.
[5] Macaulay's *Hist. of England*, vol. i.
p. 4.   Kemble, *Saxons in England*,
vol. ii. p. 280.

in the Highlands.[1] But the most formidable foes of Britain were destined to appear as pirates, and to make their attacks from the sea. While the Picts were repeating their incursions from the north, ravages were being made upon the western coast by the Scots, — the name then applied to the people of Ireland.[2] And about the time these attacks in the west began, a still fiercer race of pirates appeared upon the eastern coast, with whose origin and history we are somewhat familiar. The first recorded appearance of the Saxons as pirates in the Channel is in A. D. 287, when they are found ravaging the coast of Gaul.[3] It is not, however, until the year 364 that we hear of them as taking part in an attack upon Britain itself.[4] How serious and incessant this new scourge upon the eastern coast proved itself to be, may be inferred from the measures of defence provided against it by the provincial administration. The most vulnerable part of the coast-line, extending from the Wash on the east to the Isle of Wight on the south, was guarded by a line of fortresses, and the defence of the district so organized was committed to an officer who bore the title of " Count of the Maritime Tract," or " of the Saxon Shore." [5] With the walls upon the north, and with this semicircle of fortresses along the southeastern coast-line, the legions were able to protect the province against both Picts and Saxons up to the moment of their final withdrawal to the centre of the empire.[6] After the removal of the legions Britain was left to her own defence, and for a period of thirty years the abandoned province maintained an equal struggle with her assailants. At last, weakened by internal dissensions, her power of resistance suddenly gave

Saxons appear as pirates in the Channel in 287 ; do not attack Britain until 364.

The "Saxon Shore."

Britain left to her own defence.

---

[1] Ammianus, lib. xxvii. cc. 8, 9 ; Gibbon's *Decline and Fall*, vol. ii. p. 569.

[2] Green's *Making of England*, p. 15.

[3] Eutropius, ix. 21.

[4] Ammianus, lib. xxvi. c. 4.

[5] Palgrave (*English Com.*, p. 384), Lappenberg (*Anglo-Saxon Kings*, ed. 1881, vol. i. pp. 57, 58), Kemble (*Saxons in England*, vol. i. pp. 10–14), Skene (*Celtic Scotland*, vol. i. p. 151), and others have maintained that the "Saxon Shore" derived its name from Saxon settlements made along it of an earlier date than that assigned by the Chronicles to the begining of the Teutonic

Conquest. But the orthodox view now is that the " Saxon Shore" derived its name from its use as a barrier against Saxon invasions. See Dr. Guest's *E. E. Settlements*, p. 33 *et seq.*; Stubbs, *Const. Hist.*, vol. i. p. 59, note ; Freeman, *Norm. Conq.*, vol. i. p. 7, note 3; Green's *Making of England*, p. 19, note.

[6] In 410 Honorius, in a letter addressed to the cities of Britain, acquiesced in the independence of the province, which he instructed to provide for its own defence. — Zosimus, lib. vi. c. 10 ; Gibbon, *Decline and Fall*, vol. iii. p. 317.

way; and at that moment, according to the traditional account,[1] she appealed to the Teutonic pirates in the Channel to save her from her Celtic foes.

Importance of the period of Teutonic conquest, and dimness of its history.

2. During the century and a half which intervened between the middle of the fifth century and the end of the sixth, the Teutonic settlements in Britain were made. Within that period the whole of the island, south of the firths of Forth and Clyde, passed from the possession of the native race to that of the conquerors, with the serious exception of a broad and almost continuous strip of country extending along the entire western coast, and embracing North and West Wales,

The Welsh driven to the west.

Cumbria and Strathclyde. Within this area the entire native or Welsh population withdrew, with whatever of civilization, religion, or law they had derived from Rome. In that part of the land which the conquerors had made their own, they planted the whole fabric of Teutonic life, — social, political, and heathen,[2] — which they had brought with them in their

Out of the fusion of the Teutonic settlements grew the English nation.

blood and bone from the fatherland. Out of the fusion of the Teutonic settlements, made within the limits and during the period to which we have referred, has grown the English nation; out of the primitive political institutions embedded in these settlements has grown the English constitution. It is, therefore, impossible to exaggerate the historic importance of this period of conquest and settlement, — it is the starting-point of everything. Its importance, however, is fully equalled

Period of historic darkness and legend.

by its obscurity. A period of historic darkness and legend intervenes between the overthrow of what had been the Roman province and the beginning of the new Teutonic society. And the difficulties which arise out of this fact are greatly increased by the further fact that such light as we do possess concerning the period which follows is of the dimmest and most uncertain character. How to bridge this chasm which divides the old from the new is the most difficult problem in English history. The first step in the solution of this problem was taken when, in the last chapter, an examination was

---

[1] As to the historic value of the traditional account of the English conquest of Britain, as contained in the English Chronicles, see Freeman, *Norm. Conq.*, vol. i. p. 7, and Dr. Guest, *E. E. Settlements*, in Salisbury volume of *Transactions of the Archæological Institute.*

[2] "The proofs of such a displacement lie less in isolated passages from chronicle or history than in the broad features of the conquest itself." — Green, *Making of Eng.*, p. 132. See above, p. 85.

made of the primitive Teutonic constitution as it appeared in the home land at the end of the first century. It was, however, three centuries and a half after that time before the migrations into Britain began. Just what amount of development took place in the interval it is impossible to determine. In the light of the later evidence, there is no reason to suppose that any material advance took place in the direction of civilization.

As to the history of the conquest itself, the written evidence consists of a few scanty and uncertain fragments. Upon the part of the conquered we have only the Historia and Epistola of Gildas, really a single work, written probably about the year 560.[1] Upon the part of the conquerors we have, in the opening of that invaluable compilation generally known as the English Chronicle, much that is valuable in regard to the conquests of Kent, Sussex, and Wessex, intermixed no doubt with much that is mythical. As to the conquest of Mid-Britain, or the eastern coast, there is no written account from either side; while the fragment from the Annals of Northumbria, embodied in the later compilation which bears the name of Nennius, alone throws light upon the conquest of the north.[2] There is neither record nor tradition to guide us as to the manner in which the country was parcelled out among the conquerors; and only by the aid of local nomenclature, and by the surviving traces of the older life imbedded in the customary law, can be determined the forms in which the first settlements were made upon the conquered soil. But at the moment when the period of conquest ends, Christianity begins, and from its introduction the committing of the customary law to writing appears to have begun.[3] Of the existing laws, those of Æthelberht, Hlothere and Eadric, Wihtred, Ine, Eadward the Elder, Æthelstan, Eadmund, and Eadgar are mainly in the nature of amendments of custom; while those of Ælfred, Æthelred, Cnut, and those which bear

Fragmentary history of the conquest.

Gildas;

English Chronicle.

Nennius.

Christianity and the early laws.

---

[1] See Stubbs and Haddan, *Councils of Britain*, vol. i. p. 44; Skene, *Celtic Scotland*, vol. i. p. 116, note; Green, *Making of Eng.*, p. 24, note 3.

[2] For a complete statement of the authorities upon the early period, see Green's *Hist. of Eng. People*, vol. i., "Authorities for Book I."

[3] The promulgation of the laws of Æthelberht took place at some time between the coming of Augustine, in 596, and his death, in 605. Bæda says these laws were enacted "cum consilio sapientium." — *Hist. Eccl.*, ii. 5. Cf. Kemble, *Saxons in England*, vol. ii. p. 241; *Essays in A. S. Law*, p. 8.

the name of Eadward the Confessor, aspire to the character of codes.[1]   Just before the middle of the eighth century we have

Bæda.

the Ecclesiastical History of Bæda, from which is derived the only substantial account of the century and a half which fol-

*Archæolog-
ical and
geographi-
cal re-
search.*

lowed the coming of Augustine.   To these imperfect records have been added the fruits of the most careful and exhaustive archæological and geographical research.   Even the physical conformation of the conquered territory has been minutely examined as one of the surest of documents bearing upon the history of the conquest itself.[2]

*General
character of
the con-
quest, and
nature of
the early
settlements.*

3.   The period of piratical visitation — which began when the freebooters from the north appeared in the Channel as mere plunderers who simply came to harry the coast, and then to sail away again — gave way about the middle of the fifth century to a period of conquest and settlement.   For a century and a half after that time the coming of the Teutonic tribes into Britain assumed the form of a migration.[3]   All the

*Form of the
migration.*

evidence tends to show that the emigrants came in discon-nected bands, more or less numerous, each under its own leader or ealdorman,[4] who singled out some particular section of country for conquest and settlement.   The fact that the invaders were compelled to cross the sea in ships, capable of transporting only small bodies of men, precludes the idea of invading hordes by which the whole land could be suddenly overrun.   The weakness of the attack, and the fierceness with which it was resisted, were the dominant causes which de-termined the character of the conquest itself.   By dint of hard fighting, bit by bit, district by district, the land was won.

*Distribu-
tion of the
land.*

As we may happen to accept one or the other of two leading theories that exist as to the manner in which the land was orig-inally distributed, the conclusion may be reached, either that the invaders divided the land according to fixed rules as they advanced, or, after the first period of struggle was over, that

---

[1] Stubbs, *Select Charters, etc.*, p. 60; Cf. *Ancient Laws and Institutes of the Anglo-Saxons*, Thorpe.

[2] I refer chiefly to the works of Dr. Guest, contained in the volumes of *Transactions of the Archæological Institute ;* and to Mr. Green's *Making of England.*

[3] See Stubbs's chapter on "The Migration," *Const. Hist.*, vol. i. p. 57.

— Freeman, *Origin of Eng. Nation*, p. 65.

[4] See entries in the *E. Chron.*, a. 449, a. 495; Freeman, *Norm. Conq.*, vol. i. p. 49, and Appendix K.   The fact must, however, be borne in mind that each band of invaders constituted a part of a general migration. — Stubbs, *Const. Hist.* vol. i. p. 65.

a rearrangement took place according to established forms.[1]
No matter which theory be the true one, as to the broader
aspects of the distribution the fact remains, that the invaders
did settle down upon the land in marks or village-communities, and did possess it according to the principles of owner-
ship which that system represented.[2]   The Teutonic host not The host embodies all the elements of political organization.
only embodied within itself all the elements of political life,
but its very organization presented the most natural scheme
of allotment upon which a division of the land could be made.
The clans of kindred warriors represented the village-communities ; the hundreds of warriors, the *pagi* or *gás;* while
the host as a whole was in fact the state assembly, not in
council but in action, — the whole people in arms.   When,
therefore, the conquering host settled down upon a definite
area of land, the state reappeared as a necessary consequence.[3]
Or it may have been that the invaders often came in numbers only sufficient to constitute a single group, or even one
village-community.   Out of the union of such communities
arose *gás* or shires, which finally became organized into states
or kingdoms.   In Britain the village-community or mark is
represented by the township ;[4] the *pagus, gá,* or shire, by a
group of townships united in the district known in later times Structure of the primitive *rice* or kingdom.
as the hundred ;[5] while a union of *pagi* or *gás* is the primi-
tive *rice* or kingdom.   The political structure of the primitive

---

[1] Dr. Konrad Maurer, after discussing both theories, gives his adhesion to
the first. — *Kritische Ueberschau,* i. p.
100; *Essays in A. S. Law,* p. 57.

[2] To Kemble belongs the credit of
being the first to apply the results of
German research into the mark system
to the history of English institutions.
See ch. ii. on "The Mark," and ch.
iii. on "The Ga or Scir," *Saxons in
England,* vol. i. Cf. Freeman's *Norm.
Conq.,* vol. i. p. 66; Maine, *Village-
Communities,* lects. i., iii., v. Mr. Mo-
rier's *Essay on Land Tenure,* published
by the Cobden Club (Macmillan, 1870);
Nasse's treatise *On the Agricultural
Community of the Middle Ages,* Colonel
Ouvry's translation (Macmillan, 1871),
p. 28; Stubbs, *Const. Hist.,* vol. i. pp.
49–52, 82–85 ; Digby, *Law of Real
Property,* pp. 4–8; *Essays in Anglo-
Saxon Law,* p. 83; Seebohm, *Eng. Vil-
lage Community,* Preface, x.

[3] Stubbs, *Const. Hist.,* vol. i. pp. 31,
71.

[4] "The township (I state the matter in my own way) was an organized,
self-acting group of Teutonic families,
exercising a common proprietorship
over a definite tract of land, its mark,
cultivating its domain on a common
system, and sustaining itself by the
produce." — Maine, *Village-Communities,* p. 10.

[5] "From the first, the township or
village-community must have been regarded as forming a part of the larger
aggregate, the hundred." — Digby, *Law
of Real Property,* p. 7. This "aggregate" was originally a shire, and it
never descended to the status of a hundred until the state of which it was the
largest division became itself a shire.
— *Essays in Anglo-Saxon Law,* p. 19.

state would therefore be the same, whether it arose out of the settlement of a single conquering host, or out of the gradual coalescence of smaller settlements originally isolated and independent.

Before the historic period begins, the petty states or kingdoms, into which the settlers originally grouped themselves, had ceased to exist as independent communities,—they had become bound up in the larger aggregates generally known as the heptarchic kingdoms.[1] It is possible, however, from this condition of things to reason back, and to determine with reasonable certainty the structure of these early kingdoms before the process of aggregation began. The later evidence

justifies the assumption, which will be adhered to throughout, that these early or primitive kingdoms were reproductions, in every material particular, of the continental Teutonic states,—the *civitates* of Cæsar and Tacitus.[2] In tun-moot as in mark-moot,[3] the assembled villagers met together to regulate their own local and agricultural concerns ; in the gemot, or meeting of all the freemen resident within the *pagus* or early shire, we have in fact, if not in name, the hundred court of the continent ;[4] while the primitive state assembly is the folk-moot, the meeting of the whole people in arms. By adhering firmly to this conception of the structure of the petty states, or early kingdoms as they will be called, into which the conquerors originally grouped themselves, it will be possible hereafter the more clearly to explain the historical origin and structure of the various divisions and subdivisions which appear in the composition of the consolidated kingdom of England after the work of aggregation has been finally accomplished.

The whole fabric of the new society, which completely displaced within certain limits the older Celtic society, was purely Teutonic. Its language was made up of a set of dialects of the Low-German ; the only religion which it possessed was the religion of Woden ; its only conception of law

---

[1] Stubbs, *Const. Hist.*, vol. i. p. 169.

[2] "The *civitas* or *populus* of Tacitus, the union of several *pagi*, is in Anglo-Saxon history the *rice*, or kingdom," etc.—Stubbs, *Const. Hist.*, vol. i. p. 119.

[3] See Mr. Green's graphic description of the structure of the early kingdoms in which the conquerors originally grouped themselves. — *Making of England*, pp. 169-171.

[4] *Essays in Anglo-Saxon Law*, p. 20.

and government was a purely Teutonic conception. The witness of language, of religion, and of law, all point to the one irresistible conclusion that, within the limits which the conquerors made their own while they were still heathens, the whole fabric of Romano-British life passed away.[1]   And this conclusion is greatly strengthened by the fate of the Roman cities.   The German instinct was averse to dwelling within the confines of walled cities : in the woods and in the plain the German made his home ; his boundaries were the boundaries of the mark, his walls the mound and quick-set hedge by which his "tun" or village was surrounded.   The abandoned Roman cities went to ruin and decay, and with them perished the system of municipal life which they embodied.[2] In the course of time, it is true, the sites of many of these deserted cities were reoccupied by the conquerors,[3] but the new system of municipal life which they established had no connection with the old, — it was simply the "tun" or village life in a higher state of organization.   But it will not suffice for us simply to examine the broader aspects of the new society ; we must descend to details, and examine the specific forms in which the older life reappears when the work of conquest is done.

Fate of the Roman cities.

The new system of municipal life.

   4. The political and social life of the founders in the fatherland rested upon two fundamental conceptions, — distinctions of rank and the possession of land,[4] — two cardinal ideas which are fully developed in the life of the village-communities when Teutonic history begins.   The original basis of land-ownership was freedom ;[5] the freeman alone could possess family land[6] within the village ; and upon this possession, the badge of his freedom, depended his right to par-

Distinctions of rank :

---

[1] Freeman's *Origin of the English Nation*, part ii. ; *Four Oxford Lectures*, pp. 72–85; Green's *Making of England*, ch. iv. ; Stubbs, *Const. Hist.*, vol. i. p. 61.

[2] No one can successfully maintain the continuity, in Britain, of Roman municipal institutions. Cf. Kemble, *Saxons in England*, vol. ii. ch. vii., "The Towns;" Stubbs, *Const. Hist.*, vol. i. p. 92; Green, *Making of England*, p. 136.

[3] "And even when life returned to them, it was long before the new towns could again cover the whole area of their ruined predecessors. It was not till Cnut's time that York could cover the area of Eburacum.   It was not till after Dunstan's day that Canterbury grew big enough to fill again the walls of Durovernum." — *Making of England*, p. 138.

[4] Kemble, *Saxons in England*, vol. i. p. 35.

[5] Ibid., vol. i. p. 132.

[6] For a definition of family land see *Essays in Anglo-Saxon Law*, p. 68.

The free and the unfree.

ticipate in the enjoyment of the common lands, the property of the whole community.[1] The free were divided into two classes, nobles and simple freemen; while the unfree consisted of agrarian dependents, who occupied their masters' lands upon the basis of a fixed contribution, and of slaves, whose condition represented the full measure of servitude.[2] In the settlements made by the kindred warriors in Britain, the primitive divisions of rank distinctly reappear.   In Old-English phrase the noble is the eorl, the simple freeman the ceorl;[3] while beneath eorl and ceorl stand the unfree, representing different degrees of servitude.[4]

The free; the ceorl.

The ceorl in the new society is the basis of the village life, just as the simple freeman was the basis in the older society.[5] He is the "wæpned man," the "free-necked man," whose neck has never been bent by a master.[6] Within the village-community he possesses the "ethel"[7] or "alod," which entitles him to the enjoyment of all rights to which any other free member of the community is entitled.   But in the host and in the assembly he is simply a unit with no distinction of birth to lift him above his fellows.[8]

The eorl.

In the new life as in the old the eolas or æthelings are the highest order of freemen, distinguished above the rest of their class by reason of their noble blood, and by the possession of large estates.[9]   The eolas, the nobles of the first settlements, and their descendants, represent the ancient nobility of immemorial descent, as distinguished from the later nobility by service.

The unfree; læts.

The unfree among the settlers in Britain may be grouped in two broad divisions, — læts and slaves.[10]   The læt was a

---

[1] G L. von Maurer, *Markenverfassung*, pp. 59-62; *Dorfverfassung*, pp. 61-65; *Einleitung*, p. 71 *et seq.*

[2] Tac., *Germ.*, cc. 7, 24, 25.

[3] Kemble, *Saxons in England*, vol. i. 131-136; Freeman, *Norm. Conq.*, vol. i. p. 55.

[4] Kemble, *Saxons in England*, vol. i. ch. viii., "The Unfree; The Serf."

[5] Green, *Making of England*, p. 173.

[6] Kemble, *Saxons in England*, vol. i. p. 131.

[7] The terms *ethel* and *alod* are usually employed by the best writers to describe the land held in full ownership.

Konrad Maurer, *Kritische Ueberschau*, vol. i. p. 97; Kemble, *Saxons in England*, vol. i. p. 88. "The *ethel, hid*, or *alod:*" Stubbs, *Const. Hist.*, vol. i. p. 75. See Sir F. Pollock's criticism upon the use of *ethel* and *alod* in an article "On Early German and English Land Laws," contained in *Law Magazine and Review*, London, February 1882, p. 127.

[8] Freeman, *Norm. Conq.*, vol. i. p. 55.

[9] Green, *Making of England*, p. 174.

[10] Kemble, *Saxons in England*, vol. i. ch. viii., "The Unfree; The Serf."

dependent cultivator, whose dependence resulted from the fact that he was a landless man : he had no share in the land of the community ; he was the cultivator of the land of another. As to the lord whose land he tilled he was unfree, but, save as against him, his life and limb were as secure as the ceorl's. He had his own house and home, and the lord could not take from him the land he tilled so long as he paid his rent in labor or in kind, and performed such other services as were due to his lord. But he could leave neither land nor lord at his will ; and, as he owned no land in the village-community, he had originally no part or place in its political life.[1]

Below the læts were the slaves, whose condition repre- Slaves. sented the full measure of servitude, — a servitude as abject as the slavery described in the Germania. Slavery might result from one of many causes, and was either *casu* or *natura*.[2] The lowest condition of slavery was represented by the The *theow.* *theow*, who was either *wealh* — that is, of British extraction — or of the Teutonic stock, and a descendant of the slaves of the first settlers.[3] The *wite-theow* was the man who could not pay his debts, or who had lost his freedom through crime, and whose kindred would not make up the fine for him.[4] The *esne* served either for hire or for land, and may have been a The *esne.* little better off than the theow.[5] Then there were the men who, compelled by famine, "bowed their heads for meat in the evil days."[6] But no matter what the cause from which the slavery may have resulted, in contemplation of law the slave was the mere chattel of his lord, a part of his stock, for The slave the mere chattel of his lord, without legal rights. whose wrong-doing he answered as for the mischief done by his cattle. The slave had no legal rights, no wergild, no credibility as a witness, and a wrong done to him was only an offence as against his master.[7] At his death his status descended to his children ; and even the children of a freeman

---

[1] Green, *Making of England*, p. 185 ; *Essays in Anglo-Saxon Law*, p. 86.

[2] "The serfs *casu* comprise serfs by the fortune of war, by marriage, by settlement, by voluntary surrender, by crime, by superior legal power, and by illegal power or injustice. The remaining class are seris *natura*, or by birth." — Kemble, *Saxons in England*, vol. i. p. 194.

[3] Stubbs, *Const. Hist.*, vol. i. p. 78.

[4] Ibid., vol. i. p. 78, and note 4.

[5] Kemble, *Saxons in England*, vol. i. p. 215.

[6] This form of involuntary servitude was sanctioned by the church. Cf. Theodore's *Pentiential ;* Stubbs and Haddan, *Councils*, vol. iii. p. 202.

[7] Stubbs, *Const. Hist.*, vol. i. p. 79; Green, *Making of England*, p. 186.

by a slave mother were slaves according to the old English proverb, " Mine is the calf that is born of my cow."   But the

Practice kinder than theory.

dictates of humanity secured to the slave some rights which the theory of the law denied him.   His two loaves a day and his holidays were secured to him, and out of his savings, which in theory at least belonged to his master, he was allowed to purchase his own freedom and that of his children.[1]

The primitive village-community in Britain ;

The primitive Teutonic village-community in Britain represented, therefore, a settlement made up of eorls and ceorls, with their unfree dependents, who stood, in relation to their lords, in different degrees of servitude.   The political power of such a community was embodied in the village-moot ; in which the land-owning freemen met together, and passed all laws, or rather by-laws, necessary for the ordering of their village and agricultural life.   The title to the territory of the free community, as a whole, was vested in the community itself ; while within it each villager possessed his homestead and the right to a definite portion of arable land, which entitled him to the enjoyment of all common rights.[2]   With this conception of the primitive free community clearly before us, it will be possible to trace with more distinctness the development of an institution which grew up alongside of and at

a miniature democracy.

last overshadowed the miniature democracy.   But in order fully to grasp the nature of this institution and its development, an examination must be made into the nature of the new kingship to which the migration and conquest gave birth.

Growth of the new kingship.

From the Germania we learn that in the fatherland kingship prevailed in some of the states, while in others it did not.[3] That kingship did not prevail among the Saxons is affirma-

Invading tribes non-monarchical.

tively stated by Bæda ;[4] and the highest authorities agree in the inference that the other tribes that joined in the migration did not differ from the Saxons in that respect.[5]   Every band of invaders, great or small, that came to engage in the

---

[1] Kemble,   *Codex   Diplomaticus,* mcccli., and dccccxxxiv.

[2] As to the character of the independent village-community in Britain, see Freeman, *Norm. Conq.,* vol. i. p. 57 ; *Essays in Anglo-Saxon Law,* p. 82 ; Maine, *Village-Communities,* p. 10 ; Green, *Making of Eng.,* pp. 175, 176.

[3] Tac., *Germ.,* cc. 7, 12, 25.

[4] " Non enim habent regem iidem Antiqui Saxones, sed satrapas plurimos suæ genti præpositos." — *Hist. Eccl.,* v. 10.

[5] Royalty among the conquerors of Britain was one of the results of the migration. — Freeman, *Norm. Conq.,*

work of conquest, was necessarily obliged to intrust its fortunes to some leader or chieftain of its choice. According
to the Chronicle, the chieftains who led the first expeditions The here-
toga or eal-
into Britain bore no higher title than heretoga or ealdorman. dorman.
In A. D. 449 the Jutish war-bands landed under the command of two heretogas, Hengist and Horsa, and in A. D. 455
Horsa was slain, and Hengist and Æsc his son obtained
the kingdom. In A. D. 495 two ealdormen came to Britain,
Cerdic and Cynric his son; and in A. D. 519 they became
the kings of the West Saxons. The evidence justifies the
conclusion that each expedition was led by a chosen chieftain, who might bear as a civil ruler the title of ealdorman,
while as war leader he might bear the title of heretoga.[1]
But as the conquest advanced, and as definite districts of
country were permanently secured, and as the various groups
of conquerors within such districts felt the need of drawing
together under a permanent instead of a temporary leadership, the ealdorman was advanced to the dignity of a king Ealdorman
who could represent in his person the unity of a new national becomes
king.
life. In this wise a brood of petty kings grew up that continued to survive for centuries. In order to attach the idea
of permanency to the new kingship, the name of the son was
often associated with that of the father as a recognition of
the hereditary principle; while, in order to impart sanctity to
the person of the new king, fable at once traced his descent
in an unbroken line from Woden.[2] This recognition of the Blending
hereditary principle was attended and modified, however, of the
hereditary
by the older principle of election.[3] The right to the throne with the
elective
might be vested by the original choice in one royal house, but principle.
the question as to which member of that house should receive
the succession when a vacancy occurred was one which the
national assembly alone could determine. For centuries the
right to reject the immediate heir of the last king, in favor of

vol. i. p. 51. See, also, Appendix K,
"On the Change from Ealdormen or
Heretogan to Kings," Stubbs, *Const.
Hist.*, vol. i. p. 66. Upon this subject
Kemble says, "Kingship, in a certain
sense, seems to me rooted in the German mind and institutions, and universal among some particular tribes and
confederacies."—*Saxons in Eng.*, vol.
i. p. 137.

[1] Freeman, *Norm. Conq.*, vol. i. p. 51;
Kemble, *Saxons in Eng.*, vol. ii. p.
125.
 [2] Stubbs, *Const. Hist.*, vol. i. p. 67.
 [3] "The elective principle is the safeguard of their freedom; the monarchical principle is the condition of their
nationality."—Kemble, *Saxons in Eng.*,
vol. i. p. 137.

some other member of the same house more competent to govern, was freely exercised.   How far the power and dignity of a king exceeded that of an ealdorman it is difficult to determine, but it is quite clear that the title of king did carry with it an advance in both respects.   It is probable that the king was not chosen until a group of war-bands, each under its own ealdorman, had united in the formation of a kingdom. In this way the king was advanced to the supreme command

The ealdor-man as the head of his district.

and to national authority, while the ealdorman, descended to the status of a subordinate, although still possessing the highest command in his own district.[1]

Tribal sovereignty.

   The fact must be constantly borne in mind, that the new king was the king of a nation, the leader of his people, the head of the race, — and not the king of a country and lord of the soil.   The idea of territorial as distinguished from tribal sovereignty was the growth of later times.[2]   In war the king,

The king's powers and duties.

as leader of the host, possessed supreme command, while in peace his powers were coördinate with the national assembly, with whose concurrence he performed all important acts. He maintained, not his own peace, but the national peace, and executed justice on the breakers of it : but justice was not yet the king's justice ; it was the justice of the village, the hundred, and the folk, in whose moots was vested juris-

The dignity of kingship grows as the process of aggrega-tion advances.

diction.[3]   As the process of aggregation advanced, as the early kingdoms became bound up in the seven or eight heptarchic kingdoms, which finally united under the rule of one royal house, the institution of kingship grew with each expansion of territory.   As an heptarchic king rose in power and importance above the petty royal head of a primitive state, so did the king of all the English rise in power and

---

[1] Freeman, *Norm. Conq.*, vol. i. pp. 52, 66.

[2] " Some years ago I pointed out (*Ancient Law*, pp. 103 *et seq.*) the evidence furnished by the history of international law that the notion of territorial sovereignty, which is the basis of the international system, and which is inseparably connected with dominion over a definite area of land, very slowly substituted itself for the notion of tribal sovereignty.   Clear traces of the change are to be seen in the official style of kings.   Of our own

kings, King John was the first who always called himself King of England (Freeman, *Norm. Conq.*, vol. i. pp. 82, 84).   His predecessors commonly or always called themselves kings of the English." — Maine, *Early Hist. of Insts.*, p. 73.   " Territorial sovereignty — the view which connects sovereignty with a limited portion of the earth's surface — was distinctly an offshoot, though a tardy one, of *feudalism.*" — *Ancient Law*, p. 102.

[3] Stubbs, *Const. Hist.*, vol. i. p. 68 ; Green, *Making of Eng.*, p. 172.

importance above an heptarchic king.[1] In the process of aggregation was thus involved the growth of kingship, and in the growth of kingship were involved all the elements of constitutional life.

Reference has heretofore been made to the structure of the *comitatus*, the personal following of professional warriors who grouped themselves around a king or chief in a strange relation of fidelity and dependence which rendered them a class apart from the body of the people.[2] Each chieftain by whom a war-band was led to the conquest of Britain came attended by his *comites*, and their fortunes advanced together. In return for their fidelity and service the *comites* expected to receive from their chief whatever of bounty lay in his power to bestow; but it was a part of his absolute duty to supply them from his own board with their daily bread. The chief therefore becomes in Old-English the hlaford, the loaf-giver, a term which, by an entire departure from its original meaning, finally softened down into the modern form of lord; while the *comes*, the hlafæta, the loaf-eater, becomes the *gesið*, gesith or companion.[3] Under these names the old relations at first reappear. The right upon the part of the king to maintain a body of gesiths or household retainers has been called a very jewel in the crown: but this right was not confined to kings alone; it was enjoyed alike by all the great men of the nation.[4] As kingship advanced in power and privilege, kings were able, of course, to confer upon their dependents a status and emoluments such as no one else could bestow. And as the king grew in power and importance the companion or gesith soon changed his original title for a new one that more clearly expressed his somewhat changed relation. He became the *thegn* or servant instead of the companion of his lord. In this way originated a new nobility by service, which grew and widened until it at last

The comitatus.

The hlaford the loaf-giver.

The gesith or companion.

The thegnhood — the new nobility by service.

---

[1] Freeman, *Norm. Conq.*, vol i. p. 53.

[2] Above, p. 110.

[3] Kemble, *Saxons in England*, vol. i. p. 169. For an elaboration of the whole subject see Kemble's chapter, "The Noble by Service," in the first, and "The King's Court and Household," in the second, volume of *Saxons in England*. And also Freeman's *Norm. Conq.*, vol. i. p. 58.

[4] "The difference between the *comites* of the *princeps* and the household of the private man depends fundamentally only on the public and political position of the master. Now, the king, the perpetual *princeps* representative of the race, conveys to his personal following public dignity and importance." — Stubbs, *Const. Hist.*, vol. i. pp. 149, 150.

absorbed and superseded the older nobility of blood.[1] The ancient eorl passed away and the thegn took his place. The status of the thegn materially depended upon the status of his lord. As a king stood above ealdorman or bishop, so stood the king's thegns above their thegns.[2] The king, as *Benefits derived by the thegn from his lord.* the representative of the race, conferred upon his following, at once body-guard and council, not only dignity and importance, but substantial benefits. As no one could judge a king's thegn but his lord, the royal following became exempt from the jurisdiction of the popular tribunals.[3] The greatest boon, however, which such a thegn expected his lord to bestow was a grant of land out of the public domain, which the king had the power to make with the consent of the witan.[4] Upon estates created in this way the thegns began to dwell, and thus ceased to be members of their master's household. *The thegnhood becomes a territorial nobility:* And so the thegnhood grew into a territorial nobility,[5] into the central institution of the state. And so heavily did this institution, involving the relation of lord and man, press upon the whole social and political fabric, that it finally became a settled principle that every man should have a lord to act as his protector and surety,—the lordless man became almost an outlaw.[6] But depressing as the institution of thegnhood may have been to the simple freemen as a class, it led in the end to the firm establishment of a liberal principle of advancement that has ever abided at the root of English society. The ceorl could not become an eorl for the simple reason that "a man cannot change his forefathers." The

---

[1] Kemble, *Saxons in England*, vol. i. pp. 168, 176.

[2] "The word *thegn* became equivalent to *noble* or *gentle*. The king's thegns formed the highest rank of gentry; the thegns of ealdormen and bishops formed a lower class."—Freeman, *Norm. Conq.*, vol. i. p. 60.

[3] Kemble, *Saxons in Eng.*, vol. i. p. 176; Green, *Making of Eng.*, p. 174.

[4] Bæda complains that, in his day, so much of the folkland was bestowed upon pseudo-monasteries that there was no place where the sons of nobles or veteran warriors could receive a grant.—Epist. ad Ecgbirhtum Archiepiscopum, § 11. *Saxons in Eng.*, vol. i. p. 291.

[5] "The development of the *comitatus* into a territorial nobility seems to be a feature peculiar to English history."—Stubbs, *Const. Hist.*, vol. i. p. 152. "The dependent might be connected with the king, (1) by service, (2) by comitatus, (3) by commendation, (4) by reception of land as a benefice. Frank feudalism grew out of the two latter, the English nobility of service from the two first." Ibid., p. 153, note 1. On the growth of Frank feudalism, see Waitz, *D. V. G.*, ii. 262.

[6] On the relation of lord and man, which developed into the relation of lord and tenant, see Kenelm Digby, *Law of Real Property*, p. 20. Freeman, *Norm. Conq.*, vol. i. p. 61.

thegnhood, however, rested upon more elastic principles ; it was not an hereditary caste, but an aristocratic class, whose ranks were ever open to members from the class beneath it. The ceorl who had so thriven as to acquire five hides of land, or who had been sufficiently successful as a merchant, could become a thegn.[1]

its ranks ever open to the class beneath it.

The most important outcome of the *comitatus*, from which arose this new nobility by service, was the relation of lord and man ; a relation at first purely personal, and not necessarily connected with the holding of land.[2] This relation, therefore, represented but one element of feudalism, which implied not only the mutual relation of trust and fidelity between lord and vassal, but along with it the holding of land by the tenure of military service, — which service was due from the vassal or tenant to the lord as lord of the fief.[3] From the earliest times in England, — as soon, no doubt, as the idea of a nation as an organized political community had become fully developed, — the obligation of military service for the protection of the state was imposed upon the holding of all land by freemen as a necessary burden.[4] This obligation, which no landholder could escape, was embodied in the inevitable *trinoda necessitas*, which consisted of service in the field, and in the repair of bridges and fortresses.[5] But this service was due from the citizen to the state, or from the subject to the sovereign, and not from a vassal to his lord.[6] The two great elements of feudalism — the relation of lord and man, and the holding of land by military service — were thus embedded in an embryonic form in English institutions from the very beginning. But these elements never became inseparably welded together into a definite and harmonious system until after the Norman Conquest.[7] Not until after that event did

The relation of lord and man ;

represents but one element of feudalism.

The trinoda necessitas, — an obligation from the citizen to the state.

Feudalism in embryo.

---

[1] Creasy, *The English Const.*, p. 42 ; Stubbs, *Const. Hist.*, vol. i. p. 162.

[2] " In our own early records this relation of *princeps* and *comes* has developed into the relation of lord and man. . . . But this relation is not at first necessarily connected with the holding of land ; the relation is that of *princeps* and *comes*, of king and his thegns, of lord and man, not of lord and tenant." — Digby, *Law of Real Property*, p. 21.

[3] Freeman, *Norm. Conq.*, vol. i. pp. 62, 63.

[4] Digby, *Law of Real Property*, p. 22.

[5] " This common burden was the *trinoda necessitas*, in its origin required of all people, not resting on land, and therefore not the subject of immunity " — *Essays in A. S. Law*, p. 61.

[6] Freeman, *Norm. Conq.*, vol. i. p. 63.

[7] " The relation of lord and vassal existed, and the relation of military tenure existed ; but vassalage and mili-

the relation of lord and man fully develop into the technical relation of lord and tenant.[1]

Ownership of land, and the growth of great estates.

5. A definite conclusion has now been reached as to the general nature of Teutonic conquest in Britain, and also as to the manner in which the invaders settled down upon the conquered soil. There can no longer be any doubt of the fact that the "English kin" brought with them, and replanted, at some stage of its development, the primitive system of land-ownership represented in the fatherland by the village-community of kindred cultivators, called in the German muniments the mark, which developed in Britain into the "tun" or township. The process has already been explained through which these village-communities, or townships, became united in *pagi*, *gás* or shires, out of whose union grew the early states or kingdoms. The territory of a state, thus constituted, originally embraced three kinds of land, each one of which represented a fundamentally distinct conception.

Family land.

Within the village-community or township is found the homestead of the family, and the portion of arable land to which the family is entitled ; and these, together with the common rights appurtenant thereto, constitute the family estate. The lands that belong to the corporations, that is to the townships, to the buhrs, and to the hundreds, — as the early shires are called in

Common land.

later times — constituted the common lands. All lands that remained belonged to the people or folk in their collective capa-

Folkland.

city. The folklands were, therefore, the public domain, the lands of the state.[2] Family land, common land, and folkland all have their origin in the customary law, from which must

The ethel or alod.

be ascertained their character and attributes.[3] The history of family land cannot be severed from the history of the mark, into whose structure it entered as a component part. The

The mark.

primitive Teutonic mark consisted, as heretofore explained, of three parts, — the village, in which the mark-men dwelt ; the arable lands, which were almost invariably divided into

---

tary tenure had not yet been inseparably welded together. . . . The Norman Conquest no doubt strongly tended to promote the further development of the feudal element; but, as in every other case, it only opened and prepared the way for further changes." — Freeman, *Norm. Conq.*, vol. i. p. 63.

[1] See Kenelm Digby on the "Development of the Idea of Tenure," *Law of Real Property*, p. 37.

[2] See the invaluable essay upon Anglo-Saxon Land-Law, by Mr. H. Cabot Lodge, *Essays in A. S. Law*, p. 57.

[3] Ibid., p. 70.

three great fields; and the waste lands.   The cardinal element in the family estate was the homestead and its cur-
tilage, situated in the mark village; " *Suam quisque domum
spatio circumdat*," [1] as Tacitus has expressed it.   In the house
lands, thus set apart from the rest of the communal territory,
appears the first form of individual ownership in land; [2] a conception which the invaders transported into Britain intact.[3]
The possession of the homestead in the village entitled the
family to an equal allotment in the arable fields, while the allotment in the arable was the basis upon which depended the
enjoyment of common rights.   The house lands in the village,
the allotment in the arable, together with the common rights
appurtenant thereto, constituted the family estate, generally
called by the best writers the *ethel* or *alod*.[4]   As agriculture
improved and population increased, the principle of individual
ownership, at first represented by the house lands, broke
through the communal system by extending itself to the arable lands.   After the arable fields had been allotted in permanent instead of temporary ownership to the several households in the village, only the waste lands remained as the
common property of the community.   From the general history
of village-communities it may be safely inferred that through
this process the system of common cultivation represented
by it fell into decay.[5]   Whether the mark-men among the
first settlers in Britain cultivated the arable lands in common
as a general rule, is a question which cannot now be positively
determined.   But the fact that the system of common cultivation did exist in certain localities has been too firmly established by recent investigations to admit of serious contro-

Margin notes: The home-stead the earliest form of individual ownership; a principle next extended to arable lands. Decay of the system of common cultivation.

---

[1] Tac., *Germ.*, c. 16.

[2] G. L. v. Maurer, *Einleitung*, p. 10;
Konrad Maurer, *Kritische Ueberschau*,
i. p. 99; Digby, *Law of Real Property*,
p. 5; *Essays in A. S. Law*, p. 69.

[3] "If a ceorl and his wife have a
child together, and the ceorl dies, let the
mother have her child and feed it; let
them give her six shillings for support,
— a cow in summer, an ox in winter.
Let the kin hold the homestead until it
(the child) be grown up." — Ine, c. 38;
K. Maurer, *Kritische Ueberschau*, i. p.
99; *Essays in A. S. Law*, p. 70.

[4] See Kemble, *Saxons in Eng.*, ch.
iv. vol. i., "The Ethel, Hid, or Alod;"

K. Maurer, *Kritische Ueberschau*, i. p.
97; Stubbs, *Const. Hist.*, vol. i. pp. 75,
76.   Mr. Lodge says that he prefers the
term "family land" to ethel or alod,
for the reason that " in the family alone
can be found the characteristics which
define and separate it from all other
estates." — *Essays in A. S. Law*, p.
68.   Mr. F. Pollock, in reviewing Mr.
Lodge, says that he prefers the term
"heir land" to "family land." — *Law
Magazine and Review*, London, Feb.,
1882, p. 127.

[5] Maine, *Early Hist. of Institutions*,
p. 81; Stubbs, *Const. Hist.*, vol. i. p.
52.

Survivals
of the sys-
tem.

versy.   Lands representing the arable portion of the ancient
village-community are still found in many parts of England,[1]
and when the soil is arable they are usually called "common," "commonable," or "open" fields, or simply "inter-

Lammas
lands.

mixed" land ; when the lands are in grass they are known as
"lot meadows," or Lammas land, — Lammas-day being the
time at which the common rights begin.[2]   "One of the largest of the common fields was found in the immediate neighborhood of Oxford ; and the grassy baulks which anciently
separated the three fields are still conspicuous from the

The word
"mark" in
England.

branch of the Great Northern Railway which leads to Cambridge."[3] The word "mark," march (mearc), occurs much less
frequently in Old-English than in the German muniments, a
circumstance which Kemble attributes to the fact that "the
system, founded upon what it represents, yielded in England
earlier than in Germany to extraneous influences."[4]   And
when the word does occur, it more frequently bears the signification of a mere boundary than its full original meaning.[5]

The mark
as the
township.

The mark really appears in English history as the township,
a word derived from the "tun" or quick-set hedge by which
the cluster of homesteads in the midst of the mark was en-
circled and protected.[6] By the time the historic period is
reached, the system of common cultivation, as a general rule,
has ceased ; the arable lands have been divided ; and each
individual owns separately, as his "alod," not only his homestead, but the field which he cultivates ; the common or waste

Family
land an es-
tate of in-
heritance.

lands alone remain the common property of the community.[7]

Family land was essentially an estate of inheritance.[8]
Tacitus tells us, that among the Germans, although wills

---

[1] Maine, *Village-Communities*, p. 85.

[2] Ibid., pp. 85–89, containing extracts
from Marshall's *Elementary and Prac-
tical Treatise on Landed Property*,
London, 1804.   See the late case of
Warrick v. *Queen's College, Oxford*,
Law Reports, 6 Chancery Appeals, p.
723, by Lord Chancellor Hatherley;
Maine, *Early Hist. of Insts.*, p. 4;
Digby, *Law of Real Property*, p. 8.

[3] *Village-Communities*, p. 89.

[4] Kemble, *Saxons in England*, vol. i.
p. 36.

[5] The term "mark" occurs in its full
signification only in certain charters ;
e. g., *Cod. Dip.*, dcxxxiii.   For other

instances of its use, see Schmid, *Gesetze*,
p. 631.   Professor Stubbs says that it
is not found in its full sense in the
laws. — *Const. Hist.*, vol. i. p. 83, and
note 2.

[6] *Village-Communities*, p. 10 ; Digby,
Law of Real Property, p. 7 ; Green,
Making of England, p. 175 ; Stubbs,
Const. Hist., vol. i. p. 83.

[7] "Finally, whatever land a man can
call his own is his 'ethel' or 'alod,'
as distinguished from the common
lands, and from the folklands or public
domain." — Digby, *Law of Real Property*, p. 11.

[8] *Essays in A. S. Law*, p. 73.

were unknown, the law of inheritance was a fixed institution.[1]
But long before the period when laws and charters begin, the
family as such had ceased to hold land.   When in the course
of historical development the household was supplanted by
the individual, the family estate was probably held and administered either by individuals in that capacity alone, or as
the heads of households.[2]   The influence of the family in
historic times survived, however, in the exercise of certain
rights, and in the inalienability of family land, — a principle   Inalienabil-
which first yielded to the doctrine that lands were alienable   ity of family land.
within the limits and with the consent of the family.[3]   When
wills were introduced by the church, family land became sub-   Wills at
ject to devise, the validity of the will originally depending   first depend
for validity
upon family consent.   The force of family influence gradu-   upon family
consent.
ally gave way, however, as the idea of individual ownership,
and the use of written instruments in the alienation of land,
became firmly established.   In some cases the consent of the
king and the witan was substituted for the consent of the
family, as a confirmation of the alienation ; in other cases the
alienation was made without the consent or confirmation of
either.[4]

As the family tie weakened, and as the communal system   Common
lands, —
fell into decay, the ethel or alod of the free townsman,
embracing both house-land and arable in severalty, arose out
of the primitive family estate.   The common lands of the
marks or townships,[5] and of the other corporations, then
remained as the only pure representatives of the communal
principle.   The history of these common or waste lands is   their history coex-
coextensive with the history of the law of real property, and   tensive with
the system of common rights by which their enjoyment is   that of the
law of real
regulated is an elementary part of the common law.   In   property.

---

[1] Tac., *Germ.*, c. 20.
[2] *Essays in A. S. Law*, pp. 69, 74;
Maine, *Ancient Law*, p. 261.
[3] *Essays in A. S. Law*, pp. 75, 76.
As to the "ancient difficulties of alienation," and as to "the expedients by
which advancing communities endeavored to overcome them," see Maine,
Ancient Law, pp. 263, 264.   See the will
of a certain Ælfred (*Cod. Dip.*, cccxvii.)
in which is defined "which of my kin
and friends are the men to whom I will
my *yrfe-land* and my *boc-land*," and

comments thereon, in *Essays on A. S.
Law*, p. 76.
[4] *Cod. Dip.*, ccxxv ; *Essays in A. S.
Law*, p. 77.
[5] "The historical township is the
body of alodial owners who have advanced beyond the stage of land-com-
munity, retaining many vestiges of that
organization; or the body of tenants of
a lord who regulates them or allows
them to regulate themselves on principles derived from the same." — Stubbs,
Const. Hist., vol. i. p. 85.

regard to the possession and enjoyment of these lands arose the long controversy concerning inclosures, which has extended down to the present century.[1]

Folkland.

All the land embraced within a state which belonged neither to individuals nor to corporations was the property of the people in their collective capacity, — the folkland, the public domain.[2] The folkland rested upon the principle that royal and public are not the same.[3] Out of the folkland estates were given to the king as a private individual, and estates were given to the crown; but the residue was the public property, the property of all, subject only to the disposition of the witan acting conjointly with the king.[4]

Growth of great estates;

A special class of alodial estates now remain to be considered, — a class which probably originated, in the main, outside of and apart from the village-communities. When documentary history begins great inequality exists in the distribution of land; great proprietors are found in the possession of great estates. Nothing more substantial than conjecture can explain the origin of such estates.[5] The probabilities are, however, either that at the time the original conquests were made, large allotments of land were set apart to the king or chief and to his principal followers, to be held by them in severalty; or that as soon as states were organized large allotments were made to the king and to his followers out of the public domain. In some cases it may have been that the extinction of families and the transfer of small estates brought about an accumulation of land in the hands of certain individuals.[6] Another great factor that entered into the formation of large estates was the right of redemption from the waste, the bringing of the common lands into cultivation,

probabilities as to their origin.

---

[1] "The history of inclosures and of inclosure acts is now recognized as of great importance to our general history." — Maine, *Village-Communities*, p. 85; *Essays in A. S. Law*, p. 91; *Bentham's Works*, vol. i. p. 342.

[2] Allen and Kemble were the first to ascertain the true nature of folkland and bookland. See *Royal Prerogative*, p. 129; *Saxons in England*, vol. i. ch. xi.

[3] "The folc-land rests on the principle in the constitution that royal and public are not the same thing; that the king, not alone, but only at the head of

the whole body of the people, represents the public power; that, therefore, the public objects are the objects of all, and the public property the property of all."—Sohm, *Verfassungsgeschichte*, vol. i. p. 34. See *Essays in A. S. Law*, p. 91.

[4] Digby, *Law of Real Property*, pp. 9, 10, 14; *Essays in A. S. Law*, pp. 61, 92.

[5] Stubbs, *Const. Hist.*, vol. i. p. 73; Digby, *Law of Real Property*, p. 9; Freeman, *Norm. Conq.*, vol. i. p. 57.

[6] Stubbs, *Const. Hist.*, vol. i. p. 73.

a process which the great man with many slaves could carry on much more rapidly than his poorer neighbors.[1] The greater land-owners were the king and the crown, the great nobles and the church, — the greatest being the state, possessed of the public domain. The large estate of the great man, like the small estate of the free townsman, was his ethel or alod.[2] As population increased, and as the primitive com- munal system became inadequate to its necessities, landless men settled down upon the estates of all the great proprietors and organized thereon village-communities, whose general character was identical with that of the free communities,[3] with one vital exception. In the one case the title to the land occupied by the cultivating community was vested in the community itself, the free townsmen looked up to no superior lord; in the other the title was vested in the lord, and the dependent townsmen were his men, or, in the language of later times, his tenants.[4] The distinction is therefore appar- ent between the primitive system represented by the inde- pendent Teutonic community and the new order of things brought about by the growth of great men and great estates. The growth of the principle of lord and man drew after it a conflict between these two systems, which finally resulted in a loss upon the part of the free communities of their primitive independence.[5] Through various processes the house-lands and the arable of the free townsmen became vested in a single lord, and then the waste or common land passed as an incident. In this way the waste of the once free townsmen became the lord's waste, while the townsmen became his tenants.[6] After the Conquest the dependent township appears as the manor of the lord.

The attempt has now been made to define the general na- ture of alodial estates, of common lands, and of folkland, — in a word, of all such lands as originated in custom, and took

Marginal notes: The dependent township; title to its lands vested in the lord. The free communities lose their independence. The dependent township becomes the manor. Bookland.

---

[1] G. L. von Maurer, *Einleitung,* pp. 158–186; *Essays in A. S. Law,* p. 84.
[2] "Whatever land a man could call his own, whether it was the house and inclosure of the free townsman or the domain of the king or great man, was his 'ethel' or 'alod.'" — Digby, *Law of Real Property,* p. 11.
[3] Maine, *Village-Communities,* lec- ture v., "The Process of Feudaliza-

tion;" Freeman, *Norm. Conq.,* vol. i. pp. 57–62; Stubbs, *Const. Hist.,* vol. i. p. 85; Digby, *Law of Real Property,* pp. 8, 13, 43, "Growth of Manors."
[4] *Essays in A. S. Law,* p. 89.
[5] As to the growth of the manor out of the mark, see Maine, *Village-Com- munities,* p. 143; Digby, *Law of Real Property,* pp. 20–26, 43.
[6] *Essays in A. S. Law,* p. 90.

their character and attributes from the customary law. With a clear conception of the nature of the three kinds of ownership thus originating in one common source, it will be easier to define the nature of such estates as did not originate in custom but in written instruments, upon whose terms their character depended. Before the introduction of written instruments by the church,[1] whenever a transfer of land was to be made, the parties in interest went to the land with chosen witnesses, and there, in their presence, the actual possession was delivered by the grantor to the grantee.[2] But with the advent of the church a new method of conveyancing was introduced; written instruments were substituted for the witness of the community. These instruments, which were called books,[3] were designed with a twofold object,—first, to put in the most solemn and enduring form evidence of the fact that the claims of the nation, of the community, and of the family to the land conveyed were effectually barred; second, to establish evidence of title that would be more potent in litigation than mere oral testimony.[4] This new method of transfer was employed in the conveyance of lands both public and private, and the estate usually conveyed was the largest possible, corresponding very nearly to our fee-simple.[5] As the primitive method of transfer by actual delivery gave way to the new method of transfer by book, by which absolute estates were generally created, the term "bookland" became nearly if not quite coextensive in meaning with "alodial," which simply meant land held in absolute ownership.[6] In this way the alod disappeared in the bookland.[7] In the alienation of folkland the new method by book found a wide field for its operation. The king, with the

Marginal notes:

The witness of the community.

The new method of conveyancing.

Estate conveyed by book usually a fee-simple.

The alod disappears in the bookland.

---

[1] "Proof of its (the book's) introduction by church influence would be superfluous. Mr. Kemble accepted the fact long since, and it has not been disputed." — *Essays in A. S. Law*, p. 101.

[2] As to the ancient mode of conveyancing, see A. Heusler, *Die Gewere*, pp. 7-20; Von Bethmann-Hollweg, *Civil Process*, p. 493; *Essays in A. S. Law*, p. 101; Kemble, *Saxons in Eng.*, vol. i. p. 299.

[3] The book was divided into the Invocation, the Proem, the Grant, the Sanction, the Date, and the Teste. — *Cod. Dip.*, Introduction, p. ix.

[4] *Essays in A. S. Law*, pp. 102, 111.

[5] *E. g.*, "quam in semper possideat et post se cui voluerit heredum relinquat." — *Cod. Dip.*, cxvii. Cf. *Essays in A. S. Law*, p. 104.

[6] Digby, *Law of Real Property*, p. 13.

[7] "As the primitive allotments gradually lost their historical character, as the primitive modes of transfer became obsolete, and the use of written records took their place, the ethel is lost sight of in the bookland." — Stubbs, *Const. Hist.*, vol. i. p. 76.

consent of the witan, could carve estates out of the folkland and bestow them either upon individuals or religious corporations, and the land so granted was said to be "booked" to the grantee. In this way the king's *thegns* and the religious houses were enriched without stint out of the public domain.[1]

Family land, the alod, was primarily a "full, free, and un- burdened estate,"[2] subject only to the inevitable *trinoda ne- cessitas*, which consisted of the duty of rendering military service (*expeditio*), and of repairing bridges and fortresses (*pontis arcisve constructio*).[3] To this burden all lands were subject. As a general rule, when a grant was made out of the folkland by book, it was provided that the grantee should hold the land free from all rent or service of any kind, ex- cepting only the *trinoda necessitas*.[4] It was also generally expressed in the book that the grantee could dispose of the land as he pleased in his lifetime, or dispose of it by will at his death, or, if he died intestate, that it should descend to his heirs.[5] These powers, however, depended upon the terms of the grant, by which the right of alienation could be re- stricted to the kindred, or the course of descent limited to lineal descendants or to heirs male or female.[6] It thus be- came established in the customary law that the rights of the grantee of bookland depended upon the terms of the grant; and in some of the charters it was expressly provided that any breach of the conditions of the grant should, *ipso facto*, work a forfeiture of the estate.[7]

No special reference has so far been made to such inter- ests in land as were held by those who possessed less than an absolute estate. The general character of estates held absolutely by the great proprietors — the king, the church, and the greater nobles — has already been defined. In ad- dition, however, to their own estates, certain great individuals

Marginal notes:
Rights of a grantee of book- land, —

they de- pended upon the terms of the grant.

Laenland its origin and attri- butes.

[1] Digby, *Law of Real Property*, pp. 12, 13.
[2] K. Maurer, *Kritische Ueberschau*, i. p. 98. Cf. *Essays in A. S. Law*, pp. 78–80.
[3] Digby, *Law of Real Property*, p. 13.
[4] Kemble, *Saxons in Eng.*, vol. i. p. 301. "Hence a free hide, *hida libera*, is properly called ' án hiwisc ægefæles landes,' a hide of land that pays no gafol or tax. — *Cod. Dip.*, No. 1070."

[5] "The capacity of selling the land is often mentioned in Domesday as a characteristic of absolute ownership." Digby, *Law of Real Property*, p. 14, and note 3, citing Freeman, vol. iv. p. 732; Allen, *On the Royal Prerogative*, p. 145.
[6] *Laws of Ælfred*, c. 41; Kemble, *Saxons in Eng.*, vol. i. p. 308; Digby, *Law of Real Property*, p. 14.
[7] *Cod. Dip.*, xlvi., ccccvi., dcxli; *Es says in A. S. Law*, p. 109.

were allowed to take possession of folkland and to hold and use it upon sufferance, subject to the will of the state or of the king as its representative.[1] A person who held a loan or "laen" of a portion of the folkland in this way, held it purely upon sufferance and according to custom, and not under the terms of a book or charter.[2] Any individual or corporation possessed of proprietary rights over land could grant to another the beneficial enjoyment of the same, to be held either under the terms of a book or subject only to the terms of the customary law.[3] Land so let or loaned was called laenland. The estate or laen thus created was not a leasehold; it was not an estate for a term of years, or for a

A "laen" generally an estate for life.

fixed and limited time: it was generally an estate for life or lives. That is to say, if a man was in possession of land, although he might hold only upon sufferance, his possession was *prima facie* a possession for life.[4] If the laen was held by book, upon its terms its character and extent depended;

Occupancy at the will of the lord — an "unbooked laen."

if there was no book, the laen was held at the will of the lord, subject to the rights and limitations imposed upon that will by the customary law.[5] Reference has already been made to the dependent communities that grew up, not only upon the folkland, but upon the estates of all the great proprietors. Each group organized itself into a township, whose internal arrangements were identical with those of the free community. The title to the land so occupied by the dependent community remained in the lord; while the dependent townsmen, the lord's tenants, acquired by long occupancy, and by the payment of certain dues in services or in kind, a prescriptive right to continue in possession. A case of this kind presents a distinct illustration of what has been called an "unbooked laen," that is, of a laen or occupancy depending upon the will of the lord, as modified by the customary law. The system of letting land for fixed rent and services

---

[1] "A large proprietor, like Duke Alfred, already referred to, held extensive estates of folc-land, which he let out to poor freemen, his tenants." — *Essays in A. S. Law*, p. 59, citing *Cod. Dip.*, cccxvii.

[2] *Essays in A. S. Law*, pp. 59, 95.

[3] Digby, *Law of Real Property*, p. 16. "Such being the definition of laens, there are two classes of them, —

those which are held by book and those which are not. To the latter class belong the unbooked laens of a lord's utland, already discussed, and all estates of folc-land." — *Essays in A. S. Law*, p. 95.

[4] Ibid., p. 95; Digby, *Law of Real Property*, pp. 16, 17.

[5] *Essays in A. S. Law*, p. 86.

had become sufficiently general by the end of the seventh
century to be made the subject of special legislation.[1]

6. The growth of the township out of the mark, and the
character of the estates which the townsmen possessed, were
subjects necessarily involved in the preceding examination
of the ownership of land.   But the township, like the mark,
possessed a political as well as an agricultural aspect.   In the
states or kingdoms which arose as the conquest advanced, the
township was the narrowest form of local government, and
it has ever remained the "unit of the constitutional machinery." [2]   In the qualified members of this corporate unity
resided the power of ordering their own village and agricultural life.[3]   This power was vested in the village assembly
or tun-moot, which, in an independent township, consisted of
all the alodial owners residing within it ; in a dependent one,
of the body of tenants who had united in the formation of a
village-community upon the land of a lord.   In the tun-moot,
which could hardly have possessed more than *quasi*-judicial
functions, resided the power to regulate all the internal affairs
of the township by the making of by-laws, — a term which is
said to mean laws enacted by a "by," as the township was
called in the northern [4] shires.   The tun-moot elected its
own officers and also provided for the representation of its
interests in the courts of the hundred and the shire, where
the *gerefa* and four selectmen appeared for the township.[5]
In this arrangement appears the earliest form of the representative principle.

With the advent of Christianity the township became involved in new relations.   The limits of the political divisions
of the country were adopted as the boundaries of ecclesiastical jurisdictions.   The diocese of a bishop was usually made
coextensive with a shire or kingdom, while the limits of the
township were used to define the jurisdiction of a single
priest.[6]   In this way the township became so involved with

The town-ship and the tun-moot.

Tun-moot regulated the internal affairs of the town-ship,

and elected its own offi-cers and representa-tives.

The town-ship as the parish, —

---

[1] "If a man agree for a virgate of
land or more, at a fixed rent, and shall
plough it, if the lord wish to yield him
the land for rent and service, it is not
necessary for him to take it if he will
give him no house, nor shall he lose
the land." — Ine, c. 67. Cf. *Essays in
A. S. Law*, p. 85.

[2] Stubbs, *Const. Hist.*, vol. i. p. 82.
[3] Green, *Making of Eng.*, p. 187.
[4] Palgrave, *Commonwealth*, p. 80.
[5] Hen. I., vii. § 8. Stubbs, *Const.
Hist.*, vol. i. p. 95.
[6] Kemble, *Saxons in Eng.*, vol. ii. p.
359; Stubbs, *Const. Hist.*, vol. i. p. 227;
Green, *Making of Eng.*, pp. 332, 333.

the parish, and the meeting of the township for church purposes became so involved with the meeting of the vestry, that in small parishes the idea and even the name of the township is frequently lost in that of the parish.[1]

as the manor.

As the process of feudalization advanced, as the principle of lord and man became dominant, the free townships lost their independence, and became subject to a superior lord.[2] After the Norman conquest the dependent township appears

Jurisdiction of the tunmoot divided between the parish vestry and

as the manor of the lord, and the ancient jurisdiction of the village moot survives to this day in the parish vestry and in the manorial courts. The land-holding inhabitants of the township, considered as members of the parish, still assemble in vestry-meeting for the purpose of electing the parish officers, and for the ordering of other local interests not involved

the manorial courts.

in the manorial jurisdiction;[3] while in the court baron and customary court the land-holding inhabitants, considered as tenants of a lord, still meet together and regulate many things pertaining to husbandry and pasturage which originally belonged to the mark-moot.[4] The very existence of a manor depends upon the continuance within it of a sufficient number of freehold tenants to compose a court baron; for, as Coke has expressed it, "a court baron is the chief prop and pillar of a manor, which no sooner faileth, but the manor falleth to the ground."[5]

The hundred and the hundred-moot.

7. Having considered the origin and growth of the township and its court, it next becomes necessary in the ascending order to examine the origin and history of the district which represented a union of townships,[6] — known in later times as the hundred. It has heretofore been maintained

---

[1] "The parish, then, is the ancient *vicus* or tun-scipe regarded ecclesiastically. As many townships were too small to require or to support a separate church and priest, many parishes contain several townships." — Stubbs, *Const. Hist*, vol. i. p. 227. See, also, Ibid., p. 85.

[2] On the "Development of the Manorial System," see Digby, *Law of Real Property*, p. 43; Maine, *Village-Communities*, lecture v., "The Process of Feudalization."

[3] Digby, *Law of Real Property*, p. 8; Stubbs, *Const. Hist.*, vol. i. p. 91.

[4] "The right of the markmen to determine whether a new settler should

be admitted to the township exists in the form of admitting a tenant at the court baron and customary court of every manor; the right of the markmen to determine the by-laws, the local arrangements for the common husbandry, or the fencing of the hay-fields, or the proportion of cattle to be turned into the common pasture, exists still in the manorial courts and in the meetings of the townships." — Stubbs, *Const. Hist.*, vol. i. p. 84. See, also, Maine, *Village-Communities*, p. 139.

[5] Coke's *Copyholder*, xxxi.; Digby, *Law of Real Property*, p. 53.

[6] "The technical name for such a union is in Germany a *gau* or *bant*;

that the early English kingdoms or petty states, in which the settlers originally grouped themselves, were aggregations of *pagi, gás,* or shires, each one of which represented an aggregation of townships. It follows, therefore, that the district in which the townships were embraced was originally a *pagus,* or shire; and, as such, a division and not a subdivision of a state. This district, usually described in the earlier documents as *regio, pagus,* or *provincia,*[1] probably represented either the *pagus* or district in which the hundred warriors originally settled themselves, or a union of townships originally isolated and independent.[2] These districts were not at all uniform in size, — their boundaries generally depending upon the physical conformation of the country in which the settlements were made. In the process of aggregation, out of which the united kingdom finally arose, and which will be more fully explained hereafter, the early kingdoms descended in status one degree: they themselves became divisions of a greater whole; that is to say, *scirs* or shires. And as a necessary consequence, the shires of which they were composed descended to the status of subdivisions known in later times as hundreds. In this way the conclusion is attained, which may be accepted as a general law, that "*the state of the seventh century became the shire of the tenth, while the shire of the seventh century became the hundred of the tenth.*"[3] The word "hundred," as applied to the territorial district, first occurs in the laws of Eadgar.[4] The hundred-moot was composed of all the freeholders resident within the district, together with the representatives from the townships, and was a court of both civil and criminal jurisdiction.[5] It met frequently, and no suit could be carried to a higher

Modern hundred originally a shire.

in England the ancient name *gá* has been almost universally superseded by that of *scir* or *shire.*" — *Saxons in Eng.,* vol. i. p. 72. "The union of a number of townships for the purpose of judicial administration, peace, and defence, formed what is known as the *hundred* or *wapentake;* a district answering to the *pagus* of Tacitus, the *hærred* of Scandinavia, the *huntari* or *gau* of Germany." — Stubbs, *Const. Hist.,* vol. i. p. 96, note 2; Grimm, *R. A.,* p. 532.

[1] Terms used as equivalents for shire. — *Essays in A. S. Law,* p. 16.

[2] Stubbs, *Const. Hist.,* vol. i. pp. 71, 72, 98.

[3] This is the conclusion reached by Mr. Henry Adams, in his admirable essay upon "Anglo-Saxon Courts of Law," after a very exhaustive examination into the original authorities. — *Essays in A. S. Law,* p. 19.

[4] Eadgar, i. Constitutio de hundredis. For a comparison of Eadgar's Ordinance of the Hundred with those of Childebert and Clothaire, see *Select Charters,* pp. 68–70.

[5] "The judges of the court were the whole body of suitors, the freeholders

court until it had first been heard in the court of the hundred.[1]

The early
kingdom
and the
folk-moot.

8. While the development of Germany advanced in the path of political consolidation, that of England advanced in the path of political confederation.[2]   The course of this development is broken into two distinct and well defined epochs : the first, embracing the drawing together of the early kingdoms into the seven or eight aggregates generally known as the heptarchic states ; the second, the drawing together of the heptarchic states into the one united kingdom of all the English under the house of Cerdic.   It will not be necessary for the present to look beyond the first period, during which the early kingdoms coalesced in the formation of the heptarchic states.   In the structure of these larger aggregates one fact of paramount importance stands prominently forth, and that is that the early kingdoms descend in status without a sacrifice of their autonomy ; they

Early
kingdoms
preserve
their folk-
moot, and
for a long
time their
tribal kings.

preserve their ancient boundaries, their national assemblies or folk-moots, and their tribal kings.   The kingdom of the Mercians in Mid-Britain seems to have been a mere confederacy, which resulted from the gradual union of smaller states, whose kings, during the early days, still continued to exist.[3]   In the same way Wessex consisted of a union of kindred states, each having its own ealdorman or underking.   From the Chronicle we learn that five West Saxon kings appeared at one time in a single battle.[4]   East Anglia was made up of two settlements, the North and South Folk, whose names are still preserved in the shires of Norfolk and Suffolk, into which the kingdom was finally divided.   Kent, like East Anglia, was probably composed of two tribal divisions originally distinct ; and in the eighth century it broke up into the kingdoms of the East and West Kentings, probably upon the lines of the earlier states.[5]   And only after a

answering to the '*rachimburgii*' of the Franks." — Stubbs, *Const. Hist.*, vol. i. pp. 103, 104.

[1] Æthelstan, iii. § 3 ; Eadgar, iii. 2.

[2] *Essays in A. S. Law*, p. 21. The "confederation" here referred to must be understood to mean no more than the coalescence of the local communities into one whole, without the loss of their autonomous character.

[3] Freeman, *Norm. Conq.*, vol. i. pp. 18, 19. "In the early days of Mercia, kings of Hwiccia, Hecana, Middle Anglia, and Lindsey still subsisted." — Stubbs, *Const. Hist.*, vol. i. p. 171.

[4] *E. Chron.*, a. 626.

[5] "It is probable that from the earliest times Kent had at least two kings, whose capitals were respectively Canterbury and Rochester, the seat of two

long period of struggle did Bernicia and Deira finally unite in the kingdom of Northumbria.[1]

Such being the principle upon which the early kingdoms coalesced in the formation of the heptarchic states, the question naturally arises as to the form and structure of the national assemblies of these aggregated states. The primitive Teutonic conception of an assembly, whether local or national, rested upon one simple idea, and that was that every freeman resident within a state or district had the right to appear and represent himself in the assembly or court of such state or district. In the composition of the assemblies of the early kingdoms there was no departure from primitive traditions. The townsmen met in tun-moot, the freemen of the shire in shire-moot, while the whole people composed the state-assembly or folk-moot. And even after the early kingdoms had become bound up in larger aggregates they still firmly adhered to the original principle, so far as the composition of their own assemblies was concerned, without extending it to the national assemblies of the aggregated states. That is to say, if the right of all the people to attend in the assemblies of the aggregated or heptarchic states continued to exist in theory, it was not exercised in fact. The national assembly of an heptarchic state was not a folk-moot, but a witenagemot; it was not a great tumultuary assembly composed of the whole body of the people, but a small assembly composed of the great and wise men of the land, who met as councillors of the king. The only consistent theory upon which this changed condition of things can be explained is, that, as the process of aggregation advanced, the limits of the greater kingdoms so widened as to render a general attendance both irksome and difficult, and for this reason the mass of the people simply ceased to attend.[2] In this way assemblies purely democratic in theory, without the formal exclusion of any class, shrank up into assemblies purely aristocratic. The representative principle existed, it is true, in the lower ranges

The heptarchic kingdoms and the witenagemot.

The primitive national assembly purely democrati.

In the heptarchic states the national assembly shrinks up into a body purely aristocratic.

---

bishoprics." — Kemble, *Saxons in Eng.*, vol. i. p. 148.

[1] For the history of Northumbria, see Green's *Making of England*, chapter vi.

[2] This is the theory of Kemble as developed in his chapter (vi.) on the Witenagemot, *Saxons in England*, vol. ii.; and as restated by Mr. Freeman, *Norman Conq.*, vol. i. pp. 67-71, and Appendix Q; *Comparative Politics*, p. 232.

The representative principle not yet extended to national assemblies.

of organization,[1] but the idea had not yet sufficiently developed to be employed in national concerns. The time had not yet come for the early kingdoms which afterwards became shires to send representatives to a national parliament; that principle was destined to be the growth of later times. Such was the origin and history of the witenagemot, whether considered as the national assembly of an heptarchic state, or as the national assembly of all the English when finally united under the house of Cerdic.

[1] In the representation of the townships in the courts of the hundred and the shire.

CHAPTER IV.

THE GROWTH OF NATIONAL UNITY.

I. DURING the century and a half that intervened between the middle of the fifth century and the end of the sixth, the Teutonic invaders possessed themselves of all that part of Britain which had been embraced within the limits of the Roman Empire.[1] The same physical obstacles which had shaped the advance of the Roman invader, shaped the advance of his Teutonic successor, and thus the limits of the one became the limits of the other. The disconnected war-bands, each under its own personal leader, unconsciously united in the common design of driving the Celtic nation slowly to the west. Those of the native race who did not withdraw from the conquered soil were either absorbed or exterminated.[2] In this way the eastern portion of Britain became thoroughly heathen and Teutonic, while the western still remained in the possession of the Romanized and Christianized Celts. Britain as a country never ceased to exist, however, until the invaders, through the results of two memorable battles, were able to dismember the British nation, and to dissolve it into distinct groups of isolated peoples. By the battle of Deorham (577), the West Saxons under Ceawlin won the Severn valley, and in this way cut off the Britons in the southwestern peninsula from the main body of their race.[3] By the battle of Chester (613) the Northumbrians, under Æthelfrith, divided the district of country now known as Wales from the northern provinces of Cumbria and Strathclyde.[4] With the battle of Deorham the first period of con-

[1] "It was not the island of Britain which Engle and Saxon had mastered; it was the portion of it which lay within the bounds of the Roman Empire." — Green, *Making of England*, p. 141.

[2] This statement is repeated with the qualifications heretofore put upon it. See above, pp. 11, 85.

[3] *E. Chron.*, a. 577; Guest, "Conquest of Severn Valley," *Archæol. Journal*, xix. p. 194; Green, *Making of Eng.*, p. 124.

[4] Bæda, *Hist. Eccl.*, ii. 2; *Making of Eng.*, p. 235.

quest came to a close; with that event the period of pitiless war and extermination gave way to a period of settlement.

The conquest was far from complete, it is true, but from that time forth it assumed a new and more humane form; the conquered Welsh were suffered to remain upon the soil, not as equals, but as men and citizens whose rights, to a limited extent, were recognized by law.[1] The weakness of the Teutonic attack upon Britain, the absence of a common design among the invaders beyond that of winning the same land, the stubbornness with which the invasion was resisted, the

difficult nature of the country itself, sufficiently explain the slowness with which the land was won. As each separate warband or folk expelled or exterminated the native race within a given area, the kindred warriors settled down upon the soil with their wives, children, cattle, and slaves.[2] In this way the very slowness and thoroughness of the conquest made possible the character of the settlements that followed in its train.

The three invading tribes of Engles, Saxons, and Jutes divided the conquered area among themselves in very unequal proportions. The Jutes, who were the first to establish a permanent Teutonic settlement in Britain, founded only the kingdom of Kent, and a small principality embracing the Isle of Wight and a part of Hampshire.[3] All the remaining

English territory south of the Thames, together with some districts to the north of that river, was occupied by the three kingdoms of the South, East, and West Saxons. North of

the Thames lay the three great kingdoms of the Engles.[4] In the eastern peninsula, between the fens and the German Ocean, the Engles settled down thickly upon the soil; there the Northfolk and the Southfolk united in founding the kingdom of East Anglia.[5] Between the Humber and the Forth lay the realm of the Northumbrians, which arose out of the union of Bernicia and Deira.[6] In Central Britain the West

---

[1] "The Welshman was acknowledged as a man and a citizen; he was put under the protection of the law; he could hold landed property; his blood had its price, and his oath had its ascertained value." — Freeman, *Norm. Conq.*, vol. i. p. 23, citing Laws of Ine, 23, 24, 32, 33, 46, 54, 74, in Thorpe's *Laws and Inst.*, vol. i. pp. 119-149.

[2] Stubbs, *Const. Hist.*, vol. i. p. 64.

[3] *E. Chron.*, a. 449; Bæda, *Hist. Eccl.*, lib. i. c. 15; Guest, *E. E. Settlements in South Britain*, p. 43; *Making of England*, pp. 26, 149.

[4] Freeman, *Norm. Conq.*, vol. i. pp. 16, 17.

[5] Kemble, *Saxons in Eng.*, vol. ii. p. 3.

[6] Finally united by Oswiu, 651.

Engle, whose limits became a march or border-land against the Welsh, established the kingdoms of the Mercians, or men of the March.[1]

The disunited Teutonic settlers in Britain, who are spoken of in the very earliest records as belonging to "the English kin," must have been conscious, from an early period, of the possession of common blood, common speech, common faith, and common social and political institutions. The only differences which can be discovered among the various peoples who joined in the conquest "are differences of dialect, or distinctions in the form of a buckle or the shape of a grave mound.[2] And yet it is quite certain, in the light of the later evidence, that there was a perfect absence of anything like cohesion or national unity in the mass of separate war-bands or folks that encamped upon the conquered soil. As the conquest advanced, as definite districts of country were permanently secured, and as the groups of warriors within such districts felt the need of drawing together under a permanent instead of a temporary leadership, the heretoga or war-leader was advanced to the dignity of a king. From the military organization of the host were derived the first forms of civil organization. In this way were formed the numberless early kingdoms or petty states into which the settlers were originally subdivided.[3] For centuries one of the greatest obstacles to a union of the incoherent mass arose out of the tenacity with which the German instinct preserved the identity of these early settlements, and out of the faithfulness of each group to its ancient boundaries and to its tribal king.[4] But before the historic period begins, these early settlements or petty states have ceased to exist as independent communities, — they have taken one step in the direction of union, they have become bound up in the seven or eight larger aggregates generally known as the heptarchic kingdoms. These kingdoms are distinctly developed by the time of the conversion, when, for the first time, we are able

Formation of the heptarchic kingdoms.

The war-leader becomes king.

Early kingdoms bound together in seven or eight larger aggregates.

---

[1] Green, *Making of Eng.*, p. 82 and note.

[2] Green, *Making of Eng.*, p. 154, citing Wright (*The Celt, the Roman, and the Saxon*, pp. 481, 482), who "considers the round buckles as peculiar to the Jutes, the cross-shaped to the Engle."

[3] See above, p. 89.

[4] "Whilst the kin of the kings subsisted, and the original landmarks were preserved, neither religion, nor common law, nor even common subjection, sufficed to weld the incoherent mass."— Stubbs, *Const. Hist.*, vol. i. p. 170.

to grasp a definite idea of the form which English society in Britain had assumed.[1] The internal structure of each heptarchic kingdom clearly reveals the history of its formation.

Survival of ancient boundaries and tribal kings.

The prolonged existence of petty kings in each under-kingdom or principality, the distinctness of the ancient tribal boundaries, disclose the fact that each heptarchic kingdom represented, in some form, a union or confederacy of older states.[2]

Relation of the heptarchic kingdoms to each other.

2. By reason of certain errors and misconceptions upon the part of the older historians, the relations really existing between the heptarchic kingdoms have been, until very modern times, seriously misunderstood. According to the old theory, these kingdoms were bound together in a regular confederacy, whose affairs were regulated by an organized and systematic central authority, at whose head was placed, by election or otherwise, a recognized national chief.

The bretwaldas, — Palgrave's view of their character.

This chief or bretwalda has been presented to us by the ingenuity of Sir Francis Palgrave as an emperor of Britain, and as the bearer of the imperial titles of the Roman state.[3] But this whole fabric of error has at last broken down under the brilliant and incisive criticism of Kemble, who was the first to perceive how the original authorities had been misconceived and misunderstood. The whole

Bæda.

theory of the bretwaldadom rests upon a passage in Bæda, and upon one founded upon it in the Chronicle under the year 827. Bæda[4] tells us that Æthelberht of Kent "was indeed but the third among the kings of the Angle race who ruled over all the southern provinces, which are separated from those of the north by the river Humber and its contiguous boundaries; but the first of all who ascended to the kingdom of heaven. For the first of all who obtained this supremacy (*imperium*) was Ælla, king of the South Saxons; the second was Cælin, king of the West Saxons, who in their tongue was called Ceawlin; the third, as I have said, was Æthelbert, king of the men of Kent; the fourth was Ræd-

---

[1] "When written history first shows us the new Britain in the pages of Bæda, we find the original mass of folks and war-bands already gathered together in some eight or nine distinct peoples," etc. — Green, *Making of Eng.*, p. 153; Bæda, *Hist. Eccl.*, i. 15.

[2] Kemble, *Saxons in Eng.*, vol. ii. pp. 2–5.
[3] Palgrave, *Eng. Commonw.*, vol. i. p. 562 *seq.*
[4] *Hist. Eccl.*, ii., v.

wald, king of the East Anglians, who even during the life of
Æthelbert obtained leadership (*ducatum*) for his nation," etc.
First *imperium* and then *ducatum* are the words that Bæda
uses to describe the supremacy, predominance, or leadership
which he was striving to explain.   The Chronicler, when he The Chron-
icle.
reached his entry for the year 827, wrote : " In this year
king Ecgberht conquered the Mercian kingdom and all that
was south of Humber; and he was the eighth king that was
bretwalda."   Then, after copying Bæda's list of seven, from
Ælla to Oswiu, he adds at the close of it, " the eight was
Ecgberht, king of the West Saxons." [1]   Although this passage occurs in six different manuscripts, in one only, the
Winchester version, does the spelling bretwalda occur: " of
the remaining five, four have bryten-walda or -wealda, and
one breten-anweald, which is precisely synonymous with
brytenwealda." [2]   It required the acuteness of Kemble to Kemble's
brilliant
criticism.
perceive that the reading bretwalda was a false one, and
that the meaning attached to it of ruler of Britain or of
Britons was not the real meaning. [3]   Adopting the reading
brytenwealda, a word compounded of *wealda*, a ruler, and
the adjective *bryten*, which, in conjunction with such a word
as *wealda*, signifies nothing more than extensive, powerful,
he arrived at the conclusion that brytenwealda really indicated nothing more than a powerful king, whose dominion
was widely extended.   After a very careful and exhaustive
review of the argument of Kemble, Mr. Freeman thus ex- Freeman's
view.
presses his conclusion as to the character of the bretwaldadom : " I believe then there was a real, though not an
abiding or a very well defined, supremacy, which was often,
perhaps generally, held by some one of the Teutonic princes
of Britain over as many of his neighbors, Celtic and Teu-
tonic alike, as he could extend it over." [4]   Mr. Green, in re- Green's
view.
viewing this conclusion, has said : " The little word " Celtic "
in this very cautiously expressed passage is, no doubt, big
enough to serve as a base for the theory of an imperial

---

[1] Green, *Making of Eng.*, p. 298,
note 1.
[2] Kemble, *Saxons in Eng.*, vol. ii. p.
20.
[3] "As a piece of Teutonic scholarship Mr. Kemble is probably right, but
I doubt whether his correction of the
etymology is of much strictly historical
importance." — Freeman, *Norm. Conq.*,
vol. i., Appendix, note B, p. 367.
[4] *Norm. Conq.*, vol. i. pp. 16–19, and
Appendix, note B, pp. 366–376.

character which Mr. Freeman attributes to the rule of the later West Saxon kings through their supremacy over the Celtic people about them. Such a theory in the case of the later monarchy may be true or false; but in applying it to the kings in Bæda's list we seem to me to be going beyond the evidence we possess." [1] It is, therefore, safest to define the supremacy of bretwaldadom attained by the several Teutonic princes in Britain, before the heptarchic kingdoms were united under the final supremacy of Wessex, to be nothing more than a fluctuating and uncertain overlordship, which any one of the Teutonic kings might acquire and hold, as long as he was able, over any number of the other Teutonic states.

Supremacy of the bretwaldas only a temporary and uncertain overlordship.

When written history first reveals to us, through the pages of Bæda, the form which the new society in Britain had assumed, the seven or eight aggregates, generally known as the heptarchic states, were even then manifesting a tendency to group themselves in three great masses, soon to be known as the kingdoms of Northern, Central, and Southern Britain.[2] The limits of the northern kingdom, the realm of the Northumbrians, stretched from the Humber to the Forth. The southern kingdom of the West Saxons extended from the line of Watling Street to the coast of the Channel. Between the two lay the kingdom of Mid-Britain, destined to become most powerful under the leadership of the Mercian kings; when Æthelfrith in 593 became king of Northumbria, it is probable that this threefold division was clearly established.[3] How to destroy this threefold division so as to unite the whole English nation under the rule of a single overlord, was a problem which required for its solution a period of more than two hundred years. During this period two forces, widely different in character, were constantly working in the same direction; and through their joint efforts national unity was at last attained. These two forces were the church and the sword. The organizing and centralizing power of the one made possible and enduring the final triumph of the other.

National unity the joint work of the church and the sword.

The kingdoms of Northern, Central, and Southern Britain.

The threefold division only broken down after a struggle of two centuries.

4. In dealing with the early history of the English people

---

[1] Green, *Making of Eng.*, p. 299, note.   [2] Ibid., p. 153.
[3] Ibid., p. 212.

the fact must be constantly borne in mind that the Teutonic conquest of Britain differed in two material particulars from all other Teutonic conquests made within the limits of the Roman Empire.   In every other province the conquerors gradually accepted both the language and the religion of the conquered.[1]   But in Britain they accepted neither, — there they clung with tenacity to their native speech and to their ancient faith.   A sullen spirit of national hate seems to have forbidden any attempt upon the part of the British Christians to preach the gospel to their heathen neighbors.   For a century and a half after the conquest began the invaders of Britain remained heathen.   By the intervention of this unbroken barrier of English heathendom the Celtic Christians were entirely isolated and cut off from the continental churches of the West.   In order to break down this barrier, so as to bring Britain once more within the domain of the Christian world, Gregory sent forth a band of missionaries to reconquer for Rome what the legions had given up.[2]

The conversion and the growth of unity in the national church.

For a century and a half the conquerors of Britain remain heathen.

When Augustine landed in 597 upon the shores of Kent he found the power of its king, Æthelberht, the third in the line of bretwaldas, supreme in Mid-Britain.[3]   The Kentish overlord, who had already married a Christian wife among the Franks, received the Roman missionaries with the tolerant spirit of his race, and in a short time Æthelberht and his people were converted to the new faith.   Kent thus became the first Christian kingdom, and Canterbury, the first city centre established by the conquerors, finally became the spiritual metropolis of the English nation.[4]   But the conversion of Kent entirely failed to satisfy the comprehensive plans of Pope Gregory.   Four years after the landing of the first mission, Mellitus, Justus, and Paulinus, with other missionaries, arrived from Rome bearing a letter to Augustine in which was marked out a plan of ecclesiastical organization designed to embrace the whole island.[5]   In this scheme London and York, which had been the principal cities of Roman Britain,

Latin Christianity and its conquests.

Kent the first Christian kingdom.

---

[1] See above, p. 83.
[2] Bæda, *Hist. Eccl.*, i. 2, 5, 26.
[3] " But more than the tongue of Rome returned with Augustine.   Practically his landing renewed that union with the Western world which the landing of Hengest had all but destroyed.   The new England was admitted into the older commonwealth of nations." — Green, *Making of Eng.*, p. 215.
[4] Freeman, *Norm. Conq.*, vol. i. p. 19.
[5] Bæda, *Hist. Eccl.*, i. 29.

were designated as the centres of two archbishoprics, to each of which were to be annexed twelve suffragan sees.   In a letter which Gregory addressed at the same time to Æthelberht, the Kentish overlord was exhorted to spread the gospel

among all peoples subject to his sway ;[1] and in 604 Æthelberht entered upon the task of extending the new faith across the borders of Kent into the dependent kingdoms of which he was overlord.   In this year Justus was set as bishop in Rochester to rule a diocese whose limits mark what is supposed to have been a dependent realm of West Kent.   In

the same year Mellitus went to preach to the East Saxons, whose king Sæberct was closely allied to Æthelberht ; and so great was the success of the mission that Sæberct and his people were at once received into the fold of Christ.[2]   And, after the conversion of Essex, Rædwald, the king of the East Anglians, was induced by his overlord Æthelberht to become a Christian.   Before the death of Æthelberht, however, in 616 the overlordship of Mid-Britain had passed to Rædwald

himself, who at once threw off the new faith which his own people had steadily refused to accept.[3]   In the year in which Rædwald died (617), the kingdom of Northumbria, which the fall of Æthelfrith had for a moment dismembered, was re-

united under the Deiran house of Ælla in the person of Eadwine.[4]   In the nine years which followed his accession, Eadwine extended his overlordship over every English kingdom except Kent, to whose king he was already bound by ties of the closest character.   In 625 Eadwine was married to the Kentish princess Æthelburh, who came to the court of her Northumbrian lord attended by the priest Paulinus as her

chaplain.   After two years of hesitation Eadwine consented to accept the faith that Paulinus and Æthelburh pressed upon him, and the people of his own kingdom of Deira followed the example of their king.[5]   The zeal of Eadwine failed, however, to bring about the conversion of the East Anglians, who were not Christianized until several years afterwards, through the efforts of the Burgundian Felix.[6]   But even in Northumbria the work of Paulinus was destined to end in sudden dis-

---

[1] Bæda, *Hist. Eccl.*, i. 32.
[2] Ibid., ii. 3.
[3] Ibid., ii. 15 ; Green, *Making of Eng.*, p. 229, note 2.
[4] *E. Chron.*, a. 617.
[5] Bæda, *Hist. Eccl.*, ii. 9, 10, 12, 13 ; *Making of Eng.*, pp. 251–257.
[6] Bæda, *Hist. Eccl.*, ii. 15.

aster.   Six years after the Northumbrian witan had accepted the creed of Christ, Eadwine was slain at Hatfield by Penda, the heathen king of the Mercians.   Upon Eadwin's fall Paulinus fled with Æthelburh and her two younger children back to Kent;[1] and with their flight the effort of the Kentish church to Christianize the north came to an end.   Its imperfect work soon disappeared before the heathen reaction which at once set in.   Latin Christianity had so far accomplished nothing permanent outside of Kent.[2]   The spiritual conquest of the north was yet to be achieved by preachers who were to come from a missionary outpost of the Celtic church. Penda and the heathen reaction.

During the Roman occupation of Britain, Ireland escaped invasion ; it was never drawn within the limits of the empire.   Agricola expressed the opinion that a single legion with a band of auxiliaries would be sufficient to reduce it to subjection, but his opinion was never put to the test of a practical experiment.[3]   And so the primitive tribal life which the Celts of Ireland had brought with them from the cradle of the Aryan race went on untouched by the influence either of Roman law or Roman municipal institutions.   The Irish nation consisted of groups of tribes, connected by the ties of kinship, and loosely bound together under a graduated system of tribal government.   Traces of anything like a permanent national sovereignty are of the faintest kind.[4]   The church which Patrick founded in the midst of this primitive tribal society naturally moulded its organization upon the peculiar forms of social and political life about it.[5]   In those countries in which Roman law and municipal institutions had preceded its coming the church, modelling its organization upon the basis of the civil divisions, assumed a form at once national and episcopal.   Through the same process the Irish church became tribal and monastic.[6]   But what the Irish church lacked in compact organization it made up in a fiery missionary zeal which made it famous throughout the world. In the last half of the sixth century the Irish missionary Columba established in the Isle of Hii or Iona, off the west

Celtic Christianity and its conquests.
Tribal life of Ireland.
St. Patrick.
Elsewhere the church became national and episcopal;
in Ireland it became tribal and monastic.

---

[1] *E. Chron.*, a. 633; Bæda, *Hist. Eccl.*, ii. 20.

[2] Green, *Making of Eng.*, pp. 265, 269.

[3] Tac., *Agric.*, 24.

[4] See Maine, *Early Hist. of Inst.*, pp. 11, 132.

[5] Todd, *Life of St. Patrick*, Introd. ; Green, *Making of Eng.*, p. 276.

[6] Ibid., p. 278.

coast of Scotland, one of those monastic and tribal communities peculiar to the Celtic church as a mission station for

Celtic monastery at Hii.

the conversion of the northern Picts.[1]   In this monastery at
Hii the children of Æthelfrith found a shelter in the dark
days which followed their father's fall.[2]   Eadwine, who succeeded Æthelfrith upon the throne of Northumbria, after a
reign of fifteen years, fell before Penda at Hatfield in 633;
and upon his fall the realm of Northumbria was for a time
broken up.[3]   After two years of confusion had passed by,

Oswald.

Oswald, the second son of Æthelfrith, returned from Hii,
and, placing himself at the head of his people, reëstablished
the kingdom under the sway of his own royal house.   As
soon as Oswald was secure upon the throne, he was followed

Missionaries from Hii convert Northumbria.

by missionaries from Hii who came full of zeal for the conversion of his realm.   In 635 Aidan fixed his bishop's stool
in the Isle of Lindisfarne,[4] on the coast of Northumbria,
where a famous monastery was soon established.   Through
the efforts of the Irish missionaries Northumbria became permanently Christian.[5]   And in the very year in which the

Conversion of the West Saxons.

Celtic Aidan fixed his see at Lindisfarne the conversion of
the West Saxons was brought about by the preaching of
Birinus,[6] a missionary who had found his way into Wessex
from Northern Italy.   When, in 642, Oswald was slain in the
battle of the Maserfeld by Penda, his brother Oswiu came
from Hii to succeed him upon the throne,[7] and to unite the
two states of Northumbria in a union that was never afterwards to be broken up.   Ten years after the accession of
Oswiu the Christian house of Northumbria became allied with
the Pagan house of Mercia by the marriage of Penda's son
Peada to Oswiu's daughter.   Peada was at once baptized by
Aidan's successor, and the priests who returned with him
preached, not only among his own people, but, by Penda's

Conversion of the Mercians and East Saxons.

permission, among the Mercians themselves.[8]   In the following year the East Saxons, who had thrown off Christianity
in the days of Mellitus, received the faith anew through the

---

[1] Adamnan, *Life of Columba*, ed.
Reeves, p. 434.   As to the nature of
these communities see Sir Henry
Maine, *Early Hist. of Inst.*, p. 226.

[2] Bæda, *Hist. Eccl.*, iii. 3.

[3] *E. Chron.*, a. 633; Bæda, *Hist.
Eccl.*, ii. 20.

[4] Bæda, *Hist. Eccl.*, iii. 3.

[5] Green, *Making of Eng.*, p. 269.

[6] Bæda, *Hist. Eccl.*, iii. 7.

[7] Ibid., iii. 14.

[8] Ibid., iii. 21.

preaching of Cedd, a missionary sent among them from Oswiu at the request of their king Sigeberht.[1]   At the battle of the Winwæd in 655, between the forces of Mercia and Northumbria, Penda was slain,[2] and his kingdom for a time broken up. By the result of that battle Oswiu became supreme in Britain as no English king had been since the days of Eadwine ; and with that event the broken power of English heathenism passed forever away.[3]   The worship of Woden and Thunder was now everywhere extinct, except in the petty and isolated kingdom of the South Saxons, who accepted the faith some years afterwards at the hands of Wilfrid.[4]

Battle of the Winwæd (655) breaks the power of English heathenism

With the completion of the work of the conversion, the serious question at once arose whether the English nation, as a whole, should accept Christianity in its Celtic or its Latin form.   Should the infant church throw itself into a state of isolation by an alliance with the Celtic communions, which in certain particulars were considered heretical, or should it bring itself into relations with the rest of Western Christendom by an acceptance of the thoughts and forms of Rome ? In the Synod of Whitby called by Oswiu in 664 for the settlement of this controversy, it was determined that the nascent English church should not attempt by opposing Rome to fight against the world.[5]

Synod of Whitby, 664.

English church accepts Christianity in its Latin form.

Although each one of the heptarchic kingdoms was Christianized from a distinct source, the general aspects of the missionary work were everywhere the same.   The conversion of the king generally preceded the acceptance of the faith upon the part of his people, whereupon the missionary bishop became the royal chaplain and the kingdom itself his diocese.[6]   In this way the heptarchic divisions of the country reappeared in the earliest forms of organization which the church assumed.[7]   But it was no part of the plan of Rome to

Organization of the English church by Theodore.

---

[1] Bæda, *Hist. Eccl.*, iii. 22.

[2] Ibid., ii. 24; *E. Chron.*, a. 655.

[3] "The battle of the Winwæd had proved a delusive triumph for Northumbria ; but it was a decisive victory for the cross. With it all active resistance on the part of the older heathendom came to an end." — Green, *Making of Eng.*, p. 301.

[4] Bæda, *Hist. Eccl.*, iv. 13.

[5] Ibid., iii. 25, 26 ; Green, *Making of Eng.*, p. 313.

[6] "Accordingly the conversion of a king was generally followed by the establishment of a see, the princes being apparently desirous of attaching a Christian prelate to their comitatus, in place of the Pagan high-priest who had probably occupied a similar position." — *Saxons in England*, vol. ii. p. 360.

[7] "It might have seemed by the middle of the century that the heptarchic divisions were to be reproduced

He arrives
in Kent in
669.

permit the bishoprics thus established to remain long in a state of isolation. In 669 Theodore of Tarsus, appointed by Pope Vitalian to the vacant see of Canterbury, arrived in Kent [1] with the specific purpose of organizing the English church so that it could be brought into definite relations with the see of Rome. At the coming of Augustine, seventy-two years before, the division of the heathen English into the three kingdoms of Northern, Central, and Southern Britain was already clearly defined. Theodore upon his arrival found the political condition of the country substantially unchanged. But spiritually a great change had taken place, — the heathen English had become Christian. It was possible, therefore, for Theodore, as primate, to deal with the English nation as a whole. The first three years which followed his coming he passed in visiting all parts of the island, and he was every-where received with welcome and reverence. " He was the first of the archbishops whom the whole English church con-sented to obey." [2] After settling all personal disputes among the bishops, Theodore assembled them, together with their leading clergy, in a council which was held at Hertford in 673. [3] By the decrees of this council each bishop with his clergy was restricted to his own diocese, and, what was far more important, it was ordained that the episcopate should meet annually in council at Clovesho. [4] Soon after the meet-ing of the council of Hertford, Theodore entered upon the execution of his plans for the permanent organization of the church, which involved an increase in the episcopate, and a breaking up of the great dioceses into smaller sees. [5] The last part of the work was carried out by a falling back upon the older tribal boundaries which the English settlers were so careful to preserve. The see of East Anglia was broken up into the dioceses of the North-folk and the South-folk, [6] while Mercia and Northumbria were divided in the same

"He was
the first
of the
archbishops
whom the
whole Eng-
lish church
consented
to obey."

Annual
councils at
Clovesho.

Theodore
breaks up
the great
dioceses.

in the ecclesiastical ones." — Stubbs, *Const. Hist.*, vol. i. p. 217.

[1] Bæda, *Hist. Eccl.*, iv. 1.

[2] "Isque primus erat in archiepis-copis, cui omnis Anglorum Ecclesia manus dare consentiret." — Bæda, *Hist. Eccl.*, iv. 2. Kemble, *Saxons in England*, vol. ii. p. 364.

[3] Bæda, *Hist. Eccl.*, iv. 5.

[4] Haddan and Stubbs, *Councils*, vol.

iii. pp. 118–122; Stubbs, *Const. Hist.*, vol. i. p. 218.

[5] "It was characteristic of the care with which Theodore sought an his-torical foundation for his work that even in their division he only fell back on the tribal demarcations which lay within the limits of each kingdom." — Green, *Making of England*, p. 332.

[6] Bæda, *Hist. Eccl.*, iv. 5.

way.[1] Wessex alone of the larger kingdoms resisted ; but a few years after Theodore's death it yielded, and the whole nation was then grouped in sixteen sees subject to the metropolitan primacy of Canterbury. Within a short time afterwards, this arrangement was so modified as to allow to York the position of an archbishopric, with three suffragan sees. By the final subdivision of Wessex, under Eadward the Elder, the plan of Theodore was at last carried out, and the territorial organization of the dioceses as then fixed has remained, with a few minor changes, to the present day.[2]

Primacy of Canterbury.

York.

Theodore's work completed under Eadward the Elder.

Through the results of the work of Theodore the disunited English people found it possible, for the first time, to draw together in obedience to a recognized central authority. A people who had never yet been able to realize a sense of political unity under the sway of a single overlord were now able to realize a sense of ecclesiastical unity under the metropolitan primacy of a truly national church. Representative men from every part of the English nation had never yet assembled in a single witenagemot for the purpose of political legislation. But the existence of such an assembly was now clearly foreshadowed in the annual meetings of the episcopate for the purpose of ecclesiastical legislation. The early councils of the church were the first national gatherings in which the English nation was ever represented as a whole. The infant church thus became the nursery of a national spirit which finally ripened into a complete sense of national consciousness. The unity of the church led the way to the unity of the state, as the national councils of the church led the way to national witenagemotes.[3]

The unity of the church foreshadows the unity of the state.

The church councils the first national gatherings.

5. After the heptarchic states had grouped themselves in the three great kingdoms of Northern, Central, and Southern Britain, each kingdom attempted in turn to work out the problem of national unity by so extending its supremacy

---

[1] As to the division of Mercia, see Haddan and Stubbs, *Councils*, vol. iii. pp. 127–130. As to the work in Northumbria, see Eddi, *Life of Wilfrid*, c. 24 ; Green, *Making of England*, pp. 333, 347, 366.

[2] Stubbs, *Const. Hist.*, vol. i. p. 218, 219.

[3] " The unity of the church in England was the pattern of the unity of the state ; the cohesion of the church was for ages the substitute for the cohesion which the divided nation was unable otherwise to realize." — Stubbs, *Const. Hist.*, vol. i. p. 245. See, also, Green, *Making of England*, p. 371.

The struggle for political supremacy between Northumbria, Mercia, and Wessex.

over all the rest as to bring the whole English nation under the sway of its own royal house. The history of this struggle for supremacy occupies a period of more than two hundred years. The first effort in the struggle was made by Northumbria, a realm which arose at the end of the sixth century out of the union of Bernicia and Deira.[1] Upon the fall of Æthelfrith at the battle of the Idle in 617, the Bernician house of Ida gave way for a time to the Deiran house of Ælla, whose representative, Eadwine, at that time ascended the Northumbrian throne.[2] In the nine years which

Eadwine the first Northumbrian bretwalda.

followed his accession, Eadwine, the first Northumbrian bretwalda, extended his supremacy over all the English kingdoms except Kent, to whose royal house he became allied in 625 by a marriage with the Christian princess Æthelburh.[3] During the overlordship of Eadwine the power of Northumbria reached its height; and through the efforts of Paulinus and Æthelburh, Deira became Christian.[4] But the fabric which Eadwine had built up broke down in 633 at the battle

Overthrown at Hatfield in 633.

of Hatfield, where Eadwine was defeated and slain by Penda, the heathen king of the Mercians.[5] Upon Eadwine's fall Northumbria was broken up, and so remained until Oswald, the second son of Æthelfrith, returned from Hii to reëstablish the kingdom under the line of Ida. During the short

Oswald reëstablishes Northumbrian supremacy.

reign of Oswald the Northumbian supremacy was reëstablished, and the whole realm became permanently Christian under the teaching of missionaries from the Celtic church.[6] The power of the Christian Oswald went down at the Maserfeld in 642 before the heathen Penda, as the power of Eadwine had gone down at Hatfield nine years before.[7] After this overthrow Northumbria was again broken up, and for a time Penda's power in Britain was supreme. Upon the fall of Oswald his brother Oswiu succeeded him as king of the Bernicians, over whom he ruled for the first nine years of his reign.[8] But in due time, by an alliance between

---

[1] Green, *Making of Eng.*, p. 211.
[2] *E. Chron.*, a. 617.
[3] Bæda, *Hist. Eccl.*, ii. 9.
[4] "Though Paulinus baptized among the Cheviots as on the Swale, it was only in Deira that the Northumbrians really followed the bidding of their king." — Green, *Making of Eng.*, p. 257.
[5] Bæda, *Hist. Eccl.*, ii. 20; *E. Chron.*, a. 633.
[6] Bæda, *Hist. Eccl.*, iii. 1, 3.
[7] *E. Chron.*, a. 642; Bæda, *Hist. Eccl.*, iii. 9.
[8] Green, *Making of Eng.*, p. 288.

Oswiu and the daughter of Eadwine, Deira and Bernicia were joined in a union never henceforth to be dissolved.[1]   At the head of the united people of Northumbria, Oswiu at last grew strong enough to break the power of Penda, who was defeated and slain at the battle of the Winwæd in 655.[2]   With the fall of Penda, English heathenism came to an end, and Oswiu became one of the greatest of the bretwaldas.   Under Oswiu and his son Ecgfrith, Northumbria continued to be a great state, but its claim to predominance really ends in 659 with the revival of the Mercian power under the leadership of Wulfhere.   After that event Northumbria abandoned the struggle for supremacy to Mercia and Wessex.[3]

Oswiu finally unites Bernicia and Deira.

Northumbria gives place to Mercia.

6.   Just a century after the beginning of the overlordship of Northumbria, the Christian Mercians appear as a great power in Mid-Britain under the leadership of their aggressive king Æthelbald, who ascended the Mercian throne in 718.[4]   As long as the victorious Ine remained king of the West Saxons, his realm remained free from Mercian aggression; but, in the confusion which followed Ine's voluntary abandonment of the crown, Æthelbald overran the whole of Wessex during a war which seems to have terminated in 733.[5]   For twenty years after that event, the overlordship of Mercia was recognized by all the English south of the Humber.   But the Mercian supremacy was broken at last by the West Saxons in 754,[6] upon the field of Burford, where Æthelbald and his subject hosts were put to flight.   In 758 Æthelbald was succeeded by his great kinsman Offa, who entered with zeal upon the task of rebuilding the Mercian power.   He more than once invaded Wessex; and Kent, East Anglia, Essex, and Sussex were brought more or less under his sway.[7]   Although the power of Offa, as king of

Supremacy of Mercia.

Æthelbald.

Mercian supremacy broken by Wessex in 754.

Offa rebuilds the Mercian power.

---

[1] Green, *Making of England*, p. 289.
[2] Bæda, *Hist. Eccl.*, iii. 24. "The strife between the creeds of Christ and Woden was there finally decided; the Mercians embraced the religion of their neighbors, and Northumberland again became the leading power of Britain." — Freeman, *Norm. Conq.*, vol. i. p. 25.
[3] Green, *Making of England*, p. 298.
[4] Cf. Freeman, *Norm. Conq.*, vol. i. p. 25.
[5] *E. Chron.*, a. 733; Green, *Making of Eng.*, p. 384.

[6] *E. Chron.*, a. 752. From 752 to 849 (from the death of Bæda to the reign of Ethelwulf), the entries of the English Chronicle are wrong by two years. See Stubbs, *Roger of Hoveden*, preface to vol. i. p. lxxxix.; Freeman, *Norm. Conq.*, vol. i. p. 76, note 3; Green, *Making of England*, p. 384, note 4; Huntington, *Hist. Angl.* (Arnold), p. 121.
[7] Freeman, *Norm. Conq.*, vol. i p. 26.

the Mercians, rose high enough to tempt him to aspire to a correspondence upon equal terms with Charles the Great, he was never able to establish an overlordship over either of the rival kingdoms of Northumbria and Wessex. Upon **Cenwulf.** Offa's death in 796,[1] he was succeeded by Cenwulf, who during a reign of twenty-five years managed to hold the Mercian realm together, without being able to extend its supremacy.[2]

Final supremacy of Wessex. 7. The kingdom of the Gewissas, who became more widely known as the West Saxons, grew by degrees out of a small settlement established on the coast of Hampshire by an invading host led by the ealdormen, Cerdic and Cynric. We learn from the Chronicle, which records every step in the conquest of Wessex, that the first attack upon the coast was made in 495, and that this was followed by what seem to have been mere plundering raids in 501 and 508. Not until 514 was a landing made for the purpose of permanent conquest.[3] After five years of successful warfare, political organization took place, whereupon the ealdormen, **Cerdic and Cynric first kings of the West Saxons.** Cerdic and Cynric, were advanced to the dignity of kings of the West Saxons.[4] A long pause then followed in the advance of the invaders; for thirty years (520–552) they remained within the limits of Hampshire. At the end of that period the work of invasion was vigorously renewed, and within the next twenty years the Gewissas overran an area which roughly corresponds with that now embraced within the shires of Wilts, Berks, Surrey, Oxford, Bedford, and Bucks.[5] Wheeling then to the west, the invaders advanced from the Wiltshire Downs to the conquest of the lower **Battle of Deorham (577) secures the Severn valley.** Severn valley, which was won by the battle of Deorham in 577.[6] The conquerors, who then settled down on either side of the Severn in what is now Gloucestershire and Worcestershire, took to themselves the local name of Hwiccas. But the West Saxon advance soon received a terrible check

---

[1] *E. Chron.*, a 794 (6).
[2] Green, *Making of Eng.*, pp. 413–418.
[3] *E. Chron.*, a. 495, a. 501, a. 508, a. 514; Green, *Making of Eng.*, p. 84; Guest, *E. E. Settlements in Britain* (Salisbury volume of Archæological Institute).

[4] *E. Chron.*, a. 519.
[5] Freeman, *Norm. Conq.*, vol. i. p. 17; Green, *Making of Eng.*, p. 120.
[6] *E. Chron.*, a. 577; Guest, "Conquest of Severn Valley," *Archæological Journal*, xix. 194; Green, *Making of Eng.*, p. 124.

upon the upper Severn at a spot called Faddiley, where Ceawlin must have suffered a crushing defeat at the hands of the Welsh.[1] This defeat, which was most disastrous to the power of Wessex, was followed in a few years by a still greater misfortune in the form of a violent dissension in the royal house. Not long after the defeat at Faddiley the Hwiccas rose in revolt and took as their king Ceol or Ceolric, the son of Ceawlin's dead brother Cutha. The struggle for the throne which now arose between these rival lines continued to divide and weaken the power of Wessex for more than two hundred years.[2] And during this whole period of internal dissension, the advance of Wessex to a position of supremacy was further embarrassed by a constant dread of attack in the rear from the Welsh, who still remained unconquered in the southwestern peninsula.[3] Not until early in the ninth century did the last of the Britons in Cornwall bend to the West Saxon supremacy.[4] During this long interval of internal distraction, and war against the Welsh, the real power of Wessex only asserted itself at intervals, when some great king like Ine arose strong enough to gather for a time all the Gewissas under his sway. Near the close of the eighth century Ecgberht, a descendant of Ceawlin, made an unsuccessful attempt to wrest the West Saxon crown from the rival branch of the house of Cerdic, and, when driven into exile, found shelter for a time at Offa's court.[5] Expelled at last through West Saxon intrigue from the Mercian realm, Ecgberht sought a refuge (787) at the court of Charles the Great, where he witnessed the momentous events which transpired during the thirteen years that preceded the elevation of the mighty Frank to the throne of the Cæsars.[6] Two years after Charles had been crowned Emperor of the Romans, Ecgberht returned to Wessex (802) to mount the throne made vacant by the death of his rival, Beorhtric.[7] The first serious enterprise to which Ecgberht

Marginal notes:

Defeated by the Welsh in 584.

Internal dissensions weaken Wessex for two centuries.

Welsh in their rear remain unconquered until 815.

Ecgberht, the eighth and last bretwalda;

visits the court of Charles the Great;

ascends the throne of Wessex in 802.

---

[1] *E. Chron.*, a. 584; Guest, "Conquest of Severn Valley," pp. 196–199; Green, *Making of Eng.*, p. 200.

[2] *Making of Eng.*, p. 201.

[3] "Wessex was still engaged in its long struggle with the Welsh, and was in no position to aspire to the dominion of Britain." — Freeman, *Norm. Conq.*, vol. i. p. 25.

[4] Ibid., vol. i. p. 28.

[5] *E. Chron.*, a. 784 (6), a. 787 (9); Green, *Making of Eng.*, p. 409.

[6] Freeman, *Norm. Conq.*, vol. i. pp. 26, 27; Green, *Making of Eng.*, p. 415.

[7] *E. Chron.*, 800 (802).

Final conquest of Cornwall, 815.

devoted himself after his accession was the final subjugation of the West Welsh. In 815 he marched into the heart of Cornwall, and after a struggle of eight years the power of the Cornish Britons was finally broken and the supremacy of Wessex extended to the Land's End.[1] With all internal dissensions crushed beneath the power of Ecgberht, and with all fear of attack from the Welsh finally dispelled, the West Saxons, whose unity as a people had never been broken, were now ready to assume the leadership of the English nation. The first great conflict naturally arose with Mercia, whose

Overthrow of Mercia and Northumbria.

king, Beornwulf, invaded Wessex in 825. After the battle at Ellandun, in which Beornwulf was overthrown, the Mercian realm was deprived of all external dominion, and all of the English south of the Thames submitted to Ecgberht.[2] Four years later (829) Mercia herself was forced to yield to the victor of Ellandun, and in the same year the once great kingdom of Northumbria, now weakened by civil divisions, voluntarily accepted the West Saxon supremacy.[3] Thus,

Ecgberht unites all the kingdoms under the sway of the house of Cerdic.

after two centuries of struggle, in which the greatest kings of Northumbria and Mercia had failed, Ecgberht, the eighth and last in the list of bretwaldas, brought about a forced union of all the English kingdoms under the sway of the house of Cerdic. In the hour of victory the king of the West Saxons ventured, for once at least, to style himself king of the English.[4]

From Ecgberht to Eadgar (829–958).

8. Through the conquests of Ecgberht all the Teutonic states in Britain became mere dependencies of Wessex, as under-kingdoms, ruled either by their own royal lines or by some prince of the house of Cerdic. Each conquered state as it was annexed entered into dependent relations with Wessex, without a sacrifice of its autonomy.[5] But a century and a half had yet to pass by before these loosely united states became incorporated as integral parts of one consolidated king-

---

[1] *E. Chron.*, a. 813 (815), 823 (825); Freeman, *Norm. Conq.*, vol. i. p. 28.

[2] *E. Chron.*, a. 823 (825).

[3] *E. Chron.*, a. 827 (829).

[4] "Ecgberhtus gratiâ Dei Rex Anglorum." — *Cod. Dip.*, i. 287; Freeman, *Norm. Conq.*, vol. i. p. 26, note 4.

[5] "In his reign of thirty-six years (802–837) he reduced all the English kingdoms to a greater or less degree of subjection. The smaller states seem to have willingly submitted to him as a deliverer from the power of Mercia. East Anglia became a dependent ally; Kent and the smaller Saxon kingdoms were more closely incorporated with the ruling state (825)." — Freeman, *Norm. Conq.*, vol. i. p. 27.

dom.   The history of this process of consolidation is inseparably connected with the history of the Danish invasions, The Dan-
whose pressure had begun to be felt, even before the work of ish inva-
union had been finally accomplished.   The Northmen from sions;
the isles of the Baltic and from either side of the Scandinavian peninsula, who began about the end of the eighth century to harry and plunder the coasts of Britain and of northern Gaul, were men of the purest Teutonic blood and speech,
genuine kinsmen of the founders of the English kingdoms, —
kinsmen who had not yet emerged from the barbaric life and
from the primitive heathenism of their forefathers.   For more
than half a century after the keels of these marauders first at first
touched the shores of Britain (789–855), they confined them- mere p¹
selves to mere plundering raids in which they would secure dering
their booty and then sail away again.[1]   The Chronicler tells raids.
us that in 855 the heathen men wintered for the first time in
the isle of Sheppy.[2]   From that time to the end of the ninth Period of
century, the Danes, who now came in larger bodies, seriously conquest
engaged in the work of conquest and permanent settlement. and perma-
nent settle-
In the reign of Æthelred the First (866–871) the full force of ment.
Danish invasion broke upon the loosely united realm which
his grandfather Ecgberht had built up.   Northumbria, still
rent by internal divisions, was the first to yield to the invaders,[3] who soon completely conquered East Anglia and a part
of Mercia.[4]   The national cause now depended alone upon Ælfred
the hosts of Wessex, led by king Æthelred and by his brother and the
Danes.
Ælfred.   In the midst of the conflict Æthelred died, and the
defence of the realm passed into the hands of one who
divides with Washington alone the honor of being the most
perfect outcome of the English nation.   In 878 so over-
whelming was the force of the invasion that Ælfred was
obliged to hide as a fugitive in the marshes of Somerset;
and for a time it seemed as if the standard of Woden had
triumphed alike over the Dragon of Wessex and over the
standard of Christ.   But, after a great victory won by Ælfred Peace of
Wedmore
in the same year, the invaders entered into a solemn peace at in 878.

[1] Freeman, *Norm. Conq.*, vol. i. p.
29.
[2] *E. Chron.*, a. 855.
[3] As to the conquest of Northumbria, see Robertson's *Scotland under*

Early Kings, vol. ii. p. 430; Freeman's
Norm. Conq., Apendix KK, vol. i. p.
436.
[4] Green, *Hist. of the English People*,
vol. i. pp. 72, 73.

Wedmore, whereby "all Northumbria, all East Anglia, all Central England east of a line which stretched from Thames' mouth along the Lea to Bedford, thence along the Ouse to Watling Street, and by Watling Street to Chester, was left

subject to the Northmen." [1] Within this Danelagh, which embraced more than one half of the empire of Ecgberht, the Danes settled down among the conquered English as lords of the soil. The customary law which grew up within the Danelagh, the name applied to the region in which Danish law prevailed, varied only in small particulars from English customary law; new names rather than new customs date from the Danish occupation. [2] The settlement of a foreign foe in the land inevitably tended to consolidate, for the purpose of common defence, all that part of the English nation that remained within the limits of West Saxon dominion.

All Eng-
land out-
side of the
Danelagh
grew into a
compact
kingdom.

Under the pressure of this influence, all England southwest of Watling Street fast grew into a compact and homogeneous kingdom. Ælfred, at his death in 901, [3] left the Danes in quiet possession of the whole district ceded to them by the Peace of Wedmore; the task of reconquering the Danelagh he

transmitted to his children. Eadward the Elder, who succeeded Ælfred, did not enter, however, upon the execution of this task, until driven into war by a great rising of the Northmen in the tenth year after his father's death. [4] Before the end of his reign Eadward had recovered from the Danes the whole of Mercia, Essex, and East Anglia; and, by their annexation to his own kingdom, he became the immediate sovereign of all the English south of the Humber. [5] After the

death of Eadward, his son Æthelstan completed the conquest of the Danelagh by incorporating Northumbria as an integral part of the realm. But the reigns of Æthelstan's successors, Eadmund and Eadred (940–955), continued to be disturbed by revolts in the north, until the final extinction of the Northumbrian kings. [6] Not until the death of the last Danish

---

[1] See Ælfred and Guthrum's Peace, Thorpe's *Laws and Institutes*, vol. i. p. 152; Green, *Hist. of English People*, vol. i. p. 75.

[2] Cf. Freeman, *Norm. Conq.*, vol. i. p. 32, and Appendix E.

[3] *E. Chron.*, a. 901.

[4] *E. Chron.*, a. 910.

[5] Eadward also extended the supremacy of Wessex over the whole island of Britain. The princes of Wales, Northumbria, Scotland, and Strathclyde "chose him to father and to lord." — *E. Chron.*, a. 924.

[6] "Dogged as his fight had been, the Northman at last owned himself beaten.

king of Northumbria in 954 did the phantom of provincial royalty pass forever away. From that time forth the great realm of the north was governed by an earl or ealdorman appointed by the national king.[1] For a time after the death of Eadred (955) the kingdom was divided between his nephews, Eadwig and Edgar. Eadwig died in 958,[2] and the realm was then reunited under Eadgar the Peaceful, whose tranquil reign of seventeen years constitutes the most glorious period in the history of the West Saxon Empire. The death of Eadwig and the final extinction of all provincial royalty paved the way for Eadgar's accession to the threefold sovereignty of the West Saxons, Mercians, and Northumbrians.[3] Engle, Saxon, and Dane were united under his sway; he became the sole and immediate king of all the English; and in his time the name of Britain passed into that of Englaland, the land of Englishmen.[4] The growth of a real national unity was now complete; the consolidated kingdom of England was made not only in fact but in name. "Wessex has grown into England, England into Great Britain, Great Britain into the United Kingdom, the United Kingdom into the British Empire. Every prince who has ruled England before and since the eleventh century has had the blood of Cerdic the West Saxon in his veins."[5]

Eadgar the Peaceful unites Engle, Saxon, and Dane under his sway.

Britain becomes Englaland.

From the moment of Eadred's final triumph, all resistance came to an end." — Green, *Hist. of the English People,* vol. i. p. 86.

[1] Freeman, *Norm. Conq.,* vol. i. p. 41.

[2] *E. Chron.,* a. 958.

[3] "The last Danish king of Northumbria was killed in 954. In 959 Edgar succeeded to the kingdom of the West Saxons, Mercians, and Northumbrians." — Stubbs, *Const. Hist.,* vol. i.

p. 173, note 4. See, also, Robertson's *Hist. Essays,* pp. 203–216.

[4] "It was not till Eadgar's day that the name of Britain passed into the name of Engla-land, the land of Englishmen, England." — Green, *Hist. of the Eng. People,* vol. i. p. 96. Upon the use of the word "English," see Freeman, *Norm. Conq.,* vol. i., Appendix A.

[5] Freeman, *Norm. Conq.,* vol. i. p. 16.

CHAPTER V.

THE CONSTITUTION OF THE CONSOLIDATED KINGDOM.

The shire system, — its growth a vital element in process of national development.

1. THE growth of the consolidated kingdom, outlined in the preceding chapter, embraces three distinct periods of development: the union of the early settlements or primitive states in heptarchic kingdoms; the forced union of the heptarchic kingdoms under the supremacy of Wessex; the period of consolidation which, beginning with Ecgberht, ends with Eadgar. With the history of this process of national development the growth of the shire system is inseparably interlaced. It has been heretofore maintained that the primitive states in which the settlers originally grouped themselves in Britain were reproductions in every material particular of the continental Teutonic states as described by Cæsar and Tacitus. The unit of organization in the primitive state was the village-community, which appears in Britain as the

The early shire formed by a union of townships.

tun or township.[1] By a union of townships was formed the district generally known in Germany as a *gau* or *gá*, a name which yielded in England to that of *scir* or *shire*. By a union of *gás* or shires was formed the primitive state.[2] The scir or shire was simply what the word itself implies, a division of a larger whole; and it is now maintained, with greater or less emphasis, by the highest authorities, that scir or shire was the term originally employed in Britain to describe the district which arose out of a union of townships.[3] But the early shire, which thus represented the largest division of the primitive state, must not be confounded with the modern

The modern shire identical with the primitive state.

shire, which represents the largest division of the consolidated kingdom. The primitive states, advancing in the path of political confederation, united in forming the seven or eight aggregates generally known as the heptarchic kingdoms. Mercia seems to have grown up through the joining

---

[1] See above, p. 143.
[2] See above, pp. 119, 123.

[3] *Essays in A. S. Law*, p. 18; Stubbs, *Const. Hist.*, vol. i. pp. 96–101.

together of a number of smaller states in which the prevailing blood was Anglian. Wessex simply represented a union of kindred principalities, each one of which retained its own under-king. Out of the union of the North and South Folk arose East Anglia; Kent was probably formed by a double settlement in the same way; while Northumbria arose out of the union of Bernicia and Deira.[1] By the final triumph of Ecgberht the several heptarchic unions were forced to unite in a single comprehensive union under the sway of the house of Cerdic. In this new union the conquered states preserved their existence as such, during a long period of time, to the greatest practicable extent. Each state, while still retaining its ancient boundaries and its tribal king, simply entered, at first, into more or less dependent relations with Wessex. But with the triumph of Ecgberht begins the work of consolidation which occupies nearly a century and a half in its completion.[2] In the process of consolidation local kingship becomes extinct, and the primitive states are finally incorporated with Wessex, — they cease to exist as states and become shires. And as the primitive states thus descend in status, their own shires necessarily descend in the same way, — they cease to be shires and become hundreds. Thus it may be assumed, as a general principle, "that *the state of the seventh century became the shire of the tenth, while the shire of the seventh century became the hundred of the tenth.*"[3] The use of the word "shire "in its enlarged and modern sense seems to have been introduced during or shortly after the reign of Ecgberht;[4] but the name of the hundred does not occur until the laws of Eadgar,[5] in whose time the arrangement of the whole kingdom in shires was probably completed.[6] The map of the England of to-day clearly discloses the origin of the modern shire in what has been called the primitive state. Out of the principalities founded by the Somersætas, the Dorsætas, the Wilsætas, the Middle Sax-

With the triumph of Ecgberht the work of consolidation begins.

"The state of the seventh century became the shire of the tenth, while the shire of the seventh century became the hundred of the tenth."

---

[1] See above, pp. 146, 147.
[2] See above, p. 154.
[3] See Essay upon the "Anglo-Saxon Courts of Law," by Mr. Henry Adams, in *Essays in A. S. Law*, p. 19.
[4] Ibid., p. 20.
[5] Eadgar, i. Constitutio de hundredis.
[6] "The arrangement of the whole

kingdom in shires is of course a work which could not be completed until it was permanently united under Edgar; and the existing subdivisions of Southern England are traceable back to his day at the latest." — Stubbs, *Const. Hist.*, vol. i. p. 110.

Historical origin of certain of the modern shires.

ons, the East Saxons, the South Folk, and the North Folk, have grown the shires of Somerset, Dorset, Wilts, Middlesex, Essex, Suffolk, and Norfolk. Hampshire, Berkshire, and Devonshire are equally ancient, being mentioned in the Chronicle as shires as far back as the reign of Æthelwulf.[1] Kent and Sussex are two of the heptarchic kingdoms, whose original shires are perhaps represented by their lathes and rapes.[2] In Wessex the shire system attained its earliest and purest devolopment. The West Saxon shires retain to this day the names and boundaries of the early settlements founded by the successors of Cerdic. It is more than likely, however, from the evidence of local nomenclature, that Mercia was artificially divided into shires by the English kings after its reconquest from the Danish invaders.[3]

An outline of the constitution in the tenth century.

2. As the history of the Old-English commonwealth is incomplete and fragmentary, it is impossible to do more than define with approximate correctness the broader outlines of the several stages of growth through which it passed in the course of its constitutional development. By the end of the sixth century, the primitive states have become bound up in the seven or eight aggregates generally known as the heptarchic kingdoms. After two centuries of struggle (600–829), the heptarchic kingdoms are united under the supremacy of Wessex. A period of a century and a quarter (829–958) then ensues, during which the united kingdom of Ecgberht becomes finally consolidated under Eadgar. During the tenth century three facts stand out prominently in the general result: the incorporation of the primitive states in a single consolidated kingdom; the transformation of the prim-

Central powers of the state vested in the king and witan; local administration, in the shires.

itive state into the modern shire; the progressive consolidation and growth of the kingly power. The central and national powers of the consolidated kingdom are vested in the witenagemot and the king, while the whole system of local administration is vested in the shires. The consolidated kingdom is, in fact, a mere aggregation of shires, whose gov-

---

[1] *E. Chron.*, a. 851, 860.

[2] "Kent, however, appears as 'Cantescyre' as early as the reign of Athelstan. Essex, Middlesex, and Surrey are also ancient kingdoms." — Stubbs, *Const. Hist.*, vol. i. p. 109.

[3] "In short, the local divisions of Wessex were not made but grew. Mercia, on the other hand, has every appearance of having been artificially mapped out." — Freeman, *Norm. Conq.*, vol. i. p. 32, and Appendix, note E.

ernments represent the entire local machinery of the constitution.[1] Or, to state the matter in another form, "now the kingdom forms a new whole, of which the shires have sunk to be mere administrative divisions."[2] The primitive state, in descending to the status of a shire, preserves substantially all of its powers as a local self-governing community. The tribal king has passed away, it is true, and his place has been filled by the ealdorman, who stands in the government of the shire as the deputy of the national king;[3] but the popular assemblies of the primitive state all survive as parts of the shire system. The primitive state assembly is the folk-moot, the highest popular court of the shire, and as such it retains some traces of the ancient nationality.[4] The primitive shire court survives as the hundred-court of the consolidated kingdom; the ordinary law court in which all causes are heard in the first instance. Beneath the hundred-courts stand the tun-moots, the governing bodies of the village-communities or townships. In the organization of these local courts, the fundamental Teutonic principle is preserved intact; the administration of law, as well as local political administration, is vested in an expanding series of popular assemblies composed of the qualified freemen whose interests are directly involved. If the constitutional powers of the consolidated kingdom be classified in accordance with modern ideas, the executive power was vested in the king; the legislative, in the king and the witan; the judicial, in the witan and the local courts. In accordance with this classification the attempt will be made to present an approximately correct idea of the form in which the constitution appeared in the tenth and eleventh centuries, after the work of consolidation had been finally accomplished.

The folk-moot survives as the shire-moot, — early shire-moot as the hundred-moot.

Classification of the central state powers according to modern ideas.

[1] Speaking of the local institutions of the Old - English commonwealth, Guizot says: "Vigorous institutions were they, which feudalism could not overthrow, and which produced, at a later period, representative government in England."—*Hist. Rep. Gov.,* p. 45.

[2] Freeman, *Norm. Conq.,* vol. i. p. 67.

[3] Sohm, *Altd. R.- u. G. Verf.* i. 25, 26.

[4] The bishops of Kent and all the thegns, eorl and ceorl, of Kentshire, declare to Æthelstan in their gemot at Faversham their acceptance of measures taken in the recent witenagemot of Greatley. For the document containing this popular acceptance of a law, see Thorpe, vol. i. p. 216: for comments upon it, see Kemble, *Saxons in England,* vol. ii. p. 233, 234; Hallam, *M. A.,* vol. ii. p. 376; Palgrave, *Commonwealth,* p. 637; Stubbs, *Const. Hist.,* vol. i. p. 115.

3. The early history of Teutonic kingship has already been briefly reviewed. The fact was then ascertained that, in the home-land, kingship prevailed in some of the tribes, and in others it did not.[1] From Cæsar's sketch the conclusion has been drawn that kingship was the exception and not the rule.[2] Tacitus clearly distinguishes the monarchical tribes from the non-monarchical, without intimating the extent to which royalty prevailed.[3] Bæda affirmatively states the fact that kingship did not prevail among the Saxons, who were governed by many satraps, from whom one was chosen by lot as a leader whenever war was imminent. When the war ended, the satraps resumed their coequal powers.[4] The satrap of Bæda, who corresponds in every material particular with the *princeps* of Cæsar and Tacitus, is recognized by the great Alfred, in his translation of Bæda, as the ealdorman.[5] The highest authorities agree in the conclusion that the chiefs who led the war-bands to the conquest of Britain bore no higher title than that of ealdorman or *heretoga*.[6] In A. D. 449 the Jutish war-bands landed under the command of two *heretogans*, Hengest and Horsa,[7] and in 455 Horsa was slain, and Hengest and Æsc, his son, obtained the kingdom.[8] In A. D. 495 two ealdormen came to Britain, Cerdic and Cynric his son ;[9] and in 519 they became kings of the West Saxons.[10] As the conquest advanced, and as definite districts of country were permanently secured, and as the various groups of conquerors within such districts felt the need of drawing together under a permanent instead of a temporary leadership, the ealdorman or *heretoga* was advanced to the dignity of a

as were all
the other
tribes that
engaged in
the con-
quest.

---

[1] See above, pp. 128, 129.

[2] "In pace, nullus est communis magistratus ; sed principes regionum atque pagorum inter suos jus dicunt." — *Bell. Gall.*, vi. 23.

[3] Tac., *Germ.*, cc. 25, 44.

[4] "Non enim habent regem iidem Antiqui Saxones, sed satrapas plurimos suæ genti præpositos, qui ingruente belli articulo mittunt æqualiter sortes, et quemcunque sors ostenderit, hunc tempore belli ducem omnes sequuntur, huic obtemperant ; peracto autem bello rursum æqualis potentiæ omnes fiunt satrapæ." — *Hist. Eccl.*, v. 10.

[5] Smith's *Bæda*, p. 674 ; Stubbs, *Const. Hist.*, vol. i. p. 42.

[6] Kemble, *Saxons in Eng.*, vol. ii. pp. 2, 125 ; Freeman, *Norm. Conq.*, vol. i. p. 51, and Appendix K ; Stubbs, *Const. Hist.*, vol. i. p. 66 ; Green, *Making of Eng.*, p. 171.

[7] "Heora *heretogan* wæron twegen gebroðra, Hengest and Horsa." — *E. Chron.*, a. 449.

[8] *E. Chron.*, a. 455.

[9] "Her comen twegen *ealdormen* on Brytene Cerdic and Cynric his súnu." — *E. Chron.*, a. 495.

[10] "Her Cerdic and Cynric Westseaxena *rice* onfengon." — *E. Chron.*, 519.

king,[1] who could represent in his person the unity of a new national life.   In order to attach the idea of permanency to the new kingship, the name of the son was associated with that of the father as a recognition of the hereditary principle;[2] and, in order to impart sanctity to the person of the new king, fable at once traced his descent in an unbroken line from Woden.[3]   But the recognition of the hereditary principle was attended and modified by the older principle of election.[4] The right to the throne might be vested by the original choice in a single royal house, but the question as to which member of that house should receive the succession when a vacancy occurred was one which the national assembly alone could determine.   Just how far the power and dignity of a king exceeded that of an ealdorman it is difficult to ascertain, but it is quite clear that the title of king did imply an advance in both respects.   It is probable that the king was not chosen until a group of war-bands, each under its own ealdorman, had united in the formation of a kingdom. In that way the king was advanced to the supreme command, and to national authority, while the ealdorman descended to the status of a subordinate who still possessed the highest command in his own district.[5]   Out of the Teutonic conquest of Britain thus arose a brood of petty tribal kings whose presence in every principality retarded the growth of national unity for centuries.

Kingship in Britain an outgrowth of conquest.

Hereditary principle limited by the right of election.

The new king who thus arose out of the conquest was the king of a nation, the leader of his people, the head of the race, and not the king of a country and lord of the soil.   The idea of a territorial as distinguished from a tribal sovereignty was the growth of later times.[6]   In war the king, as leader of the host, possessed supreme command, while in peace his powers were coördinate with the national assembly, with whose concurrence he performed all important acts.   He maintained,

Growth of the new kingship.

---

[1] "The word *rice* I take to mark the change from ealdormanship to kingship." — Freeman, *Norm. Conq.*, vol. i. p. 392, Appendix K.

[2] Stubbs, *Const. Hist.*, vol. i. p. 67.

[3] "And the possession of Woden's blood was the indispensable condition of kingship." — Kemble, *Saxons in Eng.*, vol. i. p. 329.

[4] "The elective principle is the safeguard of their freedom; the monarchical principle is the condition of their nationality." — Ibid., p. 137.

[5] Upon the change from ealdormen to kings, see Freeman, *Norm. Conq.*, vol. i. pp. 51, 52; Green, *Making of Eng.*, p. 171.

[6] See above, p. 130.

Peace and
justice be-
long at first
not to the
king, but to
the folk.
not his own peace, but the national peace, and executed justice on the breakers of it : but justice was not yet the king's
justice; it was the justice of the village, the shire, and the
folk, in whose moots was vested jurisdiction.[1] As the process
of aggregation advanced, as the primitive states became
bound up in the seven or eight heptarchic kingdoms which
were finally united under the rule of a single royal house, the
institution of kingship grew with each extension of territory.
As an heptarchic king rose in power and importance above
the petty royal head of a primitive state, so did the king of all
the English rise in power and importance above the heptarchic king.   In the process of aggregation was thus involved

In the
growth of
kingship is
involved all
the ele-
ments of
constitu-
tional life.
the growth of kingship, and in the growth of kingship were
involved all the elements of constitutional life.[2]   At the time
Ecgberht united the heptarchic kingdoms under the supremacy of Wessex, local kingship was far from extinct.   But in
the process of consolidation which then set in, the smaller
royalties gradually died out.   Provincial royalty lingered,
however, in Northumbria until the death of the last Danish
king in 954.   A few years after that event, Eadgar succeeded
to the threefold sovereignty of the West Saxons, Mercians
and Northumbrians, and thus became the first sole and immediate king of all the English.   Every royal house to which
conquest had given birth was now extinct except the West
Saxon house of Cerdic : as the fittest it survived.[3]

The chieftains, ealdormen or *heretogan*, who led the war-
bands to the conquest of Britain, came attended with their
comites, and their fortunes advanced together.   In return for
their fidelity and service the *comites* expected to receive from
their chief whatever of bounty lay in his power to bestow, but
it was a part of his absolute duty to supply them from his
own board with their daily bread.   The *princeps*, therefore,
becomes in Old-English the hlaford, the loaf-giver, a term
which, by an entire departure from its original meaning,
finally softened down into the modern form of lord.   As

[1] Stubbs, *Const. Hist.*, vol. i. p. 68 ;
Green, *Making of England*, p. 172.
[2] Upon the growth of kingship see
Kemble's chapter i. (vol. ii.) on the
"Growth of the Kingly Power ;" Freeman, *Norm. Conq.*, vol. i. p. 53.
[3] "At last Edgar, having outlived

the Northumbrian royalty and made up
his mind to consolidate Dane, Angle,
and Saxon, receives the crown as King
of all England and transmits it to his
son." — Stubbs, *Const. Hist.*, vol. i. p.
173.   See, also, Robertson's *Hist. Essays*, pp. 203-216.

heretofore explained, the most important outcome of the *comitatus* was the relation of lord and man, a relation at first purely personal, and not necessarily connected with the holding of land. As the smaller kingdoms grew into a single kingdom, and as the king of the one united kingdom became the king of the whole nation, the relation of lord and man widened into the principle that the king was the lord or patron of his people.[1] In the legislation of Ælfred the relation existing between the king and his subjects is distinctly recognized as that between lord and man : "If any one plot against the king's life, of himself or by harboring of exiles, or of his men, let him be liable in his life and in all that he has. If he desire to prove himself true, let him do so according to the king's wergild. So also we ordain for all degrees, whether eorl or ceorl. He who plots against his lord's life, let him be liable in his life to him and in all that he has, or let him prove himself true according to his lord's wer."[2] The same principle is restated in the laws of Eadward the Elder,[3] and with greater emphasis in those of his son Eadmund.[4] These enactments fix the time of the transition from the old to the new relation.[5] And as the king of the nation becomes the lord and patron of his people, the national peace, which from the beginning was under his protection, becomes the king's peace, enforcible by his personal servants.[6] By imperceptible degrees the nation is merged in the person of the king, who is finally regarded as the source of all peace and law, which are supposed to die with him, and to rise again with the advent of his successor. "The sovereign was the fountain of justice ; therefore the stream ceased to flow when the well-spring was covered by the tomb. The judicial bench vacant, all tribunals closed. Such was the ancient doctrine, — a doctrine still recognized in Anglo-Norman England."[7]

The king becomes the lord of his people,—

so recognized in the early laws.

The national peace becomes the king's peace.

The king becomes the source of justice.

---

1 Stubbs, *Const. Hist.*, vol. i. p. 176. See, also, on the "Relation of Lord and Man," Kenelm Digby, *Law of Real Property*, pp. 20–26.

2 Ælfred, § 4.

3 Eadward, ii. 1, § 1.

4 Eadmund, iii. § 1.

5 Stubbs, *Const. Hist.*, vol. i. p. 176.

6 "The old folk-community, as a confederacy bound to peace, was among the Anglo-Saxons held together by the king; and what was originally *folk-*

peace became *king's* peace, without materially changing its meaning."— *Essays in A. S. Law*, p. 271.

7 Palgrave, *Normandy and England*, vol. iii. p. 193; Stubbs, *Const. Hist.*, vol. i. p. 182. There is, however, another view of this question : "Neither at the beginning nor at the end of the Anglo-Saxon time was the king considered in law as the fountain of justice. The law was administered in the popular courts, theoretically, as the act

And as the idea gained ground that the king of the whole nation was the lord of the whole people, the correlative idea developed that the folkland, which originally belonged to the people in their collective capacity, was the property of the king.[1] It has been said by a great German writer that "folcland rests on the principle in the constitution that royal and public are not the same thing; that the king, not alone, but only at the head of the whole body of the people, represents the public power; that, therefore, the public objects are the objects of all, and the public property the property of all."[2] In primitive times the distinction was plainly drawn between the lands which the king owned as a private individual — the lands which were annexed to the crown, the royal demesne — and the folklands, the land of the people.[3] The king was first permitted to make grants out of the folkland to his followers and friends, with the counsel and consent of the witan.[4] But after the time of Ælfred the charters contain less and less frequently the clause expressing the consent of the witan, who gradually sink into the position of mere witnesses of the grant.[5] In this way the people's land begins to be spoken of as the king's folkland;[6] and it finally becomes virtually the land of the king, undistinguishable from the royal demesne. In this way the actual ownership of the folkland, and a sort of suzerainty over the rest of the land of the country, becomes vested in the king.[7]

By the force of the same principle through which the king changed his relation to the folkland, the king's thegns and the great ecclesiastical persons and bodies changed their relations to the waste lands which had origininally belonged to the cultivating groups composing the village-communities

The folkland becomes terra regis.

Growth of territorial lordships.

of the freemen."— *Essays in A. S. Law*, p. 26.

[1] Digby, *Law of Real Property*, pp. 18, 25, 59; Allen, *On the Royal Prerogative*, p. 150.

[2] Sohm, in the *Verfassungsgeschichte*, vol. i. p. 34; *Essays in A. S. Law*, p. 91.

[3] Digby, *Law of Real Property*, pp. 7, 8; *Essays in A. S. Law*, p. 92.

[4] "The witan possessed the power of recommending, assenting to, and guaranteeing, grants of lands, and of permitting the conversion of folcland into

bócland, and *vice versâ*." — Kemble, *Saxons in Eng.*, vol. ii. p. 225.

[5] "It would seem to follow from this that the folkland was becoming virtually king's land, from the moment that the West Saxon monarch became sole ruler of the English," etc. — Stubbs, *Const. Hist.*, vol. i. p. 193.

[6] See Nasse, *On the Agricultural Community of the Middle Ages* (Ouvry's translation), p. 28.

[7] Digby, *Law of Real Property*, p. 19.

or townships.[1] The history of this "process of feudalization" has already been drawn out.[2] As population increased, and as the primitive communal system became inadequate to its necessities, landless men settled down upon the estates of all the great proprietors, and organized thereon village-communities, whose general character was identical with that of the free communities, with one serious exception, — the title to the land occupied by the dependent community was vested not in itself, but in the lord.[3] As the principle of lord and man grew and widened, the free communities were gradually reduced to a dependent condition.[4] Through various processes the houselands and the arable of the once free townsmen became vested in a single lord, and in that event the waste or common lands passed as an incident. In this way the waste of the once free townsmen became the lord's waste, while the townsmen became his tenants.[5] After the Conquest, the dependent township appears as the manor of the lord;[6] the thegns represent all those who appear as tenants *in capite;*[7] the free holders of the tenemental lands correspond in the main to the free heads of households composing the old village-communities;[8] while those who originally occupied the lord's domain constitute the class of tenants whose tenures were in their origin servile.[9] Both classes of tenants, the free and the servile, were necessary to the existence of the manorial group,[10] which the lord held together through the agency of the court baron. Out of the relation of *princeps* and *comes*, originally embodied in the *comitatus*, thus grew the relation of lord and man, a relation which at first was

The dependent village-community

becomes the manor after the Conquest.

---

[1] "What has been said of the king applies also, though in a less degree, to the great men of the nation, the king's thegns and the great ecclesiastical persons and bodies." — Digby, *Law of Real Property*, p. 19.

[2] See above, p. 134, on the origin and growth of great estates.

[3] *Essays in A. S. Law*, pp. 84, 89.

[4] Upon the "Rise of the Manor out of the Mark," see Maine, *Village-Communities*, p. 143; Digby, *Law of Real Property*, p. 23.

[5] "In this way were the lands of the manor substituted for those of the community." — *Essays in A. S. Law*, p. 90.

[6] Maine, *Village-Communities*, pp. 10, 133; "villas quas a manendo ma-

nerios vulgo vocamus," Ordericus Vitalis, lib. iv. c. 7; Stubbs, *Const. Hist.*, vol. i. p. 89; Digby, *Law of Real Property*, pp. 43, 53. The word *manerium* or manor appears, however, as early as the reign of Eadward the Confessor. See Ellis, *General Introduction to Domesday*, p. 225.

[7] Digby, p. 30; Stubbs, *Const. Hist.*, vol. i. p. 156.

[8] Maine, *Village-Com.*, p. 137.

[9] *Village-Com.*, pp. 134, 138; Digby, p. 50.

[10] Ibid., p. 134. If all the lands were held by free tenants the lord's authority ceased to be manorial, and became a seignory in gross, or mere lordship. — Digby, p. 50, note 3.

not necessarily connected with the holding of land. But this relation of lord and man, of king and his thegns, became intimately connected with the holding of land when the thegnhood developed in England into a territorial nobility. And the new relation which thus grew up between the king and his thegns was naturally reproduced on a smaller scale between the thegns and the great ecclesiastical persons and their dependents.[1]   As yet there is no organized feudalism; as yet there is no distinct conception of the relation of superior lord, mesne lord, and tenant; but the elements of all these relations exist, ready to be worked into that systematic feudal jurisprudence for which the Norman conquest prepared the way.[2]

All the elements of feudalism exist before the Conquest.

The movement from personal to territorial organization.

In the foregoing account of the growth of kingship is outlined the transition through which the primitive Teutonic system passed while the tribal communities, in which the settlers originally grouped themselves in Britain, were being welded into a single consolidated kingdom. The general nature of the transition has been described as a movement from personal to territorial organization,[3]—from a state of things in which personal freedom and political right were the dominant ideas, to a state of things in which these ideas have become bound up with and subservient to the relations arising out of the possession of land.[4]   In the primitive system the two hostile elements are present from the very beginning; the free, self-governing community, and the king or other lord, and his personal following.[5]   In the "process of feudalization" through which the free Teutonic communities pass, the king and the thegnhood gain the mastery and become the dominant powers in the constitution. The primitive conception of sovereign power, as originally embodied in the nation, in a great measure passes out of view, — the sovereignty of the nation becomes merged in its chief.

The free community passes through "the process of feudalization."

---

[1] Digby, *Law of Real Property*, p. 23.

[2] Freeman, *Norm. Conq.*, vol. i. p. 63.

[3] Palgrave, *English Commonwealth*, p. 62.

[4] "The Angel-cynn of Alfred becomes the Engla-lande of Canute." — Stubbs, *Const. Hist.*, vol. i. p. 166.

[5] "No wonder then if at a very early period the mark-organization, which contained within itself the seeds of its own decay, had begun to give way, and that a systematic *commendation*, as it was called, to the adjacent lords, was beginning to take place." — Kemble, *Saxons in Eng.*, vol. ii. p. 24; Freeman, *Norm. Conq.*, vol. i. p. 54.

The king becomes the lord and patron of his people ; the folkland becomes virtually the king's land ; the national peace becomes the king's peace ; the justice of the hundred and the folk becomes the king's justice ; the national officers become the king's officers ; and the national assembly — the witan — becomes more and more the king's council.[1] Every stage in the transition from the old to the new system is marked by an advance in the kingly power, and by a decrease of independence upon the part of local communities.[2]

It is now possible to estimate, in a general way, the nature and extent of the advance made by the royal power during the centuries in which the primitive tribal settlements were gradually consolidated in a single state. The growth of Old-English royalty reached its highest point in the person of Eadgar, who was not only the sole and immediate king of all the English, but also the suzerain lord of all the neighboring Celtic princes, the emperor of the whole isle of Britain.[3] A king of the consolidated kingdom, although hedged in by many constitutional restrictions, certainly occupied a position of great power and privilege. Although he could perform no important act of government without the consent of the national assembly, still he was no mere puppet in their hands, for the assembly was equally powerless to perform any act without his concurrence.[4] Although in strict theory the king was only one of the people, and as his title implied their child and not their father,[5] and dependent upon their election for his royalty, still he was the noblest of the people, and at the head of the state. The person of the king was guarded not only by the high price set upon his life as a person of royal blood, the *wergild* payable to his family in the event of his violent death, but it was also guarded by an equal amount, which was the price of his royalty, the *cynebot*, the fine due at the same time to his people.[6] The king's revenues which

Nature and extent of the royal authority.

Eadgar.

The king's wergild.

[1] See above, p. 147.

[2] "Each stage of amalgamation increased the kingly power ; each stage lessened the independence of local communities, and lessened the importance of their individual members." — Freeman, *Norm. Conq.*, vol. i. p. 67.

[3] Ibid., vol. i. pp. 44, 89.

[4] "Nothing is clearer in our early history than the personal agency of the king in everything that is done, and the unspeakable difference between a good and a bad king." — *Norm. Conq.*, vol. i. p. 77.

[5] On the origin of the word *king*, see *Norm. Conq.*, vol. i. p. 53, and Appendix L; Max Müller's *Lectures on the Science of Language*, vol. ii. pp. 282, 284; Grimm, *R. A.*, p. 230.

[6] Kemble, *Saxons in Eng.*, vol. ii. p.

Royal revenues not contingent upon legislative grants.

were not contingent upon legislative grants,[1] must have been amply sufficient to maintain the royal state and dignity. In addition to the private estates which he possessed as an individual, and which he could dispose of by will, the king enjoyed the use of the royal demesne, which belonged to him as king, and which he could neither burden nor alienate without the consent of the witan.[2] The king also received

Dues in the form of rents.

certain dues (*cyninges-gafol*) in the nature of rents, which were in their origin voluntary contributions,[3] but which finally became compulsory charges certainly upon all holders of folkland.[4] And in addition to the sums which thus accrued to the king from his private estates, the royal demesne, and the folkland, he received revenue from the following sources:

Receipts from fines, treasure-trove, and the like.

from the fines which were levied in the courts of law to the king's use, as conservator of the public peace;[5] from treasure-trove, wreck, mines, salt-works, and the mint;[6] from tolls, from markets and ports, and from transport by roads and navigable streams;[7] from the heriots which were assessed upon the estates of the king's special dependents according to their rank;[8] and from escheats and forfeitures.[9] The king had the right of maintenance for himself and suite when in public progress; and he had also the right to license the building of bridges and fortresses.[10] Thus supported and maintained by an independent revenue, the king was able to deal upon equal terms with the witan, with whose advice and consent he performed all important acts.

The legislative power: the king and the witan.

4. The supreme powers of the continental Teutonic state, whether monarchical or non-monarchical, were vested in a national assembly in which every freeman had his place.

29; Allen, *On the Prerogative*, pp. 36, 40.

[1] *Essays in A. S. Law*, p. 64.

[2] In a grant made about 980 by Æthelred to Abingdon he draws the distinction between his *propria hereditas* which he could alienate, and the *terræ regales et ad regios filios pertinentes*, whose alienation the witan had refused to sanction. — *Cod. Dipl.*, No. 1312; Kemble, *Saxons in England*, vol. ii. p. 30.

[3] Tac., *Germ.*, c. 15.

[4] *Essays in A. S. Law*, 64. See, also, Robertson, *Hist. Essays*, pp. 102,

112; Kemble, *Saxons in Eng.*, vol. ii. pp. 30, 223, 224. Kemble considers it a tax levied by the king and the witan, — a view which can hardly be correct.

[5] Kemble, *Saxons in Eng.*, vol. i. p. 151; vol. ii. pp. 54, 55.

[6] Ibid., vol. ii. pp. 55–73.

[7] Kemble, *Saxons in Eng.*, vol. ii. pp. 73–78, 94.

[8] Ibid., vol. ii. pp. 98–102.

[9] Ibid., vol. ii. p. 50; *Essays in A. S. Law*, p. 64 *seq.*

[10] Kemble, *Saxons in Eng.*, vol. ii. pp. 58, 91.

While all ordinary business was disposed of by a council composed of the *principes*, great matters were submitted by the *principes* to the general assembly of the people.[1] In the primitive kingdoms, in which the Teutonic settlers originally grouped themselves in Britain, the state assembly appears as the folk-moot, the meeting of the whole people in arms. In the structure of the folk-moot there is no departure from primitive traditions. By the time of the conversion, however, when for the first time it is possible to ascertain the form which Teutonic society in Britain had assumed, the primitive states have ceased to exist as independent communities, — they have become bound up in the seven or eight aggregates generally known as the heptarchic kingdoms. The national assemblies of these heptarchic kingdoms are not folk-moots but witenagemots ; they are not great popular assemblies of an entire nation, but small, aristocratic assemblies composed only of the great and wise men of the land.[2] In the absence of the principle of representation, it is quite possible to understand how an originally democratic assembly, into which the magnates of the land entered as the great factors, would naturally shrink up into a narrow aristocratic body composed of the magnates only, wherever the extent of territory to be traversed rendered it difficult for the mass of the people to attend. The results of this principle are practically the same, whether worked out in England or Achaia.[3] In the narrow districts of country occupied by the primitive states, it was possible for the folk-moots to preserve a continuous existence, for the reason that it was not inconvenient for the people to attend the meetings of a local assembly in which their interests were directly involved.[4] But as the process of aggregation

The folk-moot.

The witen-agemot.

Likeness between English and Achaian assemblies.

---

[1] "De minoribus rebus principes consultant, de majoribus omnes ; ita tamen ut ea quoque quorum penes plebem arbitrium est apud principes pertractentur." — Tac., *Germ.*, c. 11.

[2] See Kemble's chapter on the Witenagemot, *Saxons in England*, vol. ii. pp. 182–240; Freeman, *Norm. Conq.*, vol. i. p. 67, and Appendix Q ; Stubbs, *Const. Hist.*, vol. i. p. 119.

[3] "The Achaian assembly practically consisted of those among the inhabitants of each city who were at once wealthy men and eager politicians.

Those citizens came together who were at once wealthy enough to bear the cost of the journey and zealous enough to bear the trouble of it. . . . The congress, democratic in theory, was aristocratic in practice." — Freeman, *Hist. of Federal Government*, pp. 266, 267.

[4] "While the district whose members attend the folk-moot is still small, there is no great inconvenience in this method of proceeding." — *Saxons in Eng.*, vol. ii. p. 191.

advanced, the extent of territory to be traversed widened;
and it thus became more and more difficult for each individual freeman to attend the meetings of a national assembly
in whose proceedings he was only remotely concerned.[1] Furthermore, each advance in the process of aggregation was
attended by a corresponding increase in the power of the king
and thegnhood, and with a consequent depression of the popular power. By the combined force of these causes the mass
of the people, without the formal exclusion of any class, simply
ceased to attend assemblies in whose deliberations they could
take but a subordinate part. Thus, through a perfectly natural process, the folk-moot, the meeting of the people, was converted into a witenagemot, the meeting of the wise, in which
were considered all matters involving the general good.[2]
Such is the history of the witenagemot, whether considered
as the supreme council of an heptarchic state, or as the supreme council of the whole English nation when finally
united in a single consolidated kingdom.[3]

The folk-moot shrinks up into the witenage-mot.

It is impossible to ascertain at what exact period the change
was brought about through which the primary Teutonic assembly was converted into a narrow aristocratic body. The
change was no doubt a gradual one, which probably advanced,
pari passu, with the aggregation of the local communities.[4]
That such a change did take place, and that the whole body
of the people did retain for a long period of time the abstract
right to be present in the national gemot, may be implied
from a series of vestiges which, beginning with the Dooms of
Æthelberht, extend beyond the Norman conquest.[5] If it be
true, then, that every freeman did possess the abstract right
to be present in the national assembly, there is no reason for
the attempt to explain the presence of the great men who did

Composi-tion of the witan.

Every free-man re-tained the abstract right to be present in the national assembly.

---

[1] Kemble, *Saxons in England*, vol.
ii. p. 193.
[2] "The idea of representation had
not yet arisen; those who did not appear in person had no means of appearing by deputy. . . . By this process an originally democratic assembly, without any formal exclusion of
any class of its members, gradually
shrank up into an aristocratic assembly." — *Norm. Conq.*, vol. i. p. 68.
[3] Stubbs, *Const. Hist.*, vol. i. p. 119.
[4] "At what exact period the change

I have attempted to describe was effected is neither very easy to determine
nor very material. It was probably
very gradual and very partial; indeed,
it may never have been formally recognized, for here and there we find evident traces of the people's being present
at, and ratifying the decisions of, the
witan." — *Saxons in England*, vol. ii.
p. 195.
[5] For a collection of these vestiges
see Freeman's *Norm. Conq.*, vol. i.
Appendix Q.

in fact attend upon the theory of representation. The composition of the witenagemot is a subject which is involved in
the greatest obscurity; in no one of the ancient laws can be
found any positive enactment defining its constitution. From
the documents attested by the witan — the name by which
the members of the assembly are usually described — it appears that the great council was attended by the king, who   Witans
was sometimes accompanied by his wife and princes of the   composed
blood; by the archbishops, and all or some of the bishops and   of the king
and the
abbots, and sometimes by priests and deacons; by all or some   magnates.
of the ealdormen; and by a large number of *ministri* or king's
thegns, amongst whom were no doubt embraced the chief
officers of the royal household, as well as the most considerable of the king's personal dependents.[1] As the work of
consolidation advanced, the magnates of the conquered kingdoms became entitled to seats in the Witan of Wessex, which   Witan of
finally became the Great Council of the Empire.[2] The num-   Wessex became the
ber of the witan thus increased with the expansion of the   Great
Council of
realm. In a witenagemot held at Winchester in 934, in the   the Empire,
reign of Æthelstan, there were present the king, four Welsh
princes, two archbishops, seventeen bishops, four abbots,
twelve ealdormen, and fifty-two king's thegns, in all ninety-
two persons.[3] In another, held in 966, in the reign of Eadgar,
were present the king's mother, two archbishops, seven bishops, five ealdormen, and fifteen thegns, which is considered a
fair specimen of the usual proportion.[4] The highest number   and usually
given is one hundred and six; and it seems that from ninety   consisted
of about a
to a hundred was not an unusual attendance, after the consol-   hundred
idation of the monarchy.[5] The great council thus constituted   members.
was generally known as the witenagemot, literally the meeting of the wise; but it was also called *mycel gemot*, the great
meeting, and sometimes *mycel getheaht*, the great thought.[6]

---

[1] Kemble, *Saxons in England*, vol.
ii. p. 195; Stubbs, *Const. Hist.*, vol. i.
p. 124.

[2] Freeman, *Norm. Conq.*, vol. i. p.
70. "But just as in the case of the
assemblies of the mark and the shire,
so the gemots of the other kingdoms
seem to have gone on as local bodies,
dealing with local affairs, and perhaps
giving a formal assent to the resolutions of the central body." — Ibid., p.
70.

[3] *Cod. Dipl.*, No. 364. An act of
this witan is described as having been
executed "tota populi generalitate." —
Saxons in England, vol. ii. p. 200.

[4] *Cod. Dipl.*, No. 518; Stubbs, *Const.
Hist.*, vol. i. p. 126.

[5] *Cod. Dipl.*, Nos. 353, 364. 1107;
Saxons in England, vol. ii. p. 200.

[6] *Norm. Conq.*, vol. i. p. 70.

The meeting of the witan was generally proclaimed in advance, at some one of the royal residences.[1]

Powers of the witan. The supreme powers of the consolidated kingdom were vested in the king and the witan, who possessed the right to consider all public acts which the king could authorize,[2] including many acts which, according to modern theories, would be considered as purely executive.[3] In every act of legislation the right of the witan to advise and consent was invariably recognized.[4] The earliest of the old English enactments conform to this principle, which pervades all Teutonic legislation.[5] **King legislates with the counsel and consent of the witan.** The king enacts all laws, which are added to the existing customary law, with the counsel and consent of the witan, by whose concurrent authority they are promulgated. The laws of the Wihtræd are decreed " by the great men with the suffrages of all, as an addition to the lawful customs of the Kentish peoples." [6] Hlothære and Eadric, kings of the men of Kent, augmented the laws which their forefathers had made before them, by these dooms.[7] The laws of Ine are enacted " with the counsel and teaching of the bishops, with all the ealdormen and the most distinguished witan of the nation, and with a large gathering of God's servants." [8] Ælfred promulgated his code with the counsel and consent of his witan,[9] and Eadgar ordains with the counsel of his witan in praise of God, and in honor of himself and for the behoof of all the people.[10] **Character of the early laws.** Of the old English laws, those of Æthelberht, Hlothære and Eadric, Wihtræd, Ine, Edward the Elder, Æthelstan, Eadmund, and Eadgar, are mainly in the nature of amendments of custom. Those of Ælfred, Æthelred, Cnut, and those described as Eadward the Confessor's, aspire to the character of codes.[11] **Taxation.** Taxation, in the modern sense of the term, can hardly be said to exist until a very late period in the history of the Old-English common-

---

[1] *E. Chron.*, a. 1010.

[2] " First, and in general, they possessed a consultative voice, and a right to consider every public act which could be authorized by the king." — *Saxons in England*, vol. ii. p. 204.

[3] *Norm. Conq.*, vol. i. p. 74.

[4] " The witan deliberated upon the making of new laws which were to be added to the existing folcright, and which were then promulgated by their own and the king's authority." — *Saxons in England*, vol. ii. p. 205.

[5] Ibid., vol. ii. p. 206, note 1.

[6] Schmid, *Gesetze*, p. 15.

[7] Thorpe, vol. i. p. 26.

[8] Schmid, *Gesetze*, p. 21.

[9] Ibid., p. 69.

[10] Ibid., pp. 184 187 ; Stubbs, *Const. Hist.*, 127 ; *Saxons in England*, vol. ii. pp. 206-213.

[11] *Select Charters*, pp. 60, 61.

wealth. As the king's revenue from the public or demesne lands, from his private estates, and from other sources, was sufficient to maintain the royal state, it was not necessary to provide a royal revenue by taxation. Not until the period of the last Danish invasion did circumstances arise which required the imposition of a general tax for the public service, — with the imposition of the Danegeld the history of English taxation really begins. This extraordinary tax, which was levied by the king and the witan,[1] was imposed not only for the purpose of buying off the invaders, but for the raising of fleets.[2] The legislative powers of the king and the witan were not confined, however, to secular matters only; they embraced such subjects of ecclesiastical legislation as the appointment of fasts and festivals, and the levy and expenditure of ecclesiastical revenue. The laws abound in articles regulating the keeping of Sunday and festival holidays, the payment of tithes and other church imposts, the marrying of persons within the prohibited degrees, and the life and conversation of the clergy.[3] The great influence of the spiritual witan seems to have prevented any jealousy as to that kind of legislative interference with the government of the church. The king and the witan even possessed the power to elect bishops to vacant sees.[4] The witan, by virtue of their general power to consider every act which the king could authorize, had the right, conjointly with the king, of making alliances and treaties of peace, and of settling their terms;[5] and

Danegeld.

Ecclesiastical legislation.

Treaties and alliances.

---

[1] "The king and the witan had power to levy taxes for the public service." — *Saxons in England*, vol. ii. p. 223. For the imposition of Danegeld see *E. Chron.*, a. 991, 1002, 1007, and 1011.

[2] The assessment of 1008, *in which we find the origin of ship-money*, is thus recorded in the Abingdon and Peterborough Chronicles for 1808: "Hér bebead se Cyng þæt mán sceolde ofer eall Angelcyn scypu fæstlice wyrcan; þæt is ðonne; of þrim hund hidum and of tynum ænne scegð, and of viii hidum helm and byrnan." "The government did not levy ship-money, but required each county to find its quota of ships. This would apply as well to the inland districts as to those on the seaboard." — Mr. Earle's note, quoted in Freeman's *Norm. Conq.*, vol. i. p.

439, Appendix LL. "It may be inferred then that every three hundreds were liable to be called on to furnish one ship, whilst every ten hides were accountable for a boat, and every eight hides for a helm and breastplate." Stubbs, *Const. Hist.*, vol. i. p. 106.

[3] *Saxons in England*, vol. ii. p. 222.

[4] "The king and the witan had power to appoint prelates to vacant sees." — *Saxons in England*, vol. ii. p. 221. This was the theory; as to the practice see Stubbs, *Const. Hist.*, vol. i. p. 134.

[5] "The witan had the power of making alliances and treaties of peace, and of settling their terms."— *Saxons in England*, vol. ii. p. 213. See Ælfred and Guthrum's Peace, Thorpe's *Laws and Institutes*, vol. i. p. 152.

also of raising land and sea forces, whenever extraordinary circumstances required that the authority of the great coun-

Alienation of folkland. cil should be added to that of the king.[1]   The folkland, the national fund, was administered and conveyed conjointly by the king and the witan.   Nearly every grant professes to have been made by the king *cum consilio, consensu et licentia procerum,* or in some like formula expressing the same idea.[2] With the consent of the witan the king could carve an estate out of the folkland and vest it in a private individual or corporation, and thus convert the portion severed from the public domain into an alodial estate, heritable forever.[3]   When such a grant was made, it was usual for the land to be freed by the terms of the book or charter from all burdens except the *trinoda necessitas,* to which all lands were subject.[4]   In the same way an estate could be carved out of the folkland and vested in the king as an individual, to be held by him as a

Bookland converted into folkland. private estate of inheritance.[5]   The king and the witan could also convert bookland into folkland, and impose upon it all the burdens to which that kind of land was subject.[6]   And before the influence of the principle, which rendered family land inalienable without family consent, had fallen into decay, the king and the witan were sometimes called upon to confirm and guarantee grants of large private estates, so as to effectually bar the right of any heirs that might be cut off by the alienation.[7]   As the royal power grew, and as the monarchy became more and more consolidated, the folkland passed

The folkland becomes *terra regis.* under the control of the king alone ; the witan finally became mere witnesses of the royal grants.   In William's time the folkland had become *terra regis.*[8]

That the inherent power of the witan was, in the last re-

---

[1] "The king and his witan had power to raise land and sea forces when occasion demanded." — *Saxons in England,* vol. ii. p. 224; *E. Chron.,* a. 999, 1047, 1048.

[2] *Saxons in England,* vol. ii. p. 226.

[3] "The witan possessed the power of recommending, assenting to, and guaranteeing grants of lands, and of permitting the conversion of folcland into bócland, and *vice versâ.*" — *Saxons in England,* vol. ii. p. 225.

[4] The three duties which arose out of the *trinoda necessitas,* although distinct from the feudal services of later

times, tended "more and more to become duties attaching to the possession of the land owed to, and capable of being enforced by, the king or the great man of the district." — Digby, *Law of Real Property,* p. 14; *Cod. Dipl.,* No. 52.

[5] *Cod. Dipl.,* No. 260.

[6] *Cod. Dipl.,* No. 281; *Saxons in England,* vol. ii. pp. 226–227.

[7] See grant made by Abbot Ceolfrith, *Cod. Dipl.,* No. 127; *Essays in A. S. Law,* pp. 75-77.

[8] *Essays in A. S. Law,* pp. 99–100; Stubbs, *Const. Hist.,* vol. i. p. 193.

sort, higher than that of the king is demonstrated by the fact The witan could elect the king. that the witan had the power not only to elect [1] but to depose the king. Teutonic kingship was elective from the earliest period in its history, but the right of election was attended and modified from the very beginning by the hereditary principle. In the home-land, the king was chosen by the state assembly, but the choice was limited to those who possessed the indispensable prerequisite of noble blood.[2] In the character of the new kingship which grew out of the Teutonic conquest of Britain, there was no departure from the primitive tradition. In every kingdom there was some one royal house whose members were considered, under all ordinary circumstances, entitled to the succession ; but within the limits of that house the witan possessed the power to elect the person most competent to govern.[3] It was usual Oldest son of the last king usually chosen if fit. to give the preference to the oldest son of the last king, if he were not too young or otherwise incompetent to rule ; in that event, the witan generally elected the brother of the king, or some other kindred prince more capable of ruling.[4] But no matter who succeeded to the throne, the theory was that he succeeded by virtue of an election ; he was "*gecoren and áhafen tó cyninge,*" — elected and raised to be king.[5] Express mention is made of the act of election in the chronicles and memorials touching the accessions of the following kings : Ælfred, Eadward the Elder, Æthelstan, Eadred, Eadgar, Eadward, Æthelred, Eadmund, Cnut, Harol I., Eadward the Confessor, and Harold.[6]

The witan, who possessed the power to elect the king, possessed also the correlative right to depose him whenever his The witan could depose the king. government was not conducted for the good of his people.[7]

---

[1] "The witan had the power of electing the king" — *Saxons in England,* vol. ii. p. 214.

[2] "Reges ex nobilitate, duces ex virtute sumunt." — Tac., *Germ.,* c. 7.

[3] "The kingly dignity among the Anglo-Saxons was partly hereditary, partly elective ; that is to say, the kings were usually taken from certain qualified families, but the witan claimed the right of choosing the person whom they would have to reign." — *Saxons in England,* vol. ii. p. 214 ; Stubbs, *Const. Hist.,* vol. i. p. 135.

[4] *Norm. Conq.,* vol. i. pp. 72, 73, and Appendix S.

[5] *Saxons in Eng.,* vol. ii. p. 215.

[6] These instances in which express mention is made of the act of election have been collected by Kemble (*Saxons in Eng.,* vol. ii. pp. 215–219), Freeman (*Norm. Conq.,* vol. i. p. 591), and Stubbs (*Const. Hist.,* vol. i. p. 136, note 1).

[7] "The witan had the power to depose the king, if his government was not conducted for the good of his people." — *Saxons in England,* vol. ii. p. 219.

The greater number of cases in which this power was exercised by the witan belong to the period which precedes the union of the heptarchic kingdoms under the house of Cerdic. In the eighth century, out of fifteen kings duly elected in Northumbria, at least thirteen are said to have ended their reigns by extraordinary means.[1] In this confused history, at least one case, that of Alchred, stands out as a regular and formal act of deposition.[2] In 755 the witan of Wessex deposed Sigeberht from the royal dignity and elected his relative Cynewulf in his stead. The Chronicle says: "This year, Cynewulf and the West Saxon witan deprived his kinsman Sigeberht of his kingdom, except Hampshire, for his unjust doings."[3] Among the descendants of Ecgberht, at least two cases of deposition appear to have occurred. The Mercians reject Eadwig, sever their kingdom from his, and then elect Eadgar as their king.[4] Æthelred the Second was deposed in favor of his conqueror, and afterwards restored by the action of the witan.[5] In many of the cases it is difficult to determine whether the throne was made vacant by a legal act of deposition, or through the results of conspiracy and civil war.

Depositions of Alchred;

of Sigeberht;

of Eadwig;

of Æthelred.

The judicial power: the witan and the local courts.

All primitive Teutonic courts popular assemblies.

5. The German scholars have firmly established the fundamental historical principle, that the Teutonic race, in the earliest known period of its development, vested not only the political administration, but the administration of law, in an expanding series of popular assemblies, composed of the freemen whose interests were directly involved.[6] In the continental Teutonic state, the narrowest form of organization was represented by the mark, in whose assembly or markmoot the markmen met together to regulate all matters arising out of their peculiar system of village and agricultural life. If the markmen ever administered justice among them-

---

[1] Stubbs, *Const. Hist.*, vol. i. p. 137.

[2] " Eodem tempore, Alcredus rex, consilio et consensu omnium suorum, regiæ familiæ principum destitutus societate, exilio imperii mutavit majestatem." — Sim. Dun., a. 774.

[3] *E. Chron.*, a. 755; Flor. Wig., a. 755. The fullest account of this transaction is given by Henry of Huntingdon, *Hist. Ang.*, lib. iv.

[4] Flor. Wig., a. 957; *Saxons in Eng.*, vol. ii. p. 221.

[5] Freeman, *Norm. Conq.*, vol. i. pp. 242–247. The action of the witan relates more clearly to Æthelred's restoration than to his expulsion. — *V. S. Dunstani*, p. 35; Flor. Wig., a. 1014; Stubbs, *Const. Hist.*, vol. i. p. 139.

[6] Cf. Essay on "The Anglo-Saxon Courts of Law," in *Essays in A. S. Law*, p. 1.

selves it was in some period preceding the union of the village-communities in larger aggregates.[1] In historical times the marks appear as members of the *pagi* or *gás*, the districts known in later times as hundreds.[2] The hundred court of the Continent consisted of the regular and frequent meeting of all the freemen resident in the district; it was the court of law in which justice was ordinarily administered.[3] The state assembly possessed the judicial power to hear and determine grave public offences.[4] In the home-land, the ordinary administration of law was vested in the court of the *pagus*, *gá*, or hundred,—the extraordinary, in the state assembly. The numberless petty states, in which the Teutonic settlers originally grouped themselves in Britain, were exact reproductions, in every material particular, of the *civitas* of Cæsar and Tacitus.[5]

In the home land, justice administered in the hundred court and state assembly.

The mark appears in English history as the tun or township, a corporate unity in whose members were vested the power of ordering their own local and domestic concerns. This power was exercised by the village assembly or tun-moot, which, in an independent township, consisted of all the alodial owners residing within it,—in a dependent one, of the body of tenants who had united in the formation of a village-community upon the land of a lord. In the village assembly, which could not have possessed more than *quasi* judicial functions, resided the power to regulate all the internal affairs of the township by the making of by-laws, a term which is said to mean laws enacted by a "by," as the township was called in the northern shires. The tun-moot elected its own officers, and also provided for the representation of its interests in the courts of the hundred and the shire, where the *gerefa* and four selectmen appeared for the township.[6] In the "process of feudalization" the township finally becomes the manor of the lord; and the ancient jurisdiction of the tun-moot survives to this day in the parish vestry and in the manorial courts.[7]

The tun-moot

possessed only quasi judicial functions.

---

[1] See above, p. 104.
[2] *Essays in A. S. Law,* p. 5.
[3] Sohm, *Altd. R.- u. G. Verf.,* i. 541.
[4] "Licet apud concilium accusare quoque et discrimen capitis intendere."
— Tac., *Germ.,* c. 12.

[5] See above, p. 124.
[6] See above, p. 143.
[7] Maine, *Village - Communities,* lecture v.; Digby, *Law of Real Property,* p. 43.

The burg-
gemot

The Old-English burg or borough was nothing but a town-ship, or a group of townships, in a higher state of organiza-tion, and with defences of a more formidable character than those of the ordinary township.[1]   " It was not like an ancient Greek or Roman, like a mediæval Italian or Provençal city, the centre of the whole civil life of its district.   It was sim-ply one part of the district in which men lived closer together than elsewhere ; it was simply several townships packed tightly together, a hundred smaller in extent and thicker in population than other hundreds."[2]   The " burg " like the " tun" possessed its common lands, its own court or burg-gemot, and its head officer or *gerefa*, who was known as the *tun* or *wic-gerefa*, and in commercial places like London, Bath, and Canterbury, as *port gerefa :* [3] the burg-gerefa does not occur.[4]   The early history of the borough constitution is very obscure, but in it was undoubtedly embodied the system originally represented by the free township, which system survived as the basis of municipal authority.[5]   As the greater burgs generally represented a group of townships that had coalesced, their organization naturally resembled the constitu-tion of the hundred more closely than that of the township.

identical
with the
hundred
court.

The burg-gemot, hustings [6] or law court of the Old-English city, was nothing but the hundred court in a slightly differ-ent form ; its origin was the same and its procedure sub-stantially the same.[7]

The *pagus*, or hundred of the continental Teutonic state

[1] Stubbs, *Const. Hist.*, vol. i. pp. 92, 403.

[2] Freeman, *Norm. Conq.*, vol. v. p. 312. " The collection of geographically continuous parishes covered with build-ings, in the counties of Middlesex, Sur-rey, and Kent, which is called London in popular language, would have been a hopelessly bewildering object to an old Greek ; but of one thing he would have been sure, and rightly, — that noth-ing could well be less like a *polis*." — Sir Fredrick Pollock's *Hist. of the Science of Politics*, p. 11 (Humboldt Li-brary).

[3] Kemble, *Saxons in England*, vol. ii. pp. 174–176; Stubbs, *Const. Hist.*, vol. i. p. 93.

[4] Schmid, *Gesetze*, p. 598.

[5] It is now perfectly well understood that the origin of English municipali-ties cannot be traced to a Roman source. For authorities upon this sub-ject see above, pp. 124, 125.

[6] "This name is still preserved in the United States in the Court of Hust-ings of Richmond, Virginia." — Bige-low, *Hist. of Procedure in Eng.*, p. 141, note 2.

[7] *Essays in A. S. Law*, p. 22. " Of the influence of guilds, as a subsidiary part of town organization, there are some traces which at a later period assume great historical importance; but there is nothing to justify the notion that they were the basis on which the cor-porate constitution of the burh was founded." — Stubbs, *Const. Hist.*, vol. i. p. 94. "The various guilds were also without authority as courts of the com-mon law." — *Essays in A. S. Law*, p. 22.

is reproduced in Britain by a union of townships in the district originally known as the *gá* or shire, a term of various application.   This district, which is usually described in the earlier documents as *regio*, *pagus*, or *provincia*, represents, no doubt, either the *pagus* or district in which the hundred warriors originally grouped themselves, or a union of townships originally isolated and independent.   The early *gás* or shires were not at all uniform in size, their boundaries depending upon the physical conformation of the country in which the settlements were made.   By a union of early shires was formed the primitive state, whose national assembly was the folk-moot, the meeting of the whole people in arms.[1]   In the process of consolidation the primitive state descends in status one degree; it becomes a mere division of the greater whole, — that is to say, a scir or shire.   And as a necessary consequence the early shires[2] of which the primitive state was composed descend to the status of subdivisions, known in later times as hundreds.   In this way the conclusion is attained, which may be accepted as a general law, that *"the state of the seventh century became the shire of the tenth, while the shire of the seventh century became the hundred of the tenth."*[3]   The name of hundred, which first occurs in Old-English law in a police regulation of Eadgar's,[4] seems to have been definitely applied, during the ninth or tenth century, to the territorial district representing a union of townships, which may have been originally known as a shire. The hundred court of the consolidated kingdom and the hundred court of the Continent were, therefore, identical in fact and in name; they were the ordinary courts of law in which justice was administered in the first instance.[5]   The English hundred-moot consisted of the regular assembly of all the freemen resident within the district, together with the parish priest, the reeve, and four best men, who came as

The hundred court.

Identity of the modern hundred and the early shire.

The name of hundred first occurs in a law of Eadgar's.

Constitution of the hundred court.

---

[1] See above, pp. 123, 124.

[2] That scir or shire was the term originally employed in Britain to describe the district, which arose out of a union of townships, is maintained by very high authority. See *Essays in A. S. Law*, p. 18; Stubbs, *Const. Hist.*, vol. i. pp. 96–101 ; *Select Charters*, p. 68.

[3] *Essays in A. S. Law*, p. 19.   This statement has been repeated in the hope of emphasizing the vitally important conclusion which it embodies.

[4] Eadgar i. Constitutio de hundredis.

[5] As to the importance of this fact in establishing the historical connection between English and German institutions, see *Essays in A. S. Law*, pp. 6, 7.

representatives from every township embraced within the hundred.[1]   The judges were the whole body of suitors,[2] who, while on their way to and from the court, were under the special protection of the law.   The hundred court, which

It met monthly.

met every month,[3] could declare folk-right in every suit ; its jurisdiction was both civil and criminal ; it witnessed the transfers of land ; and no suit could be carried to a higher court until it had first been heard in the court of the hun-

Head officers of the hundred.

dred.[4]   The headship of the hundred seems to have been divided between two officers, — the one the representative of the people, the other of the king.   The hundred-man or hundreds-ealdor, who was the elected officer of the freemen of the hundred, convened the hundred court and probably presided over it.   This officer survives the Conquest, and in the thirteenth century appears as the elected representative of the hundred in the shire-moot.[5]   The representative of the king was the gerefa, who becomes after the Conquest the bailiff of the hundred.[6]

Police organization : the frithborh, or peacepledge.

Having now arrived at a definite conclusion as to the origin and structure of the township, the burg, and the hundred, it will be possible to indicate, in general terms, the relation which existed between these territorial districts and the system of police organization with which they became closely

Self-help.

interlaced.   In the most primitive periods of Teutonic society, the doctrine of self-help, the right of the individual freeman to redress his own wrongs without the aid of the judicial power, was the basis of all archaic procedure.   " The German was himself judge and warrior ; he levied execution and exacted blood for blood by the sovereign powers vested in

Right of feud.

himself by that most democratic of all constitutions." [7]   The right of feud, or private war, was a right which every Teu-

---

[1] " It was attended by the lords of lands within the hundred, or their stewards representing them, and by the parish priest, the reeve, and four best men of each township." — Stubbs, *Const. Hist.*, vol. i. p. 103, and note 1, in which is cited Hen. I., vii. §§ 4, 7 ; li. § 2. See, also, *Select Charters*, pp. 104, 105 ; Bigelow, *Hist. of Procedure*, p. 141.

[2] Stubbs, *Const. Hist.*, vol. i. pp. 103, 104, 114, note 6 ; *Essays in A. S. Law*, p. 5.

[3] " I will that each reeve have a ' gemot ' always once in four weeks, and so do that every man be worthy of folk-right," etc. — Eadward, ii. § 8 ; Eadgar, i. § 1 ; iii. § 5.

[4] Æthelstan, iii. § 3 ; Eadgar, iii. 2 ; Cnut, ii. 17, 19.

[5] Hen. I., viii. § 1 ; Palgrave, *Commonwealth*, pp. 635, cccli.

[6] Stubbs, *Const. Hist.*, vol. i. pp. 101, 102.

[7] *Essays in A. S. Law*, p. 262.

tonic freeman considered inalienable, — a right which entered with him into every political or social organization of which he was a part.　The first duty then which presented itself to every organized society that aspired to preserve the public peace was, to devise some means through which the right of every man to redress his wrongs, according to his own estimate of his injuries, might be modified and restrained.[1]　As the family in all branches of the Aryan race represented the strongest form of organization through which the individual could be governed, the state naturally invoked its aid for the maintenance of the peace and for the prevention of crime.[2] Tacitus explains the earliest attempt made by the Teutonic states to mitigate the evils of private warfare, through the agency of the family, when he says : " They are bound to take up both the enmities and the friendships of a father or relative.　Nor are their enmities implacable ; for even homicide is atoned for by a fixed number of flocks or cattle, and the whole house receives satisfaction, — a useful thing for the state, for feuds are dangerous in exact proportion to freedom." [3]　Treason and effeminacy were punished capitally ; all other offences (including homicide) could be atoned for by fines.[4]　" A portion of the fine went to the king or state, a part to the injured person or his relations." [5]　The state thus acted as mediator by guaranteeing to the person injured, or to his household, satisfaction for the injury received, and to the person paying the fine immunity from the consequences of the feud.　In this way the individual received indemnity, and the state compensation for the breach of the public peace.　As the right of feud was too deeply rooted to be eradicated by legislation, the Teutonic nations only

Agency of the family in the prevention of crime.

All fines divided between the state and the injured person or his relatives.

---

[1] " The Teutonic nations set themselves the task of regulating the *Right of Feud*. They could not entirely abrogate it, . . . but they defined, and as far as possible limited, its sphere and the extent of its action." — Kemble, *Saxons in England*, vol. i. p. 269. Kemble's tenth chapter, from which this extract is taken, has been criticised by Konrad Maurer, *Kritische Ueberschau*, iii. pp. 26–62, 1858. For a full and authoritative view of the whole subject, see Wilda's *Das Strafrecht der Germanen*, 1842.

[2] " Saxon England formed no exception to the rule. The family was not only the most important institution of private law : it stood also at the bottom of the whole police and criminal system." — Essay upon " The Anglo-Saxon Family Law," *Essays in A. S. Law*, p. 122.

[3] Tac., *Germ.*, c. 21 ; *Saxons in Eng.*, vol. i. p. 271.

[4] Tac., *Germ.*, c. 12.

[5] " Pars multæ regi vel civitati, pars ipsi qui vindicatur vel propinquis ejus exsolvitur." — Ibid., c. 12.

attempted to modify its exercise by prescribing a graduated system of compensation which embraced nearly every offence that could be committed against a man's person, honor, or domestic peace.   The unit in this system was the wergild,[1] or price set upon the life of every freeman according to his rank, his birth, or his office.   Every freeman had his wergild, from the humblest peasant to the king : its varying amount was the principal distinction between the classes ; it defined the value of each man's oath, his mund or protection, and the amount of his fines or exactions.   And after the principle was settled that the life-price could be fixed at a definite sum, the compensations for all less offences were adjusted in a corresponding ratio.   In the earliest forms of Old-English law we find every injury that a man could suffer in his person, his property, or his honor minutely assessed ;[2] and we also find the right of feud limited to the single case of guilty homicide.[3]   In the event of a man's violent death the obligation devolved upon his kindred to prosecute the blood-feud, and his wer, or life-price, was payable to them,[4] — his *maegth* or *maegburh*.   In addition, however, to the prosecution of the blood-feud, a man's *maegth* were bound to defend their kinsman before the courts, and to become responsible for him to the state.[5]   In this way the family association or *maegth* naturally supplied a system of mutual guaranty, which the state was able to employ in early times as a police organization through which it could hold lawless men to right.   In the earliest of the Old-English laws this system appears in its purity ; in the legislation of Æthelberht, Wihtræd, and Hlothære the *maegth* is still wholly responsible.[6] But the primitive system becomes greatly weakened, under the later kings, by the increasing force of public law, and by the growth of the *quasi* feudal relation of lord and

Marginal notes:

Wergild or life-price, unit in the system of compensation.

The family or *maegth* as a police organization ;

decline of its influence.

---

[1] "The wergyld, then, or life-price, was the basis upon which all peaceful settlement of feud was established."— *Saxons in Eng.*, vol. i. pp. 276, and 277–288.

[2] See the Laws of Æthelbert and Ælfred, Thorpe's *Laws and Institutes.*

[3] "Unlike some of the continental tribes, the Anglo-Saxons did not permit the exercise of the right of feud for simply corporeal injuries, but limited it to the single case of guilty homicide. When a man was slain, his kindred must avenge the murder by slaying an enemy or enemies of equal value."— *Essays in A. S. Law*, p. 143. See Æthelred, ii. 6; Cnut, ii. 56; Schmid, *Gesetze*, viii. c. 1.

[4] Schmid, *Gesetze*, vii. 3, § 4.

[5] *Essays in A. S. Law*, p. 146.

[6] Kemble, *Saxons in England*, vol. i. p. 259.

man.[1] By the time of Ælfred the right of feud had been so
far modified that a man could not fight, except in a certain
serious case, until he had first appealed to all the recognized
authorities for redress.[2] But if the offender failed to make
lawful amends after demand upon him, then the injured parties could make war upon him with the aid of the state ;
whence the Old-English proverb, "Bicge spere of síde óðer
bere,"—buy off the spear or bear it.[3] This primitive system of police, based alone upon the family tie, which originally implied the fact of neighborhood, contained within itself the seeds of its own dissolution. As the force of family
association weakened, and as the family itself became dispersed, a time came when neighbors were not necessarily
kinsmen. When that point was reached, the deficiencies in
the old system had to be supplied by a more definite form
of organization, in which the power of the family survived
as a potent influence. In the new arrangement neighbors, New police
whether related or not, were bound together in tens and hun- system embodied in
dreds, — a tithing-man for each tithing, a hundred-man for tithings and
each hundred.[4] The frithborh [5] (peace-pledge) was the mu- hundreds
as numeri-
tual guaranty by which every member of a tithing as well as cal divi-
of a *maegth* became a pledge or surety (borh) to the other sions.
members, as well as to the state, for the maintenance of the
public peace. From the time of Eadgar [6] the *maegth*, as a
police organization, no longer existed. The primitive family
system had become merged in an artificial one which was
purely political ; the police duties which at first devolved
upon the kindred passed to the members of the tithings
and hundreds. But the most difficult question yet remains :
When and in what way did these numerical and personal

---

[1] *Essays in A. S. Law*, p. 142.

[2] *Saxons in England*, vol. i. p. 271 ;
Essays in A. S. Law, p. 268.

[3] This right is thus expressed in a
formula contained in the law of Eadward the Confessor : " Emendationem
faciat parentibus, aut guerram patiatur,
unde Angli proverbium habebant :
Bicge spere of side other bere, quod
est dicere, lanceam eme de latere aut
fer eam." — Leg. Eadw. Conf., xii.,
§ 6; Thorpe, vol. i. p. 447.

[4] Kemble, *Saxons in England*, vol. i.
pp. 237, 238.

[5] Forsyth, *Trial by Jury*, p. 50.

[6] " From the time of Eadgar, the
maegth, as a police organization, no
longer existed. It had been superseded by a system of police organizations of a purely politcial nature ; and
the police duties hitherto exercised by
the kindred had passed to the members of these political organizations."
— *Essays in A. S. Law*, p. 147, citing
Eadg. iii. 6, iv. 3; Æthelr. i. 1, Pr.;
Cnut, ii. 20, Pr.; Wil. i. 25.

Numerical
divisions
merge their
functions in
townships
and territo-
rial hun-
dreds.
divisions merge their functions in the already existing territorial districts, which have been described as townships and
hundreds ?   That such a merger did take place is clearly indicated by the later laws.[1]   The functions of the tithing sink
into those of the township ; and, except in some of the western counties, even the name of the tithing is lost in that of
the township.[2]   The name of "hundred" may have extended
itself, by a perfectly natural process, to the territorial district
which the peace association protected.[3]   It is more than
probable that the development which took place in the police
system was but a part of the general process of change
through which the primitive constitution passed in the transition from the personal to the territorial system.   After the

Frithborh
(peace-
pledge)
incorrectly
translated
by the
Norman
lawyers.
Conquest the name *frithborh* was incorrectly translated by
the Norman lawyers into *liberum plegium* (frank-pledge)
instead of *pacis plegium*.[4]   The "view of frank-pledge," the
right to see that these peace associations were kept in perfect
order, ultimately became a part of the petty criminal jurisdiction of the courts leet, where it still survives.

In the process of consolidation the ancient shire becomes
the modern hundred, and the primitive state becomes the
modern shire.   The folk-moot, the national assembly of the
ancient kingdom, survives as the shire-moot, an institution
distinctly peculiar to England as compared with Germany.[5]
In descending to the rank of a shire the primitive state preserves its autonomy to the greatest practicable extent ; even
as late as the time of Æthelstan a trace of the ancient legislative authority lingers in the proceedings of the shire-moot.[6]
The government of the shire is divided between the ealdor-

---

[1] "It is well known that in the later
Anglo-Saxon law, and even to this day,
the tithing and hundred appear as local and territorial, not as numerical,
divisions. . . . I do not deny that in
process of time these divisions had become territorial," etc. — *Saxons in England*, vol. i. p. 240.

[2] "Tithings at present exist in Som-
ersetshire and Wiltshire, and according to Pearson (maps, 52) in Gloucestershire and Worcestershire, and in all
counties south of the Thames (except
Kent and Cornwall), where they answer to the townships of other coun-

ties." — Stubbs, *Const. Hist.*, vol. i. p.
86, note 2.

[3] *Select Charters*, p. 68.

[4] "An early confusion gave rise to
the reading of Freoborh, *liberum plegium*, free-pledge, frank-pledge, for
Friðborh, the pledge or guaranty of
peace, *pacis plegium*.   The distinction
is essential to the comprehension of
this institution." — *Saxons in England*,
vol. i. p. 249, note 1 ; Forsyth, *Trial
by Jury*, p. 50.

[5] *Essays in A. S. Law*, p. 21 ; Waitz,
D. V. G., ii. p. 494 ; Stubbs, *Const.
Hist.*, vol. i. p. 116.

[6] See above, p. 173.

man and the scir-gerefa or sheriff,—the one the representative of the nation, the other of the king. As the work of consolidation advances, and as the tribal kings pass away, their places are filled in the subject kingdoms by ealdormen or viceroys, appointed by the king and his witan, by whom they are removable, and to whom they are responsible for the exercise of their authority.[1] In some instances the under-kings continue to rule as ealdormen by virtue of a delegated authority.[2] "The ealdorman is a vice-king, with an independent power as opposed to the king. Not the king's pleasure, but a principle of the public constitution, determines the completeness of the ealdorman's authority. Not the king's pleasure, but only a lawful judgment, can strip the ealdorman of his office. The ealdorman excludes the king from the immediate government of the shire. The shire government is not royal but ducal."[3] The ealdorman was the leader of the military force of the shire, and, as such, he is sometimes called in the charters *heretoga*.[4] He sat in the shire-moot with the sheriff and the bishop, and received a part of the profits of jurisdiction.[5] The direct representative of the king in the government of the shire was the scir-man, scir-gerefa,[6] or sheriff, who was the administrator of the royal demesne, the judicial president of the shire-moot, and the executor of the law.[7] The most general name for every fiscal, administrative, and executive officer among the English in early times was *gerefa*, a term which was usually limited by a prefix which indicated in each case the scope of the officer's jurisdiction; as tun-gerefa, wic-gerefa, port-gerefa, and scir-gerefa. The gerefa or reeve always appears, however, in connection with judicial functions,—he is always the holder of a court of justice.[8] The scir-gerefa, who, as a judicial

Headship of the shire divided between

the ealdorman and

the sheriff.

The term "gerefa."

---

[1] Freeman, *Norm. Conq.*, vol. i. p. 52.

[2] "The under-kings of Hwiccia thus continued to act as ealdormen under Mercia for a century," etc.—Stubbs, *Const. Hist.*, vol. i. p. 112.

[3] Sohm, *Altd. R.- u. G. Verf.*, i. pp. 25, 26; *Essays in A. S. Law*, p. 21.

[4] *Cod. Dipl.*, ii. 383; iii. pp. 5, 49, 159, 259, 260, 262; Freeman, *Norm. Conq.*, vol. i., Appendix K.

[5] Stubbs, *Const. Hist.*, vol. i. p. 113.

[6] Scir-man, Ine, § 8; *Cod. Dipl.*, iv. 9. The word generally used in the laws is gerefa; scir-gerefa is found however, in charters.—*Cod. Dipl.*, iv. 10, 54, 201; *Saxons in England*, vol. ii. p. 158.

[7] Stubbs, *Const. Hist.*, vol. i. p. 113.

[8] See *Saxons in England*, vol. ii. ch. v., "The Gerefa." "I will that each reeve have a 'gemot' always once in four weeks, and so do that every man be worthy of folk-right," etc.—Leg. Eadw., i. § 2.

officer, was the executor of the law and president of the shire-moot, may have been originally its elected chief. But in historical times he is the nominee and steward of the king.[1] As a fiscal officer the scir-gerefa was the administrator of the royal demesne within his shire, and the collector of all fines that accrued to the king; and, like the ealdorman, he participated in the profits of jurisdiction. While the authority of the ealdorman might extend to several shires, the authority of a sheriff was distinctly limited to a single shire. The shire-moot was simply the ancient folk-moot, the assembly of all the freemen resident within the shire; and, like the hundred-moot, it was attended by all lords of lands (called in this aspect scir-thegns),[2] by the parish priest, the reeve, and four selectmen from each township,[3] and by the twelve senior thegns from each hundred.[4] The shire-moot was, therefore, not only a popular but a representative assembly, each township and each hundred within the shire being present in the persons of its representatives. The presiding officer of the shire-moot was the scir-gerefa, and with him sat the ealdorman and the bishop; the one to declare the law temporal, the other the law spiritual.[5] The shire-moot could declare folk-right in every suit; and as no cause could be carried to the shire until it had first been heard in the hundred, so no cause could be carried to the king until it had first been heard in the shire.[6] It must not be supposed, however, that this arrangement embodied a system of appeal in the modern sense of that term. The decision of each court was final. It was

Sheriff the nominee and steward of the king.

The constitution of the shire-moot.

The bishop sat in the shire-moot.

Ancient system of appeal.

---

[1] The right of election was asserted, however, by the constitutionalists of the thirteenth century, and it was for a few years conceded by the crown. — Stubbs, *Const. Hist.*, vol. i. p. 113.

[2] *Saxons in England*, vol. ii. pp. 234, 235; *Cod. Dipl.*, vi. 198.

[3] This fact, "left questionable in the laws, is proved by the later practice." — Stubbs, *Const. Hist.*, vol. i. p. 115; citing Henry I., vii. §§ 4, 7; li. § 2. See, also, Bigelow, *Hist. of Procedure*, p. 133.

[4] *Cod. Dipl.*, iv. 137; *Select Charters*, pp. 137, 251.

[5] By the laws of Eadgar and Cnut the shire-moot was to be held twice in the year. "And let the hundred gemot be attended as it was before fixed; and thrice in the year let a burg-gemot be held; and twice, a shire-gemot; and let there be present the bishop of the shire and the ealdorman, and there both expound as well the law of God as the secular law." — Eadg. ii. 5; Cnut, ii. 18. "It may, then, be concluded that the presence of the sheriff was necessary in any case, while that of the ealdorman might be dispensed with." — *Saxons in England*, vol. ii. p. 159; Hallam, *Middle Ages*, vol. ii. p. 283.

[6] "And let no one apply to the king in any suit unless he at home may not be worthy of law, or cannot obtain law." — Eadg. ii. 2; Cnut, ii. 17, 19; Hallam, *M. A.*, vol. ii. p. 269.

only in the event that a court failed to decide within the prescribed time that the cause could be taken to a higher tribunal.[1]

In the last resort, the witenagemot acted as a supreme court of justice both in civil and criminal causes.[2] Numerous illustrations of the exercise of civil jurisdiction upon the part of the witan can be found in the charters contained in the Codex Diplomaticus, in which the proceedings in many important trials are set forth in great detail.[3] From the same kind of evidence it is equally certain that the witan often adjudged lands of offenders, intestates, and suicides to be forfeit to the king.[4] The criminal jurisdiction of the witan extended to all such grave public offences as were originally punishable in the national assembly of the primitive Teutonic state. This jurisdiction in the time of Eadward the Confessor was substantially what it had been in the days of Tacitus.[5] By a decree of the Northumbrian witan, Wilfred was condemned to imprisonment and exile;[6] by decrees of the witan of the consolidated kingdom Ælfric, Æthelweard, Ælfgar, and Godwine were outlawed.[7] Although in theory the jurisdiction of the king and the witan might be said to extend over all persons and over all causes, yet in practice the tendency was to discourage its exercise, in order to confine litigation as strictly as possible to the local tribunals.[8]

6. As the judicial powers of the witan were exercised only at long intervals and upon extraordinary occasions, and as the

Witan a supreme court of justice in both civil and criminal causes.

[1] *Essays in A. S. Law*, pp. 25, 26; Stubbs, *Const. Hist.*, vol. i. p. 115, note 3.

[2] "Lastly, the witan acted as a supreme court of justice, both in civil and criminal causes." — *Saxons in England*, vol. ii. p. 229.

[3] As illustrations see *Cod. Dipl.*, Nos. 143, 156, 164, 220, 245, 1034, 1258.

[4] "The witan possessed the power of adjudging the lands of offenders and intestates to be forfeit to the king." *Saxons in England*, vol. ii. p. 228. See *Cod. Dipl.*, Nos. 1112, 1295, 374, 1035. Kemble also refers to a case of forfeiture for suicide, contained in a charter in the archives of Westminster Abbey,

and bearing date in the time of Eadgar.

[5] Stubbs, *Const. Hist.*, vol. i. p 132.

[6] Eddius, *V. Wilfr.*

[7] *Cod. Dipl.*, No. 1312; *E. Chron.*, 1020, 1051, 1055; *Saxons in England*, vol. ii. pp. 230-232.

[8] "Instead of enlarging their own powers by encouraging suitors to seek justice directly from the crown, the king and the witan frowned upon every symptom of popular discontent with the clumsy justice of popular tribunals, and forced suitors back upon the local courts." — *Essays in A. S. Law*, p. 25. As to the judicial powers of the witan in the Norman period, see Bigelow's *Hist. of Procedure*, pp. 20-25.

Germs of jury and representative systems imbedded in the local courts.

courts of the townships did not possess contentious jurisdiction,[1] it follows that the ordinary administration of law was confined to the courts of the shire and hundred. The business of these courts was not limited, however, to the exercise of judicial functions only. In the Old-English commonwealth, as in all other infant societies, the line of demarcation between the different powers in the state was not at all well defined; the courts of the shire and hundred were not only the judicial but the administrative workshops of the constitution. In addition to the administration of justice, these courts transacted such business as the levying of military forces, the adjustment of local assessments, and the regulation of the system of police;[2] and in their presence were performed all acts that required special publicity, such as the making of sales and the execution of important documents.[3]

Local courts survive the Conquest.

These local courts, in which were discussed and settled nearly every question in which the body of the people were directly concerned,[4] survived the shock of the Norman conquest, preserving in their organization and procedure the germs out of which the greatest of English institutions were to spring. Out of the representative principle imbedded in the courts of the shire and hundred were developed, under the influence of Norman administrative ideas, the jury system,[5] and the system of representative government.[6] In order fully to grasp the history of this development, — which involves the

Embryonic forms of representative principle.

question of questions for students of English institutions, — it will be necessary to begin with an examination of the germs of the representative principle as they appear in the primitive constitution. Such an examination can only be

---

[1] See above, pp. 104, 191.

[2] Guizot, *Hist. Rep. Gov.*, pp. 44, 49. As to the obligation of each shire to furnish its quota of ships, see the assessment of 1008 (*E. Chron.*, a. 1008), which is explained by Mr. Freeman, *Norm. Conq.*, vol. i. p. 228, and Appendix LL.

[3] Wills were often attested by the shire-moot. See *Cod. Dipl.*, vi. 198. For other acts done before the shire, see ibid., iv. 117, 137, 138, 234.

[4] "The courts of those days supplied the means by which every kind of business was transacted, and had probably a greater resemblance to a public

meeting than to a court of justice in the modern sense of the term. This was true of all courts whatever, but especially of the county court, . . . in which were transacted all the more important branches of public business, judicial, financial, and military." — Sir James Fitz-James Stephen, *Hist. Crim. Law*, vol. i. p. 77.

[5] Stubbs, *Const. Hist.*, vol. i. p. 608. "It is in the new system of recognition, assizes, and presentments by jury that we find the most distinct traces of the growth of the principle of representation; and this in three ways."

[6] Guizot, *Hist. Rep. Gov.*, p. 45.

made through an analysis of the organization of the local courts, and of the methods of their procedure. The court of the hundred, like that of the shire, consisted of the meeting of all the qualified freemen resident within the district over which its jurisdiction extended. In the hundred court appeared the reeve and four selectmen from each township embraced within the hundred; in the shire court, like representatives appeared from each township embraced within the shire.[1] Both courts were, therefore, not only popular but representative assemblies. In both courts the whole body of "suitors" (attendants) were the judges, and in theory whatever judgment was rendered was the judgment of the whole assembly.[2] But in practice it became impossible for the whole body to exercise judicial functions. The inconveniences which arose out of this state of things indicated the obvious and natural remedy. Each assembly delegated its powers to a judicial committee composed of its own members, who acted in behalf of the whole court.[3] The representatives, or "*judices*," so chosen, whose number seems to have been always twelve or some multiple of twelve, probably acted under the advice of the presiding officer, who was presumed to be familiar with all the old customs.[4] Illustrations of this principle of delegation may be found in the twelve judges elected in the shire court of Cambridge to confirm with their oaths a decision previously rendered in the same court in a case between the Bishop of Rochester and the Sheriff of Cambridge;[5] in the twelve senior thegns who appear as a representative body in the courts of both the shire and hundred;[6] and in the twenty-four "judices"[7] or the

Shire and hundred courts both representative assemblies.

The "iudices."

---

[1] See above, pp. 194, 200.

[2] "Apart from the presiding officer of the court, the judgment was theoretically given by the whole assembly; but practically, and for convenience, often by a chosen number of 'judices.'" — *Essays in A. S. Law*, p. 288.

[3] "These twelve may have been in some cases like the *scabini* or *schöffen*, a fixed body holding their appointment for life; or like the lawmen of Lincoln, the hereditary owners of sac and soc in the territory; or chosen merely for the occasion." — Stubbs, *Const. Hist.*, vol. i. p. 103. As to the scabini, see Hallam, *M. A.*, vol. i. p.

213; Savigny, vol. i. pp. 192, 217, 239; Brunner, *Die Entstehung der Schwurgerichte*, pp. 20, 21.

[4] *Essays in A. S. Law*, p. 289, note 4.

[5] "Sed cum eis Bajocensis episcopus qui placito illi præerat, non bene crederet, præcepit ut si verum esse, quod dicebant, scirent, *ex seipsis duodecim eligerent*, qui quod omnes dixerant jurejurando confirmarent." — Hickes, *Dissertatio Epistolaris*, etc., p. 33.

[6] Æthelred, iii. § 3; *Cod. Dipl.*, iv. 137.

[7] "Tandem veniens Ægelwinus Alderman ad Granteburge habuit ibi grande placitum civium et hundretano-

thirty-six "barons"[1] who were chosen in the East Anglian county courts to determine the suits of Ramsey and Ely.

Probable origin of jury of presentment.

The twelve senior thegns seem, however, to have represented the hundred or wapentake for a special purpose. Æthelred's law provides "that a gemot be held in every wapentake; and the XII senior thegns go out, and the reeve with them, and swear on the relic that is given them in hand that they will accuse no innocent man, nor conceal any guilty one." The most competent critics seem to regard the twelve thegns, not as "judices," but as inquisitors of all crimes committed within the hundred to which they belong; and, as such, they probably represent the earliest form of the criminal jury of presentment.[2]

Origin of the trial jury.

But it must not be for one moment supposed that, in the representative body of "judices" to whom the judicial powers of the popular courts were sometimes delegated, there can be discovered the beginning of the trial jury, which has its origin in an entirely different source. What that source is, cannot be discovered without a brief examination of the archaic forms of Old-English legal procedure. The modern suit represents a syllogism in which the body of judicial rules are the major, and the declaration of facts the minor, premise:

Archaic legal procedure.

the primitive Teutonic suit was a simple demand made by the actor on the defendant for compensation.[3] To such a demand, which was made in a solemn traditional form, the defendant opposed an equally solemn contradiction.[4] The demand and denial, which made up the issue, were uuattended by any allegations of fact in support of either.[5] The vitally

rum coram XXIV judicibus." — *Hist. Ely*, Gale, p. 471.

[1] "XXXVI barones de amicis utriusque partis pari numero electos ipsi judices constituerunt." — Ibid., p. 471. See Stubbs, *Const. Hist.*, vol. i. p. 103, and note 5; Forsyth, *Trial by Jury*, pp. 58, 59.

[2] Forsyth (*Trial by Jury*, p. 57) holds this view, and cites in support of it Palgrave, *English Commonwealth*, vol. i. p. 213. Bishop Stubbs assents with his usual caution. *Const. Hist.*, vol. i. pp. 103, 115, 396, 611, 618. This probable view is also adopted by Sir James Fitz-James Stephen, *Hist. of Crim. Law* (London, 1883), vol. i. pp.

68, 69. Konrad Maurer holds that Æthelred's law only related to the Danelagh, and that it is in full accord with Scandinavian law. *Krit. Ueberschau*, v. p. 389, note 2. This interpretation of the passage is disputed, however, by Brunner, *Die Entstehung der Schwurgerichte*, pp. 402, 404.

[3] *Essays in A. S. Law*, p. 183.

[4] Brunner, *Schwurg.*, p. 44.

[5] "He (defendant) did not oppose the facts on which the plaintiff rested his claim, since the plaintiff brought forward no such facts; he only attacked the assertion that he was indebted." — *Essays in A. S. Law*, p. 194.

important point in the procedure, which was conducted throughout with an iron rigorism of form,[1] was the question of proof. How the proof should be given, and who should give it, were matters settled by the judgment, which was not only rendered before the taking of the proof, but in it was declared what would happen after its completion.[2] The strange inversion of ideas involved in the rendition of the judgment before the taking of the proof can be explained, however, by the fact that proof, as understood by the Teutonic barbarian, was not a judicial means of bringing conviction to the mind of the court ; it was simply a satisfaction due and given by the party to his adversary in the form prescribed by custom.[3] It was no part of the business of the court to weigh the proof ; it simply declared who should give it, and in what manner, and then what the judgment would be after its completion.[4] Three independent means of proof were allowable, — oath, ordeal, and documents.[5] The oath, which the party having the right of proof swore in his own behalf, could be accompanied or supported, (1) by the oaths of compurgators, or oath-helpers ; (2) by the oaths of witnesses. After the party making the proof had sworn to his demand, his oath-helpers swore to their belief, not in their chief's assertion, but in his credibility.[6] The witness-proof by which a party could support his assertion was drawn either from transaction or community witnesses. Transaction witnesses, which existed in Old-English law as in all the folk laws, were official persons appointed to witness such business transactions as sales, gifts, exchanges, and the like.[7] By Eadgar's

Teutonic conception of proof.

Three independent means of proof, — oath, ordeal, and documents.

Transaction witnesses.

[1] Brunner, *Entstehung der Schwurgerichte*, p. 44.

[2] Ibid., pp. 45, 46; Siegel, *Gerichtsverfahren*, p. 148.

[3] "It follows that in the barbarian form of proof by witnesses, which was merely one particular kind of proof, as ordeal was another, the producer of the witnesses proposed not in the least to convince the tribunal of his own good right, but simply to produce the fixed number of witnesses according to the customary form, and these witnesses were to corroborate by oath the theme or statement prescribed for them in the previous judgment which had ordered the proof." — *North American Review*, July, 1874, pp. 219, 220.

[4] "The proof was regarded as a satisfaction to the claimant, and therefore was not directed to the court, but to the opponent," etc. — *Essays in A. S. Law*, p. 188.

[5] K. Maurer, *Krit. Uebersch.*, v. p. 185.

[6] *Essays in A. S. Law*, p. 186; Brunner, *Schwurg.*, p. 49.

[7] Æthelstan, v. 1, § 5. "And let there be named in every reeve's 'manung' as many men as are known to be unlying, that they may be for witness in every suit. And be the oaths of these unlying men according to the worth of the property, without election." — *Select Charters*, p. 66.

law, a given number of such witnesses were appointed in each burg and hundred.[1]

Community witnesses.   Community witnesses were such persons as could testify concerning circumstances, long-continued relations, and occurrences known to them as neighbors, or members of the community. This class of witnesses, who were chiefly employed in actions relating to real estate and status, acted in a representative capacity; they declared the witness of the community in support of the assertion of the party by whom **Inquest of proof introduced by the Normans.** they were produced.[2] After the system of inquest by proof (*inquisitio per testes*), which the Normans introduced into England under the name of assizes, became employed in legal contests between private individuals as to the possession of land, the community witnesses appear as the sworn recognitors of the assize.[3] But they appear in a somewhat changed relation: they no longer depose to the single assertion of their chief to which they were confined by the customary law; they declare the witness of the community as to the whole truth within their knowledge, in response to questions propounded to them by the judge charged with the execution of the inquiry. The conclusion is now firmly established, that out of the inquest of proof, which was chiefly employed in judicial matters in suits relating to rights in land, was developed by the lawyers of the Plantagenet period the jury of judgment, the trial jury of modern times.[4]

---

[1] Eadgar, iv. §§ 4, 5, 6; Forsyth, *Trial by Jury*, pp. 70–73.

[2] Brunner, *Schwurg.*, pp. 50–53; *Essays in A. S. Law*, pp. 186, 187. "From this class of proof arose the 'inquisitio per testes' in the Norman period, and the jury of English law," etc.— *Essays in A. S. Law*, pp. 187, 232, and note 4.

[3] "Soweit nach älterem Rechte ein Gemeindezeugniss, sei es in den Formen des fränkish-normannischen oder des angelsächsischen Verfahrens in Anwendung war, hat dasselbe unter dem Einflusse der Recognitionen und der Königsgerichtlichen Praxis allmählich den Charakter einer Inquisitio ex jure angenommen."— Brunner, *Schwurg.*, p. 382. "There was no difference whatever in principle between those inquests ['Inquisitio ex jure'] and the recognitions by the knights of assize; and it seems to me to be almost as clear as demonstration

that the idea of the latter was derived from the former. In both cases the verdict was the testimony of witnesses cognizant of the matter in dispute; and if we substitute a determinate number of knights for the *probi homines* of an ordinary inquest, we have at once the assize."— Forsyth, *Trial by Jury*, p. 112.

[4] "Henry II. expanded and consolidated the system so much that he was not unnaturally regarded as the founder of it in its English character."— Stubbs, *Const. Hist.*, vol. i. p. 614. The system of inquests by sworn recognitors has been directly traced to the Frankish Capitularies, into which it may have been adopted from the fiscal regulations of the Theodosian Code. — Ibid., p. 613; Spence, *The Equitable Jurisdiction*, vol. i. p. 178; Palgrave, *English Commonw.*, p. 271; Brunner, *Schwurg.*, p. 87.

After the church had introduced the use of documents, they were employed as a means of proof of the same character as the proof of witnesses.[1] When no decision could be reached by the use of ordinary means, a final appeal was made through the ordeal to the judgment of God.

Documents and the ordeal.

The law which was administered according to these clumsy forms of procedure was strict law, whose severity went untempered by any kind of equitable jurisdiction whatsoever. The only way in which the strictness of the common law could be avoided was by compromise, which seems to have been effected wherever it was possible.[2] Beyond these archaic forms legal procedure did not advance during the period which precedes the Norman conquest. In this procedure, and in the organization of the local courts, the representative principle clearly appears. By the reeve and four selectmen each township was distinctly represented in the courts of the shire and hundred; by the judicial committees of twelve or some multiple of that number were represented the whole body of the popular court whose powers they for the time represented; the twelve senior thegns appeared as a representative body in the courts of both the shire and hundred; the community witnesses spake as the representatives of the neighborhood as to the particular fact in question. Beyond these embryonic forms the representative principle did not advance until it developed and widened, under the influence of Norman administrative ideas, first, into the jury system, and then into the system of representative government. The several stages in the history of this development will be indicated hereafter.

Absence of an equitable jurisdiction.

Prominence of the representative principle.

7. In the preceding examination of the origin and structure of the courts of the shire and hundred, no reference has been made to the growth of a feudal innovation through which large sections of jurisdiction which had been national or royal were withdrawn from the king or state and vested in the hands of private individuals. Originally all jurisdiction

Private jurisdictions: sacu and sôcn.

---

[1] *Essays in A. S. Law*, p. 188. The document could be drawn up by a notary, or before the court. — K. Maurer, *Krit. Uebersch.*, v. p. 196.

[2] "One result followed from this absence of equitable powers, which was, perhaps, not without an ultimate influence on the fate of the whole judicial system. . . . A compromise was always effected where compromise was possible. Arbitration was, perhaps, the habitual mode of settling disputes among the Anglo-Saxons." — *Essays in A. S. Law*, p. 26.

belonged to the people in their collective capacity; the peace was the national peace, and justice was the justice of the shire and the folk in whose courts it was administered.[1] Such was the condition of things before the archaic judicial constitution was torn in pieces by the growth of the aristocratic and feudal element represented by the thegnhood, at whose head stood the king. It is admitted on all hands that, certainly before the Norman conquest, jurisdiction was granted to private individuals without stint; that private law courts did exist by virtue of royal grants made with or without the consent of the witan; and that by virtue of such grants jurisdiction ceased to be exclusively a public trust, and often became a private right accompanying the possession of land. In some instances these private jurisdictions embraced large districts, but usually only the jurisdiction of a hundred.[2] As a general rule the law court created by royal grant was simply a hundred court in private hands. How this radical departure from primitive constitutional ideas was brought about can only be explained by reference to that "process of feudalization" through which the king becomes the lord and patron of his people, through which the national peace becomes the king's peace, the folkland the king's land, the justice of the shire and the folk the king's justice, the national officers the king's officers, and the national assembly — the witan — more and more the king's council.[3] As this process advanced, the conception of sovereignty as originally embodied in the people passed out of view, — the sovereignty of the nation becomes merged in the king. The theory that the justice of the shire and the hundred was the king's justice must have preceded any attempt on the part of the crown to bestow its administration upon private individuals. The earliest royal grants touching the administration of justice seem to have been of a fiscal character only, and were confined to the granting of such interest in the profits of justice as were immemorially due to the

Private law court certainly existed before the Conquest;

product of the "process of feudalization."

The profits of jurisdiction (sôcn) first granted;

---

[1] See above, p. 130.

[2] "Some of these territories were complete states themselves, like the counties palatine of Durham and of Chester. Some were completely organized as counties. *Far the larger number, however, had only the jurisdic-* *tion of a hundred court."* — *Essays in A. S. Law*, p. 54. "In all these the machinery of the hundred or wapentake was strictly preserved, and the law was administered on the same principle." — Stubbs, *Const. Hist.*, vol. i. p. 107.

[3] See above, p. 177.

crown.[1] The effect of such grants was to transfer from the
king to the landlord all the fines and profits of jurisdiction
which accrued to the royal fisc, or to the ealdorman, from persons embraced within the exempted territory, without remov-
ing such persons from the jurisdiction of the hundred court.
The position of offenders within the immunity thus created
remained unchanged ; the amount of their fines remained the
same ; but that portion of the fine now passed to the lord
which had previously accrued to the king.[2] The word used
in the charters to convey fiscal rights of this character was
sôcn, a term which in its early technical meaning seems to
have expressed the right only to the profits of jurisdiction,
and not to jurisdiction itself.[3] The technical word which
expressed the idea of jurisdiction was *sacu* or saca, meaning
lawsuit, litigation.[4] When these terms *sacu* and *sôcn* (abbre-
viated into *sac* and *soc*) were used together in a royal grant,
the intention to convey to the grantee, not only the profits
of jurisdiction but jurisdiction itself, was clearly expressed.[5]
At what period private law courts were first established in
England is a matter difficult to determine from the existing
evidence. It is maintained by some very eminent authorities that these private jurisdictions existed in law from a very
early period, — earlier in fact than that to which they can be
traced in laws and charters ; "that they were so inherent in
the land as not to require particularization"[6] in legal docu-

*next, juris-
diction
(sacu)
itself.*

*Contro-
versy as to
the time of
the origin
of private
jurisdic-
tions.*

---

[1] As examples, see *Cod. Dipl.*, Nos.
116, 227, 236, 250, 313, 1084. "The
royal grants, so far as they affected the
ordinary course of justice, seem to
have been double in their nature. They
were, in the first place, grants of the
fines and pecuniary profits of jurisdiction, which, by the old system, fell to
the crown.   This is entirely a fiscal
arrangement, which only indirectly concerns the subject of jurisdiction." —
Essays in A. S. Law, p. 29. Professor
Stubbs seems to think that in early
times the proprietor would "as a rule
satisfy himself with the profits of jurisdiction, and transact the business of it
through the ordinary courts." — *Const.
Hist.*, vol. i. p. 185.

[2] *Essays in A. S. Law,* p. 31.

[3] "Sôcn" has generally been held to
mean "jurisdiction."   See Schmid,
Gesetze, p. 654; Ellis, *Introd.*, p. 273 ;
Stubbs, *Const. Hist.*, vol. i. p. 184, note

2.   But Mr. Henry Adams, after an
exhaustive examination of the original
authorities, concludes that, as used in
the Old-English period, "there is no
reason for supposing that jurisdiction
is implied in the word *sôcn.* The idea
expressed is always that of the charters.
*It is the profits of justice, and not the
justice itself. . . .* In point of fact, no
instance can be found, before Norman
times, in which *sôcn* means jurisdiction."—*Essays in A. S. Law,* pp. 43,
44.

[4] "Sac, or sacu, seems to mean litigation." — Stubbs, *Const. Hist.*, vol. i. p.
184, note 2.

[5] "When joined with *sôcn* in a royal
grant, the intention is to convey to the
grantee *placita et forisfacturas,* — pleas
and forfeitures, justice and the profits of
justice." — *Essays in A. S. Law,* p. 44.

[6] These are Kemble's words. *Cod.
Dipl.*, i. Introd. xliv.

ments.   It has generally been conceded, however, that there is no conclusive evidence of their existence before the reign of Cnut.[1]   But this conclusion has been assailed by a brilliant critic, who maintains that the earliest positive evidence of the existence of a private law court is contained in the charters of Eadward the Confessor, by whose sweeping grants of jurisdiction to the church they became a recognized and potent element in English judicature.[2]   However revolutionary the existence of these private jurisdictions, which could hardly have been established before the latter part of the Old-English period, may appear to be, it seems to be certain that they did not represent any serious departure from primitive ideas in respect either to their organization or procedure.

A grant of *sac* and *soc* usually conferred right to hold a private hundred court.The usual effect of a grant of *sac* and *soc* was to confer upon the lord the right to hold a private hundred court within his own territory, in which hundred law was administered according to the usual forms of archaic procedure, and subject, like all other hundred courts, to the controlling jurisdiction of the shire.[3]   The leading difference in practice between a royal or national and a private hundred court was, that in the one the freemen met together to declare the law under the presidency of a royal official; in the other, under the presidency of the lord or his representative.[4]   In either event justice was administered according to the custom of the manor, and not according to the arbitrary will of the presiding officer.[5]

Origin of the manorial system.All the elements have now been examined which enter into the constitution of the manorial system which originates

---

[1] This is the view of Kemble and Maurer. *Saxons in Eng.*, vol. ii. p. 397. Dr. K. Maurer says: "But all the more certain is it that, from the reign of Cnut, the manorial jurisdiction appears in its most complete development; innumerable charters, from his and his successors' hands, grant or confirm the same," etc. — *Krit. Ueber.*, ii. p. 58.

[2] This is the conclusion reached by Mr. Henry Adams in his invaluable essays upon "Anglo-Saxon Courts of Law," to which reference has so often been made already. *Essays in A. S. Law*, pp. 27–54.

[3] "It is probable that, except in a very few special cases, the *sac* and *soc* thus granted were before the Conquest exemptions from the hundred courts only, and not from those of the shire, and that thus they are the basis of the manorial court leet, as the mark system is that of the court baron." — Stubbs, *Const. Hist.*, vol. i. p. 185.

[4] "The machinery of the hundred court would, however, be preserved, except that the territorial court would be by the great man or his representative." — Digby, *Law of Real Property*, p. 15.

[5] "It mattered not so much to them whether the king's, the abbot's, or the lord's reeve presided over their court, as it did that whoever presided should not abuse his power." — *Essays in A. S. Law*, p. 54.

in Old-English and not in Norman law. The word "manor"[1] is of Norman introduction, but the relation of the lord of a manor and his tenants substantially existed from the time the title to the lands of the once free community passed from the community itself and became vested in a lord.[2] The tie which bound the manorial group together was the manorial court (a general name which embraced the court baron and customary court) and the court leet, which in legal theory are separate and distinct.[3] In these courts of the manor were blended two kinds of jurisdiction. As the manor was only a dependent township under a new name, the court baron, which was the principal court of the manor, inherited from the old tun-moot all of its functions, with the exception of those that had passed to the parish vestry.[4] To the administrative functions, thus inherited by the manorial court from the tun-moot, was added the jurisdiction of a private hundred court, received by the lord of the manor through the usual royal grant of *sac* and *soc*.[5] The civil hundred-jurisdiction passed to the court baron, — the criminal hundred-jurisdiction to the court leet.[6] After the copyhold or customary tenure had become established, the court baron assumes a new form in dealing with tenants of that class, and in this new relation is called the customary court baron, or customary court.[7]

Court baron.

Court leet.

Customary court.

---

[1] The word *manerium*, or manor, first appears in England in the reign of Eadward the Confessor. — Ellis, *General Introd. to Domesday*, p. 225.

[2] "It has already been seen that, although the word 'manor' is of Norman introduction, substantially the relation of lord of a manor and his tenants existed before the Conquest." — Digby, *Real Property*, p. 45. See also as to the substitution of the lord for the community, *Essays in A. S. Law*, pp. 88-91 and 54.

[3] Maine, *Village-Communities.*

[4] "The court baron is primarily the successor of the ancient assembly of the village or township." — Digby, *Real Property*, p. 53; Stubbs, *Const. Hist.*, vol. i. p. 91.

[5] "Thus, either by the creation of a franchise exempt from the jurisdiction of the hundred court, or by the amalgamation of the hundred with the manorial courts, the jurisdiction *civil and criminal* exercised by the court of the hundred comes to be exercised in the manorial courts." — Digby, *Real Property*, p. 53. Mr. Digby has thus expressed with admirable clearness the important fact that not only the criminal but the *civil* jurisdiction of the manorial court was derived from the hundred. Bishop Stubbs has been criticised for his vagueness on this point. See *North Am. Review*, July, 1874, p. 242. The critic concludes that "undoubtedly both civil and criminal jurisdiction came from the hundred, for the simple reason that there was no other source from which it could have come."

[6] "The court baron exercised civil jurisdiction especially in matters relating to the freehold lands within the manor. Criminal jurisdiction was amongst the functions of the court leet, and depended on a real or supposed grant from the crown." — Digby, pp. 53, 54.

[7] Digby, *Real Property*, p. 256.

From Eadgar to William (958–1066). National unity and the feudal tendency to destroy it.

8. The attempt has now been made to define with approximate correctness the form which the constitution of the consolidated kingdom assumed during the century that intervenes between the accession of Eadgar the Peaceful and the beginning of the Norman conquest. With the accession of Eadgar, and with the final extinction of the provincial kings,[1] it seemed as if the work of consolidating the incoherent mass of petty states, which the victories of Ecgberht had but loosely united, had been fully and finally accomplished. As the work of consolidation advanced, the royal power grew until it reached its highest point in the person of Eadgar.[2] Each step in this advance was attended by a corresponding decrease in the power and independence of the local communities.[3] The ancient states were reduced to the rank of shires, — the ancient shires to the rank of hundreds. But the local organizations, which thus descended in status, preserved their autonomy to the greatest practicable extent ; their ancient boundaries remained unchanged ; in their local assemblies was still carried on all forms of administrative and judicial business in which the mass of the people were directly concerned.[4]

Royal authority, prematurely developed, weakened by the counter-force of the provincial spirit.

The national unity which thus grew up through a premature and imperfect concentration of powers around a single throne was constantly strained and weakened by the counter-force of the provincial spirit.[5] The greatest defect in the system arose out of the weakness of the tie which bound the central powers of the state to the local machinery of the constitution. There was a want of strong organic connection between the king and the witan, as the representatives of the nation, and the system of provincial organization embodied in the shires, — a want which was never to be supplied until representatives from the local communities finally drew together in an assembly which became coördinate with the

---

[1] See above, p. 169.

[2] "But with Eadgar the glory of England sank. The reign of his elder son Eadward (975–979) was short and troubled, and the young prince himself died by violence, most probably through the intrigues of an ambitious step-mother." — Freeman, *Norm. Conq.*, vol. i. p. 45 ; Stubbs, *Const. Hist.*, vol. i. p. 207.

[3] *Norm. Conq.*, vol. i. p. 67.

[4] See above, p. 171.

[5] "The national unity was weakened by the sense of provincial unity, and individual liberty was strengthened against the time when the national unity should be, not the centralization of powers, but the concentration of all organization ; a period long distant and to be reached through strange vicissitudes. *In the maintenance of provincial courts and armies was inherent the maintenance of ancient liberty.*" — Stubbs, *Const. Hist.*, vol. i. p. 209.

king's council. While this want of organic connection con-
tinued to exist, the cohesive power of national unity, which Influence of
the per-
sonal char-
acter of the
king.
the crown embodied, necessarily depended in a great degree
upon the personal character of the national chief. Under
such rulers as Ælfred, Æthelstan, Eadred, and Eadgar the
royal power was strong and effective; under such a ruler as
Æthelred it became in a moment nerveless and inefficient.[1]
Whenever the moment of weakness came, whenever the
throne was filled by an irresolute ruler or a child, the provincial spirit asserted itself through the revolts of the ealdormen, the viceroys who were ever ready to win back from the
king a part of the sovereign power which the local communities had lost. In this form appeared in England that feudal
movement which was everywhere dissolving the continental
nations into a mass of loosely united states with nobles at
their head, who owned but little more than a nominal alle-
giance to their sovereign.[2] The political history of the cen- Struggle
between
the crown
and the
local mag-
nates,
tury that intervenes between Eadgar and William is the
history of the struggle between the power of the nation as
embodied in the crown, and the provincial power asserted by
the great ealdormen, who were ever striving in the direction
of feudal isolation. But the ealdorman never succeeded in
becoming completely independent, and his office never became hereditary. The weakest of the successors of Ælfred
were strong enough to drive the greatest ealdorman into
exile, and to supply his place with another.[3] In England the
crown proved mighty enough to preserve the national unity
which it embodied against the feudal and provincial ten-
dency to destroy it. But in the struggle the defensive power in which
the defen-
sive power
of the
nation was
broken.
of the nation was broken; the spirit of disunion and disorder
which was ever assailing the foundations of the throne was
equally ready to paralyze the national arm in the presence of
the invader.[4] At the death of Eadred in 955 the tendency

---

[1] *Norm. Conq.*, vol. i. p. 78.

[2] "The feudal movement, which in
other lands was breaking up every nation into a mass of loosely-knit states
with nobles at their head who owned
little save a nominal allegiance to their
king, threatened to break up England
itself." — Green, *Hist. of the English
People*, vol. i. p. 94.

[3] "Powerful as he might be, the

English ealdorman never succeeded in
becoming really hereditary, or independent of the crown." — Green, *Hist.
Eng. People*, vol. i. p. 94; Freeman,
Norm. Conq., vol. i. p. 52.

[4] "In the witan the king and the
church alone represented the principle
of national unity and the tendency to
centralization. The ealdormen represented an antagonistic force, the an-

towards national disintegration proved strong enough to divide the realm for a time between his young nephews, Eadwig and Eadgar. And upon the death of Eadgar the struggle between the great nobles, which his firm and peaceful reign had for a time suspended, broke out afresh over the succession of his son Eadward, whom he had designated as his successor. Eadward, whose claims were disputed by his younger brother Æthelred, was elected by the witan, but in the fourth year of his reign he was removed by a cruel murder from the path of his opponent.[1]

The last Danish invasion.

In the unhappy reign of Æthelred — whose indifference to the "rede" or counsel of the great nobles by whom he was overshadowed obtained for him the name of the "redeless" [2] — the full force of the last and fiercest of the Danish invasions burst upon the realm which a line of hero kings had built up. Under the persistent blows of Olaf, Swegen, and Cnut, the unity of the nation was for a time dissolved; everything like organized national resistance came completely to an end; the concern of each district became confined at last to its own safety. So hopeless had the condition of the

Swegen.

kingdom [3] become, about the time Swegen returned for his final attack in 1013, that there was "no headman who would gather forces, but each fled as best he might, and next no shire would so much as help other." [4] Driven out by Swegen, Æthelred sought a refuge at the court of Duke Richard of Normandy, where he was preceded by the Æthelings Eadward and Ælfred, and their mother Emma, the sister of Richard, to whom Æthelred had been married eleven years before.[5] The triumph of Swegen was, however, only momentary. Upon his sudden death in 1014 the witan recalled "their own born lord," who drove Cnut, the son of Swegen, to his ships, in which he sailed away to Denmark. Upon

---

cient constitutional rights of local independence. How strong this principle was, can best be seen in the lives of Ælfric and Eadric Streona. It made the kingdom a prey to internal treachery and foreign conquest." See review of Stubbs's *Const. Hist.* in *North Am. Review,* July, 1870, p. 238.

[1] For the details of these struggles, see Freeman, *Norm. Conq.,* vol. i. pp. 42, 177, 179.

[2] Green, *Hist. Eng. People,* vol. i. p. 97.

[3] The very best account of the Danish conquest of England, and of the Danish kings in England, can be found in Freeman's *Norm. Conq.,* vol. i. pp. 175-356.

[4] *E. Chron.,* a. 1010.

[5] Freeman, *Norm. Conq.,* vol. i. pp. 204-207, 243, 244.

Cnut's return in the following year to complete the work which
his father had begun, he found the Ætheling Eadmund levying an army to resist him.   But the power of the realm was
still broken by internal dissensions.   By the side of Eadmund
stood the arch-traitor Eadric, Ealdorman of Mercia, whose
desertion at a critical moment opened the way to the invader.
After Wessex and Mercia had been overrun, Cnut sailed
towards London, the last stronghold of the national cause.
The death of Æthelred, which now occurred (1016), was followed by a double election.   All the witan outside of the
faithful city joined in the election of Cnut to the vacant
throne, while the citizens of London, with such of the witan
as were within the walls, united in the election of Eadmund.[1]
The brilliant fight which the English king now waged for a
few months against Cnut was terminated by his overthrow
at the battle of Assandun, which was followed by a treaty
partitioning the kingdom.   Upon the death of Eadmund,
which soon followed the making of this treaty, Cnut was   His elec-
elected king of all England by the witan of the whole realm.   tion as king
After the first period of cruelty which naturally attended the   land.
conquest had passed by, Cnut suddenly rose in moderation
and wisdom to the height of the greatest of the native
kings.[2]   His first important act of administration was the   Divides the
division of the kingdom into the four great governments of   kingdom
Wessex, Mercia, Northumbria, and East Anglia, over each of   earldoms.
which he appointed a great earl, with the exception of Wessex, which he retained under his own supervision.[3]   As soon
as the work of organization was done, Cnut sent home most
of his ships, retaining only a handful of household troops or
"hus-carls" as a body-guard, — it being his purpose to reign,

[1] "We now meet with, what is so
common in German and so rare in
English history, a double election to
the crown.   Cnut was chosen at Southampton, but the citizens of London,
with such of the other witan as were
within the city, held a counter-gemót
— no doubt the earlier of the two in
date — and with one voice elected
the Ætheling Eadmund." — Freeman,
Norm. Conq., vol. i. p. 256, and Appendix TT.

[2] "His aim during twenty years
seems to have been to obliterate from
men's minds the foreign character of
his rule, and the bloodshed in which it
had begun." — Green, *Hist. Eng. People*, vol. i. p. 100.

[3] "Even the great mark of his
policy, the division of England into
four great earldoms or duchies, may be
paralleled with the state of things under Eadgar and his sons." — Stubbs,
Const. Hist., vol. i. p. 201.   The four-
fold division may be traced in a charter of Æthelred, *Cod. Dipl.*, iii. 314.
See *Norm. Conq.*, vol. i. p. 273, and
note 1.

not as a conqueror but as an English king, according to the forms of the ancient constitution.   He was therefore ready

The cry for "Eadgar's law." to hearken to the cry, which soon arose from Dane and Englishman alike, for " Eadgar's law," — not for a code of Eadgar's making, but for the law as it was administered in the peaceful days of one of the greatest of the native kings.[1] Cnut had no new ideas of government to introduce ; his laws are nothing more than reproductions of those of Eadgar and Æthelred ; and his division of the kingdom into four great earldoms simply represented the old ducal system under a more definite form of organization.   Upon the death of the great Dane the vast empire which he had built up, and of which England was only a part, fell to pieces, and the fragments were divided amongst his children.   In England his death was followed by a disputed succession.   For the settlement

Harold and Hartha- cnut: of the contest which arose between his sons, Harold and Harthacnut, the witan of the whole realm met at Oxford, and after great debate the national assembly decreed the division of the kingdom between the contestants.   Thus for

last divi- sion of the realm be- tween two acknowl- edged kings. the last time was England divided between two acknowledged kings.[2]   Upon the death of Harold the crown passed to Harthacnut, and upon his death the nation, wearied with the brutality and misgovernment of Cnut's worthless sons, reëstablished the ancient line by the election of Eadward, the son of Æthelred and Emma, to the kingdom of his fathers.

Eadward the Confes- sor. The history of the reign of Eadward the Confessor is simply a continuation of the struggles of the great nobles, whose authority completely overshadows that of the king. The feudal tendency to disruption does not prevail, simply

Godwine. because the great Earl Godwine, who is striving to win the crown for his own house, is strong enough to counteract it.[3]

---

[1] "The cry is really, as an ancient writer explains it, not for the laws which such a king enacted, but for the laws which such a king observed.   It is in fact a demand for good government in a time of past or expected oppression or maladministration." — Freeman, *Norm. Conq.*, vol. i. p. 281. The "ancient writer" referred to is William of Malmesbury, who thus concludes his explanation : "In quarum custodiam etiam Regis Edwardi juratur, non quod ille statuerit, sed quod observarit." — ii. § 183.

[2] "Once more, but now for the last time in English history, the land had two acknowledged kings.   Harold reigned to the north of the Thames and Harthacnut to the south." — Freeman, *Norm. Conq.*, vol. i. p. 326.

[3] "Policy led the earl, as it led his son, rather to aim at winning England

Upon his death (1053) the earldom of the West Saxons passed to his son Harold, who for twelve years stood forth as the real master of the realm.   When the death of the childless Eadward had removed the last obstacle from his path, the mighty son of Godwine was elected by the witan to the vacant throne. But it was impossible even for Harold to bind together the broken power of the kingdom with the great earldoms of Mercia and Northumbria in the hands of his two jealous rivals, Eadwine and Morkere, whose treacherous policy really opened the way to the Norman conquest.[1]   With the fall of Harold and with the triumph of William the royal power passed into the hands of one of the wisest and sternest of statesmen.   By his inflexible policy the tendency to disruption was checked,[2] the four great earldoms were abolished, and a real national unity at last grew up as the old provincial jealousies were gradually crushed out beneath the yoke of the foreign kings.   Under the heel of the stranger the English nation finally awoke to a full sense of its oneness.

Harold elected king.

National consolidation completed through the Norman conquest.

---

itself than at breaking up England to win a mere fief in it." — Green, *Hist. Eng. People*, vol. i. p. 105; Stubbs, *Const. Hist.*, vol. i. pp. 202, 203.   Mr. Freeman opposes this view (see *Norm. Conq.*, vol. ii. p. 32) as to the tendency to separation.

[1] " But the policy of Leofric, followed out by the lukewarm patriotism of Edwin and Morcar, opened the way to the Norman conquest by disabling the right arm of Harold."— Stubbs, *Const. Hist.*, vol. i. p. 203.

[2] " When Harold, imitating the Capetians, raised himself to the throne, the natural consequence would seem to have been that England should share the fate of France.   To have prevented this was the one great service which William rendered to mankind."—*North American Review* for July, 1874, p. 238.

BOOK II.

THE NORMAN CONQUEST.

———◆———

CHAPTER I.

THE NORMAN DUCHY AND ITS DUKES.

The king-
dom of the
West
Franks.

1. THE imperial realm which Charles the Great had built up, and whose division he had more than once in contemplation, passed unbroken at his death into the nerveless hands of Lewis the Pious, the only son who survived him. During the irresolute reign of Lewis the dismemberment of the empire really began ; but it was not until the third year after his death that the work of partition was finally accomplished. The death of Lewis in 840 was the signal for the final struggle between his three sons, Lothar, Lewis, and Charles. Lo-

Partition of
the empire
of Charles
the Great.

thar at once assumed the imperial title, and Lewis and Charles combined against him. The war which ensued was terminated in 843 by the famous Treaty of Verdun,[1] by whose terms the empire was divided into three kingdoms, — the eastern, the western, and a narrow debatable land between the two, known as Lotharingia. In the partition Charles received all of Gaul west of the Scheldt, the Meuse, the Saone, and Rhone, — an area of territory which roughly corresponds in geographical extent with that now embraced

Inroads of
the North-
men.

within the limits of modern France.[2] The kingdom of the West Franks which thus passed to Charles, afterwards called the Bald, had been for a long time subject to the ravages of Scandinavian pirates, who had dared, even in the days of the great Charles himself, to scourge the coasts of the empire. As the awe inspired by his great name passed away, and as the divided realm grew more and more incapable of united

---

[1] Sime, *Hist. of Germany*, pp. 37, 38.

[2] See G. W. Kitchin's article on France, *Enc. Brit.*, 9th ed. vol. ix. p. 534.

resistance, the inroads of the Northmen grew more serious and more frequent. As early as 841 Rouen had fallen into the hands of the pirates, and thus the whole Seine valley as far up as Paris was laid open to their assaults. In 861 Charles the Bald invested a brave adventurer, Robert the Strong, with a large district of country between Paris and the sea, which was intended to stand as the bulwark of Gaul against the invader.[1] Of this march or border territory Paris became the heart, and the descendants of Robert, as dukes of the French, grew famous as its defenders. In the terrible siege which the pirates in 885–886 laid to Paris, Odo (or Eudes), the son of Robert, maintained such a heroic and successful defence that, upon the deposition of Charles the Fat in 887, he was elected king of the French, — "*Rex Francorum.*"[2] With this event began that prolonged struggle between the descendants of Robert at Paris and the descendants of Charles at Laôn, which, at the end of a hundred years, terminated in the final overthrow of the Caroling kings. Through the results of that struggle the Duke of the French grew into a king, and his duchy into a kingdom.[3]

The bulwark of Gaul against the invader.

Hundred years' struggle between Paris and Laôn.

2. Early in the tenth century, while the great struggle between Paris and Laôn was still in its infancy, the inroads of the Northmen passed from a stage of mere piratical incursion to one of conquest and settlement. But of the many Scandinavian colonies which were then planted in Gaul, one only was destined to preserve a distinctive character, and to leave its impress upon the history of Europe. This was the Danish colony planted in 911 by Rolf or Rollo at Rouen.[4] At this moment, when the history of Rolf clearly emerges from the legends which surround it, Duke Robert of Paris stands as the vassal of Charles the Simple, who then repre-

The Danish settlement at Rouen,

planted by Rolf in 911.

---

[1] "At last a new power was formed (861), chiefly with the object of defending Gaul from their attack. A large district was granted in fief by Charles the Bald to Robert the Strong, as a march or border territory, to be defended against the invading Northmen and the rebellious Breton." — Freeman, *Norm. Conq.*, vol. i. p. 106.

[2] Ibid., p. 106.

[3] For the history of this period of

struggle, see Sir Francis Palgrave's *History of Normandy and England*, vol. ij.

[4] "This settlement, the kernel of the great Norman duchy, had, I need hardly say, results of its own and an importance of its own which distinguish it from every other Danish colony in Gaul." — Freeman, *Norm. Conq.*, vol. i. p. 110.

sented the royal house at Laôn.   It was with King Charles that Rolf made the Peace of Clair-on-Epte in 912 ;   and it was from King Charles that Rolf received the grant of the district of country on both sides of the Seine which he held already by the sword.[1]   Rolf was admitted to baptism together with his followers ; and he became the vassal of King Charles, whose natural daughter was given him in marriage. Thus the history of the Norman duchy begins.   The orig-

Origin of the Norman duchy.

inal grant to Rolf did not embrace, however, all of the later Normandy.   The Teutonic district of Bayeux[2] was not won until a few years before Rolf's death ; and it was not until the reign of his successor, William Longsword (927–943), that the limits of the duchy were extended by the acquisition of the districts of Avranches, and Coutances.[3]   The troubled reign of William, which is involved in great confusion, and which ended with his murder on an island in the Somme in 943, was followed by that of his son Richard

First collision between Normandy and England.

the Fearless, in whose time we hear of the first direct collision between Normandy and England.[4]   At the end of the important reign of Richard the Fearless, which lasted for more than fifty years (943–996) the duchy passed to his son, Richard the Good, who, as uncle of Eadward the Confessor and as grandfather of William the Conqueror, is closely connected with the causes which led directly to the Norman conquest.   Richard the Good, before his death in 1026, settled the duchy upon his eldest son Richard, and the county of Hiesmes on his second son Robert.[5]   Upon the death of Richard in 1028 the duchy itself passed to his brother,

Birth of William the Bastard in 1027 or 1028.

Robert the Devil, the father of William the Bastard, who first saw the light in 1027 or 1028 at Falaise, in Teutonic Bayeux.[6]

---

[1] But "the grant to Rolf was made at the cost, not of the Frankish king at Laôn, but of the French duke at Paris." — Freeman, *Norm. Conq.*, vol. i. p. 112.

[2] As to the history of the Saxons of Bayeux, see Lappenberg, *Anglo-Norman Kings*, p. 2.

[3] Freeman, *Norm. Conq.*, vol. i. pp. 118–123.

[4] As to the disputes between Æthelred and the Norman dukes, see Wil-

liam of Malmesbury, ii. 165, 166; William of Jumièges, v. 4; Palgrave, *Normandy and England*, vol. iii. p. 103; Freeman, *Norm. Conq.*, vol. i. p. 193, and Appendix EE.

[5] Will. Gem., v. 17; *Norm. Conq.*, vol. i. p. 312.

[6] In the *Mémoires de la Société des Antiquaires de Normandie* (1837, vol. xi. p. 179) M. Deville has attempted to fix the exact date in June or July, 1027.

3. During the centuries of Roman dominion in Gaul which
precede the conquest of Clovis, the subject nation thoroughly
assimilated the language, the laws, the political institutions,
of the conquering race.   That wonderful system of law
whose history has been so long, so unbroken, and so authentic, and which next to the Christian religion has been the
most fruitful source of the rules which have governed actual
conduct throughout Western Europe,[1] Rome imposed with
a stern hand upon all the subjects of her empire.[2] Even the
Christian church, which firmly established itself in Gaul in
the early days of Roman dominion, moulded its whole ecclesiastical organization on the political divisions of the civil
power.[3] Upon the social and political substructure which thus
grew up in Gaul, and which by the end of the fifth century
had become thoroughly Roman and Christian, was superimposed, as a whole, the scheme of Teutonic life which the Frank
conquerors of Gaul brought with them in their blood and
bone from the fatherland.   The old theory that the Frankish
conquests in Gaul were accomplished by independent *principes* each fighting with a powerful *comitatus* at his back, and
that the lands so conquered were immediately parcelled out
among the *comites* upon terms of military service and special
fidelity, seems to have passed out of view.[4]   The sounder
conclusion now is, that such "conquests were the work of
the nations moving in entire order; the *comitatus* was not
the bond of cohesion; the leudes were not *comites;* all the
people were bound to be faithful to the king; the gift of an
estate by the king involved no defined obligation of service;
all the nation was alike bound to military service; the only
comites were the antrustions, and these were few in number;
the basis of the Merovingian polity was not the relation of
lord and vassal, but that of the subject to the sovereign."[5]

Marginal notes:
Origin and character of feudalism in Gaul.

The Roman and Christian substructure.

Real character of the Frank conquests.

---

[1] Sir Henry Maine, *Early Hist. of Inst.*, p. 9.
[2] "The barbarous conquerors of Gaul and Italy were guided by notions very different from those of Rome, who had imposed her own laws upon all subjects of her empire." — Hallam, *M. A.*, vol. i. p. 153.
[3] Cf. Kitchin's "France" in *Enc. Brit.*, 9th ed. vol. ix. p. 528.
[4] This old theory, which seems to

rest upon the authority of Montesquieu, is generally followed by the
French writers. See Guizot, *Civilis.
France*, vol. i. p. 311, etc.
[5] This is the view of Waitz (*Deutsche
Verfassungsgeschichte*, ii. pp. 226–262)
as restated by Bishop Stubbs, *Const.
Hist.*, vol. i. p. 251, n. 2. "The work
of Sohm (*Altdeutsche Reichs- und Gerichtsverfassung*) completes the overthrow of the old theory by reconstruct

Frank political organization.

From the "Pactus Legis Salicæ," a collection of the customs of Frank law in the fifth century, can be obtained a reasonably clear idea of the system of political organization which prevailed among the Franks when the conquest of Gaul began.[1]

The vill.

The unit of organization in the Frank system is the vill, the successor of the mark, which is capable of holding assemblies and making by-laws.[2]

The hundred.

The next largest division, and around which the whole system revolves, is that most important and enduring of all Teutonic institutions the hundred, in whose court justice is administered with the right of appeal to the king alone.[3]

The province.

An aggregation of hundreds constitutes a district or province, whose government is intrusted to a graf, an administrative officer appointed by royal authority.[4]

The king.

The kingly office, which is distinctly recognized, is elective, with the right of election limited to a single royal house.[5] The king, who is surrounded by a *comitatus* of personal followers, appoints not only the grafs to rule the provinces, but the magistrates in the vills: he is the ruler of the nation, the

The national assembly.

supreme judge of appeal. The supreme council of the nation is the whole people in arms.[6]

Feudalism *par excellence* of Frank origin.

This simple system of political life and law, which the Franks brought with them into Gaul, settled down by the side of Roman life and law, and a struggle for the mastery was the natural consequence. Under these circumstances that peculiar system of legal and political ideas which is generally known as feudalism, and which is distinctly of Frank origin, finds its historical development upon the soil of Gaul, where it matures, not unaffected by Roman influences.[7] This system can only be clearly understood when it

---

ing in a very remarkable manner the old German system in Salian and Merovingian times." — *Const. Hist.*, vol. i. p. 252.

[1] In this law can be found no trace of a feudal nobility or a "feudal system" of any kind. Cf. Waitz (*Das alte Recht der Salischen Franken*, p. 103), who says, "Das Salische Gesetz keunt keinen Adel; auch nicht die leiseste Spur desselben findet sich."

[2] Waitz, *D. V. G.*, ii. pp. 314, 353, 354; *Das Alte Recht*, pp. 124, 210, 228, 253; Stubbs, *Const. Hist.*, vol. i. p. 54.

[3] "The court consists of all the fully qualified landowners, who bear, in their name of *Rachimburgi*, a title that shows their capacity for legal functions." — Stubbs, *Const. Hist.*, vol. i. p. 54. Cf. Waitz, *D. V. G.*, i. p. 334; ii. pp. 493-495.

[4] Savigny, *R. R.*, i. pp. 256, 265; Sohm, *Fr. R. G. Verf.*, i. p. 83.

[5] Waitz, *Das Alte Recht.*, pp. 203-214.

[6] Stubbs, *Const. Hist.*, vol. i. p. 55.

[7] "The feudal system *par excellence* is always understood to mean that special form of feudalism which was developed on the soil of Gaul by the conquering Franks." — Sir J. H. Ram-

is viewed in the two aspects in which it naturally presents itself,—as a system of land tenure, and as a system of government. Feudalism was the result of the union of two great elements ; the feudal relation implied the union of two other relations. One element consisted of the personal relation which grew up between lord and vassal, lord and man,—a relation which involved mutual service, responsibility, and protection,[1] but which at first was not necessarily connected with the holding of land.[2] By the practice of commendation the inferior put himself under the personal care of a lord, without altering his title or divesting himself of his right to his estate.[3] Another element was represented by the *beneficium*, which was partly of Roman, partly of German, origin. A practice had arisen in the empire of granting out frontier lands to soldiers upon condition of their rendering military service in border warfare.[4] But the holders of such lands stood in no personal relation to the emperor : they were not his men ; their service was only due to him as the representative of the commonwealth. This Roman custom naturally suggested to the Teutonic kings the plan of rewarding their followers out of their own estates with grants of land,—benefices or fiefs,—with a special undertaking to be faithful in consideration of the gift.[5] The Frank beneficiary system[6] originated in gifts of this character, and in the surrender of allodial estates[7] made by the owners to lay or ecclesiastical potentates, to be received back and held by them as tenants by rent or service. Through the union or interpenetration of the beneficiary system and

Feudalism as a system of land tenure,— lord and man;

commendation;

the beneficium.

---

say's " Feudalism," in *Enc. Brit.*, 9th ed. vol. ix. p. 120.

[1] " There is, in short, the old Teutonic relation of the *comitatus*, the relation of the hlaford and his thegn." — Freeman, *Norm. Conq.*, vol. i. p. 62.

[2] Digby, *Hist. Law of Real Property*, p. 21.

[3] Stubbs, *Const. History*, vol. i. p. 253.

[4] Palgrave, *English Commonwealth*, vol. i. p. 354. " Probably the conception of the tenure under which such soldiers held their lands was borrowed to some extent from the attributes of the interest in lands called *emphyteusis*."

— Digby, *Law of Real Property*, p. 30. " Emphyteusis (ἐμφύτευσις, literally an ' implanting '), is a perpetual right in a piece of land that is the property of another," etc. — Smith's *Dictionary of Greek and Roman Antiquities*, p. 400. See, also, *Inst.* 3, 25, 3, Cooper's notes.

[5] Freeman, *Norm. Conq.*, vol. i. p. 62. " Not a promise of definite service, but a pledge to continue faithful in the conduct in consideration of which the reward is given." — Stubbs, *Const. Hist.*, vol. i. p. 253, note 1.

[6] Waitz, *D. V. G.*, ii. pp. 226-258.

[7] Maine, *Ancient Law*, p. 224, " Allods and Fiefs."

Feudalism the product of the union of the beneficiary system with that of commendation.

the system of commendation, the idea of feudal obligation became complete, — both being fostered by the growth of immunities.[1] The system which thus originated spread rapidly, and all other tenures were soon assimilated to it. The *beneficia* finally receive the name of *feuda*, a word which does not appear earlier than the close of the ninth century.[2] As

Benefices become hereditary.

early as 877 Charles the Bald, by a clause in the Capitulary of Kiersi, recognized the hereditary character of all bene fices.[3] The hereditary usage, which for a long time had been growing up, had by that time no doubt become general, but by no means universal. With the Capitulary of Kiersi the growth of strictly feudal jurisprudence really begins.[4]

Feudalism as a system of government.

The principle that benefices were hereditary was soon extended to the framework of government itself. The provincial magistracies, originally received by the dukes and counts through the king's appointment, and which tended from the

Provincial magistracies become hereditary.

first to become hereditary, actually became so, as soon as the hereditary character of benefices was firmly established.[5] The local sovereignty of the official magistrate, who thus grew into a ruler by hereditary right, was greatly enhanced by grants of immunity, which were nothing less than sections of the national or royal right of judicature bestowed upon

Growth of immunities.

the receiver of a fief. Through grants of immunity the dwellers upon feudal estates were withdrawn from the jurisdiction of the national or royal tribunals, and placed under that of the lord upon whose land they dwelt.[6] To the right of judicature the hereditary provincial ruler gradually added all the other attributes of actual sovereignty. Each lord not only judged, taxed, and commanded the class next below him, but he exercised also the rights of private war and private coinage.[7] So intense did the idea of sovereignty in the pro-

---

[1] Waitz, *D. V. G.*, ii. pp. 634-645; iv. pp. 243-273. The general statements in the text as to the origin of the feudal system embody the conclusions of Waitz, which are accepted both by Bishop Stubbs and Mr. Freeman.

[2] Digby, *Law of Real Property*, p. 32. "Oddly enough, in modern use the word *benefice* has come to be used only of ecclesiastical benefices." — Freeman, *Norm. Conq.*, vol. v. p. 87, note 3. See, also, Maine, *Ancient Law*, pp. 223, 224.

[3] See Baluze, ii. p. 179; Roth, *Beneficialwesen*, p. 420.

[4] Stubbs, *Const. Hist.*, vol. i. p. 254, and note 1.

[5] "The official magistracy had in itself the tendency to become hereditary, and when the benefice was recognized as heritable the provincial governorship became so, too." — Stubbs, *Const. Hist.*, vol. i. p. 255.

[6] Waitz, *D. V. G.*, ii. pp. 634-645.

[7] Stubbs, *Const. Hist.*, vol. i. p. 256.

vincial lord become, that the doctrine was finally asserted, that a man who pledged his faith to a lord, who was the man of the king, was the man of that lord only, and not the man of the king himself.[1] The process through which the provincial potentates gradually drew to themselves all of the real attributes of sovereignty ended at last in the only result possible, — the complete attenuation of the central power. In theory the king remains the supreme lord, mediate or immediate, of every landowner, and to him great duties are due; but the royal power is reduced in fact to a mere shadow.[2] With the destructive effects of Frank feudalism upon all central or national authority, William, as Duke of Normans, became thoroughly familiar.[3] And as we shall see hereafter, he turned such knowledge to a good account. As king of the English, William was careful to devise such anti-feudal legislation as would render the disruptive tendencies of feudalism in England impossible.

4. If any records ever existed touching the details of the settlement made by Rolf and his followers at Rouen, or touching the legal and political institutions which they planted in Gaul, they have utterly perished. There are no chronicles, no charters, to guide us; of the internal organization of the Norman duchy in the early days of its history we know absolutely nothing. It seems, however, to be clear that the express condition upon which the grant to Rolf was made was, that the new settlers should become members of the Christian and Frankish commonwealth of which Charles was overlord.[4] And it also seems to be clear that the Norman dukes from the very beginning ruled, not as absolute sovereigns, but with the advice of some kind of an assembly or council of great men.[5] There is no reason to believe that

[1] Cf. Freeman, *Norm. Conq.*, vol. iv. p. 472, and note 1, in which reference is made to the refusal, at a somewhat later time, of John of Joinville, as the man of the Count of Champagne, to take any oath to St. Lewis; citing *Mémoires*, p. 37, ed. Michel, Paris, 1858.

[2] For a summing up of the results of feudalism in France, see Stubbs, *Const. Hist.*, vol. i. pp. 3, 4.

[3] Not until William had crushed a great revolt of his barons could he consider himself master in his own duchy. As to the battle of Val-ès-dunes, see Freeman, *Norm. Conq.*, vol. ii. pp. 165, 166.

[4] "The Peace of Clair-on-Epte (912) was the duplicate of the Peace of Wedmore. . . . A definite district was ceded to Rolf, for which he became the king's vassal; he was admitted to baptism, and received the king's natural daughter in marriage. — Freeman, *Norm. Conq.*, vol. i. p. 112.

[5] Stubbs, *Const. Hist.*, vol. i. p. 249, citing *Norm. Conq.*, vol. iii. p. 289 *seq.*

there was any such systematic extermination or expulsion of
the native race as attended the English conquest of Britain.
Upon the contrary, it appears that the original Gallic population, which was no doubt deeply intermixed with Roman and
Frankish elements, gradually sank down into a dependent
yet spirited peasantry, which sometimes dared to revolt
against their Norman masters.[1]   In the reign of the third
duke, Richard the Fearless, the duchy, after fluctuating in
its allegiance between the king at Laôn and the duke at
Paris, permanently attached itself to the latter ; and from

Duchy
becomes
French,
Christian,
and feudal. that time the duchy rapidly grew more French, more Christian, and more feudal.[2]   It is in the reign of Richard that we
can first trace the beginnings of the Norman nobility whose
members derive their status as nobles either from ancient
Norse descent from the companions of Rolf, or through connections, legitimate or illegitimate, with the ducal house.[3]

Relations
between the
duke and
baronage. The baronage which thus grew up held their lands of the
duke upon terms of feudal obligation, and by his strong hand
alone were they held in subjection.[4]   Over this turbulent
baronage William the Bastard, while yet a minor, was called
to rule ; and his first important victory was won in crushing
a widespread revolt headed by some of the greatest nobles
in his own dukedom.

Normandy
and Eng-
land. 5. The first direct intercourse between Normandy and
England occurred in the reign of Æthelred, who became in-
volved in a quarrel with the third Norman duke, Richard the
Fearless, on account of the friendly reception given in Norman ports to the Danish pirates who were then plundering
the coasts of England.[5]   Through the mediation of the pope
the quarrel was amicably adjusted, and an agreement entered

Palgrave holds a contrary view ; he regards William, the son of Rollo, as
absolute. " His was the law, his was
the state, his was the church." " He
spake the law, he gave the law, he made
the law, he executed the law." — *Normandy and England*, vol. ii. pp. 258,
259.
  [1] As to the peasant revolt (997), see
Freeman, *Norm. Conq.*, vol. i. pp. 115,
172, 173.
  [2] Ibid., pp. 149, 169.
  [3] " The Norman counts were at the
time of the Conquest, in most cases,
younger branches of the ducal house, or

closely connected with it by affinity. —
Stubbs, *Const. Hist.*, vol. i. p. 249,
note 3.
  [4] Richard the Fearless is regarded
as the founder of Norman feudalism. —
Normandy and England, vol. ii. p. 534.
See, also, Waitz, *Göttingische Gelehrte
Anzeigen*, Nachrichten, February 14,
1866, pp. 95, 96.
  [5] Freeman, *Norman Conq.*, vol. i. p.
192, and Appendix EE, in which is
cited William of Malmesbury, ii. 165,
166. Cf. Palgrave, *Normandy and
England*, vol. iii. p. 103 ; Lappenberg,
vol. ii. p. 154, Thorpe.

into between the two princes that neither should receive the enemies of the other.[1]   Nine years later Æthelred became involved in a dispute, probably in open war, with Richard the Good, the successor of Richard the Fearless, and again the quarrel ended in a friendly settlement.   The peace which was then made was confirmed by a marriage between Æthelred and Emma,[2] the duke's sister ; and out of that marriage grew the fatal kinship between the royal house of Ælfred and the ducal house of Rolf which led directly to the Norman conquest.   "With that marriage began the settlement of Normans in England, their admission to English offices and estates, their general influence in English affairs, everything in short that paved the way for the actual Conquest."[3] When, in 1013–14, Æthelred was driven from the throne by Swegen, he sought a refuge at the court of his Norman brother-in-law, where he was preceded by Emma, who had gone thither with the young Æthelings, Ælfred and Eadward.[4]   After the death of Æthelred, Emma, at the solicitation of the youthful king Cnut, returned to England and became his wife,[5] and thus quietly resumed her old place as Lady of the English.   The issue of the marriage of Emma with Cnut was Harthacnut, the last of the Danish kings of England.   After the marriage of Emma with Cnut, her two sons by Æthelred still found an asylum at the court of their Norman kinsman.   Ælfred perished miserably in an attempt upon the English crown in 1036 ; while Eadward remained in Normandy until 1041, when he was recalled to England by his Danish half-brother Harthacnut.[6]   Upon his death in the following year, the nation, wearied with the misgovernment of Cnut's worthless sons, resolved to restore the line of Cerdic in the person of Eadward : "Before the king buried were, all folk chose Eadward to king at London."[7]   With the election of Eadward the Norman invasion really began. The new king was a man of mature years ; he was the son

Marriage of Æthelred and Emma.

After Æthelred's death Emma married Cnut.

Harthacnut the issue of the marriage.

Election of Eadward the Confessor, Emma's son by Æthelred.

---

[1] Will. Malmes., ii. 166.

[2] *E. Chron.*, a. 1002.

[3] Freeman, *Norm. Conq.*, vol. i. p. 204.

[4] *E. Chron.*, a. 1013.

[5] Will. Malmes., ii. 180; *Norm. Conq.*, vol. i. p. 275, Appendix BBB.

[6] *E. Chron.*, a. 1041. "The invitation is distinctly asserted by the *Encomiast*, p. 39. William of Malmesbury, however (ii. 188), seems to imply that Eadward came uninvited." — *Norm. Conq.*, vol. i. p. 349, note 5.

[7] The coronation of Eadward is not recorded until the next year. See *E. Chron.*, a. 1043; Flor. Wig., 1043.

of a Norman mother; he had passed nearly his whole life in Normandy; his speech was French, and his heart was far

more French than English. Into his English realm Eadward was followed by a host of friends from the land of his exile; they swarmed about his person; they became dominant in his councils; and they were enriched with English estates, upon which they soon began to rear frowning castles.[1] In the government of the church the strangers soon became as dominant as in the government of the state; bishopric after bishopric passed into foreign hands, until at last a Norman prelate was elevated to the primatial see of Augustine.[2] The alarming influence of the Norman party, which had now reached its height, aroused a great national revolt, which was led by Godwine, the mighty earl of the West Saxons. But in the very midst of the struggle the national party dropped away from Godwine, and he and his sons were declared outlaws and banished from the kingdom. At this moment,

while the realm lay at the feet of the strangers, William the Bastard first set foot upon the shores of England.[3] He now came (1052) with great pomp to visit his cousin Eadward, and he went away loaded with gifts and honors. It is more than likely that it was during this visit that Eadward made to William the famous promise touching the succession. If

Eadward's
alleged
promise to
William, —
its consti-
tutional
value.

such a promise was ever made, if Eadward ever pledged himself to make William his heir, such a promise could not have been of any great constitutional value. The right to dispose of the English crown was vested alone in the national assembly.[4] Any recommendation which Eadward might undertake to make in favor of William, the witan were only bound to consider; they were then at perfect liberty either to accept or reject it. But slight as the value of such a promise may have been, it was sufficient, in connection with his kinship with Eadward, to enable William to construct out of it at least a plausible claim to the succession. He was ingenious

---

[1] "In all this the seeds of the Conquest were sowing, or rather, as I once before put it, it is now that the Conquest actually begins. The reign of Eadward is a period of struggle between natives and foreigners for dominion in England." — *Norm. Conq.*, vol. ii. p. 19.

[2] In 1051 Robert of Jumièges was appointed archbishop of Canterbury. — *E. Chron.*, a. 1051.

[3] *Chron. Wig.*, 1052; *Norman Conquest*, vol. ii. p. 105.

[4] As to the constitutional value of the alleged promise, see Freeman, *Norm. Conq.*, vol. ii. pp. 195–198.

enough to persuade a large part of Europe that he was the true heir of Eadward, and, what was more to the purpose, he proved himself strong enough to maintain his argument upon the field of battle. William's visit was followed by a great national reaction; the next year witnessed the complete overthrow of the Norman party, and the return of Godwine and his sons to power.[1] The king became reconciled to Godwine, and his house was fully restored to its former rank and influence.[2] In the midst of his triumph (1053) Godwine died, and the earldom of the West Saxons passed to his great son Harold, who, for the next thirteen years, became the actual ruler of the English nation.[3] Upon the death of the childless Eadward, Harold became a candidate for the royal office, to which he was hurriedly but unanimously elected by the witan of the whole realm.[4] This solemn and valid election William refused to recognize; he denounced it as hasty and illegal. William did not claim that he had an absolute right to the crown, but he did claim the sole right to present himself as a candidate to the witan as the chosen heir of the Confessor.[5] And he further claimed that Harold had bound himself by a solemn oath not to oppose but to uphold his title.[6] To win for himself the right of presentation to the witan, and to execute his vengeance on Harold for his perjury, were the ostensible objects of William's invasion.

National reaction against Norman influence.

Election of Harold, which William refused to recognize.

6. Eadward the Confessor died on the 5th January, 1066, and on the same day the witan elected Harold to be king. On the next day [7] Eadward was entombed in the West Minster, the freshly hallowed church of his own rearing; and on the same day and in the same place the king-elect was crowned and anointed, not by Stigand, the primate of all England, but by Ealdred, primate of Northumberland. The

William's conquest of England.

---

[1] *E. Chron.*, a. 1052.

[2] "To Godwine was his earldom clean given back, as full and free as he first possessed it; and in like manner to his sons all that they had before possessed, and to his wife and daughter all as full and as free as they had before possessed." — *E. Chron.*, a. 1052.

[3] Upon the accession of Harold to the earldom of the West Saxons, see Freeman, *Norm. Conq.*, vol. ii. pp. 235, 236.

[4] "A totius Angliæ primatibus ad regale culmen electus." — Flor. Wig., 1066.

[5] Freeman, *Norm. Conq.*, vol. iii. p. 350.

[6] See *Lectures on the Hist. of Eng.*, Guest (London, 1879), p. 132.

[7] "On that day began that long series of national ceremonies which has gone on uninterruptedly to our own time, and which has made the Abbey of Saint Peter the hearth and Prytaneion of the English nation." — *Norm. Conq.*, vol. iii. p. 17.

elevation of Harold to the kingdom made no vacancy, however, in the great earldom of the West Saxons.   Harold still
retained in his own hands the immediate control of the south
of England, while he continued to intrust to Eadwine and
Morkere, sons of the rival house of Leofric, the great northern earldoms of Mercia and Northumberland.   In the government of the latter Morkere had been preceded by Harold's
brother, Tostig, whose administration had been so oppressive
that, in the year preceding Eadward's death, he was deposed
and outlawed, and Morkere, the younger brother of Eadwine
of Mercia, elected in his stead.[1]   When in the ninth month
of Harold's reign the storm of the Norman conquest burst
upon the south of England, Harold was absent in the northern earldoms aiding Eadwine and Morkere to repel a great

Norwegian invasion led by Harold Hardrada, who had been
solicited to make the attack by the exiled traitor Tostig.[2]
Harold's presence in the north was at once followed by the

great fight at Stamfordbridge, in which the Norwegians were
routed, and Harold Hardrada and Tostig left dead upon the
field.   In the midst of his triumph Harold was startled by

the announcement that William had landed at Pevensey,[3] on
the coast of Sussex.   After a council had been held, Harold
at once marched towards London, after having bidden Eadwine and Morkere to follow him with the whole force of their
earldoms.   But the treacherous sons of Ælfgar held back
from their duty ; the "main forces of Northumberland and
northwestern Mercia came not to King Harold's muster."[4]
In the midst of the great crisis the cohesive power of national unity was weakened as usual by the counter-force of

the provincial spirit.   The treacherous policy of Eadwine
and Morkere, by disabling the right arm of Harold, opened
the way to the Norman conquest.[5]   Harold might not have
lost the great fight on Senlac had he been heartily sustained
by the united power of the whole realm of England.   Wil-

---

[1] "All the thegns in Yorkshire and
in Northumberland gathered themselves together and outlawed their
earl, Tostig, . . . and sent after Morkere, the son of Ælfgar the earl, and
chose him to be their earl." — *Chron.
Wig. Petrib.*, 1065; *Norm. Conq.*, vol.
ii. p. 322.

[2] Guest, *Lectures on the Hist. of Eng.*,
p. 137.
[3] "Venit ad Pevenesæ." — *Bayeux
Tapestry*, pl. 9.
[4] Freeman, *Norman Conq.*, vol. iii. p.
282.
[5] Stubbs, *Const. History*, vol. i. p.
203.

liam's victory, crushing as it was, did not put him in actual
possession, however, of more than a fraction of the kingdom ;
neither did it bring to an end all organized national resistance.   But by the death of Harold the English nation had
been deprived of the only leader under whom victory was
possible.   For the want of a more available candidate, the *Election of*
witan assembled in London now chose the almost imbecile *Eadgar*
young Ætheling Eadgar — the grandson of Eadmund Ironside *after Harold's fall.*
and the only survivor of the old line — to be king.[1] This hopeless expedient imparted no strength, of course, to the national
cause, and with the Norman duke's advance on London the
spirit of further resistance came to an end.   When William *Crown
offered to*
reached Berkhampstead he was met by a great deputation, *William ;*
headed by Eadgar, and composed of the chief men of England, temporal and spiritual, who came to offer him the
crown.[2] So far William had not claimed to be king ; he
only claimed the sole right to become king.   And even when
the crown was offered him by the deputation of great men,
who certainly had the right to represent the south of England, he pretended to hesitate ; and not until he had discussed the matter in a council of his own followers did he
express to the English embassy a decided willingness to accept it.[3] As soon as that conclusion was reached, the coronation of the king-elect was fixed to take place at London, in *his election
and corona-*
the West Minster, on the Feast of the Nativity, which was *tion.*
fast approaching.   In the church of Eadward, on Christmas
Day, amid the shouts of "Yea, yea," from his new English
subjects,[4] William, after taking the oaths usually administered
to an English king, was crowned and anointed by the hands
of the Northumbrian prelate who, less than a year before, had
poured the consecrating oil upon the head of the mighty
chief of the house of Godwine.   Thus with every outward *The duke
of the Nor-*
show of legality William, duke of the Normans, was elected, *mans becomes king
of the Eng-
lish.*
crowned, and anointed king of the English.

[1] Flor. Wig., 1066; Ord. Vit., 502 D.   [4] Green, *Hist of the English People*,
[2] *Chron. Wig.*, 1066.   vol. i. p. 115.
[3] Upon this whole subject, see *Norm.
Conq.*, vol. iii. pp. 366-369.

CHAPTER II.

THE NORMAN KINGS OF ENGLAND.

The double
origin of
William's
kingship:

1. THE great outward show of legality under which William endeavored to conceal the fact that he was a foreign conqueror, "a king only by the edge of the sword," was but a part of a deliberate policy which has marked him as one of the foremost statesmen of the world. By claiming to be the heir of Eadward, he connected himself directly with the line of national kings that had gone before him; by insisting upon his elevation to the royal office by the choice of the witan he obtained the highest confirmation of his title which could be drawn from the ancient constitution; by seeking consecration at the hands of an English prelate, and by taking the usual coronation oaths, he complied at once with every prerequisite to full kingship prescribed by ancient custom and by the national church. By means of these outward forms William clearly proclaimed the fact, not only to the conquered English but to his Norman followers, that he

Its national
aspect;

would rule in his new realm, not as a mere feudal conqueror but as a national king.[1] It was no part of William's plan to remain simply a military chieftain, wholly dependent upon the jealous and exacting host by whose aid the Conquest had been accomplished. With the prescience of a statesman, he claimed to be the ruler of a nation in which Normans and Englishmen were alike his subjects; and as such a ruler he claimed the possession of every royal right which had ever belonged to any of the kings who had gone before him. The sum of royal power which thus accrued to William as a na-

its feudal
aspect.

tional king was augmented by the addition of every feudal right[2] which tended to increase the royal revenue and to strengthen the royal authority, while every principle was

---

[1] "In that claim he saw not only the justification of the Conquest in the eyes of the church, but his great safeguard against the jealous and aggressive host by whose aid he had realized

it. Accordingly, immediately after the battle of Hastings he proceeded to seek the national recognition." — Stubbs, vol. i. p. 258.

[2] "To his elective right he added

carefully eliminated which tended to promote the disruptive tendencies of feudal institutions. As king of the English, William was careful to preserve the law of the land as it stood in the days of King Eadward,[1] and along with it those ancient assemblies of the shire and the hundred in which that law had been immemorially administered.[2] Under the authority of the old system, thus carefully preserved, the new king rigorously exacted every kind of revenue, ordinary and extraordinary, which had ever belonged to any of his English predecessors. As feudal lord, William firmly established the doctrine that the king was the supreme landowner, and that all land was held by grant from him. In his time the folk-land became *terra regis*.[3] All landowners thus became tenants of the king, and under William's successors the feudal revenue which accrued to the crown from this source was enormous. It was the policy of William to introduce but one side of feudalism,[4] — to accept it as a system of tenure, but not as a system of government. And in thus drawing to the crown all the available benefits of the system, he was careful to guard against its disruptive tendencies, first, by preventing the accumulation in the hands of any of the great feudatories of any considerable number of contiguous estates ;[5] second, by requiring from all freeholders an oath which bound them directly to the king by the double tie of homage and allegiance.[6] To every landowner the Conqueror

The national revenue.

The feudal revenue.

William's anti-feudal policy ;

the right of conquest. It is the way in which William grasped and employed this double power that marks the originality of his political genius, for the system of government which he devised was in fact the result of this double origin of his rule. It represented neither the purely feudal system of the Continent nor the system of the older English royalty: more truly perhaps it may be said to have represented both. As the conqueror of England, William developed the military organization of feudalism so far as was necessary for the secure possession of his conquests." — Green, *Hist. Eng. People,* vol. i. p. 127.

[1] With such additions as he himself made for the benefit of the English. Statutes of William, § 7.

[2] " Requiratur hundredus et comitatus, sicut antecessores nostri statuerunt." — Ibid., § 8.

[3] " The reign of the Conqueror finally changed the ancient *folkland* into *terra regis.* The doctrine was established that the king was the supreme landlord, and that all land was held by his grant." — Freeman, vol. v. p. 256.

[4] Ibid., vol. v. pp. 255–257.

[5] Thorpe's Lappenberg, vol. iii. p. 201 ; Gneist, *Self-government,* vol. i. pp. 66, 67.

[6] In the gemót of Salisbury all the landowners of England who were worth summoning, "whose men soever they were, all bowed to him and were his men, and swore to him faithful oaths that they would be faithful to him against all other men." — *E. Chron.,* 1086. As to the anti-feudal character of this oath, see Stubbs, vol. i. pp. 265, 266, and notes ; Freeman, *Norm. Conq.,* vol. iv. p. 471 ; Gneist, *Verwalt.* vol. i. p. 116.

stood in the double relation of landlord and sovereign. "After the coming of William, a king of the English remained all that he was before, and he became something else as well. He kept all his old powers, and he gained some new ones. He became universal landlord, but in so doing he did not cease to be universal ruler. At once king and lord, he had two strings to his bow at every critical moment; if one character failed him, he had the other to fall back upon."[1] During William's reign the royal power was greatly strengthened and consolidated; the tendency to provincial isolation was crushed out; the four great earldoms were abolished; and the whole realm at last united in one consolidated kingdom which was never afterwards to be divided.

he strengthens the royal authority and consolidates the kingdom.

Gradual advance of the Conquest.

2. It is a mistake to suppose that William's great victory near Hastings, crushing as it was, put him at once in possession of the whole realm of England. As the immediate result of the battle he only gained the actual possession of a few of the southern shires; but, during the month and a half that intervened between his victory and his crowning at Westminster, he received the submission of all southeastern England east of a line roughly extended from the Wash to the Southampton[2] Water. Although William was not now opposed by any rival king, the greater part of the realm held quietly aloof from him, and not until several campaigns had been fought and won was the conquest of northern and western England finally accomplished. The conquest of the west, which was first undertaken, practically ended with the fall of Exeter in 1068; and the first conquest of the north, which was provoked by the risings of Eadwine and Morkere, ended with the submission of York before the end of the same year. But the final and terrible conquest of the north, which has left an indelible stain upon the name of William, did not begin until 1069. The signal for the final struggle was the invasion of Swegen, king of Denmark, whose arrival in the Humber was followed by a general uprising not only in northern but in all western and southwestern England. After this revolt had been put down piecemeal, William,

Submission of southeastern England.

Conquest of the west and north.

---

[1] Freeman, *Norm. Conq.*, vol. v. p. 262.

[2] Green, *Hist. of the English People*, vol. i. p. 116. "He had indeed direct military possession only of certain of the southern and eastern shires." — *Norm. Conq.*, vol. iv. p. 1.

who had sworn vengeance against the north, entered upon the deliberate and systematic harrying of the whole territory between the Tyne and the Humber. Seventeen years afterwards, when the great Survey was taken, the record of the devastation was made by entries of "waste," "waste," "waste," which are attached through page after page to the Yorkshire lordships; and sixty years afterwards William of Malmesbury wrote that the country was still lying waste, and "if any ancient inhabitant remains he knows it no longer." [1] When this terrible work of policy and vengeance had been fully carried out William marched westward upon Chester, whose submission early in 1070 practically ended the Norman conquest. William was now full king over all of England in fact as well as in name.

Devastation of the north as recorded in Domesday.

Conquest not complete until 1070.

3. When the fact is borne in mind that the advance of the Conquest was gradual, it becomes more easy to understand the manner in which William dealt with the land which, district by district, became subject to his authority. The theory upon which the Conqueror claimed title to the lands of the conquered was, that he, the heir of Eadward, upon coming to take possession of his kingdom, had been opposed either actively or passively by the whole nation, who, by the customary laws of both England and Normandy, had thus become involved in the guilt of treason.[2] Under the strict letter of the law, the lands of all were forfeited to the king, but the application of this principle William undertook to regulate according to the circumstances of individual cases. While there can be no doubt that through the enforcement of this principle the bulk of all the great estates passed during William's reign into Norman hands, it seems to be equally clear that the main body of the people, the actual occupants of the soil, remained, as a general rule, undisturbed in their possessions.[3] The work of confiscation seems to have begun immediately after the great fight at Hastings, and the evi-

The work of confiscation and regrant.

Theory under which English lands were forfeited.

Main body of the people undisturbed in their possessions.

---

[1] For a full and graphic account of "The Conquest of Western and Northern England," see Freeman, *Norm. Conq.*, vol. iv. ch. xviii. See, also, Green, *Hist. Eng. People*, vol. i. pp. 116–118.

[2] Freeman, *Norm. Conq.*, vol. iv. p. 14, vol. v. p. 12; Digby, *Law of Real Property*, pp. 34, 35.

[3] "The actual amount of dispossession was no doubt greatest in the higher ranks; the smaller owners may to a large extent have remained in a mediatised position on their estates," etc. — Stubbs, *Const. Hist.*, vol. i. p. 260.

dence tends to show that the lands of all who actually took part in the battle were held to be forfeited. In this way a great fund was at once placed at the Conqueror's disposal out of which to enrich his followers. William was himself en- riched by becoming the possessor of the private estates of

Folkland becomes terra regis. his royal predecessors, and by all of the folkland becoming *terra regis.*[1] In some instances express mention is made of men's buying back their lands from the king, and from the joint witness of the Chronicle and Domesday it appears that at some time soon after the coronation of William the Eng- lish as a body redeemed their lands from him.[2] Thus as the Conquest advanced William persistently enforced with greater

Estates of great men generally forfeited. or less strictness his scheme of confiscation. In dealing with the estates of the great men, living or dead, who had actually opposed him, or who held out against him, the rule seems to have been to strictly enforce the forfeiture; but in the case of those who were willing to acknowledge him the rule seems to have been for the king to receive a surrender, and then to make a regrant upon the payment of a moneyed compensa-

No new kind of ten- ure syste- matically introduced. tion. There is no evidence, however, going to show that William directly or systematically introduced any new kind of tenure; the grantee of William, whether an old owner or a new one, held his land as it had been held in the days of King Eadward.[3] There is nothing in Domesday which estab- lishes the existence of military tenures as they were after- wards understood.[4] The powerful followers of the Conqueror who received grants of large estates received them no doubt as his tenants, bound to render military service to him. And other landholders who received their lands back from the king probably stood to him in substantially the same relation. It is not likely, however, that William's grants were made upon a definite pledge to provide a certain contingent of knights

---

[1] Digby, *Law of Real Property*, p. 34.

[2] "And he came to Westminster, and Archbishop Ealdred consecrated him king, and men paid him tribute, and delivered him hostages, *and after- wards bought their land.*"—*E. Chron.,* 1066. Domesday (ii. 360) tells of a time when the English as a body re- deemed their lands. See Freeman, *Norm. Conq.,* vol. iv. p. 16; Stubbs, *Const. Hist.,* vol. i. p. 259.

[3] Freeman, *Norm. Conq.,* vol. v. p. 249. "Domesday bears abundant traces of the growth of the idea of tenure, though we still hear of the men (*homi- nes*) of a lord rather than of his ten- ants. The land is everywhere spoken of as having been *held* of King Ed- ward or some other lord."—Digby, *Law of Real Property,* p. 38.

[4] This fact is clearly pointed out by Sir Francis Palgrave in his *Normandy and England,* vol. iii. p. 609 *et seq.*

for the king's service. The military service due from the ten- No immedi-
ate change
in the na-
ture of
military
service.
ant was probably measured at first by the old custom which
required the equipment of one fully armed man for every five
hides of land.[1] Under William as under Eadward, military
service is due, not to the lord as lord, but to the state and to
the king as its head.[2]

4. The origin and growth of the feudal elements contained Elements
of feudal-
ism im-
bedded in
the Old-
English
system.
in the Old-English system have been already explained. In
that system the relation of lord and man — a relation at first
not necessarily connected with the holding of land — was
fully developed. This relation in its primitive form was that
of *princeps* and *comes*, of king and thegn, of lord and man,
and not of lord and tenant. But in the "process of feudalization," through which the primitive system was passing at
the time the Norman conquest began, a gradual development
can be traced in which the original relation of lord and man
closely approaches that of lord and tenant.[3] The fact has Manorial
system
originates
in Old-
English
and not in
Norman
law.
been already pointed out that the manorial system originates
in Old-English and not in Norman law, and that the relation
of a lord of a manor and his tenants substantially existed
from the time the title to the lands of the once free village-
community passed from the community itself and became
vested in a lord.[4] The lord or thegn, whose men were thus
gradually becoming his tenants, looked in turn to the king as
the lord from whom he might receive the grant of a large
district to be held allodially, or simply as a possessory right in
the folkland upon the payment of dues and services. Every
landowner, whether his land was burdened or not, was subject to military service, which was regarded, not as an incident of tenure, but as a duty to the state. The Old-English
system thus contained all the elements of feudalism, and
these elements, at the time of the Conquest, were gradually

---

[1] Stubbs, *Const. Hist.*, vol. i. pp. 259–
262; Digby, *Law of Real Property*,
p. 35. "Si rex mittebat alicubi exercitum, de quinque hidis tantum unus
miles ibat et ad ejus victum vel stipendium de unaquaque hida dabantur ei
iiii. solidi ad duos menses."—"Customs of Berkshire," *Domesday*, vol. i. p.
56.

[2] Freeman, *Norm. Conq.*, vol. v. p.
249. "A principal result of the Nor-

man conquest upon the customary law
of land seems to have been the development of the idea of tenure. . . .
This result was not brought about by
any positive enactment. It was due to
the introduction of Norman customs
and ideas, and their combination with
Anglo-Saxon customs and ideas." —
Digby, *Law of Real Property*, p. 37.

[3] See above, p. 133.

[4] See above, p. 139.

becoming blended: the thegn was passing into the tenant-in-chief; the men of the dependent township were surely becoming the tenants of the lord in whom the title to lands of the community was vested. And yet these elements, which thus developed in England before the Conquest into a kind of feudalism, were never worked into a systematic shape; they were never woven into a harmonious feudal system.

Only an embryonic feudalism.

Norman feudal ideas more fully developed;

In the minds of William and his followers, who came from a continental land in which feudal ideas had reached a far higher and more perfect development, the conception of feudal tenure, of military tenure, was no doubt far more clearly defined than it had ever been in the insular English system.[1] By the coming of William two kindred systems of land tenure, both tending in the same direction, and yet in different stages of development, were brought into the closest contact, and out of the fusion between the two has arisen the feudal mode of holding land imbedded in the English common law.[2]

their influence upon the growth of the idea of tenure.

Under the invigorating influence of Norman ideas the growth of feudalism as a system of tenure was greatly stimulated; the idea of tenure, the more exact definition of the rights and duties of lord and tenant, was rapidly developed. William's endless confiscations and regrants gave a new strength to the principle that all land should be held of a lord; the folkland which had long been tending to become *terra regis* actually became so; the king's thegns who had been tending to become tenants-in-chief actually became so;[3] the dependent township became the manor of the lord, and the once free

The king becomes the supreme landlord.

townsmen became his tenants.[4] By the end of the Conqueror's reign the principle was settled that the king was the supreme landlord; that all private land was held mediately or immediately of him; and that all holders were bound to their

---

[1] "To the mass of his (William's) followers a feudal tenure, a military tenure, must have seemed the natural and universal way of holding land." — Freeman, *Norm. Conq.*, vol. v. p. 247.

[2] "From the mixture of Anglo-Saxon customary law with the Norman, the blending process beginning under the influence of the strong rule of the Conqueror, and forced on with rapid strides by the vast territorial confiscations which followed the Conquest, arose the Common Law relating to

land." — Digby, *Law of Real Property*, p. 33.

[3] "The one name gradually displaced the other, not merely because the one name was English and the other name French, but because the leading ideas conveyed by the two names now changed places." — Freeman, *Norm. Conq.*, vol. v. p. 248.

[4] "In this way were the lands of the manor substituted for those of the community." — *Essays in A. S. Law*, p. 90.

lords by homage and fealty, either expressed or implied, in every case of transfer by inheritance or otherwise.[1]   And yet the extent of the change that actually took place in William's reign must not be overestimated.   Although Domesday contains abundant evidence of the growth of the idea of tenure, the "men" of a lord rather than his tenants are spoken of on every page; the personal relation of lord and man is generally, though not always, merged in that of lord and tenant: of knight service or military tenure in its later and stricter sense we hear nothing, — "*miles*" had not yet acquired the technical sense of "knight."[2]   It was in the succeeding reign of William Rufus that the system of military tenures was hardened and sharpened by the "malignant genius" of Ranulf Flambard into a methodical system of exactions and oppressions.[3]

Feudalism hardens into a methodical system under William Rufus.

5. An examination has been heretofore made of the history of the witan, considered as the supreme council of an heptarchic state, and also as the supreme council of the whole English nation when finally united in a single consolidated kingdom.   In the Old-English national assembly all grave matters were discussed, and with its advice and consent were performed all important acts which the king could authorize.[4]

Effects of the Conquest on central organization: the king and the witan.

After the coming of William the continuity of the old national assembly went on unbroken; the witan remained, as before, the national council of the king, and during William's reign it retained much of its earlier character.   The name witan goes on in English as long as the Chronicle continues, and the new Latin name, *magnum concilium*, which grows up by its side, is simply a translation of mycel gemot.[5]   Of the constitution of the witan, either before or after the Conquest, we have no direct or formal account, but the highest authorities substantially agree in the conclusion that on all ordinary occasions the witan was a comparatively small gathering of great men, while on extraordinary occasions the assembly was sometimes reinforced by large popular bodies from every part of the kingdom.[6]   From the Chronicler, who

Continuity of the national assembly unbroken by the Conquest.

---

[1] Stubbs, *Const. Hist.*, vol. i. p. 260.

[2] Sir H. Ellis, *General Introduction to Domesday*, vol. i. p. 58.

[3] This is the conclusion of Stubbs, *Const. Hist.*, vol. i. p. 298.   Mr. Free-

man adopts this view, *Norm. Conq.*, vol. v. p. 253, and note HH.

[4] See above, p. 186.

[5] *Norm. Conq.*, vol. v. p. 276.

[6] There may be a shade of difference

Testimony
of a chroni-
cler who
had lived at
William's
court.

had evidently lived at King William's court, we learn that
"thrice he wore his crown every year, as often as he was
in England : at Easter he wore it at Winchester ; at Pente-
cost at Westminster ; at Midwinter at Gloucester ; and then
were with him all the rich men over all England, archbishops
and suffragan bishops, abbots and earls, thegns and knights." [1]
The ordinary courts or councils here referred to were no
doubt of a limited character, seldom embracing more than
the great officers of state, and the household, the bishops, the
earls, and the greater barons.   But in the great Gemot of
Salisbury in 1086 we have an example of what seems to have
been a general gathering of all the landowners in the kingdom.   What were the qualifications necessary to bestow the
right of membership in the great council, during the Norman
reigns, cannot be definitely stated : not until the reign of
Henry II. can it be confidently maintained that every tenant-
in-chief of the crown was a member of the assembly. [2]   It

The witan
as the great
council re-
tains all of
its old
powers.

seems to be admitted that the Norman conquest wrought no
formal change in the constitution of the witan : after the
Conquest the great council remains in possession of all the
powers of the old witenagemot.   In legal theory at least,
what the witan was in the days of King Eadward it seems to
have remained in the days of King William. [3]   In the forms of
legislation, change there was none.   William legislates, like
his English predecessor, "with the common council and counsel of the archbishops, bishops, abbots, and all the princes of
the kingdom." [4]   The formal right of the witan to elect the
king is still distinctly recognized ; William is elected before
he receives the crown at Westminster.   Henry admits that
he owes his election to the barons ; [5]   while Stephen rests his

---

between the masters as to the constitution of the witan after the Conquest,
but they substantially agree in the conclusion stated in the text.   See Stubbs,
Const. Hist., vol. i. pp. 356–359; Freeman, *Norm. Conq.*, vol. v. pp. 272–284.
Gneist denies the continuance of the
witan as a feudal council. — *Verwalt.*,
i. p. 224 *seq.*

[1] *E. Chron.*, 1087.

[2] Stubbs, *Const. History*, vol. i. p.
356.

[3] "As no formal change took place
in the constitution of the national as-

sembly, so no formal change took place
in its powers." — Freeman, *Norm.
Conq.*, vol. v. p. 280.

[4] "Communi concilio et consilio
archiepiscoporum, episcoporum et ab-
batum et omnium principum regni mei."
See William's ordinance separating the
spiritual and temporal courts, Thorpe,
Ancient Laws, p. 213.   "This immemorial counsel and consent descends
from the earliest Teutonic legislation."
— *Select Charters*, p. 18.

[5] See preamble to charter Henry I.,
Thorpe, *Ancient Laws*, p. 215.

claim on the broader basis of a choice by the clergy and the people.[1] At the coronation the people still formally accept the king elected by the national assembly; and the king upon his part still takes the oath of good government, whose pledges are expressed in the form of charters.[2] The elective principle survives with diminishing force until it is finally extinguished in the time of the Angevins by the new feudal theory of hereditary descent.[3] From the mention made by Henry of an aid which his barons had given him, it may be inferred that the king as of old, with the advice of the great council, laid taxes upon his people.[4] Yet the right of the council to join in taxation is nowhere distinctly stated. That the judicial powers of the witan went on practically undisturbed by the Conquest, there can be no doubt. The history of the Norman reigns furnish abundant instances of the exercise of such powers by the national assembly both in civil and criminal cases.[5] In such trials the will of the king may generally have prevailed, but the formal right at least of discussion and debate seems to have been recognized. The power of the witan to deal with ecclesiastical business also survived; but owing to the existence of the separate ecclesiastical courts and councils to which the policy of the Conqueror gave birth, it survived with diminished authority. But although the witan, under the title of the great council, outlived the Conquest, and although in legal theory it still retained all of its old powers, and although its formal right to participate in legislation was distinctly recognized, yet the fact remains that the constitution of the assembly underwent a great practical transformation. At the beginning of William's reign those who composed the council that ordinarily gathered round the king were a body of Englishmen; by the end of his reign this body had gradually changed into an

Marginal notes:

Elective kingship finally yields to the doctrine of hereditary right.

Taxative and judicial powers of the great council;

its power to regulate ecclesiastical business.

A great practical transformation.

---

[1] " Ego Stephanus Dei gratia assensu cleri et populi in regem Anglorum electus."   See second charter of Stephen, *Statutes of the Realm: Charters of Liberties,* p. 3.

[2] Stubbs, *Const. Hist.,* vol. i. p. 339.

[3] "Under the Angevins, circumstances became more favorable to hereditary succession, and such succession became, not by law but by prescription, the rule of English kingship."—

Freeman *Norman Conquest,* vol. v. p. 261.

[4] Henry I. speaks of an aid as "auxilium quod barones mihi dederunt."— *Chron. Abingd.,* ii. p. 113.   See *First Report on the Dignity of a Peer,* pp. 38, 39; Stubbs, *Const. Hist.,* vol. i. p. 371, and note 4.

[5] Stubbs, *Const. Hist.,* vol. i. pp. 371–373; Freeman, *Norm. Conq.,* vol. v. p. 282.

assembly of Normans, among whom an Englishman here and there held his place.[1] This change naturally resulted from the character of the Conquest itself. Through William's policy of confiscation and regrant, nearly all of the great estates passed from English to Norman hands; and in the same way all of the great offices in church and state were parcelled out among his followers. The king's thegns thus became his tenants-in-chief, holding their lands from him as their lord. Through this feudalizing process the national assembly of wise men gradually became the king's court of feudal vassals, whose right to exercise power was made to depend practically upon the king's pleasure.[2] The effects of the Conquest on kingship, and on the constitution of the witan, are diametrically opposite in their results. While the powers of the witan are practically reduced to a mere shadow, the royal authority becomes the central and dominant force in the constitution. The new kingship, which is built up through the consolidation of all that is strongest in both the English and Norman systems, refuses to be limited either by the constitutional action of the witan on the one hand, or to be weakened by the disruptive tendencies of feudalism on the other.

In order to discharge the vast and intricate duties which the growth of the royal power thus concentrated around the person of the king, it became necessary for the crown to organize out of the main body of the great council a smaller body, composed of the king's immediate officers and advisers, which could be specially charged with the work of administration. Owing to the scantiness of documentary evidence touching the Norman period, the early history of the constitution of this lesser council, and of its relations to the greater body of which it was a part, is vague and shadowy in the extreme. The greatest scholars substantially agree, however, in the conclusion that the lesser or inner council was what would be called in modern language a standing committee of the greater body; that it was composed of the great officers

The national assembly becomes a feudal court subject to the king's pleasure.

Growth of the inner council, — curia regis.

A standing committee of the greater body.

---

[1] "Step by step, as high posts fell vacant by death or deprivation, as great estates passed to new owners by confiscation or by marriage, Normans succeeded Englishmen at every change."

— Freeman, *Norm. Conq.*, vol. v. p. 277.

[2] "The legislative functions of the national council are, under the Norman kings, rather nominal than real." — *Select Charters*, p. 17.

of state and of the household, and of such other advisers as were specially summoned by the royal authority; and that it was charged under the king's direction with the whole work of central or national administration.[1] This inner council, which soon came to be known by the name of curia regis, seems to have been mainly occupied from the beginning with the transaction of fiscal and judicial business. Owing to the lack of direct evidence, and to the vague way in which titles are used, the growth of the great officers who stand forth most prominently among the members of the inner council is involved in the same obscurity which conceals the early history of the council itself. In the mind of the Teuton the duty of personal service involved in the *comitatus*, so far from being degrading, actually tended to ennoble those who rendered such service to persons superior in rank to themselves.[2] Upon this principle those members of a king's household who came into the closest contact with the royal person were actually honored by rendering menial services to their lord. Under the Frank kings and emperors the four great officers of the court and household were the steward, the butler, the marshal, and the chamberlain.[3] These offices, which became hereditary and which continued down to the latest days of the empire, passed with slight modifications to the lowlier court of the Norman dukes, where they had begun to be hereditary before the conquest of England.[4] The royal household of the Norman kings of England was simply a reproduction of the ducal household of Normandy; and, although it is difficult to determine the exact dates of their formation, it seems to be certain that by the end of the reign of Henry II. the offices of high steward, butler, constable, and chamberlain had become hereditary in England.[5] But whilst these great offices of the household were becoming hereditary, and whilst as offices of the household they were becoming altogether nominal and formal, the powers which had once belonged to them were gradually absorbed by a

Early history of the council obscure.

Ennobling effects of menial services rendered to royalty.

Ducal household of Normandy prototype of royal household of England.

---

[1] Freeman, *Norm. Conq.*, vol. v. pp. 283–294; Stubbs, *Const. Hist.*, vol. i. pp. 387–391, and also p. 376.
[2] See Kemble, *Saxons in England*, vol. i. ch. vii., "The Noble by Service."

[3] G. L. von Maurer, *Hofverfassung*, i. p. 189.
[4] Freeman, *Norm. Conq.*, vol. v. p. 287.
[5] Stubbs, *Const. Hist.*, vol. i. pp. 344, 345.

New
ministerial
officers:

secondary class of offices which sprang up by their side.
Among the new ministerial offices which thus grew up, and
which as a rule did not become hereditary, those of the justiciar, the chancellor, and the treasurer rise to the greatest
constitutional importance. First in power among these was

the justi-
ciar;

the justiciar, who appears in history as the lieutenant or vice-
roy of the king during his absence.[1] Under William Rufus
the office of justiciar became permanent, and its functions
were so extended as to embrace the direction of the whole
judicial and financial administration of the kingdom. After
the time of William's famous minister Ranulf Flambard,[2]
the office became a definite and well-organized institution.
In the first Henry's reign the office pased to Roger, Bishop
of Salisbury, — the first to be called " *secundus a rege*," —
who reorganized and remodelled the whole system of administration.[3] Under the second Henry the office was held by
Ranulf Glanvill, the writer of the first English law-book
which bears the name of a personal author.[4] The office of

the chancel-
lor;

chancellor, which was far older than that of justiciar, but
originally far lower in power and dignity, probably derived
its name from the *cancelli*, or screen, behind which the secretarial work of the royal household was carried on.[5] This
secretarial work was imposed upon the royal chaplains, a
trained body of men by whom all letters, writs, and accounts
pertaining to the king's immediate administration were written and kept. From the head of this body — the archi-
cancellarius, who was the official keeper of the royal seal —
the English chancellor derives his name and functions.[6] The

[1] "In this capacity Wiiliam Fitz-
Osbern, the steward of Normandy,
and Odo of Bayeux, acted during the
Conqueror's visit to the Continent in
1067." — Stubbs, *Const. Hist.*, vol. i. p.
346, citing Will. Pict., ed. Maseres, p.
151; Ord. Vit., iv. 1; Flor. Wig., A. D.
1067.

[2] " Summus regiarum procurator
opum et justitiarius factus est." —
Ord. Vit., x. 18. By Florence he is
called " negotiorum totius regni ex-
actor." — Flor. Wig., A. D. 1099.

[3] " Henry, like Rufus, found it to
his interest to vest these great powers
only in a man of his own making, a
clerk who might grow into a bishop."

— Freeman, *Norm. Conq.*, vol. v. p.
289.

[4] *Tractatus de Legibus et Consuetudinibus Regni Angliæ*, which consists
of fourteen books, is chiefly a treatise
on the forms of procedure in the curia
regis. " This book is also said to be
the first performance that has anything
like the appearance of a treatise on
the subject of jurisprudence since the
dissolution of the Roman empire." —
Reeves, *Hist. of Eng. Law*, ed. Finlason, vol. i. p. 484 and note 3.

[5] As to the etymology of the word
"chancellor," see Campbell's *Lives of
the Chancellors*, vol. i. pp. 1, 2.

[6] Stubbs, *Const. Hist.*, vol. i. p. 352.

office of chancellor, which had existed on the Continent from the days of the first Karlings,[1] was first introduced into England in the reign of Eadward the Confessor, who was the first English king that ever had a seal. The king's hoarder — the keeper of the king's hoard who received after the Conquest the Latin name of treasurer — was an important member of the household who kept the royal treasure, and received the accounts of the sheriffs in the exchequer at Westminster.

the treasurer.

The curia regis, which during the Norman reigns drew to itself the whole central administration of justice and finance, has given birth not only to every court of law or equity in which justice is administered in the king's name, but also to the entire administrative machinery of the constitution.[2] The great stages in its development may be indicated as follows : As the highest judicial tribunal in the realm, the curia regis consisted of the king sitting to administer justice in person, with the advice and counsel of those vassals who were members of the royal household, and of such others as were, on account of their knowledge of law, specially appointed as judges.[3] In the absence of the king his court was presided over by the justiciar,[4] who was at all times the supreme administrator of law and finance. As a legal tribunal the jurisdiction of the curia was both civil and criminal,[5] original and appellate. As a primary court it heard all causes in which the king's interests were concerned, as well as all causes between the tenants-in-chief of the crown, who were too great to submit to the local tribunals of the shire and the hundred.[6] As an appellate court it was resorted to in those cases in which the powers of the local courts had been exhausted or had failed to do justice. By virtue of special writs, and as a special favor, the king could at his pleasure call up causes from the local courts to be heard in his own court according to such new methods as his advisers

Curia regis the source of the entire judicial and administrative machinery of the constitution.

The curia as a legal tribunal.

---

[1] See Waitz, *D. V. G.*, ii. p. 409, and iii. p. 406.

[2] " Every court where law or equity is administered in the king's name is a fragment of the king's court of Norman times. So, again, another side of this inner council of the king survives in the privy council." — Freeman, *Norm. Conq.*, vol. v. p. 285.

[3] Reeves, *Hist. of Eng. Law*, vol. i. p. 265.

[4] *History of Procedure in England*, Bigelow, p. 87.

[5] Madox, *Hist. Exch.*, p. 70.

[6] Stubbs, *Const. Hist.*, vol. i. p. 390, citing writ of Henry I., *Select Charters*, p. 99.

might invent.[1]   Through the issuance of these special writs the king became practically the fountain of justice, and through their agency the new system of royal law, which finds its source in the person of the king, was brought in to remedy the defects of the old, unelastic system of customary law which prevailed in the provincial courts of the people.[2] The curia followed the person of the king, or the justiciar in the king's absence.   Twice in every year, at Easter and Michaelmas, the curia held sessions at Westminster in order to transact with the sheriffs the financial business of the kingdom. When engaged in this work two chambers were used : in one the reports and accounts were received and audited ; in the other the money was paid down, weighed, and tested.[3] From the chequered cloth which covered the table at which the accounts were taken, the financial session of the curia took the name of exchequer.[4]   This name does not occur before the time of Henry I., during whose reign the fiscal side of the curia was separately and elaborately organized.[5]   The same officers who sat in the curia as justices, sat in the exchequer as barons, — *barones scaccarii,* — a title which continues to belong to them after they have ceased to be chosen from the ranks of the greater vassals.[6]   With the barons of the exchequer the sheriffs accounted twice in each year for the several kinds of revenue due from or collectible in their several shires.[7]   The leading subjects of revenue to be accounted for were the "ferm of the shire ;" *i. e.* the profits of the county jurisdictions, and the rents of the royal domains let to the sheriffs at fixed sums, the Danegeld or land-tax, the proceeds of the pleas of the crown, and the fruits of feudal tenures.[8]   The record of the business of the exchequer was kept in three great rolls, by three separate officers.   One

The financial session of the curia, — the exchequer.

The leading subjects of revenue.

Exchequer records.

---

[1] As to the extraordinary jurisdiction of the king's court thus acquired by the king's writ, see Bigelow, *Hist. of Procedure,* pp. 77, 78, 83.

[2] These special writs "were the expedients by which the '*jus honorarium*' of the king, as fountain of justice, was enabled to remedy the defects of the '*jus civile*' or 'commune,' the customary proceedings of the local moots." — Stubbs, *Const. Hist.,* vol. i. p. 391. As to the connection of the Norman and English writs with the writ process of the Frankish procedure, see Brunner, *Schwurgerichte,* pp. 76–84.

[3] *Dialogus de Scaccario,* i. 2.

[4] *Dialogus,* i. 1.

[5] Stubbs, *Const. Hist.,* vol. i. p. 377.

[6] Mad., *Ex.,* p. 134; *Select Charters,* p. 17.

[7] As to the manner in which the tallies were kept, see Madox's *Ex.,* p. 708.

[8] Stubbs, *Const. Hist.,* vol. i. pp. 380–384; *Select Charters,* p. 18; Freeman, *Norm. Conq.,* vol. v. p. 294.

was kept by the treasurer, which was called the great roll of the Pipe; another was kept by the chancellor, which was called the roll of the Chancery; while the third, in which were registered matters of special importance, was kept by an officer specially nominated by royal authority.[1]

In the course of the assessment and collection of the revenue, which was the chief work of the curia as a financial body, local disputes so constantly arose that it became necessary to send detachments of justices to adjust the business of the exchequer in each shire. As early as the reign of Henry I. officers of the exchequer were frequently sent through the country to assess the revenue;[2] and in the reign of his grandson, Henry II., this custom was enforced with systematic regularity.[3] The justices while thus engaged in provincial business sat in the shire-moots, where judicial work soon followed in the path of their fiscal duties. In 1176[4] the kingdom was divided into six circuits, to each of which were assigned three justices, who are now for the first time given in the Pipe Rolls the name of *Justitiarii Itinerantes.* After several intermediate changes in the number of the circuits, it was at last provided by Magna Carta that two justices should be sent four times each year into each shire to take the assizes of *novel disseisin, mort d'ancester,* and *darrien presentment.*[5] The provincial visitations of the justices from the exchequer, whose primary object was financial, thus led to the establishment of those judicial visitations which have

Origin of the itinerant judicature.

Justices from the curia sit in the shire-moots.

Financial visitations followed by judicial.

---

[1] *Dialogus de Scaccario,* i. 5, 6. The great sources of authority for the early history of the exchequer are the Pipe Rolls and the *Dialogus de Scaccario,* a treatise written by the treasurer, Richard, Bishop of London, from which we derive an accurate idea of the administration of the exchequer as it stood in 1177. The Pipe Rolls are complete from the second year of Henry II. For the preceding period there is but one Roll extant, and that is of the thirty-first year of Henry I. The Dialogue was for the first time printed in Madox's *History of the Exchequer.*

[2] The single Pipe Roll of the thirty-first year of Henry I. exhibits a system of iters by the royal officers in regular working order. See, also, *Dialogus,* i. c. 7.

[3] "It simply needed to be organized in a more systematic shape by Henry the Second."— Freeman, *Norm. Conq.,* vol. v. p. 300.

[4] It was not until 1166 that the judicial eyres became annual and general. 2 Benedictus, pref. 64; Bigelow, *Legal Procedure,* p. 14. The division into circuits was provided for in the Assize of Northampton. For a list of the circuits, see Reeves, *Hist. of Eng. Law,* vol. i. p. 273. See, also, *Placita Ang.-Norm.,* p. 216.

[5] "Mittemus duos justiciarios per unumquemque comitatum per quatuor vices in anno, qui, cum quatuor militibus cujuslibet comitatus electis per comitatum, capiant in comitatu et in die et loco comitatus assisas prædictas."— C. 18.

ever remained an abiding feature in English judicature.[1]
Through these visitations was established that vitally important connection between the strong central system of administration embodied in the Norman curia and the ancient
system of local freedom embodied in the Old-English shire-

Fusion of Norman and Old-English judicature.

moots. "The visits of the itinerant justices form the link
between the curia regis and the shire-moot, between royal
and popular justice, between the old system and the new.
The courts in which they preside are the ancient county
courts, under new conditions, but substantially identical with
those of the Anglo-Saxon times."[2]

The break-ing up of the curia regis.

During the progressive reign of Henry II. the curia regis,
as a supreme court of justice, underwent such a rapid development, and the volume of judicial work which then came
before it became so great, that the king and his regular ministers were no longer able to dispatch it. The reasonable
inference is that this great increase of judicial work, which
grew out of Henry's legislative reforms, finally brought about
the large increase in the number of judges who are found
acting in 1178.[3] In that year, however, the staff of the
curia was reduced to five justices, and then it was increased
in the next year to six, and "these six are justices constituted in the curia regis to hear the complaints of the peo-

Beginnings of the king's bench as a distinct tri-bunal.

ple."[4] These specially selected justices, who from the year
1179 hold regular sessions "*in banco*,"[5] probably represent
the beginnings of the king's bench as a distinct tribunal.
Their sessions are still held nominally but not actually
"*coram rege ;*" and before them is brought all of the business which came at a later period before the courts of king's
bench, exchequer, and common pleas.[6] Although the business of the court is no longer conducted in the king's pres-

[1] For a more detailed account of the history of the courts of assize, see Sir James F. Stephen's *Hist. Crim. Law of Eng.*, vol. i. pp. 97–111 ; Bigelow, *Hist. of Procedure*, pp. 92–103 and 138–141.

[2] Stubbs, *Const. Hist.*, vol. i. p. 605. As to the distinction between the courts held in the counties by the royal justices and the *ordinary* county courts, see Bigelow, *Hist. of Procedure*, pp. 136–141.

[3] "It is then to these years, from 1166 to 1176, that we must refer the creation or development of the large staff of judges in the curia regis which we find acting in 1178." — Stubbs, *Const. Hist.*, vol. i. p. 600.

[4] "Isti sex sunt justitiæ in curia re-gis constituti ad audiendum clamores populi." — Benedictus, vol. i. p. 239.

[5] As to the "justiciarii sedentes in banco," see Glanville, lib. 2, c. 6, lib. 8, c. 1, and lib. 11, c. 1 ; Benedictus, vol. ii. pref. 75, *Rolls Series.*

[6] Stubbs, *Const. Hist.*, vol. i. p. 602, vol. ii. p. 266.

ence, it still follows his person, or the justiciar in his absence, until it was provided by Magna Carta that "common
pleas shall not follow our court, but shall be holden in some
certain place." [1] This provision led to the fixing of the common pleas at Westminster, which broke up the unity of the
curia. But not until the end of the reign of Henry III. was
the general staff permanently divided into three distinct
courts, each exclusively devoted to the hearing of a different
class of causes, — the exchequer to the hearing of cases
touching the king's revenue, the common pleas to the hearing of private suits of subjects, and the king's bench to the
hearing of all other suits that might fall under the general
head of *placita coram rege.*[2]

Common
pleas fixed
at West-
minster,
and the
final divi-
sion into
three dis-
tinct courts.

The three law courts to which the curia regis thus gave
birth were not, however, the last resort of suitors. "The judicial supremacy of the king is not limited or fettered by the
new rule ; it has thrown off an offshoot, or, as the astronomi-
cal theorists would say, a nebulous envelope, which has rolled
up into a compact body, but the old nucleus of light remains
unimpaired." [3] The decision of all extraordinary or difficult
causes of a judicial nature was still reserved to the king in
council.[4] The bulk of the business which thus devolved
upon the council came before it in the form of petitions,
which were divided into classes or bundles, and then severally
assigned to the consideration of the different members, according to their special knowledge of them.[5] High among
the members of the council stood the chancellor, whose con-

---

[1] " Communia placita non sequantur
curiam nostram sed teneantur in aliquo
loco certo." — Art. 17. As to the inconvenience to suitors which this provision was designed to remedy, see the
history of the plea of D'Anesty, whose
suit lasted from 1158 to 1163. Palgrave, *Commonwealth,* ii., ix.–xxvii.

[2] " The final separation of the three
courts originated in the direction of
the seventeenth chapter of Magna Carta,
but it does not appear that even then a
distinct staff of judges was appointed to
each tribunal. Probably until late in
the reign of Henry III. the same persons continued as before to sit in the
three different courts in distinct capacities." — Benedictus, vol. ii. pref. 76, *R. S.*

[3] Stubbs, *Const. Hist.,* vol. i. p. 603.

[4] " Si aliqua quæstio inter eos veni-
ret quæ per eos ad finem duci non posset, auditui regio præsentaretur et sicut
ei et sapientioribus regni placeret ter-
minaretur." — Benedictus, vol. i. p. 207.
As to the general character of the
causes reserved for the king, see *Dialogus de Scaccario,* i. c. 8.

[5] Ryley, *Pleadings,* etc., pp. 442, 459.
"Those which could not be answered
without reference to the king formed a
special branch of business, and it was
from the share taken by the chancellor
in examining and reporting on the bills
of grace and favor that his equitable
jurisdiction in the fourteenth century
grew up." — Stubbs, *Const. Hist.,* vol.
ii. p. 263. See Hardy's *Preface to the
Close Rolls,* i. p. xxviii., cited.

The chancellor ;

nection with judicial business begins with the issuance of the writs which proceed from the king as the fountain of justice.[1] This ministerial duty was not, however, his only occupation. As a baron of the exchequer,[2] and as a leading member of the curia, the chancellor had long been in possession of judicial functions, and so to him, as to the other justices, were re-

his common law jurisdiction ;

ferred a definite class of petitions. In this way the chancellor was called upon to decide a distinct class of suits as a judge, according to the rules and maxims of the common law, and hence the origin of what is called his "common law

his equitable jurisdiction.

jurisdiction."[3] The "equitable jurisdiction" of the chancellor, which has become of infinitely greater importance, must be traced to a higher source. One of the leading objects of dividing the petitions which came before the council into distinct classes was to sever from the general mass of business those special "matters of grace and favor" which could only be answered after reference to the king in person.[4] The examination of this peculiar class of petitions, which constituted a special branch of business, devolved in such a great degree upon the chancellor that finally they began to be addressed to him in the first instance, instead of being referred

The chancellor's court becomes a distinct tribunal.

to him by the king. When early in the reign of Eadward III. the chancellor ceased to follow the court as one of the royal retinue, his tribunal began to acquire a more distinct and substantive character. And from the twenty-second year of that reign, in which all petitions of grace and favor were recognized as his province, his separate and independent equitable jurisdiction began to grow in power and importance.[5] By equitable jurisdiction must be understood "the extraor-

Equity one of the agencies by which strict law is adapted to the expanding wants of society.

dinary interference of the chancellor, without common law process, or regard to common law rules of proceeding, upon the petition of the party grieved, who was without adequate remedy in a court of common law."[6] The "equitable jurisdiction" of the chancellor thus became one of the three great agencies which have adapted the old, unelastic code of cus-

---

[1] "This was the *officina justitiæ*, called chancery, and the officer who presided over it was called chancellor." — Campbell's *Lives of the Chancellors*, vol. i. p. 3.

[2] Madox, *Hist. of Ex.*, p. 131.

[3] Gilbert's *History of the Exchequer*, p. 8; Campbell's *Lives of the Chancellors*, vol. i. pp. 5, 6.

[4] Ryley, *Pleadings*, etc., p. 442.

[5] Rot. Claus., 38 Edw. III.; Hardy, *Close Rolls*, i. pref. xxviii.; Stubbs, *Const. Hist.*, vol. ii. p. 269.

[6] Campbell's *Lives*, vol. i. p. 7.

tomary law to the expanding wants of a progressive society. In order to give complete expression to this idea resort must be had to the weighty words of one who, in our own time, has made perhaps the largest and most invaluable contributions to the early history of jurisprudence : "A general proposition of some value may be advanced with respect to the agencies by which law is brought into harmony with society. These instrumentalities seem to me to be three in number, — legal fictions, equity, and legislation. Their historical order is that in which I have placed them. . . . I employ the word 'fiction' in a sense considerably wider than that in which English lawyers are accustomed to use it, and with a meaning much more extensive than that which belonged to the Roman *'fictiones.'* . . . I now employ the expression 'legal fiction' to signify any assumption which conceals, or affects to conceal, the fact that a rule of law has undergone alteration, its letter remaining unchanged, its operation being modified. . . . The next instrumentality by which the adaptation of law to social wants is carried on I call 'equity,' meaning by that word any body of rules existing by the side of the original civil law founded on distinct principles, and claiming incidentally to supersede the civil law in virtue of a superior sanctity inherent in those principles. The equity, whether of the Roman prætors or of the English chancellors, differs from the fictions which in each case preceded it, in that the interference with law is open and avowed. On the other hand, it differs from legislation, the agent of legal improvement which comes after it, in that its claim to authority is grounded, not on the prerogative of any external person or body, not even on that of the magistrate who enunciates it, but on the special nature of its principles, to which it is alleged that all law ought to conform."[1]

Maine's view.

Legal fictions.

Equity.

Legislation.

After giving birth to the system of itinerant judicature, and to the four great courts of king's bench, common pleas, exchequer, and chancery, the curia regis survived as the privy council, which has ever retained an almost indefinable reserve of administrative and judicial functions. At one period in the history of the privy council its judicial side reached an abnormal development; at another its adminis-

The privy council.

[1] Sir Henry Maine, *Ancient Law*, pp. 23–27.

trative side has become the most subtle force in the constitu-

Its judicial
functions as
developed
in the star
chamber;
tion. When under the Tudor dynasty the royal prerogative reached its height, the judicial power of the council became the handmaid of tyranny through the famous committee commonly known as the star chamber.[1] When in comparatively modern times the true principles of constitutional executive government became firmly established, — when it finally became settled that the ministry should consist of statesmen holding the same political principles, and that such ministry should depend for its authority and permanence

its adminis-
trative, as
developed
in the cabi-
net.
upon a majority of the house of commons, — the administrative functions of the privy council found their most perfect expression through that mysterious committee, undefined by law, known as the cabinet.[2] This inner circle of the privy council, which is for the time being the government of Great Britain, has been aptly styled "a board of control, chosen by the legislature out of the persons whom it trusts and knows, to rule the nation."[3]

Effects of
the Con-
quest on
local organ-
izations.
6. Having now defined the outlines of that vigorous system of central administration to which the Norman conquest gave birth, it will next become necessary to trace the effects of the Conquest on the tenacious substructure of Old-English local freedom upon which the Norman system was superimposed. As the Norman superstructure was strongest in the higher ranges of organization, so the Old-English substructure was strongest in the cohesion of its lower organism, — in the local associations of the township, the hundred, and the

The town-
ship, hun-
dred, and
shire.
shire.[4] The growth of these local associations out of the Teutonic polity of the fatherland has already been explained, — the growth of the township out of the mark, the identity

---

[1] "The original tribunal, the king's ordinary council, retained its undiminished powers throughout, changing at various times and throwing off new off-shoots, such as the court of star chamber, until it has reached our own time in the form of the judicial committee of privy council." — *Select Charters*, p. 24.

[2] "The cabinet has been formed out of the privy council by exactly the same process by which the curia regis and the later parliament were formed out

of the witenagemot. Certain members of the body are specially summoned; those who are not specially summoned stay away." — Freeman, *Norm. Conq.*, vol. v. p. 285.

[3] Bagehot, *English Constitution*, p. 78. The selection is of course formally made by the crown, but really by the house of commons.

[4] "The strongest elements of both were brought together." — Stubbs, *Const. Hist.*, vol. i. p. 278.

of the hundred with the early shire, and the origin of the modern shire in the primitive state. The fact has also been pointed out that the consolidated kingdom was but an aggregation of shires, the shire an aggregation of hundreds, and the hundred an aggregation of townships.[1] With the growth of national unity, and with the advance of the "process of feudalization," each local division and subdivision suffered a certain degree of change which necessarily curtailed its primitive freedom of action, without at all destroying its corporate identity. The greatest amount of change that took place was in the status of the township, which, in the "process of feudalization," underwent a marked transformation. The evidence seems to justify the conclusion that, before the Norman conquest, all townships had, as a rule, become dependent ; that is, the title to the land occupied by the once free community had become vested in a lord, and the dependent townsmen had become his men, or, in the language of later times, his tenants.[2] The word "manor"[3] is of Norman introduction, but the relation of a lord of a manor and his tenants substantially existed in every case in which a township had become dependent through the substitution of the lord for the community. The manorial system, which thus originates in Old-English and not in Norman law, assumed a more definite form in the hands of the Norman lawyers and justices, by whom the legal relation between the lords and the smaller holders within the manor was more exactly defined.[4] By the time of the Domesday Survey, the territorial lordship had become the rule ; there were manors everywhere ; and "the manor was a landlord's estate, with a township or village-community in villeinage upon it, under the jurisdiction of the lord of the manor."[5] At the date of the Survey, 1,422 manors were in the ancient demesne of the crown, most of which had been royal manors in the days of King Eadward.[6] After the Conquest some new manors

The township as the manor.

The word "manor" of Norman introduction,

but the manorial system of Old-English origin.

Number of manors at the date of the Survey.

---

[1] See above, pp. 170–173.
[2] *Essays in A. S. Law*, pp. 88–90 ; Digby, *Law of Real Property*, pp. 43–45.
[3] The earliest appearance of the word is in the reign of Eadward the Confessor. Ellis, *Introduction to Domesday*, p. 225.
[4] Digby, *Law of Real Property*, p. 45.
[5] Seebohm, *English Village Community*, p. 82.
[6] Ellis, *Introduction to Domesday*, p. 225.

were no doubt created; some were diminished and others added to; but upon the whole it is probable that there was **Manorial courts.** no great addition to the number of manors.[1] As the manor then was nothing but a dependent township under a new name, so the court baron, the principal court of the manor, was primarily the successor of the tun-moot, the ancient assembly of the village or township. To the functions thus inherited by the manorial court from the tun-moot, was added, by an express grant of *sac* and *soc*, the jurisdiction of a private hundred court. The criminal side of the jurisdiction thus acquired was the manorial court leet. By every grant of *sac* and *soc* — terms which are used as well after the Conquest as before — a section of jurisdiction was simply carved out of the hundred and vested in the manorial court.[2] In some instances, however, these private jurisdictions were **Liberties or honors.** organized upon a much larger scale. The greater jurisdictions, which were called liberties or honors, often embraced large districts, which were in some instances completely organized as shires, but as a general rule they were only hundreds in private hands.[3] Jurisdictions of this class which originated before the Conquest, and which were greatly multiplied during the Norman reigns,[4] constantly tended to undermine the ancient local jurisdictions by freeing suitors from all attendance upon the popular courts. And yet the leading difference in practice between a royal or national and a private hundred court was, that in the one the freemen met together to declare the law under the presidency of a royal official, — in the other, under the presidency of a lord or his representative. In either event, justice was administered according to the custom of the manor, and not according to the will of the presiding officer.[5]

Courts of the shire and hundred kept up by William. It seems to have been a leading feature in the policy of William to maintain the ancient usages of the English nation by keeping up the administration of the customary law in the popular courts of the shire and the hundred. In obedience to

---

[1] Digby, *Law of Real Property*, p. 44, note 5.

[2] See above, pp. 207–210.

[3] *Essays in A. S. Law*, p. 54.

[4] Stubbs, *Const. History*, vol. i. p. 400.

[5] "The law administered in the manorial court was hundred law; the procedure was hundred procedure; the jurisdiction, like that of the hundred, was controlled by the shire." — *Essays in A. S. Law*, p. 54. As to the manorial courts, see Digby, *Law of Real Property*, pp. 53–56.

this policy he confirmed the laws which had been in use in the days of King Eadward, with such additions as he himself had made for the benefit of the English.[1]   From the same source from which we learn this fact, we hear of the continuance by him of the courts of the shire and the hundred.[2]   The existence of these courts in the succeeding reign of William Rufus is not only proven by the expressive entry in the Chronicle which describes Ranulf Flambard as "driving all the gemots throughout England,"[3] but by writs addressed to the shire-moot through the sheriff and other leading members.[4]   From the language of the charter in which Henry I. orders the holding of the courts of the shire and hundred, it may be inferred that they had been used in the preceding reign for the purpose of extraordinary exactions.[5]   And in the same charter Henry says, "I will cause those courts to be summoned when I will, for my own sovereign necessities, at my pleasure."[6]   The use thus made of the shire-moots to raise money may account for the necessity of imposing penalties, as of old, upon those members who failed to attend.[7]   From the issuance of Henry's charter (A. D. 1108–1112) onward, the local courts are held, "as in King Eadward's day, and not otherwise." From the "Leges Henrici Primi," as they are called — a compilation later than his reign — we learn that, after the Conquest as before, the shire-moot was attended by the "thegns of the shire,"[8] by the parish priest, and the reeve and four selectmen from each township.[9]   The full court which met twice a year still possessed both civil and criminal

(marginal notes:) Employed for fiscal purposes by William Rufus and Henry I.

Composition and procedure of shire-moot unchanged,

---

[1] "Hoc quoque præcipio et volo, ut omnes habeant et teneant legem Edwardi regis in terris et in omnibus rebus, adauctis iis quæ constitui ad utilitatem populi Anglorum." — Statutes of William, § 7. See, also, Charter Henry I., § 13; *Select Charters*, pp. 84, 101.

[2] "Requiratur hundredus et comitatus, sicut antecessores nostri statuerunt." — Stat. of Will., § 8.

[3] *Chron. Petrib.*, 1099.

[4] There is extant a writ direct by the Red King to the sheriff of Northamptonshire commanding him to call together his shire to inquire into the rights of the monks of Ramsey. — Palgrave, *Commonwealth*, clxxix.

[5] For this charter, which was issued

between 1108 and 1112, see *Fœdera*, i. p. 12 : *Select Charters*, p. 104.

[6] "Ego enim, quando voluero, faciam ea satis summonere propter mea dominica necessaria ad voluntatem meam." — See Stubbs, *Const. Hist.*, vol. i. p. 398.

[7] Freeman, *Norm. Conq.*, vol. v. p. 300.

[8] "Intersint autem episcopi, comites, vicedomini, vicarii, centenarii, aldermanni, præfecti, præpositi, barones, vavasores, tungrevii et ceteri terrarum domini." — Leg. Hen. I., vii. 2. See *Norman Conquest*, vol. v. p. 301.

[9] "Si uterque necessario desit, præpositus et sacerdos et quatuor de melioribus villæ assint pro omnibus qui nominatim non erunt ad placitum submoniti." — Leg. Hen. I., vii. 7.

jurisdiction, which was exercised according to the old forms of witness, compurgation and ordeal. All transfers of land, as well as the execution of all private documents and charters, were still witnessed in its presence, and the old theory

with the exception of trial by battle.

survived that the suitors were the judges.[1] A great innovation in the proceedings of the popular courts now arose out of the introduction by the Normans of trial by battle.[2] By

Survival of the hundred court.

the so-called laws of Henry I. the court of the hundred, no less than that of the shire, was restored as it had been in the days of King Eadward.[3] In these laws the distinction is clearly drawn between the great court of the hundred, held twice a year under the sheriff for the view of frank pledge, and the lesser court held monthly by the bailiff of the hundred[4] chiefly to consider disputes about small debts, which long continued to be its sole employment.[5]

Centralization of justice and growth of immunities undermine the popular courts.

The two great forces which constantly tended to undermine and weaken the courts of the shire and the hundred were the growth of immunities and the centralization of justice, both of which had begun to assert themselves long before the Norman conquest. The growth of immunities having already been explained, the centralization of justice may next be examined. With the advance of national unity, and with the consequent growth of the royal power, the idea constantly gained ground that the national peace was the king's peace, that the national officers were the king's officers, and that the justice of the shire and the folk was the

How the king came to be regarded as the source of justice.

king's justice. In this way the principle was established that the national king was the supreme judge throughout his dominions.[6] The earliest form, perhaps, in which the assertion of this principle began to interfere in the local administration of justice, appears in a law of Cnut, in which are defined certain pleas of the crown that were specially reserved to be dealt with in the local courts, only in the king's name, by the king's officers, and for the king's profit.[7] This

---

[1] Stubbs, *Const. Hist.*, vol. i. p. 394; Bigelow, *Hist. of Procedure*, pp. 131–141.

[2] Ibid., p. 326.

[3] "The hundred courts . . . continued after the Conquest with no further constitutional change than was effected by the Conqueror's charter concerning jurisdiction of spiritual causes."—Bigelow, *Hist. of Procedure*, p. 141.

[4] Leg. Hen. I., vii. 8.

[5] Madox, *Formulare Anglicanum*, p. 40; Stubbs, *Const. Hist.*, vol. i. p. 399.

[6] See above, p. 177.

[7] Laws of Cnut, ii. § 12; K. Maurer, *Krit. Ueberschau*, ii. p. 55.

was not, however, the only form in which the royal power interfered in the local administration of justice. Several instances exist of such interference, in the later days of the Old-English commonwealth, through the issuance of the king's writ or insigel.[1] In the days of Æthelred, the king sent his writ by the hands of Abbot Ælfhere to the shire-moot of Berkshire bidding them arbitrate in a suit then pending between Wynflæd and Leofwine.[2] In Cnut's day, Tofig the Proud seems to have been sent for the same purpose on the king's errand to the shire-moot of Herefordshire, before which was pending a suit between Eanwene and her son Eadwine.[3] There is still other evidence which goes to show that the Old-English kings occasionally administered justice in the local courts either in person or by deputy.[4] It is recorded among the merits of Ælfred, Eadgar, and Cnut, that they either went about doing justice in their own persons, or else sent forth justices to do justice in their names. Two distinct records exist of the action of the royal *missi* in the reign of Æthelstan.[5] After the Conquest the interference of the king with the local administration of justice became more systematic and more frequent. The list of offences contained in Cnut's law, and which were specially reserved for the king's jurisdiction and profit, was, during the Norman reigns, greatly extended, — the king then becomes entitled for the first time to the profits of all murders.[6] The royal right to interfere with the local courts through the issuance of special writs — a right which had been occasionally exercised before the Conquest — now ripened into an established custom.[7] But the influence of the central authority over the provincial administration of justice was most effectively exercised after the Conquest through the royal representatives who presided in the local tribunals. Under the old

[marginal notes: Instances of royal interference with local justice before the Conquest. After the Conquest such interference by special writs ripened into an established custom.]

---

[1] "There is no mention in the laws of the insigel or breve, but the charters give some evidence of what has been averred." — Kemble, *Saxons in England*, vol. ii. p. 46.

[2] *Cod. Dipl.*, No. 693.

[3] Ibid., No. 641.

[4] Kemble, *Saxons in Eng.*, vol. ii. p. 41.

[5] Freeman, *Norm. Conq.*, vol. v. pp. 298, 299.

[6] *Murdrum* was the fine payable by the hundred in which the murder was committed, in the event of its being unable to prove that the party slain was an Englishman. — *Dialogus de Scaccario*, i. 10. As to Englishry, see Bigelow, *Hist. of Procedure*, p. 81.

[7] For a full history of the growth of the "writ process," see Bigelow's *History of Procedure*, pp. 147-200.

system the ealdorman and the bishop presided in the shire-moot to declare the law, secular and spiritual, while the sheriff was the constituting officer, and the executor of the law.[1]

Ancient presidents of the shire disappear.

After the Conquest the constitutional presidents of the shire-moot both disappear. The old earldoms, which were stripped of their official duties, sink into mere places of honor, while the bishop was virtually removed from the headship of the shire-moot by the ordinance which placed him at the head of a distinct ecclesiastical court.[2] In this way the headship of the shire was left alone to the sheriff, the king's ever-present and immediate representative.

Their places filled by royal officers.

In addition to this permanent officer, the crown was represented by commissioners, justices, or barons, who were periodically sent from the king's court to preside in the local tribunals. The connection between the central and provincial judicature, of which there is not the faintest trace before the Conquest, was definitely established in the reign of Henry I., who sent justices from the exchequer through the country to assess the revenue.[3] These justices while engaged in provincial business sat in the shire-moot, where judicial work soon followed in the path of their fiscal duties. In the reign of Henry II. the system of itinerant judicature became a well organized and permanent institution.[4] Through the visits of the itinerant justices was gradually brought about that vitally important union between the curia regis and the shire-moot, between the new system of royal law and the old system of popular law, out of which has been born the typical English law court, in which the witnesses depose to facts upon which the jury pass, under the guidance and instruction of a judge learned in the law.

The itinerant system firmly established in the reign of Henry II.

Effects of the Conquest on ecclesiastical organization.

7. The same general plan of reorganization which William applied to the remodelling of the state, he gradually applied to the remodelling of the church. With the councils of the

---

[1] See above, p. 199.

[2] "The chief places in the local assemblies were then open, to be filled no longer by the local chiefs, but by the immediate representatives of the king." — *Norm. Conq.*, vol. v. p. 299.

[3] As heretofore explained, the single Pipe Roll of the thirty-first year of Henry I. exhibits a system of iters by

the royal officers in regular working order.

[4] "The courts held by these itinerant justices of the king possessed a dignity altogether above that of the ordinary judicial assembly of the county. These were the king's courts held in the counties" — Bigelow, *Hist. of Procedure*, p. 137.

year 1070 the Conqueror's ecclesiastical policy actively begins.   In that year, at the request of William, Pope Alexander II. sent into England three legates[1] to aid in the work
of deposing the native bishops in order to make places for
such Norman or other foreign prelates as the new king could
trust.[2]   The metropolitan see of York, now regularly void by
the death of Ealdred, was bestowed by William upon one of
his own chaplains, Thomas,[3] treasurer of the church of Bayeux.   The primatial see of Canterbury, as soon as it could
be made vacant by the deposition of Stigand, was bestowed
upon an Italian abbot from Normandy, — the famous scholar,
theologian, and statesman, Lanfranc.[4]   By the end of the
year 1070 only two sees, Worcester and Rochester,[5] remained in the hands of native pastors, and for a long time
to come all Englishmen were severely excluded from the
rank of bishop, and but sparingly admitted to that of abbot.
The natural result of the deposition of the native bishops,
and the elevation of their foreign successors, was to draw the
English church from its position of practical independence
and isolation into closer communion with the rest of Western Christendom, and into greater dependence upon the see
of Rome.   From the accession of William, applications to
Rome, and the visits of Roman legates, became more frequent ; and questions which in earlier times would have been
settled in the national assembly now began to be referred to
the judgment of the pope, or to some one of his representatives.   William was careful, however, to provide that the
Roman pontiff should not interfere with the internal affairs
of the church, except under such restrictions and limitations
as should be fixed by him.   From the historian Eadmer we
learn that " he would not suffer that any one in all his dominions should receive the pontiff of the city of Rome as
apostolic pope except at his command, or should on any condition receive his letters if they had not been first shown to

Marginal notes:
Deposition of the native prelates.

English church drawn into greater dependence upon Rome.

William's restrictions upon the papal power.

---

[1] Bishop Ermenfrid and the cardinal priests John and Peter. — Ord. Vit., 516 A ; Flor. Wig., 1070.

[2] They came " at once to congratu-late the Conqueror on the temporal success of his holy enterprise, and to help him in carrying out his ecclesias-tical schemes for the subjugation and reformation of the benighted island-ers." — Freeman, *Norm. Conq.*, vol. iv. p. 220.

[3] Ord. Vit., 516 B.

[4] *Vita Lanfr.*, Giles, i. 19, 20, 293 ; Flor. Wig., 1070.

[5] Stubbs, *Const. Hist.*, vol. i. p. 282.

himself." [1]   But in spite of all such restrictions the English church was brought into closer connection with Rome
through the Conquest, and out of this closer connection grew
the tendency that now began to manifest itself to sever the
organization of the church from that of the state.[2]   The
direct aid which William gave to this tendency by separating
the spiritual from the temporal tribunals constitutes the leading feature in his ecclesiastical policy.   The fact has been
heretofore pointed out that the distinctive feature in the history of the church before the Conquest was its perfect oneness with the state.   The same legislative and judicial assemblies dealt alike with ecclesiastical and temporal business,
without the slightest jealousy or conflict of authority.   The
witan legislated for the church as it did for the state, and in
the witan the bishop as well as the ealdorman was elected
and deposed.   In the shire-moot the bishop and the ealdorman sat side by side as its constitutional presidents, and in
the popular courts there was no separation of secular from
spiritual causes.[3]   The primary object of the new policy,
which grew directly out of the Conquest, was to accomplish
a complete severance of ecclesiastical from temporal business by the creation of distinct courts and councils, in which
the church could judge and legislate upon its own affairs
without secular interference.

Severance of ecclesiastical from temporal business.

By an express ordinance William and his witan decreed
the separation of the spiritual from the temporal tribunals.[4]
This ordinance, after declaring the episcopal laws which had
previously been in force in England to be bad and contrary
to the sacred canons, forbids the bishops and archdeacons to
bring any cause involving questions of canon law, or questions concerning the cure of souls, before the courts of the

Creation of a separate system of spiritual courts.

---

[1] Eadmer, *Hist. Nov.*, i. p. 6. From
the same authority we learn that the decrees of an ecclesiastical council, even
when convened by the archbishop of
Canterbury, had no force until they
were confirmed by the king. See *Select Charters*, p. 82.

[2] " We must never forget that, while
Lanfranc ruled at Canterbury, Hilde-
brand ruled at Rome. . . . . The two
main objects of the great pope, two objects which in his idea could hardly be
kept asunder, were the subjection of

the civil to the ecclesiastical power,
and the establishment of the clergy as
a distinct order, animated by one universal corporate spirit, and cut off
from those ties of citizenship and
kindred which bind men together in
earthly bonds." — Freeman, *Norm.
Conq.*, vol. iv. p. 286.

[3] See above, p. 200.

[4] For the text of the ordinance, see
Thorpe, *Ancient Laws*, p. 213; *Select
Charters*, p. 85.

hundred.[1] Henceforth they are to hold courts of their own, in which causes are to be tried, not by the customary but by the canon law.[2] All interference by laymen in spiritual causes is expressly forbidden. Those who are summoned must attend, as in the courts of the civil magistrates ; and in case of continuacy the offender may be excommunicated, and the king and sheriff will enforce the punishment. Thus by the policy of William and Lanfranc was organized a distinct system of ecclesiastical courts, whose jurisdiction was destined to grow and widen with the growth of the canon law, which had not yet become a well organized system of authoritative jurisprudence.[3] Not until the reign of Stephen did the systematic study of the canon law begin in England. In that reign (1149) Vacarius began his first teaching of the civil and canon law at Oxford.[4] The bishops and clergy vigorously supported the new system, so favorable to their order, which gave to them a more distinct civil status than they had ever possessed before, and which ultimately drew into the spiritual courts a mass of business with which the church had heretofore only a remote connection.[5] Out of the new order of things soon grew up claims upon the part of churchmen to exemption from all temporal jurisdiction, and to the right of appeal to Rome, — claims which led, after bitter strife, to the adoption, in the reign of Henry II., of the restraining measures which are embodied in the Constitutions of Clarendon.

Systematic study of canon law began in the reign of Stephen.

The same general causes which led to the organization of a distinct system of ecclesiastical courts, soon led to the organization of a distinct system of ecclesiastical councils. Such a separation of spiritual from temporal affairs had occasionally occurred before the Conquest, but the custom was

Distinct ecclesiastical councils.

---

[1] " Propterea mando et regia auctoritate præcipio, ut nullus episcopus vel archidiaconus de legibus episcopalibus amplius in hundret placita teneant, nec causam quæ ad regimen animarum pertinet ad judicium secularium hominum adducant."

[2] " Quicunque secundum episcopales leges, de quacunque causa vel culpa enterpellatus fuerit, ad locum quem ad hoc episcopus elegerit vel nominaverit veniat, ibique de causa vel culpa sua respondeat, et non secundum hundret, sed secundum canones et episcopales leges, rectum Deo et episcopo suo faciat."

[3] Stubbs, *Const. Hist.*, vol. i. p. 284.

[4] " Tunc leges et causidici in Angliam primo vocati sunt, quorum primus erat magister Vacarius ; hic in Oxenefordia legem docuit." — Gervase, c. 1665. Cf. R. de Monte, A. D. 1149.

[5] For an exhaustive review of the jurisdiction and procedure of the ecclesiastical courts, see Bigelow, *Hist. of Procedure*, pp. 30–75.

looked upon with such disfavor as to evoke, in the reign of Æthelred, a solemn condemnation in a formal decree of a national assembly.[1] Under the new theories of William and Lanfranc, the holding of distinct ecclesiastical councils, so far from exciting condemnation, received open and positive approval. During the primacy of Lanfranc the meetings of such councils, which were held at the same time as the regular gemots, became frequent.[2] From an entry in the Chronicle, under the year 1085, we learn that "at midwinter the king was at Gloucester with his witan, and he held his court there five days; and afterwards the archbishop and clergy held a synod during three days; and Maurice was there chosen to the bishopric of London, William to that of Norfolk, and Robert to that of Cheshire; they were all clerks of the king."[3] It was, however, no part of William's policy to allow to these ecclesiastical assemblies the right to legislate without limitation. Eadmer tells us that "he did not suffer the primate of his kingdom, the archbishop of Canterbury, if he had called together under his presidency an assembly of bishops, to enact or prohibit anything but what was agreeable to his will and had been first ordained by him."[4] Under these circumstances, and subject to such limitations, the national councils of the English church finally became distinct bodies from the national parliaments. But it must not be inferred from this statement that it was only in national councils that the clergy met together for the purpose of deliberation and action. The character of the lesser councils can best be explained by reference to the jurisdictions into which the church, as a whole, was subdivided. At an earlier period of our inquiries the fact was pointed out that, although each one of the heptarchic states was Christianized from a distinct source, the general aspects of the missionary work were everywhere the same. The conversion of the king generally preceded the acceptance of the faith upon the part

Marginal notes:
During the primacy of Lanfranc such councils met frequently.

William limits ecclesiastical legislation.

Diocesan and provincial councils.

---

[1] Æthelred's Laws, §§ 36, 37, 38, in Thorpe's *Ancient Laws*, vol. i. p. 340; Schmid, p. 242; Freeman, *Norm. Conq.*, vol. i. p. 248.

[2] Such councils were held in 1071, 1074, 1075, 1076, 1078, 1081, 1086. See Latin Life of Lanfranc attached to the Canterbury Chronicle.

[3] *Chron. Petrib.*, 1085.

[4] "Non sinebat quicquam statuere aut prohibere nisi quæ suæ voluntati occomoda et a se primo essent ordinata."—Eadmer, *Hist. Nov.*, i. p. 6. See Stubbs, *Const. Hist.*, vol. i. p. 286.

of his people, and then the missionary bishop became the royal chaplain, and the kingdom itself his diocese. The diocesan synod was therefore, in the early days, the highest ecclesiastical assembly of an heptarchic state. In this way the heptarchic divisions of the country reappeared in the earliest forms of organization which the church assumed. When Theodore came to bind the missionary bishoprics together under a single rule, so as to bring the united church into definite relations with the see of Rome, he began his work by breaking up the great original dioceses into smaller sees. Not long after Theodore's death the work of subdivision had so far advanced as to allow the grouping of the whole nation in sixteen dioceses subject to the metropolitan primacy of Canterbury. This arrangement was in a short time so modified as to allow to York the position of an archbishopric, with three suffragan sees. By the final subdivision of Wessex, under Eadward the Elder, the scheme of Theodore was at last carried out, and the territorial organization of the dioceses, as then fixed, has remained with a few minor changes to the present day.[1] In the organization of the church as thus finally established, the narrowest ecclesiastical assemblies were the diocesan synods; the next in the ascending scale, the provincial convocations of York and Canterbury;[2] the last and highest, the general councils of the united national church.[3] The circumstances under which these general councils became, during the primacy of Lanfranc, distinct bodies from the national parliaments, have already been drawn out. The existence of such councils was destined, however, to be of short duration. Owing to the jealousy and strife between Canterbury and York, the assembling of general councils, after the independence of York had been vindicated by Thurstan, became practically impossible.[4] The government of the church thus passed to the two provincial convocations of York and Canterbury, which, as constitutional assemblies of the English clergy, have suffered no

Diocesan organization.

The system completed under Eadward the Elder.

National councils short-lived.

---

[1] Upon this subject see above, pp. 160, 161.

[2] As to the respective constitutions of the convocations of York and Canterbury, see Wilkins, *Concilia,* vol. ii. 41, 49.

[3] "The diocesan synod answers to the county court, the provincial convocation to the occasional divided parliaments, and the national church council to the general parliament." — Stubbs, *Const. Hist.,* vol. ii. p. 195; Bigelow, *Hist. of Procedure,* pp. 28, 29.

[4] Stubbs, *Const. Hist.,* vol. ii. p. 198.

Government of the church passes to convocations of Canterbury and York.

material change of organization from the reign of Eadward I. down to the present day.[1] The clergy, as a mere spiritual organization, when assembled in convocation, possessed the power to legislate for the general government of the church, subject to such restrictions, limitations, or warnings as the king or the parliament might from time to time impose. In the Conqueror's reign, as has been already pointed out, even a general council, held under the presidency of the primate himself, was not allowed "to enact or prohibit anything but what was agreeable to his will and had been first ordained by him." [2] This rule was, however, so far relaxed in practice as to allow to the convocations great freedom of action, so long as their deliberations were confined to matters of purely spiritual or ecclesiastical concern.[3] But the clergy, as a distinct body possessing class interests, stood to the state, so far as constitutional history is concerned, in another and

Representation of the clergy in parliament.

far more important relation. When, in the thirteenth century, the system of estates becomes thoroughly organized, the clergy head the list ; in the classification of estates the order is, the clergy, the baronage, and the commons. The temporal representation of the clergy in the national parliament, as a distinct estate, must be considered hereafter.

The Domesday Survey.

8. In the attempt which has now been made to define in general terms the effects of the Conquest on central, local, and ecclesiastical organization, it has been necessary to pass not only beyond the limits of the Conqueror's reign, but beyond the limits of the Norman period itself. Let us return for a moment to that early stage in the history of the Conquest at which we have heretofore examined the manner in which William dealt with the conquered soil of his English kingdom, as it passed, district by district, under his authority. It was there observed [4] that the theory upon which the Conqueror claimed title to the lands of the conquered was, that he, the heir of Eadward, upon coming to take pos-

---

[1] See Sir Travers Twiss's excellent article upon Convocation in *Enc. Brit.*, 9th ed. vol. vi. p. 325.

[2] Eadmer, *Hist. Nov.*, i. p. 6 (ed. Selden).

[3] " As a rule, the later sovereigns, in-stead of restricting the liberty of meeting, contented themselves with warning the clergy not to infringe the royal rights." — Stubbs, *Const. Hist.*, vol. iii. p. 324.

[4] See above, p. 235.

session of his kingdom, had been opposed, either actively or passively, by the whole English nation, who thus became involved in the guilt of treason.   It was claimed that under the strict letter of the law the lands of all were forfeited to the king; but the application of this principle William undertook to regulate according to the circumstances of individual cases. There can be no doubt that, through the enforcement of this principle, the bulk of all the great estates passed during William's reign into Norman hands, although the main body of the people, the actual occupants of the soil, may have remained, as a general rule, undisturbed in their possessions. In view of this vast confiscation, in view of the numberless grants and transfers of land which followed in its train, it is not strange that William should have desired to know, as his reign drew to a close, "about this land, how it was set and by what men." [1]   From the well known entry in the Chronicle, under the year 1085, we further learn that "he sent over all England into ilk shire his men, and let them find out how many hundred hides were in the shire, or what the king himself had of land or cattle in the land, or whilk rights he ought to have to twelve months of the shire.   Eke he let write how mickle of land his archbishops had and his bishops and his abbots and his earls, and though I it longer tell, what or how mickle ilk man had that landholder was in England, in land and in cattle, and how mickle fee it were worth.   So very narrowly he let spear it out, that there was not a single hide nor a yard-land, [2] nor so much as — it is shame to tell and it thought him no shame to do — an ox nor a cow nor a swine was left that was not set in his writ.   And all the writs were brought to him since."   Under this order, passed in the midwinter gemot of 1085–1086, the Great Survey was made. By Lammastide the work was done, and the result was the famous record of Domesday. [3]   The Survey was taken by royal commissioners, who went forth into every shire in order

Causes which brought it about.

Chronicler's entry under 1085

---

[1] *Chron. Petrib.*, 1085.

[2] The statement that "*næs an ælpig hide ne an gyrde landes*" was omitted from the Survey "does not mean that not a hide nor a yard of land was omitted, but not a hide or a yard-land, *i. e.*, a *virgate*." — Seebohm, *English Village Community*, p. 92. The *virgate* was the normal holding of the nor-mal tenant in villenage. — Ibid., pp. 36, 73.

[3] In order fully to grasp the nature and value of this great record, it is necessary to read Sir Henry Ellis' *Introduction*, in connection with Mr. Freeman's brilliant chapter entitled "Domesday." See *Norman Conquest*, vol. v. ch. xxii.

Manner in which the Survey was taken.

to prosecute their inquiries through the oaths of those who, in ordinary times, composed the county court. Oaths were exacted from the sheriff and all the barons of the shire and their Norman associates; every hundred appeared also by sworn representatives, and from each manor or township the priest, the reeve, and six villeins or ceorls.[1] From the testimony thus obtained was reported the name of each manor, its owner in the time of King Eadward and its present owner; its extent in hides, the number of carucates or plough-teams; the number of homagers, ceorls or villeins, cotters, and serfs; how many freemen, how many sokemen; the extent of wood, meadow, and pasture; the number of mills and fisheries; the increase and decrease since King Eadward's time, the several and collective values of every holding.[2] From this statement may be derived a very definite idea of the minuteness and exactness with which the commissioners made up the great

William treated as the immediate successor of Eadward.

rate-book of the kingdom.[3] The leading fiction which pervaded the whole work was that King William was the immediate successor of King Eadward; their reigns were established as the two great periods of legal government; and the leading inquiry as to each parcel of land was, — who was its owner in the time of King Eadward, who was its owner at

Unit of inquiry the manor.

the date of the Survey.[4] Throughout the record, "the unit of inquiry is everywhere the manor, and the manor was a landlord's estate, with a township or village-community in villenage upon it, under the jurisdiction of the lord of the manor."[5] It is therefore possible to gather from the Survey a very definite idea of the internal organization of the manorial system, and of the different classes into which each manorial group was divided. The division of the lands of the manor into

---

[1] " Barones regis inquirunt, videlicet per sacramentum vicecomitis scirae et omnium baronum et eorum Francigenarum, et totius centuriatus, presbiteri, praepositi, vi. villanorum uniuscujusque villae." — Ely Domesday, *Dom.* iii. 497.

[2] " Deinde quomodo vocatur mansio, quis tenuit eam tempore Regis Eadwardi; quis modo tenet; quot hidae; quot carrucae in dominio, quot hominum; quot villani; quot cotarii; quot servi; quot liberi homines; quot sochemanni; quantum silvae; quantum prati;

quot pascuorum; quot molendina; quot piscinae; quantum est additum vel ablatum; quantum valebat totum simul; et quantum modo." — Ibid.

[3] " By this report an exhaustive register of the land and its capabilities was formed, which was never entirely superseded." — Stubbs, *Const. Hist.*, vol. i. p. 386.

[4] Freeman, *Norm. Conq.*, vol. v. pp. 9, 10.

[5] Seebohm, *Eng. Village Community*, p. 82.

lord's demesne and land in villenage seems to have been almost universal; [1] while the manorial group was broadly divided into two classes, free tenants and tenants in villenage. The result of special investigation into the relation of the classes to each other is that the free tenants — *liberi homines*, together with the allied class of sokemen — constituted but a small part of the whole population. It further appears that the free tenants, who seem to represent the mediæval and modern freeholders, were most numerous in those counties which had been most completely under Danish influence.[2] There seems to be no doubt that the tenants in villenage constituted the bulk of the population. The three classes of tenants in villenage actually mentioned in the Survey are almost universally the (1) *villani*, the (2) *bordarii* or *cotarii*, and the (3) *servi*.[3] The *servi*, embracing less than ten per cent. of the population, and who seem to have held no land, were perhaps rather household thralls of the lord of the manor than tenants in the proper sense of the term. The real tenants in villenage, then, were the *bordarii* or *cotarii* — the cottage-tenants — and the *villani*; and these two classes seem to have been scattered over the country in nearly equal proportions.[4] The *villani*, who were at the date of the Survey somewhat more numerous than the *cotarii*,[5] were the typical tenants in villenage, who are supposed to represent the Old-English ceorls, the settled cultivators of the soil, who were no doubt in the early days the owners of the land they tilled.[6] The commissioners made careful inquiry as to every class of which mention has been made, — "*quot villani; quot cotarii; quot servi; quot liberi homines; quot sochemanni,*" are the words of the Ely Domesday.[7] The Norman lord does not seem, however, to have been willing to recognize in practice these minute distinctions between the different classes

Marginal notes:

Manorial group divided into two classes.

Fewness of free tenants.

Tenants in villenage constitute the bulk of population.

Norman lords failed to recognize in practice degrees of villenage.

---

[1] "Both at the time of Edward the Confessor and at the later date." — Seebohm, *Eng. Village Community*, p. 84.

[2] See the very interesting shaded maps, illustrating the manner in which the different classes were distributed over the country, contained in Seebohm's *Eng. Village Community*, pp. 86, 87.

[3] According to Ellis (*Introduction*, vol. ii. p. 511 *seq.*) the bordarii numbered 82,119, the cotarii 5,054, the coscets 1,749, the servi 25,156, the villani 108,407.

[4] Ibid., pp. 89, 90.

[5] "They were at the date of the Survey even more numerous than the cottier class below them." — Seebohm, p. 90.

[6] Stubbs, *Const. Hist.*, vol. i. p. 428.

[7] See above, p. 266, note 2.

of tenants in villenage : the tendency of both law and social custom was to throw the *servi, bordarii,* and *villani* into the class of born villeins, who held their lands at the will of the lord, and who were bound to perform the customary services.[1] The rising of the commons, and the breaking up of villenage, are subjects which belong to the history of the thirteenth century.

Gemot of Salisbury.

9. Immediately after the completion of the Domesday Survey, William called together the famous Gemot of Salisbury,[2] in which was carried out the most far-reaching single feature of his English policy.

Weakness of the royal authority before the Conquest.

The fact has been heretofore explained that in the Old-English system the cohesive power of national unity, which had grown up through a premature and imperfect concentration of powers around a single throne, was constantly strained and weakened by the counter-force of the provincial spirit. Whenever the moment of trial came, whenever the throne was filled by an irresolute ruler or a child, the tendency to disruption was sure to assert itself through the defections of the provincial magistrates, the great earls, who were ever striving to win for themselves a part of the sovereign power which had passed from the nation to the king. In the wasting struggle which ensued, the cohesive power of the nation was broken ; the spirit of disunion and disorder, which was ever assailing the foundations of the throne, was equally ready to paralyze the national arm in the presence of the invader.[3]

William remedies old evils and provides against new ones.

Through the inflexible policy of William the old tendency to disruption was checked, the four great earldoms were abolished, and the whole realm united in one consolidated kingdom which was never afterwards to be divided.[4] Under the heel of the stranger the English nation finally awoke to a sense of its oneness. While William was thus careful to crush out every tendency to disunion that lurked in old institutions, he was equally careful to see that the same danger should not be reëstablished in a new form by his own policy. With the tendency

---

[1] " The tendency of both law and social habit was to throw into the class of *nativi* or born villeins the whole of the population described in Domesday under the heads of servi, bordarii, and villani." — Stubbs, *Const. Hist.,* vol. i. p. 428.

[2] *Chron. Petrib.,* 1086.

[3] See above, p. 216.

[4] " The great work of William's reign was to make England for ever after an undivided kingdom." — Freeman, *Norm. Conq.,* vol. iv. p. 472.

of Frank feudalism to destroy all forms of central or national organization, William, as duke of the Normans, had become thoroughly familiar. In the Frank kingdoms, as has been heretofore pointed out, feudalism grew not only into a system of tenure, but into a system of government. As soon as the principle was established that benefices were hereditary, it was extended to the official magistracies, which also became hereditary. The local sovereignty of the official magistrate, who thus grew into a ruler by hereditary right, was then enhanced by grants of immunity, which were nothing less than sections of the national or royal right of judicature bestowed upon the receiver of a fief. To the right of judicature the hereditary provincial ruler gradually added all the other attributes of actual sovereignty. And so intense did this idea of sovereignty in the provincial lord become, that the doctrine was finally asserted that a man who pledged his faith to a lord, who was the man of the king, became the man of that lord only, and not the man of the king himself. To the disruptive tendency of this principle, more than to any other cause, can be attributed the falling to pieces of France and the imperial kingdoms.[1] In order to render the growth of this principle impossible in England, William determined to make himself immediate sovereign and immediate lord of every man in the realm. With this end in view he convened the great assembly of landowners at Salisbury, whose numbers tradition fixes at sixty thousand.[2] From the Chronicle we learn that, after the completion of the Survey, William went to Salisbury, "and there came to him his witan, and all the landowning men (landsittende men) of substance that were over all England, whose soever men they were, and all bowed down to him, and became his men, and swore oaths of fealty to him that they would be faithful to him against all other men."[3] In the statute which was passed, it was provided that every freeman should take the oath of fealty to King William, that he would be faithful to him within and without England, that he would keep his lands and honors with all faithfulness, and would defend him before all men against all enemies.[4] After the completion of this great act of precau-

margin notes: Disruptive tendency of Frank feudalism.

William makes himself every man's immediate lord.

---

[1] Upon this whole subject, see above, pp. 222-225.

[2] Ord. Vit., 649 D.

[3] *Chron. Petrib.*, 1086.

[4] "Statuimus etiam ut omnis liber homo fœdere et sacramento affirmet,

tion against the disintegrating power of feudalism in England,[1] William passed over into Normandy, where he died in
the following year.

William Rufus: the growth of feudal tenures.

10. The death of William was the signal for the first great
struggle between the crown, whose powers he had been so
careful to consolidate, and the baronage, now eager to throw
off the stern rule beneath which they had bowed. The Norman succession the Conqueror had bequeathed to his eldest
son, Robert, to whom it had been promised even before the
crown of England had been won; while the English succession was by the aid of Lanfranc peacefully secured to his
second son, William the Red. At the time of his crowning,
William promised Lanfranc that he would preserve justice
and mercy throughout the realm, that he would defend the
church, and in all things comply with his precepts and coun-

Revolt of the Norman nobles, —

sels.[2] But the peace of the new reign thus auspiciously begun was soon rudely broken by a revolt of the chief men of
Norman blood throughout England, who rose under the leadership of bishop Odo, upon the pretext of supporting the
claims of Robert to the whole of his father's dominions.
Thus deserted and defied by the bulk of the greater nobles,
William at once fell back upon his character as a national
king, and appealed to the loyalty of his English subjects. If
they would assist him in his need, he promised to grant them
a better law of their own choosing; he would instantly forbid
all unjust taxation, and would surrender his hold upon their
forests.[3] All who refused to obey the summons of their lord
the king would be branded with the shameful name of nith-
ing.[4] By the aid of the English host which William thus

quod infra et extra Angliam Willelmo
regi fideles esse volunt, terras et hono-
rem illius omni fidelitate cum eo ser-
vare, et ante eum contra inimicos de-
fendere." — *Select Charters*, p. 83.

[1] William's anti-feudal legislation
was entirely misunderstood by the
older writers, who seem to have looked
upon the law passed at Salisbury as
the definite and formal introduction of
feudalism into England. Blackstone,
speaking of this statute, says that
"this may possibly have been the era
of formally introducing the feudal tenures by law." Vol. ii. p. 49. The view
stated in the text is supported by all of

the leading modern authorities. See
Freeman, *Norm. Conq.*, vol. iv. p. 472;
vol. v. p. 246; Stubbs, *Const. Hist.*, vol.
i. p. 265. As to the direction given to
English feudalism by the oath at Salisbury, see Gneist, *Verwalt.*, i. p. 116.

[2] "Pacem, libertatem, securitatem ecclesiarum contra omnes defensurum;
necnon præceptis atque consiliis ejus
per omnia et in omnibus obtemperatu-
rum." — Eadmer, *Hist. Nov.*, i. p. 14.

[3] Will. Malmes., *G. R.*, iv. § 306;
Ord. Vit., viii. 2; Stubbs, *Const. Hist.*,
vol. i. p. 296, and note 1.

[4] This word appears in William of
Malmesbury, iv. 306, and in the Chron-

drew to his standard the revolt was crushed, and the power which is crushed by the aid of the English. of the baronage trampled under foot. The royal authority, thus left unchecked by the counter-force of the feudal power, became in the hands of William an irresponsible despotism. And in the midst of his triumph, at the very moment when his restraining influence was most needed, William was deprived of his wisest counsellor by the death of Lanfranc, who was succeeded by Ranulf Flambard, the organizer of the tyrannical policy which marks the remainder of the reign.[1] Into the hands of Ranulf, who rose from the post of royal Flambard becomes justiciar, chaplain to that of justiciar,[2] passed the management of all the fiscal and judicial business of the kingdom. To this un- and systematizes military tenures, scrupulous minister is attributed the organization of the system of military tenures, together with all the oppressive consequences which were held to flow from them.[3] The system of feudal law which he seems to have worked into a definite and formal shape was applied by him with equal severity to all feudatories, temporal and spiritual. The estate of a bishop which are applied to estates of the church. or abbot now came to be regarded as a fief or benefice, held personally of the king by the tenure of military service. When a vacancy occurred, as there was no heir to the dead bishop or abbot who could demand seisin, the king took the fief into his own hands until such time as he saw fit to admit a successor. When the new heir was admitted it was upon the payment of such a sum as the lord saw fit to impose. The profits of the vacancy and the payment from the successor were the equivalents which the church paid for being exempt from the ordinary feudal exactions which fell upon the estates of laymen.[4] From the introduction by Flambard

icle under 1088. As to the vileness of the epithet, see *Norm. Conq.*, vol. ii. p. 67.

[1] "Whether or not it is fair to ascribe to Ranulf the suggestion of the tyrannical policy which marks the reign, it is to him without doubt that the systematic organization of the exactions is to be attributed."—Stubbs, *Const. Hist.*, vol. i. p. 298.

[2] As to the offices held by Ranulf, see *E. Chron.*, 1099; Ord. Vit., 786 C; Will. Malmes., iv. 314; Lappenberg, *Norman Kings*, p. 226.

[3] This is the inference of Stubbs, *Const. Hist.*, vol. i. p. 298. Mr. Free-

man in accepting this conclusion says, "We can feel little doubt in saying that the man who organized the system of feudal oppression was that same Randolf Flambard whom we have met with as the author of so much evil, and whom a contemporary writer does not scruple to speak of as the dregs of wickedness."— *Norm. Conq.*, vol. v. p. 253.

[4] "The Church was open to these claims because she furnished no opportunity for reliefs, wardships, marriage, escheat, or forfeiture."— Stubbs, *Const. Hist.*, vol. i. p. 300.

of these new and evil customs touching ecclesiastical fiefs, it is inferred — and the charter of Henry I. confirms the inference [1] — that he was also the author of the equally oppressive charges imposed about the same time upon lay estates.[2] To the reign of William Rufus is now assigned the formal organization of that system of feudal oppression whose burdens are generally summed up under the heads of relief, wardship, marriage, escheat, and forfeiture.[3] To the reign of Henry I must be traced the origin of the feudal exaction of an aid on the marriage of the king's daughter.[4] The feudatories were not, however, the only subjects of William's exacting financial policy. The body of the people at large were oppressed not only indirectly by the burdens which were imposed upon their feudal masters, but they were also subjected to a direct exaction in the form of the old and hateful tribute of Danegeld,[5] which assumed during the Norman reigns the character of ordinary revenue. By the policy of Flambard the local courts of the shire and the hundred were turned into engines of extortion ; in the expressive words of the Chronicler, "He drove and commanded all his gemots over all England." [6] In the midst of his tyrannies William perished by the hand of a hunter or assassin, and thus made way for his younger brother Henry, the one English-born member of the house of the Conqueror.

The body of the people oppressed through the local courts.

11. At the time of William's sudden death his elder brother Robert, upon whom he had attempted to bestow the right of succession by treaty,[7] being far away from England, Henry, who was on the spot, promptly embraced the opportunity to seize the kingdom. William "was slain on a Thursday, and buried the next morning ; and after he was buried, the witan, who were then near at hand, chose his brother Henry as king." [8] The promises contained in Henry's coronation oath, whose exact words are still preserved,[9] were

Henry I. : the administrative system.

---

[1] Henry's charter, art. 2.

[2] "All are deductions from a single principle, and we can hardly doubt that he who is known to have invented one of them was also the inventor of the others." — Freeman, *Norm. Conq.*, vol. v. p. 254.

[3] As to the nature of these incidents, see Digby, *Law of Real Property*, pp. 77–86 ; Blackstone, vol. ii. pp. 63–72.

[4] Henr. Huntingd., *Hist.*, lib. vii.; *Chron. Petrib.*, 1110.

[5] Stubbs, *Const. Hist.*, vol. i. p. 301.

[6] *Chron. Petrib.*, 1099.

[7] As to the terms of the treaty of Caen, see the Chronicle, 1091.

[8] *Chron. Petrib.*, 1100. As to the election, see Will. Malmes., *G. R.*, v. § 393.

[9] See Maskell, *Mon. Rit.*, vol. iii pp. 5, 6 ; *Select Charters*, p. 99.

amplified into a comprehensive charter of liberties, which Henry's charter the parent of the Great Charter. stands not only as the immediate parent of the Great Charter of John, but as the first limitation imposed upon the despotism established by the Conqueror and carried to such a height by his sons.[1]   In this charter,[2] which was specially intended to undo the wrongs of the preceding reign, distinct concessions were made to the clergy, to the baronage, and to the people at large.   The "evil customs" through which Rufus had plundered and oppressed the church were specially renounced,[3] while to the baronage the guarantee was given that the recent feudal innovations should be limited to the exaction of customary fees.[4]   This concession was not made, however, for the exclusive benefit of the tenants-in-chief: they were admonished to extend the same concessions to their own under-tenants,[5] and to renounce all tyrannical exactions.   To the people at large were restored the laws of King Eadward, — which symbolized the ancient constitution, — with such amendments as the Conqueror had made.[6]   The hold which Henry thus acquired upon the English nation, by the accident of birth and by the grant of a charter, he strengthened in a short time by a marriage with Matilda, the daughter of Henry's marriage with Margaret. King Malcolm of Scotland and of Margaret, the sister of Eadgar Ætheling, the last king of the ancient house of Cerdic and of Woden.   Thus intrenched in the affections of his English subjects, Henry found it an easy matter to maintain himself in the face of the disaffection of his nobles, when Robert, upon his return from the Holy Land, came to challenge the English crown as the head of the Norman race.   But not until the unfaithful baronage had been trampled under foot, not until Normandy had been made an English dependency, was Henry free to devote himself to the working out of that memorable policy whose central idea seems to have been the organization of the vast powers of the crown, which Rufus

---

[1] Green, *Hist. Eng. People*, vol. i. p. 140.

[2] For the text of the charter, see Thorpe, *Ancient Laws*, p. 215; *Select Charters*, p. 100.

[3] " Sanctam Dei ecclesiam imprimis liberam facio." Art. 1.

[4] " Si quis baronum . . . mortuus fuerit, hæres suus non redimet terram suam sicut faciebat tempore fratris mei, sed justa et legitima relevatione relevabit eam." Art. 2.

[5] Art. 2.

[6] " Lagam Edwardi regis vobis reddo eum illis emendationibus quibus pater meus eam emendavit consilio baronum suorum." Art. 13.

had wielded with the caprice of a despot, into a rigorous sys-

tem of methodical administration.[1]   Upon the ruins of the
great feudatories whom he had crushed, Henry now raised up
a set of lesser nobles, whom he enriched out of the estates
which, through forfeiture, had fallen to the crown.   Out of
this new nobility, upon which the older nobles of the Conquest looked down with scorn, Henry selected the sheriffs
and judges who were to aid him in the work of administrative

reform.[2]   Chief among this new ministerial nobility dependent upon royal favor was Bishop Roger of Salisbury, who,
as justiciar, became the organizer of the new fiscal and
judicial system.[3]   It has been heretofore observed that the
vast accumulation of powers and duties, which the growth of
the royal authority after the Conquest concentrated around
the person of the king, made it necessary for the crown to
select out of the main body of the great council a smaller
body which could be specially charged with the work of
administration.   This inner council, which soon came to be
known by the name of curia regis, and which was composed
of the great officers of state and of the household, and of
such other advisers as were specially summoned, seems to
have been mainly occupied from the beginning with fiscal

and judicial business.   During the reign of Henry the curia
was organized by Bishop Roger into a strong judicial and
ministerial body, whose methodical procedure imposed upon
the despotic powers of the crown the restraints at least of
administrative routine.   From the reign of Henry I. the
curia can be distinctly traced as a supreme court of justice
containing specially appointed judges, and presided over by
the king or justiciar, who is occasionally distinguished by the
title of "*summus*" or "*capitalis*."   In this reign the financial
department of the curia, now called for the first time the
exchequer, was also made a more efficient instrument for the
collection of the revenue.[4]   Henry's reforms were not limited

---

[1] For the details of the struggle
which ended with the battle of Tinche-
brai (1106), see Freeman, *Norm. Conq.*,
vol. v., pp. 109–118.

[2] Green, *Hist. of the Eng. People*,
vol. i. p. 145.

[3] "Under his guidance, whether as
chancellor or as justiciar, the whole administrative system was remodelled;

the jurisdiction of the curia regis and
exchequer was carefully organized,
and the peace of the country maintained in that theoretical perfection
which earned for him the title of the
Sword of Righteousness." — Stubbs,
Const. Hist., vol. i. p. 349.

[4] Upon this whole subject, see above,
pp. 245, 246.

however, to the central administration. A memorable part and also in-
vigorates
the local
courts. of his policy consists of his order for the holding of the courts of the shire and the hundred.[1] Under the guidance of Bishop Roger the whole judicial and financial organization of the kingdom, both central and local, was reorganized and remodelled. The death of Henry brought to a close the reign of peace and order, and opened the way for that long period of anarchy which is called the reign of Stephen.

12. After the loss of Henry's only son in the sinking of Stephen :
the anar-
chy. the White Ship, and after he had given up all hopes of children by a second marriage,[2] he resolved to settle the succession in a way which then stood without a parallel either in England or in Normandy. So long as the old Teutonic notion of kingship prevailed, so long as kingship was looked upon, not as an estate but as an office, the idea never gained ground that it could be bestowed upon one who could discharge none of its chief duties. Not until the new feudal conception of kingship arose was it supposed that a kingdom, like any other estate, might, in the absence of a son, pass to a daughter.[3] By the aid of this growing feudal theory Henry hoped to be able to settle the succession to all his dominions upon his widowed daughter Matilda. With this The oath to
Matilda. end in view, at the Christmas gemot of 1126–1127, Henry required all the great men of the land, both clergy and laity, to swear that they would, after his death, receive his daughter as Lady over England and Normandy.[4] Before the end of The
Angevin
marriage. the year in which these oaths were taken, Matilda was married to Geoffry, called Plantagenet, the son of the one enemy whom Henry feared, — Count Fulk of Anjou.[5] But in spite of all his precautions Henry's experiment only paved the way to civil war. The death of the peace-loving king was immediately followed by an outburst of anarchy, during which

[1] "Sciatis quod concedo et præcipio ut amodo comitatus mei et hundreda in illis locis et eisdem terminis sedeant, sicut sederunt in tempore Regis Eadwardi et non aliter." For the full text, see *Fœdera*, i. 12; *Select Charters*, p. 104.

[2] Will. Malmes., *Hist. Nov.*, i. 2.

[3] "But now the feudal conception of kingship had gained such ground that it began to be thought that a kingdom, like any other estate, might, in the absence of a son, pass to a daughter." — Freeman, *Norm. Conq.*, vol. v. p. 133.

[4] *Chron. Petrib.*, 1127 ; Flor. Wig., 1126. William of Malmesbury (*Hist. Nov.*, i. 2, 3) says: "Ut si ipse sine hærede masculo decederet, Matildam filiam suam, quondam imperatricem, incunctanter et sine ulla retractione *dominam* susciperent."

[5] Upon the Angevin marriage, see Green's brilliant pages, *Hist. of Eng. People*, vol. i. pp. 146–150.

Election of Stephen, — his charters.

Stephen, the nephew of Henry and the nearest male heir of the Conqueror's blood, hastened over into England and was elected[1] and consecrated king with but little opposition. The first few years of the new reign, which was ushered in by the issuance of a charter,[2] were comparatively peaceful.

Civil war begins.

Not until the landing of Matilda in 1139 did the period of general civil war actively begin. In the protracted struggle which ensued the royal authority, which Henry had done so much to consolidate, came to an end; the administrative system, which Bishop Roger had so carefully reorganized, broke down; and England, for the first and last time in her history, sank into that state of feudal anarchy which the Conqueror by his far-sighted policy had striven to prevent. Neither party was strong enough to preserve discipline. The whole land was rent, not only by the struggle between the king and the empress, but by individual strife between the barons, who arrogated to themselves all the powers of petty despots.[3]

Wail of the Peterborough Chronicler.

From the wail of the Peterborough Chronicler we learn that "they filled the land with castles. They greatly oppressed the wretched people by making them work at these castles, and when the castles were finished they filled them with devils and evil men. . . . Many thousands they exhausted with hunger. . . . And this state of things lasted the nineteen years that Stephen was king, and ever grew worse and worse." The land thus lay helpless for a time in the hands of the barons, who even presumed to strike their own coins, and to exercise every other royal right which the feudal history of France suggested. When each of the contending parties had well-nigh reached a state of exhaustion, Henry of Anjou, the son of Geoffry and Matilda, appeared upon the scene as the champion of his own cause. In 1153 Henry came to England, raised a native army,[4] and confronted

Barons exercise sovereign rights.

---

[1] *Gesta Stephani*, p. 3; *E. Chron.*, 1135; Will. Malmes., *Hist. Nov.*, i. § 11; Gervase, c. 1340.

[2] This first charter, probably issued at the coronation, is both brief and formal. See *Statutes of the Realm: Charters of Liberties,* p. 4. In 1136 a second charter was issued, however, in which, as in the charter of Henry I., distinct promises are made to each of the three estates. In this charter he describes himself as elected by the

clergy and the people, — "Ego Stephanus Dei gratia assensu cleri et populi in regem Anglorum electus." See *Select Charters*, p. 120.

[3] "There were in England as many kings, tyrants rather, as there were lords of castles; each had the power of striking his own coin, and of exercising like a king sovereign jurisdiction over his dependents." — Stubbs, *Const. Hist.*, vol. i. p. 328.

[4] R. de Monte, 1153.

Stephen in the field.   But before a decisive battle could be fought, the barons intervened as mediators; the archbishop and the bishop of Winchester also counselled conciliation; and the result was the Treaty of Wallingford, through which the evils of the long anarchy were brought to a close.[1]   This treaty, in which Stephen was recognized as king and Henry as his heir, was attended by an elaborate project of reform which contemplated among other things the resumption of all royal rights that had been usurped by the baronage, the restitution of estates taken from their lawful owners, the razing of all unlicensed castles, the banishment of the foreign mercenaries from the country, and the appointment of sheriffs to reëstablish justice and order.[2]   The death of Stephen, within a short time after the pacification, removed the only remaining obstacle from the path of Henry, "whose statesmanlike activity, whose power of combining and adapting that which was useful in the old systems of government with that which was desirable and necessary under the new, gives to the policy which he initiated in England almost the character of a new creation."[3]

Treaty of Wallingford.

Death of Stephen and accession of Henry of Anjou.

[1] "The result was stated in the form of a treaty to settle the succession. Each of the parties had something to surrender and each something to secure." — Stubbs, *Const. Hist.*, vol. i. p. 332.

[2] The treaty itself is preserved in the form of a charter of Stephen, printed in Rymer, i. 18. But the entire scheme of reform which attended it can only be gathered from the contemporary historians.   See R. de Monte, 1153; Hen. Hunt., fol. 228; Gervase, 1375; Will. Newburg, i. 30; Roger of Hoveden, i. 212. Cf. Freeman, *Norm. Conq.*, vol. v. p. 219, and note FF.

[3] Stubbs, *Const. Hist.*, vol. i. p. 336.

CHAPTER III.

HENRY OF ANJOU.[1] — THE PERIOD OF FUSION.

The growing together of Old-English local machinery and Norman system of central administration.

1. By the death of Stephen the strictly Norman period of English history was brought to a close. The character of that period, and the immediate changes which it wrought in government, in law, and in tenure, have in the preceding chapter been briefly reviewed. The leading object of that review was to point out the fact that, although the Conquest brought with it a change of dynasty, the establishment of a new nobility, and a sweeping confiscation through which most of the great estates were transferred from English to Norman hands, yet that it did not involve the displacement of the English nation, nor a wiping out of the immemorial laws and political institutions of the conquered race. The master of the history of the Norman conquest never grows weary of enforcing the truth that the importance which belongs to it is not the importance which belongs to a beginning or an ending, but the importance that belongs to a turning point ;[2] that the coming of the Normans only gave a fresh impulse to causes already at work, only hastened tendencies to change already begun. In the Old-English system all the elements of feudalism were imbedded ; and long before the Normans came these elements were gradually becoming blended : the thegn was passing into the tenant-in-chief, the men of the dependent township were surely be-

---

[1] The most perfect sketch ever drawn of the personal and political character of this great prince is contained in Bishop Stubbs's preface to Benedict of Peterborough, whose chronicle is the leading authority for the reign. The vividness, the warmth, the brilliancy of the picture, is like an oasis in the desert to the student who has marched across the sands of the *Constitutional History*. See *Rolls Series*, Benedictus, vol. ii. Bishop Stubbs's view differs widely from that of Sir Francis Palgrave, who regards Henry's reign as a period of revolution as a second conquest. " I can find the most evident and cogent proof," says Sir Francis, " that a great revolution was effected, not by William, but by Henry Plantagenet." See *Normandy and England*, vol. iii. p. 601. For Mr. Freeman's view, which agrees in all material particulars with that of Bishop Stubbs, see *Norm. Conq.*, vol. v. pp. 436–459.

[2] Freeman, *Norm. Conq.*, vol. i. p. 1 ; vol. v. p. 434.

coming the tenants of the lord in whom the title to the lands
of the cultivating community was vested. The "process of
feudalization" which everywhere in Europe was transform-
ing the mark into the manor, the village-community into the
fief, the elective chief of the people into the hereditary lord
of the land,[1] did not fail to extend itself to the English kingdom. But in the continental land from which the conquerors came these feudal ideas had reached a far higher and
more perfect development than they had yet reached in the
insular system. By the coming of William two kindred systems of government and tenure, both tending in the same
direction and yet in different stages of development, were
brought into the closest contact, and out of the fusion be- *The mod-
tween the two has grown the modern constitution.[2] The ern constitution the
period of transition and growth which intervenes between outcome of
the fusion.*
the ancient constitution and the constitution in its modern
form has been happily divided into two stages: the first or
Norman stage, embracing the reigns of the four Norman
kings, is the stage during which the great mass of foreign
elements and influences were infused into the blood, the
language, the laws, the political institutions, of the English
nation; the second or Angevin stage, embracing the reigns
of Henry II. and his sons, is the stage during which the foreign and native elements were worked together into a new
combination which retained the strongest elements of both.[3]
The most striking single fact which an analysis of the result *Superstructure
has so far revealed is, that in the new combination the super- Norman,
structure is Norman, the substructure Old-English.[4] The substructure Old-
first or Norman stage of the transitional period has already English.*
been reviewed. In the preceding chapter the attempt was
made to define in general terms the character of the new
elements, and the amount of change or innovation introduced

[1] See Sir Henry Maine's review of
"The Process of Feudalization," *Vil-
lage - Communities*, lecture v.; *Ancient
Law*, pp. 101–108.

[2] For a more complete statement of
this whole subject with the authorities,
see the preceding chapter, pp. 238–248.
"The Anglo-Saxon and the Norman
institutions had been actually in a state
of fusion since the Conquest, and the
reign of Henry gave to the united systems the character which has devel-

oped into the English constitution." —
Preface to Benedict, *Rolls Series*, vol.
ii., xxxvi.

[3] Freeman, *Norm. Conq.*, vol. v. p.
439.

[4] "The principle of amalgamating
the two laws and nationalities by su-
perimposing the better consolidated
Norman superstructure on the better
consolidated English substructure, runs
through the whole policy." — Stubbs,
Const. Hist., vol. i. p. 278.

during the reigns of the Conqueror and his sons. The effort was then made to draw out the fact that, while the Norman kings were ever striving to consolidate and strengthen the royal authority by building up around it a new system of central administration, they were also careful to preserve by express ordinance the ancient customary law of the realm, together with the system of local courts in which that law had been immemorially administered. The distinctive feature of the Norman period, so far as constitutional history is concerned, is the development of a new system of central administration with the source of its strength in the royal authority.

Norman central system the outgrowth of the new kingship.

In order to discharge the many vast and intricate duties which the growth of the royal power after the Conquest concentrated around the person of the king, it became necessary for the crown to organize out of the main body of the great council a smaller body, which could be charged under the king's direction with the whole work of central or national administration.[1] Out of this inner council, which soon came to be known by the name of curia regis, all the administrative institutions of the kingdom seem to have sprung. During the reign of Henry I. the curia was organized by Bishop Roger into a strong judicial and ministerial body, whose methodical procedure imposed upon the despotic powers of the crown the restraints at least of administrative routine. In this reign the financial department of the curia, now called for the first time the exchequer, was also made a more efficient instrument for the collection of the revenue. In Henry's time detachments of justices were first sent from the curia to assess the revenue and to adjust the business of the exchequer in each shire.[2] In this way the new system of central adminis-

Central and local systems first drawn together through fiscal visits of the justices itinerant.

tration was first brought into direct contact with the local machinery of the constitution. But, excepting the occasional contact which thus arose out of the fiscal visitations of the justices, the central and local systems stood apart during the reigns of the Norman kings. Not until the Angevin period is reached, not until the reigns of Henry II.[3] and his sons,

---

[1] "In conformity with the system of France and other feudal countries, there was one standing council, which assisted the kings of England in the collection and management of their reve-nue, the administration of justice to suitors, and the dispatch of all public busi-ness."— Hallam, *M. A.*, vol. ii. p. 317.

[2] See above, p. 247.

[3] "His reign was the period of amal

is there anything like a growing together of the Norman system of central administration and the tenacious machinery of
Old-English local freedom embodied in the organizations of
the township, the hundred, and the shire.

The same agencies which, during the Angevin reigns, Commix-
ture of royal
and cus-
tomary
law.
brought about the amalgamation of the new administrative
system and the ancient local machinery, also brought about
a union between the new system of royal law, which radiated
from the curia regis, and the ancient system of customary
law as administered in the local courts.   A great German
writer has lately pointed out the fact that in the study of Teutonic law the distinction must be sharply drawn between such
law as flows from a royal or official source, and such as flows
from a customary or popular source.[1]   By the application of
this idea to the special investigation of the origin of the English jury, rich results have already been attained.   By keep-
ing this distinction steadily in view, Brunner has finally dem- Origin of
the trial
jury.
onstrated the fact that out of the union of a certain branch
of royal law — in the form of special commissions or writs of
inquiry issued from the curia regis — with a certain kind of
witness-proof imbedded in the customary law has been gradually developed the English jury of judgment, the trial jury
of modern times.[2]

Before attempting, however, to work out in detail the pro- Union of
races.
cess of fusion between the systems of central and local administration, and between the systems of royal and customary
law, it will be helpful to indicate in general terms the steps
by which the two races became fused into one nationality.
The effects of the Conquest on national unity were twofold.
In the first place it had the effect of uniting the English
among themselves.   By the coming of William the tendency
to provincial isolation was checked, and the whole realm
united in one consolidated kingdom which was never afterwards divided.[3]   After the time of Stephen, even the threefold division of the kingdom into the Dane law, the West

gamation, the union of the different
elements existing in the country, which,
whether it be looked on as chemical
or mechanical, produced the national
character and the national institutions." — Preface to Benedict, *Rolls
Series*, vol. ii. p. xxxiii.

[1] As to Sohm's views upon this subject, see *North American Review* for
July, 1874, p. 222.
[2] See *Die Entstehung der Schwurgerichte*, Berlin, 1874.
[3] See above, p. 217.

Saxon, and Mercian law became obsolete and disappeared.[1] No dividing lines survived except such as were drawn by slight differences in local custom.[2] Into the greater mass of the united English nation the smaller Norman mass was gradually absorbed; the "conquerors were conquered; the Normans became Englishmen." As early as the reign of Henry I. causes began to work which, before a century had passed by, had drawn together into one nation all natives of the soil, regardless of older differences of race and speech.[3] Under the pressure of common calamities, national enmities were during Stephen's reign in a great measure forgotten. And through the agency of frequent intermarriage the work of fusion so rapidly advanced that a writer of the time of Henry II. is obliged to confess that, without a careful examination of pedigree, it was impossible to ascertain in his time who was Norman and who was English.[4] It may therefore be

Fusion completed at the accession of Henry II.

safely assumed that by the time of the accession of Henry of Anjou the two races had become fused together into one nation scarcely conscious yet of its own unity. As soon as this condition of things was reached, in which it was difficult to distinguish an Englishman from a Norman, all legal distinctions in favor of one race as against the other necessarily passed out of view.[5]

The restoration of order.

2. During the protracted struggle which occupies the period of anarchy known as the reign of Stephen, the royal authority which Henry I. had done so much to consolidate came to an end; the administrative system which Bishop Roger had so thoroughly organized broke down; and England, for the first and last time in her history, sank into that state of feudal anarchy which the Conqueror by his far-sighted policy had striven to prevent. For a time the land lay helpless in the hands of the barons, who intrenched themselves in their

---

[1] "The terms are become archaisms which occur in the pages of the historians in a way that proves them to have become obsolete." — Stubbs, *Const. Hist.*, vol. i. p. 545, citing Simeon of Durham, ed. Hinde, vol. i. pp. 220–222.

[2] These, Glanvill says, are too numerous to be put on record. — *De Legibus*, lib. xii. c. 6.

[3] Freeman, *Norm. Conq.*, vol. v. pp. 98, 438.

[4] "Jam cohabitantibus Anglicis et Normannis, et alterutrum uxores ducentibus vel nubentibus, sic permixtæ sunt nationes, ut vix discerni possit hodie, de liberis loquor, quis Anglicus quis Normannus sit genere." — *Dialogus de Scaccario*, i. c. 10.

[5] As to the gradual extinction of Englishry, see Bracton, 135 *b*; Fleta, lib. i. c. 30; Bigelow, *Hist. of Procedure*, p. 81.

unlicensed castles, and arrogated to themselves all the rights of petty despots.[1] Not until both of the contending parties had well-nigh reached a state of exhaustion was the long anarchy brought to a close by the Treaty of Wallingford, which was attended by an elaborate scheme of reform that contemplated, among other things, the disarming of the feudal party, the demolition of the unlicensed castles, the banishment of all mercenary soldiers, the resumption of all royal rights that had been usurped by the baronage, the restitution of estates taken from their lawful owners, the abolition of the fiscal earldoms, and the appointment of sheriffs to reëstablish order.[2] Upon the death of Stephen in 1154,[3] Henry of Anjou, then in his twenty-second year, came to the throne pledged to the task of bringing peace and prosperity out of anarchy and exhaustion upon the lines of that project of reform which had followed the Treaty of Wallingford. To the complete performance of the work of restoration the first ten years (1154–1164) of Henry's reign were chiefly devoted.[4] During the first three years of the reign, however, the greater part of the work was actually accomplished. Within that time the feudal party — in the teeth of fierce resistance from some of its strongest members — was disarmed, the unlicensed castles were destroyed, the royal estates resumed, the mercenaries banished, the curia regis and exchequer reëstablished, and careful provision made for both central and provincial judicature.[5]

3. It was impossible, however, for Henry, the ruler of vast continental dominions, to confine his energies exclusively to the affairs of England. In 1159 he became involved in a foreign war by attempting to enforce the claim of his wife on the county of Toulouse.[6] As it was highly inconvenient to carry on military operations against the most distant province of France by the aid of feudal levies who were only bound to a limited service, Henry hit upon an expedient through which money

The institution of scutage, or shield-money.

---

[1] Cf. Green, *Hist. Eng. People*, vol. i. p. 155.
[2] As to the scheme of reform that attended the Treaty of Wallingford, see above, p. 277.
[3] Gervase, cc. 1375, 1376.
[4] Freeman, *Norm. Conq.*, vol. v. p. 441.

[5] For the details of the work accomplished by Henry in 1155, '56, '57, see Stubbs, *Const. Hist.*, vol. i. pp. 449–455. Henry did not land in England until the 8th of December, 1154.
[6] R. de Monte, A. D. 1158, 1159.

could be realized for the employment of mercenary soldiers. In the fourth year of his reign, as a financial measure to aid the meditated expedition against Toulouse,[1] Henry and Thomas devised the institution of scutage or shield-money, — a pecuniary compensation in lieu of military service. The hiring of mercenaries was nothing new, but the new device for raising money for their employment was an innovation which dates from this time.[2] Those tenants of the crown who did not desire to go to the war were allowed to pay a tax

Assize of arms.

of two marks on the knight's fee.[3] The natural supplement to this blow against feudalism was embodied in Henry's assize of arms (1181), whereby the old constitutional force was reorganized by the duty being imposed upon every freeman to provide himself, for the defence of the commonwealth, with arms according to his means.[4] By reason of the expedition against Toulouse, and a consequent quarrel with Louis VII., his feudal lord, — against whom he declined personally to bear arms,[5] — Henry was kept away from England until the beginning of the eventful year 1163.

Henry's effort to establish the reign of equal law.

4. The full scope of Henry's policy was not only to establish the reign of law, but to reduce all orders of men to a state of equality before the same system of law. The most formidable obstacles which stood in the way of the complete execution of this design were the baronage on the one hand, with their private jurisdictions, and the clergy on the other, with their far-reaching claims of exemption from the ordinary

Conflict with the clergy.

process of the temporal tribunals.[6] Not long after Henry's return in 1163 the prosecution of his scheme of reform brought him into conflict with the clerical order, at whose head now stood Thomas Becket, who, a year before, had been elevated to the see of Canterbury. At the beginning of the

---

[1] "Tolosam bello aggressurus," etc., John of Salisb. (Ep. 145), i. 223.

[2] "The hiring of mercenaries was nothing new; but to hire them with money paid as an exemption from personal service was a device of Henry and Thomas." — Freeman, *Norm. Conq.*, vol. v. p. 451.

[3] Upon the general subject, see Reeves, *Hist. Eng. Law*, vol. i. p. 247; Digby, *Law of Real Property*, p. 116; Madox, *Hist. Ex.*, ch. 16; Preface to Benedict, vol. ii. p. xcv.

[4] Benedictus, vol. i. p. 278; Hoveden, ii. 261; Gervase, c. 1459; *Select Charters*, 153.

[5] Will. Fitz-Stephen (ed. Giles), vol. i. p. 200; R. de Diceto, 531.

[6] "The former must be compelled to agree to the restriction of their hereditary jurisdictions, and the latter to allow themselves to be, in all matters not purely spiritual, subject to the ordinary process of law." — *Select Charters*, p. 21.

reign Thomas of London, the pupil of Archbishop Theobald, had been recommended by his patron as an able adviser to the young king, who at once raised him to the office of chancellor.[1] This office Thomas held until his unfortunate elevation to the primacy of the kingdom.[2] In his new station the temper of Thomas at once passed through a marked transformation; the knightly courtier now assumed the garb of the ascetic; the foremost lawyer and statesman of the kingdom now became the champion and assertor of the rights and privileges of the church.   The first dispute between the archbishop and the king — the details of which are very obscure — seems to have arisen out of the opposition of the former to the levying of a Danegeld in some new form prejudicial to the interests of the sheriffs, and in favor of the royal revenue, and in a form which would vest it as a permanent revenue in the king without any express grant by the national assembly. Thomas, as the leader of the first constitutional opposition to an English king in a matter of taxation,[3] is recorded to have said: "We will not, my lord king, saving your good pleasure, give this money as revenue; but if the sheriffs and servants and ministers of the shires will perform their duties as they should, and maintain and defend our defendants, we will not be behindhand in contributing to their aid." To which the angered king answered: "By the eyes of God, it shall be given as revenue, and it shall be entered in the king's accounts; and you have no right to contradict; no man wishes to oppress your men against your will." Thomas then replied: "My lord king, by the reverence of the eyes by which you have sworn, it shall not be given from my land, and from the rights of the church not a penny."[4] With this event the enmity between the king and the primate begins.

In the following October, in the Council of Westminster, a

Thomas as primate.

First quarrel between Thomas and the king touching taxation.

Thomas the forerunner of Hampden.

---

[1] Gervase, c. 1377.

[2] For a sketch of the life of Thomas, see Green, *Hist. of the Eng. People*, vol. i. pp. 164–170.

[3] "Even those who are most unwilling to allow any praise to one who bore the titles of saint and martyr have been driven to confess that in this matter the part of Thomas did but forestall the part of Hampden." — Freeman, *Norm. Conq.*, vol. v. p. 451.

[4] As to the obscure details of this first dispute, see Grim, *Vita S. Thomas*, vol. i. pp, 21, 22; Roger of Pontigny, *Vita S. Thom.* (ed. Giles), vol. i. p. 113; Preface to Benedict, vol. ii. p. xci.; Stubbs, *Const. Hist.*, vol. i. pp. 462, 463.

The second
quarrel
touching
clerical im-
munities,
1163.

new quarrel arose between the primate and the king touching the exemption of the clerical order from the jurisdiction of the temporal tribunals. From the time of the Conqueror's famous ordinance separating the spiritual from the temporal courts, the punishment of members of the clerical order guilty of criminal offences had been attended with great difficulty. In such cases the ecclesiastical courts would not allow the lay tribunals to take jurisdiction, and the ecclesiastical courts themselves could only inflict spiritual penalties.[1] The provision that the king and the sheriff should, under certain circumstances, enforce the judgments of the bishops, had, through the jealousies of the two estates, failed of its purpose.[2] Under these circumstances a large number of clerks guilty of serious criminal offences, besides a large number who falsely claimed to be clerks, escaped all real punishment.[3] To remedy these evils in the administration of the criminal law, Henry now resolved that all criminals, clerical as well as lay, should be tried in the ordinary tribunals. If a clerical criminal confessed or was convicted, he should first be degraded by the bishops, and then handed over to the officers of the law for punishment.[4] Henry at the same time complained of the exactions of the spiritual courts, and he finally demanded that the bishops should agree that the proceedings of their courts and the rights of the clergy generally should be regulated by the customs which had prevailed in the time of Henry I. Thomas refused to accede unconditionally to the king's demands, and the result of his refusal was a qualified assent of the bishops, "saving their order."[5] To definitely settle the controversy, Henry

Council at
Clarendon,
1164.

called together all the bishops and barons at Clarendon,[6] in January, 1164, and there renewed his demand that the customs regulating the rights of the church in use in the time

[1] "This state of things existed at its height from the beginning of the reign of Stephen until the tenth year of the reign of Henry the Second." — Bigelow, *Hist. of Procedure*, p. 34.

[2] The provision referred to was contained in the Conqueror's famous ordinance separating the spiritual from the temporal courts. Cf. Stubbs, *Const. Hist.*, vol. i. pp. 283, 463.

[3] "The clerical order in the Middle Ages extended far beyond the priesthood; it included in Henry's day the whole of the professional and educated classes." — Green, *Hist. Eng. People*, vol. i. p. 164.

[4] Hoveden, vol. i. p. 219; Gervase, c. 1384.

[5] Such were the results of the Council of Westminster which met in October, 1163. Cf. Stubbs, *Const. Hist.*, vol. i. p. 464.

[6] R. Diceto, c. 536; Gervase, c. 1385.

of his grandfather should be accepted as the law. After a second refusal from the archbishop to accept the royal demand unconditionally, Henry ordered that the customs should be reduced to writing, after their existence had first been established by the process of recognition.[1] The result of the inquiry was embodied in the famous document known as the Constitutions of Clarendon. These constitutions, sixteeen in number, were intended to codify and reëstablish the law as it had stood in the time of Henry I. In this fresh understanding between church and state the distinction between temporal and spiritual courts established by the Conqueror was distinctly recognized.[2] But it was left for the king's court to decide by which jurisdiction accused clerks were in each case to be tried; and it was further provided that in all ecclesiastical proceedings a royal officer should be present to confine the spiritual court to its proper limits, and that the spiritual court should not shelter persons who had offended against the laws of the land.[3] The curia regis was recognized as a court of regular resort, and to it were reserved all questions of presentation and advowson.[4] An appeal was still allowed from the archbishop's court to the king's court in a proper case, but no appeal to the papal court could be taken without the king's leave.[5] Direct reference was made not only to the use of juries of twelve men from the vicinage in criminal causes,[6] but also to the principle of recognition by twelve lawful men in case of a dispute as to the tenure of an estate alleged to be in franc-almoign.[7] All elections to bishoprics and abbacies were to take place before the royal officers, in the king's chapel, and with the king's assent.[8] The baronial status of the bishops was expressly recognized:[9] the prelate-elect before consecration must do homage to the king, from whom his lands must be held as a

Marginal notes: Constitutions of Clarendon:

the concordat between church and state.

---

[1] "These constitutions were, as they purport, the result of an inquiry into the customs of England existing in the time of Henry the First, grandfather of Henry the Second." — Bigelow, *Hist. of Procedure*, p. 34.

[2] Freeman, *Norm. Conq.*, vol. v. p. 452. For the text of the constitutions, see Lyttleton's *Life of Henry II.*, vol. iv. pp. 182–185; *Select Charters*, p. 140.

[3] Cap. iii.

[4] Cap. i. "De advocatione et præsentatione ecclesiarum si controversia emerserit inter laicos, vel inter laicos et clericos, vel inter clericos, in curia domini regis tractetur vel terminetur."

[5] Cap. viii.

[6] "Vicecomes requisitus ab episcopo faciet jurare duodecim legales homines de vicineto, seu de villa." Cap. vi.

[7] Cap. ix.

[8] Cap. xii.

[9] Cap. xi.

barony subject to all feudal burdens. No bishop was to leave the realm without the royal permission, and no tenant-in-chief or royal servant was to be excommunicated, nor his land placed under interdict, without the royal assent.[1] It was further provided that no villein should be ordained with-

Permanent results of the Constitutions.

out the consent of his lord.[2] The permanent results of the reform brought about by the adoption of the Constitutions have thus been summarized: " 1. All questions agitated concerning church property were relegated to the king's court, or other lay court, in one form or another. 2. All offences committed by men in orders upon laymen were to be redressed alone in the lay courts. 3. Debts and demands in favor of laymen against clerics were to be sued in the same courts. 4. Redress by clerics against laymen, when it was not pursued for the mere purpose of punishing sin, was to be sought in the lay courts. On the other hand, the Court Christian still retained jurisdiction in the following cases: 1. Over offences between the clergy alone. 2. Over small debts, and perhaps minor property causes between the clergy. 3. Over matrimonial causes, the conduct of the sexes, defamation, usury, and wills. 4. Over, it seems, crimes committed by the laity, when jurisdiction was sought for the purpose of imposing ecclesiastical censure, admonition, or penitential punishment. The jurisdiction of the Ecclesiastical Court having thus become settled before the close of the reign of Henry the Second, a way was found to keep that court within the limits fixed, to wit, by means of a writ of prohibition, issued from the king's court, — a writ in use from the time at least of Glanvill, and probably earlier, until the present day."[3] To the definitions of ecclesiastical

Thomas' reluctant assent and exile.

rights and limitations contained in the Constitutions Thomas, after a passionate refusal, was finally induced to set his seal. His reluctant assent was, however, immediately revoked, and he appealed to the pope for forgiveness for having betrayed the interests of the church.[4] This conduct greatly enraged the king, through whose violent resentment he was soon driven into exile.[5] But notwithstanding the storm which

---

[1] Cap. vii.

[2] " Filii rusticorum non debent ordinari absque assensu domini de cujus terra nati dignoscuntur." Cap. xvi.

[3] Bigelow, *Hist. of Procedure*, pp. 52, 53.

[4] Cf. Robertson, *Becket*, pp. 101–103.

[5] The fatal quarrel in which Thomas

followed their adoption, the Constitutions regulated from this time the relations of the church with the state.[1]

5. By the victory won at Clarendon in favor of administrative order, the first period of Henry's reign was brought to a close. The remainder of the reign (1164–1189), so far as constitutional history is concerned, was devoted to the reorganization of the central and provincial systems, and to the task of drawing them into closer relations with each other. The system of central administration, embodied in the national council and the curia regis, reached under Henry II. and his sons a definiteness of organization which it had never possessed before. The composition of the national council, which was now summoned at regular intervals, was that of a perfect feudal court, — an assembly of archbishops, bishops, abbots, priors, earls, barons, knights, and freeholders.[2] The constituent members of the assembly are the same as under the Norman kings, but greater prominence and a more definite position are now assigned to the minor tenants-in-chief.[3] But under the changes of form and of name the continuity of the Old-English national assembly went on unbroken. "A great council of Henry the Second undoubtedly differed widely from a witenagemot of the Confessor, and a parliament of Edward the First differed yet more widely from a great council of Henry the Second. But there is no break between any of the three. The constitution of the assembly is changed first in practice, then by direct ordinance ; but the assembly itself is the same. At no time was one kind of assembly formally abolished, and another kind of assembly formally put in its stead."[4] In the days of Henry of Anjou, as in the days of Eadward and of William, an ordinary meeting of the national assembly embraced only the witan, — the magnates of the kingdom; while on an extraordinary occa-

Margin notes: Reorganization of the central system : the national council, — a perfect feudal court, — its relation to the witenagemot.

---

perished, and which had nothing whatever to do with the Constitutions, did not occur until his return in 1170. The final quarrel grew out of the old rivalry between York and Canterbury.

[1] "In spite of denunciations from primate and pope, the Constitutions regulated from this time the relations of the church with the state." — Green, *Hist. Eng. People*, vol. i. p. 167.

[2] *Select Charters*, pp. 22, 23.

[3] "There is a growing recognition of their real constitutional importance, . . . and a growing tendency to admit not only them, but the whole body of smaller landowners, of whom the minor tenants-in-chief are but an insignificant portion, to the same rights." — Stubbs, *Const. Hist.*, vol. i. p. 564.

[4] Freeman, *Norm. Conq.*, vol. v. p. 272. See, also, Green, *Hist. Eng. People*, vol. i. p. 349.

sion it might embrace, besides these, not only the tenants-in-chief, but the whole body of freeholders. But through the influence of the practice of summons, to whose origin an exact date cannot be assigned, the tendency was fast gaining ground to limit the national assembly to those only who were summoned by the king's writ, either personally or in a body. The writs of summons were of two kinds : first, such as were specially addressed to those great personages whose presence was necessary, and who were summoned as a matter of course ;[1] second, such as were addressed generally to the sheriff of each shire, requiring him to summon in a body the lesser landowners.[2] How far this practice of summons, which was in active operation in the time of Henry II.,[3] had developed up to the sixteenth year of the reign of John, can be definitely ascertained from the fourteenth article of the Great Charter, which provides that, "to have the common counsel of the kingdom, we will cause to be summoned the archbishops, bishops, abbots, earls, and greater barons singly by our letters ; and besides we will cause to be summoned in general by our sheriffs and bailiffs all those who hold of us in chief."[4] By this clause, which no doubt expressed the then existing practice, the qualification for membership in the national assembly was at last distinctly defined, and that qualification naturally assumed a feudal shape. No one was expected to attend unless he was summoned ; and no one was summoned unless he was a tenant-in-chief. By the form of the summons a line was also distinctly drawn between two definite classes of men, — between the magnates, who were entitled to a personal summons, and the main body of

Influence of the practice of summons.

The practice as defined in the fourteenth article of the Great Charter.

Form of the summons draws the line between lords and commons.

---

[1] The earliest writ of this class extant is one addressed to the bishop of Salisbury in 1205, in which is stated the date of the assembly and the cause of the meeting. It also contains a general clause directing the bishop to warn the abbots and priors of his diocese to be present. See *Report on the Dignity of a Peer*, App. i. p. 1 ; *Select Charters*, p. 282.

[2] The presumption is, in the absence of any extant writs of this class of an early date, that "they must have enumerated the classes of persons summoned in much the same way as they were enumerated in the writs ordering the assembly of the county courts." — Stubbs, *Const. Hist.*, vol. i. p. 568.

[3] A memorable instance of a special summons in that reign is the one directed to Becket, citing him to appear in the Council of Northampton to answer the claim of John the Marshal. — W. Fitz-Stephen, i. 220.

[4] Cap. 14. "Summoneri faciemus archiepiscopos, episcopos, abbates, comites, et majores barones, sigillatim per litteras nostras; et præterea faciemus summoneri in generali, per vicecomites et ballivos nostros, omnes illos qui de nobis tenent in capite."

tenants-in-chief, who were summoned generally in the shires: in this way the distinction between lords and commons begins.[1]

Henry II. legislated in the old Teutonic form which had been immemorially employed by his Old-English and Norman predecessors. As Ine legislated with the counsel and with the teaching of his bishops, with all his ealdormen and the most distinguished witan of his people; as Ælfred promulgated his code with the counsel and consent of his witan,[2] — so Henry legislated with the advice and consent of his national council. The "counsel and consent may have been, as a general rule, a mere formality; it certainly did not imply that full and authoritative power of deliberation possessed by the witan in earlier times; and yet the very survival of the ancient form attested the fact that the theoretical right of the nation to participate in legislation was not forgotten." In Henry's time as in Ælfred's, in all public matters — legislative, judicial, political, and financial — the nation through its assembly was in theory consulted.[3] The legislative enactments, which were thus promulgated by the Norman and by some of the Plantagenet kings, assumed many different forms before they appeared in the final form of statutes. During the Norman reigns such enactments were usually cast in the form of charters;[4] in the reign of Henry II. they were generally known by the name of assizes, — a word of various application. The assizes of Henry II., considered as legislative enactments, were in the main edicts or regulations for the enforcement of new methods of legal procedure; they were not drawn up in the form of perpetual statutes, but rather in the form of tentative or temporary enactments.[5] The most important remains of Henry's legislative work survive in the form of assizes, — in the Assizes of Clarendon and Northampton, in the Assize of the Forest, and in the

King legislates as of old with the advice and consent of his council.

Charters.

Assizes.

[1] Freeman, *Norm. Conq.*, vol. v. pp. 274, 275.
[2] As to the forms of Old-English legislation, see above, p. 186.
[3] *Select Charters*, p. 23; Green, *Hist. Eng. People*, vol. i. p. 350.
[4] "The form of a charter, in which the king is considered as a person granting, was a very common way of

making laws at this time." — Reeves, *Hist. of Eng. Law*, vol. i. p. 478.
[5] "In this respect they strongly resemble the Capitularies of the Frank kings, or, to go farther back, the edicts of the Roman prætors: they might, indeed, as to both form and matter, be called Capitularies." — Stubbs, *Const. Hist.*, vol. i. p. 573.

Provisions.

Statutes
and ordi-
nances.

Assize of Arms. In the reign of Henry III. legislative enactments appear in the form of provisions;[1] in the reigns of
Edward I. and his successors they assume the form of statutes and ordinances.[2] The ancient form of royal legislation
is not superseded by the modern form of national legislation
until the ancient council of the king is transformed into a
national parliament.[3]

Taxation
under the
Old-Eng-
lish system.

6. In the early days of the Old-English commonwealth, as
the king's revenues from the folkland, from his private estates,
and from customary dues were amply sufficient to maintain
the royal state, and as the threefold duty (*trinoda necessitas*)
of rendering military service and of repairing bridges and
fortresses supplied all local requirements, there was no necessity for the imposition of taxes, in the modern sense of
that term.[4] Not until the reign of Æthelred, when money
had to be raised for the purpose of defence against the
Danes, did it become necessary for the king and the witan
to levy extraordinary taxes for the public service. With the
imposition of the Danegeld the history of English taxation

The Dane-
geld or
land-tax.

really begins.[5] This tax, which was levied not only for the
purpose of buying off the invaders but for the raising of
fleets, was necessarily a land-tax, for the reason that land, in
the early days, was the only standard of value on which an
assessment could be made. Under the famous rating of 1008,
to which can be traced the origin of ship-money, the burden
of raising a fleet was imposed upon the whole nation, but the
proportion to be contributed in kind by each district was
fixed by reference to the number of hides contained in each.
It may be inferred from the terms of assessment that every
three hundred hides were liable to furnish a ship, every ten
hides a boat, and every eight hides a helmet and breastplate.[6]
From what we know of the Old-English fiscal system, the

---

[1] Stubbs, *Const. Hist.*, vol. i. p. 574.

[2] Hallam, *M. A.*, vol. iii. p. 50.

[3] "The legislation of the Great
Charter was to a certain extent an anticipation, a type, a precedent, and a
firm step in advance, towards that consummation." — Stubbs, *Const. Hist.*,
vol. i. p. 576.

[4] As to the royal revenue under the
Old-English system, see above, p. 182.

[5] "To raise a ransom which freed
the land from the invader, the first

land-tax, under the name of the Danegeld, was laid on every hide of ground;
and to this national taxation the Norman kings added the feudal burdens of
the new military estates created by the
Conquest, reliefs paid on inheritance,
profits of marriages and wardship, and
the three feudal aids." — Green, *Hist.
Eng. People*, vol. i. p. 321.

[6] For the authorities upon this subject, see above, p 187, note 2.

conclusion may be drawn that the only tax ever levied, in the The Old-
English
unit of as-
sessment,
the hide. modern sense of that term, was the Danegeld or land-tax, and that the unit of assessment was the hide.   As the hide, then, was the unit of assessment from the earliest times, and continued to be so long after the Norman conquest, it is quite possible to understand why such great labor has been expended in the attempt to ascertain its character and extent.[1] By the light of recent researches into the early history of the English land system, something like definite results have at last been attained.   Mr. Seebohm, after a minute examination of the open-field system by the aid of the Great Survey and the Hundred Rolls, has ascertained that a virgate — the normal holding of a normal tenant in villenage — usually contained about thirty acres, and that the normal hide consisted Extent of
the normal
hide as a rule of four virgates.   Although the virgate did not always contain thirty acres, and although the hide did not always contain the same number of virgates,[2] still, as a rule, the normal hide seems to have represented about one hundred and twenty acres.   In the Hundred Rolls the assessed value of manors is generally stated in hides and virgates. The hide and the virgate thus seem to have been used as measures of assessment as well for the demesne land of the manor as for the land in villenage.[3]   After the Conquest the Danegeld or land-tax assumed under the Conqueror and his sons the form of ordinary revenue, which, like the ferm, was compounded for by the sheriffs at a fixed sum.   In the case of the towns, to which the reckoning by hides could not apply, the Danegeld seems also to have been compounded for, and the composition or aid thus derived represents no doubt the later talliage.[4]   In the ninth year of Henry II. the Dane- Talliage. geld, as such, finally disappeared from the Rolls, but was suc-

---

[1] As to the original character and extent of the ethel, hide, or alod, see Kemble, *Saxons in Eng.*, vol. i. ch. iv.; G. L. von Maurer, *Einleitung*, p. 120 *seq.*; Grimm, *R. A.*, p. 535. The hube, the ethel, the hide, originally represented the family estate, which, "in the old English community, consisted of the house and arable lands, and the rights in the common land running with them." — *Essays in A. S. Law*, p. 74; K. Maurer, *Kritische Ueberschau*, i. P 97.

[2] "There were occasionally five virgates and sometimes six virgates in the hide, . . . but the *normal* hide consisted as a rule of four virgates of about thirty acres each." — Seebohm, *English Village Community*, p. 37.

[3] Ibid., p. 38.

[4] Freeman, *Norm. Conq.*, vol. v. pp. 294, 295; Stubbs, *Const. Hist.*, vol. i. p. 381 *seq.*

Hidage.

ceeded at once by a land-tax known as aid or hidage, which must have been only a reproduction of the old impost in a new form.   In the reign of Richard I. the Danegeld reap-

Carucage.

pears in a more oppressive shape as carucage.[1]   The caru-cate — the quantity of land which could be ploughed by a plough-team in a season — seems in some cases to have been identical with the normal hide, while in others it seems to have varied according to the quality of the soil or strength of the team.[2]   Under all these names, — whether as Danegeld, aid or hidage, carucage, or, in the case of towns, talliage, — the ancient land-tax, originally imposed by Æthelred on the hide, can be surely distinguished.

Taxation
under the
Norman
system.

When William, duke of the Normans, was elected, crowned, and anointed king of the English, he succeeded to every royal right that had ever belonged to any of his English pre-decessors, and he vigorously exacted every kind of revenue, ordinary and extraordinary, that had ever been employed by any of the kings who had gone before him.   The sum of fis-cal rights which thus accrued to William as a national king was greatly augmented, in the reign of his successor, by the feudal incidents which resulted from the position of the king as supreme landlord.   The income from feudal tenures, which accrued to the Norman kings as feudal lords, may be regarded then as an addition or supplement to the taxes and dues which grew out of the ancient constitution.   But not until after the Conqueror's death, not until after feudalism as a system of tenure had been developed under William the Red, did the profit from reliefs, wardships, marriages, fines for alienation, escheats, and from the three feudal aids, begin to swell the

Gradual
develop-
ment of
military
tenures.

royal revenue.[3]   The conclusion is now established that the development of military tenures in England was gradual, and that the transition from the old military system by the thegn's service to the new system by knight-service was also grad-ual.[4]   At the time of the Conquest the Old-English system

---

[1] "Each carucate containing a fixed extent of one hundred acres." — Stubbs, *Const. Hist.*, vol. i. p. 582, citing Hove-den, iv. 47.

[2] For a definition of the "carucate or land of a plough-team, used instead of the hide for later taxation," see *English Village Community*, p. 40.

[3] For the authorities upon this sub-ject, see above, pp. 271, 272.

[4] Cf. Palgrave, *Normandy and Eng-land*, vol. iii. p. 609 *seq.* ; Stubbs, *Const. Hist.*, vol. i. p. 261 *seq.* ; Freeman, *Norm. Conq.*, vol. v. p. 249, and note HH.

was rapidly moving in a feudal direction, — the thegn was gradually passing into the tenant-in-chief, the man of a lord of a district into his tenant.[1] The name thegn is supposed to cover the whole class which, after the Conquest, appears under the name of knights, with the same qualification in land and nearly the same obligation.[2] Under the old system the thegn was not only a warrior but a landowner, and as such he was bound to render military service; but such service was due to the state and to the king as its head, and not to the king as lord.[3] There is no reason to believe that William directly introduced into England any new kind of tenure; in the language of Domesday there is no mention of military tenures[4] as afterwards understood. There is no direct evidence to show that the old obligation of military service underwent any material change in the Conqueror's time; throughout the Survey the land is divided not into knights' fees, but into hides or carucates.[5] But although William did not directly introduce military tenures as afterwards understood, still the effect of his vast confiscations and regrants was to firmly establish the principle that the king was the supreme landlord, and that all lands were held by grant mediately or immediately of him. As soon, then, as the idea gained ground that the military service due from the landowner was due to the king, not as the head of the state but as lord, the conception of feudal tenure became complete. The new military service which thus arose out of the development of tenures was probably measured at first by the existing custom which imposed the equipment of one fully armed man upon every five hides of land.[6] By degrees the older system based upon the hide was gradually superseded by a new division of the land into knights' fees, and by the fixing of the knight's fee to a particular amount of land.[7] This new scheme of distribution, which probably took a defi-

The Survey based upon hides and carucates.

Growth of the system of knights' fees out of the older system of hides.

---

[1] Digby, *Law of Real Property*, p. 35.

[2] Stubbs, *Const. Hist.*, vol. i. p. 156.

[3] See above, pp. 133, 180.

[4] Palgrave, *Normandy and England*, vol. iii. p. 609 *seq.*

[5] Seebohm, *English Village Community*, p. 84.

[6] "Si rex mittebat alicubi exercitum, de quinque hidis tantum unus miles ibat, et ad ejus victum vel stipendium de unaquaque hida dabantur ei iiii. solidi ad duos menses." — *Domesday*, (Customs of Berkshire), i. 56. See, also, Digby, *Law of Real Property*, p. 35.

[7] The knight's fee superseded the hide as the unit of taxation so far only as the knights and barons were concerned.

nite shape under Henry I., was certainly not completed before the reign of Henry II.[1] Under the new arrangement the specific obligation was imposed upon each knight's fee to furnish a fully armed horseman to serve at his own expense for forty days in the year. This duty of military service was the substantive duty due from the tenant in chivalry to his lord ; the right to aids, reliefs, wardships, marriages, alienations, and escheats were mere incidents.[2]

The army composed of both feudal and national elements.

As successors of the Old-English kings, the Norman and Angevin rulers retained the right to summon, under the lead of the sheriffs, the ancient forces of the shires ; as feudal lords, they gained the right through the growth of tenures to call upon the feudal array to perform the military service due from their lands. As the fruits of feudal tenures were an addition or supplement to the older revenues derived from the ancient system, so the feudal army was an addition or supplement to the older constitutional force of the land.[3] To the army thus made up of feudal and national elements were sometimes added mercenary soldiers. In order to raise money for the employment of mercenaries in his war against Toulouse, Henry dealt a serious blow at the feudal power by

Scutage.

the establishment of the institution of scutage, — a pecuniary commutation for personal service in the host.[4] This commutation, at first assessed arbitrarily at the king's pleasure, was finally made subject to legislative control by that clause in the Great Charter which provides that "no scutage or aid shall be imposed in our kingdom unless by the common counsel of our kingdom." [5]

Excepting the customs, all taxes fell upon the land.

Up to this point in Henry's reign — leaving out of view the receipts from the customs — *all taxation fell upon the land,* and consisted (1) of the ancient customary dues, and the tax on the hide, — survivals of the Old-English system ; and (2) of the feudal incidents, and the scutage, or tax on

---

[1] " It is, however, probable that a record of the number of knights' fees in England had been made before the death of Henry I., and that it was the basis of the computation adopted by his grandson." — Stubbs, *Const. Hist.*, vol. i. p. 383.

[2] Digby, *Law of Real Property*, pp. 35, 36, 40, 123.

[3] " The English *fyrd* went on alongside of the Norman feudal array, and the king could make use of either or both, as suited his purpose." — Freeman, *Norm. Conq.*, vol. v. p. 258.

[4] See above, p. 283.

[5] Cap. 12. " Nullum *scutagium* vel auxilium ponatur in regno nostro, nisi per commune consilium regni nostri."

the knight's fee, — products of the new system of military tenures. Leaving the old customary dues and the feudal incidents out of view, the two great burdens on land which stand prominently forth are the Old-English tax on the hide, — whether known as aid, hidage, carucage, or, in case of the towns, talliage,[1] — and the new feudal tax on the knight's fee known as scutage. These two taxes affected two distinct classes of landowners; the scutage was the tax assessed upon the lands of the tenants in chivalry, the hidage or carucage upon the lands of the freeholders. The tax last named, when applied to the towns, bore the name of talliage.[2] On great occasions, under the general name of *auxilium*, both taxes were sometimes raised at once; but as a general rule a year marked by a scutage was not marked by a carucage.[3] So long as taxation fell only on the land, and so long as the hide continued to be the unit of assessment, the Domesday Survey, whose record generally begins with the number of hides or carucates at which the whole manor was rated according to ancient assessment,[4] continued to be the rate-book of the kingdom.[5] When disputes arose as to the assessment of towns, which could not be settled by the Survey, they were specially adjusted or permanently fixed by the sheriffs, or by the detachment of barons from the exchequer during their fiscal circuits of the shires.[6] As soon, however, as the old system of rating the lands of the tenants in chivalry, based upon the hide, was superseded by the new system based upon the knight's fee, a departure from the ancient rate-book followed as a necessary consequence. The next expedient which Henry II. employed to ascertain the number of knights' fees subject to taxation was to require by writ every tenant-in-chief, lay or clerical, to report directly the number of knights' fees for the service of which he was legally liable.[7] Under this arrangement the assessment of each baron or knight depended chiefly upon his own report. After the Danegeld was superseded by the tax known as aid or hidage,

While the hide remained the unit, Domesday the rate-book of the kingdom.

New expedient for ascertaining the number of knights' fees.

---

[1] Cf. Madox, *Hist. Exch.*, p. 480; Blackstone, vol. i. p. 310 (Sharswood ed.).

[2] "The knights paid aid or scutage, the freeholders carucage, the towns talliage: the whole and each part bore the name of auxilium." — Stubbs, *Const. Hist.*, vol. i. p. 583.

[3] Ibid., vol. i. p. 583.

[4] *English Village Community*, p. 84.

[5] *Dialogus de Scaccario*, i. c. 16.

[6] Ibid., ii. c. 13.

[7] Stubbs, *Const. Hist.*, vol. i. p. 584.

Henry intrusted its assessment upon the towns and the free-holders to the officers of the exchequer. Under this system the justices were compelled to accept the sum conceded by each town or individual freeholder, or the latter had to pay whatever the justices saw fit to put upon them.[1] Not until personal property became subject to taxation was a new method of assessment employed just alike to the crown and to the tax-payer.

<small>Taxation of personal property.</small> The growth of national prosperity, and the consequent development of material wealth, which followed Henry's policy of order and reform, rapidly brought into existence a mass of personal property which presented to the Angevin financiers a new and tempting basis of taxation, — a basis <small>Assize of Arms, 1181.</small> capable of unlimited expansion.[2] By the Assize of 1181, in which each freeman was required to equip himself with arms according to his means, and in which local jurors were required to determine on oath the liability of each, the first move was made towards the taxation of rent and chattels.[3] Seven years later Henry took the final step, and brought taxation directly to bear upon personal property by decreeing, <small>Saladin tithe of 1188 assessed by local jurors.</small> with the authority of a great council at Geddington, a tithe of a tenth of movables to aid the common host of Christendom in the retaking of the Holy City from Saladin. In order to fairly assess each man's liability to the tithe, Henry resorted to his favorite institution of inquest by the oaths of local jurors. Whenever any one was suspected of contributing less than his share, four or six lawful men of the parish <small>Lands assessed in the same way in 1198.</small> were chosen to declare on oath what he should give.[4] In the reign of Richard I., when the Danegeld was revived under the name of carucage, the new principle of jury assessment was applied in a general way to the assessment of all lands subject to the tax.[5] In this way the representative principle — which first appears in the form of the reeve and four selectmen who represent the township in the courts of the shire

---

[1] *Dialogus de Scaccario,* ii. c. 13.
[2] Green, *Hist. Eng. People,* vol. i. p. 322.
[3] See article 9 of the Assize; *Select Charters,* p. 154.
[4] " Et si aliquis juxta conscientiam illorum minus dederit quam debuerit, eligentur de parochia quatuor vel sex

viri legitimi, qui jurati dicant quantitatem illam quam ille debuisset dixisse; et tunc oportebit illum superaddere quod minus dedit." — Benedictus, vol. ii. p. 31 ; *Select Charters,* p. 159; *Norm. Conq.,* vol. v. p. 456.
[5] Hoveden, vol. iv. p. 46 *seq.* ; Stubbs, *Const. Hist.,* vol. i. pp. 510, 589.

and hundred [1] — is brought into close contact with the system of taxation. In connection with that system the representative principle ascends, through three stages, from the lowest to the highest functions of government. It is first applied in a humble way, through the chosen jurors, to the assessment of the tax; it next becomes involved with the granting of the tax; and finally it determines the method of its expenditure.

Taxation and representation.

In what has so far been said in regard to the direct taxation of real and personal property, no reference has been made to indirect taxes, — the duties, toll, tribute, or tariff payable upon merchandise exported and imported, — which are included under the general name of the customs.[2] The origin of the duties on imports can be directly traced to the ancient customary right of the Old-English kings to levy tolls in harbors, and upon transport by roads and navigable streams.[3] Upon its entry into the harbor the toll or tax was imposed directly on the ship; and in the early charters several instances can be found of grants to individuals and monasteries of an exemption from toll for one ship of burden, and in the event of the destruction of the particular ship another was to receive the same privilege.[4] The toll paid by the ship was the equivalent given by the merchant for the right to bring goods into the realm, and to trade under the king's protection. The duties on imports are thus much more ancient than the duties on exports, which are said to have come into existence as a part of the general system of taxing personal property.[5] In the reigns of Richard I. and John, the receipts from the customs seem to have been considerable.[6] At the date of the Great Charter they were of sufficient importance to suggest the provision forbidding the levy of more than the ancient and

Indirect taxation, — the customs;

tax on imports;

tax on exports.

---

[1] See above, p. 143.

[2] For a definition of customs, see Bacon, Abr., under Smuggling. The word "customs" — *custuma* of the ancient records — seems to be derived from the French word *coustum* or *coutum*, which signifies toll or tribute, and owes its etymology to the word *coust*, which signifies price, charge, or, as we have adopted it in English, cost. — Sharswood's *Black. Comm.*, vol. i. p. 314, and note *v*. Cf. Worcester's Dictionary, "Custom," as applied to taxation.

[3] Kemble, *Saxons in England*, vol. ii. p. 75.

[4] See *Cod. Dipl.*, Nos. 78, 84, 95, 106.

[5] "Those on exports were only a part of the general system of taxing personal property which we have already noticed." — Green, *Hist. Eng. People*, vol. i. p. 323.

[6] Madox, *Hist. Exch.*, p. 529 *seq.*

Exclusive right of parliament to authorize taxation.

lawful customs on merchants entering and leaving the realm.[1] Not until the reign of Edward I., however, did the right to regulate the customs, together with the right to regulate direct taxation, finally pass under the exclusive control of the parliament.[2] The confirmation of the charters by Edward at Ghent, in November, 1297, contained an express pledge from the king that "for no occasion from henceforth will we take such manner of aids, tasks, or prizes but by common assent of the realm and for the common profit thereof, saving the ancient aids and prizes due and accustomed."[3] It seems to be clear that under the Old-English system the right of the witan to join with the king in the imposition of taxes was full and authoritative. In the levying of the land-tax for the purpose of defence against the Danes, the right of participation upon the part of the witan is distinctly recognized.[4] But from the dim fiscal annals of the Norman reigns it is hard to determine whether taxes were imposed by mere edict of the sovereign, or whether with the counsel and consent of the great council. The idea that the nation was in some form consulted is strengthened, however, by two records which belong to the reign of Henry I. : in the one the king describes "the aid which my barons gave me ; "[5] in the other— the charter ordering the restoration of the local courts — he

First formal discussion of a grant in the Council of Oxford, 1197.

speaks of summoning the county courts in cases in which his royal necessities required it.[6] Not until the latter part of the reign of Richard I. can there be traced anything like a formal discussion and refusal of a grant in the national assembly.[7]

---

[1] Cap. 41. "Omnes mercatores habeant salvum et securum exire de Anglia, et venire in Angliam, . . . sine omnibus malis toltis, per antiquas et rectas consuetudines."

[2] Green, *Hist. Eng. People*, vol. i. p. 365 ; Gneist, *Verwalt.*, i. pp. 393–396 ; Stubbs, *Const. Hist.*, vol. ii. pp. 142, 244.

[3] Art. vi. *Statutes of the Realm*, vol. i. pp. 124, 125. Cf. Blackstone's *Introduction to the Charter*, p. xcv. ; *Select Charters*, p. 497.

[4] See above, p. 186.

[5] "Auxilium quod barones mihi dederunt." — *Chron. Abingd.*, ii. 113.

[6] "Ego enim, quando voluero, faciam ea satis summonere propter mea dominica necessaria ad voluntatem meam."

— *Fœdera*, i. p. 12. As to the bearing of these citations upon the question of parliamentary consent to taxation, see Stubbs, *Const. Hist.*, vol. i. p. 371, and note 4, p. 398. "Henry even forestalls the constitutional language of later times when he speaks, in words half feudal, half parliamentary, of the aid which his barons had granted to him." — Freeman, *Norm. Conq.*, vol. v. p. 280.

[7] As to the successful opposition of St. Hugh, bishop of Lincoln, to the king's demand for money to carry on a foreign war, see Hoveden, vol. iv. pp. 33, 34, 40 ; *Magna Vita S. Hugonis*, p. 248 ; Freeman, *Norm. Conq.*, vol. v. p. 465.

Although the provision contained in the twelfth article of the Great Charter — that no scutage or aid, other than the three customary feudal aids, should be imposed without the common counsel of the kingdom — was a clearer statement of the right of the nation to be consulted than had ever been made before, yet not until Edward's confirmation of the charters at Ghent was the exclusive right of parliament to authorize both direct and indirect taxation fully and finally recognized.

7. Perhaps the most important part of Henry's work in the restoration of law and order was the reëstablishment of the system of central administration embodied in the curia regis, which the policy of Henry I. had so successfully built up, but which the protracted anarchy of Stephen's reign had completely broken down.   Under the organizing hand of Bishop Roger the curia was developed into a strong judicial and ministerial body, before which passed in review the whole fiscal and judicial business of the kingdom.   Under the administration of Roger the financial department of the curia — then called for the first time the exchequer — assumed such special importance that when the king was not personally present the judicial aspect of the curia seems to have been overshadowed by its fiscal character.   As reorganized by Henry II. the unity of the curia was preserved, and its financial department restored as it had been in the days of his grandfather.   But through the results of Henry's legal reforms, which tended to centralize to the utmost the administration of justice, the financial aspect of the curia was overshadowed by its development as a judicial tribunal.[1] From the Constitutions of Clarendon we learn that the system of recognitions was then in full force ;[2] that the curia regis was a court of regular resort, and that to it were reserved all questions of presentation and advowson.[3]   In the

Reorganization of the curia regis.

Its financial now overshadowed by its judicial aspect.

[1] " Whereas under Henry I. the financial character, under Henry II. the judicial aspect, of the board is the most prominent. In the former reign the curia regis, except when the king takes a personal share in the business, seems to be a judicial session of the exchequer, an adaptation of exchequer machinery to judicial purposes ; under the latter the exchequer seems to be rather a financial session of the curia regis. The king is ostensibly the head of the one, the justiciar the principal actor in the other." — Stubbs, *Const. Hist.*, vol. i. p. 596.

[2] This is the earliest mention of the principle of recognition by twelve lawful men, in a dispute as to tenure, in anything like statute law. See art. ix. of the Constitutions. *Select Charters*, p. 136.

[3] " De advocatione et præsentatione ecclesiarum . . . in curia domini regis tractetur vel termineter."   Art. 1.

twelve years (1164–1176) of legislative reform which followed the adoption of the Constitutions, the growth of the judicial business of the curia seems to have been so great that in 1176 its staff had increased to eighteen justices, who were apportioned to the six circuits into which the kingdom was then divided. In 1178 this staff, which was found to be too large, was reduced to five judges, who "are to hear all the complaints of the kingdom and to do right, and not to depart from the curia regis." In the following year a new arrangement was made, and out of a larger staff, charged with exchequer business and the work of the circuits, six justices instead of five were selected, and "these six are the justices constituted in the curia regis to hear the complaints of the people." This limited tribunal, which from the year 1179 held regular sessions *in banco*, probably represents the beginning of the king's bench as a distinct tribunal. Its sessions are still held nominally but not actually *coram rege*, and before it is brought all of the business which came at a later period before the courts of king's bench, exchequer, and common pleas. But neither the special tribunal, nor the courts to which it gave birth, were courts of the last resort : all causes too difficult for the justices were reserved for the decision of the king in his ordinary council,—a body from which at a later date the jurisdiction of the chancellor and the judicial functions of the privy council emerge.[1] Upon the internal organization of the curia as it existed in the time of Henry II. we have two famous treatises from contemporary authors whose opportunities for knowledge were singularly great. As to the history of the exchequer we have, in addition to the Pipe Rolls, the Dialogus de Scaccario,[2] a treatise written by Richard, bishop of London, great nephew of Roger of Salisbury, the reorganizer of the court, which gives us a complete picture of the administration of the exchequer as it stood in 1177. As to the procedure of the curia we have the famous treatise of the justiciar Ranulf Glanvill, which is not only the first English law-book which bears the name

In 1176 the staff consisted of eighteen justices, in 1178 reduced to five.

The king's bench as a distinct tribunal.

Dialogus de Scaccario.

Tractatus de Legibus Angliæ.

---

[1] For the authorities upon this subject, see above, p. 248.

[2] "The *Dialogus de Scaccario* has generally passed as the work of Gervase of Tilbury, but Mr. Madox thinks it was written by Richard Fitz-Nigel, bishop of London, who succeeded his father in the office of treasurer in the reign of Richard I." — Reeves, *Hist. Eng. Law*, vol. i. p. 482.

of a personal author, but, with a single exception perhaps, the first formal dissertation on jurisprudence since the fall of the Roman Empire.[1]

8. In the outline heretofore drawn of the constitution of the Old-English commonwealth, — in the form in which it appeared after the fusion of the heptarchic states into a single consolidated kingdom, — the attempt was made to explain in detail the origin and structure of the system of local machinery embodied in the organizations of the township, the hundred, and the shire. It was then ascertained that the modern shire — the shire of the consolidated kingdom — was an aggregation of hundreds; that the hundred was an aggregation of townships; and that both hundred and shire possessed its own assembly or court, in which the freemen met together to discharge such judicial or political functions as arose out of the administration of their local concerns. The courts of the shire and hundred — which were more like public meetings than like courts of justice in the modern sense of that term — were not only popular but representative assemblies. In the hundred court appeared the reeve and four selectmen as representatives from each township in the hundred; in the shire court appeared like representatives from each township within the shire; while the twelve senior thegns appeared as a representative body in the courts of both the shire and the hundred. In both courts the whole body of suitors were the judges; and, in theory, whatever judgment was rendered was the judgment of the whole assembly. But the inconvenience which arose out of the practical application of this principle to large bodies of men indicated the obvious and natural remedy. It seems to have been the custom of each assembly to delegate its powers to judicial committees of its own members, who acted as representatives of the whole court. The familiar historical illustrations of this principle of delegation are to be found in the twelve judges elected in the shire court of Cambridge to confirm with their oaths a decision previously rendered in the same court in a case between the bishop of Rochester and the sheriff of Cambridge, in the twelve senior thegns who appeared as a representative body in the courts of the shire and the hundred, and in the twenty-four

Reorganization of the provincial system: the local courts.

Shire and hundred courts not only popular but representative assemblies.

Delegation of judicial authority.

---

[1] See above, p. 244, note 4.

"*judices*" or the thirty-six "barons" who were chosen in the East Anglian county courts to determine the suits of Ramsey and Ely. The growth of the practice of delegating the powers of the popular courts to select bodies was no doubt stimulated in England, as it was upon the Continent, by an indisposition upon the part of the mass of the freemen to attend and exercise their rights in their own persons.[1] In England, as well as upon the Continent, it became necessary

Attendance enforced by fines. in comparatively early times to enforce attendance upon the popular courts by the imposition of fines. But even this expedient proved ineffectual. In the Frankish assemblies of the *gau* or hundred, in order to insure the certain attendance of a sufficient number to discharge judicial functions, it be-

Schöffen, Scabani, or Échevins. came necessary to appoint fixed bodies of Schöffen, Scabani, or Échevins, who held their appointments for life, and who were compelled to be present at the public assemblies as official personages.[2] How near the system of delegation as practised in the English popular courts ever approached the Frankish Schöffen system is a question which has often been suggested but never distinctly answered.[3] Apart, however, from the loss of vigor which the local courts sustained through the unwillingness of the general mass of freemen to attend and exercise their rights in person, their powers were further undermined, as heretofore explained, by the growth of immunities and by the centralization of justice.[4] Subject to the silent operation of these forces — all of which had begun to work before the Norman conquest — the ancient courts of the shire and the hundred continued to exist substantially unchanged in organization or procedure throughout the reigns

Ordinance separating spiritual and temporal courts. of the Norman kings. The greatest change which did take place by virtue of direct ordinance was brought about by the Conqueror's famous edict which provided that spiritual causes should no longer be tried in temporal tribunals. By virtue of this ordinance the bishop was practically, if not for-

---

[1] This whole subject is drawn out in detail in bk. I, ch. v., secs. I, 5, 6.

[2] Savigny says : "Der Unterschied lag nur darin, dass die Scabinen, als öffentliche Personen, die Verpflichtung hatten, als Schöffen den Gerichten beyzuwohnen, während es in der Willkühr der übrigen Freyen stand, zuerscheinen wenn sie wollten, nur mit

Ausnahme der drey grossen Versammlungstage in Jahr, an welchen alle erscheinen mussten." — *Geschichte des Römischen Rechts,* i. p. 197. See Waitz, iii. p. 487, iv. p. 325; Hallam, *M. A.,* vol. i. p. 213 and n. 4, p. 233 and n. 5.

[3] See *North American Review,* July, 1874, ccxliv. p. 243.

[4] See above, p. 256.

mally, removed from the joint headship of the shire-moot by
being placed at the head of a distinct ecclesiastical court.
After the practical removal of the bishop, and after the ancient earl had been stripped of his official character, the
presidency of the shire was left alone to the sheriff, the
king's ever-present and immediate representative.[1] Henry I.,
in his effort to reorganize and invigorate the provincial system, commanded "that all the people of the county go to the
county and hundred courts as they did in the time of King
Eadward," [2] and from the "Leges Henrici Primi" we learn
that the shire-moot was attended as of old by the sheriff as   Attendants
presiding officer, by the thegns of the shire, by the parish   of the shire
priest, and the reeve and four best men from each town-   and the
ship ; [3] but not by villeins, cottagers, *ferdingi* (freemen of the   hundred
lowest grade) or lower men.[4] The full court which met twice   courts.
a year still possessed both civil and criminal jurisdiction,
which was exercised according to the old forms of witness,
compurgation and ordeal. The composition of the hundred
court as restored by Henry I. was substantially the same as
that of the shire ; and in both courts the theory survived
that the "suitors" or members were the judges.[5] The
"*judices*" and the "*judices et juratores*" of the Pipe Roll of
Henry I. probably represent the body of land-holders, above
the villeins in rank, who constituted the courts of the shire
and hundred, with full power to participate in the administration of justice.[6] These fully qualified members seem to be
distinguished from the "*minuti homines*," or mean men, who
were likewise bound to attend both courts, but who probably
did not possess a sufficient amount of land to qualify them to
act in a suit in which land was in question.[7] All members
of the court, including the mean men, who failed to attend
and discharge their judicial duties, were, in the absence of a
satisfactory excuse or exemption, punished by large fines.
With fines of this character the single Pipe Roll of Henry I.

[1] Upon this subject see above, p. 258.

[2] For Henry's charter ordering the
holding of the courts of the hundred
and the shire, see *Fœdera*, i. p. 12.

[3] Laws Hen. I., c. vii. For the text
of the compilation known as Henry's
Laws, see *Ancient Laws*, pp. 216-266;
Select Charters, p. 104.

[4] "Villani vero, vel cotseti, vel fer-

dingi, vel qui sunt viles vel inopes per-
sonæ non sunt inter legum judices
numerandi." — Laws Hen. I., c. xxix.
Cf. Bigelow, *Hist. of Procedure*, p. 133.

[5] Stubbs, *Const. Hist.*, vol. i. pp. 393-
399.

[6] Pipe Roll, p. 34; Bigelow, *Hist. of
Procedure*, p. 134.

[7] Stubbs, *Const. Hist.*, vol. i. p. 397.

abounds.   In order to escape the burden of personal attendance, and the penalties consequent upon non-attendance, a
composition was sometimes entered into with the king: the
"*judices et juratores*" of Yorkshire pay one hundred pounds
for the privilege of being no longer judges or jurors.[1]   During the anarchy of Stephen's reign the local courts were no
doubt disorganized by the same disturbing influences which
shattered for a time the system of central administration, but
upon the restoration of peace and order prompt provision

was made for their reorganization.   In the scheme of reform
which attended the Treaty of Wallingford it was provided
that the jurisdiction of the sheriffs should be revived; and
we learn from a trustworthy source that, at the very outset
of his reign, Henry II. made careful provision not only for
central but for provincial judicature.[2]

Not until the twelfth year of his reign is there direct evidence of an attempt upon Henry's part to remodel the provincial administration of justice by positive legislation.   In
1166 Henry, with the counsel and assent of the "arch-

bishops, bishops, abbots, earls, and barons of all England"
issued the Assize of Clarendon, which has been called "the
most important document, of the nature of law or edict, that
has appeared since the Conquest."[3]   The two leading objects
of this Assize, whose enforcement was committed to the
justices itinerant, were to remodel the system for the presentment of criminals, and to advance the king's anti-feudal
policy by opening every franchise to the visits of the sheriffs

and justices.   The manner in which criminal accusations
were made in the popular courts, prior to the Assize of Clarendon, is a subject which is wrapped in much obscurity and
confusion.   It may, however, be reasonably inferred from the
ancient laws that, in the pre-Norman period, such accusations were made either by a private accuser, by the reeve
and four men of the township, or more often perhaps by the
twelve senior thegns in each hundred or wapentake,[4] who

---

[1] Pipe Roll, Henry I., pp. 27, 28.
"Judices et juratores Eboraciscire debent c. li. ut non amplius sint judices
nec juratores."   As to the significance
of such entries, see *Norm. Conq.*, vol.
v. p. 296.

[2] Will. Newb., ii. c. 1.

[3] Stubbs, *Const. Hist.*, vol. i. p. 469.
For the text of the Assize, see MS.
Bodl. Rawlinson, c. 641 ; *Select Char-
ters*, p. 143.

[4] Sir James F. Stephen, *Hist. Criminal Law of Eng.*, vol. i. p. 68 ; Palgrave, *Commonw.*, vol. i. p. 213.   Pal-

went out, and the reeve with them, to "swear on the relic that is given them in hand, that they will accuse no innocent man, nor conceal any guilty one."[1] There is reason to believe that after the Conquest, in the absence of a private accuser, it was generally left to the common voice of the neighborhood to make the accusation and denounce the suspected person.[2] A leading object of the Assize of Clarendon was to provide a definite system for the presentment of all persons accused of felony by public report to the courts of the sheriffs or justices. Under the provisions of the Assize inquiry was to be made on oath in every county and in every hundred, by twelve lawful men of the hundred, and by four lawful men of each township,[3] whether any man in any hundred or township had been accused of being a robber, murderer, or thief, or a harborer of robbers, murderers, or thieves, since the king was crowned. All persons so accused should be taken before the sheriffs, and by them brought before the justices.[4] All persons are required to attend the county court and join, if required, in the presentments.[5] No lord of a franchise, not even of the honor of Wallingford, shall refuse to allow the sheriff to enter his franchise either to arrest accused persons, or to take the view of frankpledge.[6] All who were presented by the inquest were required to go to the ordeal, which seems to have been substituted for the usual method of trial by compurgation.[7] If they failed to stand the test of the ordeal, they were required to accept the legal punishment; if they were successful they

The scheme of presentment contained in the assize.

The accused required to go to the ordeal.

---

grave infers that the reeve and four men had the power of accusation from a passage in a law of Cnut. See Laws of Cnut, 30, in Thorpe's *Ancient Laws*, vol. i. p. 393.

[1] Laws of Æthelred, iii. 3, in Thorpe, vol. i. pp. 294, 295. Upon this provision in Æthelred's Law see above, p. 204.

[2] Forsyth, *Trial by Jury*, p. 160.

[3] Art. 1: "Inprimis statuit prædictus rex Henricus de consilio omnium baronum suorum, pro pace servanda et justitia tenenda, quod per singulos comitatus inquiratur, et per singulos hundredos, per xii. legaliores homines de hundredo, et per iv. legaliores homines de qualibet villata, per sacramentum quod illi verum dicent. . . . Et

hoc inquirant Justitiæ coram se, et vicecomites coram se."

[4] Art. 4. This provision illustrates the fact that, "in ordinary matters at least, the duties of the sheriffs on the Eyre of the justiciars were *ministerial*, and not judicial. Thus early was the change coming about which was at last to strip the sheriffs of their ancient functions as judges." — Bigelow, *Hist. of Procedure*, p. 99.

[5] Art. 8: "Nullus remaneat pro libertate aliqua quam habeat, vel curia vel soca quam habuerit, quin veniant ad hoc sacramentum faciendum."

[6] Art. 9.

[7] Art. 4: "Ibi ante Justiciam facient legem suam." — Cf. Bigelow, *Hist. of Procedure*, pp. 297, 323.

were even then required to abjure the realm, — provided they had been accused of any grievous felony by the public voice of the neighborhood.[1] With the issuance of the Assize of Clarendon the history of the jury of presentment emerges from obscurity ; and yet the scheme of accusation contained in it cannot be considered as a new creation, but rather as a fresh and formal union of the representatives of the township and hundred in the joint discharge of a public duty with which each body of representatives had been immemorially

Assize of Northampton, 1176. connected. In 1176 the Clarendon Assize was reissued as the Assize of Northampton, "in the form of instructions to the six committees of judges who were to visit the circuits" then marked out for them.[2] In the reign of Richard I. Henry's scheme of presentment was reorganized and reëstablished upon a basis more distinctly representative. Under

Primitive form of the grand jury. the new arrangement "four knights are to be chosen from the whole county, who by their oaths shall choose two lawful knights of each hundred or wapentake, and those two shall choose upon oath ten knights of each hundred or wapentake,[3] or if knights be wanting, legal and free men, so that these twelve may answer under all heads concerning their whole hundred or wapentake." The presentment juries thus chosen were limited to the cognizance of offences com-

Its later development. mitted within their own hundreds. Not until later times was this primitive system gradually superseded by the more comprehensive one known as the grand inquest, which consisted of a single representative body of grand jurors, whose duty it was to make inquiry and presentment throughout the whole county. Not until this last stage was reached did the grand jury attain its full modern development.

Use of the petty jury in criminal cases. The jury of presentment as organized under the ordinances of Henry II. and Richard I. was a representative body whose duty it was to make inquest and presentment in each hun-

---

[1] Art. 14. Cf. Stephen, *Hist. Criminal Law*, vol. i. p. 251.

[2] *Select Charters*, p. 150; Benedictus, vol. i. p. 108 ; Hoveden, vol. ii. p. 89 *seq.* "The two assizes regulate the inquisitions to be held by the king's judges in every shire and in every hundred, without regard to local privileges." — Freeman, *Norm. Conq.*, vol. v. p. 454.

[3] "In primis eligendi sunt quatuor milites de toto comitatu, qui per sacramentum suum eligant duos legales milites, de quolibet Hundredo vel Wapentacco, et illi duo eligant super sacramentum suum x. milites de singulis Hundredis vel Wapentaccis." Hoveden, vol. iii. p. 262.

dred of persons accused of crime by public report, and all
persons so presented were required to submit the question of
their guilt or innocence to the ordeal.[1]   The procedure was
very simple.   In what is said to be the oldest judicial record
in existence are contained several illustrations of the manner
in which such prosecutions were conducted.   From the "Roll
of the Iter of Stafford in 5 John," we learn that "Andrew
of Bureweston is suspected by the jurors of the death of one
Hervicus because he fled for his death ; therefore let him
purge himself by the judgment of water."[2]   After the decree ~Trial by or-~
of the Lateran Council forbidding it, trial by ordeal became ~deal forbid-~
~den by the~
obsolete,[3] and the petty jury gradually took its place as a body ~Lateran~
~Council~
before which the truth of the presentment of the grand jury
could be finally determined.   The stages in the process by
which this result was finally worked out may be indicated as
follows : During the period which intervenes between the
Conquest and the introduction of the petty jury there were
but three modes of trial in criminal cases, — compurgation,
ordeal, and trial by battle.[4]   By the Assize of Clarendon, if ~Compurga-~
not before, compurgation as a method of trial in criminal ~tion super-~
~seded by~
cases was superseded by the ordeal,[5] and trial by battle could ~ordeal.~
only apply in a case where there was an individual accuser.
It follows, therefore, that the truth of the public accusations
made by juries organized under the Assize of Henry II. could
have been tested only in one mode, — by the ordeal.   After
the decree of the Lateran Council of 1215, in which it was
ordered that the ordeal should be discontinued throughout
Christendom, it soon became obsolete in England.   When
this point was reached an accusation by a grand jury became
practically equivalent to a conviction, for the reason that no
way remained of traversing the presumption of guilt which
arose out of the presentment.[6]   To remedy this evil, and to

---

[1] "The body of the country are the
accusers.   Their accusation is practically equivalent to a conviction subject
to the chance of a favorable termination of the ordeal by water." — Stephen, *History of the Crim. Law*, vol. i.
p. 252.
[2] This entry is from the *Rotuli Curiæ Regis* for the reigns of Richard
and John, and is published in his
"Proofs and Illustrations," by Sir

Francis Palgrave, clxxxv. – clxxxviii.
Cf. Stephen, vol. i. p. 252.
[3] "The effect of this decree, however, was not an immediate abrogation
of ordeals in England." — Bigelow,
Hist. Procedure, p. 323.
[4] Stephen, *Hist. Crim. Law*, vol. i. p.
244 and note 2.
[5] Bigelow, *Hist. Procedure*, p. 2.
[6] Stephen, *Hist. Crim. Law*, vol. i. p.
254 ; Forsyth, *Trial by Jury*, p. 165.

The petty jury takes the place of both. give to the accused his constitutional right to traverse in some form the presumption of guilt against him, trial by petty jury — a form of trial which was first introduced in civil suits involving the right to land — was gradually introduced into criminal proceedings.[1] It seems, however, that even before the abolition of ordeals the right to have the question of guilt or innocence finally determined by a petty jury had occasionally been purchased as a special boon from the royal authority.[2] The legal historians find it difficult to determine the exact point of time when a second and a different jury came into general use as a tribunal before which could be

That result reached by the end of the thirteenth century. tried the truth of the presentment made by the first. This result seems certainly to have been reached by the end of the thirteenth century.[3] But the fact must be borne steadily in mind that at the time of their introduction, and for a long period thereafter, the jurors who were allowed to disprove or sustain the accusation made by the jury of presentment were nothing but witnesses. They were therefore summoned from the hundred in which the crime was supposed to have been committed, for the reason that personal knowledge of the facts was an indispensable qualification. If any of the jurors chosen were uninformed of the matters as to which they were to swear, those who were informed were added to or afforced until at least twelve were found who could agree in a definite conclusion in favor of guilt or innocence. By degrees this clumsy system was improved by separating the informed or afforcing jurors from the uninformed jurors, who, after being relieved of their character as witnesses, became judges of evidence detailed by other persons.[4] By the end of the fifteenth century the evolution is complete,[5] and the result is

---

[1] As to the right of the court to force the new method of trial upon a prisoner who did not request it, by the proceeding known as *pèine forte et dure*, see Palgrave, *English Commonwealth*, vol. i. pp. 268–270; vol. ii. pp. 189–191.

[2] See Palgrave, "Proofs and Illustrations," clxxvi., clxxvii., and clxxxvi., No. 17.

[3] Britton wrote, it is supposed, about 1291–92. "In his time there certainly were two juries, and each was composed of witnesses." — Stephen, *Hist. Crim. Law*, vol. i. p. 258.

[4] As to the history of the process through which the jurors ceased to be witnesses, and became judges of evidence derived from others, see Forsyth, *Trial by Jury*, pp. 199 *seq.*

[5] This is a reasonable inference from the account given by Sir John Fortesque in his *De Laudibus Legum Angliæ*, which must have been written between 1460 and 1470. How jurors are informed by evidence is made plain, so far as civil cases are concerned, in ch. xxvi. p. 89 (Clermont ed.). Cf. Stephen, *Hist. Crim. Law*, vol. i. p. 264; Forsyth, *Trial by Jury*, pp. 158–167.

the jury of judgment, the trial jury of modern times. But By the end of the fifteenth century appears the trial jury of modern times. not until the present century was the ancient requirement, that the jurors in a criminal case should be taken from the hundred in which the crime was alleged to have been committed, finally abolished. Since the passage of the Stat. of 6 Geo. IV. (c. 50) the sheriff is only required to return for the trial of an issue, civil or criminal, twelve good and lawful men from the body of the county qualified according to law.[1]

Trial by battle, which was of Norman introduction,[2] has, as Trial by battle. a method of trial in criminal cases, a distinct history of its own. To the jury of presentment it stood in a perfectly independent relation, for the reason that it could only be invoked upon the accusation of an individual accuser, and such an accuser could make his "appeal" not only after indictment for the offence, but after trial and acquittal had been had upon it. Many instances may be given of trial by battle during the Norman period, but not until the thirteenth century can there be found a complete history of the procedure.[3] This is given by Bracton, who is the great authority upon the subject.[4] This method of trial seems to have been Usual method of prosecuting murder down to the close of the fifteenth century. the usual and established way of prosecuting murder down to the close of the fifteenth century. As late as the years 1768 and 1774 attempts to abolish appeals of murder by statute were unsuccessful.[5] The last appeal of murder brought in Ashford v. Thornton, 1818. England was the case of Ashford *v.* Thornton in 1818.[6] In that case, after Thornton had been tried and acquitted of the murder of Mary Ashford at the Warwick Assizes her brother charged him in the court of king's bench with her murder, according to the forms of the ancient procedure. The court admitted the legality of the proceedings, and recognized the appellee's right to wage his body ; but as the appellant was not prepared to fight, the case ended upon a plea of *autrefois* Appeals not abolished until reign of George III. *acquit* interposed by Thornton when arraigned on the appeal. This proceeding led to the statute of 59 Geo. III., c. 46, by which all appeals in criminal cases were finally abolished.

---

[1] Forsyth, *Trial by Jury*, p. 138.
[2] As to its possible existence in England at an earlier date, see Palgrave, *Commonwealth*, p. 225; *Placita Ang. Norm.*, p. 16.
[3] Cf. Bigelow, *Hist. of Procedure*, p. 327.

[4] See Bracton, vol. ii. p. 425 *seq.*
[5] Stephen, *Hist. Crim. Law*, vol. i. pp. 248, 249.
[6] 1 *Bar. & Ald.*, 405. The case was argued by Mr. Chitty and Sir N. Tindal, and the great authority relied upon was Bracton.

Assize of
Arms, 1181.
The two remaining measures of Henry II. touching the
provincial administration still to be noted are the Assize of
Arms,[1] issued in 1181, and the Assize of the Forest,[2] issued
in 1184. As has been heretofore pointed out, the primitive
Teutonic national assembly was simply a meeting of the
whole nation in arms; it was "parliament, law-court, and
army in one."[3] The national assemblies, or folk-moots, of
the numberless petty states in which the Teutonic settlers
grouped themselves in Britain, did not depart from the continental original; and when, in the process of aggregation, the
primitive petty state descended to the rank of a shire, and its
folk-moot became the shire-moot, there was still no material
departure from ancient traditions, — the assembly of the shire
was still law court and army in one.[4] A meeting of the
whole free population of the shire under the presidency of
the sheriff, the bishop, and the ealdorman made up the court
of the shire; the same freemen, marshalled under the command of the ealdorman, made up the military force of the

Ancient
military
force of the
shire,
shire.[5] The ancient landfyrd, the militia of the shire, survived the Norman conquest, and its aid was more than once
invoked in great emergencies by the Conqueror and his sons.

reorgan-
ized and re-
armed,
The object of Henry's Assize of Arms was to reorganize and
rearm the ancient force as a body safer and more trustworthy
for national defence than the feudal host. This assize was
renewed and expanded by Henry III. in conjunction with
the system of watch and ward; and through subsequent legislation by Eadward I., Henry IV., Philip and Mary, and James
I., the ancient landfyrd, the constitutional force of the shire,

the militia
of modern
times.
has been brought down in principle as the militia of modern
times.[6]

Assize of
the Forest,
1184.
As the folkland, the land of the people, silently passed into
terra regis, the wooded parts of the public domain, which had
been immemorially subject to the common use of the nation,
came to be regarded as a special possession for the king's

---

[1] Hoveden, vol. ii. p. 261; Benedictus,
p. 278.

[2] Benedictus, vol. ii. p. clix.

[3] *Essays in A. S. Law*, p. 1.

[4] "The folkmoot was, in fact, the
war host, the gathering of every freeman of the tribe in arms." — Green,
Making of England, p. 167.

[5] In his character of leader of the
host the ealdorman was sometimes
styled in the charters *heretoga*. —
Freeman, *Norm. Conq.*, vol. i. p. 51 and
note K.

[6] *Select Charters*, pp. 153-156.

exclusive profit and pleasure.   That certain forests were Royal hunt-
ing-grounds
in the days
of Cnut.
royal hunting-grounds as early as the days of Cnut is mani-
fest from that provision in his genuine laws which concedes
to every man the right to hunt on his own ground, but which
severely forbids all trespass upon the royal hunting "under
penalty of the full wite." [1]   But not until after the Norman
conquest were the uninclosed woodlands hedged about by a
definite system of stringent regulations, cruel alike to man
and beast.   Large districts of country were afforested by the Forest reg-
ulations of
the Norman
kings.
Conqueror for purposes of the chase,[2] and the forest regula-
tions which are credited to him were made, under the administration of Rufus, extremely vexatious and burdensome to
all classes of the people.   In the comprehensive reforms of
Henry I. a correction of the forest administration had no
place.   After the issuance of his charter for the reform of all
other abuses, he declared that he would keep the forests in
his own hands, as his father had before him :[3] in his reign
the forest laws were enforced with the strictest severity.
The first forest code, the Assize of Woodstock, which was First forest
code, 1184.
issued by Henry II. in 1184,[4] contains a set of stringent
ordinances, somewhat less severe, however, than the usages
which prevailed in the days of his grandfather.   The forest
administration when fully organized consisted of a set of
special jurisdictions or franchises set up by the crown in
those shires in which the royal forests were situated, each
jurisdiction or franchise being governed by the special code
of forest laws which were administered in the forest courts.[5]
"A forest is a certain territory of woody grounds and fruitful A forest a
special ju-
risdiction
or franchise
pastures, privileged for wild beasts and fowls, fowls of forest
chase and warren, to rest and abide in the safe protection of

---

[1] "And I will that every man be entitled to his hunting, in wood and in
field, on his own possession.   And let
every one forego my hunting : take notice where I will have it untrespassed
on, under penalty of the full wite."—
Cnut, *Secular Dooms,* cap. 81.   Cnut's
hunting code, which may be found in
Thorpe's *Ancient Laws* (vol. i. p. 358),
is regarded as of very doubtful authenticity.— *Norm. Conq.,* vol. i. p. 291,
note III. ; *Select Charters,* p. 156.

[2] Freeman, *Norm. Conq.,* vol. v. pp.
82, 305.

[3] Art. 10: "Forestas communi consensu baronum meorum in manu mea
retinui, sicut pater meus eas habuit."
— Henry's charter, *Ancient Laws and
Institutes,* p. 215.

[4] Benedictus, vol. ii. p. clix.

[5] "It was a jurisdiction fenced in by
heavy penalties, denounced against
man and beast.   Still it was a jurisdiction ; it had a system of law, with courts
to administer it."— *Norm. Conq.,* vol.
v. p. 306.

the king."[1]   The boundaries of the territory thus described marked the limits of the forest code, and the jurisdiction of the forest courts.   From the Dialogue of the Exchequer[2] we learn that these courts — which had exclusive jurisdiction of all offences committed in the forests in violation of the king's exclusive right of proprietorship[3] — were outside of the common law ; that they were not subject to the visitations of the ordinary judges from the king's court ; and that they were governed by their own laws and customs, which were made rather in the interest of the beasts of the chase than of the king's subjects.   The organization of the courts of the forest, like that of all other private jurisdictions, was modelled after the ordinary popular tribunals ; in shires in which these royal franchises existed, the same persons who were required to attend the shire-moot were required to do suit at the forest courts.[4]   In the courts of the forest which still exist, as in the other franchises which have lived on without being absorbed into the general judicial system, may yet be found some of the best remaining illustrations of ancient local customs.[5]   From the greatest living master of the English constitution we learn that in the courts of the Forest of Knaresborough, in the district of his own birth, each township or berewic is still represented by the reeve and four men, — the recognized representatives of the townships in the very earliest laws.[6]

9. Having now drawn out the development of the Norman system of central judicature as embodied in the curia regis down to the reorganization of that court by Henry of Anjou, and having traced in the same way the unbroken history of the Old-English system of provincial judicature as embodied in the courts of the shire and the hundred down to their reorganization by the same king, the task remains to unfold

Side notes:
outside of the common law.

Organization of the forest courts.

Courts of the Forest of Knaresborough.

Development of the itinerant judicature, and the origin of juries.

---

[1] This is the definition of Manwood, *Forest Laws*, p. 40.   Cf. Stephen, *Hist. Crim. Law*, vol. i. p. 135.

[2] *Dialogus de Scaccario*, i. II.

[3] Hen. I. c. 17 ; Bigelow, *Hist. Procedure*, p. 144.

[4] Assize of the Forest, art. 11. For details as to the organization and procedure of the forest courts, see Stephen, *Hist. Crim. Law*, vol. i. pp. 135-138 ; Bigelow, *Procedure*, pp. 144-146.

[5] "Certain it is that, within the forest jurisdictions, some of the old forms of the ancient courts have gone on with less change than they did in general." — *Norman Conquest*, vol. v. p. 306.

[6] I refer of course to Bishop Stubbs. See *Const. Hist.*, vol. i. p. 107, in which is cited Hargrove, *Hist. of Knaresborough* (ed. 1798), pp. 44, 45.

the process through which the two systems were drawn together and finally amalgamated in one composite whole which retains to this day the strongest elements of both. The visible outcome of the union between the Norman curia and the Old-English shire-moot is the typical English law court of modern times, in which witnesses depose to facts, upon which the jury pass, under the guidance and direction of a judge learned in the law. Wherever the English legal system prevails, this idea of a law court is so deeply imbedded in the minds not only of laymen but of lawyers, that it is hard for either class to realize the fact that it did not exist from the very beginning of things, and that in its earliest form it did not present the same aspect which it wears at the present day. Until this delusion is discarded it is impossible to comprehend the process of change and of growth through which the typical English law court was slowly evolved out of the union of elements alien and antagonistic to each other. Under the Old-English system, as the judicial powers of the witan were only exercised upon extraordinary occasions, and as the courts of the townships did not possess contentious jurisdiction, the ordinary administration of law was confined to the courts of the shire and the hundred. The whole tendency of the ancient system was to discourage suitors from seeking justice from a royal source: "the king and the witan frowned upon every symptom of popular discontent with the clumsy justice of popular tribunals, and forced suitors back upon the local courts."[1] As no cause could be carried to the shire until it had first been heard in the hundred, so no cause could be carried to the king until it had first been heard in the shire. It must not be supposed, however, that this arrangement embodied a system of appeal in the modern sense of that term. The decision of each court was final, and it was only in the event that a court failed to decide in a prescribed time that the cause could be taken to a higher tribunal.[2] In the light of this explanation it will be easier to understand those instances which survive of interference by writ upon the part of the Old-English kings with the local administration of justice. In the days of Æthelred the king sent his writ or insigel by the hands of Abbot Ælf-

Marginal notes:

Typical English law court the product of the union of curia and shire-moot.

Old-English judicature.

Influence of the local tribunals.

But little interference from the central authority.

---

[1] *Essays in A. S. Law* (Boston, 1876), p. 25.   [2] See above, p. 200.

here to the shire-moot of Berkshire, bidding them to arbitrate in a suit then pending between Wynflæd and Leofwine. This instance illustrates the fact that the purpose of the king's writ was not to remove the cause in question from the local court to the king's court, but to stimulate the local court into action. There is also evidence going to show that the Old-English kings occasionally administered justice in the local courts either in person or by deputy. It is recorded among the merits of Ælfred, Eadgar, and Cnut that they either went about doing justice in their own persons, or else sent forth justices to do justice in their names. It also appears that before the Conquest certain pleas of the crown were specially set apart to be dealt with in the local courts in the king's name, by the king's officers, and for the king's profit.[1]

Centralization of justice after the Conquest.

Not until after the Norman conquest did the tendency to the centralization of justice, which had but feebly manifested itself before that event, grow strong enough to enable the king's court to seriously encroach upon the local tribunals.[2] As soon as the principle was firmly established that the king was the fountain of justice, and that all courts were the king's courts, there was nothing to prevent the king from invading any jurisdiction and withdrawing from it any cause whatsoever. The means employed to accomplish this result was the king's

The writ process.

writ;[3] but such a writ, issued by a Norman king to withdraw a cause from a popular or franchise court into his own court for trial, differed widely from the writ issued by an Old-English king commanding the local court to do justice. Through the instrumentality of the writ process, in its various forms, the curia regis persistently encroached upon the local and franchise courts, until the main volume of judicial business was finally withdrawn from them into the courts of the king.

---

[1] Upon this subject, see above, p. 257.

[2] "In this way the predominant influence of the king in the judicial order was established. This was a powerful instrument in producing centralization and unity; and yet, as the royal judges only interposed their services as supplementary to the institution of the jury, and did not substitute them for it, — for questions of fact and questions of right remained distinct, — the germ of free institutions, that existed in the judicial order, was not entirely destroyed."— Guizot, *Hist. Rep. Govt.* (Scoble's trans.), p. 297.

[3] "Jurisdiction obtained by the king's court in this way may be called the extraordinary jurisdiction of the court. It was acquired by direct usurpation, in derogation of the rights of the popular courts and manorial franchises, upon the sole authority of the king."— Bigelow, *Hist. of Procedure*, p. 78.

This statement, though strictly and technically true, is apt to
be misleading, unless the fact is borne in mind that the royal
courts into which the mass of business was so withdrawn
were the king's courts sitting in the shires under the presi- The king's courts sitting in the shires.
dency of a judge or other royal commissioner detached for
that purpose from the staff of the central tribunal.[1] Each
local court so held in the king's name by a royal commissioner or justice was held by virtue of a commission in which
the classes of cases to be tried, and the limits of the local
jurisdiction, were carefully designated.[2] There is evidence
going to show that royal courts were held in the shires, away
from the king's person, by the king's immediate justiciars, as
early even as the Conqueror's reign ;[3] but not until the latter
part of the reign of Rufus can there be found any record of
anything like a judicial iter by the royal justiciars in the modern sense of that term. In 1096 the Red King sent Bishop Judicial iter of 1096.
Walkelin and his chaplain, Flambard, into Exeter, Devon-
shire, and Cornwall to hold royal pleas.[4] From the single Pipe
Roll of the succeeding reign of Henry I. we learn that the
custom of sending itinerant justices through the shires was
then in full operation.[5] In Henry's reign the officers of the
exchequer were sent through the country to assess the revenue, and while thus engaged in provincial business they sat in
the shire-moot, where judicial work soon followed in the path
of their fiscal duties.[6] It is reasonable to suppose that the
custom of sending out itinerant justices, which seems to have
been in full force in the thirty-first year of Henry I., continued until the whole system of central administration finally
broke down during the anarchy brought about by the struggle between Stephen and Matilda. As soon as peace was
restored, as early in fact as the second year of Henry II. when

[1] "The courts in which they (the
itinerant justices) preside are the ancient county courts, *under new conditions*, but substantially identical with
those of the Anglo-Saxon times." —
Stubbs, *Const. Hist.*, vol. i. p. 605.
"These were the king's courts held in
the counties." — Bigelow, *Hist. of Procedure*, p. 137.
[2] "These commissions were issued
by the Conqueror and his sons, and by
Henry II., his son and grandson to
their '*justitiarii*,' just as they are issued by her Majesty in the present
day to the judges of the High Court of
Judicature." — Stephen, *Hist. of the
Crim. Law*, vol. i. p. 99.
[3] Cf. *Placita Ang.-Norm.*, pp. 4, 16,
22, 34.
[4] Bigelow, *Hist. of Procedure*, pp.
93, 94 ; *Placita Ang.-Norm.*, p. 69.
[5] Freeman, *Norm. Conq.*, vol. v. p.
300.
[6] Stubbs, *Const. Hist.*, vol. i. pp.
392, 393.

Itinerant system became a permanent institution under Henry II.

Its complete organization generally dated from 1176.

Arrangement of circuits.

Meaning of the term Nisi Prius.

the Pipe Rolls begin again, the system of iters or circuits was reëstablished ;[1] during this reign the itinerant judicature became a well organized and permanent institution. The earlier iters, which seem to have been rather fiscal than judicial, were generally held by the sheriffs,[2] who were only occasionally superseded by justices from the curia regis. Not until 1166 — the year in which the judges were charged with the execution of the Assize of Clarendon — did the system of judicial eyres held by justices from the central tribunal become annual and general.[3] But from the year 1176 is generally dated the complete organization of the itinerant system. In that year, in a great council held at Northampton, was issued an important assize whose execution was committed to eighteen justices,[4] now called for the first time in the Pipe Rolls *"justitiarii itinerantes,"* a name which in its Anglicized form of "justices in Eyre" has continued to the present day. The eighteen justices of 1176 were divided into six detachments, and to each detachment of three justices a distinct circuit was assigned. By the Assize of Northampton the itinerant justices were instructed among other things to decide all causes involving not more than half a knight's fee, unless the matter was so important that it could not be determined but before the king, or unless it were such that the justices themselves, on account of its difficulty, chose to refer it to the king, or, in his absence, to those who were acting for him.[5] In this instruction we have a general statement of the principle that all causes of any moment were cognizable in the central court of the king, unless before (*nisi prius*) they could be heard therein the itinerant justices should be sent to pass upon them in the king's court sitting in the shire in which they arose.

---

[1] As to Henry's measures for the reëstablishment of provincial judicature, see William of Newburgh, ii. c. 1.

[2] Bigelow, *Hist. of Procedure*, p. 94. As royal justices the sheriffs "acted under special writ, managed the pleas of the crown, and conducted the tourn and leet, or the courts which were afterwards so called." — Stubbs, *Const. Hist.*, vol. i. p. 606.

[3] Benedictus, pref., vol. ii. p. lxiv.

[4] Reeves, *Hist. of Eng. Law*, vol. i. p. 273; Madox, *Hist. Ex.*, vol. i. p. 18; Stephen, *Hist. Crim. Law*, vol. i. p. 100.

[5] "Item Justitiæ faciant omnes justitias et rectitudines spectantes ad dominum regem et ad coronam suam, per breve domini regis, vel illorum qui in loco ejus erunt, de feodo dimidii militis et infra, nisi tam grandis sit querela quod non possit deduci sine domino rege, vel talis quam Justitæ ei reportent pro dubitatione sua, vel ad illos qui in loco ejus erunt." — Assize of Northampton, art. 7. The admonition as to difficult questions is repeated in 1178. See Benedictus, vol. i. p. 207.

Prior to the definite arrangements of 1176 the judicial functions of the sheriffs had already begun to decline. In 1170, after the king's return from the Continent, in response to a general complaint of their exactions, nearly every sheriff in the kingdom was removed from office, and an inquiry ordered into their collections.[1] After this event, although a few were restored to their old positions,[2] their authority became more and more circumscribed. In 1194 it was provided that the sheriffs should no longer sit as judges in their own shires, and the holding of the pleas of the crown was committed to elective officers, — the coroners of the thirteenth century.[3] By the twenty-fourth article of the Great Charter the right of either sheriffs or coroners to hold pleas of the crown was taken away altogether.[4] Although this clause does not seem to have been promptly enforced,[5] it led the way to the final settlement of the principle that the sheriff was a mere ministerial officer, and that judicial functions in the courts of assize belonged exclusively to the justices sent by the king.

Decline of the judicial powers of the sheriffs.

By the firm establishment of the system of itinerant judicature the Norman curia regis was at last brought into close and permanent union with the Old-English shire-moot. But the assemblies of the shires which were summoned by the sheriffs to meet the royal justices in order to participate with them in the administration of justice, and in the transaction of other public business, must not be confused with the ordinary and ancient county courts which met from month to month.[6] It is highly important that this distinction should be kept steadily in view, for the reason that the king's courts held in the counties, the courts of assize, have a history which is entirely separate and distinct from that of the ancient county courts, which, after having their powers transferred to

Twenty-fourth article of the Great Charter.

The courts of assize as distinguished from the ancient county courts.

---

[1] For the text of the "Inquest of Sheriffs," see *Select Charters*, pp. 148–150.

[2] Those who were restored revenged themselves upon the people. *Placita Ang.-Norm.*, p. 216.

[3] Bigelow, *Hist. of Procedure*, p. 131.

[4] "Nullus vice-comes, constabularius, coronatores, vel alii ballivi nostri, teneant placita coronæ nostræ." The sheriff's tourn, however, was not abolished; it was held for centuries. Cf. Stephen, *Hist. Crim. Law*, vol. i. p. 83.

[5] Stubbs, *Const. Hist.*, vol. i. p. 607.

[6] For a full statement of this distinction, see Bigelow (*Hist. of Procedure*, p. 137), who says, "The courts held by these itinerant justices of the king possessed a dignity altogether above that of the ordinary judicial assembly of the county. These were the king's courts held in the counties." See, also, Stubbs, *Const. Hist.*, vol. i. p. 605; Stephen, *Hist. Crim. Law*, vol. i. pp. 81–85, 97.

the royal tribunals, have kept up a shadowy existence down almost to the present day.[1] The full assembly of the shire, which was called together to meet the itinerant justices, embraced a far more perfect representation of the county than the ordinary county court. Before the coming of the judges a general summons was issued to the sheriffs commanding them to summon all archbishops, bishops, abbots, priors, counts, barons, knights, and freeholders of their entire bailiwick, and of each vill four lawful men and the reeve, and of each borough twelve lawful burgesses, and all others who by duty and custom were bound to appear before the itinerant justices.[2]   At this stage, then, of its development the king's court held in the shire is a full representative assembly of the county summoned by the sheriff to meet the itinerant justices, in order to participate with them in the transaction of all judicial and fiscal business given them in charge.[3]   By what process has the court thus constituted been transformed into the modern court of assize, in which the itinerant justices still preside, but in which the general assembly of the shire is represented only by the grand and petty jurors who are summoned by the sheriff for the trial of civil and criminal causes ?   How are we to explain the fact that " by degrees the old system of convening something like a county parliament, in which every township was represented by its reeve and four men, fell into disuse, and the sheriffs fell into the habit of summoning only a sufficient number of *probi et legales homines* to form a grand jury, and as many petty juries as might be needed, for the trial of the civil and criminal cases to be disposed of ?"[4]   How this result was finally brought about can only be explained by tracing the process through which one particular method of trial — known as trial by jury — struggled into existence, and then swallowed up all other methods of trial which prevailed in the popular courts.   To adequately explain the history of this process it will be necessary to enter the domain of legal procedure.

A full representation of the county convened to meet the justices.

The county assembly now represented only by the grand and petty jurors.

How this change was brought about.

---

[1] As to the modern history of the ancient county court, see Freeman, *Norm. Conq.*, vol. v. p. 312.

[2] See Bracton, Twiss ed., vol. ii. pp. 188, 234, 251.

[3] As an illustration of the nature and variety of the business carried on before the itinerant justices, see the *agenda* of the year 1194, Hoveden, vol. iii. pp. 262–267 ; *Select Charters*, pp. 259–263. Cf., also, Bigelow, *Hist. of Procedure*, pp. 138–141.

[4] Stephen, *Hist. Crim. Law*, vol. i. p. 253.

At an earlier stage of this work an imperfect sketch was drawn of the archaic system of legal procedure, which, in the pre-Norman period, regulated the administration of justice in the popular courts of the shire, the hundred, and the private franchises. The statement was then made that the primitive Teutonic suit was a simple demand made by the actor on the defendant for compensation. Whether the procedure was civil or criminal, its introduction lay in the hands of the person seeking justice, who was required to summon his opponent with prescribed and rigorous formalities, — personal summons being a private, extra-judicial act which the plaintiff was always required to execute without the aid of a judicial officer. To the demand, which the plaintiff was required to make at the court in a solemn traditional form, the defendant opposed an equally solemn contradiction. The demand and denial which thus made up the issue were unattended by any allegations of fact in support of either. The vitally important part of the procedure, which was conducted throughout with an iron rigorism of form, was the question of proof. After the issue was made up, this question was settled by the proof-judgment, pronounced at the issue term, in which the court determined what kind of proof should be given in the particular case, by whom it should be given, and at what time it should be given. As a general rule, after the rendition of the proof-judgment, the party upon whom the burden fell gave security to furnish such proof as was required of him at the second or trial term. Four distinct means of proof were known to the customary law, — compurgation, witnesses, documents, and the ordeal. By means of one of these methods the party having the right of proof was required to support the issue which in the particular case he was called upon to maintain.[1] Such was the procedure and such the means of proof that prevailed in the Old-English popular courts, which, with their machinery unimpaired, survived the Norman conquest.[2] After that event a new means

Old-English legal procedure.

Private summons.

The issue.

The burden of proof.

Four means of proof known to the customary law.

---

[1] For the authorities upon the subject of Old-English legal procedure, see above, pp. 204-207.

[2] "The retention of this lower machinery involved the retention of the ancient process of jurisdiction. In this, at least in its subordinate arrangements, the Conquest produced little change except in the substitution of Norman for English names and persons." — Preface to Benedictus, vol. ii. p. lv.

A new means of proof added by the Normans. of proof was added to the ancient procedure : to the four existing methods of proof the Normans added trial by battle. After this innovation the issue was made up and the proof-judgment rendered as before, and in such judgment the court determined as of old, according to the circumstances of each particular case, whether the trial should be had by compurgation, by witnesses, by documents, by the ordeal, or by battle.

How the form of trial was determined. It was not, however, within the arbitrary discretion of the judges to order such a trial as they saw fit ; as a general rule the party who had made the last good pleading was entitled to ask the court for a judgment according to law as to the form of trial to be followed.[1] With the foregoing statement of the scheme of procedure which prevailed in the popular courts down to and after the Norman conquest clearly in view, it will be possible to explain with greater clearness how still another method of proof — afterwards known as trial by jury — struggled into view, and finally superseded all other methods of proof known to the customary law. The origin and growth of this new method of proof will be considered in the following sections.

Origin and history of juries. The historical origin of trial by jury — an institution which reached its full development only upon the soil of England — has been examined from every possible point of view by scholars who represent the leading nationalities of the world.[2] By these various inquirers the origin of the institution has been traced to every source which hypothesis or analogy could plausibly suggest. The fruit of this investigation, carried on for so long a time and by so many hands, has finally expanded into a great literature, the mass of which has been rendered practically worthless through the results of the latest research. Not until a very recent period was the thread of truth discovered which has led to the removal of the endless difficulties and confusions which at one time arose out of the application to the history of the jury of a mass of false and misleading analogies. But even now that its true history has been fully worked out, and the several stages of

---

[1] Upon this whole subject, see Bigelow, *Hist. of Procedure*, ch. viii., "The Medial Judgment." See, also, p. 301.

[2] For a catalogue of the works which have been written by authors of various nationalities upon the history of juries, see Brunner, *Die Entstehung der Schwurgerichte.*

its historical development clearly defined, it is still difficult to unfold, within narrow limits, the processes of thought through which the final result was at last attained.   Upon the thresh- The trial old of the inquiry let the conclusion be accepted that the jury of judgment, the trial jury of modern times, has been slowly developed upon English soil out of the fusion of two distinct elements, — one of which can be traced to Old-English, the other to Norman law.[1]   In order, therefore, to solve the problem involved in the historical development of the jury, we must first ascertain the origin and character of the elements out of which it arose ; next must be examined the process through which these elements were blended ; and finally the after-growth of the new creation.   Before attempting, however, to trace the elements of the jury to the sources from which they were drawn, it may be helpful to emphasize the fact that, down to about the middle of the fifteenth century,[2] jurors, in all the changing relations which they were called upon to assume, were simply witnesses and nothing more ; whatever report or verdict they made upon their oaths was based, not upon the testimony of witnesses other than themselves, but upon what they derived from their own personal knowledge or from reliable report.   Not until after jurors were relieved of their early character as witnesses did they assume the character of judges, who were no longer required to furnish proof, but simply to pronounce judgment upon proof brought before them.   The historical development of the jury may therefore be divided for convenience into two epochs ; the first embracing the period in which the jurors were mere witnesses, the second embracing the period in which they became judges of facts established in their presence, without reference to their previous knowledge of the case.   The history of the jury, in the first period of its development, involves then an examination of the process by which definite issues of fact came to be submitted to organized bodies of witnesses whose unanimous deposition or report as to the fact in question was conclusive of it.

The fact has been heretofore explained that proof by wit-

Marginal notes:

The trial jury the product of the union of Old-English and Norman elements.

Jurors originally witnesses and nothing more.

History of the jury divided into two epochs.

---

[1] "That institution (the modern jury) was purely Norman-English, having come by direct lineage from the inquisition procedure introduced from Normandy by William the Conqueror." — Bigelow, *Hist. of Procedure*, p. 334.

[2] See above, p. 310.

The barbaric theory of proof.

nesses was one of the four leading methods of proof known to the customary law.[1] Such proof, in the form in which it appeared in the archaic procedure, does not satisfy, however, the modern conception of legal testimony. The witnesses of the customary law could only appear before the court when produced by the party required to make proof, and

Witnesses swore only to the assertion of their chief.

when thus produced they swore only to the truth of the assertion made by their chief;[2] they were neither required nor allowed to respond to interrogatories propounded either by the parties, or by the court itself. Their testimony was offered in obedience to that barbaric theory which regarded the proof given in a cause, not as a means of bringing conviction to the mind of the court, but as a satisfaction due to the adversary in the forms prescribed by custom.[3] The witnesses known to the Old-English customary law embraced

Transaction witnesses.

two distinct classes, — transaction witnesses, who were in the nature of official persons appointed in every town and hundred to witness sales, gifts, exchanges, and the like;[4] and

Community witnesses.

community witnesses. The latter class, whose very name goes far to explain their real character, were persons selected from the community or neighborhood who, by their long acquaintance with the locality, could testify as to long continued relations, circumstances, and occurrences known to them as neighbors, or members of the community. Such witnesses were chiefly employed in causes touching the relationship or status of an individual, or in suits in which the right to

They spoke the voice of the community as to the fact in question.

land was in question.[5] And although such witnesses were party witnesses, — that is, witnesses produced by the party to whose assertion they swore, — still the assertion made by them derived its force from the fact that it embodied the voice or knowledge of the community as to the particular

[1] See above, p. 205.

[2] Brunner, *Schwurg.*, pp. 50–53; *Essays in A. S. Law*, pp. 186, 187.

[3] "It follows that in the barbarian form of proof by witnesses, which was merely one particular kind of proof, as the ordeal was another, the producer of the witnesses proposed not in the least to convince the tribunal of his own good right, but simply to produce the fixed number of witnesses according to the customary form, and these witnesses were to corroborate by oath the theme or statement prescribed for them in the previous judgment which had ordered the proof." — *North American Review*, No. ccxliv. (July, 1874), pp. 219, 220.

[4] Eadgar's Laws, iv. 4, 5, 6; Æthelstan, v. 1, § 5; Forsyth, *Trial by Jury*, pp. 84, 85.

[5] Brunner, *Schwurg.*, pp. 50–53; *Essays in A. S. Law*, pp. 186, 187; Bigelow, *Hist. of Procedure*, p. 309.

fact or right in question.[1] If this idea is kept steadily in view, it will be possible to distinguish this important class of witnesses through all the changes of form and of name through which they pass. The principle that disputed questions of fact should be determined by the voice of sworn witnesses taken from the neighborhood survived the Norman conquest, and under the organizing hands of the conquerors this form of proof was cast into a more definite and formal shape, and was at the same time emancipated from much of the rigorous formality which had surrounded it in the primitive system. After the Conquest the community witnesses of the customary law were brought into contact with, and incorporated into, a new scheme of proof, — the *inquisitio per testes*,[2] an instrument of royal law whose introduction into England can be traced directly to a Norman source.

Community witnesses after the Conquest.

No trace of the inquest of proof (*inquisitio per testes*) can be found in Old-English legal procedure;[3] it was purely a Norman innovation, but by no means a Norman invention. It is admitted on all hands that the inquisitorial system was introduced into England by the Normans, who derived it directly from the Frank Capitularies, into which it was probably adopted from the fiscal regulations of the Code of Theodosius,[4] — a code which in 438 was promulgated as law in both the Eastern and Western Empires.[5] The inquest of proof, in the form in which it appeared in the Frank system, consisted of the instructions or special commissions issued by the kings to their *missi*, or royal commissioners, commanding them to make special inquiry into fiscal and judicial matters by the oaths of sworn witnesses in the local courts.[6] An inquisition pure and simple was an official inquiry instituted by royal authority, and executed by a judge or other royal

The *inquisitio per testes* derived by the Normans

from the Franks, who probably took it from the Theodosian Code.

---

[1] "The testimony of the neighborhood was appealed to for the purpose of deciding questions which related to matters of general concern." — Forsyth, *Trial by Jury*, p. 92.

[2] "From this class of proof (community witnesses) arose the 'inquisitio per testes' in the Norman period, and the jury of English law." — *Essays in A. S. Law*, p. 187.

[3] Brunner, *Zeugen und Inquisitionsbeweis*, p. 41.

[4] Brunner, *Schwurg.*, p. 87, citing Cod. Theod. x. 10. l. 11; Ibid., l. 29. Cf. Palgrave, *Eng. Commonw.*, p. 271; Stubbs, *Const. Hist.*, vol. i. p. 613.

[5] Cf. Smith's *Dictionary of Greek and Roman Antiquities*, "Codex Theodosianus."

[6] The roots of the Frankish inquest of proof "are not to be found in the customary or folk law; it is a creation of new or royal law." — *North American Review*, July, 1884, p. 220.

An inquisition a royal inquiry executed in a local court through the oaths of witnesses.

officer in a local court through the oaths of sworn witnesses who responded to interrogatories propounded by the judge himself.[1] As to the number of witnesses, the judge could use his own discretion; according to the sources, the number varied between two and five hundred. As every qualified member of the community was a member of the local court, the answers of the representative witnesses selected by the officer charged with the execution of the inquiry embodied the knowledge or belief of the community itself. But this method of proof, which was a creation of new or royal law, differed radically from the witness proof which existed in the old customary or folk law. The customary witnesses were narrowed down by a rule which required that they should swear only to the assertion of their chief; while the witnesses of the inquest were emancipated from the old rigor of form, and were sworn to answer all such questions as the judge should propound. The customary witnesses were *jurors*, the witnesses of the inquest were *jurati*. The Frankish inquest of proof found in Normandy a soil favorable to its development. It was in use in the duchy before the Conquest,[2] and it was there applied to both fiscal and judicial purposes. The evidence is abundant to show that the inquest of proof was a favorite instrument of law in the hands of the Conqueror which he frequently applied to the transaction of both fiscal and judicial business. The most comprehensive application ever made of the principle, perhaps, was made by William in the taking of the Domesday Survey,[3] which is nothing but the fruit of a general inquiry conducted by royal commissioners into the condition of every part of the kingdom, in order to ascertain "how it was set and by what men." The commissioners went into every shire, and before them came representatives from every hundred and from every township. Upon the deposition or verdict of these representative jurors, together with the depositions of the

Difference between customary witnesses and those of the inquest.

Domesday the result of a vast royal inquest.

---

[1] Brunner, *Schwurg.*, p. 85.

[2] Brunner, *Schwurg.*, pp. 84, 381, 382. But it was in England only that the system reached its full development; the witnesses of the Frankish inquest were never transformed in Normandy into the jury of judgment, the trial jury of modern times. After the union of

Normandy with France, proof by inquest disappeared, little by little, until it finally became extinct in Normandy, as in the rest of France.

[3] Stubbs, *Const. Hist.*, vol. i. p. 385, 611; Freeman, *Norm. Conq.*, vol. iv. p. 470, vol. v. p. 303.

sheriff and all the barons and Norman landholders of the
shire, was drawn up a detailed history of every manor or
township in the kingdom.[1]   This system of inquest by the
oaths of local witnesses, which William thus applied on so
large a scale to the accurate assessment of the land over
which he was called to govern, was frequently applied during
his reign to the trial of private causes in which the right to
real property was drawn in question.   Throughout the Norman period it seems to have been a constant practice in suits
involving the right to land to decide the controversy by ap-
pealing to the knowledge of the community in which the
parties resided and the land lay.[2]   The authority for the proceeding was the royal writ authorizing the inquiry, which was
executed by a judge or other royal officer through the answers of witnesses who represented the vicinage, and who
stated upon their oaths to which contestant the right belonged.   The case usually cited to illustrate the character of
a simple judicial inquisition of the Norman period is that one
in which William, in one of the earliest English writs extant,
directed his justiciars to summon all the shire-moots that
had taken part in a previous unsatisfactory trial as to lands
belonging to the church of Ely : that being done, they were
directed to choose a number of Englishmen who could state
how the title stood upon the day Eadward the Confessor
died; the statement thus made by them was to be confirmed
by their oaths.   The title as it was found to exist in the time
of Eadward was to prevail, except in the cases of gifts made
by the king since the Conquest.[3]   In this proceeding we have
an example of a royal writ directed to the king's justices commanding them to inquire, upon the testimony of the vicinage,
into the truth of a disputed allegation in a suit in which land
was in question.[4]   The writ which authorized the holding of
the inquiry was an instrument of royal law, while the community witnesses who responded to the inquiry represented a
form of witness proof which finds its origin in the customary

Marginal notes:

Same sys-
tem applied
during
William's
reign to the
trial of pri-
vate causes
involving
land.

A simple
inquisition
of the Nor-
man period.

---

[1] See Ely Domesday, *Dom.*, vol. iii.
p. 497.

[2] Forsyth, *Trial by Jury*, p. 108.

[3] *Placita Ang.-Norm.*, p. 24; Forsyth, *Trial by Jury*, p. 99; Dugdale's
Monasticon, vol. i. p. 478.

[4] " The essential feature of this writ
is the direction for an inquiry upon
testimony of the vicinage concerning
which had been the subject of an unsatisfactory trial." — Bigelow, *Hist. of
Procedure*, p. 176.

The
community
witnesses
now appear
in a new re-
lation.
law. But the old customary witnesses now appear in a new relation : they are no longer mere jurors who swear only to the assertion of their chief ; they are sworn men (*jurati*), who, being emancipated from the rigor of form that prevailed in the ancient procedure, answer upon their oaths such questions as are propounded to them by the officer charged with the execution of the inquiry. If this theory be the true one, it clearly explains how the community witnesses of the customary law were developed into the community *jurata*, whose existence is clear from the time of the Conquest ; [1] it clearly explains how the more perfectly organized method of proof (*inquisitio per testes*), which the Normans introduced, was engrafted upon the undeveloped witness-proof of the customary

Whether
produced
by a party
or convened
by an offi-
cer, they
were the
same body
of men.
law. In the face of all the learned refinement upon the subject, it is safe to say that the community witnesses, whether produced by a party in his own behalf, or convened to meet the officer charged with the execution of the inquest, were one and the same body of men, — they were the representatives of the vicinage through whose oaths the community spake as to the particular fact in question. The simple judicial inquisition of the Norman period may therefore be defined to be an inquiry into the truth of a disputed allegation, authorized by the king's writ, and directed to a judge, sheriff, or other royal officer, commanding him to ascertain the right in question by the oaths of witnesses taken from the neighborhood. Thus under the influence of the writ process the community witnesses of the customary law were developed into the community *jurata*, whose existence in England is clear from the time of the Conquest.

Recogni-
tions, —
how they
differed
from a
simple
inquisition.
During the reign of Henry of Anjou there was introduced into England a new species of the inquest of proof known as the recognition.[2] The distinction between a simple inquisition and a recognition was that the former consisted of an inquiry into a disputed allegation conducted by a judge or other royal officer, who propounded interrogatories to an in-

---

[1] "Forms of the community-*jurata*, so often mentioned in the law-books of the thirteenth century, had clearly been in use in England ever since the Conquest ; such for instance as the simple judicial inquisition ordered for the trial of a cause by the king's writ." — Bigelow, *Hist. of Procedure*, p. 337.

[2] Brunner, *Schwurg.*, pp. 303, 304 "On the assize as established by Henry II.," see Forsyth, *Trial by Jury*, ch vi.

definite number of witnesses taken from the body of the local
court; while the latter consisted of an inquiry made by a
definite body of chosen witnesses, who, after being duly
chosen, were summoned by an officer of the law to make
inquiry into the matter in dispute, and then to report (*recog-
noscere*) the truth to the court itself.[1] In each proceeding,
inquiry was made by the oaths of witnesses, whose answers
were supposed to embody the knowledge of the community.
But in a simple inquisition the witnesses were a part of the
court, and as such were interrogated by the judge; while the
recognitors sat apart from the court, and conducted their own
inquiry as a distinct body which stood between the parties
and the judge. The report of the recognitors was based
upon their own knowledge, and by knowledge, says Glanvill,
was meant what they had seen or heard from reliable report.[2] There seems to be no doubt that the system of recognition existed in Normandy before it was brought into England.[3] The most authoritative view is that Henry II., who is
supposed to have introduced the *recognitiones* into Normandy
between 1150 and 1152, introduced them into England, upon
his accession to the throne of that kingdom, under the name
of assizes.[4] To the student of English law, the Great Assize, and the assizes of *novel disseisin, mort d'ancester* and
darrein presentment, the leading recognitions in civil matters,
are the most familiar. The nature of the Great Assize
has been thus explained by a contemporary historian: "Now
the Great Assize is a royal benefit indulged to the people by clemency of the prince on the advice of the nobles,
whereby life and property are so wholesomely cared for that
men can avoid the chance of the combat, and yet keep whatever right they have in their freeholds. . . . This constitution arises from the highest equity, for the right which can
scarcely be proved by battle after many and long delays is
more conveniently and speedily acquired by the benefit of this
constitution. . . . Besides, this institution has in it more

Marginal notes: Introduced by Henry II. under the name of assizes.

Nature of the Great Assize.

---

[1] Bigelow, *Hist. of Procedure*, p. 175,
note 4, pp. 335, 336.

[2] Glanvill, lib. 2, c. 17, § 4.

[3] "The system of recognition existed
in Normandy before it was brought into
England, but it was developed in England, and that development probably

had a reflex influence on Normandy."—
Stubbs, *Const. Hist.*, vol. i. p. 614, note 2.

[4] Brunner, *Schwurg.*, pp. 303, 304.
"The recognition by jurors was called
an assise, because it was established by
an *assisa*, or statute of Henry II."—
Forsyth, *Trial by Jury*, p. 122, note 1.

A substi-
tute for trial
by battle
in suits for
freeholds.

equity than trial by combat in proportion as more weight is to be allowed in judgment to many fit witnesses than to one alone." [1] The primary object, then, of this beneficent institution, organized by the legislation of Henry II. out of elements existing in the jurisprudence of the time, was to furnish to those who were assailed in their freeholds a reasonable and equitable method of trial by witnesses taken from the neighborhood in lieu of trial by battle. When the right to a freehold was drawn in question, and the demandant tendered to the party in possession trial by combat, the defendant, unless some valid objection could be taken by his adversary, could escape from it by putting himself upon the Great Assize.[2] This was accomplished by the defendant's obtaining from the curia regis a writ to stop all proceedings in the local court until a recognition could be had as to the right set up by the claimant.[3] In order to obtain a trial the claimant was then obliged to obtain a writ directed to the sheriff commanding him to summon four lawful knights of the neighborhood wherein the disputed property lay, who were to choose twelve lawful knights of the same neighborhood most cognizant of the facts, who were upon their oaths to declare which of the parties litigant had the greater right to the land in dispute.[4] The proceedings in the other assizes were substantially the same, with the exception that the sheriff himself selected the twelve recognitors from those best acquainted with the facts,

Recogni-
tors mere
witnesses.

without the intervention of the four electors.[5] That the recognitors were regarded as mere witnesses is manifest from the procedure in the event that some of the number summoned were found to be ignorant of the facts in question. If any of the twelve did not possess the requisite knowledge, or if they disagreed, others were summoned until at least twelve were found who knew and agreed upon the facts.[6] It required the concurrent testimony or verdict of twelve witnesses or recognitors to be conclusive of the right.[7] Beyond

---

[1] Glanvill, lib. ii. c. 7.
[2] As to the details of the procedure, see Stephen, *Hist. Crim. Law*, vol. i. p. 256; Forsyth, *Trial by Jury*, pp. 122–129.
[3] Glanvill, lib. ii. c. 8; Bigelow, *Hist. of Procedure*, p. 269.
[4] Glanvill, lib. ii. c. 10.

[5] Glanvill, lib. xiii. cc. i., 2 *seq.*; Stubbs, *Const. Hist.*, vol. i. p. 617; Reeves, *Hist. Eng. Law*, vol. i. p. 443.
[6] Cf. Forsyth, *Trial by Jury*, p. 127.
[7] And no subsequent action could be brought upon the same claim. — Glanvill, lib. ii. c. 18.

this stage, in which the recognitors or jurors were mere witnesses, the Norman jury did not advance.   In Normandy, as
well as in the rest of France, the whole system of inquest by
proof was gradually superseded by the French *enquête*, a
procedure partly Roman, partly canonical.[1]   The remarkable
fact is that only on English soil did the jury of proof survive, and finally pass through the ultimate evolution which
has transformed it into the jury of judgment, the trial jury
of modern times.   The steps by which the trial jury, in
the form in which we now know it, was at last established,
may be briefly explained as follows : If any of the jurors
chosen were uninformed as to the matters concerning which
they were to swear, those who were informed were added to
or afforced until at least twelve were found who could unite
in a definite conclusion in favor of one side or the other.[2]
By degrees this clumsy system was improved by separating
the afforcing jurors from the uninformed jurors, who, being
thus relieved altogether of their character as witnesses, became judges of evidence detailed by others.   From the account
given of juries by Fortescue in his treatise, written between
1460 and 1470, it is quite clear that this final stage in the
development of the trial jury in civil cases must have been
reached by the middle of the fifteenth century.[3]

In England only was the jury of proof transformed into the jury of judgment.

The attempt has now been made to unfold the process
through which a certain kind of witness-proof, whose germs
were imbedded in the customary law, was slowly developed
upon English soil, first into the jury of proof, and finally into
the jury of judgment, the trial jury of modern times.   The
four stages of growth in the historical development of the
jury are represented by the community witness of the customary law, the simple inquisition of the Norman period, the
recognitions of the Angevin period,[4] and the trial jury of to-
day.   As heretofore explained, the simple judicial inquisition,
out of which the jury of proof directly arose, struggled into

Trial by jury gradually superseded all other methods of trial.

---

[1] "The *enquête*, introduced by an ordinance of Louis IX. in 1260 first into the royal tribunals, afterwards took the place of the ancient *inquisitio* both in France and in Normandy." — *North Am. Review*, July, 1874, p. 221.

[2] Forsyth, *Trial by Jury*, p. 127.

[3] See above, p. 310 and note 5.

[4] "The simple inquisition stands be-tween this mode of trial by witnesses and that species of the inquisition known as a recognition ; not in strict chronological order, for all three ex-isted side by side throughout the Nor-man period." — Bigelow, *Hist. of Pro-cedure*, p. 335.

existence after the Conquest, and took its place in the procedure of the local courts alongside of compurgation, witnesses,
documents, ordeal, and battle.   How in the process of time
and of growth this new method of trial gradually superseded
or absorbed all other methods of trial which had prevailed in
the popular courts is a question full of interest, but one which
belongs to the history of legal procedure.   Suffice it here to
say that such was the final result of the development of the
jury in England, where, rather by the silent force of its own
intrinsic excellence than by the artificial stimulus of legislation, it gradually overshadowed and exterminated all other
methods of trial which had ever been employed for the settlement of issues in which disputed facts were in question.   By

As the
fittest it
survived.

the force of the law of natural selection it outlived them all,
— as the fittest it survived.   First employed in suits in which
rights to land were in question, the jury was gradually extended by the judges to the trial of other civil causes in
which rights to land were not involved.   The decree of the
Lateran Council which led to the abolition of trial by ordeal
paved the way for the introduction of the trial jury into criminal procedure.   After ordeals were abolished in England, no
way remained of traversing the presumption of guilt which
arose out of the accusation made by the jury of presentment.
To remedy the evil by giving to the accused his constitutional
right to traverse in some form the presumption of guilt raised
against him, trial by petty jury was gradually introduced in
criminal cases.[1]   Long after the jury had thus worked its
way to a position of supremacy in both civil and criminal
causes, some of its older rivals lived on in neglect and obscurity until finally abolished by statute in the present century.   As late as 1818, in the case of Ashford *v.* Thornton,
before referred to, the judges held, after solemn argument,
that trial by battle in appeals of murder was still a part of
English criminal procedure : this decision led to its abolition
in the following year.[2]   In the case of King *v.* Williams,
which occurred in 1824, the ancient method of trial by compurgation, in the form of " wager of law," was for the last
time actually put in force ;[3] ten years later a statute ended

[1] See above, p. 310.
[2] See above, p. 311.

[3] Probably the last case in which it
was employed was that of *King* v.

its existence.   As all other methods of trial except trial by
jury gradually fell into disuse, and as the king's courts held
in the shires were gradually relieved of all fiscal and administrative work, the county parliaments, which were originally
convened to meet the itinerant justices, were slowly transformed into the modern courts of assize, in which the itinerant justices still preside, but in which the general assembly
of the shire is represented only by the grand and petty jurors
summoned by the sheriff for the dispatch of the civil and
criminal business to be disposed of.

Williams, 2 B. & C. 538.   "Wager of   c. 42, § 13.   Cf. Stephen, *Hist. Crim.*
law" was abolished by 3 & 4 Will. IV.,   *Law*, vol. i. p. 244, note **2**.

CHAPTER IV.

THE WINNING OF THE CHARTERS.

1. In the two preceding chapters the attempt was made to emphasize the fact that, although the Norman conquest brought with it a change of dynasty, the establishment of a new nobility, and a sweeping confiscation through which most of the great estates were transferred from English to Norman hands, yet that it did not involve the displacement of the English nation, nor a wiping out of the immemorial laws and political institutions of the conquered race. The Old-English system of local, self-governing communities survived; and upon that tenacious system as a substructure the Norman system of central administration was superimposed. During the four Norman reigns, upon the immutable foundations of Old-English local freedom was organized a vigorous system of central administration with the source of its strength in the royal authority. How the royal authority itself was strengthened and consolidated through the results of the Conquest has already been explained in the review which has been heretofore made of the double origin of William's kingship. It was no part of the Conqueror's plan to remain simply a military chieftain wholly dependent upon the jealous and exacting host by whose aid the Conquest had been accomplished. With the prescience of a statesman, he claimed to be the ruler of a nation in which Norman and Englishmen were alike his subjects, and as such ruler he claimed the possession of every royal right that had ever belonged to any of the kings who had gone before him. The sum of royal power which thus accrued to William as a national king was augmented by the addition of every feudal right which tended to increase the royal revenue or to strengthen the royal authority. As a national king, William claimed every kind of revenue, ordinary and extraordinary, which had ever belonged to any of his English predecessors.

As feudal lord, William firmly established the doctrine that he was the supreme landlord, and that all lands were held by grant from him. All landowners thus became tenants of the king, and under William's successors the feudal revenue which accrued from this source was enormous.[1]

In order to exercise the vast powers, and to discharge the endless and intricate duties, which the growth of the royal power after the Conquest thus concentrated around the person of the king, it became necessary for the crown to organize, out of the main body of the great council, a smaller body which could be charged under the king's direction with the whole work of central or national administration. During the reign of Henry I. this inner council, known as the curia regis, was organized by Bishop Roger of Salisbury into a strong judicial and ministerial body, whose methodical procedure imposed upon the despotic powers of the crown the restraints at least of administrative routine. In this reign the financial side of the curia, now called for the first time the exchequer, was definitely organized, and before it the whole financial administration of the kingdom passed in review.[2] The vast power thus consolidated in the hands of the crown through the centralization of finance was soon augmented by the centralization of justice.[3] Not until after the Norman conquest did the tendency in that direction grow strong enough to enable the king's court seriously to encroach upon the ancient local and popular courts. Not until the principle was firmly established that the king was the fountain of justice, and that all courts were the king's courts, did it become possible for the king to invade with his writ any jurisdiction and to withdraw from it any cause whatsoever. Through the instrumentality of the writ process in its various forms, the curia regis persistently encroached upon the popular and franchise courts, until the main body of judicial business was finally withdrawn from them into the royal tribunals. This vast concentration of powers around the person of the king, this constant withdrawal of jurisdiction from the local and popular courts into a single central and royal court,

Centralization of justice and finance.

[1] As to the double origin of William's kingship, see above, pp. 232–234.

[2] As to the growth of the inner council, see above, p. 242.

[3] For the history of the centralization of justice, see above, p. 257.

naturally and necessarily resulted in vesting in the Norman system of central administration as embodied in the crown an abnormal preponderance both in power and authority. Out of this condition of things arose the gravest political problem to which the constitutional growth of the English nation has ever given birth. That problem was so to limit the royal authority, so to combine the vigorous Norman system of central administration with the laxer system of Old-English local freedom, as to preserve the counterpoise between the two, and at the same time retain in the new combination the strongest elements of both. In the effort to work out this result the prolonged and bitter struggle for the charters had its birth. But it must not be supposed that the leaders in this struggle upon the part of the nation against the crown were political theorists intent upon bringing about a readjustment of the forces of government upon abstract lines to be drawn in paper constitutions. They were practical statesmen and patriots intent upon the redress of existing evils by winning back under new forms a part at least of the ancient freedom which the nation as a whole had lost. The struggle for the charters did not grow out of any vague apprehension of possible evils which might arise out of the unequal adjustment of the Norman system of central administration to the Old-English system of local freedom embodied in the township, the hundred, and the shire. Neither did it grow out of the mere possession, by wise and politic princes of the type of Henry I. and his grandson Henry II., of vast and unlimited powers which were never deliberately employed for purposes of oppression merely. Not until the grinding weight of the central and royal authority was actually and wantonly applied by careless despots to the oppression of all classes and conditions of men did the collective people, in the persons of the three estates, rise up as one man to grapple with the crown in a struggle for the establishment of rights which were made eternal. The two parties to the contest, whose history is now to be recounted, are therefore the central or royal authority upon the one hand, and the nation, marshalled in the ranks of the three estates, upon the other.

2. Having briefly reviewed the growth of the royal authority, it next becomes necessary to summarize the causes which

Origin and character of the struggle for the charters.

led to the division and classification of the nation in three Rise of the three estates, — the clergy, the baronage, and the commons.
estates.   The growth of the system of estates in England
was simply a part of a general movement which constitutes
an important epoch in the constitutional history of Europe.[1]
The causes which brought about the establishment of the
estate system were general in their operation, and in each
one of the European countries the result was reached about
the same time. The complete establishment of the system
is generally regarded by the historians as the work of the
thirteenth century. During that period was established in
Europe that type of a national assembly into which the
several classes or orders of society entered in the form of
definitely organized estates.[2]   The estate system itself con- Estate system defined.
sisted of the division of a nation into definite classes or
orders of men ; the outcome of the system was that type of
a national assembly in which each class or order appeared in
person or by representatives.[3]   In each country the system
has its special or local history, but as a general rule in all of
the European constitutions the three political factors are
arranged upon substantially the same principle. In the
history of the English nation the three estates appear as the Clergy, baronage, and commons, and not king, lords, and commons.
clergy, the baronage, and the commons, and not, as is often
erroneously stated, as the king, lords, and commons.[4]   In the
language of the Lords' Report, " In England . . . the clergy
have been esteemed one estate, the peers of the realm the
second estate, and the commons of the realm, represented in
parliament by persons chosen by certain electors, a third
estate." [5]   According to no mediæval theory of government
could the king be considered an estate of the realm.[6]   The

---

[1] See *Comparative Politics*, p. 230 *seq.*, and p. 233.

[2] " Notwithstanding the difference of circumstances and the variety of results, it is to this period that we must refer, in each country of Europe, the introduction, or the consolidation, for the first time since feudal principles had forced their way into the machinery of government, of national assemblies composed of properly arranged and organized estates." — Stubbs, *Const. Hist.*, vol. ii. pp. 159, 168.

[3] " The lower house of parliament is not, in proper language, an estate of the realm, but rather the image and

representative of the commons of England." — Hallam, *M. A.*, vol. iii. p. 102, and note 2.

[4] An argument in favor of this obsolete view may be found in Whitelocke's work on the *Parliamentary Writ*, vol. ii. p. 43.

[5] Vol. i. p. 118.

[6] " The king is not an estate, because there is no class or order of kings, the king being one person alone by himself. The proper phrase is the king and the three estates of the realm." — Freeman, *Growth of the English Constitution*, p. 134 (Tauchnitz ed.).

several classes into which the nation was divided represented the estates, and over all stood the king, not as a coördinate political factor, but as the head of the state itself. As Chancellor Stillington quaintly expressed it, in the 7th of Edward IV., "This land standeth by three states, and above that one principal, that is, to wit, lords spiritual, lords temporal, and commons, and over that state-royal, as our sovereign lord the king." [1]

As, in obedience to a pious courtesy, precedence was always conceded to the clergy in the arrangement of estates, the causes will be first examined which led to their withdrawal from the main body of the nation, and to their organization into a distinct estate or order. The fact has been more than once pointed out that the distinctive feature in the history of the church before the Conquest was its perfect oneness with the state. Throughout the pre-Norman period the same legislative and judicial assemblies dealt alike with ecclesiastical and temporal business without the slightest jealousy or conflict of authority. The witan legislated for the church as it did for the state, and in the witan the bishop as well as the ealdorman was elected and deposed. In the shire-moot the bishop and the ealdorman sat side by side as its constitutional presidents, and in the ancient popular courts there was no separation of secular from spiritual business.[2] The

natural result of the deposition of the native English bishops which followed the Norman conquest, and the promotion of foreign prelates to their vacant thrones, was to draw the English church from its position of practical independence and isolation into closer communion with the rest of Western Christendom, and into more direct dependence upon the see of Rome. Out of this closer connection with Rome grew the tendency that now began to manifest itself to sever the organization of the church from that of the state.[3] Upon the papal throne now sat one of the greatest of the Roman pontiffs, Gregory VII., the leading ideas of whose policy were the complete establishment of the supremacy of the

---

[1] *Rot. Parl.*, vol. v. p. 622. The treaty of Staples, in 1492 was to be confirmed "per tres status regni Angliæ ritè et debitè convocatos, videlicet per prelatos et clerum, nobiles, et commu-nitates ejusdem regni." — Rymer, vol. xiii. p. 508 ; *Middle Ages*, vol. iii. p. 103.

[2] Upon this whole subject see above, pp. 187, 200.

[3] See above, p. 259.

papacy within the church, and the supremacy of the ecclesiastical over the civil power.   In order to make effectual the assertion of the supremacy of the church over the state, Gregory labored to bring about "the establishment of the clergy as a distinct order, animated by one universal corporate spirit, and cut off from those ties of citizenship and kindred which bind men together in earthly bonds."[1]   Through the agency of the foreign prelates the ecclesiastical policy which was now impressing itself upon the whole of Western Christendom was brought directly to bear upon the organization of the English church.   The new ecclesiastical policy organized by William and Lanfranc contemplated the complete severance of spiritual from temporal business through the creation of distinct courts and councils in which the church could judge and legislate upon its own affairs without secular interference.   By an express enactment William and his witan decreed the separation of the spiritual from the temporal tribunals.   This ordinance, after declaring the episcopal laws which had previously been in force in England to be bad and contrary to the sacred canons, forbade the bishops and archbishops to bring any cause involving questions of canon law, or questions concerning the cure of souls, before the courts of the hundred.   Henceforth they are to hold courts of their own, in which causes are to be tried, not by the customary but by the canon law, and all interference by laymen in spiritual causes is expressly forbidden.[2]   In this way was brought about the organization of a distinct system of ecclesiastical courts whose jurisdiction was destined to grow and widen with the growth of the canon law.[3]   The growth of this new system of law not only gave to the clergy

Marginal notes:

Gregory VII.'s effort to make the clergy a distinct order.

Ecclesiastical policy of William and Lanfranc.

Growth of the canon law.

---

[1] Freeman, *Norm. Conq.*, vol. iv. p. 287.

[2] As to the ordinance separating the spiritual from the temporal courts, see above, p. 260.

[3] For the general history of the canon law in England, cf. Hale's *Hist. of the Common Law*, ch. ii.; Reeves' *Hist. of the English Law*, chs. xxv., xxvi. (Finlason ed.); Burn's *Ecclesiastical Law*; Phillimore's *Ecclesiastical Law of the Church of Eng.*; Stubbs, *Const. Hist.*, vol. i. p. 284; vol. ii. pp. 170, 171; vol. iii. p. 321.   The canon law is of no intrinsic obligation in England.   "All the strength that either the papal or imperial laws have obtained in this realm, or indeed in any other kingdom in Europe, is only because they have been admitted and received by immemorial usage, . . . or else because they are in some cases introduced by consent of parliament." — Blackstone, *Com.*, vol. i. pp. 79, 80.   And yet it is one of the sources of the common law; from it has been drawn, for instance, the rules regulating the descent of real property.

a more distinct civil status than they had ever possessed before, but it ultimately drew into the spiritual courts a mass of business with which the church had heretofore had only a remote connection.   Out of this new order of things soon grew up claims upon the part of churchmen to exemption from all temporal jurisdiction, and to the right of appeal to Rome, — claims which led after bitter strife to the adoption in the reign of Henry II. of the restraining measures embodied in the Constitutions of Clarendon, whose leading provisions have heretofore been drawn out.[1]   By the adoption of the Constitutions, the jurisdiction of the ecclesiastical courts was distinctly defined, and a way was found to keep them within proper limits by means of the writ of prohibition issued from the king's courts of law or equity.[2]

Ecclesiastical divisions of the kingdom:

the province;

the diocese and its subdivisions.

The ordinance of William led directly to the establishment of a distinct system of spiritual courts, whose difficult history cannot be at all clearly explained without reference to the ecclesiastical divisions into which the kingdom as a whole is subdivided.   Ecclesiastically England is divided into the two provinces of Canterbury and York, whose subdivisions closely coincide with the subdivisions of the kingdom itself. As the shire is the largest and most important division of the kingdom, so the diocese is the largest and most important division of the province.[3]   And as the shire-moots were the most important local courts in the kingdom, so the diocesan councils were the most important local courts in the church.   "These were the county courts and the burghmots of the church, and were composed of the bishop and his superior clergy, the archdeacon, abbots, deacons, and sometimes of 'all the *clerici*' and the laity."[4]   As out of the ancient county court held by the king's judges in the shire was slowly developed the modern court of assize, so out of the diocesan council was developed, by a process whose history is somewhat obscure, the consistory court held by each dio-

---

[1] As to the concordat embodied in the Constitution see above, p. 287.

[2] Bigelow, *Hist. of Procedure*, pp. 52, 53.   "From this time an inveterate animosity subsisted between the two courts, the vestiges of which have only been effaced by the liberal wisdom of

modern ages." — Hallam, *M. A.*, vol. iii. p. 129.

[3] As to the early history of the ecclesiastical divisions, see above, pp. 260, 261.

[4] Bigelow, *Hist. of Procedure*, p. 28; Smith, *Dict. Christ. Antiq.*, title "Council."

cesan bishop for the trial of all ecclesiastical causes arising in his diocese.[1] The subdivisions of the diocese roughly correspond with those of the county. As each county is divided into hundreds, and each hundred into townships, so each diocese is divided into archdeaconries, each archdeaconry into rural deaneries, and each deanery into parishes. The unit of organization in each is the same,—the parish, as a general rule, simply representing the township in its ecclesiastical aspect.[2]

The most inferior court in the ecclesiastical system is the archdeacon's court, the hundred court of the church, whose jurisdiction is sometimes concurrent with, and sometimes exclusive of, the jurisdiction of the consistory court. From the archdeacon's court an appeal lies to the bishop's court.[3] *Archdeacon's court.*

Next in the ascending scale is the consistory court held by each diocesan bishop for the trial, as before stated, of all ecclesiastical causes arising in his diocese. In this court the bishop's chancellor or commissary is the judge, from whose decree an appeal lies to the archbishop's court.[4] *The bishop's court.*

In the province of Canterbury the archbishop's court is known as the court of the arches, from the name of the church (*Sancta Maria de arcubus*) in which the court was anciently held. The judge of this court — the dean of the arches — hears and determines appeals from all inferior courts in the province. The court of peculiars is a branch of the court of arches, whose jurisdiction extends over all those parishes in the province of Canterbury which are exempt from the bishop's jurisdiction and subject to the metropolitan only. *The archbishop's court.* *Court of peculiars.*

From the archbishop's court, after the final extinction of the right of appeal to Rome, an appeal lay to the king in chancery, that is, to a court of delegates appointed by the king's commission under the great seal, by virtue of the statute 25 Henry VIII., c. 19, until the partial repeal of that statute by statute 2 & 3 Will. IV., c. 92, whereby such appeals were transferred to the king in council.[5] The ecclesias- *Court of delegates.*

---

[1] "The history of the development of these councils, and of the settlement of their judicial functions, resulting in a fixed tribunal of the English constitution, is very obscure." — Bigelow, *Hist. of Procedure*, p. 28.

[2] As to the relations between the parish and the township, see above, p. 143.

[3] By virtue of the statute 24 Hen. VIII., c. 12. Cf. Blackstone, *Com.*, bk. iii. p. 64.

[4] Ibid.

[5] See Wendell's Blackstone, bk. iii. p. 66, note 5.

System of appeal.

tical system of appeal as thus finally settled corresponds with the scheme contained in the eighth chapter of the Constitutions of Clarendon, wherein it was provided that appeals in spiritual causes ought to be from the archdeacon to the bishop, from the bishop to the archbishop, and from the archbishop to the king, without whose special license they could proceed no further.[1]

Matrimonial and testamentary causes.

One of the most important elements of jurisdiction immemorially vested in the ecclesiastical courts was the right to hear and determine matrimonial and testamentary causes.[2] This jurisdiction was taken away from them and vested in other tribunals by statutes 20 & 21 Vict., c. 77, § 3, c. 85, § 2; 21 & 22 Vict., c. 95, whereby the judicial authority of the spiritual courts was reduced to the consideration of such matters only as legitimately arise out of the administration of the affairs of the national church.

The new system of ecclesiastical councils.

The same general causes which led to the organization of a distinct system of ecclesiastical courts led to the organization of a distinct system of ecclesiastical councils. Such a severance had occasionally occurred before the Conquest, but the custom was looked upon with such disfavor as to evoke in the reign of Æthelred a solemn condemnation in a formal decree of a national assembly.[3] Under the new theories to which the Conquest gave birth, the holding of distinct ecclesiastical councils, so far from exciting condemnation, received open and positive approval. During the primacy of Lanfranc the holding of such councils, which were held at the same time as the regular gemots, became frequent. It was, however, no part of William's policy to allow to these ecclesiastical assemblies the right to legislate without limitation ; he did not permit such assemblies "to enact or prohibit anything but what was agreeable to his will and had first been ordained by him." Under these circumstances, and subject to such limitations, the national councils of the English

---

[1] "De appellationibus si emerserint, ab archidiacono debent procedere ad episcopum, ab episcopo ad archiepiscopum. Et si archiepiscopus defecerit in justitia exhibenda, ad dominum regem perveniendum est postremo, ut præcepto ipsius in curia archiepiscopi controversia terminetur, ita quod non debet ulterius procedere absque assensu domini regis."

[2] See Bigelow, *Hist. of Procedure,* pp. 51–53 ; *Placita Ang.-Norm.,* p. 311.

[3] Laws of Æthelred, §§ 36, 37, 38; Thorpe, vol. i. p. 340; Freeman, *Norm. Conq.,* vol. i. p. 248.

church became distinct bodies from the national parliaments.[1]
It must not be supposed, however, that it was only in national councils that the clergy met together for the purpose
of deliberation and action. In fact the existence of such
councils was of but short duration. Owing to the jealousy
and strife existing between Canterbury and York, the assembling of general councils of the whole church, after the independence of York had been vindicated by Thurstan, became
practically impossible.[2] The government of the church thus
passed to the two provincial convocations of York and Canterbury, which, as constitutional assemblies of the English
clergy, have suffered no material change of organization from
the reign of Edward I. to the present day. Each convocation is called by the writ of the archbishop directed to each
bishop in his province, commanding him to cause the clergy
of his diocese to assemble at a certain time and at a certain
place in order to select two proctors in the name of the
clergy, and one proctor for each cathedral and collegiate chapter, to appear in convocation as representatives.[3] The convocation of the province of Canterbury — originally including
bishops, abbots, priors, deans of cathedral and collegiate
churches, heads of religious houses, archdeacons, and proctors — is divided like the parliament into two houses. In the
upper house the great ecclesiastical magnates appear in their
own right; in the lower, appear the representatives of the
chapters and the clergy at large. As Blackstone has well expressed it, "the convocation is the miniature of parliament,
wherein the archbishop presides with regal state; the upper
house of bishops represents the house of lords; and the
lower house, composed of the representatives of the several
dioceses at large, and of each particular chapter therein, resembles the house of commons with its knights of the shire

Marginal notes:
National councils short-lived.

Provincial convocations: Canterbury and York.

Convocation "the miniature of parliament."

---

[1] See above, pp. 261, 262.

[2] "Only when the authority of a legate superseded for the moment the ordinary authority of both, were any
national councils of the church summoned." — Stubbs, *Const. Hist.*, vol. ii.
p. 198.

[3] The rule which finally determined
the basis of representation was embodied in the writ through which was
called a convocation which met at the
New Temple after Easter, 1283. — Wil-

kins, *Concilia*, ii. 93. The rule then
adopted was soon after accepted as a
canon. — Ibid., ii. 49. But the writs
through which the metropolitans convene the provincial convocations must
not be confounded with the king's
writs to the bishops individually, commanding through the "*præmunientes*"
clause the attendance of the proctors
in parliament. See Hody's *History of
Convocations*, p. 12.

and burgesses."[1] The practice of representation makes its appearance about the same time in the church councils and in the parliament,[2] and the two systems of representation develop side by side. From the Conquest down to the Reformation, the clergy as a spiritual organization, when assembled in convocation, possessed the power to legislate for the general government of the church, subject to such restrictions, limitations, or warnings as the king or the parliament might from time to time impose. Through the vicissitudes of the Reformation the English church passed with its legislative power substantially unimpaired. In the words of Mr. Gladstone: "The Reformation statutes did not leave the convocation in the same condition relatively to the crown as the parliament. It was under more control, but its inherent and independent power was thereby more directly recognized. The king was not head of convocation ; it was not merely his council. The archbishop was its head, and summoned and prorogued it. It was not power, but leave, that this body had to seek from the crown to make canons. A canon without the royal assent was already a canon, though without the force of law ; but a bill which has passed the two houses is without a force of any kind until that assent is given. Again, the royal assent is given to canons in the gross, to bills one by one, which well illustrates the difference between the control in the one case and the actuating and moving power in the other."[3]

As the administration of the vast powers which were vested in the separate courts and councils of the mediæval church was substantially controlled by the bishops themselves, who also possessed no inconsiderable weight in the councils of the king, it is by no means strange that the right of appointment to the episcopal office should have become the subject of earnest contention between the crown, the papacy, and the clergy of the national church. In the early days of Christianity

Its power to legislate.

Mr. Gladstone's view.

Election of bishops.

---

[1] *Com.*, bk. i. p. 279.

[2] As early as 1255 proctors of the parochial clergy appear in parliament at Westminster. — *Ann. Burton*, p. 360. See Hody's *Hist. of Convocations*, p. 345; Hallam, *M. A.*, vol. iii. p. 126. Bishop Stubbs does not think it clear, however, that the representative principle was at that time regarded "as an

integral part of the system of convocation." He considers that the rule for representation in convocation was first definitely fixed by the action of Archbishop Peckham in 1283. — *Const. Hist.*, vol. ii. p. 197.

[3] See Gladstone on the Royal Supremacy, p. 31.

the right to elect a bishop was, as a general rule, jointly vested in the clergy and people belonging to the city or diocese over which he was called to rule. By degrees the laity were excluded from any real participation, first in the Greek and finally in the Western church.[1] The right to join in the election which was thus withdrawn from the people was not vested in the general body of the diocesan clergy, but in the council of priests and deacons, which originally stood in the closest relation to the bishop, constituting what came to be known as the chapter of the cathedral church.[2] By the twelfth century these little senates or councils annexed to the cathedral churches had succeeded in winning for themselves throughout Christendom a monopoly of the right to make episcopal appointments.[3] In the English kingdom during the entire pre-Norman period the bishops were elected by the clergy and the laity acting conjointly in the national assembly, — it being the joint right of the king and the witan to appoint prelates to vacant sees.[4] During the latter part of this period, however, instances occur of the assertion of the right of capitular election. In the case of Ælfric and Robert in 1050 it is clear that the monks and canons of a cathedral church made an election in canonical form, and then petitioned the king and his witan to confer the bishopric upon their nominee.[5] Although at the time of the Conquest the tendency was in another direction, it suited the first two Norman kings to cling to the earlier custom. Not until the reign of Henry I. did the right to elect the bishops finally pass from the king and the witan to the chapters of the cathedral churches.[6] The right of election which thus passed to the

Origin of chapters.

Election of English bishops in the early days.

---

[1] Marca, *De Concordantia*, etc., l. vi. c. 2; Schmidt, t. iv. p. 173; Hallam, *M. A.*, vol. ii. p. 172 and notes. The clergy no doubt took the leading part in the election, but the ratification of the people was necessary to render it valid. See Father Paul on Benefices, c. 7.

[2] As to the origin of chapters, see Rev. Canon Venable's article on "Cathedrals," in *Enc. Brit.*, vol. v. p. 227, 9th ed.

[3] Fr. Paul's treatise on Benefices, c. 24; *Middle Ages*, vol. ii. p. 183 and note 2.

[4] Kemble's sixth canon states the

rule to be this: "The king and the witan had power to appoint prelates to vacant sees." — *Saxons in Eng.*, vol. ii. p. 221. As to the actual practice in particular cases, see Stubbs, *Const. Hist.*, vol. i. p. 134.

[5] As to the history of this case, see Freeman, *Norm. Conq.*, vol. ii. p. 386 (Appendix I). In this appendix the whole question of the appointment of bishops and abbots in the early days is fully discussed.

[6] "The struggle between Henry I. and Anselm on the question of investiture terminated in a compromise which placed the election in the hands of the

Their elec-
tion after
the Con-
quest.

chapters was coupled with a serious limitation in favor of the
royal authority. It was required that the choice of the chapter should be preceded by the royal license, and that it should
be followed by the presentment of the bishop-elect for the
royal approval. The necessity for the royal license preserved
in substance to the crown the right of nomination. Under
the old system the crown possessed the right to press its
nominee upon the witan ; under the new, to press its nominee
upon the chapter. But the bishop-elect, even after his due
appointment by the chapter, and after the giving of the royal
assent to his consecration, could not enter into the possession
of the temporalities attached to his office without the act of
the king as his feudal lord and sovereign. As the process of
feudalization advanced, the estates of a bishop or abbot came
to be looked upon as a fief or benefice held of the king by

The ques-
tion of in-
vestiture.

the tenure of military service.[1] It therefore became necessary under feudal ideas that the bishop-elect should be invested (from "*vestire*," to put in possession) by his lord with
the feudal estates annexed to his office. Upon the death of
a bishop the ring and staff, the symbols of episcopal jurisdiction, were delivered to the king by a deputation from the
chapter. When the vacancy was filled, these symbols were
returned to the new incumbent as evidence of the fact that
he had been fully invested by the king with his temporal possessions. Such was the general rule of investiture which
prevailed throughout Christendom down to the famous controversy between the pope and the emperor which was finally

Concordat
of Worms,
1122.

settled by the concordat of Worms (1122), wherein it was
agreed, " on the one hand, that the emperor should surrender
to the church the right of investiture by ring and staff, grant
to the clergy throughout the empire the right to free election,
and restore the possessions and feudal sovereignties which
had been seized during the wars in his father's time and his
own ; while on the other hand it was conceded by the pope
that all elections of bishops and abbots should take place in
the presence of the emperor or his commissioners, and that
every bishop-elect in Germany should receive, by the touch
of the sceptre, all the temporal rights, principalities, and posses-

chapters of the cathedrals," etc. —   [1] See above, p. 271.
Stubbs, *Const. Hist.*, vol. iii. p. 295.

sions of the see, excepting those which were held immediately of Rome."[1] The continental quarrel upon the subject of investitures which was thus settled by the concordat of Worms was fought out in England between Anselm and Henry I. Under the influence of the decrees of the Lateran Council (1099) Anselm felt obliged to refuse to do homage to Henry, or to consecrate the bishops whom Henry had invested according to the ancient custom. After years of serious controversy a compromise was reached in 1107 wherein it was agreed that the king should give up the right of investiture by the ring and staff, — symbols of spiritual jurisdiction, — and should accept in lieu thereof from the bishop a promise of fealty and homage before he should receive the temporalities of his office. It was further agreed that the election of bishops should be vested in the chapters of the cathedral churches, subject to the royal right of license or nomination.[2] This right of canonical election, which was confirmed by Stephen at his accession,[3] was recognized in turn by Henry II. and Richard I., and finally by John in a charter issued to the church a short time before the granting of the Great Charter itself.[4]

Anselm and Henry I.

An archbishop, even after his election by the cathedral chapter, and after the reception of the temporalities from the king as feudal lord, could not consider himself fully inducted into office until his right had finally been confirmed by the see of Rome. The right of the papacy to a voice or influence in episcopal appointments was first asserted in the case of archbishops, who in early times were expected to make a journey to Rome for the purpose of being invested with the pallium, — the emblem of metropolitan power, — without which no archbishop could safely venture to perform the highest functions of his office.[5] Upon the receipt of the pallium the metropolitan took an oath of obedience to the pope, with

Rome and the pallium.

---

[1] See *Enc. Brit.*, vol. xiii. p. 201, article on "Investiture."

[2] For the history of the quarrel between Henry and Anselm, see Freeman, *Norm. Conq.*, vol. v. pp. 95, 127, 146, 237; Stubbs, *Const. Hist.*, vol. iii. pp. 295, 296.

[3] For Stephen's charter see *Statutes of the Realm: Charters of Liberties*, p. 3.

[4] For John's charters, see ibid. p. 5.

[5] Lingard, *Anglo-Saxon Church*, p. 205. Gregory and his immediate successor excused the English metropolitans from so long a journey, and sent the pall by messengers. — Wilkins, *Concilia*, pp. 32, 35. See, also, Stubbs, *Registrum Sacrum Anglicanum*, pp. 140, 141.

whom he entered into the closest relations.   Not until the
thirteenth century was the papal influence brought to bear
directly upon appointments to suffragan sees.   This influence

was chiefly asserted through the medium of appeals to the
papal court in disputed elections, which constantly arose, not
only out of disputes between the clergy themselves, but out
of the attempts upon the part of the crown to force upon the
chapters the selection of royal nominees.   In such cases,
prior to the famous controversy which followed the death
of Archbishop Hubert Walter, the popes had contented
themselves with rejecting unfit candidates, and with passing
upon the canonical validity of elections.[1]   Upon the death of

Hubert a controversy as to the future incumbent of Canterbury was brought on between John and Innocent III., which
led to the assertion upon the part of the papacy of claims of
a far more aggressive character.   The bearings of this famous
controversy will be considered hereafter.

The causes have now been briefly reviewed which brought
about in England after the Conquest the establishment of the
clergy as a distinct and privileged " body completely organized, with a minutely constituted and regular hierarchy, possessing the right of legislating for itself and taxing itself,
having its recognized assemblies, judicature, and executive,
and although not as a legal corporation holding common property, yet composed of a great number of persons each of whom
possesses corporate property by a title which is either conferred by ecclesiastical authority or is not to be acquired without ecclesiastical consent.   Such an organization entitles the
clergy to the name of a ' communitas,' although it does not
complete the legal idea of a corporation proper." [2]   The principle of cohesion which thus united the church as a spiritual
organization grew out of that universal corporate spirit which
was everywhere animating the clergy of Western Christendom.   The force of that corporate spirit was organized and
strengthened by the growth of the canon law, in which the
expanding claims of the clergy were distinctly defined, and
by the application of that system by the clergy themselves,
in their own courts and councils, to the maintenance and

---

[1] See Stubbs, *Const. Hist.*, vol. iii.
pp. 303-305.

[2] Stubbs, *Const. History*, vol. iii. p.
290.

advancement of the rights and privileges of their order. Thus organized and equipped for action, the clergy entered as one of the leading constitutional factors into the prolonged struggle for the charters. In that struggle, as we shall see hereafter, while the clergy as a body were intent upon the assertion of their special rights and immunities, — foremost among which was the right to tax themselves in their own councils, — they were at the same time animated by a broad spirit of generous patriotism. Throughout the struggle of the nation against the crown, in the corporate person of the church, English freedom found a stern and resolute defender. "The historians of the age, all of them churchmen, most of them monks, are all but unanimous on the popular side. Prelates like the Primate Stephen, like Robert Grosseteste of Lincoln and Walter Cantelupe of Worcester, were foremost in the good cause ; the two latter were among the closest friends and counsellors of the patriot earl," [1] Simon of Montfort.

Having stated the causes which impelled the clergy to withdraw from the main body of the nation, and to incorporate themselves into a spiritual organization which finally takes, for a time at least, its constitutional place as an estate of the realm ; or, in other words, having explained how the line was drawn between the clergy and the laity, — the more difficult task remains to draw out the causes which led to the division of the laity themselves into the two estates of the baronage and the commons. From the reign of Edward I. down to the present day, the estate of the baronage or peerage has been identical with the house of lords.[2] The hereditary and official counsellors of the crown who constitute the upper house of parliament represent in their own persons the entire estate of the baronage, — they do not represent a wider noble class or caste of which they themselves are but

Estate of the baronage, —

identical with the house of lords.

---

[1] Freeman, *Growth of the Eng. Constitution*, p. 112.

[2] The Lords' committee conclude, "that from the twenty-third of Edward the First to the fifteenth of Edward the Second, the legislative assemblies of the country appear to have been generally, but not always, constituted nearly in the manner in which the assembly in the twenty-third of Edward the First was constituted ; that they at length consisted, as they now consist, of two distinct bodies, having different characters, rights, and duties, and generally distinguished by the appellations Lords and Commons ; the lords being all personally summoned by special writs, but distinguished among themselves as spiritual and temporal." — *Report on the Dignity of a Peer*, vol. i. p. 390.

a part. The only nobleman known to English law is he who holds the hereditary office of a peer. The right to inherit such an office the law concedes to the peer's eldest son, but it concedes no other rights to his children. The children of a peer — even the future holder of the peerage himself while the father lives — are, in the eyes of the law, commoners and nothing more. The crown may ennoble any one, but the nobility so granted belongs only to that member of the family so ennobled, — to the actual owner of the peerage himself.

Distinction between English and continental nobility. In this fact lies the marked distinction between nobility as it has existed in England and nobility as it has existed in those continental lands in which the privileges of the noble were permitted to extend to all his children and their children forever. The theory that mere nobility of blood conveys political rights or privileges has never been recognized in the English system.[1] As the hereditary peers of the realm, in conjunction with the lords spiritual, — whose special status will hereafter be explained, — constituted the entire estate of the baronage, and as the estate of the baronage is identical with the house of lords, it follows that the history of the one is the history of the other.

The witan survives as the house of lords. It is a distinctive feature in the political history of the English nation that there has never been a time when it has been without a national assembly ; the ancient witenagemot has never ceased to exist ; it has never lost its corporate identity. Despite the changes of constitution and of name through which it has passed, it still survives in the person of the house of lords. In the language of one of the masters of English history, "the house of lords not only springs out of, it actually is, the ancient witenagemot." [2] The fact of this corporate identity can only be grasped through an examination of the process through which the Old-English national assembly was transformed into the feudal councils of the Norman and Angevin reigns ; then by a further examination of the process through which, out of these Norman and Angevin councils, was finally developed, by the practice of sum-

---

[1] For a full statement of the differ-ence between English and foreign no-bility, see Freeman, *Growth of the Eng. Constitution*, pp. 125–129 ; Stubbs, *Const. Hist.*, vol. ii. pp. 176–178.

[2] Freeman, *Growth of the Eng. Con-stitution*, p. 91. See, also, *Comparative Politics*, p. 232.

mons, the hereditary chamber of the national parliament. An examination has been heretofore made of the history of the witan, whether considered as the supreme council of an heptarchic state, or as the supreme council of the whole English nation when finally united in a single consolidated kingdom.[1] After the coming of William the continuity of the old national assembly went on unbroken ; the witan remained as before the national council of the king, and during William's reign it retained much of its earlier character.[2] Of the constitution of the witan, either before or after the Conquest we have no direct or formal account, but the highest authorities substantially agree in the conclusion that on all ordinary occasions the witan was a comparatively small gathering of great men, while on extraordinary occasions the assembly was sometimes reinforced by large popular bodies from every part of the kingdom. "According to one view, the assembly was in theory open to every freeman, but in practice only a small class habitually attended. According to the other view, it was in theory confined to a small class, but in practice it was ever and anon thrown open to large classes of men besides its usual members. . . . The practical aspect of the two doctrines is the same."[3] But although the witan, under the name of the great council, outlived the Conquest, and although in legal theory it retained all of its old powers, yet the fact remains that the constitution of the assembly underwent a great practical transformation. At the beginning of William's reign, those who composed the council that ordinarily gathered around the king were a body of Englishmen ; by the end of his reign this body had gradually changed into an assembly of Normans, among whom an Englishman here and there held his place. This change naturally resulted from the character of the Conquest itself. Through William's policy of confiscation and regrant, nearly all of the great estates passed from English to Norman hands ; and in the same way all of the great offices in church and state were parcelled out among his followers. The king's thegns thus

Continuity of the witan.

Practical transformation wrought by the Conquest.

---

[1] See above, pp. 147, 148.
[2] See above, p. 241.
[3] Mr. Freeman thus states the difference, if difference there be, between his own views and those of Bishop Stubbs, as to the constitution of the witenagemot. See *Norm. Conq.*, vol. v. p. 273. For the Bishop's views, see *Const. Hist.*, vol. i. p. 121.

became his tenants-in-chief, holding their lands from him as
The ancient
assembly
becomes
the king's
court of
feudal vas-
sals. their lord.   Through this feudalizing process the ancient
national assembly of great men gradually became the king's
court of feudal vassals, whose right to exercise power was
made to depend practically upon the king's pleasure.[1]   Under
Henry II. and his sons, the national council, which was now
summoned at regular intervals, attained to a definiteness of
organization which it had never possessed before.   Its composition was that of a perfect feudal court, — an assembly of
archbishops, bishops, abbots, priors, earls, barons, knights,
and freeholders.   The constituent members of the assembly
are the same as under the Norman kings, but greater prominence and a more definite position is now assigned to the
minor tenants-in-chief.   In the days of Henry of Anjou, as
in the days of Eadward and of William, an ordinary meeting
of the national assembly embraced only the witan, the great
men of the kingdom ; while on an extraordinary occasion it
might embrace, besides these, not only the tenants-in-chief,
The prac-
tice of sum-
mons, but the whole body of freeholders.   Through the influence
of the practice of summons, to whose origin an exact date
cannot be assigned, the tendency was fast gaining ground to
limit the national assembly to those only who were summoned
by the king's writ either personally or in a body.[2]   The writs
of summons were of two kinds : first, such as were specially
addressed to those great personages whose presence was necessary, and who were summoned as a matter of course ;
second, such as were addressed generally to the sheriff of
each shire, requiring him to summon in a body the lesser
landowners.   How far this practice of summons, which was
in active operation in the time of Henry II., had developed
up to the sixteenth year of the reign of John, can be defi-
as defined
by the
Great Char-
ter. nitely ascertained from the fourteenth article of the Great
Charter, which provides that, "to have the common counsel
of the kingdom, we will cause to be summoned the archbishops, bishops, abbots, earls, and greater barons singly by
our letters ; and besides we will cause to be summoned in
general by our sheriffs and bailiffs all those who hold of us in
chief."[3]   By this clause, which no doubt expressed the then

[1] See above, p. 242.   [3] The Lords' Committee report,
[2] See above, pp. 289–291.   " That the Great Charter of John is

existing practice, the qualification for membership in the national assembly was at last distinctly defined, and that qualification naturally assumed a feudal shape. No one was expected to attend unless he was summoned, and no one was summoned unless he was a tenant-in-chief. By the form of the summons, a line was also distinctly drawn between two different classes of men, — between the magnates, who were entitled to a personal summons, and the main body of tenants-in-chief, who were summoned generally in the shires : in this way the distinction between lords and commons begins.

The greater tenants-in-chief, who received personal summons to the national council, and whose right to receive such personal summons became hereditary, represent, together with the lords spiritual, the peerage of England.[1] Every peer, whether temporal or spiritual, holds, or is supposed to hold, an ancient barony directly of the king.[2] The theory is that the holding of an estate by the peculiar tenure of barony was the original qualification which entitled the tenant-in-chief to the right of personal summons,[3] — "the baronage of the thirteenth century was the body of tenants-in-chief holding a fief or a number of fiefs consolidated into a baronial honor or qualification."[4] The difficult matter, in the absence of any early enfeoffment of a barony, is to determine what elements were necessary to constitute the baronial honor or estate. Although the characteristics and attributes of the baronial tenure have been made the subject of special investigations by Selden,[5] Madox,[6] Hallam,[7] and Stubbs,[8] no precise or satisfactory definition of a barony has resulted from the

Every peer supposed to hold a barony directly of the king.

Nature of the baronial tenure.

---

the earliest document of which authentic evidence remains, from which the constitution of that legislative assembly called the king's great council, or the great council of the realm, can be, with any degree of certainty, collected ; . . . that that assembly consisted of certain persons who by that charter were required to be personally summoned by the king's writ, and of other persons who by that charter were allowed to be summoned generally, and not personally." — *Lords' Report*, vol. i. p. 389.

[1] No reference is here made to life peerage, which will be separately considered hereafter.

[2] But the simple holding by barony was not of itself a sufficient ground for requiring attendance in parliament ; a writ of summons did not necessarily follow tenure by barony. — *Lords' Report*, vol. i. pp. 326, 342. Cf. *Blackstone*, bk. i. p. 156, as to the baronial tenure of the lords spiritual.

[3] Hallam, *Middle Ages*, vol. iii. pp. 9, 117.

[4] Stubbs, *Const. Hist.*, vol. ii. p. 178.

[5] Selden's Works, vol. iii. pp. 713–743.

[6] *Baronia Anglica.*

[7] *Middle Ages*, vol. iii. pp. 9–14, 117–119.

[8] *Const. Hist.*, vol. ii. pp. 178–184.

inquiry. The writer last named cautiously concludes that the definitions of law recognize rather than create the character of barony; that that estate, however acquired, was a

Barony by summons. barony which entitled its owner to a personal summons to the council of the king; that the baronage was ultimately defined and recognized as an estate of the realm by the royal action in summons, writ, and patent. But the status of the peer was not fully established by the mere reception of the king's writ; it was upon the hereditary right to receive the writ that the status of the peer ultimately depended. The hereditary right to receive the king's writ, rather than the tenure which was the original qualification for the writ, represents the constitutional basis upon which the peerage now

Feudal rule of primogeniture. reposes. As the process of feudalization advanced, the inherent power of the crown to determine who should be summoned as barons gradually became subject to the limitation imposed by the feudal rule of primogeniture. It is generally conceded that certainly during the reign of Edward I. the right of a baron — whose ancestor had once been summoned and had once sat in parliament — to claim the hereditary right to be so summoned was clearly and definitely estab-

The right to be summoned becomes hereditary. lished. The peers of the realm who thus acquired the hereditary right to be summoned, together with the lords spiritual, constitute the estate of the peerage which is identical with the house of lords.[1]

The lords spiritual. The political status of the lords spiritual, which was at one time involved in some confusion, has of late years been placed upon a broad and rational basis. It was for a long time contended that the spiritual lords sat in parliament by virtue of their baronial tenures only, and not by virtue of that older and higher right upon which the baronial status was simply superimposed. The fact has been pointed out over and over again that in the Old-English witan the prelates sat with the other magnates of the realm as constituent elements in the national assembly. The Conquest wrought no formal change in this condition of things, apart from that general process of change through which the witan itself was silently transformed into a feudal council. In the process of feudalization the church in its temporal relations was directly in-

---

[1] Courthope, *Hist. Peerage*, p. xli.; Stubbs, *Const. Hist.*, vol. ii. p. 184.

volved. The system of feudal law which Flambard seems to have worked into a definite and formal shape was applied by him with equal severity to all feudatories, temporal and spiritual. The estate of a bishop or abbot came to be regarded as a fief or benefice held personally of the king by the tenure of military service. When a vacancy occurred, as there was no heir who could demand seisin, the king took the fief into his own hands until he saw fit to admit a successor. The profits of the vacancy and the payment from the successor were the equivalents which the church paid for being exempt from the ordinary feudal exactions which fell upon the estates of laymen.[1] In this way the bishops and abbots were made to assume the relation of tenants-in-chief, holding baronies of the crown "*sicut barones ceteri*," and in this way the idea grew up that the bishops and abbots sat in parliament by virtue of their baronial tenure only.[2] But the sounder view seems to be that, as a part of the witan of the realm, the prelates never lost their immemorial right to sit in the national assembly. To this ancient right was simply added the new right growing out of their feudal relations; the title of "*barones*" was simply added to that of "*sapientes*."[3] That the ancient right was never forfeited is evidenced by the fact that the guardian of the spiritualities of a vacant see, who could not pretend to a baronial qualification, received the formal summons;[4] and by the further fact that even now, when the bishops no longer hold baronies, they are still summoned to the house of lords.

If we subtract from the English nation as constituted in the thirteenth century the estate of the clergy and the estate of the baronage, the remainder represents, although in a very vague and general sense, the third estate, — the estate of the commons. From the very variety and diversity of the

Estate of a bishop or abbot regarded as a fief.

Title of "barones" added to that of "sapientes."

The estate of the commons.

---

[1] See above, p. 271.

[2] As an illustration of this view see the *Lords' Report* (vol. i. p. 393), in which the statement is made that the "dignity of bishop arises from his consecration; but he does not become a lord of parliament until invested with the temporalities of the see to which he is promoted, and until then he cannot have a writ of summons to parliament to enable him to take his seat in parliament, because his right to a seat in parliament is a franchise annexed to the temporalities of his see, and not inherent in his spiritual dignity of bishop."

[3] Freeman, *Norm. Conq.*, vol. v. p. 279; Stubbs, *Const. Hist.*, vol. ii. pp. 169, 170; Hody, *Hist. of Convocations*, p. 126.

[4] Hallam, *M. A.*, vol. iii. p. 9.

elements that entered into its constitution, the commonalty necessarily lacked that force of internal cohesion, that sense of corporate identity and oneness, which bound together the clergy and the nobles. No mediæval politician would have thought of defining the third estate to be a union into one corporate body, conscious of its own identity, of all orders of men below the nobility and the clergy. Any such comprehensive definition would have been at utter variance with the facts. As an illustration of the narrow view of the "commons" that existed on the Continent in mediæval times, the fact may be cited that in France and Spain the term was then understood to embrace only the citizens of privileged towns, or of chartered communities of kindred municipal origin.[1] In England, however, the term has always borne a wider signification; it has there embraced not only freemen incorporated in towns, but freemen incorporated in shires. The term "commons," as it appears in the English political system, must therefore be understood to include all freemen organized and incorporated for government in the two leading classes of local communities, — towns and shires.[2] In the English system the commonalty as organized in shires were the first to send representatives to parliament in the persons of the knights of the shire, who appeared as the representatives of all the freeholders in their respective counties. Their example was soon followed by the commonalty as organized in communities of cities and boroughs. Out of the union of the knights of the shire, who represented the lesser landowners, with the citizens and burgesses, who represented the commercial interests of the towns, has grown the house of commons in which is now embodied a

The term "commons" as understood upon the Continent;

as understood in England.

Representatives of the shires and towns unite in the house of commons.

[1] As to France, cf. Thierry, *History of the Tiers-État*, vol. i. p. 56 (Eng. trans.); Savaron, *États généraux*, p. 74. As to Spain, cf. Schäfer, *Spanien*, vol. iii. pp. 215, 218; Zurita, t. i. fol. 71, 74. On the Aragonese cortes, see *Middle Ages*, vol. ii. p. 58 and notes. The term "commons" originally bore the same meaning in the constitution of Scotland. For the history of that constitution, and of the change made in it in 1427, whereby commissioners of shires were permitted to appear in parliament as the representatives of the minor tenants-in-chief, see *Lords' Report*, vol. i. pp. 111–124. In the language of the Report, the change then made "bearing resemblance, so far as it extended, to the system of representation long before adopted in England." — P. 114.

[2] "The commons are the 'communitates' or 'universitates,' the organized bodies of freemen of the shires and towns; and the estate of the commons is the 'communitas communitatum,' the general body into which for the purposes of parliament those communities are combined." — Stubbs, *Const. Hist.*, vol. ii. p. 166.

real representation, not of any single order or class, but of
the whole English nation.   This system of representation,
which has grown and widened from humble beginnings until
it has become the dominant force in the constitution, derived
its original vitality from the fact that the representatives of
the lesser landholders, who were for a long time the strength
of the country, severed themselves from the baronage,[1] and
then united upon equal terms with the representatives of the
towns in the formation of the third estate.   The third estate
in England thus acquired a vital element of strength which
in continental lands it did not possess.   How the representatives of the shire and town communities were chosen, and
how they were drawn together and happily united in a single
chamber, are questions which must be worked out hereafter
in connection with the growth of parliament.

From what has now been said, the fact appears that, al- Summary.
though the elements out of which the three estates were
organized existed from the very earliest times, the causes
through which these elements were finally worked into a
definite and formal shape sprang directly from the Norman
conquest.   The forces which the Conquest put in motion
brought about not only the severance of the clergy from the
laity, but the division of the laity themselves into the two
estates of the baronage and the commons.   The process of
definition which begins with the Conquest is completed by
the end of the reign of Edward I.   The parliaments of Eadward were assemblies of estates ; in them each estate or order
appeared in person or by representatives.   But the process
of definition was by no means complete when the struggle
for the charters begins.   It was in the course of that struggle, in which each class or order was fighting primarily to
establish its own special rights and privileges, that the corporate identity of each estate was definitely and permanently
defined.

3. The statement has heretofore been made that the struggle for the charters did not grow out of the mere possession
by wise and politic princes of the type of Henry I., and of

---

[1] " In most other countries the class
of men who were returned as representatives of the counties, the knights of
the shire, would have been members of
the estate of the nobles." — Freeman,
Growth of the English Constitution, p.
130.

his grandson Henry II., of vast and practically unlimited powers which were never deliberately employed for purposes of oppression merely. Not until the grinding weight of the royal authority was heedlessly and wantonly applied by careless despots to the oppression of all classes and conditions of men did the collective people, in the persons of the three estates, rise up to grapple with the crown in a struggle for the establishment of rights which were made eternal. With the wanton and irritating pressure of the royal authority upon every class in the reign of Richard I., the struggle for the charters really begins. The royal statesman and financier who preceded Richard, while engaged in the work of reorganizing the general system of administration, remodelled and expanded with special care the machinery of taxation. Until the latter part of the reign of Henry II. all taxation, excepting the customs, fell upon the land, and consisted (1) of the ancient customary dues, and the tax on the hide, — survivals of the Old-English system ; and (2) of the feudal incidents, and the scutage or tax on the knight's fee, — products of the new system of military tenures. Leaving out of view the ancient customary dues and the feudal incidents, the two land taxes that stand prominently forth are the Old-English tax on the hide, whether known as aid, hidage, carucage, or, in the case of towns, talliage ; and the new feudal tax on the knight's fee known as scutage. These two taxes affected two distinct classes of land-owners : the scutage was the tax assessed upon the lands of the tenants-in-chivalry, the hidage or carucage upon the lands of the freeholders. Only on rare occasions were both of these taxes imposed at once ; as a general rule, a year marked by grant of a scutage was not marked by the grant of a carucage. But as Henry's reign drew to a close, tempted by the great development in national wealth which had followed his policy of reform and order, he determined to widen the basis of taxation by a marked innovation. With the consent of a great council held at Geddington in 1188, Henry brought taxation to bear directly upon personal property by decreeing a tithe of a tenth of movables to aid the common host of Christendom in retaking the Holy City from Saladin. In order fairly to assess the tithe, Henry resorted to his favorite institution of

Pressure of the royal authority upon every class in the reign of Richard I.

Taxation under Henry II.

Land taxes :

hidage;

scutage.

Taxation of personal property.

inquest by the oaths of local jurors. Whenever any one was suspected of contributing less than his share, four or six lawful men of the parish were chosen to declare on oath what he should give. In this way the representative principle is first brought into contact with the system of taxation.[1] The fruit of this enlarged and improved system, embracing not only land but personal property, was a gross receipt from all sources, in the last year of Henry's reign, of £48,000.[2] And according to one chronicler, his treasure at the time of his death amounted to the improbable sum of £900,000.[3] At the death of Henry the vigorous system of taxation which he had constructed with care and wielded with moderation passed into the hands of a spendthrift knight-errant, who from the beginning to the end of his reign strained it to the limit of its capacity to support brilliant adventures in foreign lands in which his people had little or no real concern. From a constitutional standpoint, the reign of Richard I. is chiefly interesting in so far as it illustrates the improvements in the system of taxation suggested by its constant use, and the oppressions which arose out of its incessant application to all classes and conditions of men. Richard's first act after his accession was to seize upon his father's treasure, which he augmented by the sale of every available species of property, or office, or feudal right for which he could find a purchaser, from the disposal of the royal wards in marriage up to the sale of the supremacy over Scotland.[4] With the money thus hastily accumulated during the few months of his sojourn in his English kingdom, he sailed in December, 1189, for Palestine. During his absence, which, with the exception of his sojourn after his captivity, was coextensive with his reign, the administration of the kingdom was committed in turn to four justiciars,[5] who would no doubt have wielded the royal au-

Taxation under Richard I.

Administrations of the justiciars.

---

[1] For the authorities upon the subject of taxation as it existed in the reign of Henry II. see above, p. 298.

[2] Cf. Pipe Roll of the 1st Richard I. for the year ending at Michaelmas, 1189.

[3] "Et inventa fuerunt et numero et pondere plusquam nongenta millia librarum in auro et argento." — Benedictus, vol. ii. pp. 76, 77. Hoveden makes a much smaller estimate, — "excedens numerum et valentiam centum millia marcarum." — Vol. iii. p. 8; see note 2, *R. S.*

[4] Benedictus, vol. ii. pp. 90, 91. "Willelmus rex Scottorum dedit Ricardo regi Angliæ decem millia marcarum sterlingorum." — Ibid., p. 98.

[5] "The English history of the reign is, then, the history, not of Richard, but of his ministers; of the administrations of his four successive justiciars, William Longchamp, Walter of Coutances,

The effort
to raise
£100,000
for Rich-
ard's ran-
som.

thority with wisdom and moderation had it not been for the increasing pecuniary demands of their reckless master. In 1192, during the justiciarship of the archbishop of Rouen, Richard made his first great demand for money from the prison of the duke of Austria, who held him for a ransom of £100,000, double the whole revenue of his kingdom.[1] Hubert Walter, who visited his master in captivity, was appointed to the then vacant see of Canterbury,[2] and sent home to aid the justiciar in raising the ransom. Although the machinery of taxation was strained to the utmost by the taking of an aid of 20s. on the knight's fee, by the imposition of a carucage and talliage which fell upon all other lands, by the seizure of the wool of the Cistercians and the treasures — even the chalices — of the churches, and by the exaction of one fourth of movables, still the whole sum demanded could not be raised.[3] By the payment of what could be raised, and by surrendering his kingdom into the hands of the emperor and receiving it back again as a fief,[4] Richard purchased his release from captivity, which was followed in March 1194,[5] by his second and last visit to England.

Richard's
second and
last visit to
England.

The second visit, like the first, was for the purpose of putting everything salable to auction, and of collecting through the machinery of taxation every shilling that could be wrung out of every class of tax-payers. In a great council held at Nottingham in April, after putting up the offices for sale, he asked for a carucage, for a third part of the service of the knights, and for the wool of the Cistercians.[6] In addition to these demands, he directed the justices to make a visitation of the shires under a commission which contemplated a general review of the whole system of local administration.[7] Under the itinerant system as then organized, the justices

Hubert Walter, and Geoffrey Fitz Peter." — Preface to Hoveden, vol. iii. p. xxii., *R. S.*

[1] Hoveden, vol. iii. pp. 208, 210, 217, 222. See, also, Preface to Hoveden, vol. iv. p. lxxxiii., *R. S.*

[2] Elected to Canterbury, May, 1193. Hoveden, vol. iii. p. 213; becomes justiciar at Christmas, 1193. R. Diceto, c. 671.

[3] See Stubbs, *Const. Hist.*, vol. i. p. 501, and note 1.

[4] Hoveden, vol. iii. p. 202. Hove-

den adds that the emperor on his death-bed released him from the tribute of £5,000 a year.

[5] Lands at Sandwich, March 13, 1194 (Hoveden, vol. iii. p. 235), and sails for Normandy May 12 of the same year (Ibid., p. 251).

[6] For the proceedings of the council, see Hoveden, vol. iii. pp. 240-243.

[7] As to the history of the important Iter of 1194, see Hoveden, vol. iii pp. 262-267; Gervase, c. 1588; and also *Select Charters* (2d ed.), p. 258.

were charged under their commissions not only with judicial Visitation of the justices in 1194. but fiscal business.   It was their duty not only to hear causes, but, as a local court of exchequer, to inquire into and enforce the rights of the crown to all dues arising out of wardships, marriages, advowsons, escheats, sergeantries, measures, wines, franchises, and coinage, markets and tolls, together with all other proprietary and feudal rights to which the king was entitled.   The sums which arose from these sources, added to the fines, amercements, and forfeitures which resulted from the administration of the criminal law, constituted a very material item in the royal revenue.[1]   The " Iter of 1194 " is memorable not only for the relation which it bears to the constitution of the grand jury, as heretofore explained, but for its comprehensive and oppressive character. Among other things, the justices were commanded to collect a talliage from all cities, towns, and demesnes of the king.[2] In 1196 the king, being impatient at the delay in the progress of the visitation, sent over new agents to impart fresh energy to the work.[3]   In this year it was that the poorer citizens of London, under the leadership of William Fitz-Osbert, broke Popular rising under Fitz-Osbert. out into open revolt at the manner in which the talliage was collected.   The poorer people contended that as the talliage was collected by poll, instead of being assessed according to the property of each tax-payer, an unequal part of the burden fell upon them.[4]   Although Fitz-Osbert was slain and the outbreak put down, without apparent benefit to those who were engaged in it, the occurrence serves to indicate the severity of the distress among the people at large resulting from the continuous and persistent pressure of royal taxation.

Two years later a fresh demand for money from the bar- Opposition of the baronage to taxation in 1198. onage led to a revolt in a higher sphere.   In a council held at Oxford in 1198, the king demanded from the baronage through the justiciar that they should furnish him for his war in Normandy three hundred knights to serve for a year at

---

[1] All this is clearly explained by Sir James Fitz-James Stephen in his great history of the Criminal Law, vol. i. p. 101 *seq*.

[2] " (XXII.) Præterea tailleantur omnes civitates, et burgi, et dominica domini regis."— Hoveden, vol. iii. p. 264.

[3] Ibid, vol. iv. p. 5; William of Newburgh, v. c. 19.

[4] For the history of the rising, see Will. Newb. v. c. 20 ; R. Diceto, c. 691 ; Hoveden, vol. iv. pp. 5, 6, and preface, vol. iv. p. lxxxix.   See, also, Palgrave's preface to the *Rotuli Curiæ Regis*.

the daily pay of three shillings each.[1]   This great and unprecedented demand led to fierce opposition and high debate. There were some in the assembly who dared to maintain the principle that taxes were not to be imposed simply by the royal will, — that the right to consent to a grant necessarily

The patriot bishop of Lincoln.

implied the right to refuse it.   In the person of Hugh of Avalon, bishop of Lincoln, the opposition found a spokesman and a leader who was as ready to resist the demands of Richard as Thomas had been in the preceding reign to resist the demands of Henry of Anjou.   To the demand of the king for English money to pay a military force in a foreign war, the patriot bishop of Lincoln answered that his church and its pastor were bound to render military service to their lord the king within the realm, but that they owed him neither men nor money for wars in foreign lands.[2]   Hugh, supported by the bishop of Salisbury, held his ground, and the demand was withdrawn by the justiciar Hubert, who shortly afterwards resigned.[3]

Clerical opposition to taxation.

This unsuccessful attempt to tax the baronage was followed in the same year by the imposition of a carucage upon the lands of the freeholders at the heavy rate of five shillings on each carucate or hide.[4]   The imposition of this tax is important in view of the method employed for its assessment.   In the latter part of the preceding reign, when personal property became subject to taxation, Henry II. invoked the aid of his favorite institution of inquest by the oaths of local jurors in

Assessment of real property.

order to ascertain how much each one should give.[5]   With the imposition of the carucage of 1198 the same embryonic system of representation was for the first time extended to

---

[1] Ei trecentos milites uno anno moraturos secum in servitio suo, vel tantam pecuniam ei darent, unde ipse posset per unum annum trecentos milites in servitio suo retinere, videlicet unicuique militi tres solidos Anglicanæ monetæ de liberatione in die." — Hoveden, vol. iv. p. 40.

[2] " Scio equidem ad militare servitium domino regi, sed in hac terra solummodo, exhibendum Lincolniensem ecclesiam teneri; extra metas vero Angliæ nil tale ab ea deberi." — *Magna Vita S. Hugonis*, p. 248.

[3] As to the constitutional importance of this event, see preface to vol. iv.

Hoveden, p. lxxxi. ; *Norm. Conq.*, vol. v. p. 465; Stubbs, *Const. Hist.*, vol. i. pp. 509, 510.

[4] Hoveden, vol. iv. p. 46.   " In some cases the carucate seems to be identical with the normal hide of 120 acres, but other instances show that the carucate varied in area.   It is the land cultivated by a plough-team ; varying in acreage, therefore, according to the lightness or heaviness of the soil, and according to the strength of the team." — Seebohm, *Eng. Village Community*, p. 40.

[5] See above, p. 298.

the assessment of real property.   The officers who were sent
out to collect it were commanded, with the aid of the sheriff
in each county, to call before them the members of the
county court, lords and bailiffs, the stewards of barons, the
reeve and four men of each township, and two knights from
each hundred, who were to be sworn to declare how many
carucates, or what wainage for ploughs, there were in each
township.[1]   Whether the assessment or survey was fully carried out is not known,[2] but it is quite clear that the collection
of the tax itself, which was excessive in amount, met with
resistance.   The religious houses opposed it in such a spirit
as to bring upon the clergy a royal proclamation which put   Clergy
them practically outside of the law.   The effect of this meas-   practically
ure was to force the monks to purchase a reconciliation.[3]   outlawed.
Thus, by the steady and persistent pressure of taxation upon
every class during the reign of Richard I., the clergy, the
baronage, and the commons were each in turn aroused to more
or less positive resistance.   The poorer part of the commons
of London break into open revolt under the leadership of
William Fitz-Osbert ; the barons refuse a grant under the
lead of Hugh of Avalon ; while a part of the clergy go far
enough to bring upon themselves a denunciation which
amounts practically to outlawry.   By this severe preliminary
discipline, under which every class and condition of men
were made to feel the nature of the wrongs that were to be
righted, the nation was trained for action in the darker days
that were yet to come.

4. The sudden death of the childless Richard, which oc-   From the
curred in April, 1199, brought face to face two hostile   accession
claimants to his continental provinces and to his island king- of John to
the loss of
dom, at a time when the principles regulating the right of   Normandy
in 1204.
succession to the royal office were still in a state of transition
from the ancient rule of elective kingship to the new feudal
rule of hereditary right.   If the growing feudal doctrines of
primogeniture and representation had been universally recognized, the right of Arthur, the son of Richard's deceased

---

[1] " Quot carucarum wanagia fuerint
in singulis villis ; quot scilicet in domi-
nico, quot in vilenagia, quot in elee-
mosynis viris religiosis collatis." —
Hoveden, vol. iv. p. 46.

[2] As to the resemblance of this inquest to that of Domesday, see Stubbs,
Const. Hist., vol. i. p. 510.
[3] Hoveden, vol. iv. p. 66.

elder brother, would have been clearly superior to that of
John.   Upon the Continent, where the new feudal notions
had taken the deepest root, Arthur's right was admitted in
Anjou, while Philip received his homage as duke and count
of all the provinces which Richard had held of the French
crown.[1]   In Normandy and England, however, John, to whom
Richard had bequeathed, as far as he had the right to be-
queath, his island realm, with all his other lands,[2] entered
into quiet possession of dukedom and kingdom without opposition in favor of Arthur's title.   To the kingship of England
John was elected according to the ancient custom, and, if the

story told by Matthew Paris can be accepted, Archbishop
Hubert, before he poured the consecrating oil upon the head
of the king-elect, reminded him that no man had by virtue
of his birth a right to the kingship of England ; that that
right was conferred through the election of the nation after
invoking the aid of the Holy Ghost ; that the only limit upon
the elective right thus vested in the nation was the right of
the royal house to have the choice made of some one of its
own members, provided one could be found eminently fit for
the kingly office.   Richard having died without an heir, and
John being of the royal house, and possessing the other necessary qualifications, was declared elected ; and the cry of
" Vivat Rex" was the response of the assembled multitude.[3]
Thus secure in the possession of his English kingdom, John
set himself to work to wrest from his nephew such of his
continental lands as Arthur, by the aid of the king of the
French, had been able to withhold from him.   After two
years and more of war and diplomacy between Philip and
John, the latter in a sudden fit of energy surprised Arthur
while he was besieging his grandmother in the castle of Mirabel, and took him prisoner to Rouen, where he was murdered

in the spring of 1203, as all the world believed, by his uncle's

---

[1] Hoveden, vol. iv. pp. 86–94.   See,
also, Freeman, *Norm. Conq.*, vol. v. p.
466.

[2] Hoveden, vol. iv. p. 83.   " Divisit
Johanni fratri suo regnum Angliæ, et
omnes alias terras suas."

[3] Matthew Paris, vol. ii. p. 80, *R. S.*;
and in a shorter form in *Chr. Maj.*,
p. 197.   "This speech has been much

criticised, and its authenticity questioned, but it is directly referred to by
Prince Louis of France in 1216, in a
public document printed in Rymer's
Fœdera." — Preface to M. Paris, vol. iii.
p. xli., *R. S.*   For Mr. Freeman's view
of the speech, see *Norm. Conq.*, vol. i.
p. 404, vol. v. p. 466.

hand.   In the midst of the indignation aroused by this dark
and bloody deed, Philip, after having first cited John to appear
before his court to be tried by his peers upon an accusation
of murder made by the barons of Brittany,[1] declared that his
guilty and contumacious vassal had forfeited all the fiefs which
he held of the crown of France.   In the execution of his own
sentence Philip at once marched on Normandy.   Castle after
castle fell before him, city after city surrendered at his mere
summons, until the whole land, without any show of serious
resistance, passed into his hands, to be united at last to his
dominions as one of the most faithful provinces of France.
By midsummer of 1204 Philip was master not only of Normandy, but of Maine, Anjou, and Touraine, and of nearly all
of Aquitaine north of the Garonne.[2]   As a punishment for
his great crime, John was thus stripped at a blow of all of his
continental dominions, with the exception of the fragment
which he retained of his mother's inheritance.

Loss of Normandy.

By the breaking up of the vast empire of which England
was only a part, although the greater part, John was brought
into more dependent relations with the English nation than
had ever been imposed upon any of his Norman or Angevin
predecessors.   But the change which was thus brought about
in the attitude of the king was no more marked than the
change which the loss of Normandy brought about in the
attitude of the baronage.   By this time the great baronial
houses of the Conquest had to a very great extent either died
out or had been humbled by the overshadowing power of the
crown which had raised up in their places a new ministerial
nobility which had waxed strong in the sunshine of royal
favor.   The new nobility which had thus grown to greatness
on English soil, although in the main no doubt of Norman
descent, were in feelings and interests far more English than
Norman, and far less closely connected with the Norman
duchy than had been the older nobility.[3]   With the conquest

Political results of the loss of Normandy.

The new ministerial nobility.

---

[1] On this subject, see Sismondi, *Histoire des Français*, vol. iii. p. 489; Le Baud, *Hist. Bret.*, p. 210; R. Wendover, iii. p. 273; *Fœdera*, i. p. 140. Mr. Freeman says: "The French king cunningly devised for himself a jurisprudence out of the romances of Charlemagne; and by its help he professed to deprive his guilty vassal of all his lands which owed homage to the crown of France."— *Norm. Conq.*, vol. v. p. 469.

[2] Green, *Hist. Eng. People*, vol. i. pp. 189, 190

[3] See *Select Charters*, 2d ed. p. 269.

of Normandy by Philip, the last direct connection of the baronage of England with the land of their fathers passed forever away.   An election had now to be made between Philip and John, and under the pressure of this necessity those families that still retained estates on both sides of the Channel either split into two branches, each of which made terms for itself, or, renouncing their interests in one kingdom, cast their fortunes with the other.[1]   This complete severance of all connection with the Continent, whereby the barons of Norman descent who had grown up on English ground were finally transformed into Englishmen, was the completion of the great work which had been steadily going on since the Conquest, — the work of building up a united English nation.[2]

The baronage assumes the leadership of the nation.

At the head and front of the united nation, which thus arose out of the assimilation of the smaller mass of the conquerors by the greater mass of the conquered, the baronage — Norman in descent, but English in interest and in feeling — held its place throughout the prolonged struggle in which the Great Charter was won.

From the loss of Normandy to the signing of the Great Charter at Runnymede.

5. After John had been reduced by the loss of his continental dominions to the kingship of England, he set himself to work to illustrate to his English subjects, with whom he was now brought face to face, how far, in the absence of positive guarantees, the royal authority might be applied to the wanton oppression of all classes and conditions of men, when that authority happened to be wielded by the vilest, the craftiest, the ablest of despots.   " His worst enemies owned

The character of John.

that he toiled steadily and closely at the work of administration. . . . His plan for the relief of Château Gaillard, the rapid march by which he shattered Authur's hopes at Mirabel, showed an inborn genius for war.   In the rapidity and breadth of his political combinations he far surpassed the statesmen of his time. . . . The closer study of John's history clears away the charges of sloth and incapacity with which men tried to explain the greatness of his fall.   The awful lesson of his life rests on the fact that the king who lost

---

[1] Hallam, *M. A.*, vol. iii. p. 154; Stubbs, *Const. Hist.*, vol. i. p. 518.

[2] " The loss of Normandy thus once more called into being an united English nation.   It was well at such a mo-

ment that England had a king whose reign was one long series of wrongs and insults done to the English nation." — *Norm. Conq.*, vol. v. p. 470.

Normandy, became the vassal of the pope, and perished in a struggle of despair against English freedom, was no weak and indolent voluptuary, but the ablest and most ruthless of the Angevins."[1]   By the scourge of oppression in the hands of such a master the English nation was aroused not only to a sense of its oneness, but to a sense of the utter weakness of the royal authority, even in the hands of the ablest and craftiest of despots, when steadily opposed by a united people marshalled in the ranks of the three estates.   The great lesson which the struggle for the Charter teaches is embodied in the fact that, while the royal authority which towered so high over the land was more than a match in a single-handed contest with any one order in the state, it became perfectly powerless in the presence of an offensive alliance between the three.   As soon as the united nation was aroused to a realization of this fact, by the persistent warfare waged by John against the estates in detail, the royal authority was broken and the cause of the king was lost.

Powerlessness of the crown when opposed by the three estates.

The constitutional struggle, which pauses for a moment with the winning of the Great Charter, actively begins with the famous ecclesiastical quarrel which brought John into conflict not only with the clergy of his own realm, but with the greatest of all the popes, — Innocent III.   The break between John and the clergy grew out of the death of Hubert Walter, archbishop of Canterbury, which took place in July, 1205.   The right to fill the vacancy thus created in the primacy of the kingdom gave rise to an angry controversy between the monks of Christchurch, the bishops of the primatial province, and the king.[2]   The monks upon their part claimed the right to exercise all of the powers of the cathedral chapter of Canterbury; the bishops upon their part, while they conceded the right of capitular election, claimed that they should at least concur with the monks in the choice of the metropolitan; the king upon his part claimed that no valid election could be made by either or both without the royal license.   As soon as the death of Hubert was known, the junior part of the

The great quarrel over the appointment of primate.

---

[1] Green, *Hist. Eng. People*, vol. i. pp. 229, 230.

[2] For a general statement of the controversy, see M. Paris, vol. ii. pp. 104–107, vol. iii. p. 222, *R. S.* I know of no modern historian who has stated the whole matter with more clearness than Lingard. — *Hist. Eng.*, vol. ii. pp. 40–47.

monks[1] met clandestinely at night, and without the royal
license, and without the concurrence of the suffragan bishops
of the province, elected Reginald, their sub-prior, to the
metropolitan office. In the hope of sustaining this rash and
irregular proceeding, Reginald was dispatched to Rome to
seek the confirmation of the apostolic see. After his departure the wiser part of the brotherhood resolved to ignore
what had been done, and, having obtained the royal license,
proceded to hold an open and regular election. At the king's
dictation the chapter elected John de Gray, bishop of Norwich, who was at once put into possession of the archbishopric, and a delegation of twelve monks was sent to Rome to
support his title. After a year's delay Innocent first decided
the dispute between the suffragan bishops and the monks in
favor of the exclusive claim of the latter.[2] This question
being removed from the controversy, the pope proceeded to
pass upon the validity of the two elections which the monks
themselves had made, and, to the disappointment of both
parties, quashed them both.[3] The election of Reginald was
annulled upon the ground that it was uncanonical; that of
John de Gray, upon the ground that it was improperly held
while the validity of the first election was a pending question.
These judgments of Innocent, which seem to have been in
accordance with the jurisprudence of the age, were followed
by the assertion of a papal claim of a startling character.
The primatial see being vacant, and the representatives of
the chapter having the right to fill the vacancy being present
in Rome with authority to enter into a new election, the
pope proceeded to end the controversy by assuming to himself the royal right of nomination. In the exercise of this
assumption, which was contrary to all English precedent,[4]

Decision of Innocent.

---

[1] "Several of the cathedral churches
had been originally settled in monasteries, and still continued to be served
by monks, who claimed and exercised
all the rights of the chapters." — Lingard, vol. ii. p. 41.

[2] "Post multas tandem hinc inde
disceptationes, tandem a domino papa
pronunciata est pro monachorum parte
contra episcopos sententia diffinitiva."
— M. Paris, vol. ii. p. 107.

[3] Ibid., p. 111.

[4] "Hitherto the pope had done no

more than reject unfit candidates or
determine the validity of elections;
now he himself proposed a candidate,
pushed him through the process of
election, and confirmed the promotion,
although the royal assent was withheld." — Stubbs, *Const. Hist.*, vol. iii.
p. 305. The pope promised that, if
John would acquiesce, the appointment
should not be converted into a precedent injurious to the English crown.
See Lingard, vol. ii. p. 43.

Innocent commanded the monks to elect in his presence He claimed the right of nomination. Stephen Langton, an English scholar of eminence, who had been raised to the rank of cardinal, and who was then present at the papal court. Without conceding to John even the right to confirm the election, the archbishop-elect was consecrated by the pope himself at Viterbo in June, 1207.

As the theories and relations of mediæval times cannot be Theory of the mediæval empire. measured by the standards of to-day, it is impossible to understand the changing phases of the bitter and prolonged conflict which ensued between Innocent and John without some insight into that shadowy yet supreme overlordship which the Roman pontiffs then claimed and exercised over all the princes of the Christian world. The theory of the mediæval empire rested upon the magnificent notion of a vast Christian monarchy whose sway was absolutely universal.[1] The chiefs of this comprehensive society were the Roman emperor and the Roman pontiff,—the one standing at its head in its temporal character as an empire, the other standing at its head in its spiritual character as a church. The theory was that each chief in his own sphere ruled by divine right as the direct vicegerent of God, and that each possessed the hearty sympathy and support of the other. The Roman Empire Roman empire and Catholic Church two aspects of a single Christian monarchy. and the Catholic Church were, according to mediæval ideas, two aspects of a single Christian monarchy whose mission it was to shelter beneath its wings all the nations of the earth. Although this magnificent theory was never fully carried out, although the universal monarchy never extended its dominion over all mankind, or even over the whole of Christendom, yet the fact remains that the ideal empire did for ages so far Continuous existence of Roman empire the key to mediæval history. influence the thoughts and actions of men that it is impossible to understand the history of mediæval Europe if we fail to grasp the theory of its existence. No part of the system was less faithfully carried out in practice than the requirement that the pope and the emperor should exercise their concurrent sway without conflict of jurisdiction. It could hardly have been otherwise, for the reason that the very

[1] The outline here given of the theory of the mediæval empire is drawn in the main from the famous work of Mr. James Bryce, entitled *The Holy Roman Empire*, published at Oxford in 1864; and from the brilliant review of that work by Mr. E. A. Freeman. The review may be found among Mr. Freeman's select historical essays.

structure of the dual fabric necessarily provoked a struggle for supremacy between the temporal and the spiritual power. When this struggle grew into overshadowing prominence during the thirteenth and fourteenth centuries, while the disputants admitted that the papacy and the empire were both ordained of God, and that each in its own sphere had universal jurisdiction, they failed to agree upon the relations of the two jurisdictions to each other. Whether the supreme temporal ruler, who was admitted into his high office through consecration at the hands of the spiritual chief of Christendom, was in the last resort subordinate to the latter as the lesser to the greater light, or whether their dignities were coördinate and coequal, were the questions over which was fought the great battle between pope and emperor in the days of the world's wonder, Frederick II.[1] The contention which Frederick left unconcluded was continued in the next age by two

Dante and Saint Thomas as disputants.

famous disputants. Saint Thomas of Aquin, in his treatise, "Of the Government of Princes,"[2] defended the supremacy of the papacy on the one hand; while Dante, in his treatise "De Monarchia," maintained the independence of the empire on the other.[3]

Mediæval claim of papal supremacy as restated by Cardinal Manning.

The mediæval claim of papal supremacy has thus been restated in our own time by a great English cardinal: "The supreme civil power of Christendom was dependent on the supreme spiritual authority. The pontiffs created the Empire of the West: they conferred the imperial dignity by consecration; they were the ultimate judges of the emperor's acts, with power of deprivation and deposition."[4] This supremacy, which the pope claimed not only over the emperor but over all other Christian princes, taking its color from the prevailing jurisprudence, naturally and necessarily assumed a

The papal supremacy naturally assumed a feudal shape.

feudal shape. The theory was that all Christian princes stood to the Roman pontiff as great vassals to a supreme lord or suzerain, and as such supreme lord the pope claimed the right to enforce the duties due to him from his feudal subordinates

---

[1] See Pollock's *Hist. of the Science of Politics,* p. 14 (Humboldt Library).

[2] As to the authorship of the *De Regimine Principum,* see *Réformateurs et Publicistes de l'Europe,* Paris, 1864.

[3] Dante, however, puts Frederick among the unbelievers in the *Inferno,* Canto xiii. 60-68:—

"I it was who held
Both keys to Frederick's heart, and turned the wards."

[4] See a monograph by Cardinal Manning entitled *The Pope and Magna Carta,* lately published in England, and reprinted in Baltimore in 1885.

through an ascending scale of penalties which culminated at
last in the absolution of the subject from the bonds of allegiance, and in the deposition of the sovereign himself.   Such
were the claims of the papal power, and such its resources,
when John entered the lists against Innocent III.

With the consecration of Langton the trial of strength between the pope and the king openly began.   John at once declared that Stephen should never set foot in England in his
character as primate, while the monks who had taken part in
his election were made the special objects of the royal vengeance.   They were despoiled of their lands and driven across
the sea.[1]   In vain did Innocent attempt to appease the wrath
of John by the promise that, if he would acquiesce in what had
been done and receive the primate, the election itself should
not be converted into a precedent injurious to the prerogatives of the English king.   When John refused to listen to
such proposals Innocent threatened to lay the whole land
under interdict[2] if Langton were longer kept out of his see.
John responded with a counter threat that, in the event of an
interdict, he would banish the clergy, and mutilate every
Italian he could find in the realm.   Thus defied, Innocent proceeded to compel his contumacious vassal to obedience by applying to his kingdom the coercive machinery incident to his
supreme spiritual authority.   On the day appointed, March
23, 1208, the interdict which had been threatened fell upon
the land.[3]   The churches were closed; the church bells were
silent; the administration of the sacraments, save to the new-
born and the dying, were suspended; the dead were silently
buried in unconsecrated ground.   In the midst of the general
gloom John, who mocked at the pope's resentment, vented
his wrath upon the clergy by banishing the bishops who proclaimed the interdict, by confiscating the estates of those who
observed it, and by subjecting them to the jurisdiction of the
king's courts in spite of their privileges.[4]   Thus ended in anger that long alliance between the king and the clergy which
William and Lanfranc had built up, and which the quarrels of

Marginal notes:

John refused to receive the new primate.

The interdict, March 23, 1208.

John breaks with the clergy.

---

[1] M. Paris, vol. ii. pp. 112, 113; vol.
iii. p. 223.

[2] The bishops of London, Ely, and
Worcester were commanded by the
pope to make the threat. — M. Paris,
vol. ii. p. 114.

[3] Ibid., pp. 115, 116.

[4] Cf. Green, *Hist. of Eng. People,*
vol. i. p. 232.

Anselm and of Thomas had never completely broken down. The church, so long the steadfast support of the royal authority against the baronage, was now changed from a faithful ally into a dangerous enemy. John remaining obdurate under the interdict for a whole year, Innocent proceeded to inflict upon

The excommunication, 1209.

him a still more serious punishment: in 1209 he was cut off from the pale of the church by a sentence of excommunication, which, under the papal procedure, was the natural prelude to a sentence of deposition. Three years elapsed, however, before the pope resorted to the supreme and final exercise of his authority. During the interval many of the bishops fled from the kingdom, while those who remained appealed to Rome for protection for themselves and their clergy against the cruelties and oppressions to which they were subjected. In vain did Innocent seek to renew negotiations with John, who was now carrying on military expeditions in Wales and Ireland by means of the vast sums which the plunder of the church had placed at his disposal. Not until all attempts to renew negotiations had failed did Innocent take the final step.

The deposition, 1212.

In 1212 the bull of deposition was issued against John, absolving his subjects from their allegiance, and exhorting all Christian princes to unite in dethroning him.[1] What gave alarming significance to the final sentence was the fact that its execution was specially committed by the pope to John's arch adversary, the king of France, who at once gathered a great host for the purpose of an invasion. These dangers from without were soon followed by a menace from within. The Welsh princes, who had just been forced into submission, again rose in rebellion.[2] The universal discontent which prevailed throughout the host which John gathered for a fresh invasion of Wales revealed the fact that there was scarcely a man

Defection of the baronage.

upon whose loyalty the king could depend. The barons, too timid as yet to lead the nation in an open attack upon the crown, were conspiring in secret; some of them had even gone so far as to promise to go over to Philip upon his landing.[3]

[1] M. Paris, vol. ii. p. 130.
[2] M. Paris, vol. ii. p. 128.
[3] When John discovered the conspiracy he disbanded his host, and sheltered himself in the castle of Nottingham. After an interval of two weeks he arrested some of the barons and seized their castles. — Walter of Coventry, vol. ii. p. 207. Some of the nobles took refuge in France. — M. Paris, vol. ii. p. 128.

Thus menaced by conspiracies in his own ranks, John with consummate craft dealt a stunning blow to the adversaries combined against him by winning to his side as an ally the cohesive force by which they were united and directed. Behind Philip, the clergy, and the baronage stood the power of Rome; at the feet of that power John now sought deliverance from the hands of his enemies. On the 13th of May, 1213, he made an unqualified submission to Innocent, in which he agreed that Langton should be received as primate; that the exiles, clerical and lay, should return and be restored to their lands and offices; and that full restitution should be made to the clergy for the seizures to which they had been subjected.[1] On the fulfilment of these terms and conditions the sentences of interdict and excommunication were to be revoked. But this was not all. On the 15th of May John knelt before the legate Pandulf and surrendered his kingdom to Innocent, to be held of him and his successors in the Roman see at the annual rent of a thousand marks. John then took the oath of fealty to the pope in the form usual between lord and vassal.[2] As the man of the pope, John was now entitled to his protection, and to a consequent revocation of the authority under which the French king was threatening to invade his dominions. Under these changed conditions the French army was withdrawn to face another enemy, while Philip's dream of winning the English crown passed for the moment away. John's sudden and abject submission to Innocent, which entirely frustrated the plans of his enemies, was looked upon at the time as a complete settlement of all the difficulties in which he was involved. There is little or nothing in the contemporary accounts of the transaction to show that it excited anything like a feeling of national humiliation.[3] It certainly was not without precedent. John's own father, Henry II., had become the feudatory of Alexander III.,[4] while his brother, the lion-hearted Richard, had

John submits to Innocent, May, 1213.

Surrenders his kingdom and takes the oath of fealty;

and is delivered from his enemies.

---

[1] M. Paris, vol. ii. p. 135; *Fœdera*, i. p. 170.

[2] M. Paris, vol. ii. p. 135. The charter placed by John in Pandulf's hands is in Rymer, *Fœdera*, i p. 111. The homage is renewed to Nicholas, bishop of Tusculum, at London, on the 3d October. — *Fœdera*, i. p. 115.

[3] Green, *Hist. Eng. People*, vol. i. p. 236.

[4] See Lingard, vol. i. p. 417, note 1, in which reference is made to a letter written to the pope by Henry and preserved by his secretary, Peter of Blois.

become the man of the emperor.[1]　The idea that the English nation thrilled with a sense of shame and degradation when John became the vassal of Innocent seems to have been the afterthought of a later time.

John's quarrel with the nobles.

The respite which John won from the attacks of his enemies by his sudden submission to the pope was only of a moment's duration.　The defection of the baronage, which had crushed his hopes in the presence of Philip, still stood as a menace before him.　The causes of this defection reached back to the very beginning of the reign.　At his accession John had won the adhesion of the nobles by the promise that the demands made by them for the redress of grievances suffered in the preceding reign should be satisfied.[2]　The performance of this promise John had neglected; and when in 1201 the barons refused to follow him to Normandy until his pledge should be kept, he responded by seizing their castles and their children as hostages for their loyalty.[3]　The breach thus opened through John's faithlessness was widened and deepened in each succeeding year by the shameless pressure of taxation, by acts of wanton despotism in individual cases, and by an endless number of lustful assaults upon the honor

Taxation of the baronage.

of the proudest of the baronial families.[4]　In the first year of the reign the scutage — the tax which specially affected the tenants-in-chivalry — was increased from a pound to two marks on the knight's fee; in 1203 a seventh of the movable property of the barons was exacted;[5] in 1204 an aid was taken from the knights;[6] and in 1207 a thirteenth of movables from the whole country.[7]　And apart from the pressure of taxation which these demands illustrate, the baronage were constantly

Military service.

harassed by demands for military service in fruitless expeditions which were never carried out.　In 1201, in 1202, in 1203, and in 1205 armies were assembled for the ostensible purpose of foreign service, and when the time for action came the king, either from caprice or mistrust, refused to fight;

[1] See above, p. 360.

[2] Hoveden, vol. iv. p. 88.

[3] Hoveden, vol. iv. p. 161; Stubbs, *Const. Hist.*, vol. i. p. 522.

[4] "The licentiousness of his amours is reckoned by every ancient writer among the principal causes of the alienation of his barons." — Lingard, vol. ii. p. 78.

[5] M. Paris, vol. ii. p. 98. "Cepit ab eis septimam partem mobilium suorum."

[6] Ibid., p. 100.

[7] "Cepit per totam Angliam tertiam-decimam partem ex omnibus mobilibus et rebus aliis." — Ibid., p. 108.

and, after first accepting money from the forces, permitted them to disperse.[1]   But from his accession down to the eventful year 1213 the baronage sullenly yet silently submitted to every insult and oppression that John saw fit to put upon them.   While the church was being plundered, the nobles simply stood by without offering to make the cause of the clergy their own.   Not until the quarrel between John and the church had ended in a submission, in which it was stipulated that the clergy should be indemnified for all losses to which they had been subjected, did the redress of the wrongs which the baronage had suffered become a practical question. Open resistance upon the part of the nobles begins with their refusal in the summer of 1213 to follow John to France upon the ground that he was still excommunicate.   That objection being removed by a formal absolution pronounced by Langton on the 20th of July,[2] John made a second demand upon the baronage to follow him.   All admitted his right to call upon them for service at home, but the northern barons, the barons who had sprung to greatness upon the ruins of the great houses of the Conquest, now openly maintained that their tenure did not compel them to serve abroad, and therefore they refused to follow the king.[3]   In a storm of rage at their defiance John, on the 25th of August, marched rapidly northward to force them to submission.   At Northampton he was overtaken by Archbishop Langton, who reminded him that it was the right of the accused to be heard in the king's court, that not until all legal methods of redress had been appealed to in vain did he have the right to make war upon them.[4]   John continued his march, but before proceeding to extremities he yielded to Langton's suggestion, and summoned the revolting barons to appear on a certain day before the king or his justices.[5]

The barons refuse to serve abroad.

---

[1] Upon this whole subject of taxation and military service, see Stubbs, *Const. Hist.*, vol. i. p. 523.

[2] The patriot primate required John at the same time to swear not only to maintain the church, but to observe the laws of King Eadward, — "quodque bonas leges antecessorum suorum, præcipue sancti Ædwardi, revocaret, singulis reddens sua jura." — M. Paris, vol. ii. p. 140.

[3] R. Coggeshale, pp. 242, 243.   M.

Paris attributes this second refusal to the poverty of the baronage (vol. ii. p. 140), but Bishop Stubbs prefers to assign to this second refusal the reason which Ralph gives. — *Const. Hist.*, vol. i. pp. 524, note 3, 525, note 1.   See, also, Walter of Coventry, vol. ii. p. 212.

[4] " Si absque judicio curiæ suæ contra quempiam, nedum suos homines geniales, bellum moveret." — M. Paris, vol. ii. p. 142.

[5] Ibid., p. 143.

Council at
St. Alban's,
Aug. 4,
1213.

Represen-
tatives
from town-
ships sum-
moned.

Geoffry
Fitz-Peter
recurs to
the laws of
Henry I.

In the
council at
St. Paul's
Langton
reads the
charter of
Henry I.

Three weeks prior to the beginning of John's march to the north, a memorable council was held at St. Alban's, to which were summoned not only the bishops and barons, but also the reeve and four legal men as representatives from each township on the royal demesne.[1] Although the reeve and four men were summoned no doubt simply to assess the damages due to the clergy,[2] the incident is important as the first illustration of which there is any historical proof of representatives being summoned to a national council. The gathering at St. Alban's, although called simply to assess the damages due to the church, assumed in its deliberations a far wider scope. The resolves of the assembly, which were cast in the form of royal proclamations, threatened with the severest punishment all royal officers who should practise illegal exactions. But what was far more important, the laws of Henry I. — the embodiment of the laws of King Eadward as amended by King William — were brought to the attention of the assembly by the justiciar Geoffry Fitz-Peter, and proclaimed as the basis upon which the liberties of the nation were to be reëstablished.[3] The significance of the then almost forgotten laws of Henry I., brought to light by the patriot justitiar, was emphasized by the patriot primate in a second gathering of the barons held at St. Paul's in London on the 25th of the same month. In the council at St. Paul's Langton produced and read the charter of Henry I., which was warmly accepted as the basis of national action.[4] The claims of the councils of St. Alban's and St. Paul's were then laid before the king by the justiciar, who died almost immediately thereafter,[5] leaving the guidance of the baronage to Langton, under whose leadership they united, upon the basis of Henry's charter in an open demand for a definite and positive scheme of national reform. On the 7th of November the king called

---

[1] "In crastino autem misit rex litteras ad omnes vicecomites regni Angliæ, præcipiens ut de singulis dominicorum suorum villis quatuor legales homines cum præposito upud Sanctum Albanum pridie nonas Augusti facerent convenire." — M. Paris (ed. Wats), p. 239.

[2] "De damnis singulorum episcoporum et ablatis certitudinem inquireret, et quid singulis deberetur." — Ibid.

[3] "Galfridus Filius Petri et episco-

pus Wintoniensis cum archiepiscopo et episcopis et magnatibus regni, ubi cunctis pace regis denunciata ex ejusdem regis parte firmiter præceptum est, quatenus leges Henrici avi sui ab omnibus in regno custodirentur, et omnes leges iniquæ penitus enervarentur." — Ibid., p. 239.

[4] Ibid., p. 240; *Ann. Waverl.* p. 178.

[5] M. Paris, p. 243; Walter of Coventry, vol. ii. p. 215.

a council at Oxford, to which the sheriffs were directed to summon, besides the armed force of the knights, four discreet men from each shire, to share [1] "in the king's deep speech touching the affairs of his kingdom, to form, in short, the first representative parliament." [2]

First representative parliament.

The demands for reform which were made by the representatives of the church, the baronage, and the people in the council at St. Alban's, and which were repeated in firmer tones in the council at St. Paul's, were permitted to lie without action from October, 1213, when they were presented to the king by the justiciar, until October in the following year. During the interval John set himself to work to so strengthen his position as to make it possible for him not only to set the demands pressed upon him by the baronage at defiance, but also to pursue their authors with his vengeance.   In furtherance of this design John deemed it expedient to cement more closely his alliance with the papacy, and at the same time to attempt to crush upon the fields of France the military power of Philip, to whom the baronage looked not only as a possible ally, but as a possible sovereign. With this end in view John in the spring of 1214 sailed to the coast of Poitou with such English forces as would follow him.   After drawing to his standard a large number of the Portevin nobles [3] John crossed the Loire in triumph, and won back the city of Angers. Here it was he was informed by messengers from Rome that, in consideration of his acceptance of the papal award of damages to be paid to the bishops, the interdict which had now lasted for over six years should be finally removed. [4]   But in the very month in which John's reconciliation with Rome was consummated by the removal of the interdict, his hopes of military glory were shattered by Philip upon the field of Bouvines, where the English forces under the Earl of Salisbury were, together with their allies, completely routed.   Thus broken by defeat, John sought and obtained a five years' truce from Philip, after which he returned from France in October

The years 1214, 1215.

John's expedition to Poitou.

Defeat at Bouvines, and truce with Philip.

---

[1] "Quatuor discretos homines de comitatu tuo illuc venire facias ad nos ad eundem terminum ad loquendum nobiscum de negotiis regni nostri." The summons to the Oxford council may be found in the *Lords' Report*, App. i. p. 2.

[2] *Norm. Conq.*, vol. v. p. 474. "Again, however, the historians forsake us, and we do not even know that the assembly was ever held."—Stubbs, *Const. Hist.*, vol. i. p. 528.

[3] M. Paris, vol. ii. p. 148.

[4] Lingard, vol. ii. p. 57.

to renew the struggle with adversaries made stronger by his discomfiture.[1] The coming of the storm was now greatly accelerated by the king's demand of a scutage from those of the baronage who had refused to follow him to Poitou.[2] The northern barons, against whom this demand was mainly directed, were already on the alert and ready for action. In the Meeting of the barons at St. Edmund's, Nov., 1214. latter part of November these barons, under the pretext of a pilgrimage, had assembled secretly at the abbey of St. Edmund for the purpose of casting into a definite and final shape the schedule of liberties which they had resolved to force upon the king. They parted to meet again after Christmas, after having first sworn on the altar to withdraw their allegiance from John, and to make war upon him until their demands should be complied with.[3] In the presence of such dangers the king was not inactive. He not only garrisoned his castles, and brought mercenaries from Poitou, but he also attempted to break the coalition between the clergy and the baronage by spontaneously granting to the former the right to free election which had so long been withheld from them.[4] But this act of royal diplomacy failed of its purpose. Early Reassemble in arms in Jan., 1215, and make a truce until after Easter. in January, 1215, the united baronage, faithful to the pledge made at St. Edmund's, met in arms to press their demands upon the king. On the feast of the Epiphany John received a deputation from his adversaries at the Temple, and after listening to what was demanded of him he asked for a truce until the first Sunday after Easter.[5] During the interval the crafty despot made a desperate and final effort to dissolve the confederacy arrayed against him by attempting to secure the allegiance of one or more of three estates. He strove to win the adhesion of the clergy by a reissue to the church of the charter of free elections,[6] he attempted to strengthen his hold upon his tenants-in-chief by a renewal of their homage, while

---

[1] For a general description of the campaign, see Green, *Hist. Eng. People,* vol. i. p. 239 *seq.*

[2] "Dissensio orta est inter Johannem regem Angliæ et quosdam de proceribus pro scutagio quod petebat ab illis qui non ierant, nec miserant cum ipso in Pictaviam."— Walter of Coventry, vol. ii. p. 217.

[3] M. Paris, vol. ii. p. 153; R. Coggeshale, p. 246.

[4] For the charter containing the grant of freedom of election to the church, see *Statutes of the Realm:* Charters of Liberties, p. 5. This charter was reissued 15th January, 1215, and confirmed by the pope. See *Select Charters,* 2d ed., p. 287.

[5] See Stubbs, *Const. Hist.,* vol. i. p. 529.

[6] This was the reissue of January 15, 1215.

he sought to draw to himself the main body of the people by demanding that a general oath of fealty and allegiance should be taken throughout the realm.[1]   But his efforts were all in vain.   The clergy were unwavering in their devotion to the popular cause, the baronage were unshaken in their true allegiance, while the commissioners who were sent to the shire courts brought back the news that the "commons" were with the barons and against the king.[2]   In Easter week the baronage again assembled in arms at Stamford, and as soon as the truce expired they marched to Brackley in Northamptonshire.[3] The king, who was at Oxford, sent Langton and William Marshall to ascertain their demands, and when the commissioners brought back the same list of grievances that had been presented to him before, John cried out in anger, "Why do they not demand my kingdom?   I will never grant them liberties that will make me a slave."   The king's passionate refusal aroused the nation.   The baronage, when informed of it, proceeded at once to London with their forces arrayed under the leadership of Robert Fitz-Walter as "Marshal of the Army of God and Holy Church."   On the 24th of May London threw open her gates to the patriot host, and Exeter and Lincoln followed her example.   The occupation of the capital was followed by a summons from the confederates to all barons and knights who had so far stood aloof to unite themselves with the national cause, under the penalty, if they refused, of being treated as public enemies.   Nearly all of the nobles who had as yet clung to the king yielded to this final summons, thus leaving John with a mere handful of retainers to face a nation in arms.   Among those who still remained with the king, rather as mediators than as supporters, were Archbishop Langton ; Pandulf, the papal envoy ; Ranulf, earl of Chester, and William Marshall, earl of Pembroke, — all of whom urged upon the king the acceptance of the charter. Thus overcome by force from without and pressure from within, John yielded with affected cheerfulness to a necessity which he could no longer withstand.   In order to save himself from the final humiliation of unconditional surrender, he

In Easter week they meet again at Stamford.

"Army of God and Holy Church" marches upon London.

John's surrender.

---

[1] "Fecit sibi soli contra omnes homines per totam Angliam fidelitatem jurare et homagia renovare."—M. Paris, vol. ii. p. 155.

[2] Cf. Green, *Hist. Eng. People*, vol. i. p. 242.

[3] M. Paris, vol. ii. p. 155.

attempted to conceal the real nature of the submission about
to be made under the cloak of a negotiation. With this end
in view he invited the barons to a conference on an island in
the Thames between Windsor and Staines,[1] near the meadow

Great Charter signed at Runnymede, June 15, 1215.

of Runnymede. On the 15th of June the delegates met on
this island in view of the opposing forces encamped on either
bank of the river, and after going through the form of a negotiation agreed upon the Great Charter of liberties in a single
day.[2]

Analysis of the Great Charter.

6. An analysis of the Great Charter, when made in the
light of the circumstances attending its execution, clearly reveals the fact that, although it was issued in the form of a

A compact between the crown and the estates,—

royal grant, it was in substance a treaty or compact[3] entered
into between the royal authority on the one hand and the
nation marshalled in the ranks of the three estates on the
other. As the clergy, the baronage, and the general commonalty of freemen all participated in the movement which
brought about the making of the convention, and as all three
orders participated equally in its fruits, the great act at Run-

a national act,—

nymede was in the fullest sense of the term a national act,
and not the mere act of the baronage in behalf of their own
special privileges. There is nothing in the provisions of the
charter to recall obsolete distinctions of English and Norman
blood ; there is nothing to suggest differences of English and
Norman law. Upon the contrary, the very absence of such
provisions clearly shows that such distinctions had passed
forever away. It is clear that the process of assimilation,
through which the lesser mass of the conquerors had been

the consummation of the work of union,—

absorbed by the greater mass of the conquered, had been
fully worked out before the Great Charter was won. The
winning of the charter was in fact the final consummation of

---

[1] " Data per manum nostram in prato
quod vocatur Runingmede, inter Win-
delesorum et Stanes." — *Magna Carta*,
§ 63.

[2] For the general history of the crisis, see M. Paris (ed. Wats), pp. 252–
255 ; Walter of Coventry, vol. ii. pp.
219–229. The best modern statements
of the transaction are to be found in
Blackstone's preface to Magna Carta ;
Stubbs, *Const. Hist.*, vol. i. pp. 519–530 ;
Green, *Hist. Eng. People*, vol. i. pp.
230–244.

[3] M. Boutmy, in his comments on the
" Constitution Anglaise," has this to
say : " Les pactes sont au nombre de
trois : la grande Charte (1215), . . .
Le caractère de cet acte est aisé à dé-
finir. Ce n'est pas précisément un
traité, puisqu'il n'y a pas ici deux
souverainetés légitimes ni deux nations
en présence ; ce n'est pas non plus une
loi ; elle serait entachée d'irrégularité
et de violence ; c'est un compromis ou
un pacte." — *Etudes de droit constitutionnel*, pp. 39–41 (Paris, 1885).

the work of union.   In the words of the masters : " It is the
first great act of the English nation after the descendants of
Norman conquerors and Norman settlers had fully become
Englishmen, after all thought of any distinction between the
king's men, French and English, had passed away from the
thoughts of men." [1]   " The Great Charter is, then, the act of
the united nation, the church, the barons, and the commons,
for the first time thoroughly at one." [2]   This first great act of
the united nation was not in the path of political experiment.
The provisions of the charter embody no abstract theory of
government : they consist simply of a summing up of the traditional liberties of the English nation, with such modifications as those liberties had suffered through the results of the
Norman conquest.   The fact has again and again been drawn
out, that the Conquest involved neither a displacement of the
English nation nor a wiping out of the immemorial laws and
political institutions of the conquered race.   The Old-English
system of local self-governing communities, together with the
customary law, survived ; and upon that tenacious system as
a substructure the Norman system of central or national administration was superimposed.   During the century and a
half which followed the Conquest, this new system of central
administration, with the source of its strength in the royal
authority, grew and widened until it became the dominant
force in the constitution.   While the growth of the royal
authority was thus advancing and overshadowing the traditional liberties of the kingdom, the causes were at work which
finally brought about the division and classification of the nation in three estates.   By the thirteenth century the estate
system had reached its completion, and the royal authority
the limit of its growth.[3]   The tendency of that growth was
to withdraw, through the centralization of justice and finance,
the administration of all rights from the local and popular
courts, whose procedure was regulated by that ancient code
of Teutonic law which found its source in the customs of the
people, into a single central or royal court whose procedure
was regulated by the new code of royal law which found its
source in the will of the king.   The royal authority reached

*a summing
up of the
traditional
liberties of
the English
nation.*

*Completion
of the es-
tate system*

---

[1] Freeman, *Norm. Conq.*, vol. v. p.
475.

[2] Stubbs, *Const. Hist.*, vol. i. p. 543.
[3] See above, p. 337.

the limit of its growth when both Richard and John, accepting the imperialist theories of Glanvill, held that the will of
the prince was the law of the land.[1] The reckless attempts
made by John to enforce that theory finally brought about
the armed conflict between the nation and the king. Upon
the part of the nation it was claimed that the law of the
land was not the will of the prince, but the immemorial laws
of the English kingdom, with such modifications and amendments as those laws had suffered through the results of the
Norman conquest. After the coming of the Conqueror, the
Old-English system of customary law was generally appealed
to as "the laws of good King Eadward," while the changes
which it suffered through the results of the Conquest were
generally described as the amendments made by King William. This statement is clearly illustrated by that clause in
the famous charter of Henry I. in which the king promises
to restore the laws of Eadward, with the amendments which
his father had made.[2] It is therefore plain that when the
barons seized upon Henry's charter as the basis of national
action, and demanded of the king that he should enter into
a treaty with the nation upon the lines which it defined,[3] it
simply amounted to a demand upon their part that the legal
and constitutional relations between the king and the nation
should henceforth be regulated by the Old-English code of
customary law, subject to such changes in that code as the
results of the Conquest had brought about. There is no
attempt in the charter to wipe out the irrevocable effects of
the Conquest; the new system of central administration and
the system of feudal tenures are both recognized as abiding

elements in the constitution. The effort is to fix the limits
of innovation, to define the extent to which the centralizing
and feudalizing processes to which the Conquest gave birth
shall be permitted to abridge the immemorial freedom in the
time to come. In this vital question each estate is interested
as a corporate entity, and the nation as a whole is also interested as a corporate entity. Upon the basis of these several
interests the treaty is made. Each estate enters into a cov-

---

[1] See Green, *Hist. of the English People*, vol. i. p. 243.

[2] "Lagam Edwardi regis vobis reddo eum illis emendationibus quibus pater meus eam emendavit consilio baronum suorum." — Art. 13.

[3] See above, p. 376.

enant with the king as to its own special rights and privileges, while the nation in its corporate person covenants as to those general rights and immunities which are to be secured to the whole body of freemen irrespective of their division into estates or orders.   The provisions of the Great Charter, therefore, fall naturally into two broad divisions : first, those that specially relate to the rights and privileges of the three estates ; second, those that relate to the rights and privileges of the nation as a whole.   In the following statement of the contents of the charter, its leading provisions will be grouped, as near as may be, in the order which this division suggests.

Each estate covenants for its special rights, while the nation covenants for the common rights of all.

To the estate of the clergy the king promised that the Church of England should be free, and that she should have her whole rights and liberties inviolable.[1]   The right to hold free elections, which was considered first and indispensable, and which had lately been guaranteed in a charter twice issued,[2] was for the third time repeated and confirmed.

The church guaranteed free elections.

To the estate of the baronage, which consisted of the greater tenants-in-chief who held directly of the crown, the charter guaranteed many limitations and safeguards in mitigation of the feudal duties and services due by virture of their tenures to the king as supreme lord or suzerain.   But it must not be supposed that the barriers which the greater tenants-in-chief thus interposed between themselves and the king were designed for their own protection merely.   Animated by a broad spirit of generous patriotism, the barons stipulated in the treaty that every limitation imposed for their protection upon the feudal rights of the king should also be imposed upon their rights as mesne lords in favor of the under-tenants who held of them.   Upon this all-important question the charter provides that "all the aforesaid customs and liberties that we have granted to be held in our kingdom, so far as pertains to us, with reference to our vassals, all men of our kingdom, as well clerk as lay, shall observe so far as pertains to them, with reference to their men." [3]   In this way the feudal burdens are limited not only

The baronage relieved of many feudal burdens by the crown.

The same benefits extended to their under-tenants.

---

[1] "Anglicana ecclesia libera sit, et habeat jura sua integra, et libertates suas illæsas." — Art. 1.

[2] See above, p. 378.

[3] Art. 60.

in favor of the baronage as against the king, but also in favor of all under-tenants as against the mesne lords themselves. The best illustration of this statement may be found in the following clauses touching the exactions of aids and scu-

Aid and scutage limited. tages. As between the king and the baronage the stipulation is, that "No scutage or aid shall be imposed in our kingdom, unless by the general counsel of the nation, except for ransoming our person, making our eldest son a knight, and once for marrying our eldest daughter ; and for these there shall be taken a reasonable aid." [1] As between the barons and their tenants the stipulation is, that "We will not for the future grant to any one that he may take aid of his own free tenants, unless to ransom his body and to make his eldest son a knight, and once to marry his eldest daughter ; and for this there shall be only paid a reasonable aid." [2] The feudal clauses which stand next in importance are those which impose restraints upon the exactions of lords in the matter of

Relief, wardship, and marriage regulated. reliefs, wardships, and marriages. These clauses, seven in number, provide in substance that upon the death of a tenant-in-chief, whether earl, baron, or knight, the heir if of full age shall have his inheritance upon the payment of a fixed sum which is referred to as the "ancient relief." [3] If the heir is under age and the right of wardship is exercised, then, upon his majority, he shall have his inheritance without relief and without fine. [4] In the event of a wardship stringent provisions are imposed for the protection of the ward against the waste and improvidence of the keeper of his lands. [5] Express provision is made that heirs shall be married without disparagement ; and that widows shall be endowed, and shall marry again, or refuse to marry, without being compelled to pay to their lords unreasonable sums for the privilege. [6] It was further provided that no man shall be constrained to perform more service for a knight's fee, or other free tenement,

[1] Art. 12.

[2] Art. 15. And Art. 16 provides that "No man shall be distrained to perform more service for a knight's fee, or other free tenement, than is due from thence."

[3] Art. 2. Cf. Reeves, *History of English Law*, vol. ii. p. 20; vol. i. p. 382.

[4] Art. 3.

[5] Arts. 4 and 5. Upon the subject of waste, see Reeves, vol. ii. pp. 21, 22.

[6] Arts. 6 and 7. As to the older feudal law which forbade a woman to be endowed or to marry without the payment of a fine in one case, and without obtaining a license in the other, see Blackstone, *Com.*, bk. ii. p. 135.

than is due from thence.[1]   These provisions, designed to
relax the system of military tenures, were followed two years
later by a clause which tended directly in the opposite direction. In order to increase the hold of lords upon their vas-   *A restraint*
sals it was provided in the second reissue of the Great   *upon alien-*
Charter in 1217 that no tenant should give or sell to an-   *ation, 1217.*
other so much of his land as would render the remainder
insufficient to answer the services due to the lord of the fee.[2]
This restraint upon the power of alienation was designed to
check the growing practice of subinfeudation, which, as it
diminished the power of the mesne lords to perform their
services, tended directly to undermine the whole fabric of
feudal obligation.[3]

As the constitution of the commons as organized in the   *The com-*
thirteenth century can be defined only in broad and general   *mons.*
terms, it is difficult to point out definitely and precisely
those provisions of the Great Charter which relate exclusively to the third estate. As heretofore explained, according
to no mediæval theory could the "commons" be defined to
be a union into one corporate body, conscious of its own
identity, of all classes or orders of men below the nobility
and the clergy.   The term "commons," as understood on the
Continent, bore a far more restricted meaning.   In France
and Spain the term embraced only the citizens of the privileged towns, or of chartered communities of kindred municipal
origin.   The third estate in England differed, however, from
the same estate in the continental constitutions in that it
embraced not only citizens of towns, but also all landowners
below baronial rank, many of whom in continental lands
would have belonged to the estate of the nobles.   The middle   *The Eng-*
class in England consisted not only of the citizens of towns,   *lish middle*
                                                                  class em-
but also of the lesser landowners dispersed throughout the   *braced all*
                                                                  freemen be-
shires.   The term "commons," as it appears in the English   *low baro-*
political system, must therefore be understood to include all   *nial rank.*
freemen, below baronial rank, organized and incorporated for

---

[1] Art. 16.

[2] "Nullus liber homo de cetero det
amplius alicui vel vendat de terra sua
quam ut de residuo terræ suæ possit suf-
ficienter fieri domino feodi servitium ei
debitum quod pertinet ad feodum illud."
— *Magna Carta* (1217), art. xxxix.

[3] As to the place of this provision in
the history of restraints upon alienation, see Digby, *Law of Real Property*,
pp. 118, 136, 199; Reeves, *Hist. Eng.
Law*, vol. ii. p. 24.

government not only in towns, but in shires.[1] Guided by this definition it will be possible to collate, with approximate correctness, those provisions of the charter which specially relate to that great body of freemen, generally known as the middle class, that entered so largely into the composition of

Privileges of London and of all other cities and towns guaranteed.

the shire and town communities.[2] First among these provisions must be cited that clause which provides that the city of London shall have all of its ancient liberties and free customs, as well by land as by water ; and further, that all other cities, boroughs, towns, and ports shall have all of their liberties and free customs.[3] In this provision we have a definite recognition of the rights of the "commons" as organized in town communities. In the clause which provides

Rights of the shire communities.

that all "counties, hundreds, wapentakes, and tithings shall stand at the old rent, without any increase, except in manors on the royal demesne," we have a recognition of the rights of the "commons" as organized in "shire communities."[4] "Neither town nor tenant shall be distrained to make bridges or banks, unless that anciently of right they are bound so to do."[5] From such recognitions of the rights of the "commons" in their corporate relations we naturally pass to those provisions touching the rights of individuals who are unmis-

The merchant class.

takably embraced in the ranks of the third estate. In behalf of the merchant class it is provided that, except in time of war, they shall come in and go out of the kingdom without paying more than the ancient and allowed customs.[6] In the event of war, the rights even of foreign merchants are to be

The simple freeman.

carefully respected.[7] The rights of the simple freeman are also specially remembered. His horse and cart are, by an express provision, protected against the forcible requisition even of the sheriff himself.[8]

Provisions which relate to the nation as a whole.

Having now referred to those parts of the Great Charter which specially relate to the three estates, the task remains to collate those clauses which set forth the rights and immu-

[1] For the authorities upon this subject, see above, p. 356.

[2] "But in England the middle class was not confined to the towns; it spread itself, in the form of a lesser gentry and a wealthy yeomanry, over the whole face of the land." — Freeman, *Growth of the Eng. Const.,* p. 131.

[3] Art. 13.

[4] Art. 25.

[5] Art. 23.

[6] Art. 41.

[7] Ibid.   Montesquieu has praised the framers of the charter for having thus made the protection of foreign merchants an article of their national liberty. — *Spirit of Laws,* vol. i. p. 349.

[8] Art. 30.

nities of the people as a whole, regardless of their division into classes or orders. First among the provisions of this latter class stand out the great constitutional clauses which relate to the organization and powers of the national council, to the procedure of the king's court, and to the general administration of justice. The process has already been drawn out through which the Old-English national assembly was gradually and silently transformed, during the Norman and Angevin reigns, into a council of feudal tenants-in-chief. The definite results of this process of change are clearly set forth in a legal shape in that part of the Great Charter which describes the elements of·which the common council of the kingdom shall be composed, and the method by which those elements shall be brought together for national action. The constituent elements of the national council are defined to be the whole body of the king's tenants-in-chief. Out of this body the archbishops, bishops, abbots, earls, and greater barons shall be summoned by a royal writ directed to each one personally; the remainder — the lesser tenants-in-chief — shall be summoned in a body by a general writ addressed to the sheriff of each shire, in which writ shall be stated the time and place at which, and the cause for which the national council shall be called together.[1] The right of the council thus organized to consent to taxation is clearly and distinctly recognized. No scutage or aid, other than the three regular feudal aids, shall be imposed but by the common counsel of the nation;[2] and this common counsel can only be taken in a national assembly summoned in the manner which the law directs.[3] The immemorial right of the national assembly to join with the king in ordaining taxes — a right which even during the Norman and Angevin reigns had never been entirely ignored — was thus stated with a precision and clearness for which the nation itself seems to have been hardly prepared. In the many confirmations of the charter which followed during the succeeding reign, these vital clauses as to taxation and the national coun-

The constitution of the national council defined.

No taxation without its consent.

---

[1] Art. 14.

[2] "Nullum scutagium vel auxilium ponatur in regno nostro, nisi per commune consilium regni nostri," etc.— Art. 12.

[3] That direction is embodied in art. 14.

cil were invariably omitted.[1]   Not until the latter part of the
reign of Eadward I. was the right of self-taxation which they
embodied finally restored, as a part of the "Confirmatio
Cartarum," to a permanent place in the constitution.

Reforms in
the judicial
system.

The fact that the king's court was held in no fixed place
inflicted the greatest possible inconvenience and expense upon
those suitors involved in common pleas who were obliged to
follow its migrations.   In the history[2] of the plea of Richard
d'Anesty, which "followed the person of the king" for five
years, and which imposed on D'Anesty nearly thirty different
journeys, may be found, perhaps, an extreme illustration of
the evils to which suitors were exposed.   To remedy these
evils, the charter provides that common causes between party
and party shall be tried in some fixed place; that common
pleas shall no longer follow the person of the king.[3]   In
order to expedite the administration of justice in the shires, it
was also provided that two justices shall be sent four times
a year through each county, who, together with four knights
chosen by each county court for that purpose, shall take the
recognitions of *novel disseisin, mort d'ancester*, and *darrein
presentment* in their proper counties.[4]   It was further provided that no sheriff, constable, coroner, or bailiff of the king
shall hold pleas of the crown;[5] and that no one shall be appointed a justice, constable, sheriff, or bailiff except such as
are learned in the law and intend duly to observe it.[6]   The
double purpose of these provisions was to strip the sheriffs of
judicial functions,[7] and at the same time to save those charged
with criminal offences from trial before unfair and incompetent officers.   In addition to these provisions touching the
character and appointment of judicial officers, the framers of
the charter were careful to announce a series of practical
rules, both general and special, for the government of all
courts in the administration of justice.   First among these
general rules stand the famous clauses which provide that

[1] Cf. Stubbs, *Const. Hist.*, vol. i. p.
534.
[2] See Palgrave, *Eng. Commonw.*,
vol. ii. pp. ix.–xxvii; Sir James F. Stephen, *Hist. Crim. Law*, vol. i. p. 88 *seq.*
[3] "Communia placita non sequantur
curiam nostram sed teneantur in aliquo loco certo." — Art. 17.   As to the
history of this clause in its relation to

the curia regis, see Madox, *Hist. Exch.*,
vol. i. ch. xix. pp. 787–801; Reeves,
vol. ii. pp. 30–33 and notes.
[4] Art. 18.
[5] Art. 24.
[6] Art. 45.
[7] Upon this interesting subject, see
Bigelow, *Hist. Procedure*, pp. 99, 131,
137, and note.

"no freeman shall be taken, or imprisoned, or disseized, or outlawed, or exiled, or anywise destroyed; nor will we go upon him, nor send upon him, but by the lawful judgment of his peers or by the law of the land. To none will we sell, to none will we deny or delay, right or justice."[1] Among the special provisions touching particular branches of judicial administration, the following clauses may be cited. In order to restrain the king from the wanton or tyrannical imposition of amercements, — the pecuniary fines laid on those who had offended against the royal prerogative, — it was provided that the freeman shall only be amerced according to his fault, saving to him the means of maintenance; and in like manner the merchant, saving to him his merchandise; and also the villein, except he be the king's villein, saving to him his wainnage. No amercement shall be assessed in any case but by the oaths of honest and lawful men of the neighborhood.[2] Clerks shall only be amerced in proportion to their non-ecclesiastical property.[3] Earls and barons shall be amerced according to the offence, but only by the judgment of their peers.[4] As a protection to the local jurisdictions it was provided that the use of the writ of præcipe should be limited.[5] In a case involving life or limb, nothing shall be given or taken for the writ of inquisition, which shall be granted freely.[6] No bailiff shall henceforth force a man to compurgation or ordeal unless the accusation is supported by credible witnesses.[7] No man shall be taken or imprisoned upon the

General principles to govern the administration of justice.

Amercements.

Writ of præcipe.

Writ of inquisition.

Criminal accusations.

---

[1] "Nullus liber homo capiatur, vel imprisonetur, aut dissaisiatur, aut utlagetur aut exuletur, aut aliquo modo destruatur, nec super eum ibimus, nec super eum mittimus, nisi per legale judicium parium suorum vel per legem terræ." — Art. 39.

"Nulli vendemus, nulli negabimus, aut differemus, rectum aut justiciam." — Art. 40. The "judicium parium" does not refer, as has been erroneously supposed, to trial by jury, but to trial by members of the feudal and county courts. In this formula was embodied a principle which lay at the foundation of all Teutonic law; a principle which two centuries before had been announced, in an edict of Conrad II., in these terms: "Nemo beneficium suum perdat, nisi secundum consuetudinem antecessorum nostrorum et per judicium

parium suorum." In the so-called laws of Henry I. the principle is thus expressed: "Unusquisque per pares suos judicandus est et ejusdem provinciæ." — See Forsyth, *Trial by Jury*, p. 91 and note 1 *et seq.* (2d ed.); Stephen, *Hist. Crim. Law*, vol. i. p. 162.

[2] Art. 20.

[3] Art. 22.

[4] Art. 21. Upon this whole subject of amercements, see Reeves, *Hist. Eng. Law*, vol. ii. pp. 35–39.

[5] Art. 34. For the history of this writ see Bigelow, *Hist. Procedure*, pp. 77, 78, 83.

[6] Art. 36. The writ here referred to — *de odio et atiâ* — was in those days one of the great securities of personal liberty. Cf. Reeves, vol. ii. p. 47 *seq.*

[7] Art. 38.

appeal or accusation of a woman for the death of a man

Intestates. other than her husband.[1] When any freeman shall die intestate his chattels shall pass to his next of kin, subject to the claims of the church and the rights of his creditors.[2] In

Collection of the king's debts. order to restrain the severity with which debts due to the crown were exacted, it was provided that less oppressive means should be used for their collection ;[3] and also for the collection of debts due to the Jews, in which debts the crown possessed a contingent interest.[4] If, however, the king's debtor dies, no part of his chattels shall be removed until the royal demand is fully satisfied.[5] In mitigation of abuses

The forest code. which arose out of an undue expansion of the forest code, it was provided that the forest courts should not compel the attendance of those who were not directly concerned in the forest jurisdiction.[6]

Miscellaneous provisions. As a limitation upon the royal right of purveyance it was provided that the royal officers shall pay cash for all provisions taken by requisition ;[7] and that neither sheriff nor bailiff shall take a man's horse or cart, or his wood, for the king's use, without the consent of the owner.[8] Weights and measures shall be uniform throughout the kingdom.[9] All forests made in the present reign shall forthwith be disforested, and all rivers placed in fence shall be thrown open.[10] All weirs in the Thames and Medway, and throughout England, except upon the seacoast, are to be removed.[11] All evil customs concerning forests and foresters, sheriffs and their officers, rivers and their keepers, shall be inquired into in each county by twelve sworn knights, and forthwith abolished.[12]

Articles of a temporary nature. In addition to the clauses of a general and permanent nature which have now been summarized, the charter contained others of a temporary character, designed to remedy special abuses which had arisen out of recent events. All hostages and charters given to the king by his English subjects as securities for the peace shall be given up ;[13] and, as

---

[1] Art. 54. "Appeal" is here used in the sense of accusation.
[2] Art. 27.
[3] Art. 9.
[4] Art. 10. This clause was omitted in the first reissue of the charter.
[5] Art. 26.
[6] Art. 44.

[7] Art. 28.
[8] Arts. 30, 31.
[9] Art. 35.
[10] Art. 47.
[11] Art. 33.
[12] Art. 48.
[13] Art. 49.

soon as peace is restored, all foreign mercenaries shall be sent out of the kingdom,[1] and all who have been disseized or exiled shall be forgiven and recalled.[2] To the Welsh, who have been illegally disseized or dispossessed, restitution shall be made and justice done according to law.[3] The Welsh princes held as hostages shall be released, and the rights of the king of Scots shall be recognized.[4]

That the nation was fully impressed with John's faithlessness, is made manifest by the provision for the enforcement of the treaty in the event of a breach of any of its provisions upon the part of the king. The enforcement of the charter is committed to twenty-five nobles to be chosen from the whole baronage. In the event of a failure upon the part of the crown or its officers to perform any of its terms, the duty is cast upon four barons, to be chosen out of the five-and-twenty, forthwith to lay the grievance before the king. If he shall fail to do justice in due time, then the twenty-five barons, together with the community of the whole realm, — "*communa totius terra,*" — are authorized to levy war upon him, to distrain and distress [5] him, until the compact is kept and justice done.[6] The charter concludes with an oath upon the part of the barons and upon the part of the king, that all the articles of the agreement shall be observed in good faith, and according to their true meaning.

Guarantees for the enforcement of the charter.

Conclusion.

The coalition which coerced John into the execution of the charter trusted but little, however, to the good faith of a king whom no oath could bind. The only real guarantee that the principles which the charter defined should enter into the actual administration of government lay in the fact that, in the event of a breach of the compact upon the part of the king, the legal right of resistance remained to the nation in arms. The great act of the "Parliament of Runnymede" marks the beginning, not the end, of a conflict.[7] It embodies,

Signing of the charter marks the beginning, not the end of a conflict.

---

[1] Art. 51.
[2] Art. 52.
[3] Art. 56.
[4] Arts. 58, 59.
[5] "A contractual right of distress was so bound up with the legal customs of the Middle Ages, that the Committee of Resistance almost loses thereby its apparently revolutionary character." — Gneist, *The Eng. Parliament,* p. 85 (Shee's trans.).

[6] Art. 61.
[7] "For eighty years from the 'parliament of Runnymede,'" the history of England is the narrative of a strugle of the nation with the king, for the real enjoyment of the rights and liberties enunciated in the charter, or for the safeguards which experience showed to be necessary for the maintenance of those rights." — Stubbs, *Const. Hist.,* vol. ii. p. 1.

not a final statement of concessions to the nation from the crown, but rather a definite programme of reform which the nation resolves to persevere in until it is finally accepted by the crown as an irrevocable basis of government. During a period of more than eighty years the crown resists the right of the nation to enter into the full enjoyment of the rights and liberties which the charter defines. The struggle ends at last with the final confirmation of the charters at the close of the reign of Edward I. The absolute good faith with which Edward finally accepted the programme of reform announced at Runnymede closed forever the strife which finds a fresh beginning in the duplicity of John, whose one thought in the execution of the treaty was to violate its terms, and at the same time to crush in detail the elements which had so successfully combined against him. To accomplish these ends John resorted again to the tactics which he had so brilliantly employed in 1213, when by a sudden appeal to the pope he delivered himself in a moment of despair from difficulties which seemed to be insurmountable.[1] From the scene at Runnymede John dispatched envoys to Rome to plead for the condemnation of the Charter upon the ground that it had been extorted by rebellion, and in defiance of the suzerainty of the Holy See.[2] While his messengers were gone the king was busily employed in fortifying his castles, in borrowing money, in placing the county administrations in the hands of his own creatures, and in hiring mercenaries to fight under the royal standard.[3] In due time the desired answer came. In August, 1215, letters were received from the pope condemning the barons, and exhorting them to respect the royal authority, and to lay their claims before a council to be held at Rome.[4] The archbishop was commanded to excommunicate the disobedient, and upon his refusal to do so he was suspended from the exercise of his archiepiscopal functions. The sentence of excommunication which Langton refused to proclaim was published, however, by the bishops in the presence of the baronial army on August the 26th.[5] On the day before was issued the bull in which

Struggle continues for more than eighty years.

Duplicity of John.

The barons condemned at Rome.

---

[1] See above, p. 373.
[2] *Fœdera*, i. p. 202.
[3] M. Paris, p. 264; W. Coventry, ii. p. 222.

[4] *Fœdera*, i. pp. 203, 204.
[5] M. Paris, p. 270; W. Coventry, ii. pp. 223, 234. Cf. Stubbs, *Const. Hist.*, vol. ii. p. 7, and note 6.

"the pope, after deliberation at his will, by a definite sen- The pope
condemns
and annuls
the charter.
tence condemned and annulled the oft-named Charter of
Liberties of England."[1] In December a second sentence of
excommunication was issued, in which the leaders of the
national cause were mentioned by name, and the city of
London laid under interdict.[2] The open espousal of John's
cause upon the part of the pope ended the hollow truce, and
reopened the conflict between the nation and the king. In
September the foreign auxiliaries had arrived from over sea,
and with the royal standard thus strengthened, John began
hostilities in October by laying siege to the castle of Roch- The king
renews the
struggle.
ester, which fell on the 30th of November.[3] After the fall of
Rochester John intrusted the conquest of the midland counties to the Earl of Salisbury, while he marched northward,
ravaging the land as far as Berwick. After reducing the
north to subjection, he returned to the south and joined the
forces besieging Colchester, which fell in March, 1216.[4]
While John was harrying the shires of the north as they had
never been harried since the days of the Conqueror, the
barons in their desperation resolved, as a last resort, to renounce their allegiance to their faithless master and to offer
the crown to Lewis, the son of Philip of France.[5] In spite
of a threat of excommunication from the legate Gualo, the
tempting offer was accepted in April, and in May Lewis The French
invasion,
May, 1216.
landed in Kent with a formidable army.[6] John, who was
waiting on the coast to intercept him, now discovered that
the French mercenaries who composed his array could not be

---

[1] M. Paris, p. 162; *Foedera*, i. p. 136.
Cardinal Manning, in a monograph
entitled *The Pope and Magna Carta*,
has made a great effort to show "that
the Pope condemned not the charter,
but the barons; not the laws and liberties set down in the charter, but the
way and action by which the barons
had wrung it from their sovereign." —
p. 21. His Eminence clearly perceives,
however, the difficulty arising out of
the fact that Innocent denounced the
charter, in his letter of cassation, as
"compositio vilis et turpis, verum etiam
illicita et iniqua et merito ab omnibus
reprobanda." The purpose of the cardinal was to defend the Catholic Church
against the charge of being "the friend
of despotism and the enemy of liberty."

Lingard does this much more successfully by condemning the act of Innocent as a purely personal act entirely
outside of his ecclesiastical jurisdiction: "The control of ecclesiastical
matters only had been intrusted by
Christ to Peter and Peter's successors."
See Lingard, *Hist. Eng.*, vol. ii. p. 72.

[2] M. Paris, p. 277; *Foedera*, i. p. 139.

[3] M. Paris, p. 270.

[4] For the movements of John, see
Sir T. D. Hardy's Itinerary of John in
the Introduction to the first volume of
the *Patent Rolls*.

[5] *Ann. Waverley*, p. 283; M. Paris,
p. 279. The date of election of Lewis
is not given.

[6] *Ann. Waverley*, p. 285; W. Coventry, ii. p. 228.

relied upon to fight against their sovereign. Thus shorn of the power of resistance, the baffled tyrant was forced to fall rapidly back upon the Welsh Marches, while Lewis marched triumphantly into London, where he received the homage of the barons on the 2d June.[1]   After four months more of warfare and devastation John died, either from poison or debauch, at Newark,[2] on the 19th of October, leaving Lewis in possession of the greater part of his kingdom.

John dies, October 19, 1216.

Outline of the constitutional struggle during the reign of Henry III.

7. The death of the king wrought a marked revulsion of feeling in favor of the royal cause, whose hopes now centred in John's infant son, Henry of Winchester, who had just completed his tenth year.   The very helplessness and innocence of the boy-king forbade that the righteous wrath which the crimes of the father had aroused in the heart of the nation should be visited upon the head of the son.   For the first time since the days of the second Æthelred, the crown of England had fallen to a child;[3] for the first time since the Conquest had it become necessary for the representatives of the nation to appoint a guardian for the king.   The barons upon whom this duty devolved wisely chose William Marshall, earl of Pembroke, as governor of king and kingdom.[4] With him were associated as councillors Gualo, the legate of Honorius III., to whom the young king had sworn fealty as his feudal superior,[5] and Peter des Roches, bishop of Westminster.[6]   The first act of the regent was to reissue, in the name of the son and with the legate's approval,[7] the Great Charter against which the father had died fighting, with the omission, however, of all the merely temporary provisions, together with the constitutional clauses touching taxation and the national council, as well as all others that restrained the royal authority in the raising of revenue.[8]   Having thus announced the basis upon which that part of the baronial party which stood about the king would conduct the administra-

First regency since the Conquest.

William Marshall appointed regent.

Reissue of the charter with certain serious omissions.

---

[1] M. Paris, p. 282; W. Coventry, ii. p. 230.

[2] M. Paris, p. 242; *Fœdera*, i. p. 144.

[3] Æthelred was elected at the age of ten years.

[4] *Fœdera*, i. p. 215; M. Paris, p. 289. Cf. Gneist, *The Eng. Parliament*, p. 87.

[5] *Fœdera*, i. p. 145; M. Paris, p. 289.

[6] " The former, to satisfy the claims

and to secure the support of the pope; the latter perhaps, however inadequately, to fill the place that belonged to the archbishop of Canterbury." — Stubbs, *Const. Hist.*, vol. ii. p. 20.

[7] Cardinal Manning makes special reference to this fact in the monograph heretofore referred to.   See p. 20.

[8] *Statutes of the Realm*: Charters of Liberties, pp. 14–16.

tion, the earl Marshall addressed himself to the patriotic task of ridding the realm of the French invaders. For a time Lewis held firmly in his grasp the capital and the eastern shires, but the constant desertions of the English barons so weakened his forces that the regent made bold to attack him in the spring of 1217. The decisive battle was fought in May at Lincoln, where the regent was completely victorious.[1] Lewis retreated on London and called for aid from France, but his last hope of success disappeared with the destruction of the fleet upon which he was depending for reinforcements.[2] This disaster was followed by a treaty concluded at Lambeth in September, in which Lewis, after stipulating for the safety of his adherents, promised to withdraw from England and to renounce all claims upon the crown upon the payment of a sum which he claimed as expenses.[3] The pacification which followed the treaty was marked by a second reissue of the charter in a form which differed from the two preceding editions in several material particulars.[4] This second reissue was followed in November by a Forest Charter, in which the remedial provisions of John's charter touching forest abuses were enlarged and rendered more efficacious.[5] The text of the charter of 1217, though often republished and confirmed, was never afterwards materially altered. After expelling the French, and restoring peace and good government upon the general basis of reform proclaimed at Runnymede, the earl Marshall died, lamented by all, in the spring of 1219.[6]

Battle of Lincoln.

Treaty of Lambeth, September, 1217.

Second reissue of the charter.

Charter of the Forest.

The work of administration now passed into the hands of the justiciar Hubert de Burgh, who was sustained in his efforts to preserve law and order by Archbishop Langton, who had just returned forgiven from Rome.[7] The government of

Administration of Hubert de Burgh, 1219–1232.

---

[1] M. Paris, pp. 247–249; *Ann. Dunst.*, pp. 80–82; *Ann. Waverley*, p. 183.

[2] This was the achievement of Hubert de Burgh, who commanded a fleet collected in the Cinque Ports.

[3] M. Paris, p. 299; *Fœdera*, i. p. 148.

[4] *Statutes of the Realm:* Charters of Liberties, pp. 17–19. For the details see *Select Charters*, p. 344, 2d ed.

[5] The old idea that John issued a separate Forest Charter is erroneous.

The articles of the Great Charter that relate to forest abuses are the 44th, 47th, 48th, and a part of the 53d. Cf. Blackstone's *Introduction to the Charters*, pp. xxii., xli. For Henry's Forest Charter, see *Statutes of the Realm:* Charters, pp. 20, 21.

[6] *Ann. Waverley*, p. 291.

[7] As to Langton's treatment at Rome, see M. Paris, vol. ii. pp. 168, 174, *R. S.* He returned in May, 1218. — *Ann. Mailros*, p. 196.

Hubert was confronted by three difficulties which were bravely met and completely overcome. The papal legate, who represented the pope as overlord, claimed a voice in the administration ;[1] the foreign party that John had built up about him still had a footing in the kingdom ; while the remnant of the feudal party, which still longed for independence, threatened to renew the feudal anarchy which had existed in Stephen's time. Through the joint efforts of primate and justiciar, a promise was obtained from Rome that the legate should be withdrawn, and no successor appointed while Langton lived ;[2] the last of John's mercenaries were expelled ; and by a vigorous policy of coercion the attempt at feudal rebellion was finally crushed out.[3] The complete establishment of peace in 1225 was followed by a reissue of the charter by the king " *spontanea et bona voluntate nostra*,"[4] and in consideration of the concession a grant was made of a fifteenth of all movables,[5] — a foreshadowing of the principle that the redress of grievances should precede the making of a money grant. Henry, though only eighteen, had already been declared by the pope competent to govern ;[6] but not until two years later, in a council held at Oxford in January, 1227,[7] did he complete his emancipation by announcing his intention to give personal direction to the administration of the kingdom. From a constitutional point of view, the minority which was thus brought to a close is memorable as the time from which it is possible to trace the existence of a permanent royal council, composed of the king's personal advisers, — the officers of state and of the household, the judges, besides a number of bishops, barons, and others, — who constitute a resident and continual council for the dispatch of public business, apart from the greater body known as the common council of the kingdom. As the right to appoint the regent was assumed by the great council, it is more than likely that the other personal advisers who stood

Margin notes:
Third reissue of the charter, 1225.

Henry completes his emancipation, 1227.

A resident and continual royal council can be traced from Henry's minority.

---

[1] Gualo, who returned to Rome in November, 1218, was succeeded by Pandulf. Cf. Lingard, vol. ii. p. 86.

[2] *Ann. Dunst.*, p. 74. Pandulf resigned in July, 1221. M. Westm., p. 280.

[3] See Green, *Hist. Eng. People*, vol. i. p. 251 *seq.*

[4] *Statutes of the Realm:* Charters, pp. 22–25.

[5] The consideration is clearly stated : "Omnes de regno nostro, dederunt nobis quintam decimam partem omnium mobilium suorum."

[6] Honorius so declared in letters issued in 1223.

[7] M. Paris, p. 336; Stubbs, *Const. Hist.*, vol. ii. p. 39.

with him around the king were also during the minority appointed with its consent and approval. From the great council the earl Marshall received his appointment as "*rector regis et regni*" in 1216,[1] and Ralf Neville the chancellorship in 1226.[2] It is therefore probable that to the minority of Henry can be traced the beginnings of the constitutional doctrine that the king can do no wrong, and that the ministers who advise him are responsible to the assembled representatives of the nation who have a consultative voice in their appointment.[3] Years, however, elapsed, after Henry's formal emancipation in 1227, before he actually attempted to govern alone. For five years more the real direction of affairs continues in the hands of the justiciar Hubert, who is for a time aided in the difficult task of preserving peace at home and abroad, and in governing England in the interest of the English, by the patriot primate, who died in July, 1228.[4] After Langton's death Hubert found himself too weak to stand alone against the tide of papal aggression which now began to press upon the realm. Hubert's supposed connection[5] with an organized popular opposition to the collection of a tax[6] imposed for the aid of Gregory IX. in his war with the emperor broke his power with the king, whose dominant impulse was his devotion to the papacy, and led at last to his dismissal in July, 1232.[7] After the fall of Hubert, his old rival, Peter des Roches, regained the royal confidence, and became for a time dominant in the king's councils. But his power was short-lived. In April, 1234, the king commanded Bishop Peter to confine himself to his spiritual duties;[8] from that time the personal government of the king really begins.

Henry, who held with his father that the will of the prince was the law of the land, now attempted to enforce his personal rule, unrestrained by the influence of the great ministers of state who had carried on the work of administration since the days of his grandfather, Henry of Anjou. The first

Ministerial responsibility, and the doctrine that the king can do no wrong.

Langton dies in July, 1228.

Peter des Roches.

Henry's personal rule.

---

[1] W. Coventry, ii. p. 233.
[2] M. Paris, pp. 316, 430.
[3] Upon this whole subject, see Stubbs, *Const. Hist.*, vol. ii. pp. 40, 41, 255–266.
[4] M. Paris, vol. ii. p. 302, *R. S.*
[5] *Ann. Dunst.*, p. 129.
[6] M. Paris, pp. 335, 361; *Ann. Burton*, p. 245; *Ann. Waverley*, p. 305.

[7] For the charges brought against Hubert, see M. Paris, p. 377.
[8] M. Paris, vol. ii. p. 366, *R. S.* "Præcepit Petro, Wintoniensi episcopo, ut pergens ad episcopatum suum curis intenderet animarum, et de cetero regiis negotiis non interesset."

step was to abolish the ancient dignity and power of the justiciar. With the fall of Hubert de Burgh [1] the line of great justiciars comes to an end: henceforth the justiciar becomes simply the head of a law court; he is no longer "*secundus a rege.*" Henry's policy was to reduce the dignity and importance of the justiciar, and at the same time to distribute all the other great offices of state among trained administrators wholly dependent upon his personal will. In spite, however, of the king's lofty assumptions, the actual direction of affairs soon passed into the hands of the brood of foreign favorites who followed in the train of Eleanor of Provence, to whom he was married in 1236,[2] and to the Poictevin kinsmen of the queen mother who came in 1243.[3] And about the same time still another and more potent foreign influence was introduced into the personal government of the king. The one power which Henry admitted to be superior to his own was the power of the papacy, whose influence upon English affairs was formally renewed by the arrival in 1237 of the legate Otho, who came upon Henry's secret invitation to carry out projected reforms in church and state.[4] Out of the pressure of the king's personal rule as directed by the interests of the foreign favorites, and by the exactions of the papal court,[5] arose that bitter conflict between the English church and nation on the one hand, and the royal and papal authority on the other, which finally resulted, in Henry's latter days, in an open appeal to arms. The dreary waste of years that intervenes between the beginning and the end of the conflict is filled up with endless details which illustrate the growth of the royal and papal exactions on the one hand and the rising spirit of resistance on the other. The history of the conflict can be most clearly traced in the proceedings of the parliaments which meet to listen to demands for money from pope

The justiciar becomes simply the head of a law court.

Foreign influences at work.

Conflict between the crown and papacy on the one side and the English church and nation on the other.

---

[1] "Robert Burnell was the first great chancellor, as Hubert de Burgh was the last great justiciar." — Stubbs, *Const. Hist.*, vol. ii. p. 269.

[2] M. Paris, vol. ii. p. 385, *R. S.*

[3] "Henry, a good son and a good husband, could not bring himself to say No to his mother or his wife, and the land was filled with successive swarms of the kinsfolk and countrymen alike of Isabel and of Eleanor." — *Norm. Conq.*, vol. v. p. 483.

[4] "Ad reformandum statum ecclesiæ et regni." — M. Paris, vol. ii. p. 398, *R. S.*

[5] Lingard, with his usual frankness, admits that "the history of Henry's transactions with the court of Rome discloses to us a long course of oppression, under which the English clergy, by the united influence of the crown and the tiara, were compelled to submit to the most grievous exactions." — *Hist. of England*, vol. ii. p. 99.

or king, and, in turn, to concede or reject them. In the proceedings of the parliament of 1242, which were duly recorded
and which survive as the earliest authorized report of a parliamentary debate,[1] we find the representatives of the nation,
after thoroughly discussing the expediency of a foreign war,
bold enough to oppose it by refusing an aid to the king to
carry it on. To the parliament of 1244 the king was forced
to appeal with his own mouth for aid out of the difficulties in
which he had become involved by attempting to carry on war
after a grant had been denied him. To this appeal upon the
part of the king the parliament replied that they would grant
him no money unless he would first assent to a definite plan
of reform which contemplated, among other things, the confirmation of the charters, the election by the national assembly
of a justiciar, chancellor, and treasurer, and the establishment of a permanent council which should attend upon him
and supervise his administration.[2] This demand, though not
accepted at the time, defined the basis of later reforms ; it
foreshadowed the practical expedients which were afterwards
employed to force upon the king a faithful observance of the
principles which the charter defined. From 1244 to 1254
the contest is continuous. The effort upon the part of the
king is to obtain from the parliament without conditions
money enough to supply his ever-increasing wants ; the
effort upon the part of the nation is to secure the appointment of the great officers of state in order to control through
them the king's improvident administration. To the parliament of 1254 — which was convened by the regents for the
purpose of obtaining an aid for the king, who was absent on
an expedition to Gascony — the chosen knights from the
shires are summoned for the first time since the reign of
John.[3] The grant which the regents asked was made and
wasted, and at the end of the year the king returned to

Marginal notes:

Earliest authorized report of a parliamentary debate, 1242.

The proposed reform of 1244.

From 1244 to 1254.

Knights of the shire reappear in the parliament of 1254.

---

[1] M. Paris, pp. 581, 582 ; *Select Charters*, p. 368, 2d ed.

[2] M. Paris, pp. 640, 641. As to the connection of Simon of Montfort with the joint committee of bishops and barons that drew up the reply to the demand of the king, see Green, *Hist. Eng. People*, vol. i. p. 275.

[3] *Report on the Dignity of a Peer*, App. i. p. 13, and also vol. i. pp. 94, 95.

The Committee say that "it seems to have been the first instance appearing on any record now extant, of an attempt to substitute representatives elected by bodies of men for the attendance of the individuals so to be represented, personally or by their several procurators, in an assembly convened for the purpose of obtaining an aid." — P. 95.

become involved in fresh complications. While in Gascony Henry had accepted from his papal overlord, for his second son Edmund, an offer of the Sicilian crown, which was regarded as a papal fief, upon the pledge that England would send an army across the Alps, and also repay the sums which the pope was then borrowing to carry on his war with the house of Hohenstaufen.[1] In 1257 the pope presented his account to Henry, showing an indebtedness of 135,000 marks, which was duly laid before the parliament.[2] The crisis had now come. The king was so helplessly in debt,[3] and the administration of the kingdom was in such hopeless disorder, that the fact was apparent to all that the point had at last been reached at which it was necessary for the parliament to place the royal authority in commission, and to provide through its own agents for the future government of the state.

Disclosure of the king's debts to the parliament of 1257.

The work of reorganizing the system of central administration which Henry's personal misrule had completely broken down, of freeing the nation from the presence and influence of the foreign favorites whom he had quartered on the crown, and of checking the aggressions of the papal power, naturally devolved upon the barons, who were now aroused to a definite plan of action under the leadership of the great Earl of Leicester, Simon of Montfort.[4] In a parliament which met at London in April, 1258, the king in his helplessness agreed to put himself in the hands of the barons, and to submit himself to a definite plan of reform which they were to unfold in a parliament to be held at Oxford on the 11th of June.[5] At the time appointed, the baronage appeared in arms[6] under the leadership of Leicester and Gloucester, and presented a petition embodying the reforms which they had resolved to carry out.[7] In accordance with the agreement

The Barons' War, 1258-1272.

Simon of Montfort.

[1] *Fœdera*, i. pp. 297, 301, 316, 318, 336, 337. See Ranke, *Englische Geschichte*, i. 98.

[2] *Fœdera*, i. p. 354; M. Paris, p. 946; *Ann. Burton*, p. 384.

[3] "It was calculated that since his wasteful days began, he had thrown away 950,000 marks." — Stubbs, *Const. Hist.*, vol. ii. p. 71, citing M. Paris, p. 948.

[4] The best sketch of the whole career of Earl Simon is perhaps that one contained in Dr. R. Pauli's monograph

entitled *Simon von Montfort Graf von Leicester, der Schöpfer des Manses der Gemeinen*. Trans. by Una M. Goodwin, with introduction by H. Martineau, London, 1876. See, also, Blaauw's *Barons' War*.

[5] M. Paris, pp. 963, 968; *Ann. Theokesb.*, p. 164; *Fœdera*, i. pp. 370, 371.

[6] M. Paris, p. 970; Pauli, p. 91; *Lords' Report*, vol. i. p. 126.

[7] For the petition of the barons, see *Ann. Burton*, pp. 339-443.

made at London in April,[1] a committee of twenty-four were elected, half by the king and half by the barons, who drew up the articles generally known as the Provisions of Oxford.[2] Under the terms of the Provisions, the royal authority was placed under the control of three committees, who were charged with the task of reforming the entire administration. A council of fifteen were elected by four of the original twenty-four to advise the king in all ordinary matters of government; another committee of twenty-four were appointed to deal only with the negotiation of financial aids;[3] a third committee of twelve were chosen by the barons to represent the community in three annual parliaments:[4] while to the original committee of twenty-four was committed the reformation of the church.[5] It was provided that parliament should convene thrice in the year, and that in each parliament the permanent council of fifteen should meet with the body of twelve to be chosen by the barons, to discuss the common business of the whole community.[6] Hugh Bigod, the adherent of both of the baronial leaders, was chosen justiciar; and justiciar, chancellor, and the guardians of the king's castles were sworn to act only with the advice of the permanent council.[7] The provisional government, which went into operation in June, promptly expelled the foreigners, but the work of reform which it undertook to carry out proceeded so slowly that the knighthood[8] openly complained that, while the barons had looked after their own interests, they had kept none of their promises. The result of this outcry was the additional provisions known as the Provisions of Westminster, which were published in Latin and French in October,

Provisions of Oxford, 1258.

Provisions of Westminster, 1259.

---

[1] For the king's consent to the scheme of reform, and to the election of the twenty-four, see *Fœdera*, i. pp. 370, 371.

[2] *Ann. Burton*, pp. 446–453. Upon the whole subject, see *Select Charters*, pp. 378–400, 2d ed. See, also, Mr. Luard's translation of the *Ann. Burton*, pp. 501–505.

[3] *Ann. Burton*, p. 450.

[4] Ibid., p. 449.

[5] Ibid., p. 480. "The complexity of such an arrangement was relieved by the fact that the members of each of these committees were in great part the same persons." — Green, *Hist. of the Eng. People*, vol. i. p. 292.

[6] With the further provision "that the commonalty shall hold as established that which these twelve shall do. And that shall be done to spare the cost of the commonalty."

[7] *Ann. Burton*, pp. 447–449. A proclamation, the first in the English tongue since the Conquest, was issued by the king commanding the observance of the Provisions. — *Fœdera*, i. p. 378.

[8] "Communitas bacheleriæ Angliæ." — *Ann. Burton*, p. 471 ; Pauli, pp. 95–100.

1259.[1] This last effort, like the first, failed, however, to satisfy public expectation. The very complexity of the scheme of reform which the barons had devised, coupled with the existence of an open feud between the baronial leaders — Gloucester and Leicester — foredoomed the provisional system to failure and disappointment. The king, emboldened by the division of his adversaries, announced in 1260 that, as the barons had failed to keep the Provisions, they were no longer binding on him. In this crisis the king's eldest son, Edward, stood for a moment by the side of Earl Simon in behalf of the popular cause, while Gloucester went over to the king.[2] But father and son were soon reconciled, and Gloucester returned to join with Earl Simon in calling a parliament, in the fall of 1261, at St. Alban's, to which were summoned three knights from every shire south of Trent.[3] The death of Gloucester in the summer of 1262 delivered the popular cause from the difficulties of a divided leadership, leaving the great earl free to deal single-handed with his royal opponent. After raising the standard of successful revolt, Simon, in order to avert civil war, agreed in December, 1263, as a compromise, to submit the matters at issue between the nation and the crown to the arbitrament of the king of France, who, it was agreed, should pass upon the validity of the Provisions, and at the same time determine whether or no they should continue in force.[4] Early in the following year Lewis made his award, in which he solved the questions at issue in favor of the king, with the proviso, however, that his award was not intended to abridge the liberties of the nation as defined by charter, statute, or custom.[5] This award, which upon its face seemed to be a contradiction, settled nothing but the fact that the last and only hope of the nation was in civil war, which soon began. In the decisive battle fought at Lewes in May, 1264, Simon was completely victorious over Henry and Edward, who, together with their chief supporters, became prisoners in his

Knights of the shire in the parliament of 1261.

Award of St. Lewis, Jan., 1264.

Battle of Lewes, May, 1264.

---

[1] *Statutes of the Realm*, i. pp. 8–11; *Ann. Burton*, pp. 471–479. In 1267 these Provisions were embodied in the Statute of Marlborough. — *Select Charters*, p. 400.

[2] Green, *History of the English People*, vol. i. pp. 294, 295; Pauli, p. 108.

[3] Henry commanded the sheriffs to send the knights, not to St. Alban's but to Windsor. For the writ, see *Lords' Report*, App. i. p. 23.

[4] Shirley, *Royal Letters*, vol. ii pp. 249–251; *Ann. Dunst.*, p. 225; Pauli, p. 132 *seq.*

[5] The award may be found in the *Fœdera*, i. p. 433, and in the *Liber de Antt. Legg.*, p. 59.

hands.[1]   The only use which the earl sought to make of his
victory was to place fresh and binding restraints upon the
royal authority.   In the " Mise of Lewes " — the convention
between the patriot leaders and their captive lord — the Provisions were confirmed, and a new body of arbitrators appointed to settle all controversies existing between the nation
and the king.[2]   Pending the award, the royal castles were
delivered to the barons, and on the 4th of June writs were
issued appointing guardians of the peace in each county, and
summoning four knights from each shire to meet the king in
a parliament to be held on the 22d of the same month.[3]
The parliament met at the time appointed, and drew up a new
programme of government, — to last while Henry lived, — under which the king was to act with the advice of a council of
nine, to be nominated by three electors to be chosen by the
barons, — three of the nine to be in constant attendance.[4]   In
order to conclude the arrangements embraced in the " Mise
of Lewes," and in order to gain a broader popular basis for
his government, Simon, on the 14th of December, issued the
writs for his famous parliament, to which were summoned not
only the two discreet knights from the shires, but also, for the
first time in the history of English politics, two representatives from the cities and boroughs.[5]   This bold and unprecedented appeal for aid to the rising democracy of the cities
and towns did not avail, however, to save the government
of the earl, now tottering to its fall.   The weakness of the
patriot party among the baronage had undermined Simon's
strength, and this fact finally led to his overthrow when the
disaffected, under the lead of Gloucester and the Mortimers,
were joined by Edward, who escaped from the earl in May,
1265.[6]   In the person of the prince the royal cause now found

*Knights of
the shire in
the parlia-
ment of
1264.*

*Famous
parliament
of 1265:
representa-
tives for the
first time
summoned
from cities
and towns.*

---

[1] For a general account of the battle,
see Rishanger, ed. Halliwell, p. 31 *seq. ;
Ann. Waverley*, p. 356; Blaauw's
Barons' War, pp. 143–189; Pauli, pp.
144–151.

[2] The substance of the convention,
which contained seven articles, is stated
in the Chronicle of Rishanger, p. 37.

[3] *Fœdera*, i. p. 442; *Select Charters*,
p. 411 *seq.*

[4] Ibid., i. p. 443.

[5] " Item in forma prædicta scribitur
civibus Eboraci, civibus Lincolniæ, et
ceteris burgis Angliæ, quod mittant in
forma prædicta duos de discretioribus,
legalioribus et probioribus tam civibus
quam burgensibus.

" Item in forma prædicta mandatum
est baronibus et probis hominibus
Quinque Portuum." The writ is contained in the *Lords' Report*, App. i. p.
33. " The novelty was simply the assembling the representatives of the
towns in conjunction with those of the
counties." — *Select Charters*, p. 410.

[6] Pauli, pp. 183–186.

a brilliant leader, whom Simon himself had trained in the art of war. When, in August, master and pupil met at Evesham [1] as leaders of the opposing forces, the great earl went down, and with him perished for a time the patriot cause for which he had so long and so unselfishly contended. Those of Simon's followers who survived the defeat were at once made to understand the full significance of unsuccessful rebellion. The franchises of every town that had supported the earl

were held to be at the king's mercy, while a general sentence of forfeiture was issued against all who had fought under his standard.[2] These exasperating measures drove the disinherited lords to gather for resistance in the castle of Kenilworth, where they were besieged by the king from June to December, 1266.[3] During the siege a parliament was held, and with the king's consent arbitrators were appointed who were charged with the duty of preparing a plan of reconcilia-

tion. The scheme thus prepared, known as the "*dictum de Kenilworth*," provided among other things that no one should be conclusively disinherited from the mere fact of having participated in the rebellion, — that all who would submit within a given time should be spared and forgiven.[4] After the terms thus proposed had been generally accepted, and after all show of armed resistance to the royal authority had completely disappeared, the king, in November, 1267, called a parliament at Marlborough, whose spirit stands in marked contrast to that which inspired the restoration parliament which had met in October of the preceding year. Instead of decrees of forfeiture against those who had been in rebellion, a statute was now passed in which were embodied the Provisions of Westminster,[5] — a series of ordinances of a remedial character which comprised substantially all of the grievances embraced

in the Provisions of Oxford. By the enactment of this statute, known as the Statute of Marlborough,[6] the nation won, after the pacification, the legal recognition of nearly every

---

[1] As to the battle, see *Ann. Wykes*, pp. 172–175; *Chron. Mailros*, pp. 199–215; *Ann. Waverley*, pp. 362–365.

[2] *Fœdera*, i. p. 462; *Liber de Antt. Legg.*, p. 76; *Ann. Wykes*, p. 176. As to the excesses of the Royalists, see Blaauw's *Barons' War*, pp. 267, 268.

[3] *Ann. Waverley*, p. 373; *Ann. Winton*, p. 104.

[4] The ordinance known as the "dictum de Kenilworth," which is divided into 41 articles, is contained in the *Statutes of the Realm*, i. pp. 12–17. See, also, *Select Charters*, pp. 419–425.

[5] See above, p. 401.

[6] *Statutes of the Realm*, i. pp. 19–25. For a commentary on this statute, see Reeves, vol. ii. pp. 323–340.

right — excepting the appointment of ministers and the election of sheriffs — for which the baronial leaders with Simon at their head had so long and so valiantly contended.[1] The concessions thus wisely made by the crown in the hour of victory were followed by peace which remained unbroken down to Henry's death in November, 1272.

8. The period of peace which followed the policy of reconciliation inspired by the victor of Evesham was so profound that Edward took the cross and went to Palestine.[2] While on his way home the news of his father's death reached him at Capua in 1273, but he did not arrive in England until August, 1274.[3] The fact that no one questioned the right of the absent heir to succeed to the vacant throne goes far to show how the ancient doctrine of elective kingship was fast giving way to the new feudal notion of hereditary right. Without election or coronation, the reign of the new king dated, for the first time, from the death of his predecessor. On the day of Henry's funeral the baronage swore fealty to their absent lord,[4] and three days afterwards the royal council, under whose control the kingdom passed, proclaimed the new peace in Edward's name.[5] It was not, however, until the reign of Edward IV. that the new doctrine of hereditary right finally ripened into the maxim that the king never dies, from which results the correlative idea that there can be no such thing as an interruption in the king's peace.[6] The first act of the important reign which now begins was a commission of inquiry into the territorial franchises, the results of which, recorded in the Hundred Rolls,[7] led to the passage of the Statute of Gloucester, which will be considered hereafter. The work of investigation thus begun was soon followed by the work of legislation : in April, 1275, Edward's first parliament met at

From the accession of Edward I. to the enactment of Quia emptores.

Edward's reign dates from the death of his predecessor.

Maxim that the king never dies not firmly established until the reign of Edward IV.

---

[1] Stubbs, *Const. Hist.*, vol. ii. p. 97. "Except the demand for the appointment of the ministers and the election of sheriffs, the statute of Marlborough concedes almost all that had been asked for in the Mad Parliament."

[2] *Ann. Winton*, p. 109.

[3] The king arrived on the second and the coronation took place on the nineteenth. — *Ann. Winton*, p. 118 ; *Fœdera*, i. p. 514.

[4] *Ann. Winton*, p. 112 ; *Fœdera*, i. p. 497.

[5] *Liber de Antt. Legg.*, p. 155 ; *Fœdera*, i. p. 497 ; *Select Charters*, pp. 447, 448.

[6] Stubbs, *Const. Hist.*, vol. ii. p. 103.

[7] For the facts upon this subject, see the introduction to the *Rotuli Hundredorum*, published by the Record Commission. For the relation of the *Hundred Rolls* of Edward I. to the history of the manorial system, see Seebohm, *English Village Com.*, p. 32 *seq.*

Statute of
Westminster I., 1275.

Westminster. In that parliament was passed the great statute or code known as Westminster the First,[1] which, in its fifty-one chapters, seems to have embraced nearly every subject which at the moment called for remedial legislation. This statute declares that the peace of the church and of the realm shall be kept and maintained in all things, and that common right shall be done to all, rich and poor alike, without respect to persons.[2] It further provides that all elections

Free elections.

shall be free, and that no man shall by force or menace disturb them,[3] — a provision the more important in view of the fact that sheriffs, coroners, and other officers connected with the administration of justice were then elected by the people.[4] In favor of the feudal tenants, certain clauses of the Great Charter were emphasized by provisions forbidding the illegal exaction of feudal aids, the abuse of wardships, and

Reform of legal procedure.

the imposition of excessive amercements. The statute then provides for a far-reaching reformation of the whole system of legal procedure both in civil and criminal cases.[5] As a compensation for this remedial measure, the parliament made a grant to the crown of custom on wool, woolfells, and leather.[6] Wool, the then staple produce of the country, which had been for some time the subject of unrestrained royal exaction, was now protected to some extent against arbitrary seizure by being made for the first time the subject of parliamentary taxation.[7] Passing over the parliament of 1276, which is only memorable because of the attendance of

Francesco Accursi the civilian.

Francesco Accursi of Bologna,[8] the civilian whose services Edward had retained before entering upon the work of legislative reform,[9] and over the year 1277, in which the king was engaged with an outbreak in Wales, we come to the parliament of 1278, in which was passed the Statute of Glouces-

---

[1] *Statutes of the Realm*, i. pp. 26, 35.

[2] Ch. 1.

[3] "And because elections ought to be free, the king commandeth upon great forfeiture that no man by force of arms, nor by malice or menacing, shall disturb any to make free election." — Ch. v.

[4] Cf. Coke, *Inst.*, ii. p. 169; Reeves, *Hist. Common Law*, vol. ii. p. 391 *seq.* (ed. Finlason).

[5] Upon this whole subject, see Reeves, vol. ii. pp. 390–429.

[6] *Parl. Writs*, vol. i. p. 2.

[7] Cf. *Select Charters*, p. 450.

[8] *Statutes of the Realm*, i. p. 42.

[9] "Francesco was in attendance on Edward at Limoges in May, 1274, *Fœdera*, i. pp. 511, 512." — Stubbs, *Const. Hist.*, vol. ii. p. 107, note 2. He was the son of the great Accursi of Bologna, who was the writer of the glosses on the civil law.

ter,[1] a statute designed to give effect to the work begun by Statute of Gloucester, 1278. the inquiry of 1274 into the territorial franchises. As heretofore explained, the jurisdictions of the local courts were from the earliest times cut up and undermined by a network of territorial lordships, which were nothing more nor less than law courts in private hands, that stood as stumbling-blocks to the orderly and uniform administration of law by the king's justices. Against the existence of these private law courts Anti-feudal policy of Henry II. the anti-feudal policy of Henry II. had been vigorously directed,[2] and in furtherance of that policy the Statute of Gloucester was enacted. Under the authority of that statute the itinerant justices were directed to inquire into the right by which the several franchises, liberties, and privileges were held by the lay and spiritual lords who claimed them; and by virtue of the *quo warrantos* which were issued to all war was openly declared by the crown against all liberties and franchises in the kingdom.[3] Every holder of a franchise was thus driven to maintain his warrant or title. The feudal lords, who regarded the inquiry as a dangerous assault upon their local rights, angrily resisted it; and in this spirit it was that the Earl of Warenne, when called upon to show his title, produced an old sword and exclaimed to the justices, "See, my lords, here is my warrant."[4]

The blow thus dealt at the possessors of territorial franchises was followed in the next year by a memorable statute Statute of mortmain, 1279. devised in the interests of the feudal lords, with the king at their head, as against any "person religious or other, whatsoever he be, that will buy or sell any lands or tenements, or under the color of gift or lease, or that will receive by reason of any title, whatsoever it be, lands or tenements, or by any other craft or engine will presume to appropriate to himself under pain of forfeiture of the same, whereby such lands or tenements may anywise come into mortmain."[5] In order to Charter provision inadequate. prevent the cutting off of the feudal dues and services which resulted from the conveyance of lands into the "dead hands" of religious orders, it was provided in the Great Charter that

---

[1] *Statutes of the Realm*, i. p. 45.
[2] See above, p. 282.
[3] Reeves, *Hist. Eng. Law*, vol. ii. pp. 523–526.
[4] Hemingb., ii. p. 6.

[5] This is a translation of the vital part of the famous statute *De religiosis*, commonly called the statute of mortmain. — *Statutes of the Realm*, i. p. 51.

"it shall not be lawful from henceforth to any to give his lands to any religious house, and to take the same land again, to hold of the same house. Nor shall it be lawful to any house of religion to take the lands of any, and to lease the same to him of whom they were received to be holden."[1] This provision of the charter was not, however, sufficiently comprehensive to compass the evil, and for that reason the statute *De religiosis* was passed to give to the prohibition a wider application.[2]

Ecclesiastical ingenuity proved, however, to be more than a match for the skill of the legislator. The new statute was soon evaded by the bringing of actions for land, in which "the religious men and other ecclesiastical persons" sued the tenant, who, by "suffering a recovery," aided the plaintiff to evade the statute by acquiring the land, not by gift or alienation, but by process of law. To prevent this new device a clause was introduced into the Statute of Westminster II. which provided that in such cases a jury should determine whether the claimant had a right over the land sued for or not.[3] The prohibition as to mortmain imposed by the statute could only be removed by license from the crown and the mesne lords, if any, down to the passage of the statute of 7 & 8 Will. III. c. 37, whereby it was provided that such license could be granted by the crown alone, without the consent of the mesne lords, in any form whatsoever. Exceptions have also been made in favor of certain classes of corporations by act of parliament.[4]

From the congenial work of legislation Edward was called in 1282 by a renewal of the Welsh war, which, after less than a year's duration, ended in the death of Llewelyn and the annexation of the principality to the English crown. Llewelyn fell in December, 1282,[5] and in the following June his brother David, who after having received an English lordship from Edward's hands had conspired against him,[6] was captured. In an anomalous assembly or parliament which

Marginal notes: Ecclesiastical ingenuity. Remedy for evasions of the statute. Prohibition removed by license. Conquest of Wales, 1282–83.

---

[1] Cap. 43, ed. 1217.
[2] Reeves, *Hist. Eng. Law*, vol. ii. pp. 445 *seq.*
[3] Cf. Digby, *Law of Real Property*, pp. 182, 183.
[4] "When, however, no license has been obtained from the crown or has been conferred by act of parliament,

the old rule of law still prevails." — Digby, *Law of Real Property*, p. 183.
[5] *Fœdera*, i. p. 631 ; *Cont.*, Fl. Wig., p. 229.
[6] Green, *Hist. Eng. People*, vol. i. p. 332.

met at Shrewsbury in September, 1283,[1] David was tried and condemned as a traitor and immediately executed. A few days afterwards the king at Acton Burnell, in the irregular assembly which had gathered to witness David's trial, enacted the Statute of Acton Burnell, or, as it is generally called, the Statute of Merchants,[2] in which was provided a more speedy and certain remedy for the collection of that class of pressing demands which arise out of mercantile transactions.[3] In order to render secure the results of his conquest over Wales, Edward not only provided for the settlement of English barons upon the confiscated soil which rebellion had forfeited to the overlord, but he also, by statutes[4] published at Rhuddland in 1284, attempted to incorporate the principality into the body of the kingdom by introducing into the greater part of it the English shire system, together with the system of English legal administration.[5] From this time began that tendency to closer union between the kingdom and the principality which finally resulted, in the reign of Henry VIII., in the complete incorporation of Wales with England, and its representation in the English parliament.[6]

Statute of Merchants, 1283.

Incorporation of Wales with England.

In 1285, the year following the settlement of the Welsh conquest, were passed two great statutes — the Statute of Winchester and the Statute of Westminster the Second — which are justly regarded not only as the highest exhibitions of Edward's constructive skill as a legislator, but also as vitally important links in the chain that binds the ancient system of customary law which prevailed in the local courts of the people to the new system of royal or official law which prevailed in the central court of the king.[7] These statutes, in their respective spheres, not only reorganized and improved the systems of central and provincial administration, but they brought them into closer and more harmonious relations with each other. As the leading object of the second

Two great statutes.

---

[1] *Fœdera*, i. p. 630; *Parl. Writs*, vol. i. p. 16 ; *Select Charters*, pp. 463, 467.
[2] *Statutes of the Realm*, i. pp. 53, 54.
[3] Reeves, *Hist. Eng. Law*, vol. ii. p. 452.
[4] *Statutes of the Realm*, i. pp. 55–68.
[5] "They were intended to assimilate the administration of Wales to that of England, a principle which Edward had in vain attempted to enforce in his Welsh territories before he became king." — Stubbs, vol. ii. p. 117.
[6] Green, *Hist. Eng. People*, vol. i. p. 334.
[7] "If the Statute of Westminster represents the growth and defined stature of the royal jurisdiction, the Statute of Winchester shows the permanence and adaptability of the ancient popular law." — Stubbs, *Const. Hist.*, vol. ii. p. 118.

Statute of Westminster was to readjust and perfect the new system of legal administration which had sprung from the Statute of Winchester, 1285. curia regis, so the leading purpose of the Statute of Winchester[1] was to revive and strengthen the ancient system of police which had immemorially existed in the organization of the hundred, and the ancient military system which had immemorially existed in the organization of the fyrd.[2] The statute last named recites that all kinds of crime are more frequently committed for the want of a proper enforcement of existing law; and in order to remedy the special evil resulting from the concealment of crime, provision is made that "hue and cry" shall be made in all public gatherings, so that no one by pleading ignorance shall shield himself from doing his duty in the arrest of criminals.[3]

Statute of Westminster II., 1285. The provisions of the Statute of Westminster[4] the Second fall into two broad divisions: first, those which relate to the organization of the king's itinerant courts, and to the general administration of justice therein; second, those that relate to the tenure and transfer of land. Under the first head the most important single provision is perhaps that one which Bill of exceptions. grants to suitors the right to a bill of exceptions, whereby all matters of exception occurring at the trial can be reëxamined upon a writ of error, whether appearing upon the face of the record or no.[5] Under the second head, by far the most important provision is that one contained in the first chapter of *De donis conditionalibus.* the act, which chapter is generally known as the statute *De donis conditionalibus.* In order to clearly illustrate the bearings of this statute, designed as a feudal restraint upon alienation, it will be necessary to briefly review the other leading restraints upon alienation which precede and follow it.

Restraints upon alienation. In the review heretofore made of the system of Old-English land law as it existed in the pre-Norman period, the fact was drawn out that the village community or township was originally subdivided into family estates, and that the family estate consisted of house-lands in the village, the allotment

---

[1] *Statutes of the Realm,* i. pp. 96–98.

[2] *Select Charters,* p. 469. A translation of the statute is there given.

[3] Reeves, *Hist. Eng. Law,* vol. ii. p. 518 and note, Finlason ed. That part of the statute which relates to the

fyrd and the assize of arms is contained in cap. vi.

[4] *Statutes of the Realm,* i. pp. 71–95.

[5] Coke, *Inst.,* ii. p. 426; Reeves, *Hist. Eng. Law,* vol. ii. pp. 487–490 and notes, Finlason ed.

of the family in the arable fields, together with the common rights in the waste lands appurtenant thereto. As the family tie weakened, and as the communal system fell into decay, the "alod" of the free townsman, embracing both houselands and arable in severalty, ultimately arose out of the primitive family estate. But even under this changed condition of things the influence of family organization lingered in the restraints which it imposed upon the right of alienation. **Restraints in favor of the family.** The family estate was primarily an estate of inheritance, and as such inalienable. This principle first yielded to the doctrine that lands were alienable within the limits and with the consent of the family. Then, when wills were introduced by the church, family land became subject to devise, the validity of the will originally depending upon family consent.[1] With these beginnings, the doctrine that the lands of the family were alienable gradually widened as the idea of individual ownership and the use of written instruments in the alienation of land became more firmly established. As the primitive method of transfer by actual delivery gave way to the new method of transfer by book or charter, whereby absolute estates were generally created, the term "book-land" became nearly if not quite coextensive in meaning with "alodial;" in that way the "alod" disappeared in the book-land.[2] But even after this change in the evidence of title, traces of the family influence still survived. As a general rule, the grantee under **A grantee of book-land.** a book or charter had an absolute right of alienation by virtue of the terms of the book itself. In the absence, however, of the grant of such a power in the charter, the customary law stepped in and declared that the property of the family could not be wholly alienated.[3] This restraint upon alienation in favor of the heir, which survived as a relic of primitive custom down to the time of Glanvill, had disappeared by the time of Bracton.[4] With the growth of feudal ideas the primitive restraints upon alienation, based upon the duties of the ancestor to the heir, were succeeded by a new system of restraints which grew out of the duties due from the tenant

---

[1] Upon this whole subject see above, p. 137.

[2] See above, p. 140.

[3] "Si bocland autem habeat, quam ei parentes sui dederint, non mittat eam extra cognationem suam." — Leg. Hen. I. 70, § 21, in Thorpe, *Anc. Laws,* fol. ed., p. 251. Cf. Digby, p. 90.

[4] Digby, *Law of Real Property,* pp. 90, 136.

Restraints in favor of the lord.

to his lord. First among these feudal restraints stands the clause of the Great Charter which provides that "no free-man from henceforth shall give or sell any more of his land but so that of the residue of the lands the lord of the fee may have the service due to him which belongeth to the fee."[1] After a long interval this clause of the Great Charter was followed by the statute *De donis conditionalibus*, by force of which estates tail came into existence. The purpose of this statute was not only to protect the interest of the heir to a conditional estate by restraining its alienation by the ancestor, but also to prevent the defeat of the lord's right of escheat by the alienation of his tenant. By the force of this statute a new species of estates of inheritance came into existence, whose alienation was subject to a twofold restraint in favor of the heir and the lord.[2] The great inconvenience which in time resulted from the establishment of this new system of estates was in a great measure modified by a series of legal fictions established in the famous case of Taltarum in 12 Edward IV.[3]

Estates tail.

Taltarum's case.

Quia emptores, — Statute of Westminster the Third, 1290.

The crowning restraint upon alienation in favor of the feudal lords was, however, embodied in the statute of *Quia emptores,* enacted in the 18 Edward I. in the parliament of 1290. The primary object of this statute was to prevent the loss to the lords of manors caused by the granting out of lands by their tenants to be held of themselves by subinfeuda-tion. In such a case, as there could be no immediate relation of lord and tenant between the chief lord and the alienee, the feudal rights of the former over the land conveyed were consequently diminished. To remedy this evil it was provided in the Statute of Westminster the Third — *Quia emptores* — that in all future conveyances by tenants the alienee, instead of becoming the feudal dependent of the alienor, should simply step into the shoes of the alienor, and

[1] Cap. 39 (ed. 1217). "The provision in Magna Carta given above appears to be the only restraint upon alienation of lands in fee simple ever recognized by law in the interest of the lord." — Digby, pp. 136, 137. Cf. Coke, *Inst.,* ii. p. 66; Reeves, vol. ii. p. 24.

[2] Digby, *Law of Real Property,* pp. 187–195; Reeves, *Hist. Eng. Law,* vol. ii. pp. 459–463; Littleton, sec. 13.

[3] Year Book, 12 Edward IV. 19. "From this time till 1834 (3 & 4 Will. IV. c. 74) it became the common practice for tenant in tail to suffer a recovery; that is, by a proceeding similar to that adopted in Taltarum's case, to convert his estate into a fee simple." — Digby, p. 219.

become subject to all the duties and obligations under which he held the land of the chief lord.[1]   The statute *Quia emp-* Edward's fame as a legislator. *tores* was the last of that series of remarkable legislative enactments, whose far-reaching influence in defining and amending the common law has won for Edward the imposing title of the English Justinian.   Other important statutes of a political and constitutional character were passed, it is true, in the latter part of the reign, but it is rather to those statutes touching the private rights of individuals, and the general administration of justice, already reviewed, that Sir Matthew Hale alludes when he says that "it appears that the very scheme, mould, and model of the common law, especially in relation to the administration of common justice between party and party, as it was highly rectified and set in a much better light and order by this king than his predecessors left it to him, so in a very great measure it was continued the same in all succeeding ages to this day.   So that the mark or epocha we are to take for the true stating of the law of England, what it is, is to be considered, stated, and estimated from what it was when this king left it."[2]

Long before the organizing and defining hand of Edward Growth of the common law. was applied to the task of reducing through the agency of legislation the body of the customary law, as modified by the innovations to which the Conquest had given birth, to system and order, two great text-writers had been at work smoothing the path before him.   In the reign of Henry II. we have the work of Glanvill, — the first English law-book Glanvill. bearing the name of a personal author, — which, as a commentary upon the procedure of the curia regis, has been referred to already.[3]   The work of Glanvill, which is rather a treatise upon legal procedure than a systematic exposition of the corpus of the common law as it stood in Glanvill's day, was followed at the end of the reign of Henry III. by Brac- Bracton. ton's De Legibus et Consuetudinibus Angliæ.[4]   This great

---

[1] Reeves, *Hist. Eng. Law*, vol. ii. p. 527 *seq.*; Digby, *Law of Real Property*, pp. 199–204.   This act, though devised in the interest of the lords for the preservation of their estates, really afforded greater facilities for their division, and led to the multiplication of tenants *in capite*, and of socage tenants also.   "It is one of the few acts of legislation which, being passed with a distinct view to the interests of a class, have been found to work to the advantage of the nation generally." — *Select Charters*, p. 478.   Cf. *Lords' Report*, vol. i. p. 129.

[2] *Hist. Com. Law*, vol. i. p. 277.

[3] See above, p. 302.

[4] As to Bracton's life, of which little

work, which even in Coke's time was looked to as the highest source from which a knowledge of the common law could be drawn, is a comprehensive and systematic statement of the whole law of England as it stood when the reign of Edward I. begins.   Bracton's great familiarity with the imperial and pontifical jurisprudence, which had already been introduced to some extent into the English system by the clerical judges,[1] is manifest not only from his frequent quotations from the Digest, Institutes, and Code of Justinian, but also from his use of definitions and maxims drawn from Roman sources.[2]

Influence of the imperial and pontifical jurisprudence.

The tendency thus exhibited by Bracton to enrich the common law by principles and definitions drawn from the revived Roman jurisprudence was followed by Edward, who was careful to secure the services of the civilian, Francesco Accursi of Bologna, before entering upon the work of legislative reform.[3]   For Edward's own reign we have the treatises of Britton[4] and Fleta, which do little more than supplement Bracton's work, and adapt the principles which it defines to practical uses.   The Mirror of Justices, an anonymous treatise, is generally ascribed to the reign of Edward II.   For the reign of Henry VI. we have the treatise De Laudibus Legum Angliæ from the pen of Henry's chancellor, Sir John Fortescue, in which the outlines of English law are set forth in the form of a dialogue between the chancellor and the prince.[5]   In the following reign was published Littleton's treatise on Tenures, of which the first part of Coke's Institutes is but a later elaboration.   But neither to the work of the legislator, nor to the more or less scientific disquisitions of the early text-writers, must we look for the overshadowing force which for centuries has been organizing and adapting the unelastic system of English law — which has grown out of an admixture of Teutonic custom and Norman feudalism — to the expanding wants of a progressive society.   The great

Britton and Fleta.

Mirror of justices.

Fortescue.

Littleton.

Coke.

---

is known, see Foss, *Judges of England*, vol. ii. p. 251.

[1] "It seems to be a fashion to discredit Bracton, on a supposition of his having mingled too much of the civilian and canonist with the common lawyer." — Reeves, vol. ii. p. 360, note 1.

[2] Cf. *Henricus de Bracton und sein Verhältniss zum Römischen Rechte*, by

Dr. Carl Güterbock, Berlin, 1862, translated by Coxe, Philadelphia, 1866. Digby, p. 104.

[3] See above, p. 406.

[4] As to the authorship of Britton, cf. Nicholas' *Britton*, preface, pp. xviii-xxvii.

[5] See the Introduction to the Clermont ed.

organs of interpretation which have given form and consist- Judicial decisions become a source of law.
ency to the customary law are the judicial tribunals in which
that law has been immemorially administered.   The recorded
decisions of these tribunals have stood not only as expositions
of the existing law as applied to particular cases, but as
sources of law from which have been drawn rules of decision
which govern in new cases for which there is no precedent.[1]
In this way "the decisions of the tribunals come to constitute
in the strictest sense of the term a source or cause of law.
Judge-made or judiciary law henceforth gradually displaces
customary law." [2]   Records of cases adjudicated in the Eng- Records of adjudicated cases exist from the time of Richard I.
lish courts are in existence from the time of Richard I., and
have been published by the Record Commission,[3] which has
also lately published four volumes called Year Books, containing the reports of cases decided on the *itinera* of the
justices and at Westminster between the twentieth and thirty-
second years of Edward I.   The regular series of reports The Year Books.
known as the Year Books begin, however, with the reign of
Edward II., and contain reports of cases decided to the end
of the reign of Edward III., and from the beginning of the
reign of Henry IV. to the end of that of Henry VIII., — the
reports of the reign of Richard II. being contained in a volume known as Bellewe's Reports.[4]

9. The constructive genius of Edward, which was first Parliament as an assembly of estates.
employed in the work of organizing and defining the custom-
ary law, is applied, as his reign advances, to the task of
organizing and defining the constitution of parliament itself.
The process has already been drawn out through which the
Old-English witan was silently transformed, after the Conquest, into the feudal councils or courts of the Norman and
Angevin kings.   Under Henry II. and his sons, the constitution of the national council reached a definiteness of organi-

---

[1] "Il y a quatre sources principales du droit constitutionnel anglais : les traités et les quasi-traités, les précédents et usages que l'on désigne ordinairement sous le nom de Common law, les pactes, les statuts ou lois." — M. Boutmy, *Études de Droit Constitutionnel* (Paris, 1885), p. 9.

[2] Digby, *Law of Real Property*, p. 103.   That judicial decisions are a source of the common law is the doctrine of Austin. — *Jurisprudence*, lect.

xxxvii.   Blackstone holds that they are the evidence of the common law. — *Com.*, bk. i. p. 70.

[3] The edition called *Rotuli Curiæ Regis* was edited by Sir Francis Palgrave, and published in 1835.   The first publication in 1811 bore the name of *Placitorum Abbreviatio.*

[4] Cf. Reeves, *Hist. Eng. Law*, vol. iii. pp. 73, 443, 570; vol. iv. pp. 24, 160, 225, 561.   See, also, Digby, p. 175, and notes.

zation which it had never possessed before; through the influence of the practice of summons, the right to attend the national council was limited to those only who were summoned, by the king's writ individually or in a body. How far this practice had developed up to the sixteenth year of John is made clear by the fourteenth article of the Great Charter, which provides that the greater tenants-in-chief, lay and spiritual, shall be summoned individually by special writ, while the minor tenants-in-chief shall be summoned in a body by a general writ addressed to the sheriffs.[1] This provision of the Charter as to the summons of the minor tenants-in-chief did not absolutely imply representation, but it recognized a condition of things out of which representation arose as a natural and necessary consequence. The only constitutional mode in which the sheriff could execute the general writ of summons to the minor tenants was in the county court,[2] in whose organization and machinery the principles of election and representation had been imbedded from the earliest times. As heretofore pointed out, the earliest manifestation of the representative principle appears in the form of the reeve and four men who represent the townships in the courts of the shire and the hundred.[3] In the shire court the reeve and four men appeared for each township, the twelve senior thegns for each hundred. The shire court was, therefore, not only a popular but a representative assembly, — a county parliament in which each township and hundred appeared in the persons of its representatives. The representative principle, which survived the Conquest as a part of the machinery of the local courts, never entered, however, into the constitution of the national council prior to the reign of John. Not until that time did the ancient practice of sending the reeve and four men from the township to the shire-moot expand into the practice of sending the "four discreet men" as representatives of the shire to the common council of the kingdom. For the first time, in the fourteenth year of John, the writ addressed to the sheriffs provided for the return of "four discreet men" from each shire as its representatives in the national council.[4] Thus, by a change in the form

Election and representation.

The shire court.

Representatives of the shire in the national council.

---

[1] See above, p. 387.
[2] *Select Charters*, p. 39.

[3] See above, p. 143.
[4] See above, p. 377.

of the writ, a system of representation was substituted in lieu of the general summons to the minor tenants-in-chief. The practice of shire representation thus established slowly gained strength by repetition during the reigns of Henry III. and Edward I. until from the year 1295 it becomes fixed as a permanent institution. A considerable period elapsed, however, before the right of representation first conceded to the shires was extended to the cities and towns : in the famous parliament of Simon of Montfort, which met in 1265, the citizens and burgesses first appear.[1] A period of thirty years then elapsed before the experiment was repeated, — the representatives of the cities and towns are not again summoned until Edward's great parliament of 1295.[2] The principle of representation which thus gradually worked itself into the constitution of the national council must be considered in connection with the growth of the system of estates with whose history it is inseparably interlaced. As heretofore explained, the growth of the estate system in England was simply a part of a general European movement which is generally regarded by the historians as the work of the thirteenth century. During that period was established in Europe that type of a national assembly into which the several classes or orders of society entered, in the form of definitely organized estates, either in person or by representatives. In English history the three estates appear as the clergy, the baronage, and the commons.[3] The process of definition which begins with the Conquest is completed by the end of the reign of Edward I. The growth of the estate system and of the representative system therefore synchronize with each other. In the composition of the famous parliament convened by Edward at Westminster in November, 1295, the estate system in England reached for the first time its full and final development. In the parliament of 1295 each estate appears in person or by representatives. In this assembly the baronage appear in person and represent themselves ; the clergy and the commons, each as an estate of the

Representatives from the cities and towns first appear in the parliament of 1265.

Growth of the estate system.

Synchronizes with that of the representative system.

The model parliament of 1295.

---

[1] See above, p. 403.
[2] "The national councils of 1273 and 1283, and the parliament of Acton Burnell, contained representatives of the towns, but they are not allowed by constitutional lawyers the full name of parliaments." — *Select Charters*, p. 44.
[3] See above, p. 337.

realm, appear in the persons of their chosen representatives.[1]
This parliament, which stands as a model for all that succeed
it, completes the transition in the constitution of the national
assembly from a feudal council to a council of estates.[2] After
the failure of Edward's attempt to organize the clergy as a
parliamentary estate, owing to the unwillingness of the clergy
themselves to attend in a secular assembly, the lords and
commons remain as the permanent elements in the parliamentary system. Out of these elements, which the organizing hand of Edward first brought into lasting contact with
each other, has been gradually developed the parliamentary
constitution of modern times.

Close of the
constitu-
tional strug-
gle in the
final con-
firmation of
the charters
in the 25th
of Edward
I.

10. In Edward's model parliament of 1295 the representatives of the three estates met together in the face of an
emergency which, in the language of the writs addressed to
the archbishops and clergy, plainly admonished all "that
common dangers must be met by measures concerted in common."[3] These dangers were no less than rebellion in Wales,
and war with Scotland and France. To put down the Welsh
rebellion, to maintain his freshly established overlordship
over Scotland, and at the same time to defend his Gascon
possessions against the designs of Philip the Fair, were
tasks well calculated to tax to the utmost the resources of
Edward, not only as a general, but as a financier.[4] In the
face of such difficulties he appealed for aid and counsel not
only to the clergy, the baronage, and the shires, but also to
that rising branch of the commons which dwelt within the
limits of the cities and towns. To the appeal thus made, the
nation, which so far in Edward's reign had not been heavily
taxed, made a hearty response : the barons and knights gave
an eleventh ; the clergy a tenth ; the representatives of the
boroughs a seventh.[5] During the course of the year the

---

[1] The writs to the baronage are issued on the 1st October. — *Lords' Report*, App. i. p. 67. The writs to the
archbishops and clergy are issued on
the 30th September. — Ibid., App. i. p.
67. The writs to the sheriffs commanding the return of representatives
from the shires and towns are issued on
the 3d October. — Ibid., App. i. p. 66.

[2] "The thirteenth century turns the
feudal council into an assembly of estates, and draws the constitution of

the third estate from the ancient local
machinery which it concentrates." —
Stubbs, *Const. Hist.*, vol. ii. p. 168.

[3] "Sic et nimis evidenter ut commu-
nibus periculis per remedia provisa
communitur obvieter."

[4] The character of Edward's difficulties and their relation to the parliament of 1295 are clearly set forth in
the *Lords' Report*, vol. i. pp. 217, 218.

[5] M. Westm., p. 425, 426; *Ann. Wi-
gorn*, p. 522; Patent Rolls, Dec. 4.

Welsh were subdued,[1] but not until midsummer, 1296, did
Edward complete the conquest of Scotland, — an enterprise
which not only delayed his departure for the war against
Philip, but also exhausted the subsidies which had been
granted him.   To raise more money a new parliament was
summoned to meet in November, 1296, whose constitution
was in all respects the same as that of the preceding year.
In this assembly the barons and knights gave a twelfth, and
the representatives of the towns an eighth ;[2] but the clergy
now notified the king that it was impossible for them to
give anything by reason of a bull — *Clericis laicos* — which
had just been published by Boniface VIII., forbidding the
state to exact, or the clergy to pay, any taxes whatever from
the revenues of their churches.[3]   In the face of this refusal
the king at once collected what had been granted by the
baronage and the commons, giving the clergy until January,
1297, to make their final answer.   Before the end of the
month so fixed, their refusal was repeated and the clergy
practically outlawed ; and promptly thereafter writs were issued for the seizure of the lay fees of the province of Canterbury.[4]   Thus at open war with the clergy, the king resolved to appeal to the baronage alone to aid him in the
prosecution of the war in Gascony.   The barons, under the
leadership of the great earls Roger Bigod of Norfolk and
Humfrey Bohun of Hereford, met the king in February at
Salisbury,[5] where he proposed to them singly that they
should go to Gascony while he took command in Flanders.
The earls, while admitting that their tenures obliged them to
go to Gascony with the king, firmly refused to go without
him.   After bitter recrimination between Bigod and the king
the council broke up in anger, and the baronial leaders retired to their estates and prepared for civil war.   Thus exas-
perated by the refusal of the baronage to render military

Conquest of Scotland.

The bull Clericis laicos.

Attack upon the clergy, Jan., 1297.

Quarrel with the baronage.

---

[1] The third Welsh war really ended
before the model parliament met.

[2] The material facts are all stated in
the *Lords' Report*, vol. i. p. 219. See,
also, *Parl. Writs*, vol. i. p. 47 ; Hemingb., ii. p. 116 ; M. Westm., p. 428 ;
Ann. Trivet, p. 352.

[3] *Fœdera*, i. p. 836 ; Wilkins, *Conc.*,
vol. ii. p. 222.

[4] *Lords' Report*, vol. i. p. 219 ; Stubbs,
Const. Hist., vol. ii. p. 131.

[5] Hemingb., ii. p. 121 ; M. Westm.,
p. 429 ; *Parl. Writs*, i. p. 51.   "No
writs to the prelates, or for the election of knights, citizens, and burgesses,
appear on the record." — *Lords' Report*,
vol. i. p. 220.   And yet the historians
call this meeting of the baronage a parliament.

service at the critical moment when, in connection with his allies, he had planned a deadly blow against France, Edward resolved to ignore all of the restraints of legality, and by the mere force of royal edict to raise both men and money for the war.[1]

Edward's extreme measures.

In execution of this rash policy Edward arbitrarily ordered the seizure of the wool of the merchants, security for payment being given in the form of tallies ; and a like order was also issued commanding the shires to furnish a large amount of provisions to be paid for in the same manner.[2] Having thus provided for the raising of supplies, an equally unconstitutional measure was resorted to for the purpose of raising troops to cross the sea under the king's command. Writs were issued in May for a military levy of the whole kingdom to meet in London on the 7th of July, the sheriffs being enjoined to enforce the attendance in arms of all persons holding lands of the annual value of £20.[3] This proposal to employ the whole force of the kingdom in a foreign war, regardless of tenure, precipitated the crisis between the nation and the king.[4]

Resistance under the leadership of Bigod and Bohun.

When, on the day appointed, the military force met, Bigod and Bohun as marshal and constable refused to perform their official duties ; whereupon the king indignantly superseded them in their offices, and they left the court. After the departure of the earls, Edward, as a last resort, assembled the leading men who had attended the military levy, and, although they had not been summoned to a parliament, appealed to them to assume the right to act as representatives of the nation, and as such to make on the instant a money grant. In this unauthorized gathering, an aid of an eighth from the barons and knights, and a fifth from the towns, was declared to be granted ;[5] and as a reward for this concession the king promised a confirmation of the charters.

Confirmation of the charters promised.

Before attempting, however, to collect the tax thus imposed, Edward resolved to make a final attempt to come to

[1] *Select Charters*, p. 489.
[2] Rishanger, p. 169; M. Westm., p. 430.
[3] *Fœdera*, i. p. 865; *Parl. Writs*, vol. i. p. 281.
[4] " The attempt on the part of the king to require the military service beyond sea of all who held £20 a year of land, . . . occasioned great dis-

turbances." — *Lords' Report*, vol. i. p. 221.

[5] M. Westm., p. 430; *Ann. Dunst.*, p. 407 ; *Select Charters*, p. 490. " There is no evidence that this grant was made by a legislative assembly, and it seems that the manner of levying it was ordained by the king and his council." — *Lord's Report*, vol. i. p. 221.

terms with the clergy and the earls. With this end in view he made peace in a public manner with Archbishop Winchelsey,[1] who at once assumed the rôle of mediator. But the time for mediation had passed ; the time had now come when the supreme question, involving the right of the nation to tax itself, — a right which the barons of Runnymede had clearly defined, but which the struggles of eighty years had failed to confirm, — had to be settled once and for all between the nation and the king. The twelfth article of the Great Charter had expressly declared that no scutage or aid, other than the three regular feudal aids, should henceforth be imposed but by the common counsel of the nation ; and by the fourteenth article it was provided that such common counsel as to the assessment of aids and scutages should only be taken in an assembly duly summoned. These vital clauses were, however, omitted from the very first reissue of the charter, and in the numberless confirmations which took place during the reigns of Henry III. and Edward I. they were never afterwards reinstated.[2] During the reigns of Henry and Edward taxes, it is true, were generally imposed by national consent, but there was no constitutional guaranty that in the stress of a great emergency they might not be imposed simply as an effort of the royal will. In the stress of such an emergency Edward had ventured to press to the utmost the right of the crown to tax the nation without its authority, and the result was a counter-movement upon the part of the nation which made all such future attempts upon the part of the crown forever impossible. Whatever may have been their motives,[3] the fact remains that Bigod and Bohun, as the leaders of this counter-movement to bridle the royal prerogative, stood firmly by the nation and against the king. After repeated attempts, the archbishop utterly failed to bring the earls to submission ;[4] whereupon the king published a manifesto against the earls in which he appealed to the people to keep

The king makes peace with the archbishop.

The omitted provisions of the Great Charter.

Edward's extreme measures produce the counter-movement led by the earls,

---

[1] At Westminster Hall, July 14. M. Westm., p. 430.

[2] Dr. Gneist gives his reason why, during this long period, articles 12 and 14 were omitted, the essence of which is the supposed difficulty of drawing a line of demarcation between the greater and lesser nobles. See *The English Parliament*, p. 89 (Shee's trans.).

[3] Hallam pays a high tribute to the patriotism of the earls (*M. A.*, vol. iii. p. 6), while Stubbs holds that their action was prompted by "personal ambitions and personal grievances." — *Const. Hist.*, vol. ii. p. 146.

[4] As to Winchelsey's fruitless negotiation with the earls, see *Fœdera*, i. pp. 872, 873 ; Wilkins, *Conc.*, vol. ii. p. 227.

the peace during his absence.[1]   After this appeal, it seems
that the baronial leaders brought forward a formal list of
grievances, which were duly presented to the king before his
departure.[2]   Thus the issue stood at the time of Edward's
embarkation for Flanders on the 22d of August.   Before
leaving, the king appointed his son Edward regent, with

who resist the collection of the unauthorized taxes.

Reginald Grey as his chief counsellor.   On the day following
the king's departure the storm broke : on that day Bohun
and Bigod, backed by a military force in which appeared the
citizens of London, came into the exchequer and forbade the
collection of the unauthorized taxes which the king had
levied until the promised confirmation of the charters had
taken place.[3]   In the presence of such a demonstration, which
amounted to civil war, the regent was compelled to yield ;
and in order to carry out such concessions as were promised,
a parliament was summoned for the 6th of October.[4]   In this
assembly, which was irregularly summoned, and in which the
baronial leaders appeared with a strong military force at

Close of the struggle.

their backs, the prolonged struggle was brought to a close.
The earls demanded not only the confirmation of the charters, but also the adoption, as a part of such confirmation,
of certain supplementary articles that embodied the list of
grievances which prior to his departure they had presented
to the king.   The regent, with the advice of his council, at
once conceded all that was demanded of him, and then for-

Charters confirmed at Ghent, Nov. 5, 1297.— Confirmatio Cartarum.

warded the charters with the new articles to the king, who
confirmed both at Ghent on the 5th of November.[5]   The
new articles, which were thus solemnly made a part of the
constitution, not only denounced all of the unauthorized taxation which had recently been imposed by royal authority, but

---

[1] B. Cotton, p. 330; *Fœdera*, i. p. 872, 873.

[2] B. Cotton, p. 325; *Ann. Trivet*, p. 360; Rishanger, p. 175 ; *Select Charters*, p. 491.

[3] M. Westm., p. 430; Rishanger, p. 178; *Parl. Writs*, i. p. 32 ; *Lords' Report*, vol. i. p. 222.

[4] That is to say, writs were addressed to the sheriffs on the 15th September commanding them to return, by the day named, representatives of the shires, to receive the king's charters and letters patent in consideration of an eighth to

be granted him. No mention is made of representatives from the cities and towns, or of the inferior clergy. The facts as to this assembly, which was summoned in a most irregular manner, are all stated in the *Lords' Report*, vol. i. pp. 224, 225. See, also, *Select Charters*, p. 492.

[5] *Fœdera*, i. p. 880. The charters had been previously confirmed by *inspeximus* on the 12th of October. — *Fœdera*, i. p. 879; *Statutes of the Realm*, i. pp. 114–119.

they also provided that, with certain exceptions, no **taxes** should henceforth be imposed without the common consent of the realm and to the common profit thereof. The king was made to promise the clergy, the barons, and "all the commonalty of the land, that for no business from hence-forth will we take such manner of aids, tasks, nor prizes, but by the common assent of the realm, and for the common profit thereof, saving the ancient aids and prizes due and accustomed." [1] And in order to extend the limitation to indirect as well as to direct taxation, the articles further provide that the royal right of taxing wool shall not in the future be exercised "without their common assent and good-will ; saving to us and our heirs the custom of wools, skins, and leather granted before by the commonalty aforesaid." [2] Thus by the reincorporation into the charters of these vital limitations upon the royal right of taxation, which for more than eighty years had been omitted from them, the pro-longed struggle which the barons of Runnymede had in-augurated ended at last in a completely successful con-summation. The exclusive right of the national assembly to authorize taxation was now fully and finally recognized, save so far as that right was limited by the proviso, "saving the ancient aids and prizes due and accustomed." [3] How under the cover of this proviso the crown afterwards exercised the right to talliage the cities and towns upon the royal demesnes will be explained hereafter.

Provisions of the new articles as to taxation.

Exclusive right of the nation to authorize taxation finally ad-mitted by the crown.

11. Before the end of Edward's reign the struggle for the charters was brought to a close, and with the close of that struggle finally disappeared the political results of the Nor-man conquest. The fact has again and again been drawn

Summary.

[1] Art. vi.
[2] Art. vii. The supplementary arti-cles are preserved in French and Latin, and the two forms differ materially from each other. In the French form the articles have become a permanent part of English law. *Statutes of the Realm*, i. 124, 125. In their Latin form, preserved by Walter of Hemingburg (ii. p. 152), the articles are generally known as the statute *De tallagio non concedendo*. A lucid analysis and com-parison of the two forms of the articles with each other may be found in Stubbs, *Const. Hist.*, vol. ii. p. 142, 143.

"They (the Latin articles, as the stat-ute *De tallagio non concedendo*) were referred to as a statute in the preamble to the Petition of Right, and were de-cided by the judges in 1637 to be a statute." — *Select Charters*, p. 497.

[3] By this proviso the king refused "to relinquish his old exchequer-rights over the settlers on his domain lands, and over the tolls traditionally fixed (*custuma antiqua*), those, namely, on wool, hide, and leather." — Gneist, *Eng. Parliament*, note to page 136 (Shee's trans.).

out that the coming of the Normans did not involve the displacement of the English nation, nor a wiping out of the immemorial laws and political institutions of the conquered race. The Old-English political system of local self-governing communities, together with the customary law, survived the shock of the Conquest, and upon that tenacious system as a substructure the Norman system of central administration was superimposed. By the coming of William two kindred systems of government, both tending in the same direction and yet in different stages of development, were brought into the closest contact, and out of the fusion between the two has grown the modern constitution. The period of transition and growth which intervenes between the ancient constitution and the constitution in its modern form naturally divides itself into three stages: the first or Norman stage, embracing the reigns of the four Norman kings, is the stage in which the great mass of foreign elements and influences were infused into the blood, the language, the laws, the political institutions of the conquered race; the second or Angevin stage, embracing the reigns of Henry II. and his sons, is the stage in which the foreign and native elements were worked into a new combination which retained the strongest elements of both; the third or charter stage, extending from the fifteenth year of John to the twenty-fifth of Edward I., is the stage in which the work of limitation and definition was so far advanced, and the machinery of the constitution so far perfected, as to render it in outward form at least essentially the same as it is at the present day. The new system of central administration, with the source of its strength in the royal authority, grew and widened during the reigns of the Norman and Angevin kings, until it became the dominant force in the constitution. While the growth of the royal authority was thus advancing and overshadowing the traditional liberties of the people, the causes were at work which finally brought about the division and classification of the nation in three estates. By the thirteenth century the estate system had reached its completion and the royal authority the limit of its growth. This limit was reached when both Richard and John, accepting the imperialist theories of Glanvill, held that the will of the prince was the law

of the land.   Upon the part of the nation it was claimed that
the law of the land was not the will of the prince, but the
immemorial laws of the English kingdom, with such additions
and amendments as those laws had suffered through the results of the Norman conquest.   In the conflict between these
irreconcilable theories, the struggle for the charters had its
birth.   The parties to that struggle were the royal authority
on the one hand and the nation marshalled in the ranks of
the three estates on the other.   In order to make good its
cause against the crown, the nation undertook to render the
royal authority subservient to that ancient system of Teutonic law which finds its source in the customs of the people,
and which as a system of law the effects of the Conquest
were unable to wipe out.   After the Conquest the Old-English system of customary law was generally appealed to as
"the laws of good King Eadward," while the changes which
it suffered through the results of the Conquest were generally described as the amendments made by King William,
who claimed to rule, not according to any laws of his own
making, but according to the laws of his predecessor, King
Eadward.   This statement is illustrated with great clearness
in that clause of the famous charter of Henry I. in which the
king promises to restore the laws of Eadward with the
amendments which his father had made.   It is therefore
plain that when the barons seized upon Henry's charter as
the basis of national action, and demanded of the king that
he should enter into a fresh understanding upon the lines
which it defined, their action simply amounted to a demand
that the legal and constitutional relations between the nation
and the king should henceforth be regulated by the Old-
English code of customary law as modified and amended
through the effects of the Norman conquest.   The struggle
for the charters involved no attempt to wipe out the irrevocable effects of the Conquest ; in the charters themselves
the new system of central administration and the system of
feudal tenures are both recognized as abiding elements in
the constitution.   The effort was to fix the limits of innovation, to define the extent to which the centralizing and feudalizing processes to which the Conquest gave birth should
be permitted to abridge the immemorial freedom in the time

to come. Before the struggle for the charters began, the
process of assimilation, through which the lesser mass of the
conquerors was absorbed by the greater mass of the conquered, had been fully worked out. The winning of the
Great Charter was in fact the final consummation of the
work of union; it was "the first great act of the English
nation after the descendants of Norman conquerors and Norman settlers had fully become Englishmen." But the fact
must never be lost sight of that the winning of the Great
Charter was the beginning, not the end, of a conflict. It
embodied, not a final statement of concessions from the
crown to the nation, but rather a definite programme of reform which the nation resolved to persevere in until it should
be finally accepted by the crown as an irrevocable basis of
government. The struggle does not end until the charters
are finally accepted in good faith by both parties as authoritative definitions of the rights and liberties of the nation on
the one hand, and of the rights and prerogatives of the crown
on the other. The definitions of rights and liberties thus
established in favor of the nation as against the crown embody no abstract theories of government; they consist simply of a summing up of the traditional liberties of the English
nation, with such modifications and amendments as those
liberties had suffered through the effects of the Norman
conquest. When the struggle is over, when the process
of limitation and definition has been finally completed under
the master hand of Edward I., the English constitution
stands forth, in a broad and general sense, in essentially the
same outward form which it wears at the present day. During the reign of Edward the struggle of the constitution
for existence comes to an end; every vital part of the constitutional machinery exists;[1] nearly all of the great principles of English freedom have been firmly established.
Under Edward's organizing hand the Old-English system
of local administration, embodied in the township, the hundred, and the shire, is revivified and readjusted to the more
perfectly organized system of central administration to which

---

[1] It can hardly be maintained, however, that the mechanism of the constitution was complete in any full and
perfect sense until its vital organ — the
parliament — had developed all of its
powers and privileges, — a result which
was not reached until the reigns of the
Lancastrian kings.

the Conquest gave birth. And under the same hand the central system itself becomes essentially as complete as it is at the present day. Then as now the executive government was vested in the king and his council; then as now the king could not legislate without the counsel and assent of a parliament duly summoned; then as now the king could levy no tax without the authority of such a parliament; then as now the ancient code of customary law existed as a definitely organized system of jurisprudence; then as now the courts of the king's bench, common pleas, and exchequer, each with its separate staff of judges, were dispatching the several classes of business that came before them; then as now the system of itinerant judicature embodied in the courts of assize was in full operation. To a somewhat later day, however, must be assigned the full development of the equitable jurisdiction of the chancellor. But in attempting to establish an identity between the outward form of the constitution as it appeared in Edward's day and as it appears in our own, the fact must be borne steadily in mind that hidden inner changes have for centuries been going on which have completely revolutionized its practical working. These changes have taken place as certain parts of the ancient machinery which were once potent have become antiquated and obsolete, and as certain other parts, which were once undeveloped and insignificant, have grown into overshadowing importance. The changes which have thus taken place in this ever-altering constitution have been happily illustrated by likening it to " an old man who still wears with attached fondness clothes in the fashion of his youth: what you see of him is the same; what you do not see is wholly altered." This great transformation which — without making any change in its outward form — has thus taken place in the internal mechanism of the English constitution, has been brought about by the silent migration of all the real powers of government from the king and the nobles to the main body of the people. The agent employed by the nation to bring about this result was the parliament, whose mediæval growth will be traced in the following chapters.

BOOK III.

THE GROWTH AND DECLINE OF PARLIAMENT.

———◆———

CHAPTER I.

HISTORY OF PARLIAMENT FROM EDWARD I. TO HENRY IV.

Place of the English parliament in the history of institutions.

1. IN the gorgeous language of Burke, the "Parliament of Great Britain sits at the head of her extensive empire in two capacities. One, as the local legislature of this island, providing for all things at home immediately, and by no other instrument than the executive power. The other, and I think her nobler capacity, is what I call her *imperial character ;* in which, as from the throne of heaven, she superintends all the several inferior legislatures, and guides and controls them all without annihilating any." [1] A third and higher capacity still in which the English parliament may be viewed is that in which it stands forth as the accepted political model after which have been fashioned the several systems of popular government which now exist throughout the world. In this last and highest capacity its position is not more than a century old.

Representative government a "Teutonic invention :"

The political systems of all the Teutonic nations, as they appear to us when written history begins, contained the germs of the representative principle, and in every one of the modern European states that have arisen out of the settlements made by the Teutonic nations on Roman soil a serious attempt has at some time been made in the direction of representative government. The remarkable fact is that in every continental state in which such an attempt was made, it ended at last in failure and disappointment. By the sixteenth century nearly every effort in the direction of repre-

[1] Speech on American taxation, April 19, 1774. See Burke's *Works*, 4th ed., vol. ii. p. 75.

sentative government upon the continent of Europe had come to an end. In England only among the Teutonic nations did the representative system survive ; in England only has the representative principle — which has been called " a Teutonic invention " — been able to maintain a continuous existence. In this way the English nation has been able to hand down the representative principle from the barbarian epoch to modern times ; in this way England has become the "mother of parliaments," — the teacher of the science of representative government to all the world. Since the beginning of the French Revolution nearly all of the states of continental Europe have organized national assemblies after the model of the English parliament in a spirit of conscious imitation.[1] But the typical English national assembly, embodying what is generally known as the bicameral system, was not copied into the continental European constitutions until it had first been reproduced in a modified form by the founders of the federal republic of the United States. In the several colonial commonwealths founded by English settlers upon American soil, the typical English national assembly reappeared in an embryonic form as the predestined product of a natural process of reproduction.[2] These assemblies "were not formally instituted, but grew up by themselves, because it was in the nature of Englishmen to assemble."[3] A graphic statement of this fact may be found in the words of a writer upon our colonial history who tells us that in "this year (1619) a House of Burgesses *broke out* in Virginia."[4] When the colonial commonwealths in America severed the tie of political dependence which bound them to the mother country, and rose to the full stature of sovereign states, they, with a single exception, organized their several legislatures after the ancient model as it existed in the insular system. And the framers of the federal constitution of 1787, abandoning the original idea of a federal assembly consisting of a single chamber, adopted the English system of two chambers in the form in which that system had reappeared in the several states.[5]

Margin notes: It survives in England only among the Teutonic nations.

English bicameral system first reproduced in the English states in America,

---

[1] For the authorities upon this subject, see above, p. 14.
[2] See above, p. 15.
[3] Seeley, *The Expansion of England*, p. 67.
[4] These are the words of Hutchinson quoted by Prof. Seeley, Ibid, p. 67.
[5] See above, pp. 44, 45, 71.

and then in most of the states of continental Europe. Thus rendered popular by its successful reproduction in the American constitutions, state and federal, the "British political model was followed by France, by Spain and Portugal, and by Holland and Belgium, combined in the kingdom of the Netherlands ; and after a long interval by Germany, Italy, and Austria." [1]   To the student of the "science of politics" the typical English national assembly, therefore, appears not simply as the local legislature of the United Kingdom, nor even as the imperial parliament of the British Empire, but higher still, — as the accepted model of popular government throughout the world.

Continuity of the history of the English parliament.   2. To the mere student of the English constitution the English parliament appears only in the two aspects in which Burke has presented it.   Viewed in these aspects, it is all-important to grasp the persistency of its growth, — the unbroken continuity of its historical development.   The history of the English parliament is coextensive with the history of the English nation.   From the time when the several branches of the "English kin" grouped together in the heptarchic kingdoms were drawn together under the sway of a single royal house, the united nation has never been without a national assembly.   In its progress through the centuries such assembly has, it is true, passed through a long process of change and of growth ; it has taken on new forms and new The primitive national assembly survives as the house of lords. names ; and yet in all these changing phases of growth the personal identity of the primitive assembly has never been lost ; the constitutional historian can clearly explain how it still survives in the corporate person of the house of lords. Although the existence of the house of commons, which has grown up alongside of the older assembly, cannot be traced back farther than the thirteenth century, still the system of representation — imbedded in the local, self-governing communities out of which the younger body grew — can be traced House of commons the product of the representative principle imbedded in the organizations of the shires and towns. back to the very earliest times.   As surely as the house of lords is the lineal successor of the witan, the house of commons is the product of the representative principle imbedded from the beginning in the organization of the shires and towns.   In order to understand how the two distinct elements, equally ancient, which enter into the composition of

----

[1] Sir Henry Maine, *Popular Government*, p. 13.

the two houses, were at different periods of time worked into the constitution of the national assembly, it is necessary to constantly bear in mind the two great stages of transition or growth through which the Old-English witan was transformed into the feudal councils of the Norman and Angevin reigns, and through which these councils were in their turn transformed into the parliaments of Edward I.

Two great stages of transition.

At an earlier stage of this work an examination was made into the historical origin of the witan, whether considered as the supreme council of a single heptarchic state, or as the supreme council of the whole English nation when finally united in a single consolidated kingdom.[1] One of the leading objects of that examination was to explain the process through which the primitive national assembly or folkmoot, in which every freeman had his place, gradually shrank up into a narrow aristocratic body composed of the magnates only. Such was the historical origin and such the political structure of the witenagemot of the Old-English commonwealth in which all grave matters were discussed, and with whose advice and consent were performed all important acts which the king could authorize.

Historical origin of the witen-agemot.

After the coming of William the continuity of the old national assembly went on unbroken ; the witan remained, as before, the national council of the king ; and during William's reign it retained much of its earlier character. Even the name witan goes on in English as long as the Chronicle continues, and the new Latin name of *magnum concilium* which grows up by its side is simply a translation of *mycel gemót*. Of the constitution of the witan, either before or after the Conquest, we have no direct or formal account, but the highest authorities agree in the conclusion that on all ordinary occasions the witan was a comparatively small gathering of great men, while on extraordinary occasions the assembly was sometimes reinforced by large popular bodies from every part of the kingdom. What were the qualifications necessary to bestow the right of membership in the great council, during the Norman reigns, cannot be definitely ascertained ; not until the reign of Henry II. can it be confidently maintained that every tenant-in-chief of the crown was a member of the

The witan survives the Conquest.

---

[1] See above, pp. 147, 148, 183, 184.

assembly.   It seems to be clear, however, that the Norman conquest wrought no formal change in the constitution of the witan ; that, in legal theory at least, what the witan was in the days of King Eadward it remained in the days of King

The witan,
after the
Conquest,
passes
through a
great prac-
tical trans-
formation :

William.   But although the witan under the name of the great council outlived the Conquest, and although in legal theory it still retained all of its old powers, yet the fact remains that the constitution of the assembly underwent a great practical transformation. /At the beginning of William's reign, those who composed the council that ordinarily gathered around the person of the king were a body of Englishmen ; by the end of the reign, this body had gradually been changed into an assembly of Normans in which an Englishman here and there held his place. / This change naturally resulted from the nature of the Conquest itself. Through William's policy of confiscation and regrant, nearly all of the great estates passed from English to Norman hands ; and in the same way nearly all of the great offices in church and state were parcelled out among his followers. The king's thegns thus became his tenants-in-chief, holding

it becomes
the king's
court of
feudal vas-
sals.

their lands from him as their lord.   Through this feudalizing process, the ancient assembly of wise men was gradually and silently transformed into the king's court of feudal vassals, whose right to exercise power was made to depend practically upon the king's pleasure.   During the reigns of the Norman kings the legislative functions of the great council were reduced to a mere shadow.[1]   Under Henry II. and his sons the constitution of the national council reached a definiteness of organization which it had never possessed before.   The composition of the council, which was now summoned at regular intervals, was that of a perfect feudal court, — an assembly of archbishops, bishops, abbots, priors, earls, barons, knights, and freeholders.   The constituent members of the assembly are the same as under the Norman kings, but greater prominence and a more definite position is now assigned to the

Influence
of the prac-
tice of sum-
mons.

minor tenants-in-chief.   Through the influence of the practice of summons, to whose origin an exact date cannot be assigned, the tendency was fast gaining ground to limit the national council to those only who were summoned by the

---

[1] See above, pp. 239–242.

king's writ, either personally or in a body. How far the practice of summons, which was in active operation in the time
of Henry II., had developed up to the sixteenth year of John,
can be definitely ascertained from the fourteenth article of the
Great Charter, which provides that, "To have the common
counsel of the kingdom we will cause to be summoned the
archbishops, bishops, abbots, earls, and greater barons singly
by our letters ; and besides we will cause to be summoned in
general by our sheriffs and bailiffs all those who hold of us in
chief." By this article, which no doubt expressed the then
existing practice, the qualification for membership in the national council was at last distinctly defined, and that qualification naturally assumed a feudal shape. No one was expected
to attend unless he was summoned, and no one was to be
summoned unless he was a tenant-in-chief. By the form of
the summons a line was also distinctly drawn between two
definite classes of men ; between the magnates, who were
entitled to a personal summons, and the main body of tenants-
in-chief, who were summoned generally in the shires : in this
form the distinction between lords and commons begins.[1]

> The line drawn between lords and commons.

The time was now fast approaching when the constitution
of the feudal council, which the practice of summons had thus
definitely defined, was in its turn to be modified by the force
of a new principle which demanded that every national assembly should consist of representatives of all the estates or
classes of men into which the body-politic was divided. The
causes which brought about the establishment of the estate
system were general in their operation, and in each one of
the European countries the result was reached about the
same time. The complete establishment of the system is
generally regarded by the historians as the work of the thirteenth century. During that period was established throughout Western Europe that type of a national assembly into
which the several orders or classes of men entered in the
form of definitely organized estates. In each country the
system has its special or local history, but as a general rule
in all of the European constitutions the three political factors
are the same, — the clergy, the nobles, and the commons.[2]
In nearly all of the Western nations the old primary assem-

> Constitution of the feudal council modified by the growth of the estate system.

[1] See above, pp. 289–291.　　　[2] See above, pp. 337.

blies died out and were succeeded by representative assemblies founded on the principle of estates. In one important
particular the English kingdom stands as an exception to the
general rule, — in England the old primary assembly never
entirely died out. After first shrinking up into the narrow
aristocratic body known as the witan, — the witan of the
consolidated kingdom which survived the Conquest was ultimately transformed, through the practice of personal summons to the great magnates of whom it had been immemorially composed, into the house of lords. In this feudalized
form the Old-English national assembly survived, and entered
as the aristocratic element into the new system of estates.[1]

3. The ultimate effect of the process of feudalization upon
the constitution of the national council was to transform the
ancient assembly, composed of the lay and spiritual witan,
into a court or council of feudal vassals in which, according
to feudal theory, every tenant-in-chief possessed the right of
membership. In practice, however, after the Conquest as
before, the feudal councils which ordinarily gathered round
the king were composed, as the old assembly had been, only
of the territorial magnates, and of the holders of the great
offices in church and state. The greater tenants-in-chief who
thus gathered around the person of the king, and who won
for themselves the right to be personally summoned to his
council, and in whom that right became hereditary, represent, together with the lords spiritual, the peerage of England,
which is identical with the house of lords. By the practice
of personal summons, to whose origin an exact date cannot
be assigned, the line was first drawn between the greater
tenants and the mass of lesser vassals who were summoned
generally in the shires. This practice, which was in active
operation in the reign of Henry II., received positive recognition in the terms of the Great Charter itself. The difficult
matter to ascertain is the qualification of blood, or tenure, or

---

[1] "In England, . . . the primitive
Assembly never died out; it never was
trampled out; it simply — through the
natural working of causes of which I
have already spoken — shrank up into
a narrow body. Through that law of
shrinking up, the old democratic Assembly lived on to become the aristocratic element in a new form of the
constitution. That is to say, I believe
that the primitive Assembly was, by
lineal personal succession, continued
in the Witenagemót, and that the Witenagemót is, by lineal personal succession, continued in the House of Lords."
— Freeman, *Comparative Politics*, p.
232.

special privilege, which entitled the greater tenants to receive the special writ. Upon what principle were those who received the special writ distinguished above their fellows? The theory is that the holding of a feudal estate by the peculiar tenure of barony was the original qualification which entitled the tenant-in-chief to the right of personal summons, — "the baronage of the thirteenth century was the body of tenants-in-chief holding a fief or a number of fiefs consolidated into a baronial honor or qualification."[1] It seems to be clear, however, that a special summons did not necessarily follow tenure by barony, — that the holding by such tenure was not of itself a sufficient ground for requiring attendance in parliament. It follows, therefore, that the right to receive the special writ was not an incident of tenure merely. Only by the actual reception of the writ was the dignity of peerage conferred upon the holder by barony. But not until this right to receive the king's writ had become hereditary was the status of the peer ultimately fixed and determined. The hereditary right to receive the writ, rather than the tenure which was the original qualification for the writ, finally became the constitutional basis upon which the peerage now reposes. As the process of feudalization advanced, the inherent power of the king, as the fountain of honor to determine who should be summoned as barons, gradually became subject to the limitation imposed by the feudal rule of primogeniture. It is generally conceded that certainly during the reign of Edward I. the right of a baron — whose ancestor had been summoned and who had once sat in parliament — to claim the hereditary right to be so summoned was clearly and firmly established.[2] The right thus established was ultimately defined in that rule which provides that where a peerage has been created by writ the right descends by operation of law to the heirs of the person so ennobled, without words to that effect in the terms of the writ itself.[3]

The holding of an estate by barony the original qualification for personal summons;

although the special writ did not necessarily follow such tenure.

The hereditary right to receive the writ the real basis of peerage.

Feudal rule of primogeniture.

Peerage by writ descends by operation of law to the heirs of person ennobled.

---

[1] Stubbs, *Const. Hist.*, vol. ii. p. 178.

[2] For the authorities upon the subjects restated in this section, see above, pp. 353, 354.

[3] See Blackstone (Sharswood's ed.), *Comm.*, bk. i. p. 399. "The blood of a temporal lord is considered as ennobled by a writ of summons to parliament, and taking his seat under that writ; and unless the terms of the writ, or of the patent under the authority of which it issues, provide to the contrary, he now gains by the writ, and his seat in parliament thereupon, an hereditary honor, descendible to the heirs of his body, whatever may have been formerly the law on this subject." — *Lords' Report*, vol. i. p. 393.

Under this rule a barony created by writ could, in default of male heirs, descend to baronial heiresses, who, although they could not themselves sit in the king's council, conveyed to their husbands the presumptive right to receive his sum-

mons.[1] The hereditary peers thus created by writ were designated — prior to the reign of Edward III. — by the titles of earl and baron only.[2] The former dignity, which descended from the Old-English system, was generally embraced, however, in the latter term.   Upon the comprehensive title of baron, which was common to the whole peerage, the higher titles of duke, marquis, earl, and viscount were simply superimposed.[3]   In the reign of Edward III. the title of duke was for the first time conferred upon a subject, and, what is more important, the new dignity was created by

letters patent.[4]   This new method of creation by patent instead of by writ gave rise to an important innovation.   The dignity conferred by the new method did not descend generally to the heirs of the person ennobled ; its descent was prescribed and limited by the terms of the instrument by which it was created.   The result of the new method of creation was to limit the descent of the peerage to a particular line of succession, — generally to the heirs male of the person ennobled.   Prior to the reign of John, the ancient dignity of earl seems to have been generally derived from patents of the crown.[5]   In the reign of Edward III. the title of duke was so granted, and in subsequent reigns the titles of marquis and viscount.[6]   But not until the reign of Richard II. was a baron pure and simple created by patent instead of by writ.   In

1387 Richard II. created John Beauchamp of Holt, a baron by patent,[7] and from the twenty-fourth year of Henry VI., barons were generally created in that manner.[8]   To the two

---

[1] "They even sat, after the death of their wives, as tenants by the curtesy." — Hallam, *M. A.*, vol. iii. p. 119, citing Collin's *Proceedings on Claims of Baronies*, pp. 24, 73.

[2] *Lords' Report*, vol. ii. p. 65.

[3] Ibid., vol. ii. p. 240.

[4] Ibid., vol. ii. p. 186. "The dignity of duke, as a distinct name of honor, was first given by Edward the Third in the eleventh year of his reign, when in parliament he created his eldest son, Edward, before Earl of Chester, Duke of Cornwall. In the patent for this purpose the words of creation used are," etc.

[5] *Lords' Report*, vol. i. p. 69.

[6] Ibid., vol. ii. p. 240.

[7] Ibid., vol. i. p. 345.   The language of the Report is, "which is commonly considered as the first creation of a baron by patent."

[8] See Nicolas, *Hist. Peerage* (Courthope ed.), p. 291 ; Stubbs, *Const. Hist.*, vol. iii. p. 437.

ordinary methods of creating the dignity of peerage, by writ and by patent, must be added the extraordinary method of creation by the king in parliament:[1] to such creations the assent of parliament is frequently stated. As to the dignity of banneret, the better opinion seems to be that it was a mere order of knighthood and not a rank of peerage.[2] The peers of the realm, although distinguished from each other by titles expressive of different degrees of dignity, were otherwise equal both in privilege and authority.[3]

Peers created by the king in parliament.

Bannerets.

During the two centuries which intervene between the Conquest and the formation of the estate system in the reign of Edward I., the national assembly survives in the form of the feudal court or council, whose constitution has in general terms been already defined. Although this council, generally known as the *magnum concilium*, may have embraced on extraordinary occasions the whole body of the tenants-in-chief, it was no doubt composed, on all ordinary occasions, only of the greater tenants, among whom were, of course, embraced the holders of all the great offices in church and state. To the great council thus constituted passed, in legal theory at least, the sum of political, fiscal, legislative, and judicial powers which had been possessed by the ancient witenagemot.[4] The dominant force in the feudal court or council was the new kingship to which the Conquest gave birth, a kingship which refused to be limited by the constitutional action of the witan on the one hand, or to be weakened by the disruptive tendencies of feudalism on the other. That the Norman and Angevin kings were practically absolute there can be no doubt; and yet it is equally clear that they retained throughout both the theory and form of a national council, by whose counsel and consent they performed all important acts of judicature and legislation.[5] Even Dr. Gneist, who denies the survival of the witan in the form of a feudal council, and who holds that the royal power

Legislative and judicial powers of the great councils of the Norman and early Angevin kings.

---

[1] *Lords' Report*, vol. ii. p. 40, citing Co. Litt., 16 b.

[2] *Lords' Report*, vol. i. pp. 328, 329; Stubbs, *Const. Hist.*, vol. iii. p. 441.

[3] *Ibid.*, vol. ii. p. 243. The Report says : "As peers of the realm all were esteemed equal."

[4] "As no formal change took place in the constitution of the national assembly, so no formal change took place in its powers. . . . But with the powers of the assembly, just as with its constitution, while there was no formal change, the practical change was great." — Freeman, *Norm. Conq.*, vol. v. pp. 280, 281.

[5] See above, pp. 241, 291.

in Norman times was virtually absolute, admits that the form of counsel and consent in legislation was never entirely abolished, — that "in the first centuries of the Norman period is met with, occasionally, the *consensu baronum meorum*, which crops up whenever fundamental changes in the hereditary 'common law' are in question."[1] Although the legislative functions of the great council may in Norman times have been more nominal than real, the immemorial form of counsel and consent which descends from the earliest Teutonic legislation never entirely disappeared. That the great council of peers was a supreme judicial court, in the same general sense in which the witan had been, cannot be successfully questioned.

Survival of "counsel and consent."

4. The standing committee of the great council, — curia regis, — after giving birth to the four great courts of king's bench, common pleas, exchequer, and chancery, still retained a vast and indefinite reserve of administrative, legislative, and judicial functions.[2] In order to indicate, even in general terms, the domain of these far-reaching powers, it is necessary to outline the relation which existed between the great council and the smaller body which, in the language of Lord Hale, stood to the former as a *concilium in concilio.* To the great council, as heretofore pointed out, passed, in theory at least, the sum of political, fiscal, legislative, and judicial powers which had been possessed by the ancient witenagemot. To facilitate the work of administration, the ordinary exercise of these powers was committed to an inner or continual council, whose relation to the greater body, owing to the scantiness of documentary evidence touching the Norman period, is vague and shadowy in the extreme. From the existing evidence, the conclusion has been reached that the lesser or continual council was what would be called in modern language a standing committee of the great council.[3]

Judicial powers of the house of lords.

Relation of the continual to the great council.

---

[1] Gneist, *The English Parliament*, p. 60 (Shee's trans.). For the views of this writer upon "the transformation of the ancient witenagemotes into the Norman 'court-days,'" see Ibid., pp. 54–71. See, also, Gneist, *Hist. of the Eng. Const.*, vol. i. pp. 246–271 (Ashworth's trans.). "Gneist's position, that the Norman assemblies were not independent legislative or governing assemblies, needs no proof. The kings were practically absolute, but they retained the theory and the form of a national council." — Stubbs, *Const. Hist.*, vol. i. p. 356, note 1, citing Verwalt. i. 238 *seq.*

[2] See above pp. 245, 249

[3] See above, p. 242.

As such standing committee, the continual council seems to reproduce the relation which existed between the primary Teutonic assembly and the permanent council composed of the magistrates (*principes*) who decided all ordinary questions, reserving only the graver ones for the consideration of the greater body.[1] Such was the relation finally established, so far as judicial business is concerned, between the continual council and the four great courts developed out of it, on the one hand, and the great council, finally known as the house of lords, on the other. All ordinary questions of judicature pass in the first instance to one or the other of the great law courts ; a more exceptional class, to the court of the chancellor ; while another and more difficult class still is reserved to the king in his ordinary council.[2] Only causes of an extraordinary character remain for the judgment of the great council of the kingdom. In the exercise of this extraordinary jurisdiction the house of lords, as the highest judicial body in the realm, appears in three aspects : (1) as a court of peers for the trial of its own members ; (2) as a high criminal court of state for the trial of both peers and commoners who are impeached by the commons ; (3) as a supreme court of error and appeal in civil causes.

All ordinary causes decided by the continual council, or by the courts born of it.

Only extraordinary causes remain for the judgment of the peers.

As a court of peers for the trial of its own members, the house of lords was the only tribunal in which the peerage could enjoy the benefits of that principle of Teutonic law which granted the *judicium parium* to the members of every class or order. As heretofore explained, the famous clause in Magna Carta touching the "*legale judicium parium suorum*" refers rather to the general right of each estate or class to be tried by its own members than to the special right of trial by jury as afterwards understood.[3] From the very nature of the right itself, the right of a peer to be tried by members of his own order could not have antedated the organization of the peerage as a distinct estate. Although the right had been claimed at an earlier date, it was first definitely established in 1341 by the statute of 15 Edward III., which provides "that no peer of the realm, officer, or other, on account of his office, can be brought before the court,

The house of lords as a court of peers for the trial of its own members.

Statute of 15 Edward III.

---

[1] See above, p. 108.
[2] See above, p. 302.
[3] See above, p. 389, note 1.

condemned to the loss of his worldly possessions, put in arrest or prison, rendered responsible, or judged otherwise than through award of the said peers in parliament."[1] Two years later this statute was repealed, but in the repealing statute the general principle embodied in the first was distinctly recognized. The right as ultimately defined in the law of the land was restricted, however, to a narrower basis than that upon which the statute of 1341 had placed it. In that act the right of a peer to be tried by his peers was made to extend to all offences whatsoever; in the law as finally established, the right was limited to cases of treason and felony only. A peer may be tried like a commoner for the commission of a misdemeanor.[2] By statute of 20 Henry VI. the right of a peer to be tried by his peers in cases of treason and felony was extended to peeresses.[3] When an accusation is to be made against a peer, it is made by indictment in any competent court having cognizance of the offence, and if the offence charged be treason or felony the case is removed for trial by *certiorari* to the house of lords.[4] If parliament is sitting, the trial proceeds in the house of lords as such, which is usually, though not necessarily, presided over on such an occasion by a lord high steward[5] appointed for that purpose. Under these circumstances the lord high steward is simply the president of a court in which the peers are the judges. If, however, the parliament is not sitting, the indictment is tried in the court of the lord high steward, which was originally simply a select committee composed only of such peers as the steward might see fit to summon. In this tribunal the steward sits as the only judge, while the peers summoned by him — the "lords triers" — act as a jury.[6] Owing to an abuse which arose out of the power of the steward to limit his court to such peers only as he saw fit to summon,[7] an act was passed (7 and 8 Will. III. c. 3) which provides that, upon the trial of any peer or peeress for treason or misprision, all the

A peer may be tried like a commoner for a misdemeanor.

The lord high steward and his court.

[1] *Rot. Parl.*, ii. p. 132.

[2] 3d *Inst.*, 30; Hawkins, *C. P.*, bk. 2, ch. 44, §§ 13, 14; Stephen, *Hist. of the Criminal Law*, vol. i. p. 164.

[3] *Rot. Parl.*, v. p. 56.

[4] Stephen, *Hist. of the Crim. Law*, vol. i. p. 165.

[5] As to the origin of the office, Coke, 4th *Inst.*, 58.

[6] See Sir T. Erskine May, *Parl. Prac.*, p. 737–741; Campbell, *Lives of the Chancellors*, vol. iii. pp. 538 n., 557 n.

[7] See trial of Lord Delamere, 11 Howell, *St. Tr.* 539; Macaulay, *Hist. of England*, vol. ii. pp. 313–316.

peers shall be summoned, and that every peer so summoned and appearing shall have a vote at the trial.

A second and higher judicial aspect still, in which the house of lords appears, is that in which it stands out as a high criminal court of state for the trial of all persons who are impeached or accused by the commons, sitting as a grand jury of the whole nation, of the commission of high crimes and misdemeanors.   The right to thus assail the great functionaries of the realm was one of the weapons won by the commons during their struggles for political power in the fourteenth and fifteenth centuries.   The earlier instances of criminal proceedings which take place in parliament during the period which intervenes between the beginning of the reign of Edward I. and the fiftieth year of Edward III. are both irregular and ambiguous.[1]   Not until the year last named do we find, in a series of proceedings which take place in the Good Parliament, a clear instance of a parliamentary impeachment in the sense in which that term is now understood. The proceedings against the lords Latimer and Neville, and their agents and accomplices,[2] who were accused of the commission of all kinds of fraud upon the revenue, are regarded by the historians as the earliest instance of a trial by the lords upon a definite accusation made by the commons.[3]   In the early part of the reign of Richard II. (1377–1383) impeachments were directed for various kinds of misconduct against Gomenys and Weston, against Cressingham and Spykesworth, and against the Bishop of Norwich, Elmham, and others.[4]   In 1386 these cases were followed by the famous accusation against Michael de la Pole, the lord chancellor, who was impeached for grave misconduct in his office.[5] Thus by frequent repetition and employment the law and practice as to parliamentary impeachments was by the end of the reign of Richard II. established in substantially the same form in which it appears in modern times.

During the period in which the practice of impeachment by public accusation of the commons was taking on a definite

The house of lords as a high court for the trial of all persons impeached by the commons.

Proceedings against the lords Latimer and Neville.

---

[1] See Stephen, *Hist. of the Crim. Law*, vol. i. pp. 145–155.
[2] *Rot. Parl.*, ii. pp. 323–326, 328, 329; Rymer, p. 322.
[3] Hallam, *M. A.*, vol. iii. p. 56; Stubbs, *Const. Hist.*, vol. ii. p. 431.

[4] *Rot. Parl.*, iii. pp. 10–12, 153, 156.
[5] *Rot. Parl.*, iii. pp. 216–219; Knighton, c. 2684. See Hallam, *M. A.*, vol. iii. pp. 66, 67.

and final form, it was for some time rivalled by a method of private accusation known as an "appeal," whose history, as a part of the procedure in ordinary criminal cases, has been heretofore examined.[1] By an "appeal" any person had the right to bring any other to trial for any offence before the high court of parliament. In the reign of Richard II. the lord chancellor was in this manner impeached by a fish-monger who accused him of taking bribes in the form of money, and in cloth and fish delivered free at his house.[2] The strife and the bloodshed which resulted from the use of this unbridled method of private accusation by the turbulent feudal nobility were so serious that it was finally abolished by a statute passed in 1 Henry IV. c. 14, which provided "that no appeals be from henceforth made, or in any wise pursued in parliament in any time to come."

The practice of impeachment by accusation of the commons, thus left without a rival, was employed against the duke of Suffolk, who was charged with high treason in 1450,[3] and against Lord Stanley in 1459.[4] After the trial of Lord Stanley, no impeachment seems to have taken place until the trial of Sir Giles Mompesson in 1621, — an intermission of one hundred and sixty-two years. From that date down to the impeachment of Lord Melville in 1805, the impeachments which have taken place have been estimated at fifty-four.[5] Of these the most famous are those which took place in the struggle between the parliament and the crown during the first two years of the Revolution of 1640. The law of impeachment as finally settled has thus been summed up by Sir James Fitzjames Stephen : —

"1. The house of lords is a court of justice in which peers may be tried for any offence, and commoners for any offence not being treason or felony, upon an accusation or impeachment (*impetitio*) by the house of commons, which is the grand jury of the whole nation.

"2. When such an impeachment is once made, it is not abated either by a prorogation or by a dissolution of parliament, but must go on from session to session, and from parliament to parliament, till it is determined.

---

[1] See above, p. 311.
[2] *Rot. Parl.*, iii. p. 168.
[3] *Rot. Parl.*, v. p. 176.

[4] *Rot. Parl.*, v. p. 369.
[5] See Stephen, *Hist. of the Crim. Law*, vol. i. pp. 157–159.

" 3. A pardon from the crown cannot be pleaded in bar of an impeachment." [1]

The third and last aspect in which the house of lords is to be viewed as a court of justice is that in which it sits as a final court of appeal for the correction of errors in judgments and decrees rendered in civil suits by the great courts of law and equity. This supreme appellate jurisdiction in civil cases seems to have lain dormant from the time of the complete organization of the courts of Westminster down to its revival in the sixteenth and seventeenth centuries. The right to remove a law case to the house of lords by writ of error, originally derived from the crown, was confirmed by statute in the 27th year of Elizabeth ; [2] while their appellate jurisdiction in equity cases on petition to themselves, without reference to the crown, has been exercised since the reign of Charles I. [3]

House of lords as a court of error in civil causes.

5. Having now explained how the witan grew into the feudal councils of the Norman and Angevin reigns, and how out of these feudal councils was developed the house of lords, the task remains to explain the process through which a new and a popular assembly grew up, alongside of the older aristocratic body, out of the system of representation immemorially imbedded in the organization of the shires and towns. In order fully to grasp the nature of this later growth, it is all-important to bear in mind the fact that, from the time of the Conquest down to the establishment of the estate system in the reign of Edward I., all of the great powers of government were concentrated around and centralized in the person of the king acting through his ordinary council, composed of the great officers of state and the household, or through that larger body known as the great council, composed of those tenants-in-chief who won for themselves the right to be personally summoned, and in whom that right became hereditary. During a long period of time, from the person of the king acting through his lesser or greater council, — whose relation to each other is not clearly defined,

House of commons the product of the representative principle imbedded in the organization of the shires and towns.

---

[1] *Hist. of the Crim. Law*, vol. i. p. 146.
[2] See Intr. to Sugden, *Law of Real Property*, p. 2.
[3] See May, *Parliamentary Practice*, p. 56. " In 1873, indeed, their ancient appellate jurisdiction was surrendered by the Judicature Act; but before that act came into operation this provision was repealed." — Ibid., p. 56.

— emanated all the great acts of government, whether administrative, legislative, judicial, fiscal, or political.[1]   Under the highly centralized political system to which the Conquest gave birth, the main body of the people, upon whom the burden of government fell, were sternly excluded from all voice in its administration.   The great outcome of the political struggle between the nation and the crown, which extends through the thirteenth and fourteenth centuries, is embodied in the fact that during that period the main body of the nation as organized in shires and towns won for themselves the right to participate in, if not absolutely to control, the entire administration of the kingdom.   The way in which the nation worked out this result was by building up alongside of the older national assembly a new body composed of the representatives of the local self-governing communities, which, from humble beginnings, won first the right to participate in taxation, then to participate in legislation, then to impeach the ministers, and finally to participate in the control of the royal administration, and in the deposition of the king himself.   The whole process is one of struggle and of growth.   At the outset " *Vos humbles, pauvres communs prient et supplient pour Dieu et en œuvre de charité*"[2] that their petitions may be granted.   Next they establish the principle that not until their grievances as set forth in their petitions are redressed will they grant the supplies expected of them.   With this weapon in their hands they next claim the right to examine the royal accounts, to regulate the royal expenditures, and to hold responsible to themselves the ministers, who in earlier days answered not to the nation, but to the king.   The final result of this process, which has only been fully worked out in our own time, has been a virtual transfer of the fiscal, political, and administrative powers of government from the king and his council to the representatives of the people.   One great power only has never joined in the migration.   The judicial power vested in the greater and lesser councils, and in the tribunals born of them, has never passed to the popular chamber ; the house of commons persistently refused to participate in the judicature of

Sidenote: How the main body of the people as organized in shires and towns win the right to participate in national affairs.

Sidenote: The commons refuse to participate in judicature except in attainders and impeachments.

[1] See above, pp. 241–247.

[2] This, Gneist says, "is the wonted formula."   See *The Eng. Parliament* (Shee's trans.), p. 138.

the realm save so far as its participation was necessary in bills of attainder and impeachments. The process of growth through which the body of the nation, as organized in shires and towns, work their way into a partial exercise of the great powers of government, originally vested in the king and his feudal council, begins with the appearance of the shire representatives in the national council in the reign of John.[1] That tentative effort is followed in 1265 by the appearance in the national council not only of representatives from the shires, but from the cities and towns.[2] From the meeting of the famous parliament of 1295,[3] which completes the transition from a feudal council to an assembly of estates, the right of the shires and towns to send representatives to the national council becomes a permanent institution. It is, therefore, as a part of the estate system that the representatives of the English commons finally take their place in the national parliament. Who, then, were the third estate, — the commons, — as that term was understood in the politics of the thirteenth century? As heretofore explained,[4] the term "commons," as it appears in the English political system, must not be understood to imply a union into one corporate body conscious of its own identity of all orders of men below the nobility and the clergy, — it must be understood only to include all freemen organized and incorporated for government in the two leading classes of local communities, — shires and towns. In order, therefore, to present a complete statement of the origin and growth of the house of commons, it is first necessary to describe the political organization of the shires and towns; second, the successive periods at which representatives were sent from these local communities to the national council; third, the union of the shire and town representatives in one house; fourth, the process through which that house won, step by step, the right to participate in all the great functions of government.

Representatives of the commons take their place in parliament as a part of the estate system.

6. At an earlier stage of this work the historical origin of the shire, and the nature of its internal organization before and after the Conquest, were made the subjects of special examination. The conclusion was then reached that the

Origin and structure of the shire communities.

---

[1] See above, p. 377.
[2] See above, p. 403.
[3] See above, p. 417.
[4] See above, p. 356.

modern shire — the shire of the consolidated kingdom — finds its historical origin in the primitive state; "that the state of the seventh century became the shire of the tenth, while the shire of the seventh century became the hundred

The modern shire an aggregation of hundreds.

of the tenth." The modern shire is an aggregation of hundreds, the hundred an aggregation of townships.[1] The fact that the modern shire finds its historical origin in the primitive state is best illustrated by the structure of the shiremoot, which was not only a popular but a representative assembly — a county parliament[2] — in which each township and hundred appeared in the persons of its representatives.

The representative principle at work in the shire.

In the reeve and four selectmen who appear for the township in the courts of the shire and the hundred we have the very earliest illustration of the representative principle. In the shire court thus constituted, the whole body of "suitors" (attendants) were the judges, and in theory whatever judgment was rendered was the judgment of the whole assembly. In practice, however, the unwieldy body usually delegated its powers to a committee of "*judices*" who acted in behalf of the whole court. This principle of delegation, involving the selection of a chosen few to act in behalf of the whole, which is further illustrated by the action of the twelve senior thegns as a jury of presentment, and by the party-witnesses who under certain conditions declare the report of the community, runs through the whole system.[3] Into the structure and procedure of the courts of the shire and hundred the practice of election and representation entered from the very

The shire system survives the Conquest.

earliest times as an active and familiar principle. Through the ordeal of the Conquest the system of local self-government embodied in the shire system passed without material impairment. It seems to have been a leading feature in the Conqueror's policy to maintain the ancient usages of the English nation by keeping up the administration of the customary law in the popular courts of the shire and the hundred. Leaving out of view the removal of the bishop from the shire court to a court of his own, the transformation of the ancient office of earldom into a titular dignity, and the addition of trial by battle to the ancient procedure, the

---

[1] See above, pp. 145, 170–172   [3] See above, pp. 203, 303.
[2] See above, p. 303.

shire under the Norman name of county maintains unim- The shire under the Norman name of county.
paired its old position as the governing unit in the local or
district administration.   From the so-called laws of Henry I.
we learn that, after the Conquest as before, the shire-moot was
attended by the "thegns of the shire," by the parish priest,
and the reeve and four selectmen from each township.   The
full court, which met twice a year, still possessed both civil
and criminal jurisdiction, which was exercised according to
the old forms of witness, compurgation and ordeal; and the
old theory survived that the "suitors" were the judges.   The
"*judices*" and the "*judices et juratores*" of the Pipe Roll of
Henry I. probably represent the body of landholders, above
the villeins in rank, who constituted the courts of the shire
and the hundred, with full power to participate in the administration of justice.   A punishment by fines applies to all
members who fail to attend and discharge their judicial
duties.[1]

The Old-English system of local administration embodied The Old-English shire-moot brought into contact with the Norman curia regis.
in the shire-moot is first brought into contact with the system
of central administration embodied in the Norman curia regis
through the visitations of the itinerant justices, who were sent
through the shires during the reign of Henry I. to assess the
revenue.   While thus engaged in provincial business the justices sat in the shire-moot, where judicial work soon followed
in the path of their fiscal duties.   In the reign of Henry II.
the system of itinerant judicature became a well organized
and permanent institution.[2]   After that time the full assembly A full assembly of the shire meet the justices itinerant.
of the shire, summoned by the sheriff to meet the royal jus-
tices in order to participate with them in the administration
of justice, and in the transaction of other public business,
embraced a far more perfect representation of the county
than the ordinary shire court.   Before the coming of the
judges a general summons was issued to the sheriffs, commanding them to summon all archbishops, bishops, abbots, priors,
counts, barons, knights, and freeholders of their entire bailiwick, and of each vill or township, four lawful men and the
reeve, and of each borough twelve lawful burgesses, and[3] all

---

[1] Upon this whole subject, see above, pp. 252–256, 303–306.

[2] As to the growth of the itinerant judicature, see above, pp. 247, 248.

[3] "Et omnes alios qui coram justi- tiariis itinerantibus venire solent et debent."   See the form in Bracton, vol. ii. p. 188; Stephen, *Hist. Crim. Law,* vol. i. p. 101.

others who by duty or custom were bound to appear before the itinerant justices.   Of the extent and variety of the fiscal and judicial business usually transacted before the justices in

Agenda of the iter of 1194. one of these county parliaments, the *agenda* of the iter of the year 1194[1] has been frequently cited as a typical illustration.

The sheriff becomes the executive head of the shire. After the bishop was by the effect of William's ordinance removed from the shire-moot, and after the ancient earl was stripped of his official character, the presidency of the shire was left alone to the sheriff, the king's ever-present and immediate representative.[2]   The earlier iters, which seem to have been rather fiscal than judicial, were generally held by the sheriffs, who were only occasionally superseded by jus-

Decline in the judicial powers of the sheriff. tices from the curia regis.   A steady decline in the judicial powers of the sheriffs resulted, however, from the development of the itinerant system.   In 1194 it was provided that the sheriffs should no longer sit as judges in their own shires, and the holding of the pleas of the crown was committed to

Coroners of the thirteenth century. elective officers, — the coroners of the thirteenth century. Although the 24th article of the Great Charter, which forbade both sheriffs and coroners to hold pleas of the crown, does not seem to have been promptly enforced, it led the way to the final settlement of the principle that the sheriff is a mere ministerial officer, and that judicial functions in the courts of assize belonged exclusively to the king's itinerant justices.[3] But even after the loss of his judicial functions the sheriff still remained in possession of great local power and importance.   He was still the executive head of the shire; he still convened the county court, in which was transacted all of the business of the shire, whether judicial, fiscal, military, or such as arose out of the conservation of the peace.   So great were

The right to appoint the sheriffs. his powers that the right to appoint him was claimed in turn of the crown, by the baronage, and by the shire communities. In the scheme of reform known as the Provisions of Oxford, which was forced on the crown by the baronage in 1258, it was provided "that in each county there be a vavasour of the same county as sheriff to treat the people of the county well, loyally, and rightfully.   And that he take no fee, and that he

---

[1] See Hoveden, vol. iii. pp. 262–267.

[2] See above, p. 258.

[3] See above, p. 319.

be sheriff only for a year together." [1]   The right to control the nomination of the sheriffs, which thus passed for a moment to the baronage from the king, was challenged in the succeeding reign by the people of the shires, who claimed that they should have the right to choose the sheriffs by election.   This demand Edward I. in 1300 conceded to the people of those shires where they desired to have it, and where the office was not "of fee," or hereditary. [2]   This privilege, which seems to have been sparingly exercised, was withdrawn by ordinance early in the reign of Edward II. [3]   Upon a renewal of the contest in the reign of Edward III. he ordered that the sheriffs be elected by the shires ; but after a few years more it was finally provided that the sheriffs should be appointed by the officers of the exchequer, and that they should hold office for not more than one year. [4]

The office for a time elective.

Finally appointed by the officers of the exchequer

When in 1294 the sheriffs were forbidden to sit as judges in their own shires, the holding of pleas of the crown was committed to four officers, — three knights and a clerk, — who were always elected in full county court. [5]   These elected officers, whose duty it was to look after the pleas of the crown and other branches of the king's business in the shire, were the coroners of the thirteenth century. [6]   Although the coroner has been stripped of his ancient dignity, and although his chief remaining duties are the holding of inquest in case of violent or sudden death, and the discharging of the functions of sheriff in the event of the disability of that officer, the office itself is still elective.   The freeholders who in full county court elected the coroners also elected in the same manner the venderers, the officers who stood between the crown and the people in the administration of the forest laws. [7]

The coroner.

The office still elective.

Venderers.

---

[1] Cf. *Ann. Burton*, pp. 446–453; *Select Charters*, 2d ed., pp. 391, 395.

[2] "Le roi ad grante a soen poeple qil eient esleccion de leur vicontes en chescun conte, ou visconte ne est mie de fee, sil voelent."— *Statutes of the Realm*, i. p. 139.

[3] *Statutes of the Realm*, i. p. 160.

[4] *Fœdera*, ii. pp. 1049, 1099. Upon the whole subject, see Stubbs, *Const. Hist.*, vol. ii. pp. 2c6–208, 382. The Bishop concludes (p. 208) that "the real loss of his ancient importance re-sulted from the limitation of his period of office." See, also, Blackstone, *Com.*, bk. i. p. 340.

[5] "20. Præterea in quolibet comitatu eligantur tres milites et unus clericus custodes placitorum coronæ." For a list of the agenda of the "iter" of 1194, see Hoveden, vol. iii. pp. 262–267.

[6] Cf. Bigelow, *Procedure*, p. 131.

[7] See 2 *Inst.*, p. 558 ; Blackstone, *Com.*, bk. i. p. 347.

The shire, which was recognized by the state as a "*communitas*" [1] or corporation, and whose court or assembly was the place in which was transacted all local public business, whether fiscal, judicial, or administrative, was the preparatory school in which the main body of the English people were trained for the work of self-government in a higher sphere.   Under the

new order of things to which the Conquest gave birth, the principles of election and representation, which from the earliest times had entered into the structure and procedure of the shire-moot, were still employed in every branch of judicial, fiscal, or remedial work which devolved upon the shire community.   Into the new system of presentment and recognition by jury, election and representation both entered, in different forms and in different combinations, as an active and familiar

principle.   Under the Old-English procedure the presentment of criminals was probably made either by a private accuser, by the reeve and four men of the township, or more often perhaps by the twelve senior thegns of each hundred or wapentake.   By the Assize of Clarendon, under which the ancient system of presentment was reorganized and reëstablished, the representatives of the township and hundred were brought into a fresh and formal union in the discharge of a public duty with which each body of representatives had been immemorially connected.[2]   In the reign of Richard I. the presentment system was still more perfectly reorganized upon a basis distinctly representative.   Under the last arrangement "four knights are to be chosen from the whole county, who by their oaths shall choose two lawful knights of each hundred or wapentake, and those two shall choose upon oath ten knights of each hundred or wapentake, . . . so that these twelve may answer under all heads concerning their whole

hundred or wapentake." [3]   The principles of election and representation thus embodied in the system of presentment were as clearly defined in the system of recognitions.   By the terms of the Grand Assize, a writ was directed to the sheriff commanding him to summon four lawful knights of the neighbor-

---

[1] "A city or borough is, in its corporate capacity, a 'communitas;' so is a county." — Introduction to Toulmin Smith's *English Gilds*, p. xx.

[2] See above, pp. 306, 307.

[3] "In primis eligendi sunt quatuor milites de toto comitatu, qui per sacramentum suum eligant duos legales milites de quolibet hundredo vel wapentacco, et illi duo eligant," etc. — Hoveden, vol. iii. p. 262.

hood wherein the disputed property lay, who were directed to choose twelve lawful knights of the same neighborhood cognizant of the facts, who were to declare on oath who had the best right to the land in question. In the other assizes the procedure was substantially the same, with the exception that the twelve were chosen by the sheriff without the intervention of the four electors.[1] In either event the chosen recognitors, who were regarded as mere witnesses, acted in a representative capacity, — as representatives of a particular community they declared its testimony as to the fact in question. By the employment of local jurors in fiscal as well as judicial business, the representative principle was first brought into contact with the system of taxation. This contact first arose when personal property and income were brought under contribution. By the Assize of Arms, in which each freeman was required to equip himself with arms according to his means, and in which local jurors were required to determine the liability of each, the first step was taken towards the taxation of rent and chattels. Seven years later, Henry II. took the final step when with the consent of the great council he demanded a tenth of all movables to aid the host of Christendom in the war against Saladin. In order to fairly assess each man's liability to the tithe, Henry employed his favorite institution of inquest by local jurors. Whenever any one was suspected of contributing less than his share, four or six lawful men of the parish were chosen to declare on oath what he should give. In the next reign, when the Danegeld was revived under the name of carucage, the new system was extended to the assessment of real property liable to that tax.[2] Early in the reign of Henry III. a writ was issued for the collection of a carucage in which the sheriff was ordered to cause two knights to be chosen in the full assembly, and by the " will and counsel " of the county court, to take part in the assessment and collection of the tax.[3]

Representative principle comes in contact with the system of taxation, when personal property is brought under contribution.

The Saladin tithe assessed by local jurors, a method of assessment soon extended to real property.

In the review heretofore made of the primitive system for the preservation of the peace, whose difficult history extends back to the very earliest times, the conclusion was reached

The shire police system.

---

[1] See above, pp. 329, 330.
[2] See above, pp. 298, 299.
[3] " De voluntate et consilio omnium de comitatu in pleno comitatu eligentur ad hoc faciendum." — *Close Rolls*, i. 437. Cf. *Select Charters*, 2d ed., pp. 351-353.

that it survived the Conquest under a name which did not clearly express its real character. The ancient *frithborh* (peace-pledge), the mutual guarantee by which every member of a tithing as well as of a *meagth* became a pledge or surety (*borh*) to the other members, as well as to the state, for the maintenance of the public peace, was incorrectly translated by the Norman lawyers into *liberum plegium* (frank-pledge), instead of *pacis plegium* (peace-pledge).[1] The "view of frank-pledge," the right to see that these peace associations were kept in perfect order, ultimately became a part of the criminal jurisdiction of the manorial court, where it still survives. As the manor was nothing but a dependent township under a new name, so the court baron, the principal court of the manor, was primarily the successor of the tun-moot, the ancient assembly of the village or township. To the functions thus inherited by the manorial court from the tun-moot was added, by a grant of *sac* and *soc*, the jurisdiction, civil and criminal, of a private hundred court. The criminal side of the jurisdiction thus derived from the hundred survives as the manorial court leet.[2] It was not, however, in these manorial courts leet only that the jurisdiction of the hundred court was exercised. It was the duty of the sheriff to hold a hundred court twice a year in different parts of the county for the view of frank-pledge, and this court was called the great court of the hundred, or the sheriff's tourn and leet,[3] to distinguish it from the lesser court held monthly by the bailiff of the hundred chiefly for the settlement of disputes concerning small debts. The hundred court held by the sheriff on his semi-annual turn, tourn, or circuit, for the dispatch of criminal business, was the great court leet of the county, — that held by the steward was the court leet of the manor ; "one being only a larger species of the other, extending over more territory, but not over more causes."[4] The business of the courts leet was not only to take the view of frank-pledge, but to present by jury all crimes whatsoever that happened within their respective jurisdictions, and to punish all trivial misdemeanors. In the system of district administration, as

The " view of frank-pledge."

The manorial court leet.

Sheriff's tourn and leet.

Business of the courts leet as county police courts.

---

[1] See above, p. 198.
[2] See above, pp. 207–211, 254.
[3] Blackstone, *Comm.*, bk. iii. pp. 33, 34 ; bk. iv. p. 273. See, also, Viner's *Abridgment*, vi. p. 586 ; vii. pp. 3, 8.
[4] Blackstone, *Comm.*, bk. iv. p. 273.

it existed after the Conquest, the courts leet were the county police courts in which all criminals were presented, and in which those accused of trivial offences were tried and punished. By the force of legislation the jurisdiction of the courts leet, excepting the view of frank-pledge, has been gradually transferred to the court of quarter session,[1] a tribunal which grew out of the establishment of the office of justice of the peace.

The execution of the provisions of the Statute of Winchester, whereby Edward I. revived and strengthened the ancient system of police, was committed, as vacancies occurred, to conservators of the peace, who were elected, like the coroners, in full county court.[2] The election of these conservators was, however, put an end to by a statute enacted early in the reign of Edward III. (1 Edw. III. c. 16)[3] which provided that "in every county good men and lawful which be no maintainers of evil or barretors in the county should be assigned to keep the peace." By the terms of this act the assignment or appointment of conservators was vested in the crown, and the right to elect them taken away from the people. At first the authority of the conservators thus appointed was simply executive, limited probably to quelling riots and apprehending offenders. Not until 1344 were judicial functions conferred upon them by an act (18 Edw. III. stat. 2, c. 2)[4] which provided that "two or three of the best of reputation in the counties shall be assigned keepers of the peace by the king's commission . . . to hear and determine felonies and trespasses done against the peace in the same counties, and to inflict punishment reasonably." The Statute of Laborers, passed in 1350, provided that the justices should sit four times a year for its enforcement. In 1360 another statute (34 Edw. III. c. 1)[5] gave to the keepers of the peace not only

Justices of the peace.

Judicial functions conferred in 1344.

---

[1] See Sir James F. Stephen, *Hist. of the Criminal Law*, vol. i. pp. 75–85; Blackstone, *Comm.*, bk. iv. p. 273.

[2] "In pleno comitatu de assensu ejusdem comitatus." — *Parl. Writs*, vol. i. p. 390. "Probably the conservators were in the first instance appointed by the crown; the vacancies being filled by election : see *Parl. Writs*, vol. i. pp. 389–391." — Stubbs, *Const. Hist.*, vol. ii. p. 273, note 2.

[3] *Statutes of the Realm*, i. p. 257. "This put an end to the election of conservators, and was the beginning of the legislation relating to the officers who afterwards became justices of the peace." — Stephen, *Hist. of the Crim. Law*, vol. i. p. 112.

[4] *Statutes of the Realm*, i. p. 301.

[5] Ibid., i. p. 364.

the right to arrest offenders, but to "hear and determine at the king's suit all manner of felonies and trespasses done in the same county." Upon that statute rests the jurisdiction of the courts of quarter sessions for counties, and from the time of its enactment the conservators or wardens of the peace probably take the higher title of justices.[1]   Although the jurisdiction of the quarter sessions was extended by the statute to all felonies, by the terms of the commission[2] issued to the justices it was practically limited to minor offences by the proviso, "that if a case of difficulty shall arise they shall not proceed to give judgment except in the presence of some justice of one of the benches or of assize."   In this way the practice finally became settled to reserve the trial of all serious offences to the justices of assize, "only petty larcenies and misdemeanors" — originally punishable in the tourn and leet — remaining for trial in the quarter sessions.[3]

Court of quarter sessions.

By the Statute of Winchester it was provided that for the better keeping of the peace two constables in every hundred and franchise shall inspect all matters relating to arms and armor.   The high constables thus established were appointed at the courts leet of the hundred or franchise over which they were to preside, or, in default of an election in that way, by the justices at their quarter sessions.   The petty constables, first instituted about the reign of Edward III., are inferior officers in every town or parish, who act in a twofold capacity as subordinates to the high constables of the hundred.[4]

High and petty constables.

With the history of the English shire the history of the English town is closely interlaced.   The fact has heretofore been stated that the Old-English town or borough was simply a subdivision of the shire "in which men lived closer together than elsewhere ; it was simply several townships packed tightly together, a hundred smaller in extent and thicker in population than other hundreds."[5]   Although the early history of the borough constitution is very obscure, in it was

Origin and structure of the English town.

---

[1] Stephen, *Hist. of the Crim. Law,* vol. i. p. 113, citing Lambard, *Eirenarcha,* from which the author says is drawn the statements of Blackstone and other writers upon this subject.

[2] As to the form of the commission, which was first settled in Michaelmas term, 1590, see Lambard, p. 43.

[3] Cf. Stephen, *Hist. of the Crim. Law,* vol. i. p. 115.

[4] See Blackstone, *Comm.,* bk. iv. pp. 355, 356.

[5] Freeman, *Norm. Conq.,* vol. v. p. 312.

undoubtedly embodied the system originally represented by the free township, which system survived as the basis of municipal authority.   Despite the obscurity and confusion which surrounds the historical origin of the English municipal system, a definite conclusion has at last been reached, which is now generally accepted as final by the historians, and that is that the English town or borough is of purely Teutonic origin ; that it has its historical beginning in the immemorial system of local organization which is coeval with the race ; that at the outset it was nothing more nor less than a township, or a group of townships, more thickly settled and in a higher state of organization than the group ordinarily known as the hundred.   The theory that the Roman municipal system survived the Teutonic conquest of Britain, that the Roman cities preserved in the island kingdom a continuous municipal existence as they did in Italy and Provence, is a delusion which has finally disappeared in the light of the latest research.[1]   If, then, we accept the township system as the basis of the municipal system, if we regard the ordinary borough constitution as simply representing a group of townships, it follows that the town or borough was simply a hundred thicker in population than other hundreds, and for that very reason more strictly organized for the purposes of internal administration.   The burgemot, hustings, or law court of the Old-English town was usually nothing more than the hundred court in a slightly different form ; its origin was the same, and its procedure substantially the same.[2]   If this conception of the primitive constitution of the ordinary English town is kept steadily in view, it will be easier to explain the endless variations from the normal type which occur in the special histories of particular cities, each one of which seems to have advanced by its own road and at its own pace towards municipal independence.   In order to account even in a general way for the endless obscurities and anomalies which appear in the internal arrangements of the cities and towns when their histories can be studied in the charters in which their special privileges are recorded, the fact must be borne in mind that each town constitution presents not only a special phase of municipal development, but a special combina-

Marginal notes: The township system the basis of the municipal system.

Roman municipalities perish.

The burgemot another form of the hundred court.

---

[1] See above, pp. 125, 192.   [2] *Essays in A. S. Law,* p. 22.

tion of constituent elements. These elements have at least one thing in common: they are all drawn from a common source; they are all parts of the Teutonic system of local self-government and self-help immemorially imbedded in the gild, the township, the hundred, and the shire. The confusions which have to be mastered arise out of the endless variety of forms in which these elements of organization are combined in the several city and town constitutions.

As the ancient borough usually represented a group of townships, it is not strange that we should find in its constitution those phases of local administration which the township presents in its twofold aspect of parish and manor. As heretofore explained, the township as the domain of a single priest became so involved with the parish, and the meeting of the township for church purposes became so involved with the meeting of the vestry, that, in small parishes, the idea and even the name of the township is lost in that of the parish. That the township under the name of the parish entered into the constitution of cities and towns is illustrated by a writer who has graphically described that bewildering political aggregate known as the city of London as a "collection of geographically continuous parishes covered with buildings in the counties of Middlesex, Surrey, and Kent."[1] The

relation of the township to the manor arose out of the "process of feudalization," through which the free townships lost their independence, and became subject to a superior lord. After the Conquest the township appears as the manor of the lord, and the ancient jurisdiction of the tun-moot survives in the parish vestry and the manorial courts.[2] That the township in its manorial aspect entered into the borough constitution is most clearly illustrated by the fact that at the time of the Conquest we find the inhabitants of towns living upon the demesnes of the king, or some other lord, in the relation of tenants paying individual annual rents and other dues in various forms to the lord as owner of the soil. The first effort at emancipation from the jurisdiction of such lords is made when the burgesses obtain grants whereby the indi

---

[1] Sir F. Pollock, *Hist. of the Science of Politics*, p. 11 (Humboldt Library).
[2] Upon the history of the township as the parish and as the manor see above, pp. 143, 144.

vidual tributes are converted into a gross sum paid as a perpetual rent by the borough as a self-governing community.[1]
To the elements of organization thus derived by the borough from the township as parish and manor must be added those which it derived from the constitution of the hundred, which it so closely resembles. The most important local court in the Old-English system, in the sense of being that court which brought justice and police protection nearest to every man's door, was the hundred court. How the hundred jurisdiction was vested by express grants of *sac* and *soc* in the courts of the manor has been explained already.[2] At the time of the Conquest those boroughs that did not possess the right to hold a hundred court by virtue of their own organization as hundreds, often received the right by a grant of *sac* and *soc* from the crown whenever they happened to be situated upon the royal demesne.[3] When, therefore, the government of a borough appears to be vested in whole or in part in a court leet, it is easy to understand how that element of hundred jurisdiction passed into the borough constitution. In some instances the government of the town by the court leet has continued until modern times. It has been less than fifty years since the corporate (representative) body in Birmingham was the bailiffs and court leet.[4] In some of the larger towns, however, the municipal constitution widened beyond that of the hundred: such towns became counties, with a complete shire constitution of their own, and with sheriffs of their own. This form of constitution, first bestowed upon London by the charter of Henry I., was afterwards extended to Bristol, to York, Newcastle-on-Tyne, Norwich, Lincoln, Hull, Southampton, and other cities, which in time became "counties corporate."[5] In some of these instances the borough courts do not simply represent the hundred court, but the courts of the township, hundred, and

Relation of the town to the constitution of the hundred.

Sac and soc.

The corporate body in Birmingham the bailiffs and court leet fifty years ago.

Cities as "counties corporate."

---

[1] "The town was then said to be affirmed, or let in fee farm, to the burgesses and their successors forever." — Hallam, *M. A.*, vol. iii. p. 24, citing Madox, *Firma Burgi*, p. 1.

[2] See above, p. 254.

[3] "In some of the Domesday towns the sac and soc belongs, as in Lincoln, to the owners of manorial estates which are united within the walls. In some

it belongs entirely to the king, or to the earl or bishop." — Stubbs, *Const. Hist.*, vol. i. p. 408, citing Madox, *Firma Burgi*, p. 16, in which many illustrations are given. See, also, Stubbs, vol. iii. p. 564, citing *Firma Burgi*, p. 23.

[4] See Introduction to Toulmin Smith's *English Gilds*, p. xxii.

[5] Cf. Merewether and Stephens on the *History of Corporate Boroughs*.

shire under new names.   Under the charter of Henry I.,

London[1] is recognized as a distinct unity, entirely free from
and above the organization of the county in which it is situated.   As a distinct shire it has its own sheriff and justiciar,
who are elective officers; it has its own folk-moot as the equivalent of the shire-moot; each ward has its own ward-moot,
which is nothing but a hundred court; within the wards or
hundreds the burgesses were grouped together in township,
parish, or manor, to which are annexed the common lands
which everywhere enter into the borough constitutions.   Into

as a stand-
ard for im-
itation.

the civic organization of London, to whose special privileges
all lesser cities were ever striving to attain, the elements of
local administration embodied in the township, the hundred,
and the shire thus entered as component parts.[2]   Into the
constitutions of all other towns and cities, these identical
elements, in different forms and in different combinations,
everywhere entered as the constituents of municipal life.[3]

In the statement which has now been made of the elements
out of which has been gradually developed the English municipal system, an omission has been made of a vitally important factor which at one time became the dominant and
cohesive force in nearly all city and town constitutions.   Out
of that system of neighborhood association for mutual help
and protection which gave rise to the institution of "*frithborh*," or "peace-pledge," also sprang that closer form of
association for local self-help known as the gild.   In the one
form of association, men banded together in a given district
and joined in a "*borh*," or pledge for the keeping of the peace,
and performance of public duties, by themselves and all other
members; in the other, men entered into a local association
or benefit society, to which they gave their "*wed*," or individual promise, to abide by the by-laws or internal regulations
made for the common benefit.[4]   The spirit of association in

---

[1] For Henry's charter to the citizens
of London, see *Fœdera*, i. p. 11.

[2] "The city is an accumulation of
distinct and different corporate bodies,
but not yet a perfect municipality, nor,
although it was recognized in the reign
of Stephen as a *communio*, did it gain
the legal status before the reign of
Richard I."—*Select Charters*, p. 107.

[3] As to the general municipal history

of London, see Norton's *Commentaries
on London*.

[4] "A gild was the association of men
together for common objects of private
and individual benefit, in which each
man gave his 'wed' to abide by their
internal by-laws; while a frithborh was
the banding of men together, within
the limits of a boundary, in which each
joined in the 'borh,' or pledge for the

which the gild system finds its origin has manifested itself Uncertain origin of the gild system. in many lands, and its historical beginning has been traced by some scholars to the banquets and sacrificial assemblies of the heathen Teutonic tribes,[1] while others derive it from that form of association which existed in the Roman system under the name of *collegia*.[2] The gild system seems, however, to have attained its highest development in the Teutonic countries, — especially in England during the middle ages. One of the most eminent of the modern authorities has emphatically declared that he deems England the birthplace of gilds;[3] and from three English gild-statutes, probably drawn Oldest detailed account of gild organization English. up at the beginning of the eleventh century, is derived the oldest reliable and detailed account of gild organization. The earlier English gilds, traces of whose existence can be found as far back as the laws of Ine, Ælfred, and Æthelstan, seem to have been scattered through country and town wherever the pervading spirit of association united men in clubs or societies for religious, charitable, or social purposes. In cities Tendency of gilds to consolidate. and towns where population was densest, the tendency of gilds crowded together in close neighborhood was to coalesce in a single body. As early as the time of Æthelstan the gilds of London thus united for the purpose of more effectually carrying out their common objects; and at a later day the gilds of Berwick-upon-Tweed enacted "that where many bodies are found side by side in one place they may become one, and have one will, and in the dealings of one with another have a strong and hearty love."[4] "The united brotherhood or town gild" thus created, partaking of the commercial spirit

---

keeping of the peace, and performance of public duties by all others." — Introduction to Smith's *English Gilds*, by Miss Lucy T. Smith, p. xv.

[1] Wilda, who dissents from this view, finds in the family union the germ from which the gild was developed. See Wilda, *Das Gildewesen im Mittelalter*, Halle, 1831, p. 28 *seq.* See, also, Hartwig (*Untersuchungen über die ersten Anfänge des Gildewesens*, p. 153), who agrees with Wilda in the conclusion that nothing which is essential to the gild can be derived from the custom of holding feasts.

[2] Cf. *De collegiis et corporibus opificum, in Heineccii opera omnia*, tom. ii.

p. 390, Genevæ, 1766, and also Cicero, *De Senectute*, cap. 13.

[3] "The oldest reliable and detailed accounts which we have of gilds come from England; they consist of three gild-statutes." — Dr. Brentano's Essay in Smith's *English Gilds*, p. lxv. These statutes may be found in Kemble, *Saxons in England*, vol. i. Appendix D.

[4] This is the language of the "Statutes of the Gild," whose first article provides that "All separate gilds, heretofore existing in the borough, shall be brought to an end." — See Smith's *English Gilds*, pp. 338, 339, Brentano's Essay, p. xcix.

which by the time of the Conquest had become universal, begins to be known from that time as the "merchant-gild," [1] whose relation to the government of the towns becomes of the closest and most perplexing character.   The confusing relation which thus grew up between the merchant-gild and the borough, of which it was the inner circle, has been thus **Its relation to the borough.** defined: "Those sworn fraternities for the protection of right and the preservation of liberty, of which mention has already been made in Part I., arose independently of the towns.   Yet in the towns the necessity of protecting liberty, property, and trade against the violence of neighboring nobles . . . must have specially moved the small freemen to the formation of the societies above referred to.   These inhabitants of the towns were old, free landed proprietors ; partly of the neighboring estates, but chiefly of land within the territory of the towns themselves.   Most of them carried on trade ; some probably also handicrafts.   But the possession of town-land is the distinguishing mark of these earliest burghers. To this possession alone was full citizenship everywhere attached in the first movements of civic life. . . . Naturally, therefore, the whole body of full citizens, that is, of the possessors of portions of the town-lands of a certain value, the '*civitas*,' united itself everywhere into one gild, '*convivium conjuratum*'; the citizens and the gild became identical ; **Gild law becomes town law ; the gild hall becomes the town hall.** and what was gild-law became the law of the town." [2]   The gild hall became the town hall, and the merchant-gild, which arose within the town and yet independently of it, merged its organization in that of the town in such a manner as to draw to itself the real exercise of all municipal authority. [3] No one could enjoy the full status of burgher or citizen unless he were a member of the gild ; and even the villein (*nativus*) who obtained admission into the brotherhood, and remained unclaimed by his lord for a year and a day, became a freeman.

The cities and towns thus constituted, which grew up

---

[1] Green, *History of the Eng. People,* vol. i. p. 211.

[2] Dr. Brentano's Essay in Smith's *English Gilds,* p. xciii.

[3] " When the merchant guild had become identified with the corporation or governing body, its power of regulation of trade passed, together with other functions and properties, into the same hands." — Stubbs, *Const. Hist.,* vol. iii. p. 563.

within the jurisdiction of the shires, and upon the demesnes The struggle for emancipation from sheriff and lord. of the king or some other great lord, began the struggle for municipal independence with the effort to free themselves from the financial and judicial administration of the sheriff upon the one hand, and from the control of the lord upon the other. Until their severance from the general shire administration, the sheriff exercised the same jurisdiction over the towns as over the rest of the county; he collected from them the rents which formed a portion of the ferm of the shire; and he looked after the king's rights in their courts of justice. In order to render their portion of the burden thus imposed clear and definite, the towns first required the sheriff to fix the amount which they were called upon to pay apart from the general contribution of the shire. The next step was to obtain a charter from the crown permitting the towns to pay directly to the exchequer a fixed rent in lieu of the sum contributed through the sheriff. The fixed rent thus paid by the towns directly to the crown, which was known as the *firma burgi*,[1] the burghers apportioned and The *firma burgi*. collected among themselves by means of their own internal regulations. Thus freed from the financial interference of the sheriff, the next effort made by the towns was to free themselves from his judicial authority. Those boroughs which of themselves constituted hundreds, and those which by virtue of an express grant of *sac* and *soc* possessed the jurisdiction of a private hundred court, were exempt, of course, from all other forms of hundred jurisdiction. But such exemption did not relieve the burgesses from attendance upon the courts of the shire. Only by virtue of a special privilege, or exemption secured by fine or charter, could the townsmen claim the right to have all causes affecting themselves tried and finally determined within their own limits and in their own courts, according to the ancient methods of legal procedure, free from the Norman innovation of trial by battle. This exemption from the ordinary sessions of the county court did not extend, however, to the greater courts held in the shires by the itinerant justices. In these

[1] See Brady on Boroughs, p. 40 *seq.*; Madox, *Firma Burgi*, p. 18; *Hist. of the Exch.*, p. 226 *seq.* An instance of a *firma burgi* before the Conquest is afforded by the case of Huntington, in reference to which the term first appears in Domesday. See Hallam, *M. A.*, vol. iii. p. 24, note I.

The towns
appear in
full county
court by
representa-
tives.
courts each town was represented by twelve lawful[1] men; and the mixed juries before which the townsmen were tried were composed of six strangers, and six drawn from the body of which they were members.[2]   Thus practically severed from the administration of the shire, the burghers made a further advance towards complete civic organization by ob-taining from the king, or other lord, grants which widened Purchase of
commercial
privileges. their commercial privileges, exempted them from tolls, and at the same time conferred upon the body of the citizens or-ganized in the merchant-gild greater power to regulate their internal trade.   The charters which conveyed to the towns-men these precious privileges of freedom of trade, of justice, and of internal government had invariably to be purchased from the lord of the town, whether king, noble, or abbot, and paid for in hard cash.[3]

The towns
win the
right to
elect their
own magis-
trates.
In order to administer the special rights and privileges thus acquired by purchase from the king and other lords, and in order to supply the deficiency which arose out of the exclusion of the shire administration, it became necessary for the towns to acquire the further right of electing their own magistrates.   While the borough was administered as a de-pendent township, or as a group of dependent townships, the The leet
jury. reeve and his companions, afterwards called the leet jury, constituted the only magistracy, whose authority was supple-mented and strengthened by that of the gild.   The reeve or bailiff held the courts of the borough upon the same general principle of accountability to an external authority under which the steward held the courts of the manor.[4]   Not until the borough won exemption from the jurisdiction of the sheriff, did it win the further right to establish an independ-ent magistracy, and to choose as its head a reeve or bailiff, who now became an elective officer.[5]   The municipal char-

---

[1] The sheriffs were required to sum-mon " of each vill four lawful men and the reeve, and of each borough twelve lawful burgesses."   See the form of the summons as stated by Stephen, *Hist. of the Crim. Law*, vol. i. p. 101, cit-ing Bracton, ii. (Twiss ed.), pp. 234, 581.

[2] An illustration of this may be found in John's charter to Dunwich. " Et si forte amerciari debuerint, per sex probos homines de burgo suo et per vi probos homines extra burgum amercientur." — *Charter Rolls*, p. 51.

[3] In the charters granted to the cities and boroughs by Henry I., Hen-ry II., Richard I., and John, may be found ample illustration of the various privileges thus purchased.

[4] See *Select Charters*, 2d ed. p. 41.

[5] For the terms in which Richard grants the right to Lincoln to elect its own reeve (*præpositus*), see *Fœdera*, i. p. 52.   For the terms in which John

acter of the borough was not completed, however, until the The elective bailiff superseded by a "mayor."
elective reeve or bailiff was supplanted by the "mayor,"
whose advent completed the transition from the old system
of township government to the new system in which the
borough community appears as a *"communitas"* or corpora-
tion.[1] "The 'communitas' has, at common law, and with- Inherent power of the "communitas."
out any statute, full power to regulate its own affairs, and to
make 'bye-laws,' for its own governance, by the assent of its
own members. This power is inherent, and necessary to
enable it to fulfil its obligations to the state."[2] The entire
communitas was the corporation, and yet the exercise of all
real power lay in the hands of the gild-merchant, which was
in fact, if not in theory, the governing body. Acting as
such, it gave law to the corporation : "what was gild-law
became the law of the town."[3] So fully was the idea of Incorporation implied by the grant of *gilda mercatoria.*
corporate existence represented by the gild that it was de-
cided in later times, in the case of Totnes, that the incorporation of a borough was implied by the grant of *gilda
mercatoria.* When the existence of the merchant-gild became merged in the corporation, the title of alderman, which
originally belonged to the heads of the separate gilds, was
transferred to the magistrates of the several wards into which
the town was divided, or, where there was no such division,
to the mayor's sworn assistants. And what was more important, the common property held by the merchant-gild became
the property of the town corporation.[4] By the beginning of Condition of things at the beginning of the thirteenth century.
the thirteenth century the cities and towns that had made
the greatest advance towards municipal independence had
won the right to be exempt from the financial and judicial
administration of the sheriff, to pay their dues to the crown
in the form of a gross sum settled by a direct negotiation
with the exchequer, to hold their own courts under their own
officers, to elect their own bailiffs, and in some instances a

---

grants the same right to Nottingham,
see *Charter Rolls*, p. 39.

[1] "When municipal rights were
granted by the Plantagenet kings this
officer (reeve) was replaced by the
'mayor,' whose appearance is always
the sign of the establishment of an independent commune." — Elton's article
on "Municipality," in *Enc. Brit.*, vol.
xvii. p. 30.

[2] Introduction to Smith's *English
Gilds*, p. xxii., quoting from an unpub-
lished paper written by Toulmin Smith
in 1864 upon the "Origin of Corporations."

[3] Brentano's Essay in Smith's *English Gilds*, p. xciii.

[4] Stubbs, *Const. Hist.*, vol. iii. pp.
565, 566.

mayor, and, above all, the right to regulate their internal trade through by-laws enacted by their gild-merchant. Such was the general nature of the municipal rights recognized or confirmed in the charters which were granted by the Plantagenet kings. In the numerous charters issued by Richard and John, nearly every stage can be traced in the unequal march of the English towns towards municipal completeness. At the head of the column stands the great city of London, whose constitution is the model after which the privileges of all larger towns are modelled.[1] A month before the Great Charter was extorted from John, he granted to the *barones* of the city of London the right to elect their mayor annually; and in the charter itself provision was made that "the city of London shall have all its ancient liberties and free customs, as well by land as by water: furthermore we will grant that all other cities and boroughs, and towns and ports, shall have all their liberties and free customs."[2]

John's charter to London, May, 1215.

Summary. Such in general terms was the stage of development reached by the cities and towns when the parliamentary period begins. The more advanced have attained a complete municipal existence as *communes* or corporations, while the rest are advancing towards the common goal at different rates of progress. Under this condition of things there is, of course, a great variety of local usage, and an utter lack of uniformity in the internal arrangements through which the cities and towns are governed. "Roughly, however, we may divide them into two classes, those in which the local administration was carried on by a ruling body of magistrates or magnates, and those in which it remained in the hands of the townspeople in general; the former being the type of the larger and more ancient municipalities, the latter that of the smaller towns, and of those whose corporate character was simpler and newer."[3]

7. Having now indicated the stage of development reached by the two great classes of self-governing communities when the parliamentary period begins, the processes must next be drawn out through which the shires and towns appear by

---

[1] "It became a general rule to confirm the gild of a town by granting it all the liberties which another town already enjoyed." — Bretano's Essay, p. cv.

[2] *Charter Rolls*, p. 207.

[3] Stubbs, *Const. Hist.*, vol. ii. p. 217.

their representatives in the national council, and through Appearance of the shire and town representatives in the national council, and their final union in one house. which such representatives finally unite in the formation of the house of commons. The records of the year 1213 furnish the earliest authentic instance of the shire communities being called upon to send representatives to a national council. On the 7th of November the king called a council at Oxford to which the sheriffs were directed to summon, besides the Earliest writ summoning shire representatives to parliament, 1213. armed force of the knights, *quatuor discretos homines de comitatu tuo illuc venire facias ad nos ad eundem terminum ad loquendum nobiscum de negotiis regni nostri.*[1] The immemorial practice of sending the reeve and four men as representatives of the township to the shire-moot thus widened into the practice of sending "four discreet men" as representatives of the county to confer with the king in his great council touching the affairs of the kingdom.[2] The next instance in which it is clear that representatives of the shire were summoned to parliament occurs in 1254, when the The writ of 1254. sheriffs are commanded to return, *duos de uno comitatu et duos de alio, ad providendum, una cum militibus aliorum comitatuum quos ad eundem diem vocari fecimus, quale auxilium nobis in tanta necessitate impendere voluerint.*[3] In the language of the Lords' Report, this "seems to have been the first instance appearing upon any record now extant, of an attempt to substitute representatives elected by bodies of men for the attendance of the individuals so to be represented, personally or by their several procurators, in an assembly convened for the purpose of obtaining an aid."[4] In 1261 The assembly at St. Alban's in 1261. Gloucester and Earl Simon joined in calling an assembly at St. Alban's, to which were summoned three knights from every shire south of Trent. The significant words in the writ, in which the king afterwards commanded the sheriffs to send these knights, not to St. Alban's but to Windsor, are *colloquium habituros.*[5] In 1264, after his triumph at Lewes, Earl Simon caused writs to be issued summoning four knights from each shire to meet the king in parliament, — *nobiscum tractaturi de negotiis prædictis.*[6] To the famous parliament

---

[1] The writ may be found in the *Lords' Report*, App. i. p. 2. See above, p. 377.
[2] *Select Charters*, p. 287.
[3] For the writ, see *Lords' Report*, App. i. p. 13.

[4] Vol. i. p. 95.
[5] For the writ, see *Lords' Report*, App. i. p. 23.
[6] *Fœdera*, i. p. 442.

of 1265 the representatives from the shires and towns were
summoned in the same form as the magnates.[1] Passing over
the anomalous assemblies which met prior to the year 1290,
we find in that year the knights of the shire summoned *ad
consulendum et consentiendum pro se et communitate.*[2]   To

Edward's model parliament which met in 1295 — from which
time the attendance of representatives from both shires and
towns has been continuous, or nearly so — both knights and
burgesses are summoned *ad faciendum quod tunc de communi
consilio ordinabitur in præmissis.*[3]

Knights of
the shire
elected by
the whole
body of
freeholders
in full
county
court.

The writs which thus clearly explain the purpose for which
the knights of the shire were summoned to the national council fail, however, to disclose who were the electors of the representative members.   From the returns to the writs, it is
plain that they were elected *per totam communitatem,* or *in
pleno comitatu,* or *per consensum totius comitatus.*[4]   Beyond
this the record evidence does not go; only by inference from
the well established usage of the county court can be determined who were the electors by whom the shire representatives were chosen.   Despite all the conflicting views which
have been expressed concerning the representative character in
which the elected knights first appear in the national council,
the following statement may be accepted as a substantial
embodiment of the conclusions which have been established
by the latest and ripest research.   It seems to be more than

Fourteenth
article of
the Great
Charter, —
its probable
purpose.

probable that the fourteenth article of the Great Charter,
which provided that the lesser tenants-in-chief should be summoned by the sheriffs generally in the shires, was intended to
rouse the lesser baronage to the exercise of rights which had
practically passed into desuetude.   But the fact that this provision was omitted from the very first reissue of the charter
is persuasive to prove that the principle requiring the whole
body of the lesser barons to attend in person never received
more than a limited application in practice.   The fact seems
to be unquestioned that from the issuance of the Great Charter
down to the time when the representative members appear,
the great council, although occasionally attended by a few of

---

[1] *Lords' Report,* App. i. p. 33.   See,
also, *Select Charters,* p. 415.

[2] *Lords' Report,* App. i. p. 54.

[3] *Lords' Report,* App. i. p. 66.

[4] See *Parl. Writs,* i. 21–24, 38, 40,
41 ; Stubbs, *Const. Hist.,* vol. ii. p. 226.

the lesser knighthood, continued to be simply a gathering of the prelates and greater tenants-in-chief. The minor tenants-in-chief as a body fail to attend, and in their place and stead appear the elected knights chosen in the shires. If these elected knights had been chosen elsewhere than in the county court, the inference of a certain school might be a fair one, that they represented, not the community of the shire, but only the minor tenants-in-chief.[1] In order to maintain this narrow view it is necessary to show that only the lesser barons were the electors, and not the whole body of the county court. To give color to this idea, it has been claimed that the court summoned for the election of the knights was not the court leet of the county, at which all residents were required to attend, but the court baron, which, excluding the tenants of mesne lords, embraced only such tenants as owed suit and service to the king.[2] The fact has, however, been put beyond question, that the mesne tenants (the *vavassores* of the barons) did attend ;[3] and it is equally clear that if the elected knights were chosen by a mere fractional part of the shire court, the election could not have been described as the act of the whole community *in pleno comitatu*. The weight of authority, or rather of inference, sustains the conclusion that the elected knights were not only representatives of the whole shire community, but that they were chosen by the whole body of freeholders in full county court.[4] The representative character of the elected knights, as well as the qualification of the electors, were both determined by the nature of the only court or assembly in which the sheriff could constitutionally execute the writ under whose mandate the knights were

The elected knights appear instead of the whole body of minor tenants-in-chief.

Representative character of the knights, as well as the qualification of electors, determined by the character of the county court.

---

[1] This narrow and now obsolete view, which was maintained by Brady, Carte, and Blackstone, received a half-hearted assent from the Lords' Committee, who confess, however, that the whole subject "is involved in great obscurity."—Vol. i. pp. 149, 150. See, also, p. 30.

[2] "The county court, at which the elections afterwards took place, was that court which has been considered as the court baron of the county, distinguished from the sheriff's turn, at which all residents were bound to appear."—*Lords' Report*, vol. i. p. 140.

[3] See Mr. Allen's article in the *Edin-burgh Review*, vol. xxvi. pp. 341–347; Bigelow, *Procedure*, p. 142.

[4] This was the view of Prynne (2d Register, p. 50), who holds that the knights were "elected in the full county, by and for the whole county." This view has been sanctioned by Hallam, *M. A.*, vol. iii. pp. 19, 216–219, and by Stubbs, *Const. Hist.*, vol. ii. pp. 225–232. The Bishop concludes that "the theory of the election was that it was the act of the shire-moot, that is, of all the suitors of the county court assembled in the county court, irrespective of the question of whom or by what tenure their lands were held."—Page 232.

chosen. The sheriff could only act in the county court, which was composed of the whole body of freeholders, and he could only act in accordance with those methods of procedure with which the shire community had been immemorially familiar. As heretofore explained, the principles of election and representation which from the earliest times had entered into the procedure of the shire-moot were still employed, after the Conquest as before, in every branch of judicial, fiscal, or remedial work that devolved upon the shire community.[1] When

Practice of election and representation in the county court.

in the reign of Richard I. the presentment system was reorganized upon a basis distinctly representative, "four knights are chosen from the whole county who, by their oaths, shall choose two lawful knights of each hundred or wapentake." The four knights, who under the terms of the Great Charter are to assist the itinerant justices in taking the three assizes, are elected by the county court. The two knights, who by "the will and counsel" of the shire community take part in the assessment and collection of the carucage of 1220, are elected in the full assembly of the shire. And the elections of coroners, venderers, and conservators are all conducted in the same manner.[2] What, therefore, could be more natural or probable than that the knights who were to represent the shire in the national council should have been elected in full county court, as were the knights who were elected by the shire for local purpose? The force of this inference is certainly not weakened by anything that can be found in the form of a restriction either in the writs themselves or in the returns which were made under them. No legal restriction upon the right of the members of the county court to participate in the election of the representative knights can be found

First limitation upon the franchise, 1430.

prior to the statute of Henry VI.,[3] whereby the electoral franchise was limited to the forty shillings freeholders.

Representatives from townships on the royal demesne summoned to the council at St. Alban's in 1213.

The earliest instance of anything like a representation from the towns appearing in the national council occurs in the memorable meeting at St. Alban's, in August, 1213, to which were summoned not only the bishops and barons, but also the reeve and four legal men from each township on the royal demesne.[4] Although, as heretofore explained, the reeve and

---

[1] See above, p. 255.
[2] See above, pp. 303, 307.

[3] 8 Hen. VI. c. 7.
[4] See above, p. 376.

four men were probably summoned simply to assess the damages due to the plundered bishops and abbots, the incident is important as the first illustration of which there is any historical proof of representatives, either from shires or towns, being summoned to a national council. Not until the 7th of November of the same year did the king call a council at Oxford, to which were summoned, besides the armed force of the knights, the "four discreet men" from each shire.[1] The appearance of the town representatives in the council at St. Alban's cannot be regarded, however, as more than a mere indication of the brighter day that was yet to come when Earl Simon, in the hope of giving a broader popular basis to his government, issued writs, on the 14th of December, 1264, for his famous parliament, to which were summoned not only the two discreet knights from the shires, but also, for the first time in the history of English politics, two representatives from the cities and towns.[2] The writs addressed on this occasion to the cities and towns, commanding them to send up two representatives each, were not addressed to them through the sheriff of the county according to the practice which prevailed at a later day when they became a constituent element in the national parliament. After the year 1265, another long interval occurs before the representatives from the towns appear in what the constitutional lawyers concede to be a genuine parliament. Although representatives from the boroughs appear in the national councils of 1273 and 1283, and in the parliament of Acton Burnell, not until Edward's model parliament of 1295 are they regularly summoned. At that time their status was first recognized as an integral part of parliament, and from that time their representation has been continuous, or nearly so.[3] Under the writs issued for the parliament of 1295, the representatives from both shires and towns were to be chosen *ad faciendum quod tunc de communi consilio ordinabitur in præmissis,* a

Representatives from the cities and towns first summoned to parliament by Earl Simon in 1264.

Representatives from the towns first recognized as an integral part of parliament in 1295.

---

[1] See above, p. 465.

[2] "Item in forma prædicta scribitur civibus Eboraci, civibus Lincolniæ, et ceteris burgis Angliæ, quod mittant in forma prædicta duos de discretioribus, legalioribus et probioribus tam civibus quam burgensibus." To the barons of the Cinque Ports the mandate is, "Item in forma prædicta mandatum est baronibus et probis hominibus Quinque Portuum." — *Lords' Report,* App. i. p. 33.

[3] See *Select Charters,* p. 44.

form which is retained until the terms *ad consentiendum* are added in the reign of Edward II.[1]

Under the writ commanding the sheriff to return members from the towns, he could extend or withhold the privilege, as he saw fit.

The question has been raised whether the sheriff, under the writ commanding him to return representatives from every city and borough in his county, was restricted to such only as were situated on the royal demesne, or whether he could send his precept to any town, held by any lord other than the crown, which he might deem worthy of the privilege. Although the theory of restriction has been advocated by Brady[2] with his usual leaning to the doctrine of tenure, and has been in part supported by the Lords' Report,[3] the weight of authority is decidedly in favor of the more liberal view, which is fully sustained by the fact that in the parliaments of Edward I., North Allerton, Lynn, Downton, Evesham, Tunbridge, and other towns of the same class were represented, which were held in demesne by lords other than the king.[4] Under the general terms of the writ the sheriff seems to have possessed the power not only to extend the franchise to any town which he saw fit to recognize, but also to ignore others that were manifestly worthy, or even such as had once enjoyed the right of electing members. The legal fiction which the sheriff employed to conceal such an omission is well illustrated by the familiar case which occurred in the 12th Edward III., wherein the sheriff of Wiltshire, after making returns from one city and two boroughs, reported that there were no more cities or boroughs within his bailiwick, and this, too, in the face of the fact that eight other towns in his shire had sent representatives to preceding parliaments. In the 6th of Edward II., the sheriff of Bucks, after making a return from Wycomb, reported that there were no more boroughs in his county, although in that very reign three other boroughs had twice sent up representatives.[5] From the well-

---

[1] Hallam, *M. A.*, vol. iii. p. 38, citing Prynne's 2d Register, p. 92.

[2] According to his view representatives were sent only by " the king's demesne cities and burghs, such as had charters from the king, and paid a fee farm rent in lieu of the customs." — Brady on Boroughs, p. 73.

[3] See vol. i. pp. 231, 232.

[4] These instances, and others, are collated by Stubbs, *Const. Hist.*, vol. ii. p. 233. The more liberal view is sustained by Allen, *Edinburgh Review*, vol. xxxv. pp. 30, 36, 37 ; and by Hallam, *M. A.*, vol. iii. pp. 217, 218.

[5] See Brady on Boroughs, pp. 110-126 ; Prynne, 3d Register, p. 231 ; Hallam, *M. A.*, vol. iii. p. 110. To the same effect see, also, *Lords' Report*, vol. i. p. 375. To remedy this abuse a statute was passed (5 Richard II. stat. ii. c. 4) which imposed a fine upon the sheriff for such neglect. See *Lords' Report*, vol. i. p. 341.

known reluctance of the boroughs to send members to parliament, it is more than likely that such returns by the sheriff were in many instances the result of connivance upon the part of the burgesses themselves, who were more anxious to escape the expense incident to attendance, and the higher rate of taxation which such attendance imposed, than to enjoy the privilege of representation. In some instances in which the sheriff could not be persuaded to omit particular boroughs, they escaped the burden of representation by simply failing to make any return whatever to his precept or mandate.

The most difficult and obscure question connected with the representation of towns is that one which involves the inquiry : Who were the electors of the borough representatives ? The difficulty arises not only out of the utter lack of symmetry and uniformity in the internal arrangements of the towns, — in each one of which the manner of election was determined by local usage or custom, — but out of the further fact that the municipal records in which much of the mediæval history of the English towns is contained have not as yet been made the subject of thorough investigation. And strange as it may seem, it is nevertheless true, that the prosecution of such investigations is not always free from official obstruction. As late as 1862 the officers of the corporation of Bristol, in refusing access to its municipal records, stated that they conceived " it to be their duty to withhold the corporate records from the scrutiny of historical students." [1] Happily for the cause of municipal history, the conduct of the corporation of Bristol is only conspicuous as an exception. From such imperfect data as we do possess, it is possible, however, to arrive at a few definite conclusions which indicate the general nature of the process through which the borough members were chosen. The writ ordering the election of knights, citizens, and burgesses was returnable in about forty days by the sheriff himself, who was at first required to report to parliament the names of the persons chosen under the writ in the county court. Nothing more definite as to the sheriff's procedure can be positively stated until the passage

Reluctance of the boroughs to send members.

Who were the electors of the borough representatives?

Mediæval history of English towns not yet fully worked out.

The sheriffs procedure under the election writ.

[1] See Smith's *English Gilds,* p. 283, note, quoting from Mr. Samuel Lucas (*Secularia,* p. 102).

of the statute of Henry IV. (1406), which provided that the election should take place in the first county court held after the receipt of the writ, that it should be had in full court by those present, and that after the election the names of the representatives chosen shall be written in an indenture under the seals of them that did choose them, — which indenture tacked to the writ as the sheriff's return was to be sent into

The formal election of all representatives took place in the county court, — the real election of borough members in the boroughs themselves.

chancery.[1]   During this period there can be no doubt that the formal election of all representatives of the commons took place in the county court ; and it seems to be equally clear that the real election of the city and borough members took place in the several municipalities which they were chosen to represent.   From the time of Edward I. it seems to have been the custom for the sheriff to send to such towns as he saw fit to recognize a precept or mandate commanding the town authorities to prepare for the formal election to take place in the county court in which they were cited to appear. The failure of the sheriffs to do their duty by sending the precepts or mandates to the cities and boroughs entitled thereto led no doubt to the act of 1445,[2] which undertook to regulate the discharge of this duty by positive law.   In the

Sheriffs required by law to send precepts to the proper officers of cities and towns.

words of the Committee : "In cities and boroughs great irregularity probably prevailed, for want of settled rules for the conduct both of the sheriffs of counties in issuing their precepts, and the returning officers in returning writs in cities and boroughs ; and therefore it was enacted in the 23d of Henry VI., that the sheriffs should issue precepts to the proper officers of cities and boroughs, containing a direction, that in cities the election should be by the citizens of the city, and in boroughs by burgesses of the borough."[3]   By this act, — which sets forth the fact that the sheriffs have of late sometimes returned persons who were not chosen, and have failed to return persons who were chosen, and in some cases have failed to send precepts, — it was provided, that the sheriffs should send to the magistrates of each borough a

---

[1] "Soient lour nouns escriptz en endenture dessoutz les sealx de toutz ceux qui eux eslisent, et tacchez au dit brieve du parlement ; ... et electionem tuam in pleno comitatu tuo factam distincte et aperte sub sigillo tuo et sigillis eorum qui electioni illi interfuerint nos in cancellaria nostra." — 7 Hen. IV. c. 15 ; *Statutes*, ii. p. 156.

[2] 23 Hen. VI. c. 14 ; *Statutes*, ii. p. 340.

[3] *Lords' Report*, vol. i. p. 369. See, also, p. 375.

precept for the election to be held therein ; that such election should be held between the hours of eight and eleven in the morning, that the return should be made by indenture be- Return to be made by indenture. tween the sheriff and the electors, and that sheriffs, mayors, and bailiffs who failed to do their duty under the act should suffer a penalty. Such were the legal provisions touching the real election which took place in the boroughs themselves, prior to the formal election which took place in the county court on the day the boroughs were cited to appear therein. At the time appointed a delegation of burghers from each The formal election in the county court. city and town appeared in the county court and there announced the names of those chosen in the town meeting, or as deputies of the town, and with its assent they themselves there chose its parliamentary representatives.[1] Such is the reasonable inference as to the usual course of procedure which has been drawn from the existing evidence. Under this view the representatives of the borough were either elected primarily by the governing body of the town, and the fact then announced in the county court ; or a deputation was elected by the town with power to make its choice in the county court. In either event the original question remains unanswered : Who were the electors who possessed the right to take part in the primary election which took place within the borough itself ? This difficult question was vaguely answered by the Committee in the assertion that the sheriffs were directed to issue " precepts to the proper officers of cities and boroughs, containing a direction that in cities the election The electors in a city were the citizens, in a borough the burgesses. should be by the citizens of the city, and in boroughs by the burgesses of the borough. But who should be deemed citizens and burgesses seems still to have depended on *usage*, where not regulated by charter of the crown." [2] Where not Who were citizens and burgesses depended upon local usage, where not regulated by charter. expressly regulated by charter, the right of suffrage everywhere depended upon local usage or custom, and such usage was so various as to render anything like a perfect generalization, even upon sufficient data, almost impossible. The nearest approach to such a generalization is that one which has been made by the master of the constitutional history of the middle ages by the aid of the later evidence which exists

[1] Cf. Stubbs, *Const. Hist.*, vol. iii. pp. 413, 414.   [2] *Lords' Report*, vol. i. p. 369.

Generaliza-
tion of
Bishop
Stubbs.
when our knowledge of the subject really begins : " The most ancient, perhaps, of the franchises, was that depending on burgage tenure ; this was exactly analogous in origin to the freeholder's qualification in the counties ; but as the repressive principle extended, the right of a burgage vote had become in many places attached to particular houses or sites of houses, probably those which were originally liable for a quota of the *firma burgi ;* in others the right still belonged to the whole body of freeholders ; and this may be regarded as a second sort of franchise. A third custom placed the right to vote in the freemen of the borough, or of the guild which was coextensive with the borough ; the character of a freeman being personal and not connected with tenure of land or contribution to the public burdens. A fourth gave the electoral vote to all householders paying scot and lot ; that is, bearing their ratable proportion in the payments levied from the town for local or national purposes. A fifth lodged the right in the hands of the governing body, the corporation ; the constitution of which again varied from comparative freedom in one place to oligarchic exclusiveness in another. The newer the constitution of the town was, the less liberal the constitution seems to have been, . . . it is obvious that the tendency of restriction set in from the first institution of charters of incorporation in the fifteenth century." [1] The wonder is that this archaic system, under which as a general rule the right of suffrage was taken away from the main body of townsmen and vested in official oligarchies, should have so long survived as a monument of injustice and inequality. The bringing of order and equality out of this

Municipal
Corpora-
tions Act
of 1835.
chaos of antiquated custom was the achievement of the Municipal Corporations Act of 1835,[2] which reorganized all of the municipal corporations of England and Wales upon a uniform basis. The provisions of that act [3] — which recognized the principles that the government of towns should be vested in councils chosen at short intervals by the citizens and burgesses, and that in that class should be included prac-

---

[1] Stubbs, *Const. Hist.*, vol. iii. pp. 419, 420. See, also, as to the original form of the elective franchise in boroughs, Merewether and Stephens on Boroughs, Introd., xxvi.

[2] 5 & 6 Will. IV. c. 76, amended by 22 Vict. c. 35.

[3] See Dillon, *Municipal Corporations,* vol. i. p. 35.

tically all who occupied houses or shops, and paid taxes for the relief of the poor — will be specially considered hereafter.

The questions which have now been asked and answered as to the qualification of electors naturally suggest an inquiry as to the eligibility of the elected members. From the language of the writs it is evident that, so far as the shire representatives were concerned, an early effort was made to limit the honor to members of the knighthood only. Under the writs for the parliaments of 1290, 1294, and 1295, the election was to be made *de discretioribus, et ad laborandum potentioribus, militibus.*[1] The difficulty, however, of forcing the attendance of discreet and able knights made it necessary in the reign of Edward II. to so modify the terms of the writs as to allow the sheriffs to dispense with the original qualification.[2] The innovation thus brought about was definitely recognized by the statute of 23 Henry VI. c. 14, which declared that only notable knights, or such notable esquires and gentlemen of birth as may become knights, are to be elected; and by no means a man of the degree of yeoman (vadlet)[3] or under. By the statute of Henry V.[4] residence was made a qualification of both electors and elected: the knights of the shire are to be resident within the shire at the date of the writ, and the same thing is required of their choosers; and the citizens and burgesses are to be free and resident citizens and burgesses. This requirement, after having been long disregarded in practice,[5] was finally repealed by 14 Geo. III. c. 58, which made the residence of the electors and elected in their respective counties, cities, and boroughs no longer necessary. After the qualified representatives of the shires and towns were duly elected, they were required to give security for their attendance, and the names of the bailsmen or manucaptors were entered in the return,[6]

Marginal notes:

Eligibility of the elected members.

Representatives from the shires not necessarily knights.

Residence made a qualification of both electors and elected by a statute of Henry V.

Repealed by 14 Geo. III. c. 58.

---

[1] *Parl. Writs*, i. 21, 25, 29, etc.

[2] This change was brought about by adding to the older form, " seu aliis, de comitatu tuo assensu et arbitrio hominum ejusdem comitatus nominandos." See Stubbs, *Const. Hist.*, vol. iii. p. 397.

[3] Men of this class had been elected prior to the passage of the act. Upon the subject of " Valetti in Parliament," see the editor's learned note to Taswell-Langmead's *Eng. Const. Hist.*, pp. 347, 348.

[4] 1 Hen. V. c. 1. By statute of 10 Hen. VI. c. 2, it was provided that the land which gave the vote should be situate within the county.

[5] As to the statute of Henry V. perishing under the doctrine of desuetude, see Hallam, *M. A.*, vol. iii. p. 115; Peckwell, *Rep'ts of Contested Elections*, i. 53, note D.

[6] Luders' *Reports*, vol. i. p. 15.

Representatives required to give security for their attendance.
The *plena potestas*.
Wages.

a practice which continued down to the end of the fifteenth century. The members thus bound over to appear were armed in the early days with a *plena potestas*,[1] in the form of letters of attorney, authorizing them to represent their constituents, whose duty it was to provide beforehand for the payment of their wages. Such wages, which were made to cover not only the period of attendance in parliament, but the journey to and fro, and which seem to have been allowed from the very beginning of the representative system, were first reduced to a certain sum by the day in the 16th of Edward II.[2] By the writs *de levandis expensis* issued in that reign, the wages were fixed at four shillings a day for every knight, and two shillings for every citizen and burgess.[3]

From what has now been said, the fact appears that through the development of the writ process in its highest form the constitution of parliament was finally established as an assembly of estates. Although the name of parliament was not restricted in its earlier use[4] to councils containing representative members, it was finally limited only to such assemblies of estates as contained all of the necessary parliamentary elements and no more, and which were convened under the authority of writs regularly issued.[5] In a parliament thus constituted the lords spiritual and temporal appeared to represent themselves in response to the individual writs addressed to each member of the peerage; the representatives from the shires and towns appeared in obedience to the general writs directed to the sheriffs commanding their election; the representatives of the clergy appeared in obedience to the *præmunientes* clause in the writs directed to the bishops commanding them to cause the election and return of proctors armed with full powers from the chapters and parochial clergy.

The right to issue the parliamentary writs belonged primarily to the king, who, with the advice of his council, could

---

[1] For instances in which it was bestowed, see *Parl. Writs*, i. pp. 21–23, 39, 41, 59.

[2] Prynne, 4th Register, p. 53; Hallam, *M. A.*, vol. iii. p. 114, note 2.

[3] Such writs may be traced down to the end of the reign of Henry VIII. See Prynne, 4th Register, p. 495.

[4] As to the early use of the term, see *Lords' Report*, vol. i. p. 20.

[5] "The constitution of the legislative assembly of the kingdom must now be considered as resting in usage, as declared by statute in the 15th of Edward the Second." — *Lords' Report*, vol. i. p. 229.

determine, subject to the limitations imposed by custom, both the time and place at which parliament should assemble.[1]   Not long after the permanent incorporation of the representative members the custom became established that parliaments should be held annually, or oftener if necessary. Such was the rule laid down in an ordinance adopted in the fifth of Edward II., and in statutes passed in the fourth and thirty-sixth of Edward III.[2]   After the particular time within the year had been agreed upon, a choice had next to be made of the place at which the estates should be called together. During the pre-Norman period the witan, after due proclamation, was usually assembled at some one of the royal residences, generally after harvest, or on one of the great festivals of the church, — Easter, Whitsuntide, or Christmas.[3] When Westminster became, in the reign of Eadward the Confessor, the recognized residence of the king, it became at the same time the recognized home of the national council. After the Conquest, however, when the witan was transformed into a feudal court or council which followed the person of the king, councils were held at Westminster only when the king saw fit to make it his resting-place.   There the Conqueror often held his summer courts ; there William Rufus built the great hall which afterwards became the home of the courts of justice ; there Henry I. held his councils ; there Stephen founded in honor of his patron saint the chapel which finally became the meeting-place of the house of commons ;[4] and there the common pleas were held after it was fixed by the terms of the Great Charter that they should be held in some certain place.   In the reign of Henry III., who rebuilt the abbey and enlarged the palace, Westminster finally came to be considered as the customary and lawful meeting-place of parliament.   Not, however, until the following reign of Edward I., when the central administrative machinery became permanently fixed in and around the palace, did Westminster become, in the full sense of the

Parliamentary writs issued by the king with the advice of the council.

Annual parliaments.

Meeting-place of national councils.

Westminster in the days of the Confessor;

in the days of the Norman kings.

Henry III. rebuilds the abbey and enlarges the palace.

---

[1] "The writ of summons has always named the day and place of meeting, without which the requisition to meet would be imperfect and nugatory." — Sir T. Erskine May's *Parl. Practice*, p. 46.

[2] See Ibid., p. 45.

[3] Kemble, *Saxons in England*, vol. ii. pp. 192, 202, citing *E. Chron.*, a. 1010.

[4] A graphic description of the palace of Westminster, as it appeared in 1640, may be found in Hosmer's *Young Sir Henry Vane*, pp. 97, 98.

Westminster becomes the seat of government in the reign of Edward I.

term, the seat of government. From that time onward the dwelling-place of the king — out of whose household organization the national administrative system has been largely developed — was gradually devoted to the uses of government : "the chamber became a council room, the banquet hall a court of justice, the chapel a hall of deliberation." [1] After the final division of parliament into two houses, each found a meeting-place within the precincts of the palace of Westminster, "where the witan of all England still meet for judgment and for legislation." [2]

The meeting of parliament.

At the time fixed in the writs, the lords spiritual and temporal, together with the representatives from the shires and towns, were expected to appear before the king at Westminster, or at any other place that he had seen fit to designate. When a sufficient number had arrived the parliament was opened, and the names of the elected members were called over in order to identify them with those returned by the sheriffs. At a little later day it also became the practice to call over the names of the lords in order to ascertain who had come and who had not.[3] The first business in order was

Opening speech.

the opening speech, delivered by the chancellor, the primate, or some other great officer of state, in which was explained the purpose for which the estates had been called together.[4]

Triers of petitions appointed.

After the close of the speech, and after the appointment of triers of petitions, the parliament dissolved itself into its constituent elements in order that each group might deliberate apart upon the common work given them in charge. Whether there ever was a time, after the appearance of the representative members, when the three estates deliberated together in a single assembly, is a question whose discussion has drawn out diametrically opposite views from the highest authorities.[5] When all the probabilities are weighed in the dim light of the existing evidence, it seems to be more than likely that the different estates, each taxing itself upon its own basis,

---

[1] Stubbs, *Const. Hist.*, vol. iii. p. 384, and pp. 382, 383.

[2] Freeman, *Norm. Conq.*, vol. ii. p. 336.

[3] See *Rot. Parl.*, i. 350; Ibid., ii. p. 147; Ibid., iii. pp. 55, 71, 78, 184; Stubbs, *Const. Hist.*, vol. iii. p. 427 and note 2.

[4] As to the early practice, see Elsynge, *Ancient Method of Holding Parliament*, pp. 131 *seq.*; as to the modern practice, see May, *Parl. Practice*, pp. 47, 219.

[5] Prynne (1st Register, p. 233) holds that they never deliberated together; Coke (4 *Inst.*, p. 4) holds that they did.

deliberated apart from the very beginning, save when momentarily assembled in the presence of the king, or for the purpose of special conference with each other. The period of uncertainty, which begins with the permanent incorporation of the representative members in the famous parliament of 1295, ends with the definite and final division of parliament into two houses in the reign of Edward III.[1] In tracing out the causes which led to this division, it is easy to understand why the lay and spiritual baronage, long accustomed to united conciliar action in the great council, should have perpetuated their separate organization in the house of lords. The difficult matter is to determine why the knights of the shire, selected from the lesser landholders, who in continental lands would have belonged to the estate of the nobles, should have withdrawn from the baronage in order to unite upon equal terms with the representatives of the towns in the formation of the house of commons. So rapidly did this happy coalition advance that by the fifteenth of Edward II. (1322) the constitutional status of the lower house seems to have been definitely recognized in an act which provided that " matters to be established for the estate of our lord the king and of his heirs, and for the estate of the realm and of the people, should be treated, accorded, and established, in parliaments, by the king, and by the assent of the prelates, earls, and barons, *and the commonalty* of the realm, according as had been before accustomed."[2] Not, however, until the sixth of Edward III. (1332) do the parliament records distinctly mention the fact that the prelates, the lords temporal, and the knights of the shire deliberated apart, — the prelates by themselves, the earls, barons, and other grantz by themselves, and the knights from the counties by themselves.[3] In the next year we learn that the lords and the proctors sat apart by themselves, and the knights, citizens, and burgesses by themselves.[4] Finally the parliament rolls of the thirteenth and fifteenth of Edward III. make it clear that the process of division had by that time reached completion, — that the lords and commons had

It is probable that the three estates deliberated apart from the beginning, save when assembled for some special purpose.

The lay and spiritual baronage perpetuate their separate organization in the house of lords,

while the representative members unite in the house of commons.

Parliament definitely and finally divided into two houses in the reign of Edward III.

---

[1] Cf. Hallam, *M. A.*, vol. iii. pp. 38, 39; Stubbs, *Const. Hist.*, vol. iii. pp. 430, 431.
[2] Statutes 15 Edw. II. i. p. 189. See, also, *Lords' Report*, vol. i. p. 229.
[3] *Rot. Parl.*, ii. p. 66. September, 1332.
[4] *Rot. Parl.*, ii. p. 69.

In 1352 commons ordered to the chapter house.

then definitely arranged themselves in two separate and distinct bodies. In 1352 the commons were ordered to withdraw to the chapter house of Westminster Abbey, which seems to have been then regarded as their chamber.[1] In 1376 the lower house formally completed its organization as a deliberative body by the election of Peter de la Mare as foreman.[2]

In 1377 Sir T. Hungerford chosen speaker.

In 1377 Sir Thomas Hungerford was chosen, — the first to whom the title and position of speaker were definitely assigned ;[3] from that date the list of speakers is complete. Although the speaker was chosen by the votes of all the representative members, never did the honor pass to other than a knight of the shire until the election of Robert Brooke,

The chancellor presides in the house of lords.

a member from London, in 1554.[4] In the house of lords the duty of presiding generally devolves upon the chancellor,[5] whose position differs in several important particulars from that of the speaker of the commons.

The clergy as an estate of parliament.

8. The statement which has now been made of the final arrangement of the representatives from the shires and towns in one house, and of the lay and spiritual baronage in another, naturally suggests an inquiry as to the fate of the parliamentary representatives of the clergy who, under the scheme of Edward I., were to be incorporated as a substantive element in the assembly of estates. The idea of summoning the representatives of the clergy of both provinces as a constituent element in a national council was first fully developed in the writs by which Edward called together his famous parliament

The præmunientes clause.

of 1295. The præmunientes clause, contained in the writs addressed to the bishops, premonished them to cause the deans and priors of cathedrals and the archdeacons to appear in person, and each cathedral chapter to appear by one and the clergy of each diocese by two proctors, armed with suf-

---

[1] " When the commons deliberated apart, they sat in the chapter house of the Abbot of Westminster, and they continued their sittings in that place after their final separation." May, *Parl. Practice*, p. 25, citing Elsynge, p. 104. Not until the reign of Edward VI. did St. Stephen's Chapel become the meeting-place of the commons." — Bayley and Britton, p. 363.

[2] *Chronicon Angliæ*, p. 72.

[3] *Rot. Parl.*, ii. p. 374. See May, *Parl. Practice*, p. 23 and note 4.

[4] His successor in 1555 was a burgess from West Looe. Browne Willis, *Rot. Parl.*, p. 113. Stubbs, *Const. Hist.*, vol iii. p. 453.

[5] As to the status and duties of the chancellor as speaker of the house of lords, see May, *Parl. Practice*, pp. 49, 243, 246. The lord chancellor is not necessarily a peer. In 1830 Lord Chancellor Brougham sat on the woolsack as speaker before his elevation to the peerage, — one of many instances of a like kind. Ibid., p. 244.

ficient power to represent the clergy and chapters.[1] " In the
præmunientes clause, inserted in the writs of the 23d of Edward the First, a representation of the clergy in convention
was provided, bearing a strong resemblance to the representation of the laity in the legislative assembly in parliament,
provided by the writs issued for that purpose at the same
time."[2] If the English clergy had seen fit to accept instead
of oppose this arrangement, there was no reason why, in England as elsewhere, the clergy, like the nobles, should not have
formed themselves into a distinct parliamentary estate. But
from the very beginning the plan was opposed by the clergy
themselves, who preferred to vote their aids in their own provincial councils or convocations. Under the persistent force
of clerical opposition, the plan of Edward broke down and
became a mere shadow. The *præmunientes* clause itself is
still inserted in the writs, but it has been a dead letter since
the fourteenth century.[3] The clergy of the two provinces,
refusing to be jointly assembled as an estate of parliament,
continued to tax themselves in their provincial convocations
until after the restoration of Charles II.[4] The subsidies of
the clergy were voted in the convocations in the form of " benevolences," separate and apart from the aids granted by the
laity, down to the year 1664, when, by a mere verbal agreement
between Archbishop Sheldon and Lord Chancellor Clarendon, an arrangement was made under which the clergy waived
their right to tax themselves, and agreed to be assessed by the
laity in parliament. The results of this silent revolution,
which has been called " the greatest alteration in the constitution ever made without an express law,"[5] were distinctly
recognized in an act of parliament passed in the following
year (16 and 17 Car. II. c. 1), which recited the fact that the

The clergy opposed Edward's plan from the beginning.

Clergy taxed themselves in convocation until after the restoration of Charles II.

Sheldonian compact of 1664, wherein the clergy renounced the right of separate taxation.

---

[1] The language of the summons is :
" *Præmunientes* priorem et capitulum
ecclesiæ vestræ, archidiaconos, totum
que clerum vestræ diocesis, facientes
quod iidem prior et archidiaconi in pro-
priis personis suis, et dictum capitulum
per unum, idemque clerus per duos
procuratores idoneos, plenam et suffi-
cientem potestatem." — For the writ,
see *Lords' Report*, App. i. p. 67.

[2] *Lords' Report*, vol. i. p. 214.

[3] See *Select Charters*, p. 38.

[4] Cf. *Parliamentary Original and*

*Rights of the Lower House of Convoca-
tion*, by Bishop Atterbury, p. 7, 4to,
1702 ; May, *Parl. Practice*, p. 637 and
note 1.

[5] Speaker Onslow, in a note ap-
pended to Burnet's *History of his Own
Times* (Oxford ed. vol. iv. p. 308), says :
" Gibson, Bishop of London, said to
me that it was the greatest alteration
in the constitution ever made without
an express law." — See Sir Travers
Twiss' article on Convocation in *Enc.
Brit.* 9th ed. vol. vi. p. 327.

clergy had been assessed by the commissioners named in the statute, without any objection being raised on their part or behalf. In this act was embraced, however, a proviso, that "nothing therein contained shall be drawn into example to the prejudice of the ancient rights belonging to the lords spiritual and temporal, or clergy of this realm." If by this proviso the clergy intended to save the right to tax themselves, as Mr. Hallam [1] supposes, suffice it to say, that they have never since seen fit to reassert it. By their renunciation of the right of separate taxation,[2] the clergy gained the new right of voting at the election of members of the house of commons by virtue of their ecclesiastical benefices, — a right which has been more than once distinctly recognized by statute.[3]

The clergy gain the right to vote for members of the house of commons.

Early participation of the commons in taxation.

9. The refusal of the representatives of the clergy to habitually assemble as a separate estate of parliament fixed the fact that the national legislature of England should consist of two houses instead of three. Having explained how this division into two houses was finally settled, the task remains to draw out the process through which the younger body — composed of the representatives of the shires and towns — gradually won, through persistent effort, first the right to participate in taxation, then to participate in legislation, then to impeach the ministers, and finally to participate in the control of the royal administration and in the deposition of the king himself. The whole process is one of struggle and of growth, which finds its origin in the doctrine — fast gaining ground at the beginning of the thirteenth century — that the tax-payer had the right to be consulted in some form be-

Taxation during the Norman period.

fore he was taxed. This doctrine touched, no doubt, its lowest point during the Norman reigns, from whose vague fiscal annals it is hard to determine whether taxes were imposed by mere edict of the sovereign, or whether with the counsel and consent of the great council. The idea that the nation was in some form consulted, even during the Norman period, is strengthened by two records which belong to the reign of Henry I. : in the one, the king describes "the aid

---

[1] *Const. Hist.*, vol. iii. p. 243 and note.

[2] "And, till this power was given up, an ecclesiastical benefice gave no right to vote in the election of members of the house of commons." — Freeman, *Growth of the Eng. Const.*, p. 130.

[3] *E. g.*, 10 Anne, c. 23, and 18 George II. c. 18.

which my barons gave me;" in the other — the charter ordering the restoration of the local courts — he speaks of summoning the county courts whenever his royal necessity
should require it.[1]   These two documents clearly indicate the
only two methods through which the nation — prior to the
appearance in the national council of the representative
members — could be consulted in reference to taxation.   The
lay and spiritual baronage were consulted in the great council, but the grants there made did not bind absolutely the inferior clergy, nor the main body of the nation incorporated
for government in shires and towns.[2]   Before contributions
could be drawn from the clergy and the commons, separate
negotiations had first to be conducted with the archdeacons
of each diocese representing the spiritual estate, and with
the several county courts in which representatives appeared
from every portion of the shire community.   Such negotiations between the crown and the local communities were carried on by a detachment of justices from the exchequer
during their fiscal circuits of the shires.   The exchequer
officers, dealing with the shire communities in their corporate
capacity, sat in the county courts, and there debated "with
the landowners the number of hides for which they owe
Danegeld, or the number of knights' fees from which aids
and reliefs are due; they likewise assess the towns, which
are now becoming important contributors to the revenue."[3]
The county court was thus the only organ of communication
in fiscal matters between the crown on the one hand and the
shire and town communities on the other, prior to their representation in the national council.   When the organization
and procedure of the county court is considered, it is not
hard to understand why the system of representation, so long
employed therein for local purposes, should have been extended into a higher sphere.   As heretofore explained, the
county court which met the itinerant justices upon their visitations was not only a popular but a representative assembly, —
a county parliament, composed not only of the archbishops,

Side notes:
Lay and spiritual baronage consulted in the great council;

the clergy through the archdeacons, and the commons through the county courts.

The exchequer officers, when negotiating with the shires, sat in the county court.

The county court a county parliament.

---

[1] See above, p. 300, and notes 5
and 6.

[2] In the grant made by certain bishops and barons of an aid "pur fille
marier" in the parliament of 1290 the
limitation is put, in so far as in them

lay. The facts are thus stated in the
writ: "Pro se et communitate totius
regni *quantum in ipsis est.*"— *Rot.
Parl.*, i. p. 25.

[3] *Select Charters*, p. 18.

bishops, abbots, priors, earls, barons, knights, and freeholders, but also of the reeve and four men as representatives from each township, and twelve burghers as representatives from each borough in the shire.[1]   Into both the fiscal and judicial work of the shire, election and representation entered as active and familiar principles.   From a writ issued for the collection of a carucage early in the reign of Henry III. it appears that a subsidy granted in the great council was assessed in the shire, not as in the earlier days by the itinerant justices, but by two knights freely chosen in a full assembly of the county court.[2]   In 1225 a writ, issued for the collection of a fifteenth, provided that the tax should be collected by the reeve and four men in each township, who were commanded to pay over the proceeds to four elected knights of the hundred, who in their turn were to inquire by the oaths of local jurors into all disputed cases.[3]   The reeve and four men, who were thus charged with the collection of the tax, had been immemorially charged with the higher duty of representing the township in the miniature parliament known as the county court.   When John, in 1213, summoned for the first time the "four discreet men" from each county to appear as representatives in the great council, he simply applied to national purposes a system of representation that had existed from the very earliest times.   "The four men and the reeve had from time immemorial represented the township in the shire-moot ; now the four men and the sheriff represent the shire-moot in the national council."[4]   The fact can hardly be questioned that the elected knights were at first summoned to parliament, for the purpose of consenting to taxation upon the part of the shire communities, as a matter of fiscal expediency merely.   Instead of the officers of the exchequer going down into the shires to there negotiate separately as to the amount each would give, it was deemed more expedient for each shire court to send representatives to the national council armed with full power to express its corporate assent to whatever tax the general voice might there impose.

Early in the reign of Henry III. a carucage assessed by two knights chosen by the "will and counsel" of the county court.

The representative system, long familiar to the county court, applied to national purposes.

The elected knights summoned to parliament as a matter of fiscal expediency.

---

[1] See above, p. 320.
[2] See above, p. 451.

[3] *Fœdera,* i. p. 177 ; *Select Charters,* pp. 355–357.
[4] See above, p. 367.

The same general causes which brought about the appear- Representatives from the towns summoned for the same reason.
ance in parliament of the elected knights also brought about,
at a somewhat later day, the appearance of elected representatives from the cities and towns. Until the severance of the
borough communities from the general shire administration,
the sheriff exercised the same jurisdiction over the towns as
over the rest of the county ; he collected from them the rents
which formed a portion of the ferm of the shire, and he
looked after the king's rights in their courts of justice. The
borough communities which thus grew up within the jurisdiction of the shire, and upon the demesnes of the king or some
other great lord, began the struggle for municipal independ- The struggle for municipal independence.
ence with the effort to free themselves from the financial
and judicial administration of the sheriff upon the one hand,
and from the control of the lord upon the other. One of the
first steps in this process was to require the sheriff to fix the
amount of the ferm which the borough was to pay separate
and apart from the general contribution of the shire. The
next step was to obtain a charter from the crown permitting
the town to pay directly into the exchequer a fixed rent in
lieu of the sum contributed through the sheriff. The fixed The *firma burgi*.
rent thus paid by the town directly to the exchequer, which
was known as the *firma burgi*, the burghers apportioned and
collected among themselves through their own internal regulations.[1] But after this much had been accomplished the
towns were subject to another form of taxation, which depended chiefly upon the royal pleasure. Whenever the great
council made a grant to the crown, the king claimed the right
to levy upon his tenants in demesne an equivalent exaction
under the name of a "free aid." When the growing wealth The "free aid."
of the mercantile classes within the towns began to render
them tempting objects of taxation, the imposition of "free
aids" grew more and more frequent. During the reigns of
Henry III. and John, such demands were often made by royal
authority, even when no general grant had been made by
the great council. When a dispute arose over the collection
of a "free aid," the contention could only be settled after a
tedious negotiation between the town magistracy on the one
hand and the officers of the exchequer on the other. The

[1] See above, p. 461.

representatives of the towns were therefore summoned to parliament simply because the crown found it more profitable to obtain grants of subsidies from them in a national council than to collect "free aids" from them through the more tedious process of separate negotiation.[1]

Transition from special to general consent in taxation. By so reorganizing the national council as to require every order of men to appear therein in person or by representatives, Edward I. finally completed the transition from the older system of separate consent to taxation, which grew out of feudal ideas, to the more efficient and comprehensive one of general consent expressed as the corporate act of the nation in an assembly of estates. Although in such an assembly each estate taxed itself separately at first upon its own basis, the concurrent act was a national act, resting upon the consent of every class of tax-payers to be affected by it.[2]

Exclusive right of parliament to authorize taxation. 10. The corollary, which naturally followed the principle that each estate had the right to consent to taxation in an assembly of estates, was that no taxes whatsoever could be legally imposed upon the nation save such as were expressly authorized by parliamentary authority. The first great effort for the establishment of this principle was made by the baronage in the famous struggle with John in 1215 ; and the fruit of that effort was embodied in the twelfth and fourteenth articles of the Great Charter, which provided that no scutage or aid, except the three regular feudal aids, should be imposed but by the common counsel of the nation, and that such common counsel could only be taken in a national council duly summoned under writs regularly issued. The fact that these Declaration of the exclusive right of the nation to authorize taxation, contained in the Great Charter, premature. vital clauses were invariably omitted from all subsequent re-issues of the Great Charter is persuasive to show that the precise and positive definition of the exclusive right of the nation to authorize taxation, which the barons in the hour of victory forced upon John, was premature, — that for such an absolute assertion of the right, the nation itself was at the time hardly prepared.[3] It is true that during the eighty years which followed the issue of the Great Charter the im-

---

[1] All this has been restated by Green with his usual clearness. See *Hist. Eng. People*, vol. i. pp. 355, 356.

[2] "The process of transition belongs to the years 1282 to 1295, and the transition implies the admission of the commons to a share of the taxing power, together with the clergy and the baronage." — Stubbs, *Const. Hist.*, vol. ii. p. 243.

[3] See above, pp. 387, 388.

position of taxes generally received parliamentary sanction, but not until the end of that period did the nation finally win a constitutional guarantee that they should never be imposed simply by the force of the royal authority. In the stress of a great emergency Edward I. so reasserted the taxing power of the crown as to alarm the nation; and the result was a counter-revolution which made all such future attempts upon the part of the crown forever impossible. At the end of the "Barons' War," Edward I., in the *Confirmatio Cartarum*, was made to promise the clergy, the barons, and "all the commonalty of the land, that for no business from henceforth will we take such manner of aids, tasks, nor prizes, but by the common assent of the realm, and for the common profit thereof, saving the ancient aids and prizes due and accustomed." In order to extend this limitation of the royal authority to indirect as well as to direct taxation, it was also provided that the right of the crown to tax wool should not in the future be exercised "without their common assent and good will; saving to us and our heirs the custom of wools, skins, and leather granted before by the commonalty aforesaid."[1] Although Edward clearly conceded the chief subject of contention, he plainly indicated by the foregoing reservations that he did not consider his action at Ghent as a final and unconditional surrender of the right of the crown to still impose certain kinds of direct and indirect taxes. Under the terms of the first proviso — "saving the ancient aids and prizes due and accustomed" — the crown for a long time claimed the right to talliage the towns upon the royal demesnes without the sanction of parliamentary authority. In 1304 Edward himself ordered a talliage to be imposed on his cities and towns in demesne,[2] and in the next year he authorized the great lords to talliage their ancient demesnes as he had talliaged his.[3] In the sixth year of his reign, Edward II. also imposed a talliage on his cities, boroughs, and demesnes throughout the realm; and the command was to take "of their movables a fifteenth, and of their rents a tenth; and to send the assessment to the sheriffs of the city, to levy the talliage, and pay it into the exchequer."[4] The citizens of

Margin notes:
Guarantees contained in the *Confirmatio Cartarum.*

Right of the crown to talliage the towns upon the royal demesnes.

---

[1] For a full statement of this subject, with the authorities, see above, pp. 418–423.

[2] W. Hemingburgh, ii. 233.

[3] *Rot. Parl.*, i. 161, 162.

[4] *Lords' Report*, vol. i. p. 266.

London, in resisting this impost, did not dispute the general right of the crown to impose it, but defended themselves under that clause of the Great Charter which guaranteed to them their ancient immunities.[1] In 1332 Edward III. issued commissions for the collection of what was probably the last talliage ever demanded of the cities and towns. When the matter came up in the parliament of that year, a compromise was reached wherein it was agreed that the crown should recall the commissions, and accept in lieu of the talliage a grant of a fifteenth and tenth.[2]

Right of talliage becomes extinct in the reign of Edward III.

Parliamentary control over indirect taxes.

While the principle was thus becoming settled that the crown could impose no kind of direct taxes — not even talliage upon ancient demesnes — without parliamentary authority, the royal right to impose indirect taxes in the form of customs became subject to the same limitation. The origin of indirect taxes has already been traced to the customary right of the Old-English kings to levy tolls in harbors, and upon transport by roads and navigable streams. Upon entering the harbor the toll was imposed directly upon the ship, and the tax thus paid was the equivalent given by the merchant for the right to bring wine and merchandise into the realm, and to trade under the king's protection. The nature of this toll or tribute is well illustrated by the ancient hereditary duty belonging to the crown called prisage, which consisted of the right of the crown to take from each wine ship, English or foreign, entering the realm, one cask out of every ten, at the price of twenty shillings the cask.[3] The customs thus find their origin in the duties imposed upon imports, which are more ancient than those upon exports, — the latter originating, as it is said, as a part of the general system of taxing personal property.[4] The receipts from the customs, which during the reigns of Richard I. and John constituted a considerable item in the revenue,[5] had become of sufficient importance in the reign of the latter to suggest

Toll originally imposed directly upon the ship.

Prisage.

Origin of the duty on exports.

---

[1] Art. 13.
[2] *Lords' Report*, vol. i. p. 305. Upon the whole subject, see Stubbs, *Const. Hist.*, vol. ii. pp. 333, 376, 383, 518–521. Hallam, improperly assuming that the right of talliage had been expressly surrendered in the struggle of 1297, maintains that the three Edwards acted illegally in exacting it. — *Middle Ages*,

vol. iii. p. 43. The Bishop, in criticising Hallam's view, says: "Unconstitutional the exaction certainly was, but not contrary to the letter of the law." — Vol. ii. p. 519, note 1.
[3] Madox, *Hist. Exch.*, pp. 526, 532.
[4] See above, p. 299.
[5] Madox, *Hist. Exch.*, p. 529 *seq.*

that provision of the Great Charter which forbade the levying of more than the ancient and lawful customs[1] on merchants entering and leaving the kingdom. When the production of wool increased to such an extent as to render it the
leading element of national wealth, it soon became subject
to an export tax which became an important item in the royal
revenue. But not until after this tempting commodity had
been for a long time the subject of all kinds of irregular
seizures and exactions, was the export tax on wool definitely
fixed on a legal basis by the parliament of 1275, which gave
to Edward I. a custom of half a mark on each sack of wool
exported, three hundred woolfells, and a mark on the last of
leather.[2] The duty thus imposed by statute on wool, skins,
and leather (*magna et antiqua custuma*) is regarded as the
first legal foundation of the customs revenue.[3] As Edward's
reign drew to a close, the royal right of taxing wool became
subject, however, to a more positive limitation. A subject of
bitter contention in the crisis of 1297 was "the maletote on
wools, that is, to wit, a toll of forty shillings for every sack."
As a remedy for such exactions it was provided in the *Confirmatio Cartarum* that the royal right of taxing wool should
not in the future be exercised "without their common assent
and good will; saving to us and our heirs the custom of
wools, skins, and leather granted before by the commonalty
aforesaid."[4] Six years later (1303) Edward summoned to
the exchequer at York an assembly of merchants, consisting
of two or three burghers from each of forty-two towns, with
the view of obtaining their consent to an increase of the
customs on wool, wine, and other commodities to which the
foreign merchants had already assented. This increase in
the customs, to which the foreign merchants had already
assented, but to which the mercantile representatives of towns
refused to assent, was known as the *nova* or *parva custuma*,
as distinguished from the *magna et antiqua custuma* granted
in the parliament of 1275.[5] Early in the reign of Edward II.

[marginal notes:]
Export tax on wool first fixed by the parliament of 1275.

First legal foundation of the customs revenue, — *magna et antiqua custuma.*

The *nova* or *parva custuma.*

---

[1] " Ad emendum et vendendum, sine
omnibus malis toltis, per antiquas et
rectas consuetudines."—Art. 41.

[2] *Parl. Writs*, i. 2; *Select Charters*,
p. 451.

[3] See Blackstone, *Com.*, bk. i. p. 313.

[4] *Statutes*, i. pp. 124, 125; *Select
Charters*, p. 497.

[5] *Parl. Writs*, i. pp. 134, 135; *Select
Charters*, p. 500; Stubbs, *Const. Hist.*,
vol. ii. pp. 156, 192, 524, 525.

the new customs were declared illegal by the Ordainers, and their collection was suspended in 1311 ; but after the king's victory in 1322 they were promptly reëstablished. In the year which followed the accession of Edward III. the customs, as reëstablished in 1322, were confirmed ; and from that time they became a part of the king's ordinary revenue, and as such they received the sanction of parliament in the Statute of Staples, enacted in 1353.[1] Before the close of the reign of Edward III. the exclusive right of parliament to authorize every form of direct and indirect taxation was thus fully and finally established, not only in principle but in practice. As a principle, the doctrine could hardly have been more clearly announced than in the statute of 14th Edward III.,[2] which declared that the nation shall be "no more charged or grieved to make any common aid or sustain charge, except by the common assent of the prelates, earls, barons, and other magnates and commons of the realm, and that in parliament."

While the exclusive right of the nation to authorize taxation was being gradually established, the feudal councils which once gathered around the Norman and Angevin kings were silently transformed into national parliaments ; and the older feudal taxes, which rested in a measure upon individual consent, were gradually supplanted by the new national taxes, which were the fruit of general consent expressed through representatives in a sovereign assembly. Even the right of each estate to assent separately to the quota of the general contribution to be borne by it gradually passed out of view. "The last instance of separate assent to taxes is in 18 Edward III. In later reports both houses are mentioned, in conjunction with the observation 'that they have advised in common.' "[3] In this process of transition from special to general taxation, the old feudal burdens of scutage, — the tax on the knight's fee, — of talliage, — the feudal impost upon towns upon the royal demesnes, — together with the three regular feudal aids, gradually died out and became obsolete. But while the exchequer was thus being impoverished on the one hand by diminishing receipts from the old feudal burdens on land, it was being enriched upon the other by the new tax on personal

Before the close of the reign of Edward III. the right of parliament to control every form of taxation fully established.

Feudal taxation resting upon individual consent transformed into national taxation resting upon general consent.

Scutage, talliage, and the three regular feudal aids become obsolete.

---

[1] Stubbs, *Const. Hist.*, vol. ii. p. 526.
[2] *Statutes*, i. 289 *seq.*
[3] Gneist, *The English Parliament*, p. 137, Shee's trans.

property, which was first imposed in the reign of Henry II. The tax on personal property was at first levied in the form of grants to the crown of actual tenths and fifteenths of all movables. The amount of a fifteenth, which was more usually granted than a tenth, was finally reduced to a fixed basis by a careful assessment of every township, borough, and city, in the 8th Edward III. In this assessment the fifteenth part of the value of every township or parish was ascertained and recorded in the exchequer. Whenever in later years a fifteenth was granted, every parish knew that the proportion which it was expected to raise by a rate was the sum imposed upon it in the assessment made in the 8th Edward III.[1] A still more important and comprehensive form of taxation which must now be mentioned is that which came into use in the reigns of Richard II. and Henry IV. under the name of subsidy, — a tax not directly imposed upon property, real or personal, but upon persons in respect to both. When a subsidy was imposed, each tax-payer was rated according to the income supposed to be derived from his lands and goods ; so many shillings in the pound for lands, so many for goods. During the later middle ages the older feudal taxes were thus finally supplanted by subsidies and fifteenths, which were sufficiently comprehensive to embrace every form of direct taxation then imposed upon real and personal property. The lineal successor of the subsidy and the fifteenth is the modern land-tax, which, embracing both real and personal estates, " has superseded all the former methods of rating either property, or persons in respect of their property, whether by tenths or fifteenths, subsidies on land, hydages, scutages, or talliages." [2] Or, to sum up in the weighty words of a German scholar, "All the charges falling upon land get at last united into one general land-tax ;

"All personal charges, into a uniform income-tax ;

"And all customs and excise, into a general tariff, in such wise that the latter adapt themselves to a lasting revenue of the crown, which, since the reign of Henry V., gets assured to the king, by way of supplement to the diminishing revenues from the domain-lands. For a considerable time after,

Marginal notes:

Tax on personal property originally actual tenths and fifteenths.

Assessment of 8th Edward III.

The subsidy.

Older feudal taxes supplanted by subsidies and fifteenths.

A general land-tax ;

a uniform income-tax ;

a general tariff.

---

[1] Cf. Blackstone, *Comm.*, bk i. p. 309 ; citing 2 *Inst.* 77, 4 *Inst.* 34.   [2] Blackstone, *Comm.*, bk. i. p. 307.

"Tonnage"
and
"pound-
age."
the chief group of these indirect taxes is lumped together under the designation of 'tonnage' and 'poundage.'"[1]

Participa-
tion of the
commons
in legisla-
tion.
11. The fact has been heretofore explained that the primitive form of royal legislation, common to all the Teutonic nations, and which from the earliest times moulded the enactments of the Old-English kings, was retained by their Norman and Angevin successors. As Ine and Ælfred legislated with the counsel and consent of the witan, so William and Henry of Anjou legislated with the counsel and consent of the great council. During the two centuries which follow the Conquest, "counsel and consent" may not have implied that full and authoritative power of deliberation possessed by the witan in earlier times; "and yet the very survival of the ancient form attested the fact that the theoretical right of the nation to participate in legislation was not forgotten."[2] From the time of the Conquest down to the establishment of the estate system in the reign of Edward I., all the great acts of government, whether administrative, legislative, judicial, political, or fiscal, emanated from the person of the king acting through his inner council, composed of the great officers of state and the household ; or from that larger body known as the great council, composed of those tenants-in-chief who won for themselves the right to be personally summoned, and in whom that right became hereditary. The way in which

The great
functions of
government
monopo-
lized for a
time by the
king and
his feudal
council.
the main body of the nation, grouped together in shires and towns, achieved the right to participate in the great functions of government, thus monopolized for a time by the king and his feudal council, was by building up alongside of the older body a new and a representative assembly which first vindicated its right to participate in taxation, next to participate in legislation, and finally to control the administration of the state itself. How the first step was taken, how the represen-

Right of
the com-
mons to
participate
in taxation
drew after
it the right
to partici-
pate in
legislation.
tatives of the shires and towns won for themselves the right to join in the granting or withholding of taxes, has been explained already.[3] By the leverage thus established, the commons soon found themselves in a position to take the second step, — the right to participate in taxation soon drew after it the right to participate in legislation. This result was

---

[1] Gneist, *The Eng. Parl.*, p. 138, Shee's trans.

[2] See above, pp. 186, 240, 291, 292.

[3] See above, pp. 482-486.

brought about by the employment of a homely but natural expedient.   As early as the reign of Henry III. the principle was openly recognized by both the crown and the nation that concessions in favor of liberty moving from the former to the latter were legitimate subjects of bargain and sale.   Of this principle, the confirmation of the charters by Henry in 1225 may be taken as a typical illustration.   In his charter the king openly admits that "for this concession, and for the gift of these liberties and those contained in the charter of the forests, the archbishops, bishops, abbots, priors, earls, barons, knights, freeholders, and all men of the realm granted us a fifteenth part of all their movable goods."[1]   In the light of such precedents the representatives of the commons, when as a matter of fiscal expediency they were regularly summoned to parliament, were quick to learn how to insist upon the redress of grievances in return for a money grant. When such a grant was asked, it became the custom for the commons to put forward in the form of a petition to the crown such grievances as required amendment at the hands of the king and his council.[2]   The discussion of grievances became the preliminary to the discussion of the grant, which was invariably made in the expectation that the prayer of the petition would be followed by adequate redress.   Although earlier precedents of the procedure by petition may be found, the records of the early years of Edward II. (1309 and 1310) afford perhaps the earliest satisfactory illustrations of the nature of such petitions, and of the character of the complaints which they set forth.[3]   In the reign of Edward III. it became the custom for the chancellor at the opening of parliament to proclaim the willingness of the king to hear the petitions of his people.[4]   The petitions thus presented

Supply dependent upon the redress of grievances.

The procedure by petition.

---

[1] "Pro hac autem concessione et donatione libertatum istarum et aliarum libertatum contentarum in carta nostra de libertatibus forestæ, . . . omnes de regno nostro, dederunt nobis quintam decimam partem omnium mobilium suorum." — *Statutes,* Charters of Liberties, pp. 22-25.

[2] As early as 1309 the commons granted a subsidy "*upon this condition,* that the king should take advice and grant redress upon certain articles wherein they are agrieved." For the

articles, eleven in number, see Prynne, 2d Register, p. 68.   In 1301 the lords had told the king that if the demands made by them in behalf of the whole community were granted, they would increase their gift from a twentieth to a fifteenth. — *Parl. Writs,* i. p. 105.

[3] Cf. Hallam, *M. A.,* vol. iii. pp. 40-43.

[4] *Rot. Parl.,* ii. pp. 237, 309; iii. pp. 56, 71 *seq.;* Stubbs, *Const. Hist.,* vol. ii. p. 572.   In 14th Edw. III. an extra force had to be appointed to aid in

consisted either of such as required reference to the proper judicial tribunal, or to the king himself in council, or of such as demanded redress by the making of an ordinance or statute.[1]   To this latter class belonged the public petitions which were presented by the commons in behalf of the community. To such petitions the king was expected to make his answer during the session of parliament, and then " the petition and the answer were entered in the parliament rolls, and out of both, by advice of the judges and others of the king's counsel, the act was drawn up conformable to the petition and answer, and the act itself for the most part entered in a roll, called the statute roll, and the tenor thereof affixed to proclamation writs, directed to the several sheriffs, to proclaim it as a law in their respective counties."[2]   The right to participate in legislation thus won by the commons through the petition process grew to such proportions during the fourteenth century that, during that period, as the parliament rolls will show, nearly all statutes were based upon such petitions.   At what exact point of time the concurrence of the commons in legislation was deemed indispensable, it is difficult to determine.   Such could not have been the case as early as the 18th of Edward I., the year in which the statute *Quia emptores* was enacted by the king and the barons, before the day for which the commons were summoned.[3]   Not before the reign of Edward II. was the right of the commons to assent to legislation clearly established ; not until the fifteenth year of that reign was it declared by statute that "the matters to be established for the estate of the king and of his heirs, and for the estate of the realm and of the people, should be treated, accorded, and established in parliament by the king, and by the assent of the prelates, earls, and barons, *and the commonalty of the realm*, according as had been before accustomed."[4]   When the right of the commons to assent to legis-

Side notes:

Such petitions as demanded redress by the making of an ordinance or statute.

The statute coined out of the petition and answer.

Nearly all legislation based on petitions during the fourteenth century.

Right of the commons to assent to legislation not clearly established until the reign of Edward II.

---

dispatching the petitions in parliament.   See *Lords' Report*, vol. i. pp. 311, 312.

[1] As to the ancient mode of petitioning parliament, see May, *Parl. Practice*, pp. 606–608.

[2] Hale, *Hist. of the Common Law*, vol. i. pp. 16, 17.

[3] On the 14th of June the knights of the shire were summoned to meet at Westminster on the 14th of July.   On the 8th of July the king, at the instance of the magnates, enacted the statute *Quia emptores*.   For the writ of summons to the knights, see *Lords' Report*, App. i. 54 ; for the act, see *Statutes*, i. p. 106.

[4] Statutes 15 Edw. II. i. 189; *Lords' Report*, vol. i. p. 282.

lation thus became clearly established, the ancient formula was so widened as to embrace the new factor. After the permanent incorporation of the representative members, the king legislates either "by the assent of the prelates, earls, barons, and the commonalty of the realm," or "at the request of the commons, and by the assent of the prelates, earls, and barons." During the reign of Edward III. the name of the commons is rarely omitted from the enacting clause of a statute, and from that time it may be safely assumed that the concurrence of both houses in legislation was deemed necessary.[1]

The foregoing method of legislation, based upon the petitions of parliament and the answers of the king thereto, was liable in practice to so many abuses upon the part of the crown that it became necessary to supersede it by a more definite and guarded system. In the first place the grant of money had necessarily to precede the redress of grievances, — the royal promise was the only guarantee or equivalent which the parliament received when the grant was made. To obtain clear and definite answers to petitions, much less an actual redress of grievances during the session of parliament, was often attended with great difficulty. In 1344 and 1362 the commons beg, for the safety of the people, that the petitions may be examined and redress ordered before the end of the parliament.[2] Sometimes, by a qualified or evasive answer, the petition was so modified that the statute coined out of the two in nowise expressed the original intention. And even in the event of a prompt and definite answer being given during the session, it was not a certainty that the petition and answer would in the hurry of business, in the interval between the parliaments, be turned into a statute. And even if it was, the danger remained that the petition would be materially altered in the process of being transformed into an act to be entered upon the statute-book. To remedy evils of the kind last named, the commons, in 1347, pray that all petitions presented by them for the remedy of mischiefs might be an-

Abuses and uncertainties which grew out of the procedure by petition.

---

[1] Mr. Clifford (*Hist. of Private Bill Legislation*, vol. i. p. 288) says: "When the commons are not named in the early statutes, their assent may be presumed from the fact that most measures originated with their petitions." This statement may be accepted with the qualification put upon it by the editor of Longmead's *Const. Hist.*, p. 269, note 2.

[2] *Rot. Parl.*, ii. pp. 149, 272.

swered and indorsed before the commons in parliament, that
they might see the indorsements and have remedy thereon

Evils of the
old system
remedied by
the intro-
duction of
bills in the
form of
statutes.
according to the ordinance of parliament.[1]   In order to remedy the evils and uncertainties which grew out of "this extracting of the statute out of the petition and answer, about
the latter end of Henry VI. and beginning of Edward IV.,
they took a course to reduce them, even in the first instance,
into the full and complete form of acts of parliament."[2]
When this departure was made from the older form of initia-
tion by petition, when bills were introduced in the form of
statutes, — the original draughts of which could only be altered

Transition
from royal
to national
legislation.
by the parliament itself, — the transition from royal to national
legislation, which began with the reorganization of the feudal
council as a representative assembly, reached its full and final
consummation.

Difference
between a
statute and
an ordi-
nance.
It must not be supposed, however, that the right thus won
by the parliament to control the enactment, amendment, and
repeal of all the more weighty and permanent acts of national
legislation was absolutely exhaustive of the older right of the
crown to legislate in a tentative way, and with the advice of the
council, upon a certain class of subjects, by way of ordinance.
Through the maze of learned refinement, which has grown
out of the attempt to define the difference between a statute
and an ordinance, it is only possible to pass without confusion by keeping steadily in view the two distinct sources

Ordaining
power of
the king in
council, and
the enacting
power of
the king in
parliament.
from which each drew its authority.   The line must be clearly
drawn between the ordaining power of the king in council
and the enacting power of the king in parliament.   After the
organization of the estate system the effort was continuous
upon the part of the national assembly to draw to itself the
exclusive control of the taxative and legislative powers which,
at an earlier day, were vested in the king and council.   In
resisting such encroachments upon the prerogative, the effort
upon the part of the crown was to reserve to itself fragments
at least of taxative and legislative power which it could still
exercise in council free from parliamentary interference.   In
the review heretofore made of the struggle between the
nation and the crown as to the exclusive right of the former

[1] *Rot. Parl.*, ii. p. 165.

[2] Hale, *Hist. of the Common Law*,
vol. i. p. 18.   See, also, Ruffhead's

Statutes, preface; May, *Parl. Practice*,
p. 520.

to authorize taxation, the fact was developed that, even after the *Confirmatio Cartarum*, the crown, under the cover of certain reservations, for a long time reserved the right to talliage the cities and towns in demesne, and to a certain extent to regulate the customs.[1] Long after the general right of the nation to authorize taxation had been clearly admitted, an unflinching and persistent warfare had to be carried on by the parliament before the taxative power of the king in council was fully and finally extinguished. In draw-ing to itself the right to initiate and control legislation, the parliament stopped short of complete victory, — it left in the hands of the king in council an undefined residuum of legis-lative power which was for a long time exercised by the making and revoking of a class of temporary enactments known as ordinances. Whereas, before the end of the four-teenth century, the general principle was firmly established that all the great and permanent acts of national legislation could only emanate from parliamentary authority, it was equally well understood that alongside of this principle existed the ordaining power of the king in council. With this statement as a preface, it will be the more easy to grasp the full significance of the following statement of the rec-ognized distinction between a statute and an ordinance : "The statute is a law, or an amendment of law, enacted by the king in parliament, and enrolled in the statute roll, not to be altered, repealed, or suspended without the authority of parliament, and valid in all particulars until it has been so revoked ; the ordinance is a regulation made by the king, by himself, or in his council, or with the advice of his council, promulgated in letters patent or in charter, and liable to be recalled by the same authority. Moreover, the statute claims perpetuity. . . . The ordinance is rather a tentative act which, if it be insufficient to secure its object, or if it operate mischievously, may be easily recalled, and, if it be successful, may, by a subsequent act, be made a statute."[2]

12. At what exact point of time the parliament, which won for itself the exclusive right to authorize taxation and to

Margin notes: In drawing to itself the control of legislation, parliament stopped short of complete victory.

Bishop Stubbs's definition of the dif-ference be-tween a statute and an ordi-nance.

[1] See above, pp. 487.

[2] Stubbs, *Const. Hist.*, vol. ii. pp. 585, 586. On the distinction between statutes and ordinances, see, also, Hal-lam, *M. A.*, vol. iii. pp. 50–53 ; Gneist, *The Eng. Parl.*, p. 143 ; Clifford's *His-tory of Private Bill Legislation*, vol. i. p. 332.

initiate legislation, secured the more comprehensive right to deliberate in all matters of national concern, it is difficult to determine. Although such a right was no doubt claimed and exercised in some form by the council of magnates prior to the date of the Great Charter, it is not until the reign which follows that event that we find clear illustrations of the right of parliament to discuss foreign affairs, and to supervise and control the royal administration. The minority of Henry III., the first which had occurred since the Conquest, cast upon the national council the duty of appointing a guardian of king and kingdom ; and it is more than likely that the other personal advisers who stood with the regent around the king were, during the minority, appointed by the same authority. From that time it is possible to trace the existence of an inner royal council, composed of the king's personal advisers, which acts as a distinct and organized body, apart from the larger administrative body that directs the affairs of state and the household. Out of this condition of things the constitutional doctrine emerges that the king can do no wrong, and that the ministers who advise him are responsible to the assembled representatives of the nation, who have a consultative voice in their appointment.[1] The right thus established by the baronage to control the royal administration during the minority of the king was expanded, before the close of Henry's reign, into a general right of control whenever the exigencies of the state might require it. When in the crisis of 1258 the executive government was found to be in such hopeless embarrassment as to render it necessary for parliament to place the royal authority in commission, the baronage elected a board of control of twenty-four, who drew up the articles generally known as the Provisions of Oxford, under whose terms three committees were chosen, who were charged with the task of reforming the entire administration.[2] When in 1297 Edward I., under a pressure to raise money for a foreign war, attempted to subject the nation to unauthorized taxation, he was resisted by the baronial party under the lead of Bohun and Bigod, who, with an armed force at their backs, appeared in the exchequer and forbade the collection of the tax until a promised confirma-

---

[1] See above, pp. 396, 397.   [2] See above, pp. 400, 401.

tion of the charters had first taken place. In a parliament irregularly summoned in the midst of the revolution the regent was forced to concede, and the king to approve, the national demands, which were embodied in the famous *Confirmatio Cartarum*.[1] When, early in the reign of Edward II., a crisis was provoked by the offensive conduct of the royal favorite Piers Gaveston, as well as by the confused condition into which the affairs of the kingdom had fallen, a council of bishops and barons was called to meet the king at Westminster in February, 1310.[2] A condition of things similar to that which in 1258 had brought on the Barons' War seems to have suggested substantially the same procedure as was then employed. The baronial assembly, which in March met the king in arms, resolved that the affairs of the kingdom should be intrusted for a year to a body of twenty-one Ordainers, to be chosen by themselves,[3] who should ordain such things as should be "to the honor and advantage of Holy Church, to the honor of the king, and to his advantage and that of the people, according to the oath which the king took at his coronation."[4] In a parliament composed of the three estates held in London in August, 1311, the Ordainers, after reporting the six ordinances, which they had published with the king's confirmation in August, 1310,[5] issued thirty-five additional articles[6] of like tenor, designed to carry out more completely a general reform of existing abuses. In the additional articles (xiii.–xviii.) express provision was made that all the great officers of state were to be appointed by the king with the counsel and consent of the baronage; and they (xxxix.) were to be sworn in parliament. And it was further provided (ix.) that the king was not to declare war, to summon forces, or to go out of the realm, without the consent of the baronage in parliament. The right thus asserted and

Confirmatio Cartarum, 1297.

The Lords Ordainers, 1310.

---

[1] See above, pp. 419–423.

[2] The inferior clergy and the commons were not summoned. York was first designated as the meeting-place, but a change was afterwards made to Westminster. See *Parl. Writs*, i. pp. 40, 41; Stubbs, *Const. Hist.*, vol. ii. p. 325, and note 5. Cf. also, pp. 326–330. Although Hallam's text (*M. A.*, vol. iii. p. 43) would indicate a belief upon his part that the commons coöperated in the proceedings, in a note he cites the *Lords' Report* (vol. i. p. 259), which states "that the parliament which assembled at Westminster consisted only of prelates, earls, and barons."

[3] As to the election, see *Fœdera*, ii. p. 105; *Rot. Parl.*, i. pp. 443, 445; *Parl. Writs*, II., ii. p. 26.

[4] *Parl. Writs*, II., ii. p. 27.

[5] *Fœdera*, ii. p. 113; *Rot. Parl.*, i. pp. 446, 447.

[6] *Statutes*, i. p. 157 *seq.*; *Rot. Parl.*, i. pp. 281–286.

Right of
the baron-
age to the
exclusive
control of
the royal
administra-
tion.

maintained by the baronage to control all ministerial appointments, as well as the great questions of war and peace,
clearly discloses the fact that the nobles were still regarded
not only as the sole counsellors of the crown, but as the real
representatives of the nation and the guardians of its privileges.   The parliamentary status of the commons, down to
this point, seems to have been but little better than that of
mere tax-payers and petitioners for the redress of grievances.

Growing
power and
influence
of the com-
mons.

From this time, however, the parliamentary position of the
commons passes through a marked transformation; they
gradually cease to follow the lead of the barons, who in their
turn learn how to follow the lead of the commons.   By the
statute of 1322, — which provided that all matters to be
established touching king or kingdom "should be treated,
accorded, and established in parliament, by the king, and by
the assent of the prelates, earls, and barons, and the commonalty of the realm," [1] — a full and final recognition was
made of the right of the commons to participate in all forms
of legislation.   But the full right of deliberation in parliament

They win
the full
right of de-
liberation
in the
reign of
Edward
III.;

did not pass to the representatives of the shires and towns —
now fast becoming welded into a definitely organized body
under the name of the commons — until the following reign
of Edward III., whose financial necessities, occasioned by
his expensive foreign wars, rendered him continually dependent upon their bounty.   At the very beginning of Edward's

assent to
the treaty
of peace
with Scot-
land, and
are con-
sulted as to
the war
with
France.

reign, during the administration of Isabella and Mortimer,
the treaty of peace with Scotland was settled with the counsel and consent of the three estates, — prelates, earls, barons,
and commons.[2]   As soon as Edward's personal rule begins
we find him, in 1331, consulting parliament on the question
of war or peace with France.[3]   On these occasions not only
the magnates but the knights of the shire, who now deliberate
apart, are consulted.   In 1336 parliament advises the king to
declare war against Scotland, because he "could no longer
with honor put up with the wrongs and injuries daily done to
him and his subjects by the Scots."[4]   When in 1338 the

Hundred
Years'
War.

prolonged struggle known as the Hundred Years' War opens
with France, the king declares that he undertakes it with the

---

[1] See above, p. 494.
[2] *Rot. Parl.*, ii. p. 442; *Fœdera*, ii. p. 730.
[3] *Rot. Parl.*, ii. p. 61.
[4] See *Parl. Hist.*, i. p. 93.

assent of the nobles, but at the earnest solicitation of the commons,[1] — it is called, in fact, "the war which our lord the king has undertaken against his adversary of France by common assent of all the lords and commons of his realm in divers parliaments."[2]   In the parliament of 1341, when more money is asked with which to carry on the war, the lords and commons unite in the demand that commissioners be appointed to audit the accounts of those who receive the money in behalf of the king, and that the great officers of state be appointed by the king in parliament, and there sworn to obey the law.[3]   Although Edward by an act of duplicity afterwards repudiated these concessions, the vital principle had been announced by both lords and commons, fighting side by side in a common cause, that the ministers who conduct the royal administration are responsible not only to the king, but to the nation in parliament.

As incidents to the substantive right to supervise and control the royal administration, which the assembly of estates fully established during the reign of Edward III., should be noted the right to audit the public accounts, and to appropriate the supplies to special purposes.   Although the germ of the right last named can be discovered as early as the reign of Henry III. in the arrangements then made for the collection and custody of particular grants intrusted to officers specially appointed for that purpose,[4] the right of appropriation as a parliamentary right was not clearly established until the middle of the fourteenth century.   In 1346 and 1348 the practice distinctly appears in the provisions then made that the money collected from the northern counties should be applied to defence against the Scots;[5] and more distinctly still in 1353, when a subsidy on wool was granted with the express direction that it should be applied exclusively to the prosecution of the war with France.[6]   In 1380 the commons pray that the aid granted may be expended in defence of the kingdom;[7] and in 1390 a part of the custom on wool was appropriated to the expenses of the

Right to appropriate the supplies to special purposes.

---

[1] *Fœdera*, ii. p. 1015.
[2] Cf. Hallam, *M. A.*, vol. iii. p. 53.
[3] *Rot. Parl.*, ii. pp. 128, 130.
[4] See *Select Charters*, 2d ed., pp. 355, 364, 368.

[5] *Rot. Parl.*, ii. p. 161, art. 15; p. 202, art. 7.
[6] *Rot. Parl.*, ii. p. 252.
[7] *Rot. Parl.*, iii. pp. 90, 93, 94.

king, a part to the prosecution of the war.[1] The right to appropriate the supplies, thus clearly established by the parliaments of the fourteenth century, was not maintained, however, by those of the fifteenth and sixteenth. After the reign of Henry IV. the practice seems to have fallen into disuse, and it was not firmly reëstablished until 1666, when, by virtue of the Appropriation Act of Charles II., it became "an undisputed principle, recognized by frequent and at length constant practice," that "supplies granted by parliament are only to be expended for particular objects specified by itself."[2]

Closely allied to the right to appropriate the supplies, was the right to audit the accounts which contained the history of their expenditure. The struggle for the establishment of this right, which begins in the time of Edward III., is brought to a close during the minority of his successor. In the stormy parliament of 1341 both lords and commons join in a demand for the appointment of commissioners to audit the accounts of those who had received money granted to the king, and of those who had received and disbursed his money on both sides of the sea since the war began. Although Edward distinctly made the concession, it was probably annulled in the general revocation through which the statutes of 1341 were repudiated.[3] The claim is again asserted, however, in Edward's last parliament, by the commons, who prayed that two earls and two barons might be appointed as treasurers to see that the grants were properly expended.[4] In the first parliament of Richard II. both lords and commons renew the demand ; and when liberal grants are made, the condition is annexed that treasurers be appointed, to the end "that the money might be applied entirely to the expenses of the war, and no part of it in any other way." Two London merchants, William Walworth and John Philypot, were then appointed by the king and sworn in parliament to faithfully perform the duty assigned them.[5] Two years later, in the parliament of 1379, the king, of his own motion,

---

[1] This appropriation was made, says Bishop Stubbs, "in a way which anticipates the modern distinction between the civil list and public expenditure." — *Const. Hist.*, vol. ii. p. 567.

[2] Hallam, *Const. Hist.*, vol. ii. p. 356.
[3] See above, p. 501.
[4] *Rot. Parl.*, ii. p. 364.
[5] Ibid., iii. pp. 5-7.

without waiting for a petition from the commons, ordered the treasurers to lay before the parliament the accounts of the subsidy.[1] From that time the right to examine the accounts, and to appropriate the supplies, may be looked upon as clearly established.

13. Before the close of Edward's reign the doctrine of ministerial responsibility, so clearly announced in the memorable proceedings of 1341,[2] assumed a more serious and threatening aspect when the commons began to employ for the first time the new constitutional weapon of impeachment. The earlier instances of criminal proceedings, which take place in parliament during the period which intervenes between the beginning of the reign of Edward the First and the 50th year of Edward III., are both irregular and ambiguous.[3] Not until the year last named do we find, in a series of proceedings which take place in the Good Parliament, a clear instance of a parliamentary impeachment in the sense in which that term is now understood. The proceedings against the lords Latimer and Neville, and their agents and accomplices,[4] who were accused of the commission of all kinds of frauds against the revenue, are regarded by the constitutional historians[5] as the earliest instance of a trial by the lords upon a definite accusation made by the commons sitting as a grand jury of the whole realm. In the early part of the reign of Richard II. the new weapon forged by the commons is used without stint, and before the close of the reign occurs the famous accusation against the lord chancellor, Michael de la Pole, who was impeached for grave misconduct in his office.[6] From frequent repetition and employment, the law and practice of parliamentary impeachment was, by the end of Richard's reign, established in substantially the same form in which it appears in modern times. Through the establishment of this means of punishment, the doctrine of ministerial responsibility, which appears in an embryonic form during the minority of Henry III., was finally placed upon a definite constitutional basis. As the constitution prescribed no

The right of impeachment.

First clear case of a parliamentary impeachment, 1376.

Impeachment of Michael de la Pole, Earl of Suffolk.

Doctrine of ministerial responsibility placed upon a definite constitutional basis.

---

[1] *Rot. Parl.*, iii. pp. 56, 57; Stubbs, *Const. Hist.*, vol. ii. pp. 567–569.

[2] See above, p. 501.

[3] Stephen, *Hist. of the Crim. Law*, vol. i. pp. 145–148.

[4] *Rot. Parl.* ii. pp. 323–326 and 329.

[5] Cf. Hallam, *M. A.*, vol. iii. pp. 54–57; Stubbs, *Const. Hist.*, vol. iii. pp. 430, 431.

[6] *Rot. Parl.*, iii. p. 216; Knighton, c. 2684. Precise and formal charges were presented against Suffolk.

mode, short of deposition, through which the king could be made personally amenable for any act of maladministration,

it became necessary to accept the legal fiction that the king in his political capacity could do no wrong, or rather that in the conduct of public affairs nothing could be imputed to his bad intentions. In order to give efficacy to this fiction, which excused the king while it punished the minister, it became necessary for the law to deny to the minister either the right to claim immunity from punishment by pleading obedience to the commands of his sovereign, or a pardon granted by him under the great seal pending the impeachment.[1]

14. The ever-widening power of parliament which thus drew to itself the right to control the royal administration, and to impeach and punish the ministers guilty of misconduct, did not reach the limit of its growth until the doctrine was finally established that, in the presence of a great emergency, the assembly of estates possessed the right to lay hands upon the throne and to depose the king himself. From the annals of the Old-English commonwealth the fact appears that

the witan, which possessed the power to elect the king, possessed also the correlative right to depose him whenever his government was not conducted for the good of his people. Although the greater number of instances in which this power seems to have been exercised belong to the period which precedes the union of the heptarchic kingdoms under the house of Cerdic, there are at least two well authenticated acts of deposition which occur after that event. In 958 the unity of the realm was broken by a revolt in which the Mercians reject Eadwig, sever their kingdom from his, and elect Eadgar as their king. Early in the next century, Æthelred the Second was deposed in favor of his conqueror, and after-

wards by act of the witan restored to the throne.[2] Such acts of supreme authority, occasionally performed by the Old-English national assembly, were never repeated, however, by the less authoritative feudal councils which, during the two centuries that follow the Conquest, gathered around the Nor-

---

[1] As to the law of impeachment as finally settled, see above, pp. 442, 443; as to the practice, see May, *Parl. Practice*, ch. xxiii.

[2] See above, pp. 189, 190.

man and Angevin kings.   Not until after such feudal councils were transformed into an assembly of estates did the representatives of the nation dare to revive that highest of all rights which the witan had occasionally exercised from the very earliest times.   To Edward I. belongs the honor of having transformed the feudal council into an assembly of estates; within thirty years of the first meeting of such assembly at Westminster, the limit of its sovereign power was reached in the deposition of his son.   By the deposition of Edward II. the parliament, for the first time since the Conquest, asserted the right to rid the nation of a worthless and incompetent king.   The first serious conflict which Edward provoked, by making himself subservient to the favorite Piers Gaveston, resulted in a practical transfer of the royal power for a time to a committee of prelates and barons called the Ordainers.[1]   The fatal conflict which at a later day arose out of the choice of new favorites, in the persons of the Dispensers, led Edward into a revolution in which his foes were marshalled under the leadership of his wife Isabella, and her paramour Mortimer.   Deserted in the hour of his need by all upon whom he had the right to rely, the king sought safety in flight, leaving the kingdom to the queen and Mortimer, who began their administration by having the young Edward, with the assent of the assembled magnates, proclaimed guardian of the realm on the 26th October, 1326.[2]   In November the king was captured, and in a parliament which met on the 7th January, 1327, the question of his fate was submitted by the partisans of the queen to an assembly to which were summoned, in addition to the usual constituents, forty-eight representatives from Wales.[3]   To the parliament thus constituted the question was put, whether they would have the father or the son to be king?   In answering this question in favor of the son, the parliament expressed, in six articles drawn up by Stratford, Bishop of Winchester, the reasons

Right revived by the assembly of estates.

Deposition of Edward II.

The Lords Ordainers.

Edward's fate settled by the parliament of 1327.

Six articles drawn up by Bishop Stratford.

---

[1] See above, p. 499.
[2] *Fœdera*, ii. p. 646; *Parl. Writs*, II. i. p. 349.
[3] "No attempt to procure representatives from either North or South Wales appears to have been afterwards made until the act passed for the purpose in the reign of Henry the Eighth."—

Lords' Report, vol. i. p. 289.   By 34 and 35 Hen. VIII., c. 26, Wales was divided into twelve counties, with the right to send one knight each to parliament; every borough which was a shire town being allowed to send one burgess.

why Edward of Carnarvon should cease to reign. His incapacity to govern, his heed of evil counsellors, his neglect of good counsel, the loss of Scotland, Ireland, and Gascony, his oppression of the church and baronage, his violation of his coronation oath, and the general mischief which he had wrought to himself and the realm, — were the specific accusations preferred against him.   As no formal trial was had, or proof taken upon the charges, it was considered a prudential measure to send a deputation of the parliament to obtain

Edward as-
sents to his
son's elec-
tion.

Edward's consent to the election of his son.[1]   After the discrowned king had meekly yielded to his fate, Sir William Trussell, as proctor of the whole parliament, after renouncing the homage and fealty of those he represented, said : " I now make protestation in their name that they will no longer be in your fealty and allegiance, nor claim to hold anything of you as king, but will account you hereafter as a private person, without any manner of royal dignity."   Sir Thomas Blount, the steward of the household, then broke his staff of office in token of the fact that the king had ceased to reign.[2] This final ceremony, used only on the occasion of a king's death, was the omen of Edward's murder which occurred in the following September.

Deposition
of Richard
II.

The deposition of Edward II., which was the result of mere weariness upon the part of the nation with a worthless and incompetent king, was followed, after an interval of seventy-two years, by the deposition of Richard II., which stands out as the culmination of a conflict in which the royal authority, after having defied the constitution by an assumption of absolute power, was completely mastered and overcome by

Richard's
temper in
youth.

the irresistible supremacy of parliament.   The candor, the liberality, the courage, manifested by the youthful Richard at the outset of his reign, when in the midst of revolution he was brought face to face with the miseries of his people, gave no token of the imperious and fanatical spirit which in his maturer years provoked his deposition and murder.   The brilliant reign of Edward III., during which the military renown of England reached perhaps its highest point, was the nursery of a social discontent which began to manifest itself

[1] T. de la Moor, p. 600.
[2] A clear account of the whole trans-   action, with the authorities, may be
     found in Lingard, vol.

for the first time in the ranks of the common people. The
peasant revolt, which Richard was called upon to quell upon
the threshold of his career, was the result of causes which the
pressure of perpetual war, and the visitations of the great
plague, had set to work in his father's time. When, at the
close of 1348, the Black Death began its desolating march
through the English kingdom, the laboring classes, amongst
whom its results are historically most prominent, had for a
century or more been moving from the lower stages of serf-
age, in which the duties of the villein to his lord were discharged by personal services, to a state of comparative freedom, in which personal services were commuted by money
payments. So rapidly had the process of enfranchisement
advanced, that lords of manors were obliged to rely for
the cultivation of their lands upon hired laborers who took
the places of the villeins, who were now discharging their
duties to their lords by rentals in money in lieu of base services. Upon this hopeful condition of things the great plague
fell like a blight. By its ravages the total population was so
reduced that hired labor, which had heretofore been cheap
and abundant, now became dear and scarce. It is probable
that not much less than half of the entire population was
destroyed,[1] and the number of laborers was so reduced that
those who survived demanded double the old rate of wages.
As a remedy for this condition of things, which threatened
ruin to the great landowners, and to the wealthier craftsmen
of the towns, the council in 1349 passed an ordinance which
attempted to regulate the price of labor by providing that all
laborers should be forced to serve at the rate of wages which
had prevailed before the plague began.[2] This ordinance, published in June, was afterwards turned into the statute known
as the Statute of Laborers.[3] This measure the parliament of
1351 rendered still more stringent by denying to the laborer
the right to quit his parish in search of better employment.[4]
When the villeins refused to accept the starvation wages thus
held out to them, the landlords fell back upon their demesne

Causes of the peasant revolt.

Condition of the laboring classes at the beginning of the Black Death in 1348.

Population so reduced that hired labor became dear and scarce.

The council attempts to regulate the rate of wages by ordinance.

Statute of Laborers, 1349.

[1] Cf. Rogers, *History of Prices*, i.
p. 60.
[2] Knighton, c. 2600; *Fœdera*, iii. c.
198; *Statutes*, i. 307.
[3] 23 Edw. III. "This ordinance was
afterwards by stat. 3 Rich. II., st. 1, c.
viii., made an act of parliament, and
constitutes stat. 23 Edw. III." —
Reeves, *Hist. Eng. Law*, vol. iii. p.
128.
[4] 25 Edw. III.

rights, which when contested were tried in the manor court, presided over by the steward, whose interest it was to have the judgment given against the villein and in favor of the lord.[1]

Conflict between capital and labor intensified by the teachings of the Lollard preachers.

The wide-spread irritation and discontent among the lower classes which grew out of this bitter conflict between capital and labor was also quickened and intensified by the teachings of some of the Lollard preachers, who went about not only inveighing against the right of the clergy to hold property, but against the whole system of social inequality, which during the middle ages held the rich and the poor so wide apart. Foremost among agitators of this class stood John Ball, "a mad priest of Kent," who openly proclaimed a new doctrine of social equality, based upon the natural rights of man, which found quaint yet pointed expression in the popular rhyme: —

> When Adam delved and Eve span,
> Who was then the gentleman?[2]

The poll-tax.

The social discontent which thus smouldered at the end of Edward's reign broke into flame when, shortly after the accession of his son, the pressure of taxation was applied with fresh force, and through a new device, to every hearth and home in the realm. In the last year of Edward's reign the parliament of 1377, in order to meet the urgent need of money to carry on the war with France, devised a new form of general taxation by granting to the crown a poll-tax of a groat a head.[3] Two years after Richard's accession the parliament of 1379, in response to another pressing demand for money, granted a second poll-tax, under which every man was charged with a direct contribution in proportion to his rank or dignity.[4] In the next year still another and severer

Rising of the commons begins on the 5th June, 1381.

poll-tax was granted.[5] The collection of this last tax in June, 1381, was the signal for revolt, — on the 5th of June the rising of the commons began. Although the grounds of discontent seem to have varied somewhat in every district, two great motives for revolt stood out above all the rest, clearly

The political grievance.

and distinctly defined. The first was the political grievance which grew out of the imposition of the poll-tax, whereby the

---

[1] As to such proceedings, see Seebohm, *Eng. Village Community*, pp. 30. 31; Reeves, *Hist. Eng. Law*, vol. iii. pp. 130–132, notes, Finlason, ed.

[2] Cf. Green, *Hist. of the Eng. People,* vol. i. p. 440.
[3] *Rot. Parl.*, ii. p. 364.
[4] Ibid., iii. pp. 57, 58.
[5] Ibid., iii. p. 90.

pressure of the war was brought home to the laboring classes, already in a state of seething discontent, by subjecting them to a burden which had not before been imposed upon them. The second was the social grievance which grew out of the attempts of the landlords to exact work from the laborer at low wages, or, in default of that, to revive their demesne rights to base services from men who had begun to regard themselves as no longer villeins. The first actual outbreak, which began in Kent on the 5th of June, was provoked by the collection of the poll-tax; this seems to have been the main grievance of the hundred thousand Kentish men who gathered around Wat Tyler of Essex to march upon London: their cry was for the suppression of the poll-tax and better government. On the other hand, the grievance of the men from Essex and the eastern counties seems to have been rather social than political; their demand was that bondage should be abolished, that tolls and other imposts on trade should be done away with, that the native-born villein should be emancipated, and that all villein service should be commuted for a rent of fourpence the acre.[1] When, on the morning of the 14th of June, Richard rode from the Tower to Mile-end to meet the Essex men, their cry was, "We will that you free us forever, us and our lands; and that we be never named nor held for serfs." In reply the king promptly pledged his royal word that their demands should be granted; and as soon as the charters of freedom and amnesty could be drawn, the mass of those seeking emancipation withdrew to their homes. The same happy result followed when, on the next day, Richard, meeting the Kentish men, made to them the same pledges of freedom, coupled with the reminder that he was their captain and their king. In a little more than a fortnight the revolt was over, and then came a period of reaction, during which the confiding peasants were taught to feel how little trust could be placed even in the written pledges of a king. On the 30th of June a royal proclamation was issued ordering all tenants of land to continue their accustomed services;[2] on the 2d of July the charters of freedom and pardon were revoked,[3] and on the 18th the local

The social grievance.

Wat Tyler and the Kentish men.

The men from Essex and the eastern counties.

Richard's pledges to the Essex men.

Revolt lasted little more than a fortnight.

---

[1] For a full statement of the crisis and its causes, see Stubbs, *Const. Hist.*, vol. ii. pp. 449–463.

[2] *Fœdera*, iv. p. 126.

[3] Ibid., iv. p. 126.

courts were ordered not to release their prisoners.[1] Tres-silian, the chief justice, then began to bring the law to bear upon the insurgents, who were punished with the greatest cruelty.   And yet, in spite of all the cruelty and repression thus applied by the government to the laboring classes dur-ing the period of reaction which followed the revolt, the great purpose of the revolution was fully accomplished.   The can-cellation of charters upon the part of the crown, the attempt upon the part of the landlords to revive their old demesne rights, could not conceal the fact that villeinage had received its death-blow.[2]   The process of enfranchisement, so hope-fully progressing when the advent of the plague arrested its progress, advanced again so rapidly that, at the end of a century and a half from the time of the rising, villeinage was looked upon as a rare if not an obsolete institution. And as the work of enfranchisement advanced, the number of small freeholders was so increased by the constant ac-cession of new freemen that the yeoman class soon came to be regarded in every shire as the basis of the electoral system.[3]

In spite of cruelty and repression, the purpose of the re-volt fully accom-plished.

Within a century and a half after the rising, villeinage an obsolete institution.

Yeoman class be-comes the basis of the electoral system.

In 1394 the queen, Anne of Bohemia, died, and two years thereafter the king married a second wife, Isabella, the daughter of Charles VI. of France.   From that time dates the marked change of temper which prompted Richard to drop all disguises, and to exhibit his purpose of ruling as an absolute monarch, surrounded by a profuse and profligate court.   While the king was in this mood an effort was made by the parliament of 1397 to reform, among other things, the royal household.   When the bill of complaint upon that sub-ject, which originated with the commons, was presented to the lords, the king sent for them,[4] and requested them to inform the lower house of the offence they had given in pre-suming to "take on themselves any ordinance or governance of the person of the king, or his hostel, or of any persons of estate whom he might be pleased to have in his company."

The marked change in Richard's temper dates from the French marriage in 1396.

[1] *Fœdera*, p. 128.

[2] "The landlords gave up the prac-tice of demanding base services: they let their lands to leasehold tenants, and accepted money payments in lieu of labor; they ceased to recall the emancipated laborer into serfdom, or to oppose his assertion of right in the courts of the manor and the county." — Stubbs, *Const. Hist.*, vol. ii. p. 462.

[3] Green, *Hist. of the Eng. People*, vol. i. p. 486.

[4] *Rot. Parl.*, iii. pp. 338–340.

Not content with this rebuke, he also commanded the Duke of Lancaster to demand of the house, through the speaker, to give up the name of the member who had dared to bring forward the offensive proposal. In response to the demand the obsequious commons gave up the name of Sir Thomas Haxey, a prebendary of Southwell, who was condemned by the lords to suffer the death of a traitor,[1]—a fate from which he was saved by being claimed as a clergyman by Archbishop Arundel.

Richard rebukes the commons, and demands the name of the offending member.

In the new parliament, which met in September of this year, the crime of treason, which with its penalty had first been defined by a law passed in 1352,[2] received a fresh definition in a statute which declared the four articles of treason to be, the compassing of the king's death or deposition, the levying of war against him, and the surrendering the liege homage due to him.[3] After the king had procured such further legislation as enabled him to punish his enemies,— chief among whom were the appellants Arundel, Gloucester, and Warwick,— this parliament, which had been elected under the open pressure of royal influence, was adjourned to Shrewsbury, where it sat for three days. During these days, through parliamentary action which purported to be voluntary, Richard was transformed into a practically absolute monarch, and parliamentary government for a time brought to an end. After granting a subsidy on wool, woolfells, and leather to the king for life,[4]—such a grant as had never been before made,—the parliament terminated its existence by delegating its authority to a committee of eighteen members, who were empowered not only to hear petitions, but also "to examine and determine all matters and subjects which had been moved in the presence of the king, with all the dependencies thereof."[5] In this wise, by bringing about the surrender of the authority of parliament into the hands of a committee, selected from those who were supposed to be his faithful adherents, Richard accomplished for a time the great constitutional change to which his policy since the French marriage had been openly directed.

A fresh definition of the crime of treason, 1397.

Parliament of Shrewsbury, Jan., 1398, made Richard practically absolute.

Grant of a subsidy for life.

---

[1] Haxey was condemned under an *ex post facto* ordinance passed by the lords and the king. *Rot. Parl.*, iii. pp. 339, 341, 407, 408.
[2] Ibid., ii. p. 239.

[3] *Rot. Parl.*, iii. p. 343. See Reeves, *Hist. of Eng. Law*, vol. iii. pp. 187, 315.
[4] *Rot. Parl.*, iii. p. 368.
[5] Ibid., iii. pp. 369, 372, 385.

Reaction
which
followed
Richard's
usurpation
cost him his
crown and
his life.

Although this daring usurpation, through which the king struck down the power of parliament, and secured for himself a revenue for life, was not at the moment resisted, the reaction which followed it led directly to his deposition, and to the transfer of the crown to the house of Lancaster. The opportunity for the counter-revolution grew out of a quarrel

Quarrel be-
tween Nor-
folk and
Hereford.

which occurred in December, 1397, between the Duke of Norfolk and the son of John of Gaunt, Henry of Lancaster, now Duke of Hereford. The settlement of the quarrel was referred by a committee of parliament[1] to a court of chivalry, which met in April, 1398, and in which it was decided that the quarrel between the two dukes should be settled by single combat at Coventry in the following September. When at the time appointed the dukes entered the lists, Richard forbade the combat, and sentenced Norfolk to banishment for life, and Henry of Lancaster to exile for six

Henry of
Lancaster
exiled, and
his estates
confiscated.

years. The exile thus forced upon the heir of Lancaster was soon followed by an act of confiscation. In January, 1399, John of Gaunt died, and although special leave had been given Henry to receive his inheritance on the death of his father, Richard, under an ordinance passed by the parliamentary committee,[2] annulled the permission and seized the Lancastrian estates. Two months after that event the king left the realm in charge of his uncle, Edmund, Duke of York, as regent, and went to Ireland for the purpose of reducing it to complete subjection. An opportunity was thus promptly offered to the exiled and disinherited Henry not only to redress his own wrongs, but to become the leader of the counter-revolution through which the nation was to reëstablish, more firmly than ever before, the supremacy of parlia-

Henry
lands in
Yorkshire
on the 4th
July, 1399.

ment. On the 4th of July, 1399, Henry landed in Yorkshire, and as he marched rapidly to the south, with an army that grew at every step, all show of resistance broke down, the forces gathered by the regent refusing to oppose him. By the first of August, Henry was so completely in possession of the realm that when Richard landed in Wales all chance for a struggle was over. On the 2d of September the king was brought to London and placed in the Tower, and on the 30th

---

[1] *Rot. Parl.*, iii. p. 383.
[2] Ibid., iii. p. 372; Rymer, viii.   pp. 49, 51; Stubbs, *Const. Hist.*, vol. ii. pp. 500, 501.

of that month the parliament met in which his fate was to be decided. The procedure which was now employed was a substantial reproduction of that which seventy-two years before had attended the deposition of Edward II. On the day before the parliament met, Richard was required to sign a deed of resignation in which he fully renounced his right to the crown, and absolved his people from their oaths of homage and fealty.[1] The parliament not only accepted the resignation, but in addition thereto pronounced a judgment of deposition, upon written articles presented against the king in which he was formally charged with every possible act of illegality and malversation.[2] The throne having thus been made vacant, not only by Richard's own act, but by the act of parliament, the all-important question of the succession remained to be determined. If that question had depended only on the strict rule of hereditary descent which the feudal lawyers applied to the succession of estates, the crown would have now passed to Edmund Mortimer, the infant son of Roger Mortimer, Earl of March, son of Phillippa, the daughter and heiress of Lionel of Clarence, the third son of Edward III. But the strict rule of hereditary descent had not yet received positive and formal recognition in the case of the crown; it had not yet superseded the immemorial right of the national council to choose, in the presence of a great emergency, that member of the royal household whom it deemed most competent to govern.[3] And yet the notion that the right to the throne depended upon the hereditary principle had sufficiently advanced to prompt Henry, when he stood forth before the parliament to challenge the crown, to claim it " as that I am descended by right line of blood coming from the good lord king Henry III."[4] But this shadowy claim, which depended upon a false tradition, was too flimsy to conceal the patent fact that the new monarch had been raised to the throne through a parliamentary revolution, —

Procedure upon the deposition of Richard II.

The question of the succession.

Strict rule of hereditary descent not yet applied to the crown.

Henry's elevation the result of a parliamentary revolution.

---

[1] *Ann. Ricardi*, pp. 252, 255 *seq.*; *Mon. Evesh.*, pp. 157 *seq.* On the next day the resignation was accepted. *Rot. Parl.*, iii. p. 416 *seq.*

[2] *Rot. Parl.*, iii. pp. 416–424.

[3] " The strict rule of hereditary descent had never received any formal recognition in the case of the crown, and precedent suggested a right of parliament to choose in such a case a successor among any other members of the royal house." — Green, *Hist. of the Eng. People*, vol. i. p. 521.

[4] See what Mr. Freeman has to say as to the growth of the hereditary doctrine, in *Enc. Brit.*, 9th ed. vol. viii. p. 320.

that the royal authority was for the future to rest upon a parliamentary title. And so it came to pass that the audacious attempt made by Richard to subvert the constitution, by rendering the crown independent of the assembly of estates, not only became abortive the moment the nation under a competent leader was aroused to action, but it also fell out, as a consequence of the struggle, that the crown was placed in such a position of dependence upon the two houses as to render all such future attempts doubly perilous.

Authority of parliament reached the limit of its growth through the results of the revolution.

Through the results of the counter-revolution, the authority of parliament reached the limit of its growth when, after a struggle of scarcely two months' duration, it deposed the ruling sovereign; and then, after ignoring the pretensions of the claimant who really represented the hereditary title, awarded the throne to another member of the royal house, whom it deemed more competent to govern.[1]

---

[1] During the memorable crisis of 1386 the parliament had warned the king that a time might come when it would be "lawful for his people, by their full and free assent and consent, to depose the king himself from his royal throne, and in his stead to raise up some other of the royal race upon the same." — Knighton, c. 2683; *Parl. Hist.*, i. p. 186.

CHAPTER II.

1. A POINT has now been reached from which it is possible to review the general advance made by the parliament during the period which intervenes between the Norman conquest and the end of the fourteenth century. During that period the feudal councils which gathered around the Norman and Angevin kings, with authority too vague and shadowy for precise definition, are gradually transformed into an assembly of estates which wins not only the right to participate in taxation and legislation, but to supervise and control the entire system of national administration. At the beginning of the period all of the great powers of government are centralized in the person of the king, acting ordinarily through his continual council composed of the officers of state and of the household, from which body emanated all the important acts of government, whether administrative, legislative, judicial, fiscal, or political. At the end of the period we find that the sum of governmental power originally vested in the king in council has been vastly reduced through the operation of two distinct processes of subtraction. In the first place, by the growth out of the continual council — which soon came to be known as the curia regis [1] — of the common law courts of king's bench, common pleas, and exchequer, the greater part of the judicial work of the council was permanently transferred to three distinct tribunals, each devoted to the hearing of a definite class of causes. And when at a later day, out of the residuum of judicial power retained by the council, was developed the equitable jurisdiction of the chancellor, the judicial functions of the crown were confined within a still narrower circle. By the transfer thus brought

Review of the growth of parliament from the Conquest to the accession of Henry IV.

The sum of governmental power originally vested in the king in council reduced by a double process of subtraction.

Greater part of the judicial work of the council transferred to the courts of law and equity.

---

[1] The term *curia regis*, which for a long time after the Conquest was applied not only to the continual but to the national council, finally became the exclusive designation of the court of king's bench, after the final division into three distinct courts — which took place at the end of the reign of Henry III. — of the limited tribunal created out of the council by Henry II. in 1179. See above, pp, 248, 249.

about of the greater part of the judicial business originally dispatched by the king in council to the great courts of law and equity, the central administration, in its judicial aspect, was transformed into a government of law as distinguished from a government of functionaries.[1] In this way the principle became settled that judicial controversies should no longer be determined by the mere force of royal authority, but by due process of law, — that is, by law administered in fixed tribunals by trained judges governed by principles and precedents drawn from the Old-English code of customary law as modified by Norman innovation. That the judicial work of the kingdom should be thus conducted was as late as the reign of Henry IV. made the subject of a special demand in parliament : in 1406 the commons, as a part of the scheme of reform pressed upon the king in that year, demand that the council shall determine nothing cognizable at common law unless for reasonable cause and with the consent of the judges ; that the council and officers of state shall be sworn to observe the common law and all statutes, specially those recently enacted.[2] In the second place, while the law courts were upon the one hand drawing to themselves the control of the bulk of the judicial work which had originally belonged to the king in council, the assembly of estates was upon the other struggling to draw to itself the exclusive control of the legislative, taxative, and fiscal business of the kingdom. But before the national assembly was in a position to essay so great a task, a reorganization had first to be effected in its own constitution, a result which was brought about by the building up alongside of the older feudal council of a new and a popular body composed of representatives from the shires and towns. How these representative members were called up to confer with the king upon the business

Marginal notes:
Due process of law defined.

The assembly of estates draws to itself the control of the legislative, taxative, and fiscal business of the kingdom.

---

[1] "The guarantee of the supremacy of the law leads to a principle which, so far as I know, it has never been attempted to transplant from the soil inhabited by Anglican people, and which, nevertheless, has been, in our system of liberty, the natural production of a thorough government of law as contradistinguished to a government of functionaries." — Lieber, *Civil Liberty and Self-Government*, p. 91.

[2] *Rot. Parl.*, iii. pp. 585-589. A series of petitions begin as early as 1351 against the judicial usurpations of the council. See *Rot. Parl.*, ii. pp. 228, 239, 295. In 1390 the commons petitioned that no one should be summoned before the chancellor or the council by the writ *quibusdam de causis* to answer in any case in which the common law gave a remedy. — *Rot. Parl.*, iii. p. 267.

of the kingdom as a matter of mere fiscal expediency, how they coalesced in the formation of the lower house, and how that house gradually won the right to participate in taxation and legislation, to impeach the ministers, to participate in the general control of the royal administration, and in the deposition of the king himself, has been drawn out already. In the parliament thus reconstructed the commons soon ceased to be mere auxiliaries of the baronial body : they became the more active and aggressive force in the new combination.[1]

By the end of the fourteenth century the parliament as an assembly of estates had won for itself the possession of five substantive rights which embraced all of the higher functions of government : 1. The exclusive right to authorize both direct and indirect taxation ; and as an incident thereto the commons claimed the right to make the grant of supplies dependent upon the redress of grievances. 2. The right to concur in the enactment, amendment, and repeal of all permanent acts of national legislation. 3. The right to supervise and control the royal administration ; and as incidents thereto (*a*) the right to appropriate the supplies to special purposes, (*b*) and to audit the accounts which explained the method of their expenditure. 4. The right to impeach and punish the ministers. 5. And finally the right to depose the king himself, and to vest the succession in another member of the royal house more competent to govern.

The five substantive rights possessed by parliament at the close of the fourteenth century.

And yet, when a summing up is made of the results of the two processes of subtraction through which the bulk of the judicial business was transferred from the king and council to the great courts of law and equity on the one hand, and the virtual control of the legislative, taxative, and fiscal business of the kingdom to the parliament on the other, the important fact remains that neither process was exhaustive. After the jurisdictions of the four great courts at Westminster had been fully and finally established, an undefined reserve of judicial power still remained to the king in council, —a reserve out of which at a later day grew the court of star chamber, a reserve which has reached our own time in the form of the judicial committee of the privy council. In the same way, and about to the same extent, the parliament,

Neither process of subtraction exhaustive.

An undefined reserve of both judicial and legislative power remains to the king in council.

---

[1] See above, pp. 482-504.

in its effort to draw to itself the exclusive control of taxation and legislation, stopped short of complete victory. After persistent warfare, the assembly of estates finally extinguished, it is true, the taxative power of the king in council. But the effort made by parliament to win the exclusive control of legislation was less conclusive. At the end of the struggle there still remained in the hands of the king in council an undefined reserve of legislative power which was for a long time exercised in the making and revoking of a class of tem-

A definition of the prerogative.

porary enactments known as ordinances. When to the inherent right of the crown to conduct the executive business of the kingdom are added the personal privileges incident to kingship, and the two remnants of judicial and legislative power which remain to the king in council after the full development of the law courts and the parliament, the sum thus made up represents the aggregate of royal authority generally known in mediæval and modern times as the prerogative.

Definition of parliamentary privileges the work of the fifteenth century.

2. By the end of the fourteenth century all of the substantive powers of parliament had reached their full growth. During the fifteenth, no new powers are added. Nothing in fact transpires in the history of parliament during the latter period more important than the settlement of its principal forms of procedure, and the assertion and definition of privileges [1] which belong either to the parliament as a whole, or to the respective houses of which it is composed, or to its individual members.

Privileges belonging to parliament as a whole : origin of the modern form of legislation.

Chief among the privileges belonging to parliament as a whole, which received final definition during the fifteenth century, was that which involved the form in which the estates should concur with the king in the enactment of legislation. After the principle was settled that the concurrence of both houses in legislation was necessary, the common form of legislating throughout the fourteenth century was that initiated by the petitions of the commons, to which the king

[1] "During this epoch, the parliament gained none of those signal victories which distinguished the reigns of Edward III. and Richard II. ; no really new right, no fundamental and previously unknown guarantee, were added to those already possessed. . . . The internal constitution of the parliament, especially during the course of this period, made important progress ; from this time we may date, with some degree of accuracy, its principal forms of procedure, and its most essential privileges." — Guizot, *Hist. Rep. Government*, pp. 509, 510 (Scoble's trans.).

was expected to reply during the session of parliament.
When the answer came it was entered, together with the petition, in the parliament rolls, and out of the two, after the
adjournment, the act itself was drawn and entered in the
statute rolls.   The manifold abuses and uncertainties which
grew out of this loose and unguarded system have been explained already.   To remedy the evils which grew out of this
uncertain method of "extracting of the statute out of the
petition and answer, about the latter end of Henry VI. and
beginning of Edward IV. they (the commons) took a course
to reduce them, even in the first instance, into the full and
complete forms of acts of parliament."[1]   After the passage
of bills thus introduced in the lower house, they were sent to
the lords, and if passed there they were presented to the king
for approval or rejection without alteration.   The new method
of legislation thus inaugurated by the commons was soon
adopted by the lords ; and in time it became the settled law
of parliament that, with the exception of money bills, which
must originate with the commons, and bills touching the
peerage, which must originate with the lords, all bills upon
other subjects may originate in either house.[2]

Bills may originate in either house, excepting money bills, and bills touching the peerage.

In considering the privileges which belong to each house
as a constituent part of the high court of parliament, the
fact must be remembered that, although each house exercises
its own privileges and usages independently of the other, they
are enjoyed, not by any separate right peculiar to each, but
solely by virtue of the law and custom which appertains to
parliament as a single body.   "As every court of justice
hath laws and customs for its direction, — some the civil and
canon, some the common law, others their own peculiar laws
and customs, — so the high court of parliament hath also its
own peculiar law, called the *lex et consuetudo parliamenti*."[3]
All parliamentary privileges rest upon the ancient law and
custom of parliament considered simply as a part of the unwritten law of the land, or upon that law and custom as

Privileges belonging to the two houses separately, all depend upon a single code.

---

[1] Hale, *Hist. Com. Law*, vol. i. p. 18.
See, also, Ruffhead's *Statutes*, preface.

[2] As to the ancient mode of enacting laws, and the transition therefrom
to the modern system, see Sir T. Erskine May, *Parl. Practice*, ch. xviii.

[3] Coke, 4 *Inst.*, 15.   "Each house,

as a constituent part of parliament, exercises its own privileges independently
of the other.   They are enjoyed, however, not by any separate right peculiar
to each, but solely by virtue of the law
and custom of parliament." — May,
Parl. Prac., pp. 71, 72.

defined by statute.   It has been said that the lords enjoy the privileges possessed by them simply because "they have place and voice in parliament."[1]   An enumeration of the most important of these privileges will do much to point out not only the difference in the usage of the two houses, but also the difference in the privileges possessed by the individual members of the house of lords, as compared with the privileges possessed by the individual members of the house of commons.

Privileges of the lords: right of audience.   Foremost among the privileges possessed by the lords should be noted the right of each individual peer, as an hereditary counsellor of the crown, to have audience with his sovereign.   As the corporate successor of the great council, the upper house possessed from the beginning the right to give counsel; and only by personal access to the sovereign could that right be rendered efficacious.[2]   By reason no doubt of this close relation, the presidency of the upper house *Presidency of the lord chancellor.*   became vested in the officer most closely connected with the crown, the lord chancellor, or lord keeper of the great seal, who is prolocutor or speaker of the house of lords by prescription, although not necessarily a member of that body.[3]   When a member he is invested with no more authority than any other peer; when he is not, his office is limited to the putting of questions, and other merely formal proceedings. All speeches are addressed, not to him, but to the whole *Right to vote by proxy.*   house.[4]   From the earliest times down to a very recent date, when the peers by a standing order voluntarily abolished it,[5] every lord possessed the right to appoint another lord of parliament as his proxy to cast his vote, — a right originally exercised by virtue of a royal license which was seldom *Right to be tried by peers, and freedom from arrest.*   refused.[6]   Every peer possesses not only the right to be tried by his peers,[7] but also immunity from arrest, not merely as a member of the house of lords, but as a baron of the realm, — an immunity which is not limited to the session of parliament, for the person of a peer is "forever sacred and inviolable."[8]

---

[1] Hakewell, p. 82.
[2] See *Diary and Correspondence of Lord Colchester*, vol. iii. pp. 604–607.
[3] See above, p. 480 and note 5.
[4] May, *Parl. Practice*, pp. 243–246.
[5] On the 31st May, 1868, the house of lords agreed to a standing order, "that the practice of calling for prox-

ies, on a division, shall be discontinued."
[6] For a list of the occasions upon which the permission to appoint proxies was withheld, see Elsynge, *Ancient Method of holding Parliaments*, p. 117.
[7] See above, p. 389, and note 1.
[8] Stubbs, *Const. Hist.*, vol. iii. p. 498.

Although each house is equally entitled to its own peculiar privileges under the same code of parliamentary law, the term "privileges of parliament" is generally understood to relate more particularly to those which were won by the lower house during the period in which the united representatives of the commons were striving to win recognition as a coördinate factor in the assembly of estates. From the custom upon the part of the commons of submitting their privileges to the crown for confirmation, it would appear that such privileges were at first mere matters of royal favor. "But whatever may have been the origin and cause of this custom, and however great the concession to the crown may appear, the privileges of the commons are nevertheless independent of the crown, and are enjoyed irrespective of their petition."[1] First among the privileges established by the representative members was the right to organize as an independent corporate body and to elect a speaker. As early as 1376 the lower house formally completed its organization as a deliberative body by the election of Peter de la Mare as head officer,[2] but the title of speaker was not then assigned him. In the next year the parliament rolls contain the first mention of a speaker of the house of commons expressly named as such: "Monsieur Thomas de Hungerford, chivaler *qi avoit les paroles* pur les commons d'Engleterre en cest parlement."[3] From that year the list of speakers is complete. The choice of a speaker was made by the commons under a command from the crown usually expressed at the close of the opening speech. After the election the speaker-elect was presented by the commons to the king as their chosen "*parlour et procuratour.*" After the speaker had expressed his insufficiency for so great an office, it was usual for the crown to approve and confirm him as a speaker. After his confirmation it became his duty to claim of the crown, on behalf of the commons, all of their ancient and undoubted rights and privileges, and at the same time to request that his utterances might be considered as their utterances, that no offence should be taken at his words, and that all his shortcomings should be equitably considered. The usage has

Marginal notes:
Privileges of the commons.

Right to elect a speaker.

His demand of the rights and privileges of the house.

---

[1] May, *Parl. Practice*, pp. 69–71.   [3] *Rot. Parl.*, ii. p. 374.
[2] See above, p. 480.

The modern form of the demand and response.

been, since the sixth year of Henry VIII., for the speaker, "in the name and on behalf of the commons, to lay claim by humble petition to their ancient and undoubted rights and privileges, particularly that their persons and servants might be free from arrests and all molestations; that they may enjoy liberty of speech in all their debates; may have access to her majesty's royal person whenever occasion shall require; and that all their proceedings may receive from her majesty the most favorable construction." To this the lord chancellor replies, that "her majesty most readily confirms all the rights and privileges which have ever been granted to or conferred upon the commons by her majesty or any of her royal predecessors."[1]

Freedom of speech.

Although it may be reasonably assumed that freedom of speech was inherent in the constitution of parliament from the very beginning, it is nevertheless a fact that only after a long period of struggle with the crown was the privilege finally established upon a secure legal foundation. From Elsynge we learn that the "commons did oftentimes, under Edward III., discuss and debate amongst themselves many things concerning the king's prerogative, and agreed upon petitions for laws to be made directly against his prerogative, as may appear by divers of the said petitions; yet they were never interrupted in their consultations, nor received check for the same, as may appear also by the answers to the said petitions."[2] In the 20th of Richard II., however, when Sir

Haxey's case.

Thomas Haxey ventured to introduce a bill for the reformation of the royal household, that imperious monarch was quick to show that he was not animated by the tolerant spirit of his grandfather. The speaker was forced to give up the name of the offending member, and Haxey was condemned by the lords as a traitor. After the counter-revolution had placed Henry IV. upon the throne, Haxey exhibited a petition to the king in parliament to reverse the judgment against him as being "against the law and custom which had been before in parliament," and the prayer of the petition was granted with the assent of all the lords spiritual and temporal.[3] Not content with this adjudication by the king

[1] See May, *Parl. Practice*, pp. 68, 69.

[2] *Ancient Method of holding Parliaments*, p. 177.

[3] *Rot. Parl.*, iii. p. 430.

and lords, the commons in the same year again took up the case and presented it in a petition to the king which prayed that the judgment should be reversed, "as well for the furtherance of justice as for the saving of the liberties of the commons." By the assent of the king and lords to the petition of the commons it was agreed by the whole legislature that the condemnation of Haxey, being in derogation of the privileges of parliament, "should be annulled and held to be of no force or effect."[1] In the 33d of Henry VI., Thomas Young complained to the commons that five years before that time he had been imprisoned in the Tower "for matters by him showed in the house," which "matters" consisted of a motion that, as the king had no issue, the Duke of York might be declared heir-apparent. The petition was transmitted to the lords, and the king "willed that the lords of his council do and provide for the said suppliant, as in their discretion shall be thought convenient and reasonable."[2] The question of freedom of speech next arose in the 4th of Henry VIII. in the case of Strode, a member of the house, who was prosecuted in the stannary court, fined and imprisoned, for having proposed certain bills to regulate the tinners in Cornwall.[3] This violation of privilege led to an act which not only pronounced the proceeding against Strode void, but also declared that all similar proceedings that might be begun in the future against "the person or persons that now be of the present parliament, or *that of any parliament thereafter*, shall be . . . utterly void and of none effect."[4] Thirty years later the petition of the commons at the opening of parliament for the first time includes freedom of speech among their "ancient and undoubted rights and privileges."[5] After frequent violations occurring after that time, the right of free debate was for the last time directly impeached in the famous case against Eliot, Holles, and Valentine, against whom a judgment was obtained in the king's bench in the 5th year of Charles I. for their conduct in parliament. In 1641 the

Young's case.

Strode's case.

Case of Eliot, Holles, and Valentine.

[1] *Rot. Parl.*, iii. p. 434.
[2] Ibid., v. p. 337.
[3] *Parl. Hist.*, vol. iv. p. 85. "The court of the stannaries of Cornwall and Devon is a court of special jurisdiction . . . in derogation from the general jurisdiction of the courts of

common law, for the local redress of private wrongs." — Taswell-Langmead, *Eng. Const. Hist.*, p. 325, note 2.
[4] 4 Henry VIII., c. 8.
[5] *Rot. Parl.*, 33 Henry VIII.; Elsynge, *Ancient Method*, etc., p. 176.

house of commons declared the proceedings in the king's bench to be against the law and privilege of parliament;[1] and finally in April, 1668, the judgment of the king's bench was reversed, on a writ of error, by the house of lords.[2] By

Question finally settled by Bill of Rights. the ninth article of the Bill of Rights it was declared, "That the freedom of speech, and debates or proceedings in parliament, ought not to be impeached or questioned in any court or place out of parliament."[3]

Supply made dependent upon the redress of grievances. The statement has heretofore been made that during the fourteenth century parliament established the exclusive right to authorize both direct and indirect taxation, and that as an incident thereto the commons claimed the right to make the grant of supplies dependent upon the redress of grievances. The claim thus set up by the commons to make supply depend upon redress did not ripen, however, into a settled parliamentary privilege until the reign of Henry IV. As early

Doctrine announced in the reign of Henry III. as the reign of Henry III. the principle was openly recognized by both the crown and the nation that concessions in favor of liberty moving from the former to the latter were legitimate subjects of bargain and sale. Of this fact Henry's confirmation of the charters in 1225, in which the king openly admits that the concessions made to the three estates are in consideration of a grant of "a fifteenth part of all their movable goods," may be cited as a familiar illustration. But in parliamentary practice the difficulty was to secure for the principle a practical operation. When a grant was asked, it became the custom for the commons to put forward in a petition to the crown such grievances as required amendment at

Originally the grant preceded the redress. the hands of the king and his council. The discussion of grievances thus became preliminary to the discussion of the grant, which had to be made simply upon the hope that the prayer of the petition would be followed by adequate redress.[4] To obtain definite answers to petitions, much less actual redress of grievances, before the close of parliament, was an undertaking always attended with great difficulty. It was usual for the king to wait until the last day of the session, and then to give such answers as he saw fit after the grants

[1] *Com. Journal*, ii. p. 203.
[2] *Lords' Journal*, xii. p. 223.
[3] 1 Will. and Mary, sess. 2, c. 2.

Upon the whole subject, see May, *Parl. Practice*, pp. 118–123.
[4] See above, p. 493.

had all been made. Any attempt to change this order of proceeding was declared by Richard II.'s judges to be high treason.[1] In the third year of Henry IV. the lower house grew bold enough, however, to attempt to bring about the desired change by availing themselves of the king's necessities. When, in the parliament of 1401, supplies were asked, the commons put forward many demands, and, among others, that before they made any grants, answers should first be made to their petitions. Although the king promised to confer with the lords on the subject, he withheld his reply until the last day of the session, and then answered "that this mode of proceeding had not been seen or used in the time of his progenitors or predecessors, that they should have any answer to their petitions before they had shown and done all their business of parliament, whether it were matter of a grant or otherwise; the king would not in any way change the good customs and usages made and used of ancient times."[2] The effect of this peremptory refusal seems, however, to have been soon overcome by the practice which grew up shortly after that event of delaying the grant until the last day of the session, by which time all the more important petitions were probably disposed of.[3] The right to make supply depend upon redress was thus finally established by the employment of a simple yet potent expedient.

Finally the grant is withheld until the petitions are answered.

At a little later day in the same reign (9 Henry IV.) a collision took place between the two houses which gave rise to the earliest declaration of two principles of parliamentary law which have since become of primary importance : First, that all money bills shall originate in the house of commons; second, that the king shall not take notice of matters debated in parliament until after a conclusion is reached in both houses, and such conclusion brought before him by their consent and authority. After a debate by the lords in the presence of the king upon the state of the kingdom, the former undertook to specify what subsidies were necessary for the national defence. Whereupon the king requested the commons to send a committee to the lords to ascertain their views and to report the same to their house, "to the end that they

All money bills shall originate in the commons; king shall not take notice of matters debated in parliament pending the debate.

---

[1] Hallam, *M. A.*, vol. iii. p. 85.
[2] *Rot. Parl.*, iii. p. 458.

[3] This is the inference of Bishop Stubbs, *Const. Hist.*, vol. iii. p. 263.

might take the shortest course to comply with the intention of the said lords." A deputation of twelve from the commons then attended upon the lords and reported to their fellows. But when such report was received the lower house was not slow to manifest its alarm at the proceeding, "saying and affirming it to be much to the prejudice and derogation of their liberties." From the entry in the roll it appears that "after that our lord the king had heard this, not willing that anything should be done at present, or in time to come, that might anywise turn against the liberty of the estate for which they are come to parliament,[1] nor against the liberties of the lords, — wills and grants, and declares, by the advice and assent of the lords, in manner following : that it shall be lawful for the lords to commune amongst themselves in this present parliament, and in every other in time to come, in the absence of the king, of the state of the realm, and of the remedy necessary for the same. And that in like manner it shall be lawful for the commons, on their part, to commune together of the state and remedy aforesaid. Provided always that the lords on their part, and the commons on their part, shall not make any report to our said lord the king of any grant *by the commons granted, and by the lords assented to*, nor of the communications of the said grant, before the lords and commons shall be of one assent and one accord in such matters, and then in manner and form accustomed, that is to say, by the mouth of the speaker of the commons, in order that the lords and commons may have their will of our said lord the king." [2]

Right of the commons to regulate elections.

As all members of the house of commons were chosen under the writ directed to the sheriff of each county commanding him to return two knights from the shire, and two citizens or burgesses for each city or borough within his bailiwick, it came to be a matter of vital importance to the lower house to regulate by law both the procedure of the sheriff under the writ, and the qualification of the electors by whom the representative members were chosen. The conclusion has

---

[1] " The true position of the house of commons, as not being in itself an estate of the realm but the representative of the estate of the commons of England, is here expressed." — Taswell-Langmead, *Eng. Const. Hist.*, p. 313,

note 1. To the same effect, see above, p. 337 and note 3.

[2] *Rot. Parl.*, iii. p. 611 ; *Middle Ages*, vol. iii. pp. 100–102. See, also, *Lords' Report*, vol. i. pp. 358, 359.

heretofore been reached that from the beginning of the representative system the right to choose the elected knights was not limited to the lesser tenants-in-chief, but was vested in the whole body of freeholders assembled in the county court.[1] When in 1376 the commons, in order to prevent the malpractice of the sheriffs in returning members without due election, petitioned that the knights of the shire should be chosen by common election of *the better folk of the shires*, Edward III. answered that the knights should be chosen by the common assent of the whole county.[2] This declaration of what was no doubt the earlier custom [3] was first incorporated into a positive law when the statute of 7th Henry IV. c. 15 undertook to fix the franchise upon a definite and popular basis by providing "that at the next county (court) to be holden after the delivery of the writ, proclamation should be made, in full county (court), of the day and place of the parliament, and that all they that be there present, as well suitors duly summoned for the same cause as others, shall attend to the election of the knights for the parliament; and then, in full county, they shall proceed to the election, freely and indifferently, notwithstanding any request or command to the contrary." This statute, which recognized the fact that the franchise was vested not only in all freeholders but in the whole body of persons assembled in the county court on the day of the election, was seriously modified, however, by the statute of 8th Henry VI. c. 7, which is said to be the first disfranchising act to be found on the statute-books of England. This act, after complaining that the election of knights of the shire had lately been made " by very great, outrageous, and excessive number of people dwelling within the same counties, of the which most part was people of small substance and of no value," restricted the qualification of county electors not only to freeholders, but to such only as " have free land or tenement to the value of forty shillings by the year at least above all charges." The qualification of county electors, thus fixed at the end of the middle ages, remained

The franchise regulated by statute in 7th Henry IV.

The disfranchising statute of 8th Henry VI. c. 7.

---

[1] See above, pp. 467, 468.
[2] *Rot. Parl.*, ii. p. 355.
[3] As to the effect of this act as a declaration of the earlier custom, see Stubbs, *Const. Hist.*, vol. iii. p. 406 and

note. It has been contended, however, that the act of 1406 extended the suffrage. See Homersham Cox, *Ancient Parliamentary Elections*, p. 105.

The com-
mons regu-
late by law
the sheriff's
procedure
in elec-
tions.

unchanged until late in the first half of the present century. The omissions and commissions of which the sheriffs were guilty in the execution of the writs under which the representative members were chosen soon brought about legislation designed for their correction. In the 5th of Richard II. a statute was passed which provided that if any sheriff should fail to make return to a parliamentary writ, or should omit from such return any city or borough which had been formerly accustomed to send members to parliament, he should be punished by fine.[1] In the next reign this regulation was followed by the notable statute of 1406 (7th Henry IV. c. 15), made "on the grievous complaint of the commons of the undue election of the knights of shires for parliament," which provided that the election should be held in the first county court holden after the receipt of the writ ; that the election should be made in full county court by those present ; and that after the election the names of the persons chosen "shall be written in an indenture under the seals of them that did choose them."[2] Prior to this statute it was the duty of the sheriff to report to parliament the names of the elected members, together with the writ ; afterwards the return, which was declared to be the indenture tacked to the writ, was sent into chancery. A little later in the same reign (11th Henry IV. c. 1) an act was passed which gave to the justices of assize the power to inquire into the returns, and to fine the sheriffs for returning persons not duly elected. This measure was supplemented and rendered more effective by the act of 1445 (23d Henry IV. c. 14), to which reference has been made already.[3]

Right of
commons
to try con-
tested elec-
tions.

At a time when it was necessary for the crown to require security from the elected members for their appearance in parliament, it is hardly to be expected that we should find instances of contested elections in the sense in which that term is now understood. Such instances of disputed or contested elections as the mediæval records do contain clearly disclose the fact that the house of commons in the early days did not presume to claim for itself the right to

[1] 5th Richard II. st. ii. c. 4.
[2] See above, p. 472 and note 1. For specimens of these indentures, see Prynne, 2d Register, pp. 128–132.
[3] See above, p. 472.

determine contested elections ; that such right was originally Right origi-
nally vested
in the king
in council. claimed, and for a long time exercised, by the king with the aid of his council, or with the help of the lords. After the return was made the king, with the aid of the council or of the lords, took cognizance of all disputes which grew out of the election.[1] The earliest instance of the commons being associated with the consideration of such questions occurred in the 7th Richard II. (1384), when the borough of Shaftes-bury petitioned the king, lords, and commons, complained of a false return wherein the sheriff of Dorset had substituted the name of a person not elected, and prayed remedy.[2] Twenty years later (1404) the commons prayed the king and lords in parliament that an improper return, wherein the sheriff of Rutland had returned a person as elected who had not been elected, might be examined in parliament, and pun-ishment inflicted in the event the sheriff should be found guilty. The lords, after sending for the sheriff and the two contestants, and after due investigation, ordered the return to be amended by the substitution of the name of Thorp, the person really elected, in lieu of that of Ondeby, improperly returned by the sheriff, who, by reason of his misconduct, was removed from office.[3] Two years after this occurrence the act of 1406 was passed requiring the sheriff to make return by indenture, which, together with the writ, were sent into chancery. After the arbitrary power of the sheriffs was thus cut off by a regulation which virtually permitted the electors themselves to make the return, the act of 1410 was passed, which gave to the justices of assize the power to Justices of
assize given
power to in-
quire into
the return inquire into the returns, and to fine the sheriffs for returning persons not duly elected.[4] But even after the passage of this act placing the conduct of elections under the supervision of the justices of assize, it is probable that the ultimate right to pass upon the validity of the return remained to the king, assisted by the lords, or by the judges only. It seems to be clear that down to the end of the fifteenth century the com-mons had never thought of claiming the right to hear and determine all matters touching the validity of their own

[1] Cf. Stubbs, *Const. Hist.*, vol. iii. pp. 421–423.

[2] Prynne, 4th Register, p. 261 ; *Carew on Elections*, p. 118.

[3] *Rot. Parl.*, iii. p. 530; Hallam, *Middle Ages*, vol. iii. p. 110.

[4] See above, p. 528.

Right to
determine
validity of
election
first as-
serted by
the com-
mons in the
reign of
Elizabeth.
elections. In the reign of Elizabeth this right was for the first time distinctly asserted in a case in which the lower house ventured to examine into the circumstances attending an irregular election that had occurred in the county of Norfolk. Owing to some defect in the first return from that county, the chancellor had issued a second writ, under which a different member was chosen. Although the queen, after the matter had been noticed by the commons, directed the speaker to express her displeasure that "the house had been troubled with a thing impertinent for them to deal with, and only belonging to the charge and office of the lord chancellor," a committee was nevertheless appointed to investigate the matter, and a report was made in favor of the members elected under the first writ. In their report, which was agreed to by the whole house, the committee took occasion to say that "they had not thought it proper to inquire of the chancellor what he had done, because they thought it prejudicial to the privilege of the house to have the same determined by others than such as were members thereof."[1]

An important issue again arose between the crown and the commons when upon the accession of James I. a royal proclamation was issued which undertook to specify what kind of persons should be chosen, "bankrupts and outlaws" being specially excepted. Under the terms of the exception the clerk of the crown refused to receive the return of the election of Sir F. Goodwin, chosen for the county of Buckingham, for the reason that some years before he had been outlawed. A second writ was issued, under which Sir John Fortescue was chosen. When the matter was brought before the house the election of Goodwin was sustained, and he was ordered to take his seat. In the course of the controversy which followed, the king maintained not only that outlaws had no right to sit, but that the house had no right to meddle with returns which were made into the court of chancery, and which were within its exclusive jurisdiction. James further declared that "he had no purpose to impeach their privileges, but since they derived all matters of privilege from him, and by his grant, he expected that they should not be turned against him." He then invited the commons to confer with

[1] D'Ewes, *Journal*, p. 393; Hallam, *Const. Hist.*, vol. i. p. 275.

the judges, and upon their failure to do so he attempted to force them to confer by commanding them as an absolute king. Finally, as a compromise of the whole matter, the commons brought in a bill prohibiting outlaws from sitting in parliament in future, and as a personal favor to the king the elections of both Goodwin and Fortescue were set aside ; James admitting on his part, in an interview with a committee of the commons, that they were the proper judges of the returns.[1] From that time the commons never failed to assert their exclusive right to decide upon the legal validity of the returns, and the conduct of the returning officers in making them, — a right which was recognized and affirmed in turn by the house of lords, by the courts of law, and finally by an act of parliament (7 William III. c. 7) which declared that "the last determination of the house of commons concerning the right of elections is to be pursued." [2]

Leaving out of view the immunity from arrest which the peers enjoy, not merely as members of the upper house but as barons of the realm, a brief statement will be made of the origin of the right of freedom from personal molestation and legal arrest which, from the earliest times, has belonged to members of the English national assembly. From the very beginning of national councils in England, the persons of those who attended such assemblies were protected by law while going to and fro. By a law of Æthelberht, provision was made that "if the king called his 'leod' (people) to him (*i. e.* to the gemot) and any one there do them evil, let him compensate with a twofold 'bot' (satisfaction) and fifty shillings to the king." [3] This law, made at the end of the sixth century, was succeeded early in the eleventh by a law of Cnut, which provided "that every man be entitled to grith (freedom from molestation) to the gemot and from the gemot, except he be a notorious thief." [4] The same immunity was recognized in the laws of the Confessor in favor of persons going to and from the synods.[5] After the Conquest, the

Immunity of members of councils and parliaments from personal molestation.

Laws of Æthelberht, Cnut, and Eadward.

[1] *Commons Journal*, vol. i. pp. 149–169; *Parl. Hist.*, vol. i. pp. 993–1017; Gardiner, *Hist. of Eng.*, vol. i. pp. 185–188.
[2] See Taswell-Langmead, *Eng. Const. Hist.*, p. 341, citing *Barnardiston v. Soame*, 6 Howell St. Tr. 1092; *Ons-*

low's case, 2 Ventris, p. 37; *Prideaux v. Morris*, 2 Salkeld, p. 502.
[3] Æthelbert, § 1; *Select Charters*, p. 61; Kemble, *Saxons in England*, vol. ii. p. 33.
[4] Cnut, § 83; *Select Charters*, p. 74.
[5] Ll. Eadw. Conf., art. 2, cl. 8. Cf. Blackstone, *Comm.*, bk. i. p. 165.

persons who responded to the writs under which the parliaments were convened still retained without any fresh enactment the protection guaranteed by the earlier laws, — the sovereign who issued the writs placing under his protection, while going to and fro, the persons who obeyed them. This protection extended not only over the period occupied by the parliament, but, as was generally claimed, over a period of forty days before and after each session.[1] And it was held that this immunity extended not only to the members themselves, but to their servants. Such the privilege was declared to be by statute in the 5th Henry IV. c. 6, in the special case of Chedder, a member's servant beaten by one Savage, who was required to surrender in the king's bench, and in default to pay twofold damages to the party injured, besides the fine to the king.[2] By a general law passed in 11th Henry VI. c. 11, a penalty identical with that imposed by the law of Æthelred was fixed in all cases of affray or assault upon any member of either house coming to council or parliament under the king's command.[3]

Immunity extended to servants.

Stat. of 11th Henry VI.

The immunity from personal molestation thus enjoyed by the members and their servants was also held to exempt both, together with their property, from legal arrest, and distress in civil suits, during the period over which the privilege extended. When Edward I. was petitioned by the Master of the Temple for leave to distrain for rent of a house held of him by the Bishop of St. David's, he replied that "it does not seem fit that the king should grant that they who are of his council should be distrained in time of parliament."[4] And Edward II. in 1315 recognized the privilege by resenting the arrest of the Prior of Malton while on his way from parliament, not only as an offence to the prior, but as a breach of the king's peace and dignity.[5] But in spite of frequent prior recognitions, this privilege was openly violated in the famous case of Thomas Thorpe, speaker of the commons, who, during a prorogation of parliament, was in 1453 imprisoned on

Exemption from legal arrest and distress.

Cases of Bishop of St. David's and Prior of Malton.

Thorpe's case.

---

[1] For the authorities touching the duration of the privilege, see May, *Parl. Practice*, p. 139.

[2] *Statutes*, ii. p. 144; *Rot. Parl.*, iii. p. 542.

[3] *Statutes*, ii. p. 286; *Rot. Parl.*, iv. p. 453.

[4] *Rot. Parl.*, i. p. 61. See, also, Coke, 4th *Inst.*, 24 E; Hatsell, *Precedents*, i. p. 3.

[5] Hatsell, *Precedents*, i. p. 12.

an execution issued out of the exchequer for the non-payment of a fine due the king for a trespass committed in the seizure of certain property belonging to the Duke of York. When the commons complained to the king and lords, and demanded the release of their speaker, the judges were consulted, and they, after protesting that "the determination and knowlegge of that Privelegge belongeth to the Lordes of the Parlement, and not to the Justices," nevertheless took occasion to assert that "if any persone that is a membre of this high Court of Parlement be arested in suche cases as be not for treason or felony, or suerte of the peas, or for a condempnation hadde before the Parlement, it is used that all such persones shuld be relessed of such arrestes, and make an Attourney, so that they may have theire fredom and libertee frely to entende upon the Parlement." In spite, however, of the opinion of the judges, the lords — influenced no doubt by the fact that Thorpe was an enemy of the Duke of York, who was then dominant — held that notwithstanding his privilege he should remain in prison ; and the commons were directed in the king's name to proceed to the election of a new speaker, which they did the next day.[1]

The practical difficulty under which the commons labored, and which the case of Thorpe disclosed, was that, although the right to freedom from arrest had been established by the highest legal authority, the house itself possessed no independent means for its enforcement. Not until the middle of the sixteenth century did the commons ever attempt to deliver a member out of custody by virtue of their own unaided authority. Prior to that time, when "members were in execution, in order to save the rights of the plaintiff, they obtained special statutes to authorize the lord chancellor to issue writs for their release ; and when confined on mesne process only, they were delivered by a writ of privilege issued by the lord chancellor." [2] In 1543 the commons first asserted their right to release a member by their own authority in the case of Ferrers, a member held in custody in a civil suit

Authority of the mace.

Writs of privilege at first issued by the lord chancellor.

Ferrers' case.

---

[1] *Rot. Parl.*, v. pp. 239, 240. It was afterwards said in parliament that this case was "begotten by the iniquity of the times." — *Commons Journal*, i. p. 546.

[2] May, *Parl. Practice*, p. 130, citing cases of Larke, Clerk, Hyde, and Atwyll; *Rot. Parl.*, iv. p. 357; Ibid., v. p. 374; Ibid., vi. pp. 160, 191; Sadcliff's case, Hatsell, *Precedents*, i. p. 51.

under a writ issued from the king's bench. When the house, hearing of the arrest, sent their sergeant to demand the release of the member, he was at first resisted by the jailers and sheriffs of London, but when the sergeant was sent a second time the prisoner was promptly surrendered. As a vindication of its dignity, the house committed for contempt not only the jailers and sheriffs, but even the plaintiff in the suit. When these energetic measures were reported to the king, he earnestly commended the action of the commons in the presence of the judges, the speaker, and other leading members of the house; and, when he had finished, his views were confirmed by the lord chief justice.[1] Although after that time members were released by writs of privilege when obtained by the permission or warrant of the speaker, the case of Ferrers may be regarded as establishing the right of the commons to release a member from custody by the war-

The privilege as defined by statute in 1770.

rant of the mace alone. The privilege in its widest form, giving rise to many abuses, was restricted from time to time by statute,[2] until at last, in 1770, an act[3] was passed by which it was reduced to its ancient limits; that is to say, freedom from arrest was guaranteed to the persons of members only, their servants and their property being left subject to ordinary legal procedure. At no time was the privilege ever allowed to interfere with the administration of criminal justice, — imprisonment for treason, felony, or for security of the peace at all times being excepted from its operation.[4]

Right of conference with the lords.

In the parliament of 1402 the commons made a fresh and formal demand for the exercise of a privilege which had no doubt existed in some form from the very organization of the parliamentary system, — the privilege of conferring with the lords upon all pending questions of importance which called for concurrent action. Although the lords claimed that it

[1] This case rests upon the authority of Holinshed (i. p. 824), and not upon parliamentary records. As to the accuracy of the account, see May, *Parl. Practice*, p. 132.

[2] 12 & 13 Will. III. c. 3; 2 & 3 Anne, c. 18; 11 Geo. II. c. 24.

[3] 10 Geo. III. c. 50. It has been held that the arrest of a member is irregular *ab initio*, and that he may be discharged immediately upon motion in the court from which the process is-

sued. See Colonel Pitt's case, Strange, vol. ii. p. 985.

[4] As to the limits of privilege in case of open contempt of a court of justice, see May, *Parl. Practice*, p. 160. In the case referred to, Cockburn, C. J., after fining two members for contempt in connection with the "Tichborne Case," said if he had seen fit to commit them, he would not have been restrained by privilege.

was the duty of the commons to debate among themselves and then to report their views to them, and although the commons often claimed the right when a conference was to be had of selecting the lords with whom they were to confer, the usual course seems to have been for each body to appoint a committee to confer with a similar committee from the other, and then after consultation each committee reported the result to its own house. In 1373 the first instance occurs of the commons requesting the lords to appoint a select body to confer with them.[1] In 1383 the commons renew the request for a committee of conference from the lords, and couple with it the request that they be allowed to elect the lords of whom the committee should be composed. Richard II., in yielding to the request as a matter of grace, was careful to assert that the right of selection claimed belonged, not to the commons, but to the king himself.[2] When, in the parliament of 1402, the commons demanded of Henry IV. the right to confer with a select committee from the lords touching certain important matters he had given them in charge, he yielded to the request, but with the express statement that he did so as a matter of favor and not as a matter of right.[3]

3. The effort made in the preceding chapter to outline the history of parliament during the fourteenth century concluded with the statement that its authority reached the limit of its growth when, after a struggle of scarcely two months' duration, it deposed the ruling sovereign in the person of Richard II., and then, after ignoring the claimant who really represented the hereditary title, awarded the crown to another member of the royal house whom it deemed more competent to govern.[4] After Henry of Lancaster had stood forth in the assembly of estates at Westminster Hall, and had challenged and claimed the kingdom of England and the crown thereof, by reason of conquest, inheritance, and Richard's resignation,[5] the estates there assembled were con-

The house of Lancaster.

---

[1] *Rot. Parl.*, ii. p. 317.
[2] Ibid., iii. p. 145; Hallam, *M. A.*, vol. iii. p. 66.
[3] *Rot. Parl.*, iii. p. 486. Cf. Stubbs, *Const. Hist.*, vol. ii. pp. 426, 465, 593; vol. iii. pp. 37, 457. As to the modern practice when conferences occur be-

tween the houses, see May, *Parl. Practice*, pp. 490–496.
[4] See above, p. 514.
[5] These are the three grounds as stated by Froissart, iv c. 116. Henry rose in the assembly and stated his own claim in English, as follows : " In

sulted, singly and collectively, as to what they thought of such claim; "and thereupon the lords spiritual and temporal, and all the states, with the people, consented that the duke should reign over them."[1] And so while Henry as the leader of the counter-revolution through which the change of dynasty was brought about, was careful to put forward every claim but the true one, the estates, by whose united action the revolution was made effective, were equally careful to make it the occasion for the assertion of a constitutional principle which became the corner-stone upon which the throne of the new dynasty was erected. Although Henry challenged the crown by a threefold claim of title, which carefully excluded the theory of election, his confused assertion of right could not conceal the fact that he was the mere creature of a parliamentary revolution, that he was destined to reign by

Its right to rule based upon a parliamentary title. virtue of a parliamentary title. In spite of all disguises the fact stood out that from his election by the assembly of estates Henry derived the right to reign, and in his first parliament the new sovereign was careful to admit his real constitutional status by declaring through the mouth of Archbishop Arundel that he did not desire to be governed by his own will and purpose, but by the common advice, counsel, and consent of the wise and ancient of the kingdom.[2] The victory which the assembly of estates thus won over the

The succession four times regulated by parliament during the reign of Henry IV. monarchy was emphasized upon four different occasions during Henry's reign when the parliament saw fit to regulate and limit the succession to the crown which their election had bestowed. In the first parliament, which met on the 6th of October, 1399,[3] the Prince of Wales, with the assent of

---

the name of Father, Son, and Holy Ghost, I, Henry of Lancaster, challenge this realm of England and the crown, with all the members and the appurtenances, as that I am descended by right line of blood, coming from the good lord King Henry Third, and through that right that God of his grace hath sent me with help of my kin and of my friends to recover it, the which realm was in point to be undone for default of governance and undoing of the good laws." — *Rot. Parl.*, iii. pp. 422, 423. See also *Ann. Ric.*, p. 281; *Mon. Eves.*, p. 209. The substance of the statement is the same in the several versions.

[1] *Lord's Report*, vol. i. p. 349. The Report goes on to say: "It is to be collected from the language of the roll, that this general acclamation was considered as having made the Duke of Lancaster king."

[2] *Rot. Parl.*, iii. p. 415.

[3] This parliament, which had deposed Richard II. on the 30th of September, and which was supposed to be dissolved by his deposition, was reassembled under the new king's writs on the 6th of October. As to the short notice, see *Rot. Parl.*, iii. p. 423; as to the writs, see *Lords' Report*, vol. iv. p. 768.

the lords spiritual and temporal, and all the commons, was "created and ordained heir apparent, to have and enjoy the realm in time to come when God it should will."[1] Four years later the succession was limited to the prince and the heirs of his body, and in default upon his brothers in the order of seniority.[2] In 1406 the crowns of England and France were resettled upon the king and the heirs *male* of his body.[3] In the same year, however, this restriction was removed, and the crown finally settled upon Henry and the heirs of his body without limitation.[4] In thus accepting the crown for himself and his descendants through the choice of the three estates, Henry was not only compelled to assume a relation of dependence upon the parliament as a whole, but he was also obliged to enter into special obligations to each estate separately, from which he found release only in the grave.

While the parliament was careful to require that the new sovereign should reign as a constitutional king, the prelates, as the special defenders of the national church, were no less careful to demand that he should become the champion of orthodoxy, and the scourger of the growing heresy. The canon law, the ecclesiastical law of mediæval Europe, regarded heresy as a crime; and while the church undertook to visit the offence with such spiritual penalties as excommunication, it also looked to the state to supplement its work by the infliction of civil penalties in the form of imprisonment and capital punishment. Such a conception of heresy and its punishment seems to have been imbedded from the earliest times in the civil and ecclesiastical law of the English kingdom. Prior to the enactment of the statutes against heresy, although an English bishop could excommunicate, the offender could not be put into prison save by the king's writ of *de excommunicato capiendo;*[5] and although heresy was an offence punishable by death, the heretic could only be burned, if at all, by virtue of the writ *de hæretico comburendo.*[6] The scantiness of material illustrative of the earlier

Henry IV. and the church: the statutes against heresy.

State of the law prior to the statutes.

---

[1] *Rot. Parl.*, iii. p. 434.
[2] Ibid., iii. pp. 525, 575.
[3] Ibid., iii. pp. 575, 576.
[4] Ibid., iii. p. 581.
[5] As to the nature of this writ, some-

times called, from the bishop's certificate, "significavit," see Blackstone, *Comm.*, bk. iii. p. 102.

[6] "We find among our ancient precedents a writ *de hæretico comburendo,*

practice can be easily accounted for in light of the fact that the English mediæval church, down to the close of the fourteenth century, was exceptionally free from heresy and consequent religious persecution. Not until after the advent of Wycliffe — out of whose teachings grew the host of dissenters from the orthodox creed of the ancient church generally known as Lollards — was the machinery for the suppression of heresy in England put into active operation. During the period of reaction that followed the Peasant Revolt, which the disciples of Wycliffe were supposed to have instigated, the first appeal was made to parliament for the suppression of heresy by statute. In the parliament which met in May, 1382, Archbishop Courtenay procured the enactment of a statute which provided that commissions should issue out of chancery, directed to the sheriffs and other officers in pursuance of certificates from the bishops, to arrest all persons certified by the bishops to be preachers of heresy, and their abettors, and to hold them in prison until they should justify themselves "according to reason and the law of holy church."[1] But in the parliament which met in October of the same year, the commons petitioned that this statute should be annulled, for the reason that it had never received their assent; and the king returned a favorable answer to their petition.[2] After that event the prelates possessed no means for the punishment of heresy save such as were contained in the old canon law process. Thus the law stood at the time of Wycliffe's death in 1384. The death of the great schoolman and pamphleteer did nothing, however, to check the spread of the new doctrines which he had propounded not only to the learned in the universities, but to the rank and file of the English people. So widespread and threaten-

Marginal notes:

Wycliffe and the Lollards.

Statute of 1382 to which the commons did not assent.

Wycliffe died in 1384.

which is thought by some to be as ancient as the common law itself." — Blackstone, *Comm.*, bk. iv. p. 46. As to this statement Bishop Stubbs says: "Although Blackstone declares that a writ of the kind is found among our ancient precedents, and refers to Fitz Herbert, *Natura Brevium*, p. 269, the only example of the writ given there is the writ in Sawtre's case." — *Const. Hist.*, vol. iii. p. 358, note 4. Sawtre was the first of the Lollards executed for heresy in England. He was ex-ecuted by virtue of the king's writ, and not under the statutes.

[1] Stat. 5 Ric. II. st. 2, c. 5; *Statutes*, ii. p. 25.

[2] *Rot. Parl.*, iii. p. 141. In the statute the assent of the lords and commons is not expressed. Hallam says, "Nevertheless, the pretended statute was untouched, and remains still among our laws, unrepealed, except by desuetude, and by inference from the acts of much later times." — *Middle Ages*, vol. iii. p. 87.

ing had the religious revolt become by the end of the reign of Richard II., that Archbishop Arundel, the bitter foe of the Lollards, in supporting the revolution through which Henry IV. was raised to the throne, was careful to commit the new sovereign to a policy of active persecution. In 1399 a convocation was held in which articles denouncing the Lollard doctrines were drawn up,[1] and in 1401 Arundel procured the passage of the famous statute *De hæretico comburendo*,[2] in which it was provided that no one should presume to preach or teach, in public or private, in any diocese, without the license of the diocesan first obtained, except curates in their churches; that no one should write any book or teach in any school or conventicle the new doctrines; and that all who possessed forbidden books or writings should in a given time deliver them up. All offenders against the act the bishops were permitted to arrest and detain in their prisons until they should make canonical purgation, or abjure their opinions; and if convicted they should be imprisoned and fined in proportion to their offence. If after conviction the offender should refuse to abjure, or after abjuration should relapse, the sheriff of the county, or the mayor or bailiff of the nearest borough should, when required by the diocesan, be present at the sentence; and after it was pronounced it became his duty to receive the condemned, and before the people in a high place cause him to be burned as an example and terror to others. The practical effect of this act was to confer upon the bishop the power to try and convict one accused of heresy, without the assent of a synod, and the further power to require the sheriff to burn the condemned without the consent of the crown.[3] And yet, comprehensive and cruel as were the powers thus bestowed, another statute still more comprehensive and cruel was yet to come. In the midst of the excitement and alarm which followed the attempted insurrection of the Lollards under the leadership of Sir John Oldcastle, a statute[4] was passed in the second year of Henry V. which naturally divides itself into two parts. The first part, after repeating in substance the provisions of

The statute De hæretico comburendo, 1401.

The final and most cruel statute passed in the 2d of Henry V.

---

[1] Wilkins, *Conc.*, iii. p. 238 *seq.*

[2] 2 Hen. IV. c. 15; *Statutes*, ii. p. 125.

[3] As to the tenor of the act, see

Reeves, *Hist. of Eng. Law*, vol. iii. pp. 425–428.

[4] 2 Hen. V. st. i. c. 7; *Statutes*, ii. pp. 181 *seq.*

the act of 1401, added to the penalties to which the Lollards were previously liable by providing that those who should be convicted before the ordinaries, and delivered over to the secular power, should forfeit lands, goods, and chattels, substantially as in case of felony. The second part of the act entered a new field by providing that justices of the king's bench, of the peace, and of assize are now empowered to inquire (that is, take indictments) of heretics and their maintainers, and to award process for their arrest. Within ten days after arrest the accused were to be delivered to the ordinary by indenture for trial in the church courts.[1]   Under and by virtue of this final statute against the Lollards took place most of the fanatical executions which disgrace the records of the fifteenth and sixteenth centuries.

Henry IV. and the commons.

The conclusion has been heretofore reached that by the end of the fourteenth century the commons had not only won the right to participate in all the higher functions of government, but that they had become the more active and aggressive force in the national council reconstituted as an assembly of estates.[2]   During the first thirteen years of the fifteenth century, occupied by the reign of Henry IV., the rising influence of the commons reached the highest point of its mediæval growth, a point which it did not again reach until after the lapse of two hundred years.   Although the commons, as an estate of the realm, assented in the parliament of 1399 that the Duke of Lancaster should reign over the kingdom, it was less from the fact of their participation in the election of the new sovereign than from their right to

Their growing influence based upon the money power.

assent or dissent when grants of money were asked that their influence throughout the reign was made effective.   The new king was poor, and the demands upon him for money were great.   In this condition of things the commons were not slow to perceive their opportunity.   As early as the parliament of 1401 the lower house, taking advantage of the king's necessities, began to insist upon a clear and final concession of the constitutional principle that the grant of supplies should be preceded by answers from the crown to petitions for the redress of grievances.   Although this de-

---

[1] Cf. Reeves, *Hist. Eng. Law,* vol.   [2] See above, pp. 500–504.
iii. pp. 452, 453.

mand was met by a peremptory refusal, the effect of the refusal was soon overcome by the practice which grew up shortly after that event of delaying the grant until the last day of the session, by which time all the more important petitions were probably disposed of.   The right to make supply depend upon redress was thus secured by the employment upon the part of the commons of a simple yet irresistible expedient.[1]   Six years later (1407) a collision occurred between the two houses that led to a declaration on the part of the crown which " seems to have placed the king and the two houses of parliament each in the separate and independent situation in which they now respectively stand."[2]   The outcome of this collision, which has been heretofore considered at length, was the definition of the two vital principles of constitutional law which declare, first, that all money bills shall originate in the house of commons ; second, that the king shall not take notice of matters debated in parliament until after a conclusion has been reached in each house, and such conclusion brought before him by their consent and authority.[3]   And yet, in spite of the serious encroachments which the parliament thus made upon the monarchy under the new dynasty, Henry IV. was bold enough to declare in 1411, when a quarrel arose with the commons over some measure that had passed in the preceding parliament, that he intended to enjoy all the liberties and prerogatives which had ever belonged to any of his predecessors.[4]

The right to make supply depend upon redress finally established.

Two vitally important principles of constitutional law defined in 1407.

4. Some account must now be given of the growth of the continual council which during the reigns of the Lancastrian kings comes prominently into view, not simply as a dependent body of councillors who assist the king in conducting the executive business of the kingdom, but rather as a distinct corporate entity, which stands midway between the king and the parliament, through which the latter is able to limit and control the exercise of the royal authority.   In order to execute the mass of fiscal, judicial, and administrative work which the growth of the royal power after the Conquest concentrated around the person of the king, it became necessary to organize out of the great council a smaller body composed

The continual council

---

[1] See above, pp. 524, 525.   [3] See above, pp. 525, 526.
[2] *Lords' Report*, vol. i. p. 359.   [4] *Rot. Parl.*, iii. p. 658.

of the king's immediate officers and advisers, who were charged, under the king's direction, with the whole work of central or national administration. From the existing evidence as to the relation of the two bodies to each other, which is vague and shadowy in the extreme, the conclusion has been heretofore reached that the lesser or continual council stood to the greater as a *concilium in concilio;* or, in modern language, that the lesser council was a standing committee of the greater body.[1] The continual or "permanent council under the early Norman kings consisted of the great officers of state, — the chancellor, the great justiciary, the lord treasurer, the lord steward, the chamberlain, the earl marshal, the constable, and any other persons whom the king chose to appoint; and of the two archbishops, who claimed a right to form a part of every council, public or private."[2] This group of councillors, whom the Norman kings frequently changed, appears as a definitely organized governing body when, upon the accession of the child king Henry III., it became necessary for the first time after the Conquest to form a council of regency for the government of the state. From that time it is possible to trace the existence of a permanent royal council composed of the king's personal advisers, who constitute a resident governing body for the dispatch of public business, separate and apart from the greater body known as the common council of the kingdom. As the regent and other great officers of state who composed the permanent council during the minority of Henry III. were chosen by the great council, it is probable that from that time can be traced the beginnings of the constitutional doctrine that the king can do no wrong, and that the ministers who advise him are responsible to the assembled representatives of the nation who have a consultative voice in their appointment.[3] So firmly did the idea that the royal authority should be wielded with the advice of an organized and responsible body of state officials become established during the earlier part of the reign of Henry III. that, when he attempted after his emancipation to enforce his personal rule with the aid of foreign favorites and dependent clerks, the baronage resented the attempt by an open appeal

Margin notes:

A standing committee of the greater body.

Can be traced as a definitely organized body from the minority of Henry III.

Beginnings of the doctrine of ministerial responsibility.

---

[1] See above, pp. 242–245, 438.
[2] Dicey, *The Privy Council,* p. 7.
[3] See above, pp. 396, 397.

to arms. One of the leading concessions which Henry was required to make, after he had surrendered himself to the baronage under the lead of Leicester and Gloucester, was that a committee of fifteen, under the control of the parliament, should advise him in all ordinary matters of government.[1] During the reigns which follow, the principle that the royal power could thus be limited and controlled by the action of the council, and that the council itself could be controlled by the parliament, was brought into requisition whenever a weak or wayward king rendered its assertion necessary and expedient. Although the authority of the council, as a limitation upon the royal prerogative, naturally waned in the presence of so great a king as Edward I., even Edward seems to have recognized its existence as a part of the general political scheme,[2] and in his day it became more definitely organized as the constitutional centre of the highest state government.[3]

Growth of the doctrine that the crown should be controlled by the council, and the council by the parliament.

After the parliament had established its right to enact all the more important and permanent acts of national legislation, and after the three law courts, and the court of the chancellor, had won the right to hear and determine all ordinary litigation, a mass of legislative and judicial work still remained to the council in addition to its executive business.

General scope of the council's duties.

1. The residuary right of legislation, which remained to the king after the establishment of the parliamentary system, is generally known as the ordaining power of the king in council. It was a part of the duty of the council to advise the king whenever the issuance of an ordinance became necessary.

Its legislative functions.

2. In like manner it was the duty of the council to advise the king in the exercise of the extraordinary judicial powers which remained to the crown after the complete organization of the great courts of law and equity. Such authority was exercised either by the issuance of special commissions of "oyer and terminer," or by the direct decision of knotty cases by the king in council.

Its judicial functions.

3. Although the council was thus called upon to discharge

---

[1] See above, p. 401.
[2] Stubbs, *Const. Hist.*, vol. ii. p. 258.
[3] See Gneist, *The Eng. Parliament*, p. 115 (Shee's trans.).

Its executive functions.

both legislative and judicial duties, the fact remains that it was primarily an executive body charged with the duty of carrying out, at home and abroad, the diplomatic, financial, and military work which devolved upon the king as chief executive. As an administrative body it became the duty of the council to pass upon the vital questions of war and peace, and to make treaties with foreign nations; to manage the finances by providing the best means to raise revenue, and at the same time by looking after the method of their expenditure; to summons the feudal army and county militia, and to provide means for the maintenance of paid armies; to control aliens, and at the same time to a certain extent to regulate trade; and to preserve the king's peace by the assertion of the royal authority whenever the ordinary process of law proved inadequate. In addition to these duties the council was also called upon to pass upon a mass of miscellaneous business brought before it by petitions in which complaints were made of all such abuses as naturally arose out of an imperfect and inadequate system of judicial and financial administration.[1]

The council during the reigns of Edward II. and Richard II.

During the weak and troubled reigns of Edward II. and Richard II. the council was again employed, as in the days of Henry III., as an intermediary body through which the parliament at one time supersedes, at another limits and controls, the exercise of the royal prerogative. When in 1310–1311 Edward provoked a conflict with the nation by putting himself in the hands of the favorite Piers Gaveston, the royal power was for a time practically transferred to a committee of prelates and barons called the Ordainers, who provided, in a scheme of reform which they devised for the future government of the realm, that the king should appoint the great officers of state only with the counsel and consent of the baronage, and that all such officials should be sworn in parliament.[2] When in 1386 a serious breach occurred between the parliament and Richard II. upon the demand of the for-

---

[1] A definite idea of the extent and variety of business which came before the council can only be formed by a study of the minutes of the council itself. As illustrations, see *Proceedings of Privy Council*, i. 128, 289; ii. 165, 167, 168; iii. 115, 210, 355; iv. 76, 114, 281; v. 35, 173, 191, 290; vi. 40–45, 66, 67, 68. See, also, Dicey, *The Privy Council*, pp. 49–68; and Palgrave, *Authority of the King's Council*.

[2] See above, p. 499.

mer that certain offensive ministers should be removed from
office, the king was at last compelled not only to yield to that
demand, but also to submit to a practical transfer of the royal
power to a committee with Gloucester at its head.   This
committee, which was to hold office for one year, was not only
empowered to regulate the royal household, but also to undertake the reform of the entire administration of the kingdom.[1]

After the accession of Henry IV. the estates were not
slow to reassert the principle that the exercise of the royal
authority should be limited and controlled by the action of
the council, and that the council itself should be controlled
by the parliament.   It is not the baronage, however, as in
the days of Henry III., Edward II., and Richard II., who
take the initiative, but the commons, who now appear as the
more aggressive element, which demands that the executive
government shall be conducted in accordance with the views
of the national assembly.   In the parliament of 1404 the
commons ventured not only to attack the organization of the
royal household, but also to request the king to appoint in
parliament the servants who were to compose his great and
continual council, a request which was promptly complied
with.[2]   Two years later, after the selection of a council under
like circumstances, the commons informed the king that their
motive in making the grant then asked was not only their
fear of God and their love for him, but "the great confidence
which they had in the lords elected and ordained to be of the
continual council."[3]   Passing over the reign of Henry V.,
during which the absence of conflict between the crown and
the parliament rendered the restraining power of the council
unnecessary, a period is reached during which the council attained its highest point of activity and authority.   The minority of Henry VI. threw the executive government into the
hands of a council which derived its existence, not from royal
nomination, but from parliamentary election.[4]   The council of regency thus organized at once assumed a position of

The council after the accession of Henry IV.

Commons request in 1404 that the members of the council be appointed in parliament.

The council thus appointed upon the accession of Henry VI.

---

[1] *Rot. Parl.*, iii. p. 221; *Statutes*, ii.
pp. 39–43. The commission issued to
the committee of reform in November
was turned into a statute dated 1st December.

[2] *Rot. Parl.*, iii. pp. 525, 526, 530.
[3] Ibid., iii. p. 568.
[4] *Lords' Report*, vol. i. p. 368.

commanding importance,—an importance not unfettered, however, by restraints imposed by the power that created it. The parliament, not content with controlling the nomination of the councillors, claimed the further right to regulate their procedure by the imposition of rules and regulations which they were bound by oaths [1] to obey. A series of regulations of this character, beginning with the reign of Edward I., reappears in an improved form in the parliament rolls for 1406, 1424, and 1430,[2] as well as in the records of the privy council itself. In addition to the restraints imposed by such regulations, the parliament also retained in its hands the right to regulate the pay of the councillors. As early as the reign of Richard II., there existed a body of regularly paid and sworn councillors; during the reign of Henry IV. the commons pray that the lords of the council be suitably rewarded;[3] and during the minority of Henry VI. their pay was regulated by a scale which guaranteed to each member a fixed sum according to his rank or dignity.[4] During the period last named, it is possible to distinguish the sworn and paid councillors, who attend regularly to the king's business, from the main body of the council, which, upon special occasions, also embraced the judges and justices, and such other advisers as the king might see fit to specially summon. The sworn and paid councillors who thus devoted themselves regularly to the king's business began to be known, during the reign of Henry VI., as the "privy council,"—the private or inner circle of the greater body generally known as the "ordinary council," or simply as "the council." Or, to express the distinction in the words of one who has made the history of the privy council the subject of special investigation: "The minority of Henry VI., by flinging the whole government into the hands of the sworn councillors, must have rendered the distinction between the habitual members of the council

Parliament imposes regulations upon the council and fixes the pay of its members.

The sworn and paid councillors come to be known as the "privy council," during the reign of Henry VI.

---

[1] Steph., *Comm.*, vol. ii. (8th ed.), p. 460.

[2] "Those of 1406 were enacted in parliament and enrolled as an act; those of 1424 were contained in a schedule annexed to the act of nomination; those of 1430 were drawn up in the council itself, approved by the lords, and read in the presence of the three estates, after which they were subscribed by the councillors." — Stubbs, *Const. Hist.*, vol. iii. p. 251, citing *Rot. Parl.*, iii. pp. 585-589; iv. p. 201 *seq.*, 343, 344; *Ordinances*, i. p. 297; iii. p. 148-152; iv. 59-66.

[3] *Rot. Parl.*, iii. p. 577.

[4] *Proceedings of the Privy Council*, iii., Preface xix., and p. 154; *Rot. Parl.*, iv. p. 374.

and those, whether nobles, lawyers, or others, who were only
occasionally summoned, much more marked. . . . It is,
therefore, sufficiently apparent that under Henry VI. a select
council was gradually arising from the midst of the general
council; that a change was taking place precisely analogous
to the process by which, in a later age, the privy council itself
gave birth to the cabinet." [1]   Having traced the growth of
the council, viewed as a restraining influence upon the royal
authority, down to that point in its history at which the separate existence of the inner circle known as the "privy council" distinctly appears, its further consideration will be post
poned until it can be hereafter viewed in the new aspect
which it assumes as an irresponsible engine of tyranny in the
hands of the York and Tudor kings.

5. While the absence of conflict between the crown and
the parliament during the reign of Henry V. obscures for a
time the history of the council as a restraining influence
upon the royal prerogative, the vigorous revival of the French
war which followed Henry's accession brings the council as
an administrative body into fresh prominence as the active
agent of the executive power.   The minutes of a meeting of
the council held in May, 1415, reveal through the mass of
business then pending the full scope of its activity.   From
the consideration of matters touching an alliance with the
Duke of Burgundy, the council passes in turn to questions of
finance, matters of police, measures for the suppression of
the Lollards, and, last and most important of all, to provisions
for national defence through the issuance of commissions of
array, and orders for the equipment of the army and the
fleet. [2]   At this point the account heretofore given of the
mediæval system of military organization [3] may be conveniently supplemented by a brief summary of the history of
the admiralty.

Origin of the admiralty.

The office of admiral, which finds its origin upon the shores
of the Mediterranean, whence it was transferred to the North
European countries by the returning crusaders, seems to

Office of admiral.

---

[1] Dicey, *The Privy Council*, pp. 44,
45.   The same author says (p. 43),
"Reasonable doubts may be enter-
tained whether, prior to Henry VI. the

'Privy' and 'Ordinary' council were
in any sense distinct bodies."
[2] *Proceedings of the Privy Council*,
ii. p. 167.
[3] See above, p. 296.

have made its first appearance in England when, in the year 1286, Edward I. appointed William Leyburne captain of all the portmen and mariners of his dominions under the title of *Admiral de la mer du Roy d'Angleterre.* In 1306, from which time there is an uninterrupted succession of admirals, Edward Charles appears as captain and admiral from the mouth of the Thames northward; and Gervase Allard as captain and admiral of the fleet of the Cinque Ports and of all other ports from Dover westward.[1] This division of the maritime jurisdiction between two admirals of the North and West continued down to 1360, when a single high admiral of England was appointed in the person of Sir John Beauchamp. During the remainder of the mediæval period the office of admiral is at one time divided, at another reunited in a single person.[2]

Beginnings of the navy.

The obscurity which conceals the early history of the admiralty renders it alike difficult to ascertain how the national fleets were at first constituted, and how the sovereignty of the sea was practically secured to the king as lord thereof against the claims of the privileged seaport towns, and of private individuals who carried on sea adventures of a semi-piratical character.   The beginnings of the English navy can be faintly traced in the fleets which were raised in the latter part of the pre-Norman period for the protection of the kingdom against the incursions of the Danes.   Under the scheme then employed each shire was required to furnish ships in proportion to the number of its hundreds, — an arrangement which applied to the inland shires as well as to those on the seaboard.   Each shire sent its quota of ships to the fleet, as it sent its quota of fighting men to the host.[3]   This primitive system, which did not long survive the Norman conquest, was succeeded after that event by a new arrangement based upon different principles.   In order to supply the lack of a regular navy, and to protect the southern seaboard against attack, the Conqueror incorporated the Cinque Ports and endowed them with certain special privileges,[4] upon condition

Old-English fleets.

The Conqueror and the Cinque Ports.

---

[1] *Fœdera,* i. p. 990.

[2] A full statement may be found in Rowsell's article entitled "Admiral," in *Enc. Brit.,* 9th ed. vol. i. pp. 155, 156.

[3] See above, p. 187 and note 2. As to the history of the Old-English fleets, see *Norman Conquest,* vol. i. pp. 226–230.

[4] From the time of the Conquest the

that they would furnish a given number of ships and men for so many days in case of an emergency. The naval force thus contributed by the privileged towns for local defence was augmented, when the crusades created a necessity for a large number of ships for foreign expeditions, by fleets of mercenaries, which were maintained, like the mercenary element in the army, out of the royal exchequer. In the naval force of mercenaries thus raised and maintained out of the royal revenue the permanent fleet finds its origin.[1] The organization and government of the fleet, thus dependent upon the king's bounty, devolved during the mediæval period upon the admiral, the king's lieutenant and highest naval representative.

Origin of the permanent fleet.

In addition to his position as the executive head of the naval administration, the admiral was also the president of a sovereign court — the high court of admiralty — in which he sat in person or by deputy to assert the king's lordship over the seas, and to hear and determine all maritime causes arising outside of the limits of any county, that is, beyond the reach of the common law tribunals. The code of sea laws, which defined the jurisdiction and regulated the procedure of this high prerogative court, consisted of a collection of the usages of the sea, which during the mediæval period acquired, through the consent of the maritime nations, the force of customary law. Through the fame acquired by the judgments of a maritime court of the island of Oléron, in which were defined the sea usages of the Atlantic, such usages came to be known as the " Laws of Oléron."[2] It is probable that a record of these judgments was brought into England and published as law by Richard I. upon his return from the Holy Land.[3] Certain it is that the earliest collection of such usages and judgments of the sea received in England is described in the Black Book of the Admiralty as the " Laws of Oléron;" and the earliest known text is contained in the

The admiral as the president of the high court of admiralty.

Code of sea laws which defined its jurisdiction.

Laws of Oléron.

Cinque Ports are found in the possession of many special privileges. See Samuel Jeake, *Charters of the Cinque Ports*, London, 1728.

[1] "The permanent fleet then was, from its very origin, a fleet of mercenaries, and was maintained from the royal revenue, just as a band of Brabançons might have been. . . . John's naval ar-

mament was organized on this plan." — Stubbs, *Const. Hist.*, vol. i. p. 594.

[2] As to the cause which brought about the collection of the judgments of the maritime court of Oléron, see Cleirac's introduction to his work on *Les Us et Coustumes de la Mer*, first printed in Bordeaux in 1647.

[3] Such is the statement of Cleirac.

Liber Memorandorum, contained in the archives of the Guild-hall of the corporation of London.[1]   So marked did the tendency of the admiralty jurisdiction which grew out of the enforcement of these sea laws to encroach upon the domain of the common law tribunals become, that it became necessary as early as the reign of Richard II. to check its advance by very stringent legislation.   The statute of the 13 Richard II., after reciting in the preamble that "a great and common clamour and complaint hath been oftentimes made before this time, and yet is, for that the admirals and their deputies hold their sessions within divers places of this realm, as well within the franchise as without, accroaching to them greater authority than belongeth to their office, in prejudice of our lord the king and the common law of the realm," etc., directs that the admirals and their deputies shall not meddle henceforth with anything done within the realm, but only with things done upon the sea, according to the custom in the time of Edward III.   Two years later the statute of 15 Richard II. provided that, by reason "of the great and grievous complaint of all the commons," the court of admiralty shall have no cognizance of any contract, plea, or quarrel, or of any other thing done or arising within the bodies of counties, whether by land or water, nor of wreck of the sea ; but that the admiral shall have cognizance of the death of a man, and of mayhem done in great ships being and hovering in the main stream of the great rivers ; yet only beneath the bridges of the same rivers nigh to the sea.[2]   In the next reign it was provided by statute of 21 Henry IV. that, if the admiral or his lieutenant exceed their jurisdiction, the statute and common law may be holden against them ; and if any man wrongfully pursues in the admiralty court, his adversary may recover of him double damages at common law.   The instance jurisdiction of the admiralty was permanent ; the prize jurisdiction was

Encroachments of the admiralty court upon the common law tribunals : Stat. 13th Richard II. st. 1, c. 5.

Stat. 15th Richard II. c. 3.

Stat. 21st Henry IV. c. 11.

---

[1] See Sir Travers Twiss's excellent article entitled "Sea Laws," in *Enc. Brit.*, 9th ed. xxi. pp. 583–586.   "The Laws of Oléron, as they were called, might constitute a national code of maritime law for the direction of the admiral ; and whatever was defective therein was supplied from that great fountain of jurisprudence, the civil law, which was generally adopted to fill up the chasms that appeared in any of the municipal customs of modern European nations."— Reeves, *Hist. of Eng. Law*, vol. iii. p. 389.

[2] As to the statutes of Richard, see Reeves, *Hist. Eng. Law*, vol. iii. pp. 388, 389.

temporarily bestowed by virtue of a special commission which was usually issued at the commencement of hostilities.

When the English colonies in America were established, vice-admiralty courts were created whose civil and maritime jurisdiction "extended to the same subjects and was exercised under the same limitations in the colonies as in Great Britain. 'Upon the establishment of colonial governments,' says a learned judge of one of those courts, 'it was deemed proper to invest the governors with the same civil and maritime jurisdiction; and therefore it became usual for the lord high admiral or the lords commissioners to grant a commission of vice-admiral to them.' The office thus conferred on the governor was precisely the same with that of the vice-admirals in England, and was confined to that civil and maritime jurisdiction which was the original branch of his authority. (Stewart's V.-Ad., 394, 405.) These courts were subordinate to the admiralty court of England, and until the late reign of William IV. it received appeals from them. (1 Dod. Adm. R., 381.)"[1]

Vice-admiralty courts in the English colonies in America.

Colonial governors made vice-admirals.

Long after the Federal Constitution of 1787 had extended the judicial power of the United States "to all cases of admiralty and maritime jurisdiction,"[2] a famous controversy arose, involving the question whether the ancient rule, which excluded such jurisdiction from waters within the bodies of counties in the old land, should likewise exclude it, in the new, from the mighty rivers which constituted great highways of commerce, and from the vast lakes that were no less than inland seas. Authority and precedent, which blindly refused to recognize changed geographical conditions, fought for the ancient rule on the one hand, while an invincible logic, which demonstrated that the reason of the ancient doctrine had ceased, contended for a new and more convenient rule on the other. Guided by that marvellous prescience which has ever directed American statesmen and jurists in adapting the institutions of the mother land to the changed conditions of the new, the supreme court of the United States finally abolished the ancient rule with all of its

Admiralty jurisdiction as ultimately defined in the United States.

[1] Opinion of Mr. Justice Campbell in *Jackson et al.* v. *Steamboat Magnolia*, 20 Howard, pp. 329, 330.

[2] Art. 3, sec. 2.

inconveniences, and established in its stead a new one which makes the navigable character of the water, and not the relation of the water to the land, the test of jurisdiction.[1]

Henry VI.
and the
dynastic
struggle
known as
the War of
the Roses.

6. The Hundred Years' War, which grew out of the assertion by Edward III. of his claims to the French crown, reached its highest point of success when Henry V., after the victory of Agincourt and the conquest of Normandy, was able in 1420 to force on Charles VI. the treaty of Troyes, wherein it was agreed that Catherine, the eldest of the French princesses, should be given him in marriage; and that he should become regent of the kingdom during the life of Charles, and his heir at his death. Two years thereafter Henry V. died, leaving his English kingdom, and the vast continental possessions which he had secured by inheritance, treaty, and conquest, to Catherine's infant son, then scarcely nine months old, The infant Henry VI. at once succeeded to the English throne, and, upon the death of his maternal grandfather two months later, to that of France. For the fourth time since the Conquest the duty then devolved upon the national council to provide for the actual administration of the sovereign power during the minority of the king, as the common law of the realm neither contemplated nor provided for any such contingency.[2] How upon the accession of Henry III. the exercise of the royal authority was vested in the earl marshal, the elected representative of the baronage, who carried on the government with their advice under the title of *rector regis et regni*, has been explained already.[3] After the deposition of Edward II., and the coronation of his son, then but fourteen years old, the parliament, which was immediately summoned, vested the administration of the sovereign power, not in a protector or regent, but in a standing council of bishops, earls, and barons, which has been

Henry
VI.'s, the
fourth mi-
nority since
the Con-
quest.

---

[1] The early doctrine which limited the admiralty jurisdiction to tide waters may be found in *The Thomas Jefferson,* 10 Wheat. 428; *Peyroux v. Howard,* 7 Pet. 324; *United States v. Cooms,* 12 Pet. 72. These cases were overruled in *The Genesee Chief v. Fitzhugh,* 12 How. 443, the principles of which were reaffirmed in *The Magnolia,* 20 How. 296. The doctrine as finally settled is, that the admiralty jurisdiction in the United States is not limited to tide waters, but extends to all public navigable lakes and rivers where commere is carried on between the several states or with foreign nations.

[2] "In judgment of law the king, as king, cannot be said to be a minor." — *Co. Litt.,* p. 43.

[3] See above, p. 394.

aptly termed "a sort of parliamentary regency."[1]   The same
general plan was followed at the accession of Richard II.,
who was at the time but eleven years old.   Although he was
permitted to take the great seal from the hands of its old
keepers, and to hand it over to a new custodian who, by its
magic influence, could legalize all acts of government, the
direction of affairs actually passed to a council of twelve originally appointed by the lords, and afterwards modified by the
authority of the whole parliament.[2]   In providing for the
minority of Henry VI. the estates were careful to emphasize the exclusiveness of their jurisdiction by ignoring the
directions of the dead king, who had expressed the wish that
his eldest brother, the Duke of Bedford, should become
regent of France, while his younger brother, Gloucester,
should act as regent in England.[3]   As soon as parliament
assembled it "proceeded to authorize by its act the appointment of the Duke of Bedford, whilst in England, protector
and principal counsellor of the king, and the Duke of
Gloucester to execute the same functions in the absence of
the Duke of Bedford ; and a council, consisting of the Duke
of Gloucester and several bishops, dukes, earls, and barons
was appointed to assist in the government."[4]   The council,
which ordinarily stood as an intermediary body between the
crown and the estates, thus became the depositary of the royal
authority, — upon its ordinary executive functions the duties
of a regency were superimposed.   As the infancy, incompe-
tency, and imbecility of the unfortunate Henry rendered the
regency thus established practically perpetual, the dramatic
history of his troubled reign is no more nor less than the
record of a series of struggles carried on between the leading
statesmen of the time for supreme influence in the council,
which was equivalent to the substance of royalty itself.

The three great actors who first come upon the scene are
Bedford, Gloucester, and Henry Beaufort, Bishop of Lincoln.
During the prolonged absence of Bedford on the Continent,
where he wore his noble life out in the effort to hold the

*A parlia-
mentary
regency es-
tablished.*

*The strug-
gle for su-
premacy in
the council.*

---

[1] Knighton, c. 2556; *Rot. Parl.*, ii. p.
52. Cf. Hallam, *M. A.*, vol. iii. pp.
175-181.

[2] *Rot. Parl.*, iii. p. 386.

[3] This is the account contained in
the *Gesta Hen. Quinti*, p. 159. According to Wavrin, p. 423, Henry committed England to the Duke of Exeter,
and France to Bedford.

[4] *Lords' Report*, vol. i. p. 368.

French conquests which Henry V. had won, a struggle began between Gloucester and Beaufort for supremacy in the English administration.   The Beauforts, the natural allies of the house of Lancaster and ever the mainstays of its fortunes, were the illegitimate descendants of John of Gaunt by his mistress, Catherine Swinford, who were legitimated by act of parliament in the reign of Richard II.[1]   In the original patent of legitimation the right to succeed to the crown was not given in express terms, and from that fact the inference was drawn that they were excluded by implication.   In 1407, however, Henry IV., in confirming Richard's act of legitimation, expressly excluded the right to the succession by inserting the limitation, "*excepta dignitate regali,*"[2] — words, which were found interlined in Richard's grant on the patent rolls, but which did not occur in the document upon which Richard's parliament had acted.[3]   The fact that the express words of exclusion were introduced into the original patent through an illegal interpolation left to the Beauforts, in the event of the extinction of the legitimate branch, a pretension at least upon which to found a claim to the crown of Lancaster.   The Henry Beaufort, bishop first of Lincoln, then of Winchester, who now comes prominently into view, was a son of John of Gaunt by the Swinford alliance, who had in both of the preceding reigns held the office of chancellor.   In 1424 Beaufort was again elevated to that office,[4] and from that time his rivalry with Gloucester continues with varying fortune until it was suspended by Bedford, who returned from France in 1433 to personally assume the direction of the home administration.   In the next year, however, Bedford was recalled to France, and in 1435 he died at Rouen.   After that event Gloucester still struggled to maintain his hold upon power, until the condemnation of his wife[5] for witchcraft in 1441

Legitimation of the Beauforts.

---

[1] *Rot Parl.*, iii. p. 343.

[2] *Excerpta Historica*, p. 153.

[3] "In the original patent of legitimation, and in the copy entered on the rolls of parliament, there was no reservation of the *royal dignity*.   In the copy on the patent rolls there is such reservation, but it is interlined, and in a different ink, though the hand is nearly the same.   In the exemplifica-

tion by Henry IV., in 1407, the exception occurs without interlineation.   See Sir Harris Nicolas, in *Excerpta Hist.*, p. 153.   It appears, however, to me, that the original patent, though it omits, nevertheless implies the exception." — Lingard, vol. iii. p. 50, and note 1.

[4] *Fœdera*, x. p. 340.

[5] She is styled "Eleanor Cobham, lately called Duchess of Gloucester."

broke his prestige in the council, and left Cardinal Beaufort[1] in undisputed possession as chief minister.   To end the French war, which was a continual drain upon the national resources, now became the prime object of Beaufort's policy.   With that end in view a truce[2] was concluded in 1444 through the English ambassador, the Earl of Suffolk, William de la Pole; and by the same agent a marriage was negotiated between Henry and Margaret of Anjou, which was duly celebrated in April, 1445.   In February, 1447, Gloucester died suddenly at Bury St. Edmunds, and six weeks thereafter his old rival, Cardinal Beaufort, followed him to the tomb.   Suffolk, the negotiator of the Angevin marriage, and the trusted friend of Henry and Margaret, now comes upon the scene as chief counsellor, and assumes the burden of maintaining the French war, fast approaching an inglorious close under the leadership of Edmund Beaufort, Duke of Somerset.   In 1448 the surrender of Maine and Anjou[3]— the price of Henry's marriage with Margaret — was finally made; in 1450 the second French conquest of Normandy was completed; and in 1451 the conquest of the English possessions in the south ended with the fall of Bordeaux.   For a moment the tide was turned, when in 1453 the great Earl of Shrewsbury came as a deliverer and changed defeat into victory.   But the end had now come.   The earl was slain at Castillon in July, and in October Aquitane, the splendid inheritance of Eleanor, was lost to England forever. From that time England "constantly takes part in continental affairs; but she holds no continental possessions save such outlying posts as Calais, Boulogne, Dunkirk, or Gibraltar."[4] In 1450, in the midst of these disasters, which in rapid succession tore from the English crown all of its important continental dominions, Suffolk fell, leaving the supremacy in court and council to be fought for by the Duke of Somerset, the representative of the Beauforts, then lieutenant of France, and Richard, Duke of York, then lieutenant of Ireland.

Marginal notes:
Beaufort, who in 1424 had been made chancellor, in 1441 became chief counsellor.

Suffolk.

England loses her continental possessions.

The struggle between Somerset and York begins.

---

[1] He was first nominated to the cardinalate in 1417 (*Ang.-Sax.*, p. 800), but the king forbade him to accept.   He accepted a second nomination made in May, 1426.   Cf. Lingard, vol. iii. p. 188.

[2] *Fœdera*, xi. pp. 59–67 ; *Rot. Parl.*, v. p. 74.

[3] *Fœdera*, xi. pp. 210, 214.

[4] Mr. Freeman, in *Enc. Brit.*, "England," 9th ed., vol. viii. p. 321.

Pedigree of
Richard of
York:
The pedigree of this Richard of York, who now comes prominently into view, takes us back to the great genealogical controversy which arose between the children of Edward III. when, upon the deposition of Richard II., the crown passed by authority of parliament to Henry IV., the son of John of Gaunt, Duke of Lancaster. If the doctrine had then been firmly settled that the strict rule of hereditary descent, applied by the feudal lawyers to the succession of estates, governed the descent of the crown, it would have passed, not to the heir of John of Gaunt, the fourth son of Edward III., but to Edmund Mortimer, the heir of Edward's
his relation
to Lionel,
Duke of
Clarence;
third son, Lionel, Duke of Clarence.[1]   Whatever rights the house of Clarence possessed, under a law of succession which in that day was not at all clearly defined, were transmitted from Lionel to his daughter Phillipa, who became the wife of Edmund Mortimer, third Earl of March.   Roger Mortimer, the son of this union, fell fighting in Ireland in 1398, leaving an infant son, whom the childless Richard II. declared his heir-presumptive.   This infant son was the Edmund Mortimer, fifth Earl of March, whose claim was ignored in the revolution which elevated Henry IV. to the throne.   At his death without issue, the latent claim of his house survived to his sister Anne, who married the Earl of Cambridge, by whom she became the mother of Richard, Duke of York.[2]   In addition to the right which Richard thus derived through the house of Mortimer, a right embarrassed by the fact of its transmission through female descendants, he also claimed
his relation
to Edmund
of Langley.
descent in the male line from Edmund of Langley, a son of Edward III., younger than John of Gaunt.   Under this claim Richard stood next in the line of succession in the event of the death of Henry IV. without issue, provided the Beauforts were excluded by the terms of their legitimation.[3]   Such were the rival claims of the houses of York and Beaufort to the tottering throne of the childless Henry VI. when, in the autumn of 1450, Somerset returned from France and York from Ireland to contend for the station of chief minister, made vacant by Suffolk's fall.[4]   When the struggle for su-

[1] See above, p. 513.
[2] Richard married the daughter of the Earl of Westmoreland, Cecily Neville, the mother of Edward IV.,
George, Duke of Clarence, Richard III., etc.
[3] See above, p. 554.
[4] As to the condition of things upon

premacy between the rival dukes was at its height Henry became imbecile, and a few months thereafter the hopes of both were clouded by the birth, in October, 1453, of an heir to the demented king.   Somerset's unfortunate connection with the disasters in France, which at this juncture resulted in the final loss of Aquitaine, now turned the tide against him.   His arrest in December broke his power with the council, and in March of the next year York, whose influence was supreme, was chosen protector.[1]   The advantage thus gained by York was, however, of but short duration ; early in 1455 the king recovered, the protectorate was terminated, and Somerset released from custody.   No recourse now being left to York but arms, with Salisbury and Warwick at his back he marched upon the king, and in May the first battle of St. Alban's was fought, in which Somerset was slain and York completely victorious.   With this fight, which was but little more than a skirmish, the civil war begins.

An heir born to Henry VI., Oct., 1453.

York protector.

With the first battle of St. Alban's, May, 1455, civil war begins.

York, timid to the last in putting forward his claim to the royal office, demanded no more after his victory at St. Alban's than the first place in the council, and the calling of a parliament to which he could appeal for an approval of his policy.   The parliament which met in July [2] was prorogued until November, and in the interval the king again became insane, rendering necessary a second protectorate.   At the request of the commons the lords nominated York as protector, and the king confirmed the nomination, with a subsequent proviso that the government should be vested in the council, with the duke as its head.[3]   The ascendency thus secured by York, who now held in his grasp the royal authority, the demented king, and the infant heir, forced the leadership of the Lancastrian cause upon its natural defender, the indomitable and despotic Margaret of Anjou.   Fortune favored her at the outset : in February, 1456, the king recovered his reason, and the duke's second protectorate came suddenly to an end.[4]   The three years of peace which now ensued, during which a great formal pacification took place in March, 1458,[5]

York's second protectorate.

Margaret assumes the leadership of the Lancastrian cause.

their return, see Lingard, vol. iii. p. 209.

[1] *Rot. Parl.*, v. p. 242.

[2] *Lords' Report*, iv. p. 936.

[3] *Rot. Parl.*, v. 284–290 ; *Fœdera*, xi. pp. 369, 370.

[4] *Rot. Parl.*, v. pp. 321, 322 ; *Fœdera*, xi. p. 373. See *Paston Letters*, i. 378, as to the queen's disposition towards the duke.

[5] Fabyan, p. 464 ; Hall, p. 172 ; *Paston Letters*, i. pp. 424–427.

between York and Margaret, at St. Paul's, were simply the prelude during which both factions were marshalling their forces for the final appeal to arms.   Despite the victory won

Battle of Bloreheath, Sept., 1459. Flight of York, Salisbury, and Warwick.

by Salisbury over the forces of Lord Audley at Bloreheath, in September, 1459, the duke was soon driven through desertions to seek shelter in Ireland, while his great lieutenants, Salisbury and Warwick, took refuge at Calais.   From these safe retreats York and Warwick were busy concerting a fresh attack upon the kingdom, while Margaret, in the parliament which met at Coventry in November, was striving to complete the ruin of the Yorkist lords by bills of attainder.[1] In June, 1460, Warwick and Salisbury, with York's eldest son, the future Edward IV., landed in Kent, and, after publishing a manifesto[2] severely arraigning the royal advisers, marched with a great popular following at their backs upon London, where they were joyfully received early in July.   On

York triumphs at Northampton, July, 1460, and states his claim to the crown.

the 10th of that month a decisive battle was fought at Northampton[3] which resulted in a great slaughter of the Lancastrian lords, the capture of the king, and the flight of Margaret to Scotland.   Richard's hour of triumph had now come, and with it came the necessity of propounding to the nation the definitive claim of his house to the royal office.   In an assembly of estates which met on the 7th of October, after the repeal of the acts of the Coventry parliament,[4] Richard, whose right as heir-presumptive to the crown by virtue of his descent from Edmund of Langley had been cut off by the birth of a son to Henry and Margaret, finally rested his claim to the crown solely upon his descent from Edward III. through the house of Mortimer.[5]   To Richard's claim as thus propounded the lords, who were consulted as to its sufficiency, stated five objections,[6] which were scarcely so convincing as that of the king himself, who when questioned upon the subject thus replied: "My father was king; his father was also king; I myself have worn the crown forty

[1] *Rot. Parl.*, v. pp. 346–350.
[2] Stow, pp. 407, 408; *Eng. Chr.*, pp. 86, 87.
[3] *Eng. Chr.*, pp. 95–97; Worc., p. 773; Gregory, p. 207.
[4] *Rot. Parl.*, v. p. 374.
[5] Ibid., v. p. 375.
[6] Ibid., v. p. 376.   The judges were

consulted, but they replied that it was not a question for them to decide.   On this subject it was that Sir John Fortescue afterwards wrote his *Defensio Juris Domus Lancastriæ*, which may be found in the first volume of the Clermont ed., 1869, pp. 505–516.

years from my cradle : you have all sworn fealty to me as your sovereign, and your fathers have done the like to mine. How, then, can my right be disputed ?"[1]   The answer to this cogent question was found in a compromise wherein it was agreed that Henry should "keep the crown and his estate and dignity royal during his life, and the said duke and his heirs to succeed him in the same" at his death.[2] This settlement, which forever cut off the rights of her son, was accepted by Margaret as a fresh challenge to arms. Rapidly gathering forces in the north in the king's name,[3] in December she met York and Salisbury at Wakefield, and after a bloody fight York was slain and Salisbury captured and beheaded at Pomfret.[4]   But the fall of the duke was no overthrow of the cause of York, — it was simply an incident through which the leadership of that cause was transmitted to a more crafty, a more merciless, a more brilliant defender. The young Edward, who at the time of his father's fall was gathering forces on the Welsh marches, now took the lead, and in February, 1461, won a battle at Mortimer's Cross,[5] just two weeks prior to Warwick's defeat in the second battle at St. Alban's.   After that event Edward and Warwick joined forces and entered London, where on the 1st of March Chancellor Neville explained to an assembly of citizens the nature of Edward's title.   On the 4th, after seizing the crown and sceptre of Edward the Confessor, he was proclaimed king at Westminster under the title of Edward IV.[6]   Thus, not only without the authority of parliament, but in open defiance of the acts through which it had settled and confirmed the succession in the house of Lancaster, the heir of York seized the crown and entered into possession of the royal office as an estate which he claimed belonged to him by the unaided force of his hereditary title.   Although parliamentary sanction followed, Edward's reign, in contemplation of law, dates from the day upon which he asserted his hereditary

Margin notes:
A compromise which secures the succession to the house of York after Henry's death.

York slain at Wakefield in Dec., 1460.

Edward IV. seizes the crown and sceptre at Westminster, March 4, 1461, by virtue of his hereditary title.

[1] Blackm., 305; Lingard, vol. iii. p. 223.
[2] *Rot. Parl.*, v. 375-383.
[3] Whethamstede, i. p. 381.
[4] *Eng. Chr.*, p. 107.
[5] W. Worc., pp. 775, 776; *Eng. Chr.*, p. 110.
[6] Hardyng, p. 406; *Eng. Chr.*, p. 110; Whethamstede, i. pp. 405-407;

Gregory, *Chr.*, p. 215. Cf. Stubbs, *Const. Hist.*, vol. iii. p. 189.   Although there may have been no formal parliamentary election, the authorities clearly show that the technical claim of indefeasible hereditary right drew its practical vitality from the general approval expressed through the forms of a popular election.

claim by the seizure of the crown and sceptre at Westminster. But although Edward was now king at London and in the south of England, the decisive struggle of the civil war was yet to come. Robbed of the capital, Margaret had withdrawn with her army to Yorkshire, the Lancastrian stronghold in the north, and there on the 29th of March, 1461, was fought the bloody battle of Towton Field, in which the two armies numbered together nearly one hundred and twenty thousand men.[1] After a desperate conflict Edward was completely victorious : the Earl of Northumberland and the lords Wells and Neville were among the slain ; the earls of Devonshire and Wiltshire were taken and executed ; Margaret, with the king and heir, was forced to seek refuge in Scotland ; the war of the succession was practically at an end,[2] — the cause of Lancaster was lost.

Decisive battle of Towton Field, March 29, 1461.

7. No attempt to outline the form which the English constitutional system assumed during the fourteenth and fifteenth centuries should fail to embrace some allusion to the accounts given of that system by Sir John Fortescue, the great Lancastrian lawyer, who attended Queen Margaret in her exile on the Continent, where he seems to have undertaken, for a time at least, the political education of the heir-apparent. From the *De Laudibus Legum Angliæ*, which was designed to instruct the prince how he should rule over the English ; from the *De Dominio Regali et Politico*, a Treatise on Absolute and Limited Monarchy, and in particular on the Monarchy of England ; and from the *De Natura Legis Naturæ*,[3] — it is possible to draw something like a definite idea of the extent to which the English kingship had become limited towards the end of the fifteenth century by the growth of the parliament on the one hand, and by the growth of the system of legal administration on the other. Under the influence of mediæval political ideas, the writer divides all governments into three classes ; the first of which he describes as regal government (*dominium regale*), the second as political government (*domin-*

Outline of the constitution by Sir John Fortescue.

All governments divided into three classes.

---

[1] See Green, *Hist. Eng. People*, vol. i. p. 575.

[2] "By the surrender of Berwick to the Scots, in April, the fall of the house of Lancaster was recognized as final." — Stubbs, *Const. Hist.*, vol. iii. p. 190, citing Hall, p. 256.

[3] These three treatises are contained in the first volume of the sumptuous edition of the works of Sir John Fortescue, printed for private distribution by Lord Clermont in 1869 in two volumes quarto The first volume of this, the only complete edition of the works of Sir John,

ium politicum), and the third as government of a mixed nature, regal and political (*dominium regale et politicum*).[1] To
the third class England belongs. The contrast is then sharply
drawn between the absolute regal government of France,
where the civil law prevails, and the limited regal and political monarchy of England, where the common law prevails.[2]
The maxim of the civilians, that "what has pleased the
prince has the force of law,"[3] has no place in the English
system. The king of England is a *rex politicus :*[4] he cannot,
"at his pleasure, make any alterations in the laws of the
land, for the nature of his government is not only regal, but
political. Had it been merely regal, he would have a power
to make what innovations and alterations he pleased in the
laws of the kingdom, impose talliage and other hardships
upon the people, whether they would or no, without their
consent, which sort of government the civil laws point out
when they declare *Quod principi placuit legis habet vigorem :*
but it is much otherwise with a king whose government is
political, because he can neither make any alteration or
change in the laws of the realm without the consent of the
subject, nor burden them, against their wills, with strange
impositions ; so that a people governed by such laws as are
made by their own consent and approbation enjoy their properties securely, and without the hazard of being deprived of
them, either by the king or any other."[5] In England the
king "cannot by himself or his ministers lay taxes, subsidies,
or any imposition of what kind soever, upon the subject ; he
cannot alter the laws, or make new ones, without the express
consent of the whole kingdom in parliament assembled."[6]
Sir John, who had been chief justice of the king's bench,
while explaining how the liberties of the nation as a whole
were protected by the parliamentary system, did not forget to
point out how the life, liberty, and property of the individual
subject were guarded by the system of legal administration.

[margin notes:]
King of England a rex politicus.

Quod *principi* placuit *legis habet* vigorem, *not an English maxim.*

Limitations imposed upon the crown by the parliamentary system.

---

bears the title, "The Works of Sir
John Fortescue, Knight, Chief Justice
of England and Lord Chancellor to
King Henry the Sixth, now first collected and arranged by Thomas (Fortescue) Lord Clermont."

  [1] *De Natura Legis Naturæ*, i. 16 ; *De
Dominio Regali et Politico*, c. 1.

  [2] *De Laudibus*, cc. 35, 36.
  [3] Ibid., cc. 9, 35 ; *De Nat. Leg. Nat.*,
i. 28.
  [4] *De Nat. Leg. Nat.*, i. 16.
  [5] *De Laudibus*, c. 9.
  [6] Ibid., c. 36.

In the account given of the provisions made for the local administration of justice, a careful statement is contained of the
procedure in jury trials both in civil and criminal cases.[1]   In

*The jury
system.*

a civil case the issue is tried by an impartial jury taken from
the neighborhood; in a capital case the jury is not only selected impartially from the neighborhood, but the defendant is
given a large number of challenges, for which he need assign
no cause or reason. "In a prosecution carried on in this manner there is nothing cruel, nothing inhuman; an innocent
person cannot suffer in life or limb: he has no reason to
dread the prejudice or calumny of his enemies; he will not,
can not, be put to the rack to gratify their will and pleasure.
In such a constitution, under such laws, every man may live

*Parliament-
ary and jury
systems the
practical
guarantees
of liberty.*

safely and securely."[2]   Thus by the middle of the fifteenth
century the personal and political rights of the English people, which had long before been defined in statutes and charters, were permanently and practically guaranteed to the nation as a whole by the parliamentary system on the one hand,
and to the individual subject by the jury system on the other.[3]

*The house
of York, —
its acces-
sion marks
the begin-
ning of a
long period
of reaction.*

8. Through the exercise of the ultimate power of parliament the house of Lancaster was raised to the throne, and
for more than sixty years it reigned by virtue of a parliamentary title.   To the ascendency which the parliament thus
won over the monarchy, in the hands of that branch of the
royal house which may be regarded as its own creation, must
be added the advantage which accrued to the estates by reason of the continual dependence upon them of the ruling
house for the means with which to maintain a never-ending
foreign war.   Under the favorable conditions thus presented
by the period of Lancastrian rule, the powers and privileges
of parliament were so far defined and consolidated as to warrant the hope that in the assembly of estates the English nation had at last found a defender constant enough and strong
enough to maintain its liberties as against the monarchy in
all the years of struggle and of change that were yet to come.
And yet this hope, apparently well founded, ended in failure
and disappointment the moment that the immature parliamentary system was called upon to maintain itself amid the

---

[1] *De Laudibus*, cc. 26, 27.
[2] Ibid., c. 27.

[3] This is well put by M. Duruy, *Hist.
du Moyen Age*, Paris, 1864, p. 450.

vicissitudes of a dynastic struggle between two factions which it was powerless to control. By the fall of the house of Lancaster the first period of parliamentary growth, which had been steadily progressing for nearly two centuries, was brought suddenly to a close. With the accession of the house of York began that prolonged period of reaction which reached its highest point under the house of Tudor, — during which the monarchy, released from the fetters and safeguards which the growth of the parliamentary system had put about it, resumed in substance, if not in form, the exercise of that system of royal autocracy which it had wielded before the charters were won. The great fact which the dynastic struggle known as the War of the Roses teaches, so far as constitutional history is concerned, is embodied in the failure of the parliamentary system to maintain itself when subjected for the first time to a crucial test of its strength in the storm and stress of civil war. The question which this failure naturally suggests is this: Why was it that the monarchy, upon the accession of the house of York, was able to suddenly free itself from the limitations and restraints with which the framers of the charters had so carefully hedged it about ; why was it that the parliamentary system, upon which the practical enforcement of these restraints really depended, should have suddenly given way at the very moment when its existence as a conserving and arbitrating force had become a great national necessity? The political struggles of the thirteenth century had demonstrated the fact that the monarchy, when relying solely on its inherent strength, could not resist the might of the united nation marshalled in the ranks of the three estates. So long as the elements composing the estate system remained intact, so long as these elements acted in concert against the monarchy in the national parliament to which the estate system gave birth, so long the monarchy lay helpless in the hands of a coalition which could grant or withhold its supplies, which could dictate its policy and punish its ministers, and which, as a last resort, could lay its hands upon the throne and depose the king himself. The causes which, upon the accession of Edward IV., led to the reëstablishment of the monarchy, and to the suspension of the system of parliamentary life by which it had been over-

Collapse of the immature parliamentary system.

The monarchy, powerless when faced by a coalition of the three estates,

awed for more than a century, must be found in the processes
of dissolution and decay which by that time had undermined
not only the corporate vitality of each of the three estates,
but which had also dissolved that spirit of union and inter-
dependence, born of a common oppression, which in the earlier days had bound them to each other.

is emanci-
pated
through the
decay of the
estate sys-
tem.

Decline of
the baron-
age.

The Conqueror, warned by experience in his own duchy,
and enlightened by observation of the disruptive tendencies
manifested by feudalism in France, where it existed not only
as a system of tenure but as a system of government, was
careful to fetter its growth in his English kingdom by all
the safeguards which could be devised for the protection of
the central authority.   In the continental system, where
large sections of territory were granted to the greater vassals, such vassals, through the process of subinfuedation,
became powerful local magnates with bands of tenants at
their backs bound to them by a tie of fealty which was direct
and immediate, while that which bound them to the king as
supreme lord was only indirect and mediate.   Under this
system the tenants of the mesne lords, who owed no direct
fealty to the state or the king as its head, were ever ready
when occasion required to follow the standards of their immediate lords even against that of the king himself.[1]   In
the hope of changing this aspect of feudalism in England,
William was not only careful to so distribute the great
estates as to prevent the vesting of large sections of contiguous territory in the hands of any one great magnate, but he
was also careful in the great Gemot of Salisbury to impose
an anti-feudal restraint upon all landowners by requiring each
and all of them, in accordance with the old English practice,
to take an oath of fealty directly to the king as the head of
the state.[2] And yet in spite of all such precautions the
feudal element waxed strong upon English soil, and throughout the Norman reigns the national authority as embodied in
the new kingship was continually menaced by the great
vassals of the Conquest, who were ever eager to establish in
the new land all the special privileges and jurisdictions to
which they had been accustomed in the old.   And during
the period of anarchy which fills up the greater part of

Continental
feudalism.

William's
anti-feudal
policy.

---

[1] See above, pp. 224, 225.   [2] See above, pp. 233, 268, 269.

Stephen's reign, it seemed as if the hopes of the feudal party in England were to be fully realized. As soon as the royal authority gave way in the struggle for the crown, the land was rent by strife between baron and baron, who arrogated to themselves all of the powers of petty despots. They fortified their castles, they engaged in private war, they struck their own coins, they exercised private jurisdiction, — in a word, they reproduced for a time all the evils of continental feudalism which the Conqueror, by his far-sighted policy, had hoped to render impossible in England.[1] In the light of these events Henry II., after the restoration of order, made it the prime object of his policy to strengthen in every possible way all anti-feudal restraints, and at the same time to reduce the feudal party, as well as all other orders in the state, to obedience to a uniform system of law which the royal authority could both mould and administer. The most striking single feature of Henry's anti-feudal policy was that embodied in his scheme of commuting personal military service for the money payment called scutage,[2] — a scheme which made possible the hiring of mercenaries for foreign wars, a kind of warfare to which the feudal array with its short term of service was but illy adapted. And yet, in spite of the foresight of the Conqueror, in spite of the anti-feudal policy of Henry II., the baronial body held its own as the most powerful order in the state, and as such took the lead and maintained it throughout the prolonged struggle with the crown in which the charters were won. The leadership thus conceded to the baronage rested in the main upon its superiority as a military power: the feudal array, composed of the greater barons with their vassals at their backs, constituted a force with which no other in the kingdom could successfully compete. The bands of mounted and heavily armed knights, who were bound to their baronial chiefs by a sacramental tie which arose out of the ownership of land, could never be successfully confronted by an array of unarmored footmen until there was first a change in the art of war. As the strength of the feudal array grew out of the power of the great lords to command the services of the trained knights by virtue of their ownership of great estates, and upon the

The feudal anarchy of Stephen's reign.

Anti-feudal policy of Henry II.

Scutage.

Strength of the baronage as a military body.

---

[1] See above, pp. 275, 276.   [2] See above, pp. 283, 284.

superiority of the armored host thus organized to every other military force, the wreck of the baronage as a military body must be found in the operation of two causes, — one of which gradually dissolved its cohesion from within, while the other suddenly destroyed its military prestige from without. By the breaking up of the great estates, which the process of sub-infeudation and the elevation of the villein into a freeholder steadily advanced, the great lords were gradually deprived of their military followings, whose numbers depended upon the extent of their territorial possessions. So marked had this tendency become in the reign of Edward I., that we then find the baronial body attempting to arrest its progress by special legislation devised in the interest of their order. And yet such legislation certainly failed of its object. It seems to be no more clear that the statute *Quia emptores* was de-signed to protect the baronage against the undermining influ-ence of subinfeudation, than it is certain that the practical effect of that act was to advance the progress of the very evil which it was designed to prevent.[1] While the expedients of legislation were thus failing to check the growth of the causes which were gradually depriving the baronial body of their actual vassals, an attempt was made to nourish the dying feudalism by an artificial process of adoption, which consisted of the giving of their liveries by the baronial house-holds not only to the smaller gentry and farmers of the neigh-borhood, but to the vagrant or the outlaw who was willing to swell the retinue of the great man and to wear his livery in consideration of his maintenance and protection.[2] The arti-ficial vassalage which thus grew up filled the houses of the

Baronage weakened by the breaking up of great estates through subinfeuda-tion.

An attempt to nourish the dying feudalism by an artifi-cial process, — giving of liveries.

---

[1] As to the design and practical ef-fect of this statute see above, pp. 412, 413, and note 1. The statute *De religiosis* was also designed to protect the king and other feudal lords from the loss of services due them by the conveyance of estates to persons or institutions incapable of discharging the legal obligations. See above, p. 407.

[2] "The feudal bond between lord and vassal had been of late years grow-ing weak; and we find now that vil-leins and land-tenants had begun to break into violent demands for an ex-emption from the servitude in which they were held by their tenures. . . . The condition of the times, and the turn of manners which now prevailed, made it desirable and necessary for great lords to supply this defection in their tenants by other expedients. It accordingly had become the custom to *retain* persons in their service to be at call when their lords' affairs needed their support; and in order to distin-guish different partisans, as well as to give a splendor to such retinue, they used to dress them in *liveries* and *hats* of a particular make or color." — Reeves, *Hist. Eng. Law*, vol. iii. pp. 351, 352, Finlason, ed.

greater barons with a riotous force, equally ready for service in time of war and for acts of lawless outrage in times of peace.   When the baron could no longer demand the military service of his vassals for private war, "he could, if he chose to pay for it, support a vast household of men armed and liveried as servants, a retinue of pomp and splendor, but ready for any opportunity of disturbance ; he could bring them to the assizes to impress the judges, or to parliament to overawe the king ; or he could lay his hands, through them, on disputed lands and farms, and frighten away those who had a better claim.   He could constitute himself the champion of all who would accept his championship, maintain their causes in the courts, enable them to resist a hostile judgment, and delay a hazardous issue." [1]

This custom of the strong man undertaking to maintain the cause of his weak dependent, although it might be undertaken without pecuniary interest in the result, was so abused to the detriment and disturbance of the common law that, as early as the reign of Edward I., the maintainers of false causes were made the subject of severe repressive legislation, the scope of which was greatly widened by a series of statutes passed in the reign of Edward III. [2]   When the maintenance of a cause was undertaken upon an agreement that a part of the matter in controversy should be paid to the maintainer as a compensation for his service, it was called champerty, [3] — in simple maintenance, [4] the question of compensation not entering into the account.

Champerty and maintenance.

In this connection may be noted another evil growing out of the giving of liveries, which finally expanded into an elaborate system known as heraldry, whose organization and supervision was committed to a body of heralds, regularly organized under the presidency of the earl marshal.   The term "livery," which originally embraced the allowance both of food and clothing given by the lord to his dependent, was gradually restricted to the giving of clothing only, which took the shape of a uniform, or badge of service. [5]   When these

Heraldry.

[1] Stubbs, *Const. Hist.*, vol. iii. pp. 530, 531.
[2] See Stat. Westm., i. cc. 25, 28, 33; r Edw. III. st. 2, c. 14; 20 Edw. III. cc. 4, 5, 6.
[3] *Co. Litt.*, 38 b; 2 *Inst.*, p. 208.   As

to the distinction between champerty and maintenance, see, also, *Bell* v. *Smith*, 7 D. & R. 846, 5 B. & C. 188.
[4] *Co. Litt.*, 368 b; Blackstone, *Comm.*, bk. iv. p. 136.
[5] "Livery was originally the allow-

Badges of
service be-
come hered-
itary.
badges of service, which were looked upon as most valuable possessions by those having the right to bestow them, became hereditary, their descent was regulated by a system of complicated rules designed not only to prevent the use of similar bearings by different families, but also to determine the relative rights to the paternal coat as between different members of the same family.[1]   The administration of this complicated heraldic system, and the adjudication of the controversies which grew out of it, was committed to the earl marshal, whose jurisdiction was defined by statute in the reign of

The heralds
incorpo-
rated into a
court under
the presi-
dency of
the earl
marshal.
Richard II.[2]   Not until the reign of Richard III. were the heralds definitely incorporated into the college of arms[3] under the presidency of the earl marshal.   This court, which survived the fall of the house of Stuart, and which adjudicated a few causes as late as the last century, was not finally abolished until very recent times.

Power of
the baron-
age as a
military
force
broken by
the discov-
ery of gun-
powder.
While the cohesion of the baronial body was thus being weakened by the operation of causes working from within, its strength as a military force was rudely broken from without by a revolution in the art of war.   By the discovery of gunpowder and its application to actual warfare, which took place during the reigns of the Lancastrian kings, the impregnable feudal castle and irresistible feudal knights were shorn at once of their terror and their power.   "The introduction of gunpowder ruined feudalism.   The mounted and heavy-armed knight gave way to the meaner footman.   The 'Last of the Barons,' as Warwick has picturesquely been styled, relied mainly on his train of artillery.   It was artillery that turned the day at Barnet and Tewkesbury, and that gave Henry the Seventh his victory over the formidable dangers

---

ance (*liberatio*) in provisions and clothing which was made for the servants and officers of the great households. . . . The term livery was, however, gradually restricted to the gift of clothing; . . . the clothing took the character of uniform, or badge of service."— Stubbs, *Const. Hist.*, vol. iii. p. 531. As to the legislation known as the statutes of liveries (1 Rich. II. c. vii.; 16 Rich. II. c. iv.; and 20 Rich. II., c. i.), which were designed to prevent the many evils which grew out of the system, see Reeves, *Hist. Eng. Law*, vol. iii. pp. 352, 353.

[1] "As this right was strongest in the eldest son, he alone bore the paternal arms unaltered (in French heraldry, 'sans brisure'); and the other sons were obliged to introduce some sufficient change, called in heraldry a 'difference.'"— Clark, "Heraldry," in *Enc. Brit.*, 9th ed. vol. ix. p. 687.

[2] 13 Richard II. c. 2.   As to the limits of the jurisdiction, see Blackstone, *Comm.*, bk. iii. pp. 104, 105; Hale, *Hist. Com. Law*, vol. i. pp. 52, 53.

[3] Cf. Coke, 4 *Inst.*, p. 125.

which assailed him.   The strength which the change gave to the crown was in fact almost irresistible.   Throughout the middle ages the call of a great baron had been enough to raise a formidable revolt.   Yeomen and retainers took down the bow from their chimney corner, knights buckled on their armor, and in a few days a host threatened the throne. Without artillery, however, such a force was now helpless, and the one train of artillery in the kingdom lay at the dis posal of the king." [1]

The influences which thus undermined the power of the baronage during the period which closes with the accession of Edward IV. were scarcely more marked in their results than those which, during the same period, broke the patriot spirit of the church, and led the clergy to seek shelter and protection for their wealth and their privileges at the feet of the monarchy.   How in the struggle for the charters the clergy, as a corporate body organized for action, took an earnest part in behalf of the nation as against the crown, has been explained already.[2]   In that struggle the church, so far as its own special privileges were concerned, was completely victorious.   In the hope of breaking the coalition between the clergy and the lay estates John, a short time prior to the making of the treaty of Runnymede, specially guaranteed to the church free elections, while in the Great Charter itself express provision was made that the Church of England should be free, and should have her whole rights and liberties inviolable.[3]   By John's surrender of his kingdom to the pope, and by his receiving it back again as a fief,[4] all controversy was for the time removed as to the right of the English Church to submit itself to the papal supremacy which was firmly asserted throughout the reign of Henry III.   Not until the reign of Edward I. was the papal overlordship as admitted by John, both in the ecclesiastical and political or- der, challenged by the crown and the parliament.   When Boniface VIII., claiming to be feudal lord over Scotland, commanded Edward to withdraw his troops from that king- dom, the parliament, before whom the bull was laid by the

The church loses its patriot spirit.

Struggle between the crown and the papacy begins in the reign of Edward I.

---

[1] Green, *Hist. Eng. People*, vol. ii. pp. 14, 15.
[2] See above, pp. 348, 349.
[3] See above, pp. 378, 379, 383.
[4] See above, p. 373.

king, claimed the right to make answer and emphatically denied the pope's asserted jurisdiction.[1]   The repudiation thus announced 'of the feudal supremacy of the pope over the political relations of the crown, was followed by a series of statutes which were designed to cut off to a certain extent papal interference with the church's internal administration.

Stat. *De asportatis religioso-rum.*

The first of the series, the statute *De asportatis religiosorum* (35 Edward I.),[2] which forbade the carrying or sending of "any tax, rent, or talliage imposed by the superiors, or assessed amongst themselves, out of the kingdom," was designed to prevent alien priors from drawing tribute from English religious houses.   In the 25th Edward III. was

Stat. of Provisors.

passed the great Statute of Provisors, which, after declaring that the elections of bishops and others should be free as in time past, denied to the pope the right to make nominations to benefices within the kingdom, and also imposed severe penalties upon all "provisors" who should obtain them from

Stat. for the protection of the king's court.

him by purchase or otherwise.[3]   Three years later was passed a statute designed to protect the jurisdiction of the king's court by forbidding, under severe penalties, any person from withdrawing any cause from its cognizance by means of a citation to the court of Rome.[4]   The attempt to defy or evade all such statutes as were designed to hinder the assertion of the papal claims, by procuring excommunications directed against those who dared to obey them, led to an enactment,

Stat. 13th Richard II.

in 1389, which imposed heavy penalties upon all persons who should bring or send such excommunications into the kingdom, or attempt to enforce their mandates.[5]   In the conflict which then ensued between the crown and the papal court, when Boniface IX. declared all such statutes null and void,

Stat. of Præmunire.

the commons stood resolutely by the king.   Upon their petition was passed the famous Statute of Præmunire (16 Rich.

---

[1] *Fœdera*, ii. pp. 873–875; Richanger, pp. 208–210; Hemingb., ii. pp. 209–213; M. Westminster, pp. 443, 444. See Lingard's account of the transaction, vol. ii. pp. 184–188.

[2] 25 Edw. I. st. 1, c. 1–4. As to the relation between this statute and the Statute of Provisors, see Reeves, *Hist. Eng. Law*, vol. ii. p. 452.

[3] 25 Edw. III. st. 4. This statute was passed upon "the grievous complaints of all the commons of the realm."

[4] 27 Edw. III. st. 1. In order to enforce this and like statutes, it was necessary to obtain a writ *præmunire facias*, commanding the sheriff to warn the accused to appear and answer for his contempt. In this way the name "præmunire" became fixed to this kind of legislation. See Gibson, *Codex*, p. 80.

[5] 13 Rich. II. st. 2. c. 3.

II., c. 5), in which it was provided that if any one shall obtain from the Court of Rome, or elsewhere, any sentence of excommunication, ecclesiastical process, or any other thing touching the rights of the crown, or bring the same within the realm, such a one shall be put out of the king's protection, shall be subject to forfeiture and to be attainted, and shall also be subjected to process to "be made against them by *præmunire facias*, in manner as it is ordained in other statutes of provisors against those which do sue in the court of another in derogation of the regality of our lord the king."

During the period in which the king and parliament were thus defending by means of penal statutes the rights of the crown as against the claims of the papacy, the clergy were maturing and strengthening their internal corporate organization, and steadily increasing their enormous wealth, which could only be reached for the purposes of taxation through the two legislative bodies or convocations in which the whole clerical order appeared either in person or by representatives. "The clergy as a body were very rich; the proportion of direct taxation borne by them amounted to nearly a third of the whole direct taxation of the nation; they possessed in the constitution of parliament and convocation a great amount of political power, a majority in the house of lords, a recognized organization as an estate of parliament, two taxing and legislating assemblies in the provincial convocations; they had on their great estates jurisdictions and franchises equal to those of the great nobles, and in the spiritual courts a whole system of judicature parallel to the temporal judicature — but more inquisitorial, more deeply penetrating, and taking cognizance of every act and every relation of men's lives." [1] In this terse and graphic statement the master of the history of the middle ages has epitomized the elements which made up the aggregate social and political weight possessed by the clergy at the end of the fourteenth century, when the spiritual influence of the church was assailed by the Lollard revolt on the one hand, and its immense wealth threatened by a sweeping confiscation on the other. The first of these assaults grew out of the great religious rebellion which, taking color and form from the teachings of Wyc-

Growing wealth and influence of the clergy.

The Lollard revolt.

[1] Stubbs, *Const. Hist.*, vol. iii. pp. 365, 366.

liffe, moved under his stirring influence not only large sections of the common people, but many among the baronage
and the clergy themselves, to break away from the teachings
and authority of the older dogmatism. The response made
by the church to this assault was embodied in the series of
statutes, heretofore described as the Statutes of Heresy,[1]
which were the equivalent paid by Henry IV., after his accession, to the prelates, with Arundel at their head, for their
aid and assistance in the revolution which raised to the
throne the house of Lancaster. While the clergy by means
of these cruel statutes were engaged in crushing out the
growing heresy, through which the Lollards were undermin·
ing the church's spiritual authority, they were startled by a
fresh attack made by the commons upon their temporal possessions. In the "Unlearned Parliament"[2] which met in
1404, certain knights of the shire ventured to suggest that
the land of the clergy be taken into the king's hands for one
year as an aid in the prosecution of the war;[3] and in the parliament of 1410, the knights reasserted this suggestion in the
shape of a formal petition addressed to the king and lords
recommending a sweeping confiscation of the lands of the
bishops and religious houses, and a permanent endowment,
out of the proceeds, of fifteen earls, fifteen hundred knights,
six thousand esquires, and a hundred hospitals, — with the
further suggestion that £20,000 be reserved for the king.[4]
This radical proposal, distasteful to the lords, was earnestly
opposed by the Prince of Wales and rejected.[5] The well-
founded alarm thus excited in the minds of the clergy by the
assaults made in turn upon their spiritual authority and their
temporal possessions was naturally deepened and intensified
by the general sense of insecurity which oppressed all classes
at the end of the civil war. At the end of the struggle the
one political force that seemed to have survived, the one force
that stood out above the turbulence of the times with power
to guarantee protection and order, was embodied in the royal
authority. Moved, therefore, by a sense of insecurity, and

Marginal notes:
Statutes of Heresy, designed to protect the church's spiritual authority.

The church threatened with confiscation.

---

1 See above, pp. 537-540.
2 So called from the fact that the
king directed in the writs that no lawyers should be summoned.
3 *Ann. Henr.*, pp. 393, 394.

4 Walsingham, ii. pp. 282, 283;
Fabyan, p. 575.
5 Stubbs, *Const. Hist.*, vol. iii. pp.
47, 64.

not unmindful of the assistance it had received when as- saulted by heresy on the one hand, and threatened by confis- cation on the other, the church, which in the charter days had been the steadfast ally of freedom, turned its back upon its great traditions, and, upon the accession Edward IV., meekly sought shelter and protection at the feet of the monarchy.

In the first chapter devoted to the growth of parliament the attempt was made to draw out the fact that, from the time of the Conquest down to the establishment of the es- tate system in the reign of Edward I., all of the great pow- ers of government were centralized in and concentrated around the person of the king acting ordinarily through his continual council, or through that larger body, known as the great council, composed of those tenants-in-chief who won for themselves the right to be personally summoned, and in whom that right became hereditary. Under this highly cen- tralized system the main body of the people, upon whom the burden of government ultimately fell, were sternly excluded from all voice in its administration. Only through the per- sistent struggles of the thirteenth and fourteenth centuries did the main body of the people finally win for themselves the right first to participate in and then to control both the fiscal and political administration of the kingdom, by build- ing up alongside of the older feudal assembly a new cham- ber composed of elected representatives chosen by freemen organized for government in the shires and towns. The strength of the new body as originally organized lay in the fact that it was truly representative : at the outset the right to participate in the election of the representative members was probably extended to all, or nearly all, of the freemen embraced in the corporate organizations of the local commu- nities from which they came. The causes which led to the decline in the position and influence of the representative body thus built up must be found in the processes through which it ceased to be really representative, — through which, in the shires, the franchise, which was the birthright of the many, was finally limited to the few ; through which, in the towns, the suffrage was taken away from the main body of townsmen, to whom it had originally belonged, and vested in official oligarchies.

Elected
knights
originally
chosen by
the whole
shire com-
munity.

The weight of authority supports the conclusion that the elected knights were not only representatives of the whole shire community, but that they were chosen by the whole body of freeholders in full county court.[1] When in the parliament of 1376 the commons, intent upon correcting the evil practices of the sheriffs, petitioned that the knights of the shire might be chosen by common election of *the better folk of the shires,* and not nominated by the sheriffs without due election, Edward III. replied that the knights should be

Franchise
fixed upon
a broad
popular
basis by
Stat. 7th
Henry IV.

elected by *the common assent of the whole county.*[2] When the first statute (7th Hen. IV. c. 15) was passed regulating the election of the knights, — a statute which is regarded as simply confirmatory of the then existing custom, — the franchise was fixed upon a broad popular basis by the provision "that all they that be there present [in the county court], as well suitors duly summoned for the same cause as others, shall attend to the election of the knights for the parliament; and then, in full county, they shall proceed to the election, freely and indifferently, notwithstanding any request or command to the contrary." This statute — under which the right of suffrage reached its highest point by being recognized as the privilege of all freemen present in the county court, whether

Stat. 8th
Henry VI.
the first dis
franchising
statute in
English
history.

freeholders or not — was followed in the eighth year of Henry VI. by the first disfranchising statute of which there is any record in English history.[3] By the terms of this statute the suffrage was not only limited to the freeholders, but to such only of them as "have free land or tenement to the value of forty shillings by the year at least, above all charges." Thus before the fall of the house of Lancaster the parliament itself, impelled by the reactionary spirit of the times, consented to the weakening of its own constitution by authorizing a measure that must have resulted in a wide disfranchisement. When the difference in the value of money is taken into account, the forty shillings qualification was equivalent to a modern real property qualification of from thirty to forty pounds annual value.

    The same general tendency which, before the close of the

---

[1] See above, pp. 466, 467.

[2] *Rot. Parl.,* ii. p. 355. See above,
p. 527.

[3] 8 Hen. VI. c. 7.

middle ages, must have brought about the disfranchisement of the landless freemen and the lesser freeholders within the shires, likewise pervaded the municipal electoral systems and brought about a still more sweeping restriction of the franchise in the cities and towns. In the effort heretofore made to ascertain who were the electors of borough representatives, the general conclusion was reached that the electors in a city were the citizens, in a borough the burgesses. Who were citizens and who were burgesses seems to have depended everywhere upon local custom, and such custom was only uniform in its tendency to take away the suffrage from the main body of townsmen and vest it either in a self-elected governing body, — generally known as the mayor and common council, — or in a still smaller circle of "selectmen," nominated and controlled by them.[1] This general tendency both in the higher and lower ranges of government has been thus happily described : "While the aristocracy was encroaching upon popular power in the government of the state, it was making advances, no less sure, in local institutions. The few were gradually appropriating the franchises which were the birthright of the many. . . . The common law, in its grand simplicity, recognized the right of all rated parishioners to assemble in vestry and administer parochial affairs. But in many parishes the popular principle gradually fell into disuse ; and a few inhabitants — self-elected and irresponsible — claimed the right of imposing taxes, administering the parochial funds, and exercising all local authority. This usurpation, long acquiesced in, grew into a custom which the courts recognized as a legal exception from the common law."[2] That kind of usurpation, consecrated by custom, which secured the government of parishes to select vestries, likewise took away the government of the towns from the main body of townsmen and vested it in self-elected governing bodies, who gradually assumed the exercise of the electoral rights which had originally belonged to the whole community. In the charters of incorporation which began to be issued to the municipalities after the accession of the house of Tudor,[3]

Tendency in the towns for the few to appropriate the franchises which were the birthright of the many.

---

[1] See above, pp. 473, 474.
[2] Sir Thomas Erskine May, *Const. Hist.*, vol. ii. pp. 460, 461.
[3] The policy of the Tudors was con-tinued by the Stuarts. See Hallam, *Const. Hist.*, vol. iii. pp. 74, 75; May, *Const. Hist.*, vol. ii. p. 465.

the right of electing representatives in parliament was generally vested in the municipal governing body usually styled the
mayor and common council. When the fact is remembered
that these governing bodies were, as a rule, nominated by the
crown in the first instance, and then perpetuated by self-elec-
tion, it is quite possible to understand how the electoral rights
of many boroughs passed under royal control, or under that
of the local magnates known as high stewards, in whom the
royal or aristocratic influence finally came to be vested.

Revival of
the mon-
archy under
Edward IV.

As the parliamentary system was the outcome of the estate system, the collapse of the one naturally followed the
collapse of the other. The attempt has now been made to
draw out in some detail the processes of disintegration and
decay which, by the end of the civil war, had not only undermined the corporate vitality of each of the three estates, but
which had also broken that spirit of union and interdepend-
ence which in the earlier days had bound them to each other.
In the process of disfranchisement, which gradually withdrew the suffrage from the main body of freemen in the
shires and towns, can be discovered the chief cause which
undermined the growing strength of the house of commons ;
in the decay of the baronage, and in the weakening of the
prelacy, can be found the causes which broke the power of
the house of lords. Only in this way can be explained how
it was that the parliamentary system, which had reached its
highest point of authority at the accession of the house of
Lancaster, touched its lowest point of impotency and exhaustion at the close of the dynastic struggle which ended in its
overthrow. Under the favorable conditions then presented,
by the paralysis of the constitutional forces by which it had
been so long held in check, the monarchy, upon the accession
of Edward IV., lifted up its head, and casting off the fetters
by which it had been bound by the parliamentary system on
the one hand, and by the system of legal administration on
the other, entered upon a fresh career of autocracy which
was not destined to be broken until the days of the Stuart
kings. And yet the new system of absolutism thus reëstablished by the house of York, and perpetuated by that of Tudor, did not aim at the abolition of the older forms of legal
and constitutional life by which the monarchy had been over-

Forms of
the older
constitu-
tional life
retained.

awed for more than two centuries, — it simply strove to extinguish forever the vital spirit which in the better days had made them actual restraints upon the royal authority. With the despotic powers of the crown reorganized and reëstablished in a royal council, which was practically unlimited save by the authority which created it, the monarchy had more to gain than to fear from the perpetuity of a set of lifeless institutions which it could override at its pleasure, or manipulate at its convenience. The reëstablishment of the monarchy did not end the existence of the parliament; as a shadow of its former self it lived on as a convenient place in which acts and decrees dictated or permitted by the council could be registered, and business of minor importance transacted. Neither was the ordinary administration of law in the central and local tribunals radically modified or suspended, — the whole judicial system was simply overawed by and made subservient to the unrestrained and despotic powers of the council, in which the royal will was omnipotent. The forms of the older constitutional life were retained, and yet the monarchy as reëstablished by Edward was in substance the monarchy as it had existed under the Norman and early Angevin kings, — a monarchy still limited by the self-imposed restraints arising out of administrative routine and orderly legal procedure, and yet absolutely unlimited by the coercive constitutional restraints which had been put upon it by the patriots an statesmen of the thirteenth and fourteenth centuries.

In the reëstablishment of the monarchy Edward was careful to emphasize the fact that, as the right of the house of Lancaster to the throne had rested solely on a parliamentary election, that of the house of York rested solely upon an indefeasible hereditary title, — a title which he claimed the Lancastrian parliaments had no right to ignore, no power to set aside.[1] Upon that assumption, then for the first time practically asserted in English politics, Edward held that the Lancastrian kings were only kings *de facto non de jure*[2] —

Edward claimed that the Lancastrians were kings de facto non de jure.

[1] "The doctrine of indefeasable hereditary right, the doctrine that there was some virtue in a particular line of succession which the power of parliament itself could not overthrow, was first brought forward as the formal justification of the claims of the house of York." — Freeman, *The Growth of the Eng. Const.*, p. 194. See, also, Sir Michael Foster, *Crown Law*, p. 403, in which the author shows that the only hope of the house of York was in the assertion of "a title *paramount* to the power of parliament."

[2] The theory was that Edward IV. succeeded to the rights of Richard II.,

that their judicial acts were valid and binding only so far as he and his parliaments saw fit to ratify them.[1]   The strength which the monarchy drew from the self-sustaining theory embodied in this new doctrine of indefeasible hereditary right, Edward was careful to supplement by every practical expedient which he could devise for its protection against that most dangerous of all the restraining measures to which the parliamentary system had given birth, — the power of the estates to coerce the crown through the withholding of supplies.   What had given edge to this weapon in the hands of the Lancastrian parliaments was the continual need of the kings of that house of the means with which to carry on strife with Scotland, and at the same time to maintain the never-ending war with France, which was only brought to a close by the final loss of Acquitane late in the reign of

Edward's policy of peace. Henry VI.   The financial relief which the ending of the Hundred Years' War then brought to the monarchy was made permanent by a policy of peace which, throughout the reigns of Edward IV. and Henry VII., remained unbroken.   While the treasury was thus protected from the drain of war on the one hand, its coffers were filled on the other by various expedients which, although they involved the agency of parliament in the first instance, did not involve its annual assent or coöperation.   In the flush of victory which followed the

A sweeping bill of attainder, and a life grant of the customs. battle of Towton, Edward obtained the passage of a sweeping bill of attainder[2] through which the crown was enriched by forfeiture of the estates of fourteen lords and more than a hundred knights and esquires.   Four years later, after the victory at Hexham, he obtained from parliament a grant of tunnage and poundage and the subsidy on wool for life.[3]   After this life grant of the customs made in 1465, the meetings

Meetings of parliament grow less and less frequent. of parliament grew less and less frequent.   The long established right of the nation to express its will at least once a year through the national council was first suspended during the later years of Henry VI., when elections were avoided as

and that the three Lancastrian kings were usurpers: "Henry Usurpour, late called Kyng Henry the sixt," is the language of the act of 1461.   See Reeves, *Hist. Eng. Law*, vol. iv. p. 12, note, Finlason ed.

[1] *Rot. Parl.*, v. pp. 489 *seq*.   The validity of laws passed during the Lancastrian reigns was not questioned.

[2] Ibid., v. pp. 467-475.

[3] Ibid., v. p. 508.

much as possible, and when such parliaments as were called were rather armed assemblies of the greater nobles, with their liveried partisans at their backs, than authoritative meetings of the king's advisers. The blow thus directed at the authority of parliament during the confusion resulting from civil war was now followed by a studied contempt of its influence in times of peace. During the quarter of a century of Yorkist rule the nation was but seven times called upon to elect new parliaments, and in the brief periods during which such parliaments sat their deliberations were confined to the registry of such acts as the king in council saw fit to dictate, or to the enactment of statutes touching the growing commerce of the realm which it was his interest to promote.[1] In the words of Hallam: "The reign of Edward IV. is the first during which no statute was passed for the redress of grievances or maintenance of the subject's liberty."[2] As a part of the policy through which Edward thus freed the monarchy from all actual dependence upon the parliamentary system must be noted that most despotic of all the expedients of royal taxation through which the crown extorted gifts of money from particular subjects under the name of benevolences. Although this unconstitutional device, through which the subject's money was taken without parliamentary consent, may have been practised in substance in preceding reigns,[3] its active employment by Edward IV. has put upon him the odium of its authorship.[4] To the wealth which the crown thus derived from forfeitures, confiscations, acts of resumption, from the life grant of the customs, and from benevolences, must be added the profits which Edward derived from his adventures as a private trader, — adventures which bore the fame of the merchant king as far as the ports of Greece and Italy.

No statute in favor of liberty during Edward's reign.

Benevolences.

While Edward was thus emancipating the monarchy from the financial and political restraints which the growth of the parliamentary system had put about it, he was also careful to

Expansion of the judicial powers of the council.

---

[1] "In the reign of Edward IV. the parliament seemed to be principally taken up with the arrangement of the commercial system." — Reeves, *Hist. Eng. Law*, vol. iv. p. 9.

[2] *Middle Ages*, vol. iii. p. 189.

[3] "The collection of benevolences, regarded even at the time as an innovation, was perhaps a resuscitated form of some of the worst measures of Edward II. and Richard II." — Stubbs, *Const. Hist.*, vol. iii. p. 274.

[4] Reeves, *Hist. Eng. Law*, vol. iv. pp. 26, 261.

impart a fresh force to the judicial powers of the council which the growth of the law courts and the rise of the equitable jurisdiction of the chancellor had contracted without exhausting. In the explanation heretofore made of the process through which these courts were evolved out of the council, the fact was emphasized that a supreme and undefined residuum of judicial power still remained after their creation.[1] The necessity for protecting the ordinary administration of justice, in the subsidiary tribunals thus organized, from encroachment upon the part of the supreme and undefined judicial power[2] retained by the council, led to the enactment of a series of restraining statutes which extend from the reign of Edward I. to that of Henry IV.[3] Not until the reign of Henry VI. did a new legislative policy begin whose aim was, not to narrow the judicial powers of the council, but to give to them a wider expansion. The uniformly weak and inefficient system of internal administration which prevailed throughout the Lancastrian reigns, and which even in times of peace could neither preserve order nor guarantee a firm administration of law, almost completely gave way during the protracted confusion of the civil war. And yet at the very time when the peace of the kingdom was most poorly kept, at the very time when the steady enforcement of law was scarcely attempted, the law as a science reached a very high degree of theoretical perfection. During the reigns of Henry VI. and Edward IV. the science of pleading reached the limits of its mediæval growth:[4] the law schools known as inns of court and of chancery were filled with zealous students, while the bench was adorned by able judges who discussed the law with great learning and elaboration.[5] The difficulty lay not in the scientific perfection of the law, but in the want of administrative power adequate to its enforcement. As heretofore explained in connection with the subject of main-

Such powers first restrained,—

then expanded by statute.

Scientific perfection of the law in the reigns of Henry VI. and Edward IV.

---

[1] See above, p. 249.
[2] " This authority had been exercised in two ways: first, by issuing special commissions of ' oyer and terminer ; ' secondly, by summoning accused persons. The first process had, after repeated remonstrances from parliament, been abandoned, before Richard II. ascended the throne. The second certainly survived, and even received extension."— Dicey, *The Privy Council,* p. 69.
[3] See above, p. 516 and note 2.
[4] Reeves, *Hist. Eng. Law,* vol. iii. p. 577.
[5] Cf. Ibid., pp. 621–627. As to the history of the inns of court, see Fortescue, *De Laudibus,* c. 49.

tenance, the provincial administration of justice was para-
lyzed by the turbulent local magnates, who with their liveried
retinues at their backs could overawe the judges at the assizes,
delay a hazardous issue, seize upon the lands in dispute, or
even resist the enforcement of a hostile judgment after it was
rendered.[1]   The remedy finally proposed for evils of this character took the form of statutes which authorized the council
to draw before it all persons and all causes which could not
be dealt with in the ordinary local tribunals.   With this end
in view, the Act of 31st Henry VI. c. 2, was passed, enlarging
the powers of the council,[2] whose "judicial authority had, to
judge by the minutes of Henry VI.'s reign, been exerted
chiefly in cases where, from the might of the offenders, the
courts were powerless to enforce justice." [3]

Its practical inefficiency owing to the turbulence of the times.

Extraordinary powers of the council invoked for the preservation of order in the reign of Henry VI.

The effort thus made in the reign of Henry VI. to
strengthen the hands of the council, in order to make it the
defender of order against anarchy, was followed in the reign
of Edward IV. by an attempt to convert the judicial power
of the king in council into an irresponsible engine of tyranny.
By the patents issued by Edward, first to Tiptoft and then to
Rivers, the jurisdiction of the high constable was extended,
in contempt of the common law, to cases of high treason.
The accused were thus deprived not only of the right of trial
by jury, but their acquittal or conviction was committed,
without appeal, to the high constable, who, as the king's vicegerent, was authorized to hear, examine, and conclude all
such causes, however begun, even summarily and plainly,
without noise and show of judgment, on simple inspection of
fact.[4]   Through the judgments of this unconstitutional tribunal, which in some cases adopted the law of Padua as the
rule of its procedure, Edward made way with many of his
Lancastrian opponents.

Edward IV. converts the council into an engine of tyranny.

Jurisdiction of the high constable.

During the period in which the high constable, in contempt

---

[1] See above, p. 567.

[2] As to the relation of the council as thus invigorated to the body afterwards called, under the Tudors, the "Star Chamber," see Reeves, *Hist. Eng. Law*, vol. iii. pp. 469, 470, and notes, Finlason ed.

[3] Dicey, *The Privy Council*, p. 72.

[4] " Audiendum, examinandum et fine debito terminandum, etiam summarie et de plano sine strepitu et figura judicii, sola facti veritate inspecta." Such are the terms rehearsed in the patent issued by Edward to Rivers, Aug. 24, 1467. *Fœdera*, xii. pp. 581, 654. The powers enumerated in the patent had been originally conferred upon Tiptoft in 1462. Cf. Stubbs, *Const. Hist.*, vol. iii. p. 282 and note 2.

Construc-
tive treason.

of English precedent, was thus taking jurisdiction of cases of high treason in his novel tribunal, the English law upon that subject was itself being grossly abused in the common law courts through an unwarrantable expansion of the doctrine of constructive treason. Despite the famous Statute of Treasons (25 Edw. III.),[1] which attempted to fix the law upon a definite basis by an explicit enumeration of the cases to which it should be applied, there was a constant tendency upon the part of the courts in these evil times to extend the act to cases not enumerated in it.[2] In Edward's reign also appears the first clearly authenticated instance in the history of English law of the employment of torture as a means of forcing accused persons to confess or to betray their accomplices.[3]

Torture.

Bills of at-
tainder.

In connection with the despotic practices which at this time pervaded the administration of justice in the ordinary tribunals, should also be noted that gravest of all judicial abuses which, during the reigns of Henry VI. and Edward IV., recurred with shocking frequency in the proceedings of the high court of parliament itself. Although bills of attainder had been employed at a much earlier day,[4] it was during the period of passion engendered by the civil war that the summary power of parliament to punish criminals by statute was for the first time perverted and abused. The calm and deliberate exercise of the judicial power of the whole parliament by process of impeachment, wherein the commons as the grand inquest of the realm were required to maintain their accusations by sufficient evidence adduced before the lords sitting as judges, but illy satisfied the necessities of a dynastic struggle in which the victors were ever eager for the heads of the vanquished. Far better adapted to this condition of things was the proceeding by bills of attainder, in which, if the parliament saw fit to refuse to hear the accused in his defence, the validity of the judgment could never be questioned in any court whatsoever.[5] The accused, even

[1] The crime of treason, which was first defined in 1352, received a fresh definition in 1397. See above, p. 511.

[2] See Blackstone, *Comm.*, bk. iv. pp. 79, 80; Reeves, *Hist. Eng. Law*, vol. iii. pp. 397–400; Hale, *P. C.*, p. 115.

[3] In 1468 an accused person, by the name of Cornelius, was burned in the feet to make him betray his accom-

plices.—W. Worcester, p. 789. For early instances of the use of torture, see first volume of Mr. L. O. Pike's *History of Crime;* Coke, 3 *Inst.*, p. 35.

[4] Such was the procedure employed by parliament in the banishment of the two Despensers in 1321. See 1 *St. Tr.* pp. 23, 38.

[5] See Coke, 4 *Inst.*, p. 37.

under a bill of attainder, was, however, as a matter of grace, usually permitted to defend himself both by counsel and witnesses. "The proceedings of parliament in passing bills of attainder, and of pains and penalties, do not vary from those adopted in regard to other bills. They may be introduced in either house, but ordinarily commence in the house of lords: they pass through the same stages; and when agreed to by both houses, they receive the royal assent in the usual form. But the parties who are subjected to these proceedings are admitted to defend themselves by counsel and witnesses, before both houses; and the solemnity of the proceedings would cause measures to be taken to enforce the attendance of members upon their service in parliament."[1]

The procedure thereunder

9. The emancipated monarchy, which under the ruthless leadership of Edward had trampled upon the parliament and overawed the entire system of legal administration, passed at his death in April, 1483, to his infant son, known in English history as Edward V. The royal authority thus transmitted by the unaided force of the hereditary principle was destined to abide only for a moment in the person of the boy king. Edward, who had dyed his hands in the blood not only of his Lancastrian foes, but in that of his own house, had, through the irony of fate, left his helpless brood as a stumbling-block in the path of his ambitious brother, Richard, Duke of Gloucester, who had been drawn into tempting proximity to the throne through the murder of Clarence. The tragic episode — during which Richard overawed the council and secured the protectorship through the overthrow of Hastings, and then the crown itself through the murder, as all the world believed, of Edward's children — was of but short duration. On the 4th of May Gloucester was declared protector; on the 24th of June his right to the crown was proclaimed at Guildhall by his co-conspirator, the Duke of Buckingham;[2] on the next day an informal assembly of notables met at Baynard's Castle and presented him a petition,[3] in which he was solicited to accept the crown as the only lawful heir of Richard, Duke of York; and on the 6th of July[4] he and his

Usurpation of Richard III.

Richard declared protector on 4th May, and crowned 6th July, 1483.

---

[1] May, *Parl. Practice*, p. 744. All references to this work are to the 9th ed.

[2] See Lingard, who gives the details with the authorities, vol. iii. pp. 275–282.

[3] *Rot. Parl.*, vi. pp. 240, 241.

[4] *Cont. Croyl.*, p. 567.

consort Anne, the daughter of Warwick, were crowned at
Westminster.   Within three months after that event the
crown which Richard had forcibly taken away from his
brother's children was challenged by a new and dangerous

Henry Tudor challenges the crown, — his pedigree.
pretender, — Henry Tudor, Earl of Richmond, who, in the
absence of a better claimant, assumed to represent the house
of Lancaster.   With the death of Henry VI. and his son, the
legitimate male line of Lancaster had become extinct, — its
claims survived only in the bastard branch represented by
the house of Beaufort.   And the male line of that house had
also been extinguished by the fall of the last Duke of Somerset at Tewkesbury.   Henry Tudor, who traced his descent
through the female line of the house of Beaufort, was the son
of Margaret Beaufort — the great-granddaughter of John of
Gaunt — and Edmund, Earl of Richmond, the son of Catherine, widow of Henry V., who had married a Welshman by
the name of Owen Tudor.   The new claimant, who had found
shelter in Brittany during the reign of Edward IV., now

His first attempt in Oct., 1483, unfortunate.
threatened invasion.   In October, 1483, Henry sailed with a
fleet from Brittany, and at the same time Buckingham, who
had broken with Richard, together with the Woodvilles and
the Courtenays, raised the standard of revolt in England
But the enterprise was both premature and unfortunate.   A
storm delayed Henry's arrival ; the confederates failed to join
forces ; and Buckingham, the chief of the conspiracy, lost his
head.   In the proclamation which the new claimant put forth
at this time, a fact was announced which until then seemed
to have been carefully concealed, — the murder of the princes
in the Tower.[1]   With his popularity menaced by this ghastly
disclosure, and with his right to the crown challenged by a
resolute though baffled opponent, Richard, in the hope of
winning the support of the nation, was not slow in calling

Richard's only parliament met in Jan., 1484.
a parliament, which met in January, 1484.[2]   In this his
only parliament, the usurper made every effort not only to
strengthen his hold upon the crown by means of a parliamentary election, but also to win popular favor by consenting
to a series of measures designed in the interest of commerce
and reform.   In the act passed for the settlement of the

[1] See Green, *Hist. Eng. People*, vol.
ii. p. 62.

[2] *Rot. Parl.*, vi. p. 237 ; *Cont. Croyl.*,
p. 570.

succession the attempt was made not only to vest the crown in Richard and his issue, but to restate, as a matter of history, the circumstances and the claims under which he had accepted it in the first instance. "This act recites that a roll had been presented to Richard, as Duke of Gloucester, before his coronation, on behalf and in the name of the three estates of the realm, . . . but that neither the three estates, nor the persons who presented such roll, were assembled in form of parliament; and therefore it was ordained and established in parliament, that the tenor of the said roll, and the contents thereof, should, by the three estates then assembled in parliament, and by authority of the same, be ratified, etc., and be of the same force as if the same things had been done in parliament. The roll is then set forth, in which, after stating the right of Richard, as undoubted son and heir of Richard, Duke of York, in right king of England by way of inheritance, and asserting the bastardy of the children of Edward the Fourth, and the disability of the children of the Duke of Clarence by reason of the attainder of their father, it is stated that the persons presenting such roll had chosen in all that in them was, and by that writing chose, Richard unto their king and sovereign lord; and prayed him, that according to this election by them, as the three estates of the land, and by his true inheritance, he would accept and take the crown and royal dignity, etc., as well by inheritance as by lawful election."[1] In this statement, put forward in the first instance by the notables, and then adopted and ratified in a regular parliament, a studied effort was made to strengthen Richard's title by blending in its support the waning doctrine of elective kingship and the new feudal theory of indefeasible hereditary right. As the representative of the house that impersonated the hereditary theory, Richard was compelled to employ every pretence, however specious, to remove from his path the prior claims of the children of Edward and of Clarence; and yet the very weakness of his pretences drove him to seek shelter under the sanction of a parliamentary election.

Statement of Richard's title in the act passed for the settlement of the succession.

Blending of the doctrine of elective kingship with the feudal theory of hereditary right.

That the nation, although silent under the despotic policy of Edward IV., did not patiently acquiesce in the result of

[1] *Lords' Report*, vol. i. p. 371.

An outcry
against the
extortions
and imposi-
tions of the
preceding
reign.
the revolution through which its liberties had been overthrown, clearly appears from a petition addressed by the citizens of London to Richard III., in which the declaration is
made that "We be determined rather to adventure and commit us to the peril of our lives and jeopardy of death than to
live in such thraldom and bondage as we have lived some
time heretofore, *oppressed and injured by extortions and new
impositions* against the laws of God and man and the liberty
and laws of this realm wherein every Englishman is inherited." [1] In this outcry against "extortions and new impositions" can no doubt be found the motive for the statute [2]
now enacted, in which the evil practice of extorting benevo-
**Benevo-
lences for-
bidden, and
popular leg-
islation en-
acted.**
lences was not only forbidden, but denounced as a new and
unlawful invention.   In addition to the guarantee thus given
against the most obnoxious form of illegal taxation, other
statutes were passed of a popular character, — chief among
which may be noted those designed for the promotion of the
growing interests of English commerce, for the reform of
legal procedure, and for the prevention of the mischief arising from secret feoffments which the perils of the civil war
**Statute
upon the
subject of
uses.**
had greatly multiplied. [3]   Another statute [4] was also passed
at this time which bears an important relation to the history
of uses.   Owing to the fact that the king was incapable of
holding to a use, it was enacted that, where Richard was en-
feoffed to uses jointly with other persons, the land should vest
in the co-feoffees ; where he was the sole feoffee, it should
vest in the *cestui que use*, — an early statement of the principle, afterwards embodied in the great Statute of Uses (27
Henry VIII. c. 10), that the position of the *cestui que use*
should in all cases be assimilated to that of legal owner. [5]   As
a recognition, no doubt, of the concessions made by the king
in the interest of reform, parliament on the last day of the
**Tunnage
and pound-
age and a
subsidy on
wool
granted for
life.**
session granted him tunnage and poundage, and a subsidy on
wool for life. [6]   A few days later Richard by charter confirmed
to the clergy the privileges which had been secured to them
shortly after the accession of Edward IV.

---

[1] See Green, *Hist. Eng. People*, vol.
ii. p. 63.
[2] 1 Rich. III. c. 2.
[3] 1 Rich. III. c. 1.
[4] 1 Rich. III. c. 5.

[5] See Gilbert on Uses, ch. i. sect. 1 ;
Digby, *Law of Real Property*, p. 291,
note 1, and pp. 310, 311 ; Blackstone,
Comm., bk. ii. p. 332.
[6] *Rot. Parl.*, vi. pp. 238–240.

But the boldness, the craft, the subtilty of Richard, who under more favorable conditions might have made a great king, were powerless to avert the doom now fast descending upon him.   Not only had he shocked the moral sense of the nation by a usurpation which had culminated in a ghastly deed of blood, but he was also weighted down by the short-comings of a dynasty whose despotic policy had deprived the nation of its liberties without securing in return the one boon which every despotic power was expected to bestow, — admin-istrative order.   The weakness of the royal authority under the Lancastrian kings, their powerlessness to preserve order, their failure to maintain a steady enforcement of law, had ex-hausted the patience of the nation, and had paved the way for their overthrow.   In the hope of escaping from this con-dition of things, the nation had submitted to a transfer of the crown to the house of York from that of Lancaster.   And yet after years of waiting the expected change had not come ; the "want of governance," which had worn out the patience of all classes under one dynasty, remained as a standing re-proach to the other.   The house of York had broken down all the barriers in favor of liberty which the nation had so patiently built up, and yet it had failed to curb the spirit of lawlessness which had been steadily gaining strength during a long period of foreign and domestic war.   It may have been that the administrative machinery, which the monarchy had not yet been able to strengthen and consolidate, was itself in-adequate to cope with the chronic disorders which naturally arose out of the decay of an expiring social system.   How-ever that may have been, the fact remained that the nation was worn out by an experiment which had robbed it of nearly every political right, and which had in return given it practi-cally nothing.[1]   The spirit of discontent which grew out of this condition of things, the disposition to seek relief by still another change of dynasty, the conciliatory proceedings of Richard's parliament had failed either to allay or avert.   His

Fall of the house of York, — it establishes tyranny, and yet fails to guarantee order.

---

[1] "The house of Lancaster had reigned constitutionally, but had failed by lack of governance.   The house of York succeeded, and, although they ruled with a stronger will, failed alto-gether to remedy the evils to which they succeeded, and contributed in no small degree to destroy all that was destructible in the constitution. . . . England found no sounder governance under Edward IV. than under Henry VI." — Stubbs, *Const. Hist.*, vol. iii. p. 273.

fair promises were no doubt estimated at their true value. As subsequent events proved, his legislation in the interest of re-

form was not seriously intended. When in December, 1484, it was known that Henry Tudor was preparing for a second invasion, Richard began to collect benevolences,[1] in open violation of the statute, passed less than a year before, in which they were not only forbidden, but denounced as a new and unlawful invention. The utter faithlessness, the cruelty, the craft, the mistrust, which characterized the conduct of Richard, no less in public administration than in private intrigue, sufficiently explain why it was that his bad cause was wrecked at the critical moment by the desertion of the great military chiefs upon whose fidelity he relied. Henry, who had not

yet reached his thirtieth year, landed at Milford Haven on the 7th of August, 1485, with a small force, which was increased through the influence of his Tudor connections among the Welsh, and then by constant adhesions as he advanced towards the centre of the kingdom. On the 22d

of August he was met by Richard at Market Bosworth, in Leicestershire, where the decisive battle was fought. In the midst of the battle the Stanleys and Northumberland, upon whom the king mainly depended, deserted his standard and went over to the enemy. In his despair Richard, the last representative of a house that had produced more than one tyrant but not a single coward, threw himself into the thick of the fight, and perished while hewing his way to the presence of his opponent. Thus, by the fate of a single battle, lost through treason, the crown of England passed away from the last of the Plantagenets, — from the last king of the great house of Anjou.

---

[1] *Cont. Croyl.*, p. 572.